P9-DUC-730

BECOMING JUDY CHICAGO

ALSO BY GAIL LEVIN

Ethics and the Visual Arts (coeditor and contributor)

Aaron Copland's America (coauthor)

Edward Hopper: An Intimate Biography

Edward Hopper: A Catalogue Raisonné

Silent Places: A Tribute to Edward Hopper (editor)

The Poetry of Solitude: A Tribute to Edward Hopper (editor)

Theme and Improvisation: Kandinsky and the American Avant-Garde, 1912–1950 (principal coauthor)

Marsden Hartley in Bavaria

Twentieth Century American Painting, The Thyssen-Bornemisza Collection

Hopper's Places

Edward Hopper

Edward Hopper: The Art and the Artist

Edward Hopper as Illustrator

Edward Hopper: The Complete Prints

Abstract Expressionism: The Formative Years (coauthor)

Synchromism and American Color Abstraction, 1910–1925

BECOMING JUDY CHICAGO

A Biography of the Artist

GAIL LEVIN

HARMONY BOOKS
NEW YORK

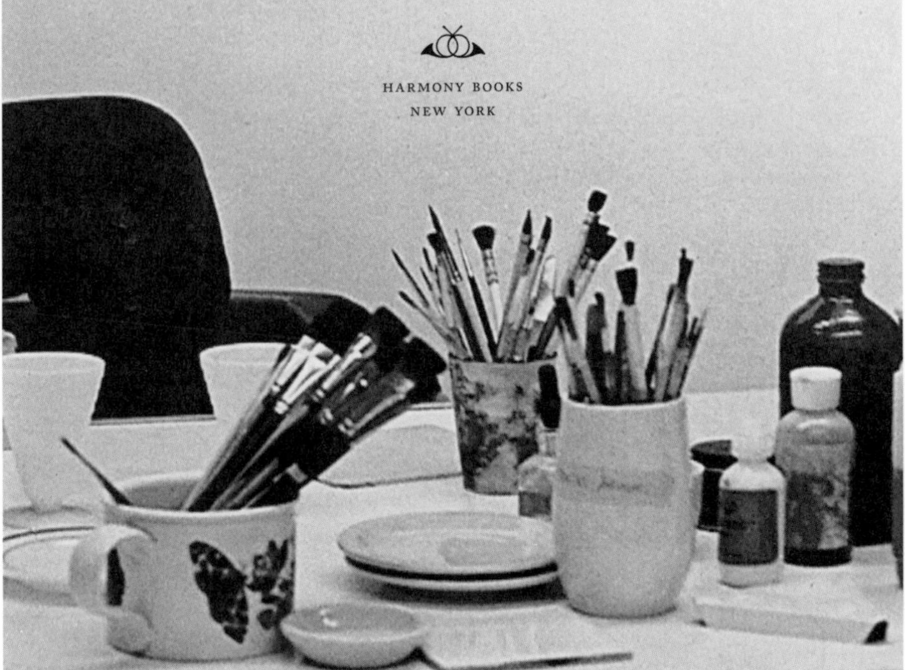

Copyright © 2007 by Gail Levin

All rights reserved.
Published in the United States by Harmony Books, an imprint of the Crown Publishing Group, a division of Random House, Inc., New York.
www.crownpublishing.com

Harmony Books is a registered trademark and the Harmony Books colophon is a trademark of Random House, Inc.

Library of Congress Cataloging-in-Publication Data
Levin, Gail
Becoming Judy Chicago : a biography of the artist / Gail Levin.
p. cm.
Includes bibliographical references and index.
1. Chicago, Judy, 1939–. 2. Artists—United States—Biography.
3. Feminism and art—United States. I. Title.
N6537.C48L48 2007
700.92—dc22 2006026158

ISBN 978-1-4000-5412-1

Printed in the United States of America

DESIGN BY BARBARA STURMAN

10 9 8 7 6 5 4 3 2 1

First Edition

For John

and

In memory of Josephine Nivison Hopper
and all the other erased women artists

CONTENTS

BECOMING JUDY CHICAGO

INTRODUCTION **What's in a Name?**

The photograph shows a petite young woman in boxing trunks and sweatshirt, her dark hair cropped short, leaning on the taut ropes at the corner of a boxing ring. She scowls slightly but maintains her poise, draping her arms over the ropes, small hands weighted down by massive gloves. Her feet—angled like a ballerina's on the dirty, bloodstained canvas floor—sport lace-up boots.

Behind her in the ring stands a taller woman wearing long pants, a T-shirt, and sandals. Her left hand dangles languidly over the top rope, and her head tilts toward the figure of the fighter. She strikes the supportive pose of a trainer but with a hint of sensuality. To the left, just outside the ring, is an elegantly

▲
Judy Chicago as a Boxer, to announce her name change and show at Cal State Fullerton, 1970. Photograph by Jerry McMillan.

dressed and groomed young man, wearing a geometrically patterned bow tie and a sports jacket, its sleeve pulled back to reveal a stiff white cuff pierced with a cuff link. With arms crossed, one leg raised above the lower rope, the other foot planted on the floor, he confidently plays the role of manager.

Above and behind the ring, visible on the wall, appear two cut-out figures of black male boxers with chests bared. The larger, who postures in fighting stance, jabbing his fists in the air, is the charismatic Sugar Ray Robinson. The smaller is a profile of the legendary Jack Johnson, who in 1908 was the first black man to win the heavyweight boxing championship of the world. His victory prompted race riots; his penchant for white women provoked prosecution under the Mann Act for transporting women across state lines for "any immoral purpose."

The scene staged for this photograph in 1970 Los Angeles also flouted custom and law. Boxing was traditionally a male domain—"part circus act, part performance art, part psych job, part street hustle."[1] California, like many other states, still barred women boxers from the ring. It would license women as boxers only in 1976, and only in 1979 would it allow them to go more than four rounds.

The figure draped on the ropes wears a sweatshirt emblazoned JUDY CHICAGO. The natty manager is her art dealer, Jack Glenn. The alluring trainer is Alona Hamilton Cooke. Glenn orchestrated the photograph to advertise both a coming show of Chicago's art at California State College at Fullerton, and a change in her name, from Gerowitz, inherited from her late husband, to Chicago, where she was born.

For the Fullerton show she declared: "JUDY GEROWITZ hereby divests herself of all names imposed upon her through male social dominance and freely chooses her own name JUDY CHICAGO."[2] By legally changing her name, Chicago publicly embraced her female identity in growing awareness of issues of gender and sexuality as the women's liberation movement gained momentum.

Other factors also favored the change. "I'm a nice Jewish girl from Chicago," she told an interviewer, who added: "She chose the name Chicago because friends tended to identify her as 'Judy from Chicago' ('I couldn't avoid it. I had a very distinct Chicago accent.')."[3]

Credit for the new name may belong to her previous dealer, Rolf Nelson, who had given her a solo show in 1966, her first, when she was just twenty-six.[4] Struck by her pronounced midwestern accent, he began calling her "Judy Chicago."[5] At the time it was an in-joke among L.A. artists to use "underground names," such as "Ben Luxe" for Larry Bell; "Eddie Russia" for Ed Ruscha; and "José Bueno" for Joe Goode.[6] Some, like Chicago, even listed their pseudonyms in the telephone book, though she alone went on to make the change legal.[7]

The change and the defiant manifesto fit the character still recalled by Cooke: "Judy was very grounded . . . she would stick up for whatever she thought . . . she wouldn't back down."[8] Cooke, who studied art and industrial design at Cal State Long Beach, met Chicago through mutual friends, the artists Laddie John Dill and Chuck Arnoldi (then Cooke's boyfriend), who recalls her as very good looking; he fantasized that "Judy had the hots for Alona." He describes Judy as "huggy and feely and touchy; she had lots of energy; her ambition was kind of a pain in the ass . . . very aggressive. She was really trying to make a name for herself."[9] Cooke recently reflected that Chicago "was a minor thorn in the side of these guys, but I have the impression that they really respected her. . . . They respected how hard she worked."

The idea of posing Judy as a boxer had come from the photographer Jerry McMillan.[10] They had met through his sometime model and her friend and neighbor, Janice Johnson, when both women lived in Topanga Canyon in the early 1960s. "I was at the deli up the street from my studio with Joe Goode, telling him I had to do something for Judy Gerowitz and that she was changing her last name to Chicago," he recalls. "We both had known her for years, and our discussion was around what a scrapper she was—maybe I should dress her like a boxer?"[11]

The role fit the figure she cut at the deli, Mayer's, where she could "embarrass a sailor who had just gotten into town," McMillan recalls, with her typical friendly greeting, "Ah, there's my three motherfuckin' artist-friends"—McMillan and his artist buddies from Oklahoma City, Ruscha and Goode, who all had studios on Western Avenue in Hollywood. "She was blunt and abrasive; that was the charm; she wasn't mean."[12]

When Nelson closed his gallery, Chicago migrated eventually to Glenn, who arrived from Kansas City and opened his gallery in May 1970. Whether Glenn or Chicago asked for the publicity shot the photographer cannot recall; but since Chicago liked his proposed theme, he encouraged Glenn to dress her in complete boxing attire, including a customized robe, to be made especially for the occasion at a sporting goods store. Meanwhile McMillan approached Howie Steindler, a notorious boxing manager who owned the Main Street Gym downtown, which was the most prominent training site for local boxers. Its alumni included Muhammad Ali, Rocky Marciano, and Jack Dempsey.[13]

The cantankerous Steindler (thought to have inspired the gruff trainer played by Burgess Meredith in the 1976 movie *Rocky*) grudgingly agreed to the photo shoot but only after being convinced that it was not a big commercial shoot and that he would receive a cash payment in advance.[14] Steindler carried a large wad of cash in his pocket and was often generous with the guys working out when they had hard luck, recalls McMillan, adding that Glenn agreed that the gallery would pay Steindler's fee, which was large for the time, "maybe $100 or $150." As for the robe, either it would take too long to produce, cost too much, or cover too much leg. Instead they ordered the sweatshirt labeled JUDY CHICAGO.

The second-floor gym was already open when Jack, Alona, Jerry, and Judy got there, but Steindler was late and his staff would not let them in. Tension grew when Jerry learned that Judy had just flown in from Fresno, where she was teaching, and had to catch a noon flight back to meet her afternoon classes. While waiting for Steindler, Jerry posed Judy, Alona, and Jack out front under the awning that read, MAIN STREET GYM WORLD'S LEADING BOXERS TRAIN HERE DAILY. He had ventured a few shots when Steindler drove up and saw them working. "He was madder than hell," Jerry remembers. He gave them only ten minutes for the shoot in the ring itself, ordering the men in training to step down. "Judy," he remembers, "seemed a little scared . . . you could tell that she was pretty intimidated." But she got her act together, and he got the photograph that would become an icon.

The name change led at least one writer to accuse Chicago of a "public erasure of her Jewish identity . . . [switching] from the ethnically marked Gerowitz to the more ethnically neutral Chicago."[15] The evidence tells a different story. In the catalog for the Fullerton show, where Chicago explained the change, she chose to include, along with her own brief statement, quotations from three women: the French feminist Simone de Beauvoir, the African-American abolitionist Sojourner Truth, and the English novelist George Eliot. The latter two had also changed their names (Isabella Baumfree to Sojourner Truth, Mary Ann Evans to George Eliot).

The quote from Eliot bears directly on the issue of Jewish identity, since it comes from the 1876 novel *Daniel Deronda,* which is noted for its sympathetic treatment of Jews. The novel features a crafty but generous pawnbroker named Ezra Cohen, his son Jacob Alexander Cohen, and the rest of their family. This would be an odd work to cite if one were trying to hide the fact that one's family name was Cohen, as Judy Chicago's was.

Three years later (in 1973) Chicago would manifest her regard for Eliot's novel again in a set of drawings, which she intended as studies for lithographs and called *Compressed Women Who Yearned to Be Butterflies.* She dedicated the third drawing to Madame Deronda and fully transcribed her bitter protest: "You are not a woman. You may try—but you can never imagine what it is to have a man's force of genius in you, and yet to suffer the slavery of being a girl. To have a pattern cut out—this is the Jewish woman! This is what you must be;

this is what you are wanted for; a woman's heart must be of such a size and no larger, else it must be pressed small, like Chinese feet."[16]

This quote is obviously self-referential, implying that Chicago too identified with male artists who had a "force of genius" while rejecting stereotypical restrictions imposed on women, including those of orthodox Judaism. Chicago was, however, proud of having been reared in the secular Jewish culture that figures repeatedly in her memoir, *Through the Flower: My Struggle as a Woman Artist,* published in 1975. There she recounts how, when she was still a small child, her mother's stories of going "to the Jewish People's Institute," where she had mingled with "creative people," became the context through which May Cohen encouraged her young daughter's love of drawing and nurtured her desire to become an artist.[17]

By adopting the name of her native city rather than a familiar name with Anglo-Saxon associations, Chicago replicated a practice long traditional among Jews. Examples of city-based Jewish surnames include London and Berlin, as in the case of Meyer London, the early twentieth-century American labor leader, who became the first Socialist Party member elected to Congress; the philosopher and historian Isaiah Berlin; and the songwriter Irving Berlin, to cite just three prominent examples. Though she may not have considered this parallel, she clearly did not choose a name that would mask her Jewish identity.

Chicago's militant stance for McMillan's photograph mingles the strains of traditional Jewish and new feminist identities, both emphasizing the courage to stand up for deeply held beliefs. Her life reflects typical patterns of Jewish activists in America, as she began in the civil rights movement campaigning for equality for African-Americans and moved on to the struggle for equal rights for women.

The photograph appeared not only on the announcement for the Fullerton show but as an ad in the magazine *Artforum* in December 1970, where it ran for free, since the editor Philip Leider had admired the photograph but could not convince Glenn to pay to run it. Chicago brought a copy of the *Artforum* ad to a party given by Laura Lee Woods celebrating Goode's calendar of L.A. artists, which featured various male friends whom he had photographed in their cars, Joe Goode recalls. When Goode learned that she really had changed her name, he thought she did so to seem more "macho, like a boxer."[18] The artist Billy Al Bengston quipped to her that she should have changed her first name, not her last. As for McMillan, he reveled in the intensity of the moment and credited Judy's "cool sense of humor" and "quick wit" with the success of their endeavor at the gym: "Judy Chicago! What an opening punch!"[19]

Early Childhood in Chicago

1

Judith Sylvia Cohen was born on July 20, 1939, the first child of a couple who typified the secular idealism of a generation that struggled to forge a new kind of Jewish identity. They not only rejected the religious strictures of immigrant parents who themselves had fled czarist anti-Semitism, but they also battled injustice in American society. Judy's mother was an eldest daughter who sacrificed her own artistic development to help support younger siblings; her father was a rabbi's independent-minded youngest son who was pampered by his older sisters; both were reared by strong mothers who sustained households when their husbands proved less able than they to cope with the new world. The birth took

▲

Family Passover seder, Chicago, c. 1921. Arthur Cohen, Judy's father, is second from the right, seated next to his father, Rabbi Benjamin Cohen.

place in Michael Reece Hospital, which German-Jewish philanthropists had founded in 1880, before the massive Jewish flight from czarist oppression and which had been "inundated by the poor" during the Great Depression of the 1930s.[1]

Poverty had long fueled political and cultural ferment among the immigrants, who attacked new injustices with ideas and actions tested against the czars; and their activism went with them when they migrated from the squalor of Chicago's near West Side to neighborhoods farther north and west, like Lake View (where Judy Cohen would grow up), Humboldt Park (where her father's family settled), and North Lawndale (a focus for her mother). Humboldt Park recalled Brooklyn's Brownsville, a place where the local Jews were vested strongly with Yiddish culture and radical philosophies.[2] Among the speakers on soapboxes who could be heard at the corners around the park were secularists and Zionists; leftist-oriented schools (a legacy of Eastern European radicalism) and Yiddish theater contributed to the ferment.

Judy's mother frequented the Jewish People's Institute in North Lawndale. From the moment in 1927 when the institute moved into a new building that was remarkable for an exterior that showed Byzantine influence (visually interpreting the Middle Eastern origins of Judaism), it became a focal point for one of the nation's largest Jewish communities.[3] Its social, recreational, and arts activities attracted children and adults. Lectures and classes, a library, an orchestra, museum exhibits, and plays performed by a resident company drew left-leaning, secular, Yiddishist Chicagoans like Judy's parents. Dancing on the roof garden every Sunday evening sparked many a romance free from the traditional control of family and religious arrangements.[4]

Despite the hardships of the Great Depression, Arthur Melvin Cohen and May Levinson married on March 14, 1936.[5] He was twenty-six, she was twenty-four. May's mother, Bertha Casan Levinson, had left Poland for the United States in 1906, at the age of twenty-three, only to suffer in an arranged marriage that proved unhappy.[6] Bertha's husband, Judy's maternal grandfather, Harry E. Levinson, left little impression on Judy as a child. She recalls her father telling her that Harry was known "to take off from time to time, walking across the country."[7] Despite this family lore, the United States census implies a somewhat different story.

Harry Levinson, who was nearly four years younger than his wife, took the trouble to specify to the census taker in 1920 that he was born not just in Russia, but in the province of Kurland, in the city of Riga. The Russian Empire had annexed Kurland, which had been a part of Latvia, in 1795. By 1897, Kurland was home to more than fifty thousand Jews, despite the fact that it was not part of the area in the Russian Empire called the Pale of Settlement (the former Polish territories of central Poland, Ukraine, Byelorussia, and Lithuania) where Jews were allowed to live. Kurland's Jews proudly blended secular Western culture from Germany and Jewish religious education from such renowned Lithuanian yeshivot (religious academies) as Slobodka, Mir, and Volozhin.[8] Even poor Jews were said to educate their children well, and most were said to have a command of the German language. Jews in Kurland were well placed to participate in the Jewish intellectual and literary movement known as the Haskalah, or "enlightenment," which began in Germany and by the mid-nineteenth century was spreading through Eastern Europe. Its proponents believed that Jewish emancipation and equality would result if Judaism could be reconciled with modern Western ideas and customs. Increasingly, they produced secular literature in both Hebrew and Yiddish.

When the Russian Revolution of 1905 began, it soon spread to Riga, the industrial center where Levinson lived.[9] Jewish youth took an active role in this antigovernment upheaval. About eighty strikers were killed in Riga and, a few days later, the government shot dead a hundred protesters in Warsaw, then also part of the Russian Empire. The government sent in troops to execute Latvian peasants and Jewish revolutionaries, causing Jews to rally together to form self-defense forces. The assassination of government officials caused retaliation and executions of Jews and others. The uproar sufficed to prompt both Harry Levinson and Bertha Casan to emigrate. Yet their meeting in the new world, the product of a *shadchen* (matchmaker), was not destined for harmony.

According to the U.S. census for both 1920 and 1930, Harry worked in the leather goods business. During his lengthy absences, however, his wife and three children had to fend for themselves. Bertha supported her family for a time by making silk flowers—an occupation that would pique the interest of her artist granddaughter.[10] Needlecraft like Bertha's had been frequently practiced in such cities as Minsk, Vilna, or Riga by Jewish women, who carried these same arts to the new world, often continuing the work in New York or Chicago.[11] Sewing skills figured in many a Jewish immigrant's visual memories of life in the old country, such as "a wall covered with pictures that Mother had embroidered as a girl."[12]

May Cohen told her daughter about the time when she saw her mother go out in the snow to sell her silk flowers; May knew then that as the eldest child she had to leave high school after only two years and go to work to help support her siblings—her sister, Dorothy, who was four years younger, and her brother, Herbert, who was eleven years younger. He would grow up to become an orchestral musician, while May would have to subordinate her interest in dance to help keep the household afloat. By 1930, she was already working as a stenographer in the advertising industry.

May was "a tiny person, slim and lovely . . . very clothes and style conscious," recalled a friend of her daughter, who remembered her as "a warm, exceedingly bright, direct, and interesting woman—a former dancer I believe . . . part of a large group of artistic intellectual left-wingers who remained friends from their twenties until members of the group died."[13] The daughter could identify with her mother's artistic side.[14]

While May was the eldest in her family, Arthur Cohen was the youngest (ninth surviving) child of his immigrant parents—Benyamin (Benjamin) Guttman Cohen (1862–1934), already forty-seven, and Anna Landau Cohen, forty-five, when their third son came on June 23, 1909. His older sisters adored the baby of the family, showering him with attention and considering him the brightest of their three brothers. Arthur proved to be very sensitive and caring, to the scorn of his older brothers, who resented their sisters' preference for the youngest.

The family name Cohen belongs to the rabbinical class—*Cohanim*—in Jewish custom; and Arthur's father (Judy's grandfather), Benjamin, was a practicing rabbi, said to be "the twenty-third in an unbroken tradition."[15] Short in stature, he had expressive eyes, dark hair, and a beard. Both his parents—Abbe Moishe Avrum (Abraham M.) Cohen and Chiah Pippa Landau—came from relatively prosperous families who lived in settlements around Kovno, which under czarist rule was the provincial capital and administrative seat for much of central Lithuania and was said to be a beautiful, clean city full of nice shops, even equal to those in some German towns across the border.

The Jewish community in Kovno supported an active embroidery trade and the klezmer music of Elyokum Zunser.[16] There were freethinkers, writers, and poets, drawn in part by a fine library named after a beloved fellow townsman, Avraham Mapu, the secular Jewish novelist and author of *Ahavot Tzion* (*Love of Zion*); they were influenced too by the Haskalah movement.

Although Kovno offered an urban life, with all its allures, worldly pleasures, and secularizing temptations, Benjamin Cohen, with his eight siblings, actually hailed from Slobodka, which was an impoverished little shtetl (small town), across the banks of the River Vilya from Kovno. Most of the residents led simple, working-class lives, earning meager livelihoods from hard work on the river, loading and unloading barges with merchandise, or from driving log-rafts. But some, such as Benjamin's rabbinical family, earned their living from the many boys who flocked there to study in the town's yeshiva (rabbinical academy). In addition to their income from religious education, the Cohens raised their own food and were better off than many families struggling under restrictions that the czar imposed on Jews.

Benjamin's younger brother Meyer liked to tell how he had learned about farming as a boy in Slobodka and that chickens ran through the family house.[17] He told of opening the door for the imagined visit of the Prophet Elijah, a tradition on the spring holiday of Passover, only to see their goat wander in, provoking laughter.

A boy like Benjamin received a Jewish education in two stages: elementary Hebrew language study in the *kheyder* beginning sometimes as early as age three, but surely by the age of six, until the age of twelve or thirteen, then the yeshiva, which stressed a rigorous intellectual discipline and what is sometimes referred to as a "Talmudic bend of mind" that would ponder any problem from multiple perspectives. Such a religious upbringing emphasized social responsibility and the "striving for moral ideals."[18]

Yeshiva education itself, however, was the object of a religious reform movement known as the Mussar (Moral) School, motivated in part by the secular humanistic challenge of the Haskalah. Reformists urged moral and ethical rejuvenation and emphasized the ethical and homiletic strain of teaching and preaching in Jewish tradition.[19] The Mussar's founder, Israel Lipkin Salanter (1810–83), stressed humility and taught the precepts of leading a "perfect ethical life, exemplified by compassion for the poor."[20] Salanter's doctrine embraced "the teachings and the path of the *gaon* of Vilna." The *gaon*, or "eminence," was Rabbi Elijah ben Solomon Zalman (1720–97) who had helped to shape the course of modern Jewish history. Like his illustrious eighteenth-century rabbinical predecessor, Salanter "championed the centrality of Torah study," the Jewish scripture—the five books of Moses, in the form of a handwritten scroll read in the synagogue each year from start to finish.[21]

Many stories of Salanter have come down. Once, during a cholera epidemic, he commanded his congregation to eat on the holy day of Yom Kippur, when fasting is required. In the hagiographic version of the story, the rabbi ate at the pulpit in order to set an example that life is more sacred than ritual and rules.[22] To overcome resistance to violating the ban against Sabbath work, which is permitted to save life, Salanter worked tirelessly seven days a week against the cholera outbreak. Salanter also advocated vocational training for Jewish youth and favored translating the Talmud (the authoritative body of Jewish tradition comprising the once oral law of the Mishnah and its commentary, the Gemara) from its original Babylonian Aramaic into Hebrew.

Salanter's principles inspired the new Yeshiva Knesset Yisroel, founded at Slobodka in 1882 as an advanced school for graduates of other schools, such as the yeshiva where Benjamin had been studying.[23] The new academy gave Benjamin, who was then twenty years old, a rare opportunity to pursue further studies without leaving his hometown. Despite Slobodka's short, muddy lanes and small, one-storied wooden houses, the new academy quickly became world famous wherever Torah study was revered.

The teachings of the new yeshiva were designed to complement the intellectual study of the Talmud and to encourage students' moral self-examination. Benjamin's exposure to such altruistic Judaic humanism, which is acknowledged to contain "potentially radical values," eventually enabled him to pass them on to his children, especially his youngest son, Arthur.[24]

Within those peripheral communities around Kovno, the families of Benjamin's father (the Cohens) and mother (the Landaus) were relatively well off. It was among his Landau cousins that Benjamin found his future wife, who lived just a few miles away in Kedainai (today Kedainiai)—like Slobodka, a shtetl. Through what may have been an arranged marriage, he wed his mother's niece, his first cousin, Khana (Annie) Etel Landau (1864–1950), a daughter of his mother's brother, Arye [Arthur David] Landau.[25] The couple's shared grandfather was Haskell Landau, and both prided themselves on descent from the Vilna *gaon*. Her Jewish name, Khana, was the same as that of the *gaon*'s first wife, perhaps reflecting the Jewish custom of naming children after deceased relatives, thus passing names down for generations. Her own father's name, Arthur, would pass to her last son, the father of Judy.

The young couple benefited from the comfortable dowry that the bride's family could afford to offer and the support they continued to provide. The Landaus were in the business of manufacturing ladies' clothing. They had taken the untraditional step of educating their daughter; as a result, Annie could read Yiddish well. In quite traditional fashion, however, she bore Benjamin three children in quick succession—Gertrude in 1884, Rose in 1886, and Tillie in 1888.

So many daughters posed a potential problem, for how would the young couple ever provide dowries at a time when economic prospects for the Jews under the czars looked increasingly bleak as political unrest grew? Already in the mid-1870s, the Jews' discontent with their status had begun to contribute to revolutionary ferment,[26] which the government vainly attempted to check. After the assassination of Czar Alexander II in 1881, conditions for the Jews deteriorated under his son, Alexander III. Pogroms began—organized killing sprees aimed at reducing the number of Jews by death or by flight. In 1882 a government policy known as the "May Laws" further attempted to drive Jews from the countryside. More and more of the Jews in the Russian Empire were being reduced to extreme urban poverty.[27] They faced harsh working conditions, long hours, and low wages in the factories and small workshops where many of them labored as artisans.

By 1886, when the Cohens produced their second daughter, socialist propaganda was flourishing among the masses and radical political activity increasing year by year. Clandestine groups of five to ten people, known as "circles," met in private homes to drink tea, read, and discuss revolutionary ideas.[28] They studied radical writings smuggled illegally from Western Europe and produced Yiddish pamphlets to organize their fellow workers. It has been suggested that Jews were "less docile, more argumentative, and keener on what they perceived to be their rights and their dignity and, perhaps above all, more liable to form cohesive groups for common action. Jewish workers, notably in Lithuania, had a tradition of self-help and pooling of resources in bad times."[29] The workers were beginning to learn that they could strike for economic benefits or better conditions such as shorter working hours.

By the beginning of the 1890s, "emigration fever" took hold among the Litvaks, as the Jews in Lithuania were known.[30] The decision to emigrate and risk an uncertain fate in the new world reflected a desire to escape the continual dangers of the growing revolutionary movement and the increasing misery of their daily lives under the czars.

Benjamin Cohen watched his three older brothers, Isaac, Eber, and Louis, emigrate to the United States, where they worked as peddlers out of Topeka, Kansas, a city founded in 1854, when it catered to wagon trains heading west to California.[31] Often a pair of Jews would journey to America and lay the groundwork so that their families, friends, and neighbors might later join them. The brothers' decision to settle in Topeka may have been the legacy of a settlement of Jews initially sent to Kansas during the 1880s by the Hebrew Union Agricultural Society, a failed attempt to establish a Jewish agricultural society for immigrants from Eastern Europe.[32] Anticipating mass Jewish migration to the United States, urban Sephardic and German Jews who had arrived earlier feared that the poor, Yiddish-speaking Eastern European Jews, so visible in their distinctive garb, would settle in crowded urban tenement houses and only barely eke out a living. One distinguished Sephardic Jew published this warning in 1887: "If 500,000 Jews come into the city within the next thirty years, there will creep up a spirit of enmity . . . as in old Europe today. There will be no safety, there may be dishonor, disgrace, and misery on every side."[33]

Despite the fears harbored by Jews who had settled in America earlier, news of a better life there circulated in Lithuania and fueled further emigration. Tales of life in America entered Yiddish fiction. In one novel, a woman interjects: "they really say . . . that the very poorest people there eat meat and rolls every day." The man's response tells us volumes about what men in his milieu thought of women: "Women speak only nonsense! You mere woman, you,—where are your brains? How could you believe such folly? Now listen, . . . if he eats meat and rolls every day, what does that show? That he is not a poor man. And if he *is* a poor man, then he can't eat meat and rolls every day. Fool!"[34]

Word came back from the older brothers that there was indeed opportunity in America. Benjamin determined to make the journey, hoping perhaps that the growing Jewish community in the new world would need rabbis and be able to support him. The painful decision was made for Benjamin to emigrate in advance of his wife and daughters, so that he could earn money to bring them over. He entered through New York's Castle Garden, joining his older brothers in Topeka about 1892. The town did not yet have a synagogue.[35] Benjamin had to work with his brothers as a peddler.

Annie and the three daughters followed Benjamin to the United States in 1893. Gertrude (1884–1950s) was nine, Rose (1886–1973) seven, and Tillie (1888–1964) five.[36] It was a year of depression and unemployment that prompted Yiddish poets to respond with poems of social protest to the hardships of American immigrant life.[37] For Annie, who had lived among her parents and siblings in relative comfort, the new circumstances must have come as a shock. In the culture she knew, it was considered a mitzvah (good deed) when a wife worked so that her husband could take part in the religious cultural elite. So Annie took charge of the family fortunes, putting to practical advantage her education and family business experience. She founded a store, Anna Cohen Clothing, which suggests that she produced or at least sold clothing, since ready-to-wear clothing was being manufactured already by this time.

Her enterprise allowed her husband to leave off peddling and return to traditional male occupations at home. Benjamin Cohen's training had prepared him only to study religion, which did not contribute to the family economy in a town like Topeka, which had neither a yeshiva nor a synagogue where he could earn a living. Like Annie, many immigrant Jewish women supported their families and rabbinical husbands, but secular Jewish literature and socialist ideologies had begun to challenge the subordinate status of women.

The plight of women like Annie informs a satirical Yiddish song: "He runs to the synagogue / And reads all the laws" while "To market she must hurry, / Wood to buy and worry. / Bread she must bake; / kindling she must break; / the children she must care for . . . / A baby every year."[38]

Scarcely a year after reaching Benjamin in Topeka, Annie gave birth to their fourth baby, the first of six born in America and their first son, Harry (1894–1949), who was born on January 23, 1894. He was followed in rapid succession by a brother Jack at the end of 1894 and sister Molly on December 23, 1895. Yet Anna also continued to run the store, above which the family lived. Inevitably some domestic responsibilities fell on little Gerdie and Rosie. Rose later recalled a time when she and her older sister were scrubbing the floor while their infant brother Jack's baby buggy was parked outside. A cat attacked him and "tried to suck the baby's breath" to get the milk he had been fed, she told her daughter, falling into the pattern of an old wives' tale.[39] Rose remained forever fearful of cats, which came to embody the many threats, imaginary and real, that the family confronted in the strange new land.

Although life in the new world might be hard, news from their friends and family back in Lithuania was even more grim. By 1895 a small group of Jewish students in Vilna, who were in touch with similar Russian circles in St. Petersburg and Moscow, formed a group that identified with leading revolutionaries such as Prince Peter Kropotkin and Nicholas Chaykovsky.[40] The Allgemeyner Idisher arbayterbund in Lita, Poylen un Rusländ (General Jewish Workers Union in Lithuania, Poland, and Russia), known simply as the Bund, was founded in Vilna in 1897. Meeting secretly to avoid the vigilant police, eleven delegates (nine men and two women), came from Vilna, Warsaw, Minsk, Bialystok, and Vitebsk. Representatives of the movement's paper, *Arbayter Shtimme* (*Workman's Voice*), produced in Vilna by a secret printing press, were also present.[41] The new central committee issued a new and popular newspaper, *Der Bund* (*The Union*), aimed at the working masses. Jews, and Jewish women in particular, were active in revolutionary work. From March 1903 to November 1904, 54 percent of those sentenced for political transgression were Jews, but over 64 percent of the women who received such punishment were Jews.[42]

What began as an economic campaign soon became revolutionary in character, and Bundists joined very soon with Russians who sought political liberty and constitutional government. Risking arrest, imprisonment, and being shipped off to Siberia, the partisans began to hold their meetings in cemeteries by imitating funerals or in synagogues under the pretext of religious services.[43] As a result, even a devout Jew very slightly concerned with worldly matters was inadvertently exposed to revolutionary ideas and activity. Although opposed by rabbinical authorities, whom they considered "reactionary elements," adherents nonetheless came from circles of students and pious scholars who had been induced to give up the Talmud for the teachings of Karl Marx.[44] The Bund then saw itself as the "Jewish antithesis of Zionism," which was the search for a Jewish homeland either in Palestine or elsewhere; Bundists considered Zionism a "bourgeois and reactionary nationalism."[45]

Benjamin and Annie's immediate concern was not with politics but with the survival of their own growing family. The struggle to support their children became easier when they moved from Topeka to Cedar Rapids, Iowa, in 1896, where Benjamin was called to teach Hebrew by a group of Jewish settlers from Russia and Poland who had reached Cedar Rapids in 1895.[46] Calling themselves Eben Israel (Rock of Israel), the group had established a cemetery association to assure proper Jewish burial. Their next step was hiring a kosher butcher and a Hebrew teacher.[47]

Whether Benjamin Cohen was hired only as the group's Hebrew teacher or also as their rabbi remains unclear, but Cedar Rapids had no synagogue until thirty-seven families founded Beth Jacob in 1906, ten years after his arrival in Iowa. The new orthodox synagogue was located in a former Episcopal chapel, which the small congregation remodeled.[48] Benjamin Cohen became the first rabbi of this tiny community. The synagogue displayed for many years a drawing that he had made of praying hands, which symbolize the *Cohanim,* or rabbinical caste.[49]

After the Cohens moved to Cedar Rapids, their life was somewhat more settled. Annie continued to run a tiny store, this one selling "notions" and once again in the same building as their home, located at 43 16th Avenue West. While "Annie Cohen, notions" was listed in the city directory from December 1896, it was not until 1900 that the listing included Benjamin G. Cohen, with his wife, Annie, followed by the word *notions,* at this same address. Their eldest child, Gertrude, by then sixteen years old, is listed separately at this address as "Gerty, student."[50] This reflects noteworthy respect for educating girls, like that which Annie had enjoyed as a child herself, since many immigrant families, including Jews, required daughters to drop out of school (at least by the legal age of fourteen) in order to become wage-earners.[51]

Only in 1902 did the Cohens produce a fifth daughter (seventh child), Shirley (Sarah), who later told her son stories of the family's poverty. Since she never had any toys, she used the washboard as a sled. Among all the children, she considered herself her father's favorite.[52] By 1904–05, "Mrs. Anna Cohen, dry goods" is listed at 76 16th Avenue West, and the family's home was also at that same address, since they lived behind the store.

By that time all three of the eldest daughters, although still living at home, were listed separately: Gertrude, then aged twenty, was working as a "bookkeeper" at Clark-MacDonald Co.; Rosa (Rose, spelled to conform to its Yiddish pronunciation), then aged eighteen, was a "clerk" at W. Howard; and Tillie, aged sixteen, did not yet have any listable employment.[53] A sixth daughter, Enid, who was originally called by her Jewish name, Esther, arrived on December 26, 1905. In 1906 Gertrude remained at the same job, but none is listed for

Rosa, while both Tillie and the eldest son, Harry, then nearing his bar mitzvah at age thirteen, are listed as students.[54]

Because Cedar Rapids offered few chances to find Jewish spouses, the three elder daughters dreamed of going to Chicago, the nearest big city. Rose went first (neither she nor Harry is listed as living at home in the U.S. census for 1920). Gertrude and Tillie also moved there on their own, got jobs, looked for husbands, and saved money to move their parents and siblings. At the time Benjamin had other, more pressing responsibilities, including joining together with his elder brothers to bring over their father, Abbe Moishe, and youngest brother, Meyer. Their mother, Chiah Pippa, did not live long enough to leave.[55] One sister, Italaya, married and remained in Lithuania, but Benjamin's two youngest sisters also emigrated.

Not until 1909 did the ninth child and third son arrive—Arthur, on whom his father pinned hopes for continuation of the Cohens' rabbinic tradition. Family lore makes Arthur the smartest of the nine children, but he rebelled early, so much so that Benjamin is said to have chased him around the house with a belt in a futile effort to make him behave.[56] Arthur even refused to attend *kheyder,* the traditional school that taught Hebrew to young boys. The curriculum that he refused was narrowly limited, focusing only on reciting from the Torah. In the context of American life, neither the primitive pedagogical methods—recitations en masse, the drill and repetition of texts—nor the strict discipline appealed.

A hint of what Arthur must have felt comes from an exact contemporary, also the son of an immigrant rabbi: "We had nothing . . . but my father had the Lord, the Lord made him ferocious. Me, I hated the Lord. All I knew was the Lord wouldn't let me play baseball, the Lord wouldn't let me go out with girls, the Lord wouldn't let me *live.*"[57]

In 1913, when the older girls managed to get the entire family to Chicago, the midwestern metropolis was second only to New York in the size of its Jewish population. Crammed tenements teemed with poor immigrants and their progeny, while early skyscrapers marked the city as modern and dynamic. So many Jews from Eastern Europe and even from Lithuania had preceded the Cohens to Chicago that settling there seemed easier, especially after the family had endured the hardships of Topeka and relative isolation of Cedar Rapids. They found lodging at 847 North Oakley Boulevard in the growing Jewish neighborhood of Humboldt Park on the northwest side.[58]

Annie's grandchildren recall that until her death she kept up with the news in the Jewish papers, such as the (Yiddish) Chicago edition of the *Jewish Daily Forward.* Secular influence, so pervasive in popular Yiddish novels during her youth, increased in the new world. Leon Kobrin's novel of Yiddish realism, translated as *A Lithuanian Village,* comments on this phenomenon: "many a maiden, in company with a girl chum, read one of Shomer's or Blaustein's novels, a couple of which had blundered hither from the city and passed from one girl to the other until the leaves were tattered; and once in a while a young man would get hold of it, too. Almost every girl in the village, indeed, had read these novels a couple of times."[59] More prophetic for Annie were Kobrin's words: "Yonder, in that unknown land, the Jew may prosper; he enjoys full rights; there his children may make a place for themselves, both his sons and his daughters."[60] The idea of equality for women was afoot in the Jewish immigrant community and in the Cohen family as young Arthur was growing up.

Political activism and radical politics had long been a tradition for Chicago Jews. In 1917, four years after the Cohens moved there, the city witnessed food riots, as Jewish women organized a boycott on meat and were arrested in front of butcher shops.[61] Jewish labor remained immigrant in composition and "Yiddish in culture."[62] "It seems to me that there is no better thing in the world than a strike," begins a story by Sholem Aleichem, who goes on to compare striking "to the pleasure of walking out on an especially nasty and abusive Hebrew *(kheder)* teacher."[63] In Arthur Cohen's case, the too-strict teacher was his own father.

Rabbi Cohen, by then in his fifties, worked tutoring boys preparing for their bar mitzvahs. Annie, later described by a grandson as shrill but as ever the good provider, made it her business to drum up work for him, whether officiating at circumcision ceremonies or performing weddings and other Jewish rituals.[64] Still, the rabbi struggled to earn enough to support so large a family. He sometimes annoyed his wife by accepting a chicken as payment, as had often been the custom in the old country, rather than insisting on much-needed cash.[65]

Rabbi Cohen's situation improved when the Zechmans, a wealthy family in the lumber business, became so pleased with his work tutoring their three sons that they endowed a small synagogue for him just a block away from their lumberyard: the Grand Avenue Synagogue located at Grand Avenue and Hoyne Avenue on the old West Side, sometimes called "West Town."[66] Orthodox synagogues had to be within walking distance of their members' homes, and many were quite small *shtiebl,* or house synagogues.

Perhaps as much for economic reasons as for their desire to assimilate to the new world, most of the Cohen children rejected their parents' religious orthodoxy.[67] The eldest girls at last began to realize their goal of getting Jewish husbands, first Rose in 1919, at the age of thirty-three. Of all the siblings, only she and Shirley kept kosher homes.[68] Arthur followed his elder brothers, Harry and

Jack, in refusing to continue the family's rabbinical tradition, eventually becoming an atheist.

The Cohen brothers' secular desires reflected the choice of an increasing number of Jewish youth who responded to the forces of socialism and Zionism instead of religion.[69] This generation in Chicago has been called "ignorant of, and largely unsympathetic to, many things Jewish."[70] In their rush to become real Americans, younger immigrants and first-generation Americans were apt to reject religion because they identified it with other trappings of the old country such as the beard, boots, and *kapote* (a long black coat), all of which they quickly discarded.[71] Popular culture, including Yiddish cinema, featured rebellious "jazz babies" who renounced the backwardness of their parents, adopting instead dreams of being American and individual.[72] Those, like Arthur Cohen, who were just entering adulthood at the beginning of the depression, identified with the most exploited workers. They read Langston Hughes and other poets and writers of the Harlem Renaissance, listened to jazz and blues, and longed for a "people's culture."[73]

Despite his sons' rejection of religion, Rabbi Cohen's judgment and wisdom seem to have been respected and appreciated in his family. When his daughter Rose bobbed her hair in the 1920s, her husband Louis was aghast, perhaps anxious that his wife was turning into a flapper with all the loose morals that the style implied. Her father mediated the couple's rift by asking Louis: "Do you cut your hair?" "Well, then," he calmly reasoned with his full rabbinic authority, "she can too."[74]

Nonetheless, the wish to become American, combined with his family's precarious economic existence, served to turn young Arthur away from the orthodox Judaism he knew at home. To a young Jewish man just getting started, synagogues seemed to offer much less hope than the Arbayter Ring (Workman's Circle), founded in Chicago in 1903 as a socialist, anti-Zionist organization closely linked with the Bund in Russia. Also in Chicago, in 1919, when Arthur was only ten, two Communist parties were founded: the Communist Labor Party and the Communist Party of America, making the city a center for immigrants who joined the party, many of them Jews from Eastern Europe.

When Arthur finished high school at the age of sixteen, he had to support himself, for his family was in no position to help him. He continued his education at Crane Technical High School (later called Crane Junior College), part of the city of Chicago's free public education system. On October 1, 1925, when he passed the civil service and physical examinations, he began to work as a substitute postal clerk, working nights at the Chicago Post Office. Until the post office made him a regular clerk in November 1929, he was also working at the

James S. Curts Company, about which nothing is known.[75] Located at Canal and Van Buren, Chicago's post office, said to be the largest in the world, offered tedious jobs sorting and stamping mail. The night shift ended at four-thirty A.M. In 1928 the pay was seventy cents an hour, enabling the worker to earn $5.60 on an eight-hour shift.[76]

Among Arthur Cohen's classmates at Crane High School was Arthur Goldberg, who like him worked nights in the post office but would eventually become a justice on the United States Supreme Court.[77] At the time young people with aspirations who worked nights at the post office dubbed it "the University." Both Cohen and Goldberg grew up in poverty, the youngest children of large immigrant families. More entrepreneurial than Rabbi Cohen, Goldberg's father, a peddler of fruits and vegetables, even bought a blind horse, the only one he could afford, in an effort to enlarge his business.[78] Both of their sons became committed to public service, and their lives would reflect both liberal Jewish social ethics and the intense poverty that they both had experienced in boyhood.

While night work in the post office was a boon to a student working his way through school, it offered little more than steady employment and job security—and even that was threatened in times of economic adversity. Arthur Cohen left no record of what he observed at the post office, but his contemporary, Richard Wright, did. Hired as a substitute clerk at Chicago's central post office in 1929, Wright turned the unpleasant experience of the post office bureaucracy into fiction in his posthumously published novel, *Lawd Today!,* which he submitted to publishers without success between 1935 and 1937: "For eight long hours a clerk's hands must be moving ceaselessly, to and fro, stacking the mail. At intervals a foreman makes rounds of inspection to see that all is going well. Under him works a legion of catfooted spies and stoolpigeons who snoop eternally. Along the walls are slits through which detectives peep and peer."[79] According to Wright, supervisors routinely screamed at clerks, and inspectors further harassed them. From his perspective as an impoverished African-American, he observed how racism and sexism affected the tenor of human relations among workers whom Wright described as "nervously exhausted from years of racking labor."[80] Blacks rarely became supervisors and never over whites. He painted a glum picture indeed: "In the faces and attitudes of the clerks the strain of the workday had begun to tell. Limbs moved with increasing listlessness. Slight puffs appeared beneath eyes that looked out with beaten, hangdog expressions."[81]

So things were already rough when the overwhelming economic downturn began that became the Great Depression. At the time of the stock market crash in October 1929, radical politics made much more sense than religion to Arthur, who was just twenty, and to Wright, just twenty-one, who lost his post office job in 1930 because the volume of mail declined after the crash. The young men struggled for a livelihood in a city and a country coping with anxiety and despair, shaken by loss of jobs, evictions from apartments, and even suicides.[82]

In January 1930 nearly nineteen thousand Chicago municipal employees were working without pay.[83] By April of that year the number of unemployed Chicagoans had grown to 147,440, and others had jobs but were on layoff without pay.[84] That summer five thousand homeless men camped in hobo villages in Chicago, and bread lines and soup kitchens supported by charities fed thousands daily. In October 1931 estimates suggested that 40 percent of those fit for gainful employment lacked work.[85] In January 1933 half of the potentially employable workforce in Chicago was unemployed. In such uncertain times it was ideal to have a paycheck from the federal government.

Fueled by the hardships of economic collapse, the American Communist Party achieved its largest impact during the 1930s. It organized the unemployed, protested evictions and cuts in relief aid, and led hunger marches. The tumult stimulated "a renaissance of American and Jewish radicalism," during which class consciousness and class struggles intensified.[86] Workers joined unions by the millions. In America both the Communist Party and its sympathizers grew in numbers. Those Jews who chose Communism as their vehicle for protest relied upon Jewish identity to attract fellow Jews. Many of the Jewish intellectuals in the party used Yiddish and included Jewish content in their cultural and educational activities.[87]

In 1931 Chicago's Communists led an interracial funeral procession for two black workers who, while protesting an eviction, had become victims of police brutality. Depending on whether the party or the *Chicago Daily News* is accurate, either 60,000 or 15,000 people marched.[88] Many viewed the party as standing for racial justice and the fair treatment of workers, not the overthrow of the United States government. These were the concerns about which Arthur Cohen later spoke to his daughter and which led him to join the Communist Party. Little did he (along with many others) realize at the time that he was exchanging one orthodoxy for another—his father's religion for Marxism. The party's popularity grew during the Popular Front of the late 1930s, especially among intellectuals, artists, and writers.

The workforce at the post office included underemployed intellectuals and aspiring writers, some of whom may have steered Cohen toward Communism, just as fellow postal workers introduced Richard Wright to the party and to the

John Reed Club, a Communist organization for writers and artists.[89] Wright, reluctantly working as a journalist for the party, would write for its newspaper, the *Daily Worker*, in 1937: "There is absolutely no difference between the Negro and white in the Communist Party."[90] In Cohen's milieu, the party seemed to profess the humanistic values that were associated with both his father's yeshiva training and the dominant political and social values of his immigrant neighborhood.

During the 1920s the Communist Party had created the Young Pioneers of America to nurture revolutionary consciousness in children. It is not known if young Arthur attended one of the summer camps under the aegis of the Young Pioneers, but he must have had classmates and neighborhood pals who participated in these free or nearly free two-week summer programs for urban children.[91] During his teens Arthur, like many young people, would have been attracted by the active social life of the Left as much as by its ideology. The Communist Party recruited through local social clubs, folk-dancing societies, musical groups, and affordable vacation resorts.[92] From social activities and friendships forged with those of shared values, it was but a small step to political activism.

Such activism could give hope and purpose even to those forced to live in the poorest of circumstances. Vivian Gornick, who grew up among Communists, has written about the intense passion that Marxism elicited: "Once encountered, in the compelling persona of the Communist Party, the ideology set in motion the most intense longings, longings buried in the unknowing self, longings that pierced to the mysterious, vulnerable heart at the center of that incoherent life within us, longings that had to do with the need to live a life of meaning."[93]

Arthur, hoping to improve the lot of the postal clerks, eventually became an active member of the postal workers' union, known as the National Federation of Post Office Clerks. The empathy for blacks that he later communicated to both his daughter and his nephew may have first developed through friendships made on the job, which occasionally reached across racial lines, for neighborhoods were still segregated in Chicago. The national union held a convention in Chicago in September 1933. At the time there were 15 million unemployed Americans, and postal revenues had fallen by 40 percent. The post office resorted to "payless furloughs" to cope with the shortfalls of funds.[94] Arthur's sister Enid recalled that her youngest brother gave speeches and lectures at union meetings.

Yiddish radicalism was more than a secular religion. It represented "a synthesis of Jewish culture and proletarian politics . . . constructed from the kind of messianic sense of purpose often contained within more conventional Jewish culture."[95] In 1934 Jewish socialists and trade unionists in Chicago formed the Jewish Labor Committee to "acquaint the American labor movement with the plight of European Jews, and impress upon the Jewish masses that they must fight hand in hand with the general forces of democracy."[96] The Jewish Labor Committee's concerns were clearly larger than just the immediate needs of workers in Chicago. This development coincided with the death of Benjamin Cohen at the age of seventy-two. His son Arthur may have rejected his father's religious calling, but not the clear humanitarian goals his father had drawn in his youth from the Mussar movement, his desire to make the world a better place.

Politically aware, Arthur was sensitive not only to economic exploitation but also to the need to fight racism. His sister Enid's son, Howard Rosen, recalls that around 1941 his uncle Arthur, who knew how much he loved baseball, took him to see the Negro League play an "all star game" in Chicago's Comiskey Park. His uncle wanted him to understand how terrible racism was and showed him in a way that he could appreciate: the inequity that prohibited talented African-American athletes from playing major league baseball.

The transition from immigrant rabbi's child to radical was hardly unique to Arthur Cohen. His life fits something of a cultural pattern. For example Anna Rappaport, called "the first woman social poet," was the daughter of a famous rabbi in Kovno who also immigrated to the United States. Forced to go to work in a sweatshop and outraged by the miserable conditions, she became a socialist and wrote Yiddish poetry of the social protest genre. She voiced the frustrations of immigrant Jewish women who struggled to adjust to their lives in a new and terrifying world.[97]

Another child of Jewish immigrants in Chicago, Saul Bellow, just six years younger than Arthur, has recalled how the children "eagerly Americanized themselves. . . . The country took us over. . . . It *was* a country then, not a collection of 'cultures.' We felt to be here was a great piece of luck."[98] But the children of immigrants in his Chicago high school considered themselves Russian as well as American, he said, and while they studied their *Macbeth* and other monuments of English literature, they also read Tolstoy and Dostoyevsky, before inevitably moving on to Lenin's *State and Revolution* and the works of Trotsky.[99]

According to Bellow, his high school's debating club discussed *The Communist Manifesto,* and immigrant intelligentsia populated his neighborhood, lecturing on soapboxes and holding debates among Socialists, Communists, and anarchists that "attracted a fair number of people. This was the beginning of my radical education. For on the recommendation of friends I took up Marx and Engels."[100] Bellow recalled:

> The October Revolution was a great reverberator whose echoes of freedom and justice you could not choose but hear. That revolution was for many decades the most important, most prestigious event in history. Its partisans held that it had brought to an end the most monstrous of wars and that Russia's revolutionary proletariat had made mankind the gift of a great hope. Now the oppressed everywhere, under communist leadership, would destroy capitalist imperialism. In Depression Chicago, boys at heart—and girls as well—were putting their revolutionary thoughts in order. The program was not very clear but the prospect was immensely thrilling.[101]

Soapbox orators, who were Communists, Trotskyists, Socialists, anarchists, and Zionists, thrived in the Jewish neighborhoods where Arthur Cohen and May Levinson grew up. At the Jewish People's Institute in North Lawndale,[102] young people could mingle freely, brought together by their political and personal passions rather than by family. Arthur must have been attracted to May's dancer's figure and to the fiery and creative personality that would go "unfulfilled," as her daughter would later regret.[103]

In the Levinson household, the often-absent father and overburdened mother kept May from fulfilling her desire to dance, although she studied it for a time.[104] One of May's closest girlhood friends, Lela Zimberoff Fizdale, told her daughters how she and May had performed in Chicago with the same modern dance troupe.[105] May told a friend of Judy's, Leoni Zverow, that she and Leoni's mother, Millie, had studied dance together.[106] Because of May's limited finances, she studied at the Jewish People's Institute and took part with Lela and Millie in the institute's performance program for modern dance. There young women raised in Yiddish-speaking homes shared the "burning aspirations for emancipation of the masses and of themselves as artists."[107]

May might also have enrolled in the dance program of the WPA, which in Chicago was under the direction of Ruth Page. In 1934, when Page was ballet director of the Chicago Grand Opera Company, she commissioned music from Aaron Copland for *Hear Ye! Hear Ye!*, a modern ballet that satirized the American justice system. Like Copland and Page, May, Millie, and Lela also shared a strong interest in leftist politics.

The economic crisis during the 1930s took a toll on both May and Arthur despite his job at the post office. Postal workers had to cope with wage cuts and furloughs. From April 1 through November 1, 1937, the young couple were living in one room at the Donmoor Apartment Hotel at 921 West Eastwood Avenue in Chicago; they were evicted for nonpayment of rent, which was only too common at the time. When they managed to establish themselves a few blocks away in an apartment at 940 West Windsor Avenue, off North Clarendon in the uptown district, they began to feel confident enough to think of having the child who arrived in July 1939. In September 1940, however, they relocated to 934 West Windsor Avenue, only to move again in October 1941—less than a mile away to a second-floor apartment at 757 West Bittersweet Place and North Clarendon Avenue, a block north of Irving Park. It was here on the North Side of Chicago, near the lakefront in the Lake View neighborhood, that Judy would live until she left for college. May's mother, Bertha, also lived nearby, until she later moved out to Los Angeles, to be near May's sister, Dorothy.

The Cohens had begun to feel relatively prosperous by the time of Judy's birth, even though the hard times of the Depression dragged on. While Arthur worked nights in the post office, May, having long since tabled her dreams of becoming a dancer, was employed by day as a social worker. Arthur also worked as a labor organizer for the postal workers' union but spent some time at home with his new daughter. His own attitude toward women was a liberal one, in keeping with the American Communist milieu's stated distaste for female oppression. (Despite this open attitude, the Communist working-class papers and magazines were more puritanical than the socialist papers, which carried more sensuous stories.) Nonetheless, in the 1930s women writers in radical circles began to attack discrimination against them in their own organizations.[108]

Arthur did not approve of May staying home after the baby arrived. He had married an independent woman and thought that she should resume working. He told her that she was becoming boring, "because all she could talk about was the baby."[109] When he got off work in the middle of the night, he began to hang out with musicians, prostitutes, and others on the fringes of society. He also visited a woman friend who was a psychiatrist and who, he claimed, was "intellectually stimulating."[110] This upset May so much that she returned to work. Judy recalls: "My first memory is when I was a year and a half old. I see myself in my crib red-faced and crying, and my mother, dressed in a navy blue suit and matching beret, going out the door, despite my screaming protests. My mother went back to work that day."[111]

To look after Judy, the Cohens hired an African-American woman by the name of Oradie Blue. Her name prompted Judy's father to create the following story, which he repeated to her as he bounced her on his knees: "Oradie Blue was walking down the street and met John Green. Then they continued walking together and met Norman White, to whom they talked for a while. Then Oradie Blue and Norman White left John Green and went to a restaurant where they met Mary Black," etc. The purpose of his story, as she sees it, was to help her "understand that color was not a significant factor in dealing with people."[112]

Judy did not talk until she was two and a half years old, raising concerns in her parents, who were both very verbal. But after this delay, she recalled, "I learned early the value that my parents placed on talking, and after my reluctant beginning, began to talk in such a way that grownups always remarked at my precociousness, which pleased my parents enormously."[113] Her parents did not send her to nursery school (although their friends the Zverows sent their daughter Leoni to the school affiliated with the Jewish People's Institute, which included Yiddish culture in its curriculum, teaching the children Yiddish songs and how to read and write Yiddish letters).

On her own Judy began drawing when she was three (Figure 1). Proud of her daughter's artistic talent, her mother saved finger paintings that Judy did at the age of five. One is clearly a landscape, but another, called *Fun in the Sun,* depicts a figure jumping over a rock. The ability to represent movement was rather advanced at such a young age. Impressed, May arranged to borrow a friend's membership card and took her daughter to the large classes for parents and young children offered to members by the Art Institute of Chicago. Judy boasts: "I took the No. 53 bus to the Art Institute, started going when I was five. I always wanted to be an artist—never wanted to be anything else."[114] She has recalled how as a child "I drew in the air while I stared at faces on the bus, as if trying to trace out the people I saw around me."[115] Her ambition was already formed. Since her mother valued her artistic efforts, Judy looked to May for affirmation, but she brought her intellectual achievements to her father.

The Cohens were "very casual about nudity," and at the age of two or three Judy took baths with her father. She once pointed to his penis and exclaimed, "When I grow up, I'm going to have one of those." He laughed and said, "Yes, if you're a good girl, you'll have one of those. If you're a bad girl, you'll have a lot of them." Arthur liked to repeat this story to his friends in his daughter's presence, which she interpreted as an attempt to make her "feel guilty about wanting to be like my father."[116]

Judy described herself as having been "a chubby, cheerful little girl," who "retained a certain naiveté, despite the fact that I learned to perform intellectually and charmingly, in response to grownups' expectations. . . . I guess that I learned this way of performing from my mother, who, even now [in 1971–73] performs for everybody, particularly men, always showing off and flirting."[117]

Evidently her father liked to show off her mother, whom Judy describes as "a very attractive woman." Her parents dancing together at home, while singing, "My Sweet Little Alice Blue Gown," left a lasting impression on the little girl. The lyrics of this song, from the long-running Broadway musical *Irene,* describe a dress in a new fashion, so beloved that it was literally worn to shreds. The song appealed to the couple who scraped by on a very modest income, metaphorically reinforcing the lasting mutuality of their love:

'Til it wilted, I wore it,
I'll always adore it.[118]

Judy's father danced with her too, when she was only about three, by having her place her tiny feet on top of his. "I was so proud of him, especially when he did the Charleston for me," she remembered.[119]

The birth on February 22, 1945, of her brother, Ben, when Judy was five and a half, made a lasting impression: "I remember the day when my mother brought him home from the hospital . . . red-faced and screaming, on my parents' big bed, which, every Sunday afternoon, I claimed as my own when my father and I listened to radio programs like *The Shadow* and *The FBI in Peace and War.* That was my favorite time of the week."[120] Another time she recalled how she liked to listen on her parents' "big bed" to the radio program *The Lone Ranger* on Sunday nights with her father.[121] These rituals were disrupted by the new arrival. As she put it: "My brother's birth marked a change in my home life. He was born with a vestigial stomach, which made it impossible for him to eat, and his frequent crying made life very difficult for all of us."[122]

From Judy's vantage point, her father appeared to reject his son, who had to contend with being her younger brother and was continually compared to her. "The result was a developing alienation between us," she remarked of her brother.[123] She associated her brother's birth with memories of her parents' arguments and discord, as if her life too were being disrupted, only to understand years later that other, more complex issues were involved. Evidently Arthur had not wanted to have a second child but May had insisted upon it.[124] The family named the baby after Arthur's father, Benjamin, but called him Bobby in memory of a young cousin who died during the war.

The wartime aims of the United States and the Soviet Union converged in the desire to stop Hitler. As a result, the American Communist Party reached a new peak in membership, which, however, was to be short-lived. Taking its cues from Stalin's diplomatic maneuvers, the American Communist Party (CPUSA) actually dissolved itself into the Communist Political Association in 1944, while its leader, Earl Browder, preached class collaboration. If workers' demands clashed with the war effort, the Communists saw to it that the workers deferred.[125] There was, however, an intense debate in 1945 Chicago over the membership of the Chicago Civil Liberties Committee, which though affiliated with the American Civil Liberties Union was at the same time an autonomous group. The national organization of the ACLU accused the Chicago group of partisanship and Communist leanings, threatening it with expulsion.[126] Such was the deep animosity between adherents of Communism and others.

Between 1946 and 1949 the CPUSA gradually changed its position that working-class women were the only women who suffered oppression. Like feminist organizations of the day, the CPUSA accepted the idea that women's oppression affected all women, without regard to class or color.[127] At the same time, it argued that gender oppression was not the only cause of women's problems. The party specifically tried to redress the problems of black women.[128] From reading leftist literature, Arthur and May Cohen were both aware of all of these issues, which on some level they communicated to their daughter.

Judy had once felt "protected from all but the emotional ramifications of the events in my parents' lives. To me, it meant, at the age of five or six, the introduction of tensions, arguments, and difficulties that were unknown to me as a young child."[129] She later reflected: "Very early in my life, I developed a compensatory personality, one which performed & pirouetted & 'came on strong' because my parents needed that."[130] Her cousin, Howard Rosen, who is nine years older than Judy, recalls that when his family moved into a new neighborhood on Chicago's West Side, May and Arthur arrived to visit, bringing along five-year-old Judy, who was so outgoing and friendly that she introduced him to everyone in his own neighborhood.

Judy's gregariousness enabled her to embrace both school and other social experiences. "I was urged to talk when I was a child, I learned to leave my body & ascend into the stratosphere of words."[131] Her emphasis on words paid off at the local public school, Le Moyne Elementary, where she excelled.[132] Her positive outlook was reinforced at the time of her sixth birthday, which she spent "at a college where my father was teaching a course in Union Organizing. The entire school celebrated my birthday in the cafeteria and I felt myself to be a fortunate child to have such as famous father."[133]

Daddy's Little Girl

2

May and Arthur marked every Fourth of July by going to a fireworks display in a big stadium. One year the Brazilian samba star Carmen Miranda, who brought the exoticism of South America to North American wartime audiences, made a big impression on little Judy. She later recalled her delight at Miranda's "flowered, feathered, and fruited costumes."[1] After the fireworks she always relished the union dinners, where she and her family "stuffed ourselves with kosher food."[2] Since they did not own a car, streetcar rides also became an occasion for amusement, when the family "played games, identifying objects on the street, counting animals, cars, people."[3]

Judy wrote that her parents "basically rejected all things Jewish," adding, "I

▲
Arthur Cohen in a festive costume.

learned less than nothing about Jewish history and culture from my parents."[4] Yet the Cohens' milieu among leftist intellectuals was populated by Jews, including their close friends Isadore and Millie Zverow, who were planning to name their daughter Leni, for Lenin. After the Hitler-Stalin Non-Aggression Pact of 1939, the Zverows decided that "Leni" was too similar to the name of Hitler's filmmaker, Leni Riefenstahl, and called her Leoni instead.[5]

While admitting the lack of Jewish ritual at home, Chicago insisted: "I was raised in a household shaped by what might be called Jewish ethical values, particularly the concept of *tikkun,* the healing or repairing of the world."[6] The legacy of her paternal grandfather's rabbinical training and values did not go the way of ritual observance, although through her extended family and her mostly Jewish classmates at Le Moyne Elementary School Judy experienced Jewish observance, culture, and ritual. Speaking of two classmates named Sandra, one Jewish and one not, she noted: "That was a big thing when I was growing up—the difference between Jews & Gentiles."[7]

Her father told her proudly that the family had the "blue blood" of her ancestor, the Vilna *gaon,* making a strong impact on his daughter: "Totally devoted to my father, I believed him & was mortified when I bled common red when I first cut myself."[8]

The Jewish community in Vilna had a rich tradition, even before the eighteenth century and the *gaon,* who himself came from a famous rabbinical and scholarly family. Learned in the religious texts of the Torah and the Talmud, the *gaon* gained renown for emending ancient texts, correcting errors of transcription, and vigorous teaching; he dealt also with secular subjects, including grammar, science, and mathematics, although Eastern European Jewry showed as yet virtually no secularizing influence. The enlightenment movement, Haskalah, arose only toward the end of his life and in distant Berlin.[9] The scholarly *gaon* opposed the Hasidim, a movement emphasizing the primacy of prayer and mysticism over rigorous study that began in Poland during the century's second half. Encouraged by the *gaon,* the Vilna community issued a document in 1772 attempting to excommunicate the Hasidim, complaining that they "behave in a crazed manner . . . belittle study of the Torah . . . And while standing during their false prayers, [they] voice sounds that are different, and there is a loud commotion in the town."[10]

At a time when many women received no formal education, the *gaon,* five of whose eight children were daughters, urged that fathers "train" their daughters, who should read "moral books," especially on the Sabbath, and that women see that their sons attended school.[11] Advising men to make only brief visits to the synagogue, the *gaon* preferred praying at home in order "to escape envy and the hearing of idle talk," warning: "It is also better for your daughter not to go to synagogue, for there she would see garments of embroidery and similar finery. She would grow envious and speak of it at home, and out of this would come scandal and other ills."[12]

The *gaon*'s renown as a sage helped make Vilna an important intellectual center, indeed "the heart of all of Belorussian and Lithuania Jewry."[13] But the citizens of Vilna were soon subject to growing Russian dominance, which led to the partition of Poland and Lithuania. In October 1795, after the Russians defeated a Polish uprising, Vilna and Kovno came under Russian rule. Because of its importance, Vilna was early to attract adherents of the Haskalah, who reached the city by the 1840s.[14] Some historians have indeed viewed the *gaon* as a harbinger of the Haskalah movement in Eastern Europe.[15] But for Judy, the *gaon* stood only for the impressive aura surrounding her ancestor, motivating her to set a goal for her own ambition in life.

"Being Jewish for me was always identified with high aspirations, which for me was expressed through artistic achievement," she would comment. "I was not oppressed as a child as a girl; in my family there was a lot of respect for being smart, and it did not matter what gender I was, and I was a smart kid. I know there have been a lot of stories about how patriarchal Judaism is and how many women have felt very oppressed by it. That was not my experience. I have always felt very connected as a Jew—connected to the cultural and intellectual tradition, to the fights for social justice in which so many Jews participate."[16]

"The discussions & ideas of my childhood are more vivid than any of the matzoh ball soup. My father may have rejected the rabbinic pulpit but he was Jewish to the core. His worldview, his values, & his political ideals were rooted in Tikkun & he passed that on to me. In certain ways I had no choice in what I became—it is interesting to me now to examine those parts of my identity that have to do with being a Jew," she commented, after reading an editorial in a new magazine called *Tikkun.*[17]

Jewish religious ritual and culture were conspicuous in Judy's extended family. She recalls that her father's was "a large quarrelsome family" and that they visited one or another of her father's sisters regularly.[18] She remembers that her aunt Rose and uncle Louie ran a kosher noodle truck.[19] Typical meals of Eastern European Jewish cooking featured "boiled chicken, matzoh ball soup, and my favorite, vanilla pudding with frozen strawberries, served by my aunt Rose, whose hand shook so nervously that, when she served the soup, I always expected a catastrophe."[20]

Speaking of her father's sister Shirley and her husband, Herman, Judy recalls: "We always had Passover seders at their house. He was stern & overly serious & insisting [sic] on droning away over every page of the Haggadah. As the evening grew late & everyone became bleary-eyed not to mention starving, my aunt would stand behind her husband, trying to skip pages so we'd be done sooner & able to eat the chopped liver, matzohs & matzoh ball soup & of course roast chicken she'd worked on cooking all day."[21]

Although her parents never once lit a candle for the Jewish Sabbath, the Cohens celebrated Christmas with a large family party until she was eight. May had observed Christmas since her childhood, because her family lived in "a gentile neighborhood" and her mother did not want her children to feel excluded. They filled stockings with oranges and treats.[22] After May and Arthur married, she asked if she could buy Christmas gifts for his sister Enid's children, Howard and Corinne. Since he did not mind, their Christmas celebrations began.

Some years later, at the insistence of one of her aunts, who still maintained a kosher home, Christmas was banned and replaced with Hanukkah, which, according to Judy, "was never as much fun . . . At the Christmas parties, everyone would bring presents, which made a big heap on the floor, and as my father read the tags, I would deliver them, squealing with excitement."[23] Later she wondered whether the cessation of observing Christmas "had anything to do with the Holocaust and my parents having to face their Jewishness in a rather overwhelming way."[24]

When the Cohen cousins were celebrating Christmas, their grandfather, Rabbi Benjamin, was long dead—he died in 1934, five years before Judy's birth; but she well remembers his widow, Annie, who lived until 1950 and was an important presence in her life. Judy very strongly recalls her grandmother's strength in the large family and the fact that all of Annie's nine children called her every day. Judy used to travel with her parents by streetcar to visit Grandmother Annie, who lived on the West Side of Chicago with her aunt Molly, who never married. Her grandmother called Judy by her Yiddish name, Yudit Sipke.[25]

Despite her grandmother's Yiddishkeit, Judy, especially between the ages of six and nine, found Christmas and all things Christian very attractive. For three years she had a crush on Charles, a little Catholic boy who lived in the neighborhood. She once accompanied him to church and then began to emulate his Catholicism, praying in her room and kneeling while listening to sermons on the radio, a practice she soon abandoned only because it was "too hard on my knees."[26] She recalled the abrupt end of the friendship: "He locked me in a car and tried to molest me. I screamed and cried and threatened to tell his mother.

He finally relented and let me go. I went home and just stopped playing with him. I never told my mother what had happened. When he grew up, Charles became a priest."[27]

When she was nine, Judy recalls, she heard about sex for the first time, although her mother insisted that she had explained the facts of life to her when she was only six. The informant she remembered was her close friend and neighbor across the street, Paula Levine, who was then eleven. A third girlfriend mentioned the word *rape* in their presence, and Judy demanded to know what it meant. To explain the violent concept, Paula used the word *fuck,* which she also had to define for her younger friend: "when a man puts his thing in your thing." Judy reflected later that Paula thoughtfully added: "People do it when they love each other."[28]

In 1947, when Judy was eight, May enrolled her in the Art Institute's Junior School.[29] The teacher was Emanuel Jacobson, whom Judy adored. He held off beginning "classical training" until students were at least eleven, because he wanted to avoid inhibiting the child's natural creative impulse. Judy enthusiastically advanced to this classical training by Jacobson, whose instruction included "rigorous training" in anatomy, still-life drawing, and the study of both human and animal bones, the latter through regular trips to the Field Museum of Natural History.[30] Judy remembers that as a child she painted and drew realistically.[31] *Bittersweet* (Figure 2), a painting that she made at the age of nine, indicates her early proficiency. Depicting the vista from her family's apartment on Bittersweet, it presents a bird's-eye view with a lively play of sunlight and deep shadows cast by the massive structures and shows that she had already acquired an understanding of linear perspective.

Already in September 1950, just after her eleventh birthday, the School of the Art Institute sent a letter to Judy Cohen, telling her: "Your work as a student in the Junior School was given an Honorable Mention by your teacher. This is a high honor which is given only to a few of the outstanding students in each class."[32] A drawing (Figure 3) from this time shows her command of composition and ability to render figures. Although she already planned to become an artist, she later recalled how she had "vowed allegiance to Miss Sypes, the fat, gray-haired teacher [at Le Moyne Elementary School] whose skirts rustled when she walked, and . . . promised to become a fifth and sixth grade teacher."[33]

Despite such avowals to her teacher, she never gave up her dream of life as an artist. This goal was reinforced by frequent letters of praise from the Art Institute, which survive from the autumn of 1951 and from 1956, when she again received an honorable mention in two classes.[34] In March 1956 a letter from the Junior School of the Art Institute informed her: "You have been awarded a scholarship in the Junior School on the sketchbook that you submitted . . . only three sketchbooks of the students in the Junior School were selected."[35] The award of seventeen dollars covered full tuition for one term of Saturday classes.

Classes in the institute's Junior School were much more professional than is usual for children's instruction. Jacobson held art history lectures in Gunsaulus Hall, where his pupils studied works of art firsthand. Other Junior School classes included general drawing and painting, outdoor sketching, figures and faces, and people and their clothes. Jacobson would use Judy's work to "exemplify what he wanted to teach," recalled Judy's classmates, Leoni Zverow and Esther Boroff.[36] One among those who preceded Judy in studying at the Junior School and later made a name for himself was Walt Disney, whose success would enable him to fund a new private art school, the California Institute of the Arts, which would later mark a turning point in Judy's career.[37]

Art was not Judy's only interest, for at this time she also found her first boyfriend, the bespectacled Sandy Kornbluth, who was, like her, a very good student in their seventh-grade class at Le Moyne. He took her to the Chicago Theater to see a movie with a stage show, and during the movie, he put his arm around her, giving her the sensation of "a burning ember" on her shoulders. She was anxious, she said, that people there might see and think she was "a terrible girl, because, despite my parents' liberal attitudes, I had remained very naive about sex."[38]

Along with her impressions of stirring sexuality and her pleasure in the new art lessons, Judy had her first encounter with death. She was nine when her father's oldest brother, Uncle Harry, died at only fifty-five. The family had traveled to southern Illinois to visit him when he was very ill and was paralyzed by Lou Gehrig's disease. She recalls that her aunt made her kiss her sick uncle and that he died the very next day.[39] Her cousin Howard remembers that his mother (Enid) attributed blame for her older brother's death to her sister-in-law, who had cooked lobster although Jewish dietary laws held that it was not fit to eat.[40]

Another trauma loomed, although she would learn about its full dimensions from her mother only years later. In 1946, when she was only six, she was briefly at home alone with her infant brother when an FBI agent dropped by. Before he could question her about her father's friends and activities, her mother suddenly returned and chased him away.[41] The unwelcome visit was an early instance of the American obsession with domestic Communism. This fixation began during the early years of the Cold War and, according to one historian, "outran the actual threat and gnawed at the tissue of civil liberties."[42]

For many of Arthur Cohen's generation, the stock market crash of 1929 and the ensuing Great Depression raised doubts about the validity of capitalism and made the professed idealism of Communism seem compelling and attractive. Making money had never really engaged Judy's father, any more than it had his father before him; Arthur also inherited his father's intelligence and love of history (in the view of his doting sisters, as reported by their children, his nieces and nephew).[43] His wife, years later, would ruefully reflect: "My husband was a very smart man. He tried to teach me not to cling to 'ephemeral things'. We fought about that."[44]

"My parents' politics were extremely left wing," Chicago would later write, "although how radical I only knew when I was twelve or thirteen years old. They had been involved in radical politics throughout the thirties and early forties. . . . Shortly after my brother's birth, my parents began to be harassed for their political activities."[45]

At the same time her father's progressive beliefs were shaping Judy's own later concern with women's rights: "There was an expressed commitment to equal rights for women, something I not only heard stated but saw demonstrated by the way in which my father always made sure to include the women in these lively discussions. Moreover, I saw it manifested in the way he treated me."[46] She remembers listening at home to heated political discussions in which her older cousin, Corinne Rosen, took part and had her ideas accepted: "The passion of these discussions shaped my idea of the human condition and the complicated notion that the world could be changed was embedded in my earliest memories."[47] She recalls that her childhood was filled with "parties for various causes, including the Spanish Civil War. People of all races mingled in our second-floor apartment to engage in near-constant political arguments."[48]

During the Spanish Civil War, which began in 1936, the U.S. Congress, in an isolationist response, enacted an embargo on arms sales to any nation involved in a war. Prominent among those who volunteered to fight, joining the Abraham Lincoln Brigade, or who raised large sums of money for humanitarian and technical assistance to the Spanish Loyalists, were Communists, who opposed the extreme nationalists led by the Spanish army general Francisco Franco and backed by Nazi Germany and Mussolini's Italy.[49] For a number of Jewish intellectuals, their main reason for volunteering for the Lincoln Brigade was their hatred of Hitler and his support for Franco. Judy's cousin Julien Schwartz remembers his uncle Arthur talking to him about the Spanish Civil War and believes that he would have gone over to fight had he not been married.[50]

Just a month after Judy's birth in July 1939, the Hitler-Stalin Non-Aggression Pact was signed. Some Jews refused to support the pact, while others, like Cohen (at least according to accusations gathered by the FBI) remained loyal to the party.[51] At the time loyal Communist Party members understood that

Britain's Neville Chamberlain had made a pact with Hitler in Munich in 1938, sacrificing Czechoslovakia, which some argued was necessary to save Western civilization because Britain was not yet prepared to go to war and would have lost to the Nazis had it done so then. Likewise, Stalin needed time to shore up Soviet defenses against the anticipated attack from Hitler. The American Communists rationalized the shock of making a pact with an anti-Communist fascist as realpolitik, the diplomatic philosophy that puts national interest ahead of idealism. The twenty months gained enabled the Soviets to mobilize against the Nazis' June 1941 invasion. When Hitler invaded Poland from the West in September 1939, the Soviet Union was able to invade from the East, forestalling the Germans' organized death camps in the Eastern section.[52]

Cohen's support for the underdog, for the common man, extended to his workplace. He served as a "member of the Grievance Committee of the Post Office Clerks Union, American Federation of Labor."[53] "During the dark years of 1932 to 1935 . . . under the impact of 15 percent wage cuts, furloughs, mass layoffs of subs, and the shattering effects of the depression, badly worried postal employees were naturally susceptible to the will-o'-the-wisp lure of ONE BIG UNION," states the official history of the National Federation of Post Office Clerks, which was written in 1945, after the war, when the United States turned its attention to the threat of Communism. This account, notable for its shrill tone and transparent anti-Communism, tells how in 1935 "all revolutionary paper unions were to be liquidated and their members ordered back into the A.F. of L. once more to 'bore from within.' "[54]

This same official publication attacked "the unsavory activities of the Communists in the postal unions," warning: "They will ceaselessly carry on every variety of communist work, forcing open and unadulterated communist propaganda down the throats of uninterested workers at every opportunity and yet if called Communists they will fly into well simulated anger and offended dignity and denounce their accusers as 'vicious company spies, fascists, and red-baiters.' "[55]

The next year, during the 1946 midterm election campaign, the national Republican Party successfully raised the specter of a Democratic administration in alliance with the forces of Communism. Right-wing crusades sought to stir up anti-Communist rhetoric during these early days of the Cold War. They saw an opportunity to exploit the new "Red Scare" in the presidential election coming up in 1948.

The FBI had geared up to combat "subversives" at home, especially within the federal government, maintaining that individual Communists might conduct espionage, influence policy, or bring other "subversives" into the government.[56] J. Edgar Hoover, as director of the FBI, sought to convince President

Harry S. Truman who had assumed office after Franklin Delano Roosevelt's death on April 12, 1945, of the internal dangers that the American Communist Party posed for the United States. Hoover argued against the establishment of even minimal safeguards to protect accused employees, insisting that "the Bureau has steadfastly refused to reveal the identities of its confidential informants" or its methods of "technical surveillances."[57]

Truman, aware that the new Republican majority in Congress would try to exploit the anti-Communist tide and that public pressure to stop government infiltration by Communists was mounting, issued a series of executive orders that were intended to quell this fear. On March 21, 1947, he signed Executive Order 9835, which declared that federal employees must have "complete and unswerving loyalty to the United States."[58] This decree gave the FBI the authority to check all current civil servants for indications of possible "disloyalty," although loyalty was never defined. The Civil Service Commission vetted only the loyalty of prospective employees, while all current civil service employees, even postal workers, were directly subjected to scrutiny by the FBI.

All employees considered "disloyal" could be dismissed not just for committing sabotage, espionage, treason, or some other menacing offense but also for being affiliated with any group "designated by the Attorney General as totalitarian, fascist, communist, or subversive."[59] To enforce Executive Order 9835, the attorney general drew up a list of ninety "subversive" organizations, which was made public and would grow within three years to nearly two hundred.[60] Affiliation with any of these organizations was tantamount to guilt by association. Even innocently joining a group that might have subsequently become Communist was dangerous.[61] With the announcement of this list, public anxiety gained momentum.

Historians of the period have noted that even one's reading became fair game for the loyalty boards, as did the ownership of recordings of music by Russian composers. The fact that the accusers remained anonymous made refuting charges very difficult. FBI files collected gossip, often malicious, from coworkers or neighbors. Those who might tattle to the FBI included rivals at work, jilted lovers, or neighbors outraged by parties to which they were not invited or where people of other races showed up.

Cohen became caught up in this investigation of the loyalty of federal employees almost as soon as it began in 1947. Critics of this program pointed out that the hearings were held in secret without a public record; that "the accused persons could not directly cross-examine informants," who were not identified and did not testify under oath; that local review boards often demonstrated racial or religious bias; and that "the program inhibited free thinking and expression by Federal employees."[62]

FBI records show that Arthur Cohen was a clerk in the Outgoing Mails Division of the Main Post Office in Chicago in August 1946, when the following letter arrived:

> As a good American citizen, I feel it is my duty to let you know of the activities of one of our supposed good Chicago peoples, who is nothing but a rank Communist.
>
> I wish to make a report on Arthur M. Cohen, 757 W. Bittersweet, Chicago, Illinois, a permanent employee of the United States Government Post Office, in the new building, who carries on Communist meetings in his home, is an active member of the organization, who has books upon books based upon Communism in his home, and yet works for the Post Office in a high position, and is a representative of the Union there, sent on trips for the Union, paid for by the U.S. Government.
>
> It would pay you gentlemen to investigate this person, who is in disguise an enemy of our country, and yet is permitted to have a wonderful job, while many of our wounded war veterans can obtain nothing, and are true Americans, while a good for nothing Communist is allowed to ruin our Country, and our government.[63]

The letter was signed, "A true American mother, who lost two sons in the war, one in France, and one at Iwo Jima."

In the copy of the letter released by the FBI, the woman's signature has been censored, but the text invites inferences as to her motives—a possible combination of anti-Communist hysteria, jealousy, racial or ethnic prejudice, and personal animus in someone familiar enough with the post office to be a fellow worker and with Cohen's home life to be an acquaintance. No doubt she was emboldened by the new executive order that aimed to destroy "Communist and subversive influence in the nation."[64] The FBI's investigation of Cohen later stated, "The Communist Party, formerly known as the Communist Political Association, is an organization designated by the Attorney General of the United States on November 24, 1947, as coming within the purview of Executive Order 9835." The agency also noted that Cohen had not signed a "Loyalty Form."

According to the FBI, the Chicago Police Department, Industrial Division, had recorded that Cohen was a member of the Robert Morse Lovett Branch of the American League for Peace and Democracy during April–June 1940.[65] Yet the American League for Peace and Democracy had dissolved after Stalin and Hitler signed their nonaggression pact in 1939.[66] A registration card dated

January 22, 1945, obtained by the FBI "from a confidential and reliable informer," lists Cohen as a member of the 48th Ward Club of the Communist Political Association, a member of the American Federation of Labor, and a subscriber to the *Daily Worker,* described by the FBI as "an East Coast daily Communist newspaper."[67]

Following the August letter, in December 1946, the FBI's "confidential and reliable informant" advised that Cohen was a member of the "Enlarged Labor Commission of the Communist Party, District 8." As a result, the FBI interviewed his fellow employees and neighbors, most of whom believed him to be "loyal to the U.S. Government."

One coworker, who claimed to know Cohen for about a year, reported that he had heard Cohen say that "the United States is the best country in the world and that he would never want to see Communism in the United States." But the same person also claimed that Cohen had "made statements criticizing the public newspapers because he believed that the newspapers were attempting to place Communism in an unfavorable light in the United States." That talkative employee also noted that Cohen had since "changed his position in that regard since that time and is now 'all out for the United States and its policies.' "

Another employee interviewed alleged that the "general tone" of Cohen's statements indicated to him that his fellow worker "was not in favor of Communism or had ever been a member of the Communist Party." Still another coworker stated that he believed Cohen "to be a 'leftist,' meaning that he 'acted and spoke like a Communist'; however, he was unable to point to any specific statements or actions of the employee during the years that he has known him other than his general association with" another worker, who was evidently either also suspect or under investigation.

A coworker, who reported having heard "continuous statements favoring the Russian system, stated that he believed Cohen was a Communist but had no positive proof." Others suspected that Cohen was a Communist. One advised that though he could not recall Cohen declaring that he was a Communist, based upon their conversations and "in view of the books which he knew Cohen had read, as well as the associates which Cohen had at his residence in 1939 or 1940, there was no doubt in my mind that Cohen was a Communist when I knew him, and I believe that he was a Party 'card holder' although I never saw a Party Card."

Most neighbors interviewed maintained that Cohen seemed to be "loyal to the U.S. Government." One, however, volunteered that although she believed that Cohen was loyal to the United States, he was "a liberal" and had "campaigned for certain Progressive candidates who were running for political office." She explained to the inquiring FBI agent that by "Progressive" she meant "candidates who were in favor of social changes."

The pursuit of Cohen coincided with the campaign leading up to the 1948 national election. The American Communist Party, which supported Henry Wallace's newly established Progressive Party against President Truman (who would surprise the pollsters and defeat Dewey), included in its platform the complaint that the nation faced "instead of greater democracy . . . mounting Jim-Crowism and anti-Semitism, and a conspiracy to undermine our sacred democratic heritage. We have anti-Communist witch hunts, the arrest and conviction of anti-fascist leaders, the harassment and intimidation of writers, artists and intellectuals. We have phony spy scares, the hounding of government employees."[68]

Arthur Cohen was one of those hounded. But the FBI ended its investigation of him on December 27, 1948, with the conclusion "that the examination of the Bureau's reports . . . failed to disclose any available evidence of a violation of Title 18, Section 1001 (18 USC 80, 1946 Ed.), or any other federal statute. In the circumstances the Department is closing its file, subject to reopening in the event additional information so warranting is received."[69] Yet, on October 14, 1949, Seth W. Richardson, the chairman of the Loyalty Review Board of the U.S. Civil Service Commission, reported to FBI director J. Edgar Hoover that Arthur M. Cohen had resigned from his federal job.

Cohen had been continually tormented by the specter of anti-Communist witchhunts fomented by the House Committee on Un-American Activities, and according to his daughter, he was "driven out of the union by the threat of an investigation that would probably have resulted in a jail sentence"; in short, he was "forced out of the post office and the union work he loved."[70] Deprived of his livelihood, Cohen was reduced to an uncertain income as a life insurance salesman, working on a commission basis.

As late as October 16, 1951, the Chicago Police Department reported to the FBI on an investigation on Cohen that they had just conducted. The report lists his wife and inaccurately gives the ages of their two children, "a daughter about ten years old, and a son about eight years old." The same report notes that "an anonymous source who has furnished reliable information in the past, advised on May 3, 1946, that MAE [May] COHEN, 757 Bittersweet, was a member of the 48th Ward Club of the CP [Communist Party]." This report concludes that "there is insufficient information to place COHEN on the SI [Security Index] of this office. This case will be placed in a closed status and in the event additional pertinent information is received, the Bureau and interested offices will be advised."[71]

With hindsight, Judy has attributed her parents' arguments to "their differing opinions as to how this situation should be handled." Relatives have since explained that her father "wanted to fight openly against the threats, even to the point of going to jail, if necessary." This conflicted with her mother's plea that he "should consider his wife and children and be responsible" to their needs.[72] Perhaps May worried that they might both end up in prison, leaving the children at the mercy of relatives. Eventually between six thousand and nine thousand government employees were fired under the loyalty programs and at least eight thousand, like Cohen, were driven to resign. Only three went to prison, but at least seven others were driven to suicide.[73]

Before the FBI's investigation, Arthur and May Cohen had made no attempt to conceal their political beliefs. Not only the books they read but even the art they displayed at home revealed their leftist sympathies. "I knew that I wanted to be an artist, and I used to look a lot at two reproductions of paintings by Diego Rivera that were hanging in my house," Judy recalled. "I think his round shapes affected my concept of form, but at that time, I just looked at them often."[74] Only later did Judy realize that the Rivera reproductions "reflected my parents' political and moral committments [sic] and that my father was undergoing a personal tragedy which reflected a period in America in which hundreds of people were suffering for their humanity and their beliefs."[75] The Cohens certainly would have known of the notorious destruction of Rivera's mural for Rockefeller Center because he refused to remove the image of Lenin. One suspects that they also knew that Rivera was considered a "fallen Communist" who had allied himself with the anti-Stalinist Trotsky and the "October" group of artists who defended Trotsky's dissident point of view.[76] In January 1928 Rivera had been in Moscow to celebrate the tenth anniversary of the October Revolution, and while he was there, Stalin expelled Trotsky from the party; the Latin American secretariat of the Comintern ordered Rivera back to Mexico that April.[77]

Rivera was not the only visual artist on the Left whose work Judy saw growing up. If, in fact, the Cohens subscribed to the *Daily Worker,* Judy would have read its comics, such as *Pinky Rankin,* whose eponymous hero taught the lessons of Socialism to fellow workers and others.[78] Her parents counted in their circle of friends Mitchell Siporin (1910–76), a social realist painter, illustrator, and muralist for the Federal Art Project. Siporin was her parents' contemporary and had, like Arthur, attended Crane Junior College, where they probably met. Like them, he was born to Jewish immigrant working-class parents and raised in Chicago; his father, a labor organizer, must have influenced his own politically charged work.

The political fallout that Judy experienced as a child sometimes confused her. "When I was about ten [in 1949]," she has recalled, "I began to find my father at home when I returned from school, sitting in the rust-colored chair, dressed in a bathrobe, with his white legs protruding, smoking Chesterfields, reading or listening to the radio. I didn't know why he was home, but I knew that other fathers didn't do that."[79] His behavior began to cause her anxiety: "I began to think that there was something wrong with him, especially when I overheard my aunts talking to him or my mother, implying that my father's statements about not feeling well . . . were not true. All this made me doubt my father, but at the same time, I loved him deeply, and at school I began to say 'My father thinks this' and 'my father thinks that,' as if to reinforce his declining authority."[80]

Arthur Cohen was suffering from depression. Having resigned his job and feeling excluded from all work that was consequential to him, he had also developed stomach ulcers. Although the date he left the Communist Party remains uncertain, that break, along with his inability to work as a labor organizer, must have represented a loss of meaning in his life. Another former Communist put it this way: "the day I left the Communist Party was a very sad one for me. It was like a day of deep mourning, the mourning I felt for my lost youth."[81]

The tensions of such persecution and the loss of his job did not help Cohen's health. Just before he was scheduled to go to the hospital for an operation for his stomach pain, he took his adolescent daughter aside to tell her about his political identity, asking her if she knew what a Communist was. He explained to her that Communists were trying to improve the world. He spoke that night "about his desire to change the condition of black people in America, to abolish poverty, to expand educational opportunities for poor people, and to try to make the place he worked more humane."[82] He then informed her that he was a Communist and asked her if she believed that all Communists were "bad." Despite the horrific depictions of Communists shown "bayoneting handsome American boys" that she saw at school in *My Weekly Reader,* she replied that "people like him *couldn't* be bad because they were only trying to make the world a better place."[83]

While their father was in the hospital, Judy and Ben were sent to stay with his sister, their aunt Shirley. Judy recalls that another of her father's sisters, her aunt Enid, arrived and told her that her father was "very sick." She remembers asking: "He couldn't die, could he?" expecting to be reassured, but only to hear a blunt yes. A few days later the children learned that their father had not survived surgery to relieve the intense pain caused by an infected ulcer.[84] On July 15, 1953, when she was only thirteen, Judy had to face the death of her father, who was only forty-three.[85]

In her mind, he would never age; her idealized view of him would be forever preserved.[86] She would never engage with him in a typical teenager's rebellion. Instead, her father's ideals and revolutionary zeal would remain intact inside her. This sense of what was right and her heartfelt duty to fight for justice would eventually lead her to wage her own battle for equal rights.

Judy and her brother were not allowed to attend the funeral. Some of Arthur's doting sisters were so grief-stricken that they lashed out and blamed May for his death, accusing her of "murder," since it was her doctor who had performed the unsuccessful operation.[87] Through all the extended family's misery and the ensuing accusations, no one considered that Judy and her brother, by missing the funeral, would have no chance for communal grieving. "It was as if my father simply walked out of our life and, with his departure, the three of us became alienated from each other," she recalled. "At night we would sit down to dinner together with my father's palpable absence filling the room, my mother's refusal to discuss his death a wall between us."[88] Even decades later Judy would write in her journal: "I found myself besieged with all the old feelings of hatred toward my mother I had when I was young."[89]

Her mother's silence prevented Judy from resolving the tremendous loss and beginning to heal. Judy needed to grieve and to make sense of the meaning of her father's life. But under the circumstances, it was not possible. As one psychologist puts it, when a child depends on an adult who has experienced unresolved loss, it can spill over onto the child in many ways.[90] Trying to cope, Judy sought solace in art. Her mother, despite the new tenseness between them and increased financial hardships, continued to encourage and support Judy's artistic ambitions.

◂ May Cohen with the infant Judy—the only extant photograph of the two of them during Judy's childhood.

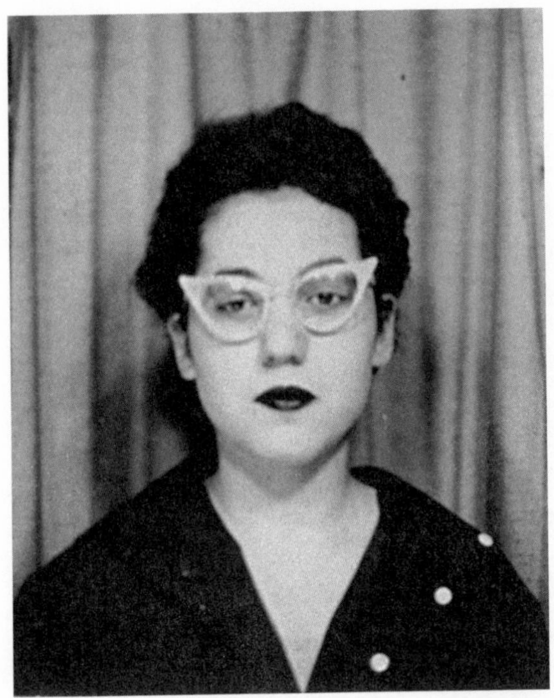

Inklings of Identity

3

"I was left grief-stricken beyond imagination and totally dazed by the loss of my most beloved parent," Judy would write, although she thought that her brother, Ben, suffered more, even if it was not apparent at the time: "He and I became even more distant, perhaps separated by the sorrow we could not share. And for many, many years, I was deeply and bitterly enraged at my mother because in my estimation and for whatever reasons, I felt that she had totally failed both me and my brother at this terrible time."[1] Like many daughters, Judy vainly sought to deny the extent of her loss[2]: it was her father who had made her feel bright and special, entitled to achieve whatever she desired; now it was hard to keep up her confidence and not to feel undermined by her mother.

▲
Judy Cohen in junior high school.

May, now a widow with two children to support, began to suffer from epileptic seizures, induced by a botched hysterectomy. As distraught as she was, she was simply unable to discuss her husband's death with the children. To what extent she was trying to protect them also from political pressures is hard to say. Her father "had apparently promised my mother that he would not tell me that he was a Communist," Judy writes, believing that he "ceased to be a party member in 1939" and that her mother never joined the party.[3]

Not only had May Cohen lost her husband, but much of his family was blaming her for his death. As a result, Judy no longer saw most of her aunts and uncles. To compound the family tensions, just eight months after Arthur's death the husband of his youngest sister, Enid, Judy's uncle Willy Rosen, was robbed and shot to death in a liquor store that he owned.

Judy continued to see her aunt Enid and her children Howard and Corinne. She also saw Peggy Strickland, the daughter of her aunt Gertrude, who often invited her to sleep over at her home near the University of Chicago, where she and her husband were graduate students. "We would engage in intense discussions about my father, by whom she, like some other cousins, had been inspired," Judy remembers. "For some reason, I found these talks comforting, if only because, at least for short periods of time, I could remember him as he had been when he was alive."[4]

Psychologists compare the "panic, terror, and confusion of a grieving child" to a sudden calamity that is absolute.[5] There is total discontinuity and a resulting insecurity that is terrifying. What seemed safe now appears threatening. What seemed settled now appears uncertain. The world itself looks profoundly empty.[6] The once-confident explorer has now lost the guide she counted on for making her way in life.

So lost was this adolescent that despite her secular upbringing, she turned to the Jewish religion, searching for solace. After her father died, she remembers that she sought out the Anshe Emet Synagogue, a congregation of the Conservative movement, on North Broadway, less than half a mile from home. She recalls going "on and off to temple in Chicago until I was 16. I went to yisker services for my father and was horrified when they sent around this piece of paper asking me to 'pledge so many dollars so that my parent could rest in peace.' My idealistic nature was shocked. I left the temple and never went back."[7] Yizkor (or Yisker) means literally in Hebrew "May God remember." It is the memorial service that Jews conduct for the dead.

At that time the prayer book used in Conservative synagogues offered the following prayer to be recited in memory of a father: "O heavenly Father, remember the soul of my dear father whom I recall in this solemn hour. I remember with esteem the affection and kindness with which he counseled and guided me. May I ever uphold the noble heritage he transmitted unto me so that through me, his aspirations shall be fulfilled. May his soul be bound up in the bonds of eternal life and his memory ever be for a blessing. Amen."[8] Elsewhere a typical prayer for deceased parents and other family members is: "Their desire was to train us in the good and righteous way, to teach us Thy statutes and commandments, and to instruct us to do justice and to love mercy. We beseech Thee, O Lord, grant us strength to be faithful to their charge while the breath of life is within us."[9]

Those reciting Yizkor promise to do "acts of charity and goodness" in the memory of the person deceased. The concept is that a person lives on through their children and grandchildren, as their memory keeps them "alive." Although the synagogue's attempt to raise donations alienated this teenager in mourning, who had no funds to offer, she nonetheless, either consciously or unconsciously, accepted the lesson of the prayer. She took to heart the humanitarian goals of her father's prematurely abridged life, which continued to inform her own: "To say that my father adored me would be an inadequate description for all the love and attention he showered upon me, and I cannot emphasize enough the pivotal role he played in my development."[10]

The loss of her father, compounded with Judy's burgeoning adolescent rebellion, further strained her relationship with her mother: "My separation from my mother was so traumatic & needlessly painful (because she couldn't allow me to go my own way) & I felt so guilty about it."[11] Their interaction was somewhat ameliorated by her mother's commitment that she should continue to study art despite the family's strained finances. From the age of fourteen Judy worked after school in a candy store to earn money to augment what her mother could afford.

Judy's Saturday trips to the Art Institute became the focus of her life. In its comprehensive collections, she came to see colors as emotive states and to admire Toulouse-Lautrec's use of reds. Other favorites were Monet's haystacks and Seurat's *Sunday Afternoon on Le Grande Jatte.* Art was opening before her another world, one that offered possibilities far beyond what she had known. As a teenager Judy moved up to the classes in the Art Institute's High School division, where her favorite teacher, Emanuel Jacobson, taught; there she could study figure and portrait drawing as well as advanced drawing and painting. Jacobson encouraged her and praised her work, although he frequently reminded her to make an effort to fit her subject within the confines of the page.

At the same time Judy studied art at Lake View High School, which she began to attend in the fall of 1953, upon entering ninth grade. Her exceptional ability stood out, recalls Philip Krone, who was in the class a year behind Judy and became friendly with her when she was about fifteen. He recalls that Judy studied with teachers Helen Wick and Edna Crowley, both of whom loved her work, and that Judy was very good at drawing with charcoal and loved doing figures.[12] Another Lake View student, Marjie Kaplow, who was in the same homeroom as Judy all four years, recalls: "It was very obvious that she was an enormous talent and one that I admired very much. Our art teacher, Miss Wick, always said she was very gifted. She was extremely bright and well read and when we graduated, her class rank was very high."[13] At the same time Miss Wick also taught others who would pursue art professionally, including the future artist Gladys Nilsson, who published her first cartoon sketch in the school newspaper.[14]

Another classmate, Anita Nelson, now a graphic designer, remembers Miss Wick as "exceptional . . . she developed a special class for her 'artists,' where we were able to focus on the human figure."[15] Miss Wick's "life sketching" class, where two fully clothed female student models posed, was the subject of a yearbook photograph for Judy's sophomore year in 1955. One model is standing and another is reclining on a table placed among the students at their easels. At one easel, in the center of the photograph, Judy sits poised with her sketching hand held up to her clearly accomplished figure drawing as she gazes out toward the photographer. Judy's talent, combined with all the practice that she had had in years of study at the Art Institute, gave her an advantage over most of the other students.

The recognition she received was not enough to satisfy her craving for it. "Even when I was a child," she would recall, "I always had to struggle & in every situation I started out behind the eight-ball, with people not recognizing my worth. Agonizingly, I would struggle until I received my rewards & people would acknowledge my worth."[16]

In a photograph of her sophomore class, Judy, her dark hair cropped short, stands smiling in the second row, near Cecilia "Ceci" Honet.[17] The two girls, who were both excellent students, often got together after school during their senior year. They took an adult education course, titled "Beyond the Pale," together at night at the College of Jewish Studies. Honet, who is now a psychologist, recalls that it was very intellectual: "I was too young for it."[18] Judy, who remembers that the course was about Zionism, did not find it to her liking. Her response was in keeping with her family's embrace of leftist politics rather than the nationalist solution of a Jewish state. Honet also had suffered the death of her mother, but she does not think that the two girls ever discussed their parents' untimely deaths.

According to Honet, Judy was "an outspoken person." Honet's father became concerned that her friend was too "radical." Asked what that meant, she quipped: "She probably wore long earrings." But one can easily imagine that Honet's father had heard something about the leftist activities of Judy's father, perhaps from the neighbors whom the FBI had questioned, and he was therefore wary of his daughter's association with the family. Senator Joe McCarthy was still aggressively trying to unmask Communists in the U.S. government, from the State Department to the Voice of America radio.[19] Their classmate Gladys Nilsson recalls watching the McCarthy hearings on television, so clearly students at Lake View High School were aware of the tense political situation.[20]

Around this time, Judy met Tommy Mitchel at a party at her friend Leoni Zverow's house. Tommy went to Sullivan High School in the West Rogers Park neighborhood. "We were sitting and talking without an introduction," he recalls, adding: "She saw the ring I was wearing (my father's high school graduation ring from Harrison Technical) and asked what the initials stood for. I said my name. I told her my name was Teck Harrison, a lie, which was pretty common in those days when you met a girl from another school who you don't expect to see again. Judy thought my name was Teck Harrison for about a week until I told her the truth. I liked her and wanted to date her so I had to."[21]

Judy identifies him as her "first real boyfriend, not counting my seventh-grade romance with Sandy." Tommy must also represent her first encounter with someone who took another name, however briefly. "Tommy went to an upper-middle-class high school and was older than I, giving me a little status at my school and also an excuse for my lack of popularity."[22] She recalls that "he had a swell car, a '53 turquoise and white Chevy, in which he would pick me up after my Saturday classes at the Art Institute."[23]

"I thought Judy was a little flakey. You know, artsy and all, but she was really impressed with me, which made me feel important. . . . We talked for hours on end about everything. We did love each other. . . ."[24]

Judy has also recounted how she had her first orgasm while petting with Tommy, although at age sixteen she didn't know what it was: "Everyone petted and everyone denied it, asserting that they only necked. If anyone admitted to petting, it was only to say that they petted above the waist. No one, but no one, went all the way."[25] From these tentative experiences in high school, Judy would go on in college to insist upon women's right to sexual pleasure.

Although she admits that she was not part of the "popular" crowd, Judy recalls "having lots of friends" and spending time with "other Jewish boys and girls who were not accepted into the Jewish clique. We read books and listened to music."[26] Her reading matter came right off the bookshelves at home, including

Dos Passos, Fitzgerald, Hemingway, Faulkner, Dostoyevsky, and other Russian novelists. But when she tried to write book reports on them, her English teachers would not accept them, expressing doubts that she had really read those books. "I had to dumb down to pass and review from *Reader's Digest.*"[27]

Among the other reading that Judy recalled and enjoyed most was Irving Shulman's novel *The Amboy Dukes: A Novel of Wayward Youth in Brooklyn.* This 1946 teenage drama was then popular with the age group it represented. It featured secular Jews in street gangs, at make-out parties, and in conflicts with their parents. But most striking is its treatment of politics: the "Socialist speaker, flanked by the American flag, stood on a ladder and hoarsely harangued the crowd. On Pitkin and Hopkinson, the speaker was a Communist, on Pitkin and Bristol, a Socialist-Laborite."[28] The novel's central character, Frank Goldfarb, "had to take a thousand dollars' worth of crap about his father who'd rather remain unemployed and on relief than work in a non-union shop."[29]

Nothing Judy read, however, could compete with her passion for art. During her junior year at Lake View, she joined the art staff for the yearbook—*The Red and White.* A photograph staged for the 1956 edition shows her meeting with the rest of the staff—just eight in all.[30] She appears again with the Alpha Chapter of the French Club,[31] not with the Fine Arts Club, although her friend Phil was a member, or the Laurels Club. The latter was considered the "Jewish club," she recalled, but she was not asked to join, "probably because I couldn't afford the number of cashmere sweaters that was required."[32] Unlike so many of her female classmates, she never did pose in a sweater with pearls. As her quip suggests, the Cohen family finances were too pinched.

Judy continued to hang out with Leoni and her friends from Von Steuben High School in the neighborhood known as Albany Park, sleeping over for slumber parties, styling their hair, dressing up, and posing for snapshots.[33] When prom season arrived, Leoni did not have a date, so Judy volunteered that her boyfriend, Tommy, with whom she went to his senior prom at Sullivan High, could also take Leoni to her prom, which he did.

After her junior year Judy spent much of the summer at Wilson Dunes on the Indiana side of Lake Michigan. She divided her time between the cabins of two family friends, the Silbers and the Zverows, Leoni's parents. Her mother made occasional weekend visits. Life at the lake was simple; the cabins had no running water but offered access to the beach and plenty of opportunity to hang out with a group of teenagers. Mrs. Zverow took Judy aside and told her that she should not plan to go off to college because her mother had to work too hard. But Judy thought otherwise: "I knew that I had a destiny." And she knew that her mother would agree.

That same summer her mother let Judy travel by train with Leoni to Los Angeles. The ride, on the *El Capitan,* then took thirty-nine and a half hours. The two teens passed time in the lounge car, drinking Cokes, before arriving in the exotic pink stucco of Los Angeles's Union Station. Each stayed with her own relatives, Leoni in Beverly Hills and Judy with her aunt Dorothy and uncle Herman in Culver City, although they got together for at least one night out with Leoni's cousin and some of his pals. Leoni recalls that Judy was "definitely assertive, bold, impatient at times (with me—she always said I was too middle-of-the-road in our various arguments about life, etc.) She was also a very good friend, someone vibrant who enjoyed life and had a great laugh."[34]

Judy also visited her maternal grandmother and met Jessica Fizdale, the daughter of Lela Zimberoff Fizdale, who had been May's best friend from their days before marriage. Like May, Lela came from a radical Left background in Chicago; as young women they had danced with the same troupe at the Jewish People's Institute. Jessica, who was just a year ahead of Judy in school, had a boyfriend who arranged a double date, bringing along a friend for Judy. When she subsequently went out with him on her own, she recalls with disgust that he drove her to the top of Mulholland Drive and tried to force her to have sex with him. Caught without her shoes on, she nonetheless extricated herself from the car and threatened to walk home rather than submit to him. He finally drove alongside her, apologized, and agreed to take her home.[35] While interested in sexual pleasure, Judy did not intend to have sex with someone she did not love.

Back in Chicago, Judy also maintained her friends at Lake View. Phil Krone recalls her as active in the student council, for which she campaigned and got herself elected vice president. Before she announced her intentions, she consulted him to see if he was running. Since he planned to run for president, he suggested that she try for secretary, only to have her dismiss the idea as "a girl's job."[36] In the end she won her campaign, while he lost his. She recalls going with several classmates to a statewide convention of students active in student councils, where she roomed with several girls from another school. They told her she was the first Jew they had ever seen and asked her to remove her clothes so they could see how she was different from them. This incident sticks in Chicago's mind as the first time she encountered anti-Semitism.[37]

Another time she remembers that Lucy McMillan, the teacher of her honors English class, which was almost 95 percent Jewish, made a comment about Franklin D. Roosevelt and "the Jewish conspiracy," calling him "a Jew lover." This prompted all the Jews to walk out. Judy recalls that there was never a discussion about this incident either at home or in school.[38] In the class behind Judy, Louise Abbell Holland recalls that she too encountered anti-Semitism in

Mrs. McMillan, who also served as the school's college guidance counselor. When Louise requested an application for the College Boards, Mrs. McMillan retorted: "Why? You're not Jewish." Not shy about her prejudice and stereotypes, Mrs. McMillan was known, according to Louise, to point to New York City on a map of the United States that she had hanging in her classroom and remark: "Most Jews live in New York. I hate New York."[39]

Mrs. McMillan, who was also the teacher for Judy's division and the adviser for the National Honor Society, was just getting adjusted to a student population that had suddenly grown to about 25 percent Jewish in just one year. In 1956 the Lake View yearbook included the banner headline: "Social Clubs Create Happy Memories, Develop Poise and Personality, Promote Ideals of Christian Living."[40] The yearbook for 1955, before Judy joined the art staff, also featured a photograph of an art student putting "finishing touches to models of nativity."[41] By Judy's senior year, however, an adjustment had been made and decorations commemorated both Christian and Jewish holidays.

Prior to 1953 Jewish students in the neighborhood could and usually did request "a pass" to attend Nicholas Senn High School, located outside their district but where the student population was mostly Jewish. Just before she was to begin high school and shortly before the pass system, which perpetuated segregation, was abandoned under legal pressure, Judy had wanted to apply for a pass, but her father, without explanation, had forbidden her to do so. She later reflected: "My father's reluctance to explain the political basis for the pass system was probably linked up to the larger issue of his dilemma as a radical in the America of the fifties."[42]

When she first entered Lake View High, she saw signs scrawled on the walls that read "Kikes, go home," but she reflected later: "I had no context for this."[43] Jewish identity ran strong at Lake View, even if religious observance did not. Since Krone, also Jewish, lived around the corner from the Cohens, he remembers that Judy's mother stood out as a good cook in the neighborhood that he describes as "family-oriented, Jewish." He recalls Judy as "not pretty, but attractive, with a very round face and a hair-do that reminded me of Nancy" in the comic strip. He met several of Judy's boyfriends, who included guys already in college.

One of these boyfriends was Allen Podet, who was already beginning rabbinical training at Hebrew Union College when he and Judy dated in her senior year. Introduced by a friend of her mother's, who brought Allen to her home, Judy described herself at age seventeen: "I trotted out the behavior I had developed for my father. I performed intellectually, dazzling him with my use of long words, and in general coming on in a way that must have been ridiculous. However, he *was* duly impressed, and I began to see him."[44] Allen recalls that he taught her about Bach and she took him to look at Impressionist paintings at the Art Institute, where, he says, "Thanks to Judy, I learned to see."[45] He also recalls that they had just listened to some music at a downtown record store, when she told him that she intended "to become an artist of renown." She went to her senior prom with him.[46]

Judy's senior year at Lake View brought her membership in the National Honor Society and the Gold Pin Society, recognition of her artistic achievement.[47] Along with Anita Nelson, she contributed line drawings to the yearbook, produced under the direction of Edna Crowley, the book's art sponsor. On the page that introduces the advertising section, the names of both Judy and Anita appear, implying that both contributed some of these drawings, which are grouped around two large letters, L and V for Lake View High. Anita recalled recently that "Judy did the speaker at the podium in the 'V' of LV . . . and the two people at the desk at the left, center."[48] Judy, who no longer remembers which drawings are hers, reflected: "my work was always too big, too dark, and too much; I'll accept that those are by me."[49] In fact her drawings are darker, heavier, and less cartoonish than Nelson's, which appear more lighthearted and include an anthropomorphic car complete with a grinning fender and pop-eyed headlights. Perhaps there is already a clue that Anita would become a successful graphic designer, while Judy would make art history.

All the joys of high school graduation were blotted out by the death of Judy's good friend and neighbor from across the street, Paula Levine, who perished with most of her family "when their car was hit by a train at a blind crossing." The two girls had been best friends throughout their childhoods, and their families had been close. Death had once again insinuated itself into this teenager's life. Already before this tragic accident, Judy had offered her classmate in figure drawing, Anita Nelson, a motto that she took from James Dean: "Live fast, die young, and have a good-looking corpse."[50] Not yet eighteen, she had become all too acutely aware of the precariousness of life and of the "fickleness of fate."

Anticipating going to college, Judy applied to the Art Institute of Chicago; the University of Chicago, which then had a joint program with the Art Institute; and the University of California at Los Angeles (UCLA), which was known for its art program. She also applied for scholarships, which she both needed and merited. For the Art Institute, she took the scholarship exam on a Saturday, during which the competing students drew and painted all afternoon. She felt confident about her chances but did not receive the scholarship, which went instead to Anita Nelson.[51] Judy did, however, receive a scholarship for

$500 awarded by her high school that was applicable anywhere. It was enough to pay for an entire year's out-of-state tuition at UCLA. That summer between high school and college, Judy worked at the sales counter of a local commercial art shop.[52]

Judy's only association with Los Angeles was with her maternal grandmother, her aunt Dorothy, and her uncle Herman Polin, as well as Jessica Fizdale, whom she had just visited the previous summer. Just as she was preparing to take the scholarship exam for the University of Chicago, Jessica arrived from Los Angeles, where she was attending UCLA. During the course of a day's excursion around Chicago that extended from the Art Institute to the red-light district on Mansfield Street, Jessica's enthusiasm, vivid tales of bohemian life, and sophistication made an enormous impression on Judy, who had been keenly disappointed not to win the scholarship to the Art Institute. It did not hurt matters that Jessica too came from a radical family; her maternal grandfather had been a Wobbly, a member of the Industrial Workers of the World, an international organization that struggled to unite all workers within a single union.[53]

Soon Jessica convinced Judy to return with her to Los Angeles. She discussed the decision with her mother, who gave her permission, and with Allen, who encouraged her to go, probably, she thought, so that he could get her to go to bed with him. Within just three days, without any planning, she gave up her notion of staying in Chicago, where everything was so familiar. She packed her bags and left with Jessica on a plane for Southern California, twenty-three hundred miles away. With no advance plans and few resources, her only option was to stay with her aunt and uncle. She had only a few possessions to take to California, but she did not lack ambition. Perhaps her most valuable asset was "determination to make something of myself."[54]

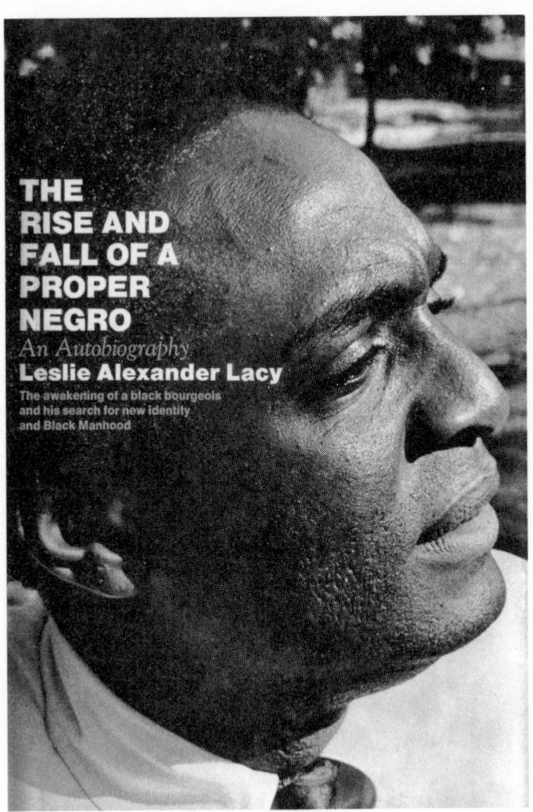

Out West: Contending with Men 4

Judy Cohen entered the College of Applied Arts at UCLA in September 1957, paying tuition with the scholarship awarded her by Lake View High School. She joined some sixteen thousand other students, about two-thirds of them male and most of them commuters to the sprawling campus in the Westwood neighborhood. Judy too lived off campus, "boarding" with Aunt Dorothy and Uncle Herman at 3638 Glendon in the Culver City neighborhood, which she described as "a squat, desolate part of the city."[1] Dorothy painted china for a hobby and hung her plates proudly on the walls, but her niece gave them scant notice.[2] She was too busy scheming to stretch her budget to move into an

▲
Leslie Lacy's memoir, *The Rise and Fall of a Proper Negro.*

apartment, which she initially hoped to share with Jessica Fizdale, who was still living with her parents.

They would furnish their apartment, Judy wrote to her mother, with some "*schmata* furniture."[3] In her letters home she frequently used Yiddish words such as *schmata,* which means "raglike." This habit of speech was second nature to her, but her unself-conscious use of Yiddish with her mother also suggests comfort with, and even pride in, their shared Eastern European Jewish heritage.

Despite her hope of moving out on her own, Judy informed her mother that her aunt and uncle, who were childless, "have allowed me comparative freedom of social life" and that her uncle had been driving her around Los Angeles. Among their excursions were visits to her grandmother, Bertha Levinson, about whom she wrote to her mother: "despite her *mishagas* [craziness], she's kind of cute."[4]

About her studies, Judy initially commented that she found French and astronomy "terrifically rough." She was also taking courses in English, physical education, and art. Before long she would write, "My art classes are becoming increasingly interesting . . . we're beginning to do more creative work."[5] With the art club she visited the private collection of the actor Vincent Price and, another time, the home of Saul Bass, whom she described as "a big *Macher* [someone with connections, a big wheel] . . . he doesn't call himself a Commercial Artist, but an Advertising Designer."[6] She also wrote about meeting Natalie, "a charming girl in scientific illustration as her husband is a doctor. She is only about nineteen, and we get along famously. For the first time in a long time I found someone who could understand all my artistic feelings and responses."[7]

The UCLA art department was the result of a merger in 1939 of faculty from the former Teachers College into the newly created College of Applied Arts. Holdovers included female artists such as Annita Delano, who had imbibed the influence of Arthur Wesley Dow's curriculum at Columbia Teachers College in New York. That curriculum, which influenced UCLA's foundation (freshman) courses, stressed composition and the harmonious division of pictorial space over "mere representation" or realism.[8]

Judy, despite her determination to become an artist, later commented that at this time she had not considered studying in New York City, the home of an American avant-garde and the center of the art market: "What did I know from New York? I was a young, idealistic, old-fashioned girl. I believed in art and truth and beauty. I didn't know anything about 'making it.' I was such a protected girl."[9]

From the beginning of her first semester in college, Judy not only focused on art but also devoted herself to political activism. UCLA was nicknamed "the Little Red School House" because of its large contingent of students engaged in radical politics.[10] During her first semester the school newspaper—the *UCLA Daily Bruin*—carried the headline: "Socialists Stir at UCLA/Radicals Pass Out Colored Circulars," and reported that "UCLA Campus is becoming a focal point for a new movement among radical students and young people from all over, who are supporters of the Socialist movement. Yellow and pink colored circulars, accompanied by copies of the 'Young Socialist' are being passed around campus by workers in this movement." The article further cited concern with "infiltration onto this very campus."[11]

The *Daily Bruin* itself was embroiled in controversy over what constituted "clear and readable" news. Several of its front-page stories that month resulted from the intervention of the House Committee on Un-American Activities and the U.S. Attorney General's Office. Apparently the *Bruin* turned reactionary and supported the student council in welcoming a state legislative committee that meant to investigate subversion on the campus.[12]

The "leftos" and bohemians hung out on campus in the Annex, a large, one-story building intended to handle overflow crowds from the main cafeteria in Kirkhoff Hall. Students and occasional faculty members spent hours on end "talking politics, plotting 'revolutions,' arguing philosophy, theories of art, the finer points of Marxism, etc."[13] There were tables for Trotskyists, Stalinists, and Socialists and a lot of mixing. The National Association for the Advancement of Colored People also had a presence. It had been founded in 1909 and was chartered "to promote equality of rights and to eradicate caste or race prejudice among the citizens of the United States: to advance the interest of colored citizens; to secure for them impartial suffrage; and to increase their opportunities for securing justice in the courts, education for the children, employment according to their ability and complete equality before law."[14] "Being a member of the NAACP was considered radical," and the organization, which was "extremely controversial on campus," was deemed subversive by the UCLA administration.

Judy's instinct for political activism led her to make like-minded friends, one of whom was Estelle Gershgoren, an English major who wrote poetry, whom Judy described to her mother as "really a marvelous person."[15] Estelle's father, Milton Gershgoren, Judy described as "a rather prominent West Coast artist," whose studio she soon visited together with her friend.[16] The studio, then located in a remodeled garage behind the family's home, was one of the first that Judy ever saw. Estelle's brother Sid Gershgoren, about two years older than his sister and also a poet, was studying at UCLA as well. With Estelle and her friend Ray, along with Mike Janusz, who was a folksinger and a fellow student in her design class, Judy attended a benefit at which the actor and folksinger Theodore Bikel performed.[17]

The benefit was organized by "the Committee for the Protection of the Foreign Born, and primarily to repeal the Walter-McCarran Act."[18] The Immigration and Nationality Act of 1952 had for the first time granted Asian immigrants the right to become citizens but also provided for the deportation of noncitizens, who were subject to being prosecuted for proscribed political beliefs and associations or being deemed "subversive" without due process.[19] Judy's political sympathies with powerless minorities echoed those of her father, about whom she wrote her mother from college: "How proud I am to have had a Father such as I did."[20]

Judy's pride in her father and his values led her to model her own politics and beliefs on his. She told her mother that she found her uncle Herman "too reactionary" after he remarked that "Communism is the worst evil man has ever seen."[21] Honoring her father's stated goal of changing "the condition of black people in America," she eagerly joined the struggle for civil rights. Others before her had linked "the twin evils of race-baiting ('nigger lover') and red-baiting ('commie sympathizer')."[22] She would have none of it.

Meanwhile the UCLA student newspaper praised President Eisenhower's "decisive and dramatic action" in forcing the central high school in Little Rock, Arkansas, to integrate.[23] Just two years after Rosa Parks had refused to give up her seat to a white man on a bus in Montgomery, Alabama, the civil rights movement was gearing up. Judy and Estelle both joined the NAACP.

Judy soon began to use her experience and skill in graphic design to make posters for the NAACP. In November she wrote home that she was going to the UCLA homecoming parade and then to an NAACP party.[24] Another time she reported going to a "huge NAACP party at the sponsor Dr. Council Taylor's house," referring to a black anthropologist from Jamaica who was then on the faculty.[25] Known as "the Count," the popular professor gave parties with lots of interesting people and lots of alcohol.[26] In early December Judy announced to her mother that she had become the corresponding secretary of the Westwood chapter of the NAACP. She observed that UCLA lacked "Negro professors" and that "Westwood Village, the area immediately surrounding the campus, has no apartments available for Negroes, & there are Barber Shops, restaurants, stores, etc. in this 'elite' neighborhood that won't serve them."[27]

The struggle in America for racial equality, as historians have noted, has twice "been midwife to a feminist movement."[28] In 1946, the growing presence of women in the workforce prompted by the war caused many men to react. "Just as the white race likes to raise its own prestige by detracting from and minimizing the abilities of the Negro race, so men in general "like to build up their superiority by minimizing all women," stated Susan B. Anthony II, who was the grandniece of the late nineteenth-century suffragist.[29] Many of the suffragists had already been active before midcentury in the movement to abolish slavery. Then and again in the civil rights movement of the 1960s, women began to think of themselves less as isolated individuals than as members of a collaborative social and political movement. As women worked for racial justice and human rights for others, they learned valuable skills as organizers and gained an understanding of the value of collective action. They also became motivated to work for their own rights as women. The lessons of working in the NAACP were valuable for the women who founded the National Organization for Women (NOW) in the 1960s. Judy, having grown up in a liberated leftist home, already knew that she wanted to work for equality in society. At UCLA, she soon experienced society as according women less than the equal status she had known at home.

Throughout her freshman year, although busy with her classes, social life, and activism, Judy kept abreast of current political and cultural events. After the launch of Sputnik, the Russian satellite that began the space race, she wrote to her mother: "we all dashed outside to see if we could spot the Russian renegade that usurped America's position (at least in American eyes.)"[30] Portraying a struggle for meaning in the face of meaninglessness, a production of *Waiting for Godot,* by the Irish playwright Samuel Beckett, impressed her so much that she wrote to her mother and brother: "This play was just marvelous—a very modern abstract thing reminiscent of Abstract Art—extremely exciting, funny almost to absurdity, with an underlying current of Existentialist-type philosophy."[31]

Judy's adjustment to college and to moving away from home inevitably had ups and downs: "In my inconsistent life of oscillating between Elation & Depression, I am now in a rather elated state. I got all kinds of nice surprises, like an A on my big Design project."[32] After her first semester Judy flew home to Chicago, happy to have done well. A few years later she looked back on the move to Los Angeles and confessed: "I had forgotten what I went thru before I could even contemplate remaining there."[33]

For her first-semester grades, Judy received half A's (in physical education, beginning drawing and painting, and English composition) and half B's (in beginning design, astronomy, and intermediate French). The next term she registered for most of the same courses but substituted general anthropology for astronomy and added life drawing.[34] She found the design course difficult and commented: "It seems that painters have a mental block against pure Design—it's so mechanical."[35]

During her second semester at UCLA Judy started to date Leslie Alexander Lacy, a handsome philosophy student at the University of Southern California. She wrote about him to her mother, connecting him to her reading of an existentialist novel in her French class. Leslie, she claimed, shared her view that existentialism "is the product of a decadent society."[36] She elaborated: "the only type of philosophy that would be allowed to flourish in the contemporary western system is one that would ultimately benefit the system. It is very interesting theory that if Existentialism ever became a potent movement . . . it is declining now . . . the result would probably be a group of very dissatisfied, aimless individuals—who, having lost the unity essential for progress, would be very happy to fall back into a system of conformity where they would have little responsibility." While she admitted that "responsibility is so tedious," she understood that "looking at the philosophy in another light, one sees some rebellion against the conformity that so characterizes our time." Existentialism, she argued, "develops from the idea that you were put on earth with no apparent purpose & in Jean Paul Sartre's works . . . 'Man is condemned to freedom.' This, of course, gives man a great many responsibilities—but to himself."

Judy's and Leslie's backgrounds could not have been more different. Leslie, the middle child and second son of a physician, spent his early childhood in Franklin, Louisiana. There his family lived in a "big comfortable house" with "a spacious yard with a garden," with rosebushes shading the front and back porches. As children, Leslie and his two siblings all had their own nursemaids. His mother's only role was to oversee these and the other servants; she did no housework since there were usually about five "hired girls" for that purpose.[37] The children attended a private Methodist school, before the Lacy family moved to Shreveport, and later Leslie was sent away to prep school in North Carolina. Shortly after he left for college, his parents divorced.

Their friendship was complicated by the fact that Leslie was an African-American. "This was the last straw for my uncle, with whom I was now fighting openly," Judy recalls.[38] Eager to move into an apartment rather than live with her aunt and uncle, Judy tried to gain her mother's support. She reported speaking to the school's counselor, who "agreed that it would be a fine idea," and implored, "I hope that you realize that I would not subject myself to any sort of unpleasant, unrewarding, or non-developmental situation, as I'm too damned selfish. I want to develop, intellectually, socially, emotionally, etc."[39] In the meantime she arranged to hold an NAACP executive board meeting at her aunt and uncle's house on February 7, 1958, openly challenging what she viewed as her uncle's prejudices. The following Saturday she attended a party given by

Walt Williams, the social chairman of the organization, who dated her friend Julie Ross for a time.

Her defiant actions seem to have had their desired effect. She moved out of her aunt and uncle's home and began to room with another art student. Her relationship with Leslie flew in the face of racism's most rigid boundaries; particularly in the Old South, "the most brutally repressed assault upon white authority became a sexual liaison between a black man and a white woman—culturally defined as 'rape' regardless of the circumstances."[40]

More than a decade later Leslie recounted his friendship with Judy in a well-regarded "fictionalized" memoir, *The Rise and Fall of a Proper Negro.* At their first meeting, at a demonstration on campus, she offered him a sign to carry that read, "Down with Capital Punishment," and in smaller letters, "Only a new social and political system can eliminate the causes of killing."[41] Although she is recognizable in Lacy's book, Judy Cohen morphed into "Judy Goldman: white, rebel, sixteen, a nervous surrealist Jew, learning how to paint at the University of Southern California in Los Angeles." He quips that on his first day of school, he met his first representative of the American Left.[42] In Judy's account, published five years after his, she recalls having fun at NAACP dances, going to folk concerts, and doing well in school: "My Chicago life seemed a million miles away. I was madly in love with Leslie and imagined him as a black prince."[43]

Judy found Leslie quite attractive, evidently much more attractive than he had considered himself to be. He described how "she took my head in her hands and told me something that I had never heard: 'Your face is beautiful.' I believed her. But it was a little strange because in the colored world I was not even handsome. Only the girls were beautiful, and the light-skinned ones at that."[44]

Lacy reflected on his experience: "Judy and her morally indignant young friends sold me not to a cause, but exposed me to the ethics of their character. Their vitality filled me with astonishment, and I respected their courage. What they said and did politically was less important than the day-to-day, week-to-month-to-year content of their lives. They shared easily, and always with a smile, the voices and thoughts of their insides."[45] He found them to be unafraid of intimacy and painfully honest.

Lacy remembers that picketing in Los Angeles in 1956 was "not fun": "We took every conceivable abuse, including the lack of police protection. Judy and I always walked together. But that proved to be dangerous, so I changed positions."[46] He maintains that he was "scared, uninvolved politically, singing foreign folk songs, tired, embarrassed, walking happily hand in hand with a blond Jewish white girl of German descent—who got you hit in the head at least once a week because she stuck out her tongue and called a Southern-born white policeman . . . a 'fascist cop.' "[47] Although he changed a few details of Judy's appearance and background, she remains remarkably recognizable. In her own account she did not disguise Leslie but omitted giving his surname.

"Singing foreign folk songs," as Lacy recalled it, was characteristic of this radical milieu, which relished singing and listening to traditional music and ethnic songs. This music became a means of connecting the world of the Communists to the traditions and culture of the United States and often featured themes of social justice, cross-cultural communication, and international peace. During the 1930s and 1940s such singers as Woody Guthrie, Leadbelly, and Pete Seeger found their first audiences through the radical labor movement.[48] Sid Gershgoren recalls that Judy and her friend Julie Ross, a self-described "red diaper baby" from Brooklyn, earned money by babysitting for the folk-singer Cynthia Gooding.[49] Gooding, who performed with Theodore Bikel, sang "world" music and from 1953 recorded folk songs in various languages with the Elektra label.

Historian Paul Buhle has suggested that "perhaps those Jewish semi-Communists who did so much to create the audience for folk music and jazz during the 1930s–1950s really *were* consciously and semiconsciously seeking to subvert an America that wouldn't let them in—as their successors, who are scarcely political, are still trying to pry open doors for something lurking outside."[50] Judy carried on this great subversive tradition, but would transfer it to a feminist context, paying homage to the legacy of her father.

Her friends and their activities attracted the attention of the FBI, and the Bureau's overzealousness led it to create a file on Judith Sylvia Cohen, investigating her between November 11, 1958, and January 27, 1959.[51] The investigation included a "pretext interview" by a confidential informant, which evidently took place at her residence on January 27, 1959, and prompted the conclusion that she did not "fall within the Security Index criteria."

The FBI claimed it was investigating a number of events that Judy had attended. One, a public meeting, held at 5925 South Figueroa Street in Los Angeles, on August 9, 1958, featured a speech by Vincent Hallinan about "the United Socialist Ticket of New York." Hallinan, a tough left-wing lawyer from San Francisco and a fighter for progressive causes, had been the Progressive Party's candidate for president of the United States in 1952, a campaign he ran largely from his jail cell.[52] According to the FBI, Hallinan referred to his previous criticism of the Communist Party as "political and constructive" and said that it "should not be considered as slander of the Communist Party." Another event that attracted the FBI's attention was a class sponsored by the local Socialist

Workers Party on August 17, 1958. In its report the FBI described the main talk at the class as "a Marxist analysis of historical developments from slavery to the present, which was termed as financial capitalism."

The FBI also claimed that Judy Cohen attended a conference of Young Socialists in Los Angeles and that the organization, which they claimed was formed and dominated by the Socialist Workers Party, "circulated a leaflet announcing a meeting" to be held on August 24, 1958, at 1930 New England Street in Los Angeles. "This Leaflet stated that the topic for the meeting was to be 'Which Way for Socialist Youth' and that JUDY COHEN, from UCLA, would be one of the members on the guest panel consisting of students." She was also observed attending a meeting of the Los Angeles Preparatory Committee for the Seventh World Youth Festival (which was to be in Vienna, Austria, and to which she did not go).

After taking the trouble to collect information about Judy's father from its office in Chicago, the FBI concluded its report by noting, "Logical informants advised they have no Communist Party information pertaining to JUDITH COHEN, or SWP [Socialist Workers Party] information." Judy has only the vaguest recollection of attending any such events; perhaps, she thinks, she may have gone to some with Estelle Gershgoren and her older brother, Sid. Estelle speculates that the FBI's interest in Judy was triggered by people whom she hung out with, in a case of guilt by association.[53]

Judy found some of her other activities with Estelle Gershgoren worth writing home about, including a Ballet Russe production of *Swan Lake* and movies such as *Citizen Kane* with Orson Welles, *Hamlet* with Lawrence Olivier, and *The Hunchback of Notre Dame* with Charles Laughton.[54] Of the latter two films, which she saw with Estelle and Sid (whom she described as "a very nice and interesting guy"), she commented: "They were both so great that I even somewhat averted the usual *schpilkes* [nervous energy or anxiousness]."[55] Her passing reference to her high energy level suggests one reason she was able to work so hard and achieve so much. Indeed, the immense energy that she dedicated to her work, combined with her passion, direction, and ambition, often provoked jealousy in those less motivated.

Finally Judy moved out of her aunt and uncle's home and into an apartment at 825 North Alfred with her friend Natalie (who by then had separated from her husband) rather than with Jessica (who she had decided was too selfish and in any event was preoccupied with a boyfriend whom she would marry that June at age nineteen). In early spring Judy exclaimed to her mother and brother, "Life is exciting . . . Leslie is exciting . . . living with Natalie and being free is exciting . . . and to sum it all up . . . I lead an exciting life."[56]

Later that year Judy moved into an apartment on La Mirada in Hollywood with Julie Ross and Estelle Gershgoren. The three girls managed to collect "linen enough for three weeks without washing," "dishes enough to serve 5 or 6," and "pots and pans enough to cook a 7 course meal." Judy boasted to her mother, "The source for this conglomeration of unmatched, but usable jazz is varied—from all corners we scrounged, even stealing a few knives from the School Cafeteria."[57] They divided the chores. Julie recalls coming home to see that Estelle, whose assigned chore was laundry, had hung the wash on the line. It seemed rather gray: Estelle had not known, it seems, that she had to put in soap.[58]

Observing Judy's friend Leslie visiting the three girls' apartment, their landlord told them that they had to move out.[59] For many in segregated Los Angeles during the 1950s, just the sight of whites associating with African-Americans raised eyebrows and suspicions. Thus rebuffed, the girls moved to the neighborhood called Elysian Park, where they rented an aluminum Quonset hut of World War II vintage. Estelle recalls the place as hot and unpleasant, but the rent was so cheap that she earned her share by modeling for life drawing classes at the Chouinard Art Institute, where the pay was three dollars an hour. Judy, who had to paint outside, was so unhappy, Estelle recalled, that she took no interest in contributing to the decor of their one-room hut.[60]

In the meantime, in Leslie's words, Judy and his "friendship extended into love."[61] They were both virgins at the time but had often shared a bed together and "went through the usual kissing, holding, touching, pushing—wanting."[62] He recalled that Judy had hitherto abstained because "she would have sex before marriage only if it was an act of love."[63] His account: "the nonsexual rituals were no longer bilateral. Judy was ready; I was not. I tried to ignore it. Judy understood. We stopped sleeping together. I told myself all kinds of things: we are too young; she will get pregnant; love is not enough; she's white—never. But her open and my repressed desires did not pass."[64]

Leslie's account does not exactly mesh with Judy's: "After a while, partly because of pressure from Leslie, I decided to give up my virginity. I was so alienated from my own sexual needs . . . that I dealt with the whole issue intellectually, saying to myself that it was not worth maintaining my virginity if I lost Leslie. To make love because I wanted to was not within my vocabulary."[65] She later described at length the difficulty that they had consummating their love: "It wasn't until years later that I discovered that he was a virgin, too, and just as scared and as inept as I."[66] She recounted bleeding so profusely that she had to stay in bed for two days afterward, putting ice packs on her abdomen. Thereafter the two made love regularly, without his ever asking if she enjoyed it. She allowed that he nonetheless "succeeded in giving me some pleasure" and reflected: "Why I was so mad about him, I am not sure, although we had long, philosophical discussions and danced a lot, which I enjoyed. I think there was something about him that reminded me of my father. There was also some strange identification between us."[67]

When her mother suggested to her that her relationship with an African-American man could prove too difficult over the long term, Judy responded with surprise and disappointment. Familiar with bigotry, May Cohen even worried that her daughter's interracial relationship might evoke "social pressures" that would damage her chances at receiving a scholarship from UCLA. Judy, however, confidently informed her mother that only her grades and recommendations would affect her chances of receiving a scholarship, adding, "The Regents, or Scholarship Committee, have neither the time nor the interest to explore the personal lives of each of the scholarship applicants."[68] She had her budget all figured out and explained that since the tuition for her sophomore year would be $120, plus about $80 for books, she would be able to manage: "Even without a scholarship, I'll be able to stay in school with the money I'll save during 3 months of summer employment."[69]

Judy was determined to make her mother understand that she couldn't abandon Leslie just because he was African-American: "it is just because I understand the necessity for self-interest & above that, self-respect, that I cannot let this relationship end because Leslie is black and I'm white."[70] She explained: "You see, Mother, perhaps you & Daddy made a mistake in developing in me the basic need for living according to one's principles—but, regardless of whether, in our society, it is a mistake, we must both recognize that this need exists in me. I have a great deal of faith in Man—perhaps I am too young and too idealistic—but the fate of this society and of its people is dependent upon the strength of its dissenters." She proclaimed that she was "in love with Leslie" but assured her mother: "Don't misunderstand—I am not continuing this relationship with any altruistic or martyr-like feelings—but because I am selfish." She asked: "Is the power of society such that personal desires, principles, ideas must bow to it—in order to further a system that these people feel is wrong?" Despite such convictions, her relationship with Leslie was on and off.

At the beginning of her sophomore year, Judy was eager to broaden her horizons. Her attitude was to take difficult courses "just for the stimulation," telling her mother, "I've decided that I can be neither strictly goal or grade oriented, forgetting my basic purpose in college, i.e., to become a broadened, enlightened human being, and a sensitive artist."[71] She was taking courses in philosophy, the American novel, American intellectual history, art history, and design. The dean sent her a letter informing her that she was in the "upper five percent" of students in the College of Applied Arts.[72]

In early October Judy reported to her mother that "Leslie & I have broken up for good."[73] This breakup did not dampen her support for the NAACP, which she continued during her sophomore year. That fall she wrote to her mother that she was working to organize protests and raise money for the NAACP's student march on Washington, scheduled to take place on October 25, 1958, "to protest present integration measures." She reported: "So we, here in this apathetic town, are trying to send a West Coast representative delegation."[74]

By this time Estelle had moved back home to save money, and Judy and Julie were rooming together in an apartment on North Serrano, near Western Avenue. Julie, who was in the same American intellectual history course as Judy, recalls her friend as "very lively, smart, interested," and as having "a big mouth."[75] Judy had the bedroom, in which she painted, and Julie had the front room, complete with a piano, which she played. Julie bought a cheap record player, and the two had at first just two records, which Julie played continually: *Madama Butterfly* and Bach, which Julie acquired for Judy, who wrote to her mother asking her to send her classical record collection, "especially Bach, Tartini, Brahms's Fourth, Bartók, the one with the Preludes to *Traviata* . . . Stravinsky."[76] When Judy, failing to take care, spoiled her roommate's clothes with paint, Julie sometimes despaired, but Julie was taking piano lessons and "Judy was terrific about listening to me bang away with it."[77]

Judy and Julie had just moved to the new place, when Judy's old beau, Allen Podet, arrived for a visit. Judy wrote to her mother that Allen hoped to visit L.A. during Christmas vacation as well. She pronounced him "a complete doll," boasting that "he bought almost all the food, my cigarettes, paid for practically everything, cleaned house, did dishes, ran around with me and for me, and really made me realize how nice it is to have a man around the house, which I suppose was probably his motive."[78] But then she quickly switched to thoughts of Leslie: "I saw him one night last week for a couple of hours. He is in pretty bad shape, being still much upset by out [our] breaking up. But, then, he is not alone. Until Allen came in and began to take my mind off Leslie, much as I tried not to, I thought of him continually, being able to shake off the thoughts only by running around, which is really no solution."[79] But she reflected: "Although I think that ending the relationship was my only choice under the problems created by two people of essentially the same temperament, despite the opposing backgrounds, I find it a very difficult situation to maintain. I am still very much involved with him, so we'll have to see what will be."[80]

Around the same time as Judy and Julie were hosting a housewarming party, Judy told her mother that they were "fighting off the men. I have reached the point where I am no longer interested in going out for the sake of going out. I would rather stay home and paint," she insisted, preferring to date only men "that I am first interested in as people."[81] In that category she placed fellow UCLA painter Lloyd Hamrol, whom she mentioned to her mother as "one doll of a guy," whom she had invited over for dinner. "Another guy is coming over to work with me," she wrote to her mother another time. "The one thing I have is men, no money, but men galore. I'm almost becoming an expert in getting rid of them, but not without a few broken hearts. So, who tells 'em to fall in love with me?"[82]

Lloyd Hamrol, born in San Francisco in 1937, was nearly two years older than Judy. He grew up in Los Angeles, to which his middle-class Jewish family had moved in 1940. His father was a podiatrist, but Lloyd was encouraged to take an interest in art by his mother's sister, his aunt Helen, an amateur ceramicist and folk dancer. He transferred to UCLA in the fall of 1957, after two years at Santa Monica City College. He eventually studied painting and drawing with William Brice, Jan Stussy, and Sam Amato and sculpture with Oliver Andrews. During the summer of 1958, at UCLA summer school, he studied painting with the abstract expressionist Adolph Gottlieb, learning about the New York avant-garde more than a year before Judy discovered it for herself.

That first spring at UCLA Lloyd organized an art club and remembers that Judy showed up at the first meeting. He recalls her as "outspoken, cute as a bug. She was not like the girls that I had known. She was from Chicago . . . she was one of the most opinionated persons I knew, not offensive."[83] Lloyd recalled learning a lot about Judy's father's belief system—"he was a real hero in her eyes and in her life; he gave her so much approval and support. She was a descendant of the Vilna *gaon.* I thought, oh my God, I've run into this cultural treasure. She was a child student at the Art Institute of Chicago. I was really as infatuated by what she represented as who she was."[84]

Lloyd still remembers his first "date" with Judy, when she was an undergraduate living in the Quonset hut in Elysian Park. He was impressed by her involvement with the NAACP, since he had not known many African-Americans before. Another night, Lloyd recalls, he and Judy went to a party at Suzi Wolfe's house, drank a lot of wine, and spent the night at the party in their underwear. He remembers how impressed Judy was that he didn't make a move on her.[85]

But Lloyd did not share Judy's political and intellectual bent. At this time she and a group of friends formed a discussion group that would meet every other week "centered around Marxist-Leninist principles for the sake of educating and broadening ourselves."[86] Her own self-education process often included attending the theater, about which she wrote to her brother, telling him that she had seen the play *The Diary of Anne Frank* and agreeing that "you're right, it was wonderful."[87] Written by Frances and Albert Hackett, the award-winning play about a young girl's tragic experience during the Holocaust was touring after its 1955 Broadway debut.

Judy and Julie coexisted in relative harmony. Once when Julie invited her philosophy professor, Anna Mather, to dinner, she forgot all about it and slept over at her boyfriend's. "Judy," she remembers, "got hold of me and she put the dinner together for me. A mixed blessing as she had not one cooking or domestic skill. The roast beef when it emerged was a tiny burnt dry sad little thing. But she really did try."[88] Often strapped for cash, Julie and Judy held Pay the Rent parties, charging everyone a dollar and often collecting enough to pay their rent. Judy wrote to her mother about one of these parties, telling her that they took in fifteen dollars, which would cover their food expenses for a week.[89] Others recall going to these parties on La Mirada and at the Quonset hut.[90]

On November 4 Judy wrote to her mother that she was "improving student/faculty relations by dating two teaching assistants": Charlie Moskos, in sociology, whom she met while working at the UCLA bookstore, and Scott Littleton, in anthropology, the study of which she had just dropped because of "sheer boredom."[91] Describing Scott as "short, stocky, and intellectual," she gushed: "He is fantastic! On top of being brilliant—working on his Ph.D. without getting his master's on recommendation of the Anthro. dept., the guy is a writer, working on a novel, knows more about Art & Art History than I do, loves music, including folk music and kind of semi-plays the guitar, is funny as hell, knows about all the same people that I do & is one hell of an exciting guy."[92] Littleton and Moskos actually shared a department and an office, but soon only Scott was in the picture. Six years older than Judy, he describes himself as "a goy [non-Jew] who hung out with activist Jews." He remembers her as "zaftig [buxom, well-rounded]," with a sunny disposition, very witty, extremely verbal, and outspoken: "She spoke her mind. She wasn't the 50s-type female. You knew where she was coming from. She was very straightforward."[93] He recalls that Judy used to quote her mother: "What's important is not IQ, but do-Q."

Littleton, whose father was a blacklisted screenwriter, was also a member of the NAACP and politically active on the Left. The shadow of the Hollywood Ten still hung over Los Angeles: seven writers, two directors, and one producer, who when called before the House Committee on Un-American Activities (HUAC) to be questioned about membership in the Communist Party, challenged the committee's right to probe their personal beliefs. After a second round of questioning, when some named names, HUAC finally left Hollywood in 1952, leaving behind more than three hundred blacklisted people, who were then unable to work in the motion picture industry.

With such a background, Littleton was clearly sympathetic with those of a leftist persuasion. Judy told her mother how he helped her "ditto postcards for the NAACP."[94] She had dinner with Scott and Julie, "after which the 3 of us, all broke, pooled our money & went to a Coffee Shop where we got involved in a fantastic discussion with Tom McGrath, famous West Coast poet, & Scotty & I ended up having Breakfast together Sat. morn."[95] Littleton recalls taking Judy home, only to walk in on McGrath, reclining nude on their couch, half covered by a sheet, just having made love with Julie, who had taken refuge in the bathroom. McGrath was divorced and, at forty-two, was more than twice the age of Judy and Julie, but they sympathized with his politics. Brought before HUAC in 1953, he had lost his job as a professor at Los Angeles State College, where he taught from 1951 to 1954. In his statement to HUAC he wrote: "I must refuse to cooperate with the committee on what I can only call esthetic grounds. The view of life which we receive through the great works of art is a privileged one—it is a view of life according to probability or necessity, not subject to the chance and accident of our real world and therefore in a sense truer than the life we see lived all around us. . . . I would prefer to take my stand with Marvel, Blake, Shelley and García Lorca."[96]

Years later Estelle Gershgoren wrote of McGrath, "He wanted revolution, but lacking that, he would take poetry." To protest his firing at L.A. State, McGrath's students put together a collection of his poems, for which he wrote a preface: "The poet always has the task, it seems to me: to bear witness to his times; but now especially when the State is trying by corruption, coercion, and its own paltry terror to silence writers, or dupe them or convert them into the bird sanctuaries of public monuments—now especially the artist should be responsible to the world."[97]

Scott and Judy became lovers, but the relationship was short-lived. Once when Scott stayed overnight at Judy's apartment on Serrano, in a Jewish neighborhood, Littleton recalls his car, a four-year-old yellow VW Beetle, was "attacked by another car that had to have struck it deliberately several times in different spots."[98] He suspected that someone in the neighborhood decided to avenge the Holocaust by attacking his German car. "Judy," he recalls, "thought so, too, and was somewhat disturbed by the incident."[99] He noted: "This was one of those rare occasions when I spent the whole night. In those days . . . even liberated girls like Judy never seriously considered living together."[100]

Littleton, who had fought in the army during the Korean War, was ready to settle down, but Judy had not totally forgotten Leslie, whom she was still seeing as a friend.[101] Littleton remembers that "Judy was definitely the one who broke it off," but she felt he was too little concerned with her sexual satisfaction.[102] She wrote to her mother about Scott, telling her, "I discovered I had gotten myself into another one of those situations in which I got involved fast, & by the time I realized I wasn't involved, he was completely sucked in. And of course, I had to Be Honest at all costs—so for a few days it was bad, but all is better now & far more honest. Also the relationship is a little more relaxed, & we're not going to be going out 3 & 4 times a week as we had been."[103]

Although Judy and Leslie had "broken up," their friendship still occupied a lot of her emotional and mental energy. She wrote to her mother about him at length, even though she said in the same letter that she was "still dating Scott, & pretty exclusively": "You see, Leslie always used to kid Estelle & me on all the theories that we would devise—a theory a week. So every time I say, 'New theory'—we both crack up. In fact, Les & I were discussing the concept of Self, as he is hung up in Youngian [Jungian] Psych., & I promised him a theory by the end of the week. We both laughed, but I have the theory, & I am very excited by it." She reflected and rationalized: "By implication, you can see that I still see Leslie, but it's on a very nice, warm Friendship basis, & I enjoy him very much, & I'm slowly getting over all my old feelings, which I must say, are taking a long time to disappear completely—but then, emotions are still my nemesis—it's my incongruous levels that are killing. Oh, well."[104]

Despite her active social life, Judy was engaged by her classes, especially by the paper that she was writing for her intellectual history class, called "Creativity, What It Is, Where It Comes From." She became absorbed with this theme and devised a theory that she planned to explore, involving the work of the early twentieth-century pragmatist philosopher and social psychologist George Herbert Mead, whose theory of self or the individual seemed significant to her.[105] Mead's theories encouraged analyzing the mind and personality as something people actively create in symbolic interaction with one another.

Discussing the relationship of the individual to the community, Mead wrote: "Persons of great mind and great character have strikingly changed the communities to which they have responded. We call them leaders."[106] He theorized that the behavior of the genius was both unique and "socially conditioned," explaining that "it is this uniqueness and originality of his response to a given social situation or problem or project—which nevertheless conditions his behavior no less than it does that of the ordinary individual—that distinguishes the genius from the ordinary individual."[107] When the reaction of the individual was "over against the situation in which the 'I' finds itself, . . . important social changes take place," he wrote, adding: "We do not know when the great artist, scientist, statesman, religious leader will come—persons who will have a formative effect upon the society to which they belong. The very definition of genius would come back to something of the sort to which I have been referring, to this incalculable quality, this change of the environment on the part of an individual by himself becoming a member of the community."[108] Mead's pronouncement about "artistic creation" struck a resonant chord with Judy, an as-yet-unformed bundle of creative energy: "the artists also reveal contents which represent a wider emotional expression answering to a wider society. To the degree that we make the community in which we live different we all have what is essential to genius, and which becomes genius when the effects are profound."[109] Already in her sophomore year, Judy had found a theoretical basis for her own future artwork. Developing creative potential would also become a central concern for her in teaching. Ten months earlier she had written to her mother that she was thinking of a teaching career and going for a master's degree.[110]

The art courses that Judy had taken so far at UCLA had not thrilled her, and she considered transferring to another institution. In fact, her grades reflected her dissatisfaction with her basic design course, for which she received her first C ever. Her other grades were better: A's for courses on the American novel, intellectual history, and philosophy, and a B in art history. She had been stuck taking lower division art courses but looked forward to taking subjects she considered more interesting—ceramics, sculpture, printmaking, painting, and advanced drawing, among others. While still engaged with academics, she was "getting the urge to paint again" and felt "continually frustrated due to my lack of time."[111]

The lack of studio space was frustrating. In December 1958 she explained to her mother that she needed not only materials but room to paint: "it is not only painting that is the problem, but sculpting such things as Plaster, which leaves a marvelous white, snow-like residue all over the Living Room Rug, despite the newspaper, or the wood splinters thru which Julie & I waded after I finished my woodcarving—& this is with only 1 art class—imagine this 3 fold, as I am going to be taking *3* Art Classes next semester."[112] She and Julie planned to move again, this time into an unfurnished apartment with a garage so that she would have a place to work, which she expected they could find for about $60.

Although she characterized Los Angeles as "apathetic," by the time she arrived in the city as a freshman, a lively art scene had already developed in Venice Beach, a town technically outside the city limits and therefore beyond the reach of the city council's repressive cultural politics. While not as notorious as New York's Greenwich Village or San Francisco's North Beach, Venice became an important enclave for art circles of the Beat generation. A group of young male artists, including Billy Al Bengston, Ed Moses, Craig Kauffman, Robert Irwin, Ed Ruscha, and Larry Bell, organized an informal cooperative around Walter Hopps and Edward Kienholz's Ferus Gallery, founded in 1957, on La Cienega Boulevard. These artists drew inspiration from the Southern California milieu of teenage hot-rods and exotic car designs with their bright, tropical colors and highly polished surfaces.[113]

In the city itself Judy frequented the Los Angeles County Museum of Art, where, in December 1958, she saw a Daumier show, which she pronounced "great."[114] She skipped the museum's Van Gogh show because it was too crowded. Her need to earn money kept her busy during college—her various jobs included working with recreation groups of children at the Los Feliz Jewish Center in the Silver Lake area of Hollywood and working in the UCLA bookstore. Unable to afford a trip home to Chicago, Judy spent Christmas with her friend Julie and her mother, who was a Communist Party functionary and an amateur painter; she had purchased a painting from Judy for twenty dollars, which Judy saw at the dinner. She wrote to her own mother, exclaiming: "Over their couch hangs one painting by Judy Cohen, framed no less. It's the first time I've ever been framed and glassed . . . veddy impressive, I'm sure."[115]

Despite her tight budget, Judy and another friend, Linda, took their pal Bob Kaufman out for his birthday to see Arthur Miller's *A View from the Bridge*, a tragedy set in a working-class neighborhood in Brooklyn, which metaphorically condemned the McCarthy trials and those who named names.[116] Judy had not forgotten her own father's agony at the accusations that forced him from the work he loved. This awareness shaped her youth, especially her choice of friends and her intellectual pursuits. Miller's belief that "meaning is the ultimate reward for having lived" also inspired her life and work.[117]

Despite her high ideals, Judy was sometimes as preoccupied as the next teenager with her appearance. Though cash-strapped, she admitted to her mother that she had foolishly "bought a dress for $6, reduced from $15, size 8, mother, dear. It's a casual little black knit semi-chemise . . . I shouldn't have, but I haven't bought anything for such a long time, that I feel great about it. So I'll wait a little while longer to have my hair cut, and I won't eat so good next week. It was silly, but worth it. Thank my lucky stars that I wear small sizes . . . all those nice sales." Later on during summer vacation she took a trip with Kaufman to "Las Vegas, otherwise termed Lost Wages." She managed to lose money in the slot machines, when what she needed was a scholarship.[118]

During the break between semesters, Judy spent most of her time painting. She felt that she was "finally beginning to produce some interesting things. I found myself not wanting to return to school, but rather, wanting only to stay home & paint. My artistic mind was beginning to come alive. Everywhere I looked, I got an idea for a painting. I began feeling as I had never before felt—sensitively, quietly, and simultaneously, an inner excitement & yet a total quietude pervaded me, mystic tho it sounds."[119] She talked her friend and classmate Mike Janusz into coming over and posing for her one Saturday afternoon, wearing "his now-famous Cossack shirt. I've been wanting to paint him for some time."[120] She produced a full-length portrait of him and quickly began another one. She reported to her mother: "The painting came out rather well, I'm quite pleased. In fact Mike wants it, but I think I'll keep it for just a little while, & then give it to him for a birthday present or sumpin'."[121]

Mike, Bob, and Lloyd were some of the male friends whom Judy nurtured since, she later reflected, "I noticed that most of the serious students were men, and because I wanted to be taken seriously, I sought the friendship of these men. They often told me that I was 'different' from other women. I felt a warm glow of pride in my 'specialness' and enjoyed the status that I had as the result of being the only woman they took seriously."[122] She sometimes joined in with the men when they put down other women, and though occasionally she felt "a little guilty," her desired to be "in" with them trumped her empathy for other women.[123] Like many creative and intellectual women of the day, she bought individual success for the price of male supremacy disguised as gender blindness.

She herself chose not to study in classes taught by the few women on the faculty, Annita Delano (1897–1979) and Dorothy Woodhead Brown (1899–1973). In her view, "the respected members of the studio faculty were all male. There were two older women teaching in the painting department; however, they were discounted by the male teachers and students. I can remember talking to one of the women [Annita Delano] and discovering that she was a fascinating person. She had lived a very independent life, had studied with John Dewey [and Arthur Wesley Dow at Columbia University] and traveled widely."[124] The other female instructor collected women's art, Judy remembered, but everyone laughed at the idea and never went to see it. At the time gaining respect necessitated following her male peer group. According to Lloyd Hamrol, Dorothy Brown, with whom he studied, favored male students.[125]

But memory seems to have eclipsed at least one female art instructor who taught Judy in foundations, one of the two art courses that she was required to take to finish her lower-division requirements. She described this woman's painting course as "just awful." She disliked the instructor, whom she described as "a short, plump, gray-haired, very un-arty-looking artist, who paints, as you would expect, in small areas, delicately & nebulously, insists upon such strong disciples as indicated by our weekend assignment: 'Paint Anything.' (Of course, she loves Abstract & Non-objective painting, which is what we've been doing.)"[126] This instructor was probably Annita Delano, since Dorothy Brown painted conventional representational landscapes. Delano evidently was a fan of Galka Scheyer, who promoted Kandinsky, Klee, Feininger, and Jawlensky in California, as well as of Hilla Rebay, the painter who had dictated the program of the Museum of Non-Objective Painting in New York, which later became the Solomon R. Guggenheim Museum.

Judy, at the time, clearly already felt the need for content in art: "as far as I am concerned, we haven't been doing anything—just wasting a lot of paint by throwing, doodling, scrawling—in a way totally without understanding meaning."[127] She complained too that her two-dimensional design class was back to painting gray squares, although she found the assignment to make a scratchboard with India ink over a white clay substance worth investigating for a figure drawing.

By early March 1959 Judy was dating Frank Mecoli, a twenty-five-year-old premedical student.[128] Although this relationship would be short, Frank made her "very happy," and she told her mother: "I think that we have a love between us . . . the love of living—that we share again & again . . . we can spend hours just talking about a tree that we saw and got excited about. I've never been able to do this with anyone, and it's all new and wonderful for me, but it hurts, too. But I know that the hurt will go away, and I'll become more of a full human being because of him."[129] When Frank told her that he had become interested in another girl, she took it in stride: "Frank & I had nothing more to give each other, so we broke up. . . . Why are people so afraid to admit to this simple fact—that they grow, & in growing, they out-grow."[130]

Drama began to figure in Judy's life. In her work with the girls' club at the Jewish Center, she organized the girls to present "a Creative play, which they wrote themselves, for family and friends. . . . What a marvelous group of girls—creative, responsive, individual. The club has really developed, grown & unified & I'm really pleased."[131] Teaching novel forms of creative drama to females would eventually figure importantly in her pedagogy, and she would later draw on this experience. In order to hold this job, she also had to lead these preteen girls from the center on bike trips, causing her to miss some of her art classes. She got her instructors to agree that she could just produce extra paintings and drawings on her own.[132]

Her agreement to make extra artwork on her own suggested that she had both self-discipline and drive. Neither quality made her a typical college student. In late March Judy wrote to her mother that she would like to try living alone: "The older I become the more I require a great deal of quiet and time alone. . . . As much as I like Julie, there are many things that we cannot share."[133] Judy wanted to move to Santa Monica, where her boyfriend Frank lived, which she described as "probably the closest thing to Greenwich Village in L.A. . . . replete with student & Artist Colony & the Ocean. And I love the ocean and all of its tempestuous serenity . . . it's such an interesting neighborhood . . . with all sorts of marvelous shops and buildings and scenery—very 'genre'—& Paradise for the kind of artist I am. Faces that are inconceivably fascinating, houses of all sorts from tumbledown shacks to modern structures. It's alive like no other area of L.A."[134]

Judy's mother and brother were about to move to L.A., and she recommended that they move "around the Westside Jewish Community Center, which is kind of halfway between Santa Monica & UCLA," noting "if you're interested in Center activities, that's the place to be."[135] She confided to her mother that she sometimes felt very sorry that they were not together and implored, "Please, mother, do come to L.A. before we lose so many of the things that we can share. Distance and time are so hard to transcend. We'll have to get to know each other all over again. And I really want to get to know my brother. He must be a wonderful, grown-up person by now."[136] This unusual request, which seems curious given the tense relationship she had usually had with her mother, may reflect the fact that she felt homesick.[137]

Judy was self-aware but also confused: "This is a very difficult, but very interesting period in my life. I am beginning to realize myself as an emotional, feeling person—and it is very exciting, although I find myself fighting to prevent other people from seeing me like this; at the same time I want very much to share these things inside me. Sometimes I look around me & feel so empty when I see the Emptiness & loneliness of Life . . . and then I smell the warmth of the day, and I feel good again."[138] But she understood what she wanted to do: "I want to put into my paintings all these feelings that are inside of me, and slowly I am learning to do it, but it's hard, because I've defended & hidden these things for so long . . . I'm changing so fast inside that I don't really know what I am."[139] At the end of March, although she had just broken up with Frank, she exclaimed to her mother and brother: "I love life. This is perhaps the most that any parent can do for his child—to make him love life & not be afraid of living."[140]

In early May Judy was trying to figure out how to borrow enough money ($300 to $500) to go to Israel with Allen Podet, who planned to study there in preparation to become a rabbi. She anticipated that she would travel to New York for three weeks after her finals in order to see him before he left for Israel.[141] Just a week passed, and she wrote to her family, "I guess the last you heard I was flying off into Never Never land on a talis [Jewish prayer shawl for men], or sumpin' to that effect. Well plans have changed."[142] She felt sorry for "Poor Allen," she said, who "is the one who is going away, and ironically, he is also the more involved emotionally." They had realized that her accompanying Allen to Israel was not "a good idea" because she would be going only because of him, and if their relationship did not work out, "he would feel great responsibility towards me for having schlepped [dragged] me to a place only because of my feeling for him . . . Therefore, we could not go unless we were to get married, first, which we both realize we are not ready to do."

Judy and Allen agreed that she should go instead to France if she could get a scholarship from UCLA to study for a year at the University of Paris—UCLA was then contemplating a new foreign study program. Clearly restless and confused, she still planned to travel to New York in June to see Allen off. But by the end of June she had broken off with him, deciding that she was not in love with him and could never "make his way of life mine, although I respect both him and his choice highly."[143] Even in her confusion she knew that she could not be a rabbi's wife, with all the demands that supportive role involved.

Writing in early June, she announced that she was moving to Santa Monica and planning to work at a day camp in Brentwood. "I have to get a fairly large place, as I am planning to set up a studio for myself. An artist friend of mine and I are hoping to work together all summer on some experimental stuff which will take up quite a bit of room. I have a choice . . . either I can get a small place and suffer claustrophobia and also rent a studio to work in or I can get a place large enough to both work and live, and I think I'll probably settle for the latter."[144]

Judy later described how her roommate, Julie, had "brought home a tall, lean, intense-looking fellow named Jerry," whom she had met at Café Fresco, a local spot that they all frequented.[145] Although Judy and Jerry felt an immediate attraction to each other, she initially resisted him. But after several months, they paired off. This may have been why, as she told her mother, "Julie and I are splitting up for the summer, and probably, for good. Living with another girl for more than a year is quite a feat."[146] Judy told her mother that she was ready to try living on her own for the summer.

Her new love interest, which had been building over several months with uncharacteristic caution, eclipsed her plan to go to see Allen in New York. She finally confided in her mother: "for the past couple of months I've been hung up behind a guy named Jerry Gerowitz, whose parents you might know . . . Edie and Ralph come from Chicago, know such people as Josh Zverow, were in the Rep group and lived the same kind of life as you and Daddy."[147] "The same kind of life" implied a leftist political bent with humanitarian values and a simple, nonmaterialistic lifestyle.

At the end of June Judy boasted that her landlady has branded her a "beatnik" and evicted her from her roach-infested apartment.[148] She moved to 2435 Third Street, paying a rent of $60 a month. Meanwhile she was working five days a week at the day camp with six- and seven-year-old girls for a salary of $55 a week and trying to save $300 by the fall semester. All these worldly concerns paled beside the fact that, as she proclaimed to her mother, she was in love with Jerry.

At twenty-four, Jerry Gerowitz exuded charm, brilliance, and "a great sense of humor," but he was also "mixed up and rebellious."[149] An extant photograph reveals an attractive young man with a beard, dark curly hair, and a hairline that already shows signs of receding. The elder of two sons in a secular Jewish family that was both radical and bohemian, Jerry had been born in Chicago, but his family moved to Los Angeles by the time he was in high school. The entire family loved music so much that even though they were struggling financially and often moved, they had a custom-made hi-fi system during the 1950s.[150]

Jerry's father had tried without success to be an actor and worked unhappily as an encyclopedia salesman.[151] His mother, Edie Solon Gerowitz, was a would-be writer who played the piano but worked, like Judy's mother, as a medical secretary. Jerry played the clarinet in high school and later taught himself to play the flute and oboe. He played jazz improvisation, according to his close friend, Frank Mecoli, whom Judy had briefly dated before she met Jerry.[152] Frank admits that Jerry, whom he describes as "anti-establishment," disdained stupidity and conventional behavior. He was an original who was "too damned brilliant for his own good; he was alienated and depressed, unable to find many people who understood him." Tall and athletic like his father, Jerry shared the deep cultural interests of his mother and liked to write songs. Judy wrote to her mother about Edie Gerowitz: "His mom has sort of taken me into the house, and provides real maternal interest in your absence."[153]

Four years older than Judy, Jerry was drafted into the army at the age of eighteen in 1953, then was court-martialed after he refused to sign the required loyalty oath during the height of the red-baiting McCarthy era. Lew Merkelson, a friend of Jerry's from high school, recalls that the two of them and another guy "were sitting in a car when we heard on the radio that the Rosenbergs got zapped," referring to the execution by electric chair of Julius and Ethel Rosenberg on June 19, 1953, for "conspiracy to commit espionage."[154] Jerry subsequently attended both Los Angeles City College and UCLA, from which he never graduated, but he once got into trouble there for arranging a concert by Pete Seeger, who at the time was blacklisted.[155]

When HUAC interrogated Seeger about his performing before Communist groups, he refused to invoke the Fifth Amendment, protecting citizens from self-incrimination, and asserted instead that the committee had no right to question him regarding his political beliefs or associations: "I have sung for Americans of every political persuasion, and I am proud that I never refuse to sing to an audience, no matter what religion or color of their skin, or situation in life. I have sung in hobo jungles, and I have sung for the Rockefellers, and I am proud that I have never refused to sing for anybody."[156] Jerry and Judy had the same kind of heroes.

Judy later reflected: "If Leslie bore a vague physical resemblance to my father, Jerry was his intellectual reflection, and I couldn't seem to stop myself from becoming involved with him."[157] Jerry's refusal to sign a loyalty oath also echoed her father's behavior. But the similarity to her father also encompassed some of the more problematic aspects of Jerry's personality, as Judy later realized: "Jerry was extremely gifted and completely undirected. He wandered from job to job, lived on unemployment, borrowed money from his parents, or gambled and won. He was brilliant and witty and terribly self-destructive, and I tried again and again during the next two years to break up with him, but I kept going back."[158]

While she was seeing Jerry, Judy had become pals with Lanny Meyers, about whom she wrote home: "He is just what I need right now . . . a sensitive male companion, with whom there is no tension, no big romance, just a warm and wonderful friendship." Their ongoing exchange was reminiscent of her earlier exchange with Allen: "I am teaching him how to look at pictures (primarily Modern Abstract) and he is teaching me how to listen to music. It's great."[159]

In the middle of July Judy was anticipating the move of her mother and brother to Los Angeles, just as she was getting settled in the Third Street apartment in Santa Monica. She characterized her new apartment as "marvelous" and described a large backyard, a large room, which was to be a study and studio, a small living room, a kitchen, a great bathroom, and a small service porch. This apartment set a pattern for the future: studio space would always receive priority over living space. She still had not finished painting her apartment, she reported, but Jerry had been staying with her while he looked for work, and she had "sucked him into helping me."[160] She told of doing a little drawing and almost finishing one painting since moving into the new place.

Over one recent weekend she reported that her time had been taken up by Paul, Jerry's ten-year-old brother, whom his parents had left with them. "What a kid!" she wrote to her mother. They had taken him to see the movie *The Horse's Mouth,* a comedy about which she exclaimed: "It was an extremely well-done thing, dealing with an artist, played by [Alec] Guinness. The movie was so stimulating to both Jerry & me that we left immediately, not wanting to interfere with the effects by seeing another film & came home, only to stay up all night, I painting, he, writing—it was a really exciting night."[161] Based on Joyce Cary's novel, with a screenplay by Alec Guinness, *The Horse's Mouth* tells the tale of a down-and-out artist who convinces wealthy people to pay him for paintings they didn't actually commission, a story reminiscent of Thomas Hart Benton's scheme in 1932 to get the Whitney Museum to buy murals for its library that he began without having received a commission.[162] In the film the artist actually gets people to come and work on his large painting as paying apprentices.

Jerry and Judy both related to the image of the struggling artist. While her mother had had to give up her own artistic ambition to dance, Jerry's father, Ralph, had never quite given up his dream of being an actor. Judy and Jerry went to see Ralph in a play, she wrote her mother, "the first he's done in a few years, altho, for a while, he was acting quite a bit."[163] The play was Clifford Odets's *Waiting for Lefty,* a Depression-era story about the ill effects of capitalism and the plight of the common man. On the whole, Judy had few complaints about her life. Jerry appeared not only to understand her need to create but also to have a comparable need of his own. Although she regretted not having enough time to do more painting, she did not mind the imposed babysitting: "I'm happier than I've ever been & I feel as if I'm beginning to build the kind of life I want, & obviously, Jerry is an intrinsic part of this life."[164] Less than a year later she would reflect on her landing in L.A.: "In my two years there, I became quieter, more subdued—in my personality, my living habits, et al. This was no mere growing up. Because L.A. is what it is, I was forced to depend upon internals, rather than the more external type of life I had led in Chicago. It takes a long time to grow accustomed to a place where there are few pressures, other than your own psyche produces, & few immediate outlets for your energies!"[165]

Judy's mother calmly took her daughter's pronouncements from college in stride, commenting to a friend, "Judy is just about what expected—20, emancipated half-baked college educated."[166] Her daughter's radical politics, her African-American boyfriend, her ambition, her decision to live on her own—none of it had so far caused serious discord between Judy and May. May knew her daughter well and recognized her strengths.

Soon after Judy announced her plan to move into her own studio and paint, she chose instead to move in with Jerry, who was undirected and unemployed, toyed with the idea of writing, and liked to gamble.[167] Out of money, the young couple elected to hitchhike to New York in the late summer of 1959, just as her mother and brother were finally, after much discussion and encouragement on her part, moving to L.A.[168] Only her daughter's decision to drop out of college caused May Cohen to despair: "the waste of a good mind, a good child's potential."[169] Judy, caught in the pull of Jerry's magnetism, put her academic goals aside and elected to have an adventure in the capital of the art world. She had no taste for middle-class security and convention. Instead, she believed in her own destiny and planned to go where her talent, ambition, energy, and resolve would take her.

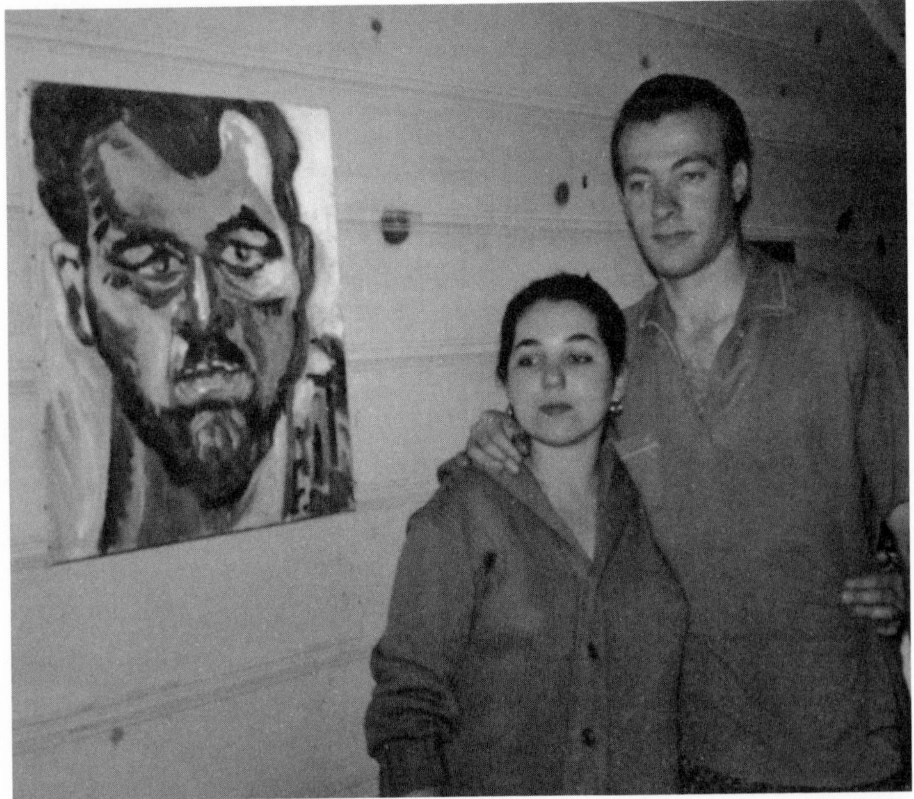

Rebellious Odyssey

5

Judy and Jerry reached New York City in early September after hitchhiking across the country. They had "encountered a series of bizarre and frightening men," she later recalled, "who stopped at the sight of a young couple on the road, an unusual sight in 1959."[1] After their midnight arrival on the back of a pickup truck, huddled under a tarp to protect themselves against the rain, they spent the first few days with her friend Lanny Meyers, at the apartment of his family, who were all out of town. Judy sent a postcard to her mother and brother, who, having moved to Los Angeles, were staying with Dorothy and Herman Polin: "Arrived Sat. morn. Went to the Museum Sat. aft. Boy it was worth the 3000 mile trip for

▲
Judy and Jerry with her portrait of him.

this. What a place."[2] The postcard reproduced Miró's *Dutch Interior,* from the Museum of Modern Art's collection.

A week later she wrote to her mother: "I begin to understand why there are so many 'starving young artisans' in New York for it is a hard, cold, brusque city."[3] At the same time she was not wholly uncritical of what she was seeing: "Jerry & I, armed with my sketch book, attended & then walked around looking at the Village Art Fair. I never realized there were so many bad painters in the world. It makes me feel like Michelangelo or thereabouts!"[4]

They managed to sublet the railroad flat of a sick friend named Peter Rosenberg, at 203 East 33rd Street, paying him $40 a month, since he had temporarily moved back to his parents' home in Connecticut. Although she found New York "hard," Judy exclaimed, "it is really a city. Whenever I go anywhere, I go in a somewhat catatonic state—there is so much to see. Jerry & I just walk & walk & walk."[5] Another time she rated the city: "With or without money, there is absolutely no place like it in the world."[6]

Almost as soon as she arrived, Judy went searching for an art school where she could continue her studies for the next school year, but she quickly ran up against inflexible admission requirements. She had wanted to enroll at Cooper Union, a tuition-free school of art and architecture, but was told she had to wait until the entrance exams were given in the spring. She could attend City College, Hunter College, or Brooklyn College for free, but having missed fall registration, she could not begin classes until February. She already knew which artists were important in New York: "Motherwell, one of the leading painters in America, teaches at Hunter, so that has definite possibilities."[7] The Hans Hofmann School had moved to Provincetown. She rejected the Art Students League because she had heard that "old people go there."[8] She decided to stay in New York until June and then return to UCLA as an "in state" student, paying lower tuition, since her mother had now moved permanently to California.

Judy had dropped out of college but definitely not out of art. If anything, her ambition to be an artist was strengthened by her arrival in the center of the art world. She was eager to learn new techniques and experiment with new media. She had completed four paintings in her head, she informed her mother, but would have to wait to realize her vision until her materials were shipped. In the meantime she purchased a dollar's worth of brown paper and charcoals and used the apartment wall as her easel.[9] She went job hunting, hoping to make enough money to pay for some art instruction: she interviewed at the Henry Street Settlement House and applied to the Museum of Modern Art as a teacher.

Having received "raves and laurels" from her old boss at the Los Feliz Jewish Center in L.A., she got the job as leader of preteen activity clubs at the

Henry Street Settlement House. Founded in 1893 by the nurse and social reformer Lillian Wald as a neighborhood-based social service agency to help immigrants in education and the arts, the house was also, in 1909, the site of the founding of the NAACP (called the National Negro Committee until 1911), in which Judy had been active in Los Angeles.

Working at a place that had long held values she cherished, Judy supported herself modestly by working five afternoons a week. She was fascinated by the neighborhood around Henry Street, which she described as "80% tenement, 20% co-op and public housing. Middle-class, Jewish families mixed with Italians, Negroes, Puerto Ricans who are not quite so middle-class (economically speaking—I do not vouch for anyone's moral!)."[10] She told her mother that she planned "to work from a base of Creative Arts, as I did last year," but would have preferred a job as an "arts & crafts" specialist, which was difficult to get.[11]

Before long Judy announced with enthusiasm that she had enrolled at the New School for Social Research in painting, drawing, and composition classes "under a well-known New York painter—Raphael Soyer," a social realist painter then nearly sixty who came of age during the 1930s. She described her teacher, who had immigrated from Russia with his family, when he was only twelve, as "a small, quiet, skinny little man who insists that we must find a 'new-realism,' whatever that means—it obviously excludes non-representational art."[12] Soyer was by then a very experienced teacher, having begun teaching about 1930 at the John Reed Club in New York. With deep roots in leftist politics, he believed in "realist and humanist art" and was strongly opposed to abstraction.[13] He had painted workers and homeless men during the Depression. Along with representational artists as diverse as Edward Hopper and Jack Levine, he was a founding member of the editorial board of the journal *Reality,* which first appeared in 1953.[14]

Soyer was then living on Second Avenue in the East Village, the center of the city's artistic and literary avant-garde. To add authenticity to the scenes he painted of the area, he liked to have young artists and writers pose in his studio, located on Second Avenue and Third Street. He may have had his eye on Judy for this work. By October 9 she was feeling good about Soyer's class: "My painting class is much improved. The instructor is letting me go my own way, but making a concerted effort to 'get to' me. His criticisms are few, but succinct. I've finally started good, & it's positively sensuous. I'm happy indeed."[15]

Elated at being in New York, Judy needed no assignments to make art. "I finished a new, & very exciting drawing," she boasted, "tho it looks more like a painting. I spent 60¢ on brown butcher paper (Oh, for Walter's Meat Market) & some charcoal, conti crayon etc. & slaved for about 3 days. Jerry and Lanny both flipped over it. My work is developing rapidly. I've already filled up the sketchbook I bought before I left L.A. I really hope this deal at the New School works out, because, altho I am painting without external discipline, I could certainly reap many benefits from the school situation."[16]

By October 20 Judy had completed her first painting and was almost finished with the second one; she was already starting two more paintings. She was painting just three hours a day, five days a week, which, she complained, was not enough. Ever industrious, she had gotten herself another part-time job, teaching painting on Friday afternoons to people over sixty at a community center.[17] But the really big news was that a local framing and painting shop had offered to sell her pictures. Progress was tentative, however, for she soon wrote to say, "I've been painting badly lately—I did three paintings in one week. I'm still having some trouble with the instructor who now has a new approach. He likes my paintings, thinks I'm very talented, but would like to see me do a factual painting. Oh well—facts are always different, depending upon who compiles them."[18] Soyer was insisting on realism, while Judy was becoming increasingly interested in exploring abstraction.

Employment took up a lot of her time, since an apartment cost more in Manhattan than in Los Angeles. "We're beginning to find nice places, fairly inexpensive," she finally wrote to her mother with relief.[19] The job at Henry Street began in October and included four groups of preteen girls (ages eleven to thirteen) and one group of fourteen-year-old African-American girls, two of whom, she noted to her mother, "had already aided the world's population directly."[20] She had also been working hard at a clerical job for six to nine hours a day at a poor salary, just to buy art materials. In California she had obtained boards on which to paint from Jerry's father and had forgotten how expensive canvas was. But she knew that when she was painting, she was developing. Though she found it novel, she relished being her own master.[21] A few weeks later she began working nights as a theater usher to pay for art materials, remarking that she had not anticipated the cost of painting, especially given her propensity for thick paint.[22]

Judy's industry and drive impressed her mother. May Cohen told her friend Pearl Cassman about Judy's adventure, reflecting: "When I think of the many parents who are uneasy because their children do not have a sense of direction, I cannot help but feel that this one has a strong independent spirit. Some kids are still dependent upon their parents even after they are married."[23]

Working at the settlement house on the Lower East Side, Judy encountered real poverty. "Americans have an ability to shut their eyes & deny the existence of anything that would shatter or even damage their security," she wrote her mother. "I suppose it's understandable—the great god Security stands for no second bests in our culture or in any others—which I suppose is in itself indicative of the Insecurity of Man."[24] The Lower East Side was cruel: "This is a world where stealing is a pragmatic, not a moral issue—where society & its mores as we know it just does not exist. And yet I find that children are children—regardless."[25] Still she had five different adolescent groups to lead. Some she found easy, but on Wednesdays her group had four "YENTAS, not potential Yentas [a busybody or gossip, usually an older woman], full-fledged members of the club, & it's nerve-wracking."[26]

Judy's job allowed her enough freedom and stimulation to hold her interest. On occasion her life in Los Angeles had been "a bit of struggle," she admitted to her mother.[27] She had occasionally fibbed about how she felt so as not to bother her mother, who had plenty of worries of her own. But her mother had seen through her ruse. Now she acknowledged that her life was sometimes rough but insisted that she was so excited by the possibilities, challenges, and rewards that lay ahead that she had no time to succumb to the adversity.[28] She felt that her work at Henry Street was improving all the time. She was constantly encountering something new there, which she enjoyed, and she felt her groups were making progress.[29] Jerry, who was working for RCA (thirty hours a week—four and a half hours every night and Saturday), was writing a short story, while she was "drawing madly, reading voraciously & going to free concerts."[30]

Despite their constant struggle to earn enough to survive, Judy soon proclaimed New York her "soul city." Her mother wrote to Pearl: "Judy is managing well, I think, but she is working like a horse . . . she is definitely on an 'art' kick now."[31] Once she had found the clerical job to tide her over before work at the settlement house began, she eagerly took in a wide range of cultural events.

Judy was so impressed by the Museum of Modern Art that she felt that it alone made her entire trip to New York worthwhile. On long-term deposit there was Picasso's monumental painting *Guernica,* which, she told her mother, "floored us—we sat in front of it for hours."[32] For someone who grew up hearing about the Spanish Republican cause from her parents and their radical friends, Picasso's mural was much more than just a famous painting. Produced for the Spanish Republican government's pavilion at the Paris World's Fair in 1937, it represented the power of art to shape public opinion. Its simple black and white forms, which memorialized those killed by the Germans' brutal bombardment of the Basque town of Guernica on market day, April 26, 1937, had caused many to focus on the immense tragedy of the Spanish Civil War.

Exciting art experiences and new people were everywhere in the city. Judy went to her first opera, *La Forza del Destino,* although she was disappointed by a poor production. But she saw dance performances by both Alvin Nikolais and Merce Cunningham, the latter with musical compositions by John Cage, Morton Feldman, and Christian Wolff; she referred to it all as a "remarkable exploration of Dance and Movement." She frequented the theater, seeing *The Connection* at the Living Theater, Beckett's *Waiting for Godot,* and Shakespeare's *Henry IV, Part I.* Although she told her mother, "I am mainly interested in contemporary work in all the fields of the arts," she allowed that "Shakespeare is always worth seeing."[33] Her favorite films included those directed by Ingmar Bergman, whose symbolic content was then much in vogue.[34] Judy's exposure to music ranged from hearing Leonard Bernstein conduct Beethoven and Shostakovich at Carnegie Hall to Jerry Gerowitz's own attempts at songwriting.

Although most often she and Jerry were alone exploring New York, she told her mother, they had met "some rather exciting people—one, an actor, Greg (Gene Gregory), who is sort of sick when it comes to women, but interesting & fun. I've met two gals—one, a model for my art class, another, a painter—both of whom I've spent time with."[35] She befriended the budding young art critic Lucy Lippard, who retroactively described herself as "a proto-hippy." Lippard has described Judy as "very emotionally honest and confrontational; it's nice but terrifying." Working in the library at the Museum of Modern Art, she could get Judy and Jerry in for free.[36]

"Our friends consisted primarily of people from the Village," Judy later wrote, "most of whom did nothing and proclaimed themselves artists of one sort or another. Many of them were involved with drugs, and a few of the women turned tricks. I experimented a little with drugs, but I was too frightened to risk doing more than that, preferring my regular work schedule to the artificially induced highs that my friends were experiencing."[37] They continued to see their friend Lanny, who told Judy that her cooking was not up to his level.[38] In mid-November Judy and Jerry finally settled down in their own "cockroach-infested apartment on [329] East Sixth Street" in Greenwich Village, where the rent was only $53 a month for three rooms, including a bathtub in the kitchen.[39] The bathroom, which lacked a shower, was out in the hall.[40] Julie Ross, who visited them there, recalls that their furniture was quite spartan: a mattress on the floor.[41]

Judy and Jerry sent his folks a handmade greeting card with "Season's Greetings" and a bold modernistic figure on the front. The back contains the phrase: "An Original J & J Creation." The interior has a poem:

Now that the first snow has fallen—
Its whiteness has wiped
palm trees from mind
As we trudge though slushy streets
we realize the year is ending
As we sit and write in radiatored,
steam apartments 3,000 miles away:
As always we are with you

Soon after this collaboration, Judy decided to leave Jerry and live alone. She felt that their the relationship was over and told her mother that she planned to move out. But she admitted that she had not told Jerry yet, because she had not yet made actual plans.[42] Despite the great sexual tension between them, they often argued, mostly over what she perceived as Jerry's lack of direction. She saw herself as "a disciplined hard-working girl" and resented his relaxed pace: "He often sat around reading, watching TV, and I guess the resemblance to my father's patterns, much as they attracted me, also frightened me."[43] Only later, after years of therapy, could she write: "It is clear that in my relationships with men, there was a high component of searching for a father figure with whom I could work out some of the unresolved issues from my father's death."[44]

Once Judy and Jerry were splitting up, Peter Rosenberg, whom she had first met in L.A. through a mutual friend, began to spend time with Judy. She saw Peter as "27, very attractive, very bright," and cautioned, "I don't know if anything will develop but I almost don't care—I like him & I like being with him, & that is enough for me right now."[45] Peter, she reported, was always "feeding me," and not just with food, for it was with Peter that she first visited Frank Lloyd Wright's new Guggenheim Museum.

Judy was enchanted by the new building, which she compared to a work of sculpture. She could hardly believe how wonderful it was: "It's based on a spiral & is all white. You know the feeling you have going up in an elevator—of moving space with a sort of strange sensation at the pit of your stomach—that's the feeling I got at the Museum—of great moving space."[46] The negative response that the building elicited from critics annoyed her: "I tell you—all the art critics, etc., can go to hell—they felt obliged, as usual, to be pedantic & picyune [*sic*]—when all they should have done was bow to the master of American Architecture. (There, I just vented my feelings towards critics, who like teachers & philosophers, of esthetics, *talk,* and talk can become quite boring.)"[47] She reminded her mother of the saying that she had often quoted to her friends: "Your little homely philosophy, i.e. I.Q. without Do-Q = Phew-Q, has become increasingly more meaningful throughout the years."[48]

While looking for an apartment for herself, she discussed her situation with Soyer, who, after she prodded him a bit, turned out to be a pretty good teacher, egging her on to make more work. She did not enjoy working in the classroom, which she felt could stifle creativity, and preferred working at home alone.[49] She planned to continue her job at Henry Street, where her groups were going well and she was learning a great deal, but she planned to supplement her income by modeling for art classes.

Soyer quickly recognized Judy's exceptional talent, energy, and ambition and told her that she drew so well that she might learn more from working with a printmaker than from being in a class.[50] He then set her up with an etcher who was also supposed to print her etching plates. He had arrived from Italy just seven months earlier and was married, which relieved her because, as she told her mother, "I am in no mood to have any sorts of erupting relationships."[51] She made her first etching plate, only to discover that her Italian instructor fancied her. She wanted nothing more from him than lessons in etching—which now became impossible for her to obtain.[52]

In January 1960 Judy, who found Soyer too conservative, complained that he wanted her to paint his version of art.[53] She rejected his "new realism" and his emphasis on communicating a humanistic message. Like so many other young artists in New York, she found that work by Jackson Pollock, Mark Rothko, Willem de Kooning, and others seemed much more appealing. She embraced abstract expressionism, the gestural painting style that had emerged during the 1940s and that dominated the city during the 1950s, becoming known as the "New York School." "I'm sure you've heard the term Abstract Expressionism—well, that's the kind of painting I'm doing," she wrote to her mother. "It took a little while for me to learn to see this way, but it's coming slowly. I do believe it is today's way of seeing the world and that is very important."[54] She considered "De Kooning's series of paintings entitled 'Woman' . . . great. He has one called 'Marilyn Monroe' which kept me laughing for a week."[55]

She started another job, teaching art to children for the Police Athletic League at the Miccio Center in Brooklyn, for two dollars an hour, five nights a week. Together with her job at the Henry Street Settlement, she earned $55 a week, enough for her to live on without any contribution from Jerry or any roommate.[56] But it left her only until two-thirty or three o'clock in the afternoon to paint. The Police Athletic League took the children to whom she taught art on excursions to "ritzy-type places," where some of the women she encountered so annoyed her that she complained that they were "T.S. Eliot types who talk about Michelangelo at Cocktail parties. I do believe that one of the things that the emancipation of women has produced, aside from a lot of crazy women, is an abundance of brilliant comments on American womanhood, ranging from Eliot to Lawrence to De Kooning."

But as before, it was not the women but the men who made the brilliant comments, and with whom Judy identified. "I slowly and unknowingly began to absorb the culture's contempt for women," she later reflected, "rationalizing my own femaleness, as the men did, by the fact that I was somehow 'different.' "[57] Her friends in the city were predominantly men, "for men are much more interesting than women it seems to me."[58]

Apartment hunting was discouraging, and Jerry was still living at their apartment and trying to hold on to her.[59] But she was so busy that she did not think that the wait for Jerry to leave would be so bad, reassuring herself, "I make it no matter where I am—Old Rubber Ball Cohen, they call me!"[60] By the end of December, however, she had become impatient that Jerry was still hanging on in their apartment, although she understood that he was not leaving until he got paid for his part-time job. She looked forward to becoming a free woman again: "it's been so long, but I love it."[61] Three weeks later Jerry moved uptown, she decided to stay on in the apartment, and he wanted to maintain a friendship. They saw each other occasionally.[62]

Judy enjoyed the challenge of teaching art to teenagers at night for the Police Athletic League: "It's very interesting how Modern Art has taken hold. The boys seem to see abstractly. No longer do they have to draw faces & houses—they just draw. I find their conceptions very exciting. . . . My major effort at night is to loosen up some of the older teenagers, who suffer from high school art inhibitions."[63] She was also enjoying making girls' costumes for one of her clubs at Henry Street, telling her mother that she had inherited her knack and "find it great fun. In fact I'd love to do some costume design for the stage."[64] A few weeks later she complained, "All my money goes for paint & supplies, & I can't bother about clothes."[65]

In the spring, Judy was upset that a colleague at the Henry Street Settlement House was planning "a big Easter play, with kids hanging from crosses & ascending to heaven." She believed that a settlement house, especially one that was attempting to maintain the participation of the neighborhood's rapidly dwindling Jewish community, should not sponsor another Christian religious production, especially so soon after its Christmas play.[66] From her point of view, all of these religious stories were just myths, so why not have a Passover play now? It would be more interesting to stage than the Easter story. But it was too late for her to do anything about it, since she was committed to working on whatever production her colleague chose. The clubs she supervised were taking "an active part in set design."[67]

Despite her disapproval, Judy made thirty costumes for the play, "each different. They have to be well-made, as they are for repertory & will be used again. The play has been cut down to readings, so I have [to] have complete sketches for about forty-five costumes—each of these take [*sic*] an hour to complete, plus 1 hour to fit . . . I've been quite a perfectionist about them."[68] Her care predicts the creativity she would put into costume design in future teaching assignments.

Judy was becoming much more interested in abstract art, although she had scorned it in college. "I seem to be getting more abstract," she wrote to her mother, sending her a drawing that she described as "still quite realistic & its major function is a decorative one . . . there are 2 figures—male & female. Look at them & try to see as I saw—distortion & abstract have a purpose & it is up to you, the viewer, to try to understand what the purpose is . . . it is a subconscious understanding, usually. As Picasso says, no one tries to understand a bird, why does everyone insist upon understanding painting?"[69]

Judy disagreed with her mother's opinion of the abstract painter, Piet Mondrian, arguing: "his contribution was of vital importance to the growth of contemporary art, & this is outside of any feeling I have for him as an artist. It is only lately that I have really begun enjoying him."[70] As she attempted to absorb the latest styles, she went gallery-hopping with a friend named Marcia. Through her friend Peter Rosenberg, she was invited to spend the night at the West Redding, Connecticut, home of Graydon and Emily Walker, art collectors whom she described as having "beaucoup money, own a Rolls Royce, and 11 Jackson Pollock paintings."[71] But it was her own painting that mattered most to her. "When I don't paint, my whole life loses its meaning," she told her mother.[72]

Despite having dropped out of college, Judy was reading more than she had in school. She devoured D. H. Lawrence, whom she declared "the recurrent rage," Carson McCullers, whom she pronounced "great," and Thomas Wolfe, whom she called "that emotional crybaby prose writer who makes the English language reach new heights."[73] Soon she was also reading Henry Miller, whom she viewed as "probably one of the greatest contemporary American writers."[74] In January, starting her second semester in New York, she was contemplating returning to UCLA.

While in New York, Judy also renewed her interest in existentialist writers, revising her earlier dismissive comments. Her friend Greg had a part in a Broadway production of *Caligula* by Albert Camus, and she read many of his works. In Camus's *The Rebel* she would have read about the agony at the heart of radicalism: "The act of rebellion affirms the value and the dignity common to all men."[75] In Camus, one learns about the limitations of human existence and the injustices of life: "So many injustices suffered, a sorrow so unrelieved, justify every excess."[76]

Jean-Paul Sartre, whom Judy identified as "the French Existentialist," had also attracted her attention.[77] Sartre's embrace of the humanist ideas in the early work of Karl Marx, his empathy with Communist idealism, and his championing of causes as a politically engaged activist had their appeal for Judy. She could see that Sartre's creative work in the theater served as a vehicle to convey his philosophical ideas, including that humanity is what we ourselves make it.

The literature and philosophy of existentialism was an intellectual source for many of the generation of the New Left during the 1960s. Historian Todd Gitlin has argued, "All breathed the air of existentialism; action might not avail, but one is responsible for choosing. And so from the dead hand of history, they leaped to a paradoxical conclusion; that history was alive and open."[78] Gitlin has theorized that Judy's generation was "haunted by history"; that they "had been taught that political failure or apathy can have the direst consequences; they had extracted the lesson that the fate of the world is not something automatically to be entrusted to authorities. The red-diaper babies among them were often especially eager not to be cowed; their own passivity might confirm their parents' defeats."[79] Judy had already observed her father's undoing. Now she was determined to change history.

Again contemplating her return to Los Angeles and to UCLA, Judy wrote to her mother—who was complaining after having moved there—that it had taken her two years to adjust, despite her youth, her studies, and her active social life. She acknowledged that she had "developed from the experience of L.A. as a city—without pressures, without mad, bustling activity—conducive to quieter, more introspective, self-sufficient living."[80] "When I got to L.A., she admitted, I oscillated from elation to deep depression, I lay down only one rule—*I will have no regrets!* I made my choice, & now—I will look ahead, rather than behind—for I can't go back even if I want to."[81]

Another time Judy wrote to her mother: "I am learning, for the first time in my life, how to be alone. In some ways, I am very lonely, as I don't go out very much, mainly because I don't want to. But being lonely is good for me—I must learn to be lonely without being unhappy. I don't mean the loneliness that can be assuaged by seeing a friend—that's aloneness. I mean the loneliness that never goes away—& is often increased in effect when I am alone."[82] But she assured her mother: "I really feel better today than I've felt in a long time . . . I'm pretty happy."[83]

In the spring Judy's friend Myrna, who had broken up with Greg, the actor, was staying with her for several weeks, but she looked forward to the return of her "blessed solitude."[84] She was annoyed when word got around that it was "Open House at Judy's after 11 PM—so it started to resemble Grand Central Station here."[85] She had difficulty kicking the visitors out and regretted losing about two weeks of painting time. She determined to end this socializing, not because she did not like people but because all the partying bored her. Finally, in disgust, she left one night at about two in the morning and went across the street to a friend's place, where she fell asleep, awaiting her guests' departure. "I'm becoming a positively anti-social type," she concluded.[86] Usually gregarious, she enjoyed people only when she felt that she was doing "all the things I have to do, at which point they expand rather than infringe upon my life."[87]

By late April she returned to living with Jerry, whom she claimed to have "rediscovered." Each was finding that the other had evolved and grown.[88] What seemed to be most changed in Jerry was his new sense of purpose; he now seemed less like her father after he lost his job and was adrift and depressed. Judy was pleased that Jerry "had established a sort of partnership with another writer—they've started on a play, outlined a film script, but lately have been writing songs for 2 singers," namely "Paul and Art who record for Columbia," and who planned to use their song on their next record.[89] After seeing her work on children's play costumes, the two singers asked her to design a costume for them, promising her $80 after their next record. She described it as "a brilliant design even by my stringent standards."[90]

Jerry's mother, Edie, whom Judy described as "*mad* (in a pleasantly insane way)," came and stayed with them for a week.[91] Judy was obviously fond of Edie, for whom she made a series of clever greeting cards, revealing that she could laugh about stereotypical women's traditional roles, even while rejecting them for herself. On a card entitled "Som[e] Mothers" that depicts three women, the imagery is clearly Judy's. Inside are phrases and sentences cut from magazines. One reads: "I've been told I can't cook. I can't sew, and I'm not fit to be a wife . . . It's OK; I'm playing along with the game, and when the right moment comes I'll let him have it right between the eyes."

Another visitor was her friend Julie Ross, who arrived in New York from L.A. Julie recalls that they went to some jazz clubs in the East Village.[92] Judy still enjoyed talking to her former roommate but felt that they had "grown in different ways."[93] By now Judy saw her future as involved with Jerry, whom Julie did not like at all and considered very selfish. Judy viewed Julie as lacking "any real direction in life."[94] Judy told her mother that she and Jerry were still planning to return to L.A. in September so that she could continue with school, but she also might decide to study with some New York painter or "Jerry will be involved in working with someone here, so we'll see."[95] At this point she could envision deferring to Jerry's needs and putting her own degree on hold. Two weeks later, however, she wrote her mother to say that UCLA had awarded her a scholarship of $3,000, so that "barring any great new development," she planned to return to L.A in the fall.[96]

Judy was elated that she landed an even better summer job than Henry Street: she became the arts and crafts specialist for Wel-Met Camp in the Catskills, where the campers were the "Golden Age group—this means old people—which may be quite an interesting change from little ones."[97] She was excited that she was getting paid room and board plus $525 for the season and that they had a kiln—she anticipated making ceramic sculptures and jewelry while there. Before she left for camp, she wrote to her mother that she and Jerry were baking a pie. For the moment their domestic bliss appeared better than ever.[98]

"I am tired of giving all of my creativity & energy to others," Judy complained from the camp in Narrowsburg, New York; it took too much of her life, although she admitted that she was learning a lot.[99] She reported her success to her mother but added that she had literally collapsed and was still exhausted. The staff was short one counselor, which kept her very busy, serving as a "group worker" and also organizing the dramatics program, which produced a play written by one of the campers. Once again she gained valuable experience teaching drama. She could only anticipate the time when she could paint again, although she did manage to fit in some sculpture, drawing, and a little painting. Her twenty-first birthday took place at the camp, marked only by two long-distance phone calls, one from Jerry and the other from her friend Tippy (Lena Tipton), Lanny's girlfriend. Judy spent her day off making a trip to New York City to see Jerry. Once again their tumultuous relationship changed course, and the bliss that she had reported to her mother ended: "We resolved some of our problems, but I am pretty sure I'll be coming to L.A. alone—perhaps he'll come out later."[100]

Back in L.A. in the fall of 1960, Judy resumed her studies at UCLA. For a few weeks she lived with her mother and brother, who had settled in the Fairfax area. She then moved alone into a small house. Her mother wrote to a friend, "Judy has already moved out and Bob wishes she wouldn't even come around at all. Apparently there is no rapport between them at all. While I was gone, he told me she ran around or had people in all the time, and treated him (I gather) as if he didn't exist."[101] She also reported that Judy was determined to learn and explore: "she doesn't want to skim the surface. . . . She *hocks a chinek* [talks a great deal or talks nonsense], and you know, my dear, I find her wearing. Am I showing my age?"[102]

After several weeks Jerry returned to L.A., no doubt aggravating the stress that Judy was feeling after returning to school. She and Jerry made another try at getting together and suffered another breakup. This time she relocated to a small house at the beach, in the Ocean Park neighborhood, between Santa Monica and Venice. The house came with a small backyard, where she cast concrete sculptures and worked on large clay pieces.[103] She shared this place with Joan D'Angelo and her boyfriend Fernando Nevarez. Both Jerry and Lloyd Hamrol were on the scene, but Jerry infuriated Fernando. Julie Ross describes an incident at the Lucky U. bar in which Jerry poured an entire pitcher of beer on Judy's head. This outburst reveals his temper and suggests that he may have had too much of Judy trying to coax him to return to school. Jerry had no college degree, but at the time he was not particularly interested in taking that route, which then preoccupied Judy, Joan, Fernando, and Julie.

At school Judy noticed more than ever that "girl students weren't taken too seriously in the art department."[104] She was having a difficult time in the painting department but found the sculpture teacher, Oliver Andrews, "more encouraging and sympathetic."[105] Andrews had joined the faculty at UCLA in 1958, at the age of thirty-three, having studied at Stanford and with Jean Hélion in Paris. Perhaps Andrews's progressive attitude toward women resulted from the fact that his own role model had been a woman. He was very proud of the career of his grandmother Lila Tuckerman as a painter. She had studied in New England around the turn of the century and produced postimpressionist paintings working with a palette knife, which he viewed as "incredibly daring at that time."[106] Andrews's own sculpture encompassed many techniques, and he was constantly open to innovation, eventually involving electricity, neon, water, and air. He was concerned with environments and later made giant floating mylar sculptures. He also wrote a book called *Living Materials: A Sculptor's Handbook.*

At the time Andrews gave his students encouragement and a sense of endless possibilities. Judy took to Andrews's teaching, as did her old friend Lloyd Hamrol, who began graduate work in the fall of 1959, working with Andrews, and finished four years later, getting his MFA in 1963.

Taking one sculpture course that fall and two more in the spring, Judy saw a lot of Lloyd. Indeed, when she seemed to have broken up with Jerry, she and Lloyd became romantically involved. Their relationship really got started in the fall of 1960 in her mother's house, when she was just back from New York. Judy later wrote, "We used to joke about being Braque and Picasso. We dated occasionally, and Lloyd always wanted to have a serious relationship. But I tended to see him as my 'soul mate,' which somehow, in my eyes, precluded the possibility of any romance."[107]

They began helping each other with their work, Lloyd recalls. Judy modeled for him, and he also posed for her.[108] She was doing figurative drawings at the time. Joan D'Angelo, her classmate and friend, remembers that Judy's "very visceral drawings" inspired her own work. She recalls that Lloyd helped Judy a lot with her work since he had building and technical skills.[109] He adored Judy, she observed, but she thought Judy was using him. Lloyd, however, recalls that they spent a lot of time together and that she wanted to get back together with him. He recalls how much Judy offered: "I could pursue art making, gossip . . . she was never stingy with her feelings—part of the attraction . . . I wasn't quite sure about how I felt about her as an equal . . . I needed time to catch up, to work on myself."[110] From her perspective, she was still longing for Jerry, and Lloyd was hurt when she and Jerry got back together.

In early November May wrote to her friend that Judy had not been feeling well. Back in New York she had been having acute abdominal pains, and now they began to recur quite frequently.[111] Tests were conducted at UCLA Medical Center, where, as her mother reported, "she was seen by a female gynecologist who was anxious to probe her for emotional problems, but Judy blandly remarked: 'I don't have any.' I may not quite agree, but I can't help but be most amused by this response."[112]

Judy then experienced stomach pains so horrific that Jerry took her to the UCLA hospital, where they hospitalized her for bleeding ulcers.[113] That was at the end of November, and she remained in the hospital for an entire month. Her mother described the situation to her friend after she had been there about two weeks: "The abdominal pains were the result of a large gastric ulcer which created quite a stir in the hospital. Surgery may be indicated. However, Judy was her old bouncy self when I saw her last, so I am hopeful that she is improving."[114]

By December 31 Judy was out of the hospital, but her ulcer had spread to her pancreas, and it would take thirty days to see if it had healed properly. "Don't tell Enid about Judy," her mother cautioned her friend in Chicago, because she didn't want her sister-in-law to be anxious that Judy now had the same illness from which her father had died.[115]

In early February her mother wrote to her friend: "About Judy—I think she is getting better, although she looks bad. Remember how lovely she was . . . she's sort of heavy looking and isn't doing anything to make herself attractive. She looks just like weird distortions of what a Beatnik is supposed to look like . . . Judy is not coming home to live . . . quite a bit of apprehension on both sides . . . So instead I shall subsidize her as long as it is possible for me to do so, in order for her to take it a little easier and not go scrounging around for jobs, etc."[116] May Cohen understood that Judy "would like to finish school" and felt that she probably should, but, she told her friend, "why I'm not sure."[117] Judy's mother, once upset that her daughter had dropped out of college, was no longer sure about her daughter's direction.

At the end of March May reflected that Judy was "beginning to become the Judy of old . . . she still has pain from the ulcer, but is generally feeling better. She is even beginning to look more like my daughter, although she is heavier than she and I would like her to be."[118] May understood that her daughter was happy when she was painting or drawing or sculpting.[119] But she worried that Judy's health remained fragile. In early May she was back in the hospital. Her mother, who worked days as a medical secretary, visited her every night. Although Judy's ulcer had healed, she suffered from "severe gastritis which they think is the result of anxiety about herself. . . . as soon as she was discharged, after having been in the hospital for a month, she went right back into her hectic way of life, working at peak . . . dating . . . so they're starting psychotherapy, I guess. I'm beginning to think it's a good idea, for she has to learn to develop some insight into this mad motivation."[120]

Judy was so frightened by the experience that she began therapy under the auspices of the UCLA student health service, seeing Elizabeth Bradshaw Sturgeon (1913–1989), a psychiatrist who, according to Judy's mother, had an interest in "creative people."[121] One of the graduate students who interned with Dr. Sturgeon at UCLA recalls that she was "particularly interested in students with artistic talent of one kind or another" and was "a very intelligent, warm and empathetic person, unusually friendly with the young interns. I believe that she worked in what we would now call a psychodyanamic framework, focusing on introspection and insight."[122] Dr. Sturgeon was married to another physician, Judy remembers, and once explained to her that "their relationship was like two kitties; they played together or something to that effect that challenged the idea of a highly intellectual relationship being the only possibility for two professionals."[123] Though this surprised her then, she later came to understand the idea.

The psychotherapy was successful enough that Judy got her life back on track and did not suffer more serious trouble from the ulcer. "Therapy was an uphill battle that lasted two and a half years," she later wrote. "After seven weeks, I began to cry, and the tears brought relief to the bottled-up grief from my father's death, which I had literally turned inward on myself, eating my own stomach away in an effort to become my father and, in that way, keep him alive. As my painful secrets came out, I looked at the stories I had told myself: that I was guilty of my father's death."[124] For a thirteen-year-old, the death of her father and the way her immediate and extended families had handled it had been too difficult to work through. She had imagined that her "thoughts and wishes had the power to kill," fantasizing that her kiss had killed her uncle Harry and that she had killed her father by arguing with him or even by disappointing him.[125] During this extremely difficult time, filled with tears, she gradually tried to reconstruct the life history shattered by her father's untimely death.

Therapy was also good for Judy's relationship with Jerry. She was anxious that he become more responsible and work regularly, since her depressed father had stayed home from his job as an insurance salesman, which he detested. She wanted Jerry to find a direction in his life, since her father had lost his direction when he had had to resign from both the post office and union work. In her view of Jerry, "he loved me and wanted to make the relationship work and agreed to make changes in himself and his life."[126]

They married in the spring of 1961 at the Los Angeles County Courthouse. Jerry got a job, and though they still fought, they started to work things out. He had been very alienated as a teenager and bored by high school. He had spent his teens at the movies but was extremely lonely and once told Judy that he preferred to be alone than to compromise with a relationship that left one lonely.[127] A rare snapshot shows the couple posing before Judy's portrait of Jerry, which is boldly and skillfully rendered, a symbol of her devotion to him. While he has his beard in the portrait, by the time the snapshot was taken, he had shaved it off, perhaps a sign of his intention to join the workforce as she hoped he would. Their facial expressions, like their relationship, were quite somber. Judy appears rather stout; her hair is dark and pulled back from her face, creating an austere look.

Judy insisted on an equal division of housework, to which he initially agreed, although they later argued about his messy habits. She once exploded over his habit of leaving his socks on the floor and exclaimed: "What makes you think that because, by a biological accident, I was born with a cunt, I am supposed to pick up your socks?" She recalls that Jerry looked shocked, then laughed and admitted that she was right.[128]

Jerry's cooking and cleaning seemed natural to Judy, since they both worked. Several of her friends, however, including Joan D'Angelo and Fernando Nevarez (who were living together), disliked Jerry. Both couples lived in Ocean Park and socialized together. "From the moment I met Judy," D'Angelo recalls, "she had confidence, knew she would be a famous artist." She was "burning at a high temperature."[129] On the other hand, she experienced Jerry as depressed, very intense, arrogant, selfish, and combative. Nevarez recalls that D'Angelo once spent the day preparing a wonderful dinner for Judy and Jerry, but when they arrived, fiercely bickering, they spoiled the evening for everyone, reducing D'Angelo to tears. In sharp contrast, Frank Mecoli says of Jerry, "I loved him like a brother," and maintains that Judy was "in awe of his brilliance."[130] It was Frank whom Judy consulted when she searched for a doctor to perform two abortions. Neither she nor Jerry then wanted to have children. Photographer Ralph Gibson, then just out of the navy, recalls Jerry as "smarter than anyone else; very witty, more erudite than others."[131]

Jerry had plenty of reasons to be distressed. Several months after he and Judy married, his parents' marriage had unwound. The strain on Jerry was so obvious that Judy's mother reported the breakup with the comment: "I'm glad my Judy is in therapy. . . . I feel she will gain a good deal of insight which she will need because of Jerry's involvement in a miserable relationship between his parents. Jerry's father had been working very little & I guess the strain was telling on him and his wife."[132] Jerry also had to worry about his younger brother, Paul, who was then only twelve years old. Paul recalls that their mother, Edie, was quite fond of Judy and had been happy that Jerry had found Judy because he had told her that "he doubted he'd ever meet the right person."[133]

While Jerry had no use for school, Judy was determined to graduate. She also genuinely enjoyed her classes. During her first semester back she received B's for her courses in painting, printmaking, and advanced drawing, and A's for sculpture and theory and criticism of art. During the spring term she switched her emphasis to sculpture, taking two courses, as well as painting, life drawing, and courses in American art history and theory and criticism of art. She earned all A's except a B in the art history course. Determined to make up for lost time, she enrolled in summer school in 1961, where she took English courses in poetry and the age of Alexander Pope and Samuel Johnson, as well as a philosophy course in religion and literature. That July she received a letter from UCLA informing her that she was on the dean's honors list for the fourth time.[134]

At the time there were few women on the faculty of the College of Fine Arts. A note in the yearbook explained, "A shift in emphasis in the College of Applied Arts, now Fine Arts, accents the aesthetic rather than the practical. Business education and Home Economics, under the new plan, will be eased out of the college in the next three years."[135] Judy's undergraduate years encompassed the beginning of a time of dramatic change in women's roles. The few women professors taught the design courses required of freshmen, a holdover from when normal school curricula offered teacher training for art in elementary and secondary schools.

Continuing her studies in the fall of 1961, Judy took two classes in life drawing, one in sculpture, one in theater, a philosophy course in laws and morals, ancient drama in the classics department, and modern European art history. Her grades were all A's except for a B in philosophy. Her mother boasted, "She's coming along beautifully . . . she's happy," proudly announcing that Judy's first piece of sculpture was then being shown in an exhibition for artists, not students, in a small town in California. A lot of artists had submitted, and many were rejected. Judy was also offered a teaching assistantship for the next year, which paid about $2,000, and she also taught some extension classes. They were in "sculpture, which she seems to think is her real field," bragged her mother. "She considers it a real triumph for very few women get TAs in that area."[136]

During her final semester, the spring of 1962, she took theater, Chinese art history, a course in Slavic studies on Dostoyevsky, a printmaking course, and social history. Her mother noted that while Judy had no phone, Jerry was working and had bought a car. Despite the distractions of Jerry and his troubled family, Judy was elected to Phi Beta Kappa when she graduated from college in 1962.[137] She was the first art major at UCLA to receive this award, since she had minored in the humanities. Thus even while Judy and Jerry were part of the youth culture of the early 1960s, she remained focused and did not drop out. She may have shared his defiant attitude, but she did not shirk responsibility and was not about to fall short of achieving her goal of becoming an artist.

Looking back years later, she recalled: "When I got out of college, I moved into 'serious' art-making . . . being affected by abstract expressionism and minimal art . . . I developed as an artist, but I was not satisfied because I felt that I was only using a part of myself. Yet there was almost no model for making art 'as a woman,' except a degrading one . . . you know, 'ladies' paintings.' But I was determined to be all that I could be and to find a way to be myself in my work."[138]

After about a year of marriage, in the spring of 1962, Judy and Jerry moved to a house in Topanga Canyon, a mountainous area of Los Angeles. Friends recall that for the first time the couple took pride in their home, set in its attractive natural environment, and were fixing it up.[139] That fall she began graduate study in art at UCLA, taking two sculpture courses and one in painting. The garage at their house in Topanga served as her studio, and she worked on stone-carvings outside behind the house. Jerry began therapy and went back to school, deciding that he wanted to be a writer. That was their best year so far. They had worked out a lot in their relationship and were both doing well in their individual lives.[140]

With marriage to Jerry, Judy kept old friends and made new ones. Lloyd

Hamrol finally accepted that he and Judy would only be friends. Judy and Jerry fixed him up with a friend of hers, Nancy Gowans, a classmate in the UCLA art department. Lloyd and Nancy soon married and held their wedding party at Judy and Jerry's Topanga Canyon home. Lloyd reflects, "Maybe I got married because Judy and Jerry got married."[141]

During this same period Judy became close with Janice Johnson, who also lived in Topanga Canyon and whom she had first met at UCLA. The daughter of a doctor, Janice had a comfortable childhood in Los Angeles, during which she studied dance with Lester Horton and Bella Lewitzky. It was in the latter class that Janice became close friends with Elaine Kusnitz (the future author Kim Chernin), whose mother, Rose, was a Communist. Janice recalls vividly when the FBI showed up unannounced at her elementary school and got to question her about who she had seen having dinner at Elaine's house. Janice graduated from Fairfax High School, where her classmates were mostly Jewish, although she was African-American. Despite their different backgrounds, she and Judy had a lot in common and would form a strong and long-lasting bond.

Janice, Judy, and Jerry used to drive to UCLA together. Janice, who says she liked Jerry, recalls him as a struggling writer who was "very bright, articulate, rather unhappy."[142] She sees Judy as "very strong, very direct, self-assured, self-directed," but adds that she was very blunt: "her diplomatic skills were nil." Perhaps this contrast of personalities alone was enough to create difficulties for the young couple. Nonetheless, after they were married for a while, Judy discovered on her regular Saturday afternoon gallery strolls that "there seemed to be too many other artists named Cohen,"[143] whereupon she took the name Gerowitz.

In early June 1963 Judy and Jerry returned home in their recently purchased pink and white Mercury to find Cleo, their four-month-old Labrador retriever puppy, dead on the road, hit by a car. Both were upset, but Jerry was particularly devastated, for he relived the experience of watching, when he was only six, his puppy get hit by a car. Depressed, the couple buried the dog behind their house. A few days later, at a gathering at the beach, one of their friends began to make observations about their marriage to Judy, telling her that she gave Jerry much more than he gave her. When she tried to talk to Jerry about this at home later that evening, "he became very defensive," and she failed to communicate to him that what she wanted was more emotional contact with him.[144]

The next morning, June 10, was bleak, gray, and rainy. But Jerry's mood had improved, because before he drove off to his therapy appointment, he joked with her, signaling that he was not still upset about the previous night's conversation. When he did not return by noon, an hour later than expected, Judy became anxious and called his doctor's office, only to be told that he had not arrived for his appointment. Two of their friends had spent the night, and they began calling the police and local hospitals, looking for Jerry. As Judy's anxiety mounted, Janice came over and decided to go out and look for Jerry herself. She recalls that she had a compulsion to stop at one particular curve in the two-lane road. It was the only place she looked.

There, well below the road, which lacked guardrails, at the bottom of a canyon where many other cars had previously landed, she saw Jerry's wrecked car turned upside down in a stream; his body had been thrown from the car. She flagged down another car and asked the driver to go and get help. Frantic, Janice climbed down the steep incline and rolled over Jerry's body, which was covered with ants. He had been dead for a while. When the firemen arrived, they could not imagine how she had made her way down the steep canyon walls.[145] It was left for Janice to break the news to Judy who, when she saw her face, knew before she could say the words: "He's dead, Judy. Jerry's dead." Judy screamed "no, no, no and collapsed into her friend's arms."[146] Judy had to tell Jerry's parents.

Janice took Judy to her mother's and then to Dr. Sturgeon, her therapist, who canceled her other appointments that afternoon to focus on Judy. Although she had by now recognized that her feeling of guilt surrounding her father's death had been based on fantasy, Judy "couldn't help feeling guilty about Jerry. Was I to blame? We had had an argument the night before. Perhaps I had made too many demands on him. It was almost ten years to the month since my father died. Did I kill everyone I loved?"[147] Her therapist reassured Judy that she had killed neither Jerry nor her father. She reflected, "I had to face that it was outside of my control, and that was what was so awful."[148]

When Judy visited Jerry's therapist, he told her that the last two years of Jerry's life had been the best. But he thought Jerry's death had been an unconscious suicide because "he couldn't face the struggle" he had ahead of him to make himself "healthy."[149] Judy's therapist disagreed and argued that Jerry's therapist was feeling guilty because he had not been able to prevent this tragic accident: "It was an unfamiliar car, a slippery road, a hairpin curve, it could happen to anyone."[150] Judy nonetheless retained a residue of guilt: "I was beginning to emerge from the nightmare void of my childhood experience of death. I was beginning to see myself in new ways, to want new things. I guess that I felt that I was beginning to outgrow Jerry. I didn't want that to happen, I wanted him to grow too. When he died, I felt that my need to develop had killed him."[151]

For a long time Judy had to deal with grief. The sudden, unexpected trauma of Jerry's loss caused her to relive her father's death, and she finally began to mourn for him as well as for her dead spouse. Such delayed mourning is often triggered by another death.[152] Faced so early with the repeated loss of loved ones, she would be more likely than most to associate love with the pain of abandonment. It was for her to figure out how to love someone when the possibility of loss was so real.[153] But she did not return to her maiden name, choosing instead to continue to be known as Judy Gerowitz.

The Dance of Loss and Love

In mid-June 1963 Judy fled to New York and was staying with her old friend Lanny Meyers and his wife Tippy in an apartment on West 46th Street. She was in miserable shape and sought comfort from Lanny, who had been close to both her and Jerry. She had left Topanga Canyon so swiftly that she even abandoned her cat.[1] The situation in New York turned out to be very difficult, as she wrote at length in separate letters to Janice Johnson and Lloyd Hamrol. Judy felt that her presence threatened Tippy, who also worried what would happen to her if Lanny died: "She has always been threatened by Lanny & my friendship, but before there was Jerry, & that made it better. But now I am alone, & I think

▲
Judy with *Sunset Squares* at the Rolf Nelson Gallery, Los Angeles, 1966. Photograph by Jerry McMillan.

that she believes that if I asked Lanny, he would go away with me. This, of course, is absurd, but last night she really was flipping out. She wanted Lanny to choose."[2]

Judy was in a desperate situation. She wrote to Janice that she would try to remain in New York, at least until there was a place to go to in L.A. Janice had even sent her a loan to tide her over, for which she expressed her gratitude and relief. She poured out her anguish in a letter: "It seems so unfair to have to face this, too—but Hell is hell—& it doesn't seem to get better or worse. I'm very frightened of the pain that is with me all the time. It's like someone is squeezing my intestines & bowels all the time. I want Jerry not to be dead, but I know he is, & I can't run away from it. But, oh, Jan, it hurts so bad. I can't hardly even feel anything else."[3] She explained that as bad as the scene with Tippy the previous night had been, her own hurt was so great "that there is no room for anything else." She was struggling to try to learn how to cope with it, but she admitted, "There are still times when I don't want to live, but it's not so often."[4] Judy apologized to Janice for crying on her shoulder and promised to be stronger by the time she returned.

Returning to Los Angeles, Judy moved into a building in Santa Monica at Pier and Fourth owned by Frank Gehry, at the time a struggling young architect whose sister was then married to art dealer Rolf Nelson. Nelson had only recently moved from San Francisco, where he had directed an art gallery, and would soon open the Rolf Nelson Gallery in Los Angeles. That fall, as she struggled to put her life back together, Judy resumed her graduate studies, working as a teaching assistant in the department.[5] She divided her course of study between sculpture, working with Oliver Andrews, and painting, working with Sam Amato and Elliot Elgart.

Amato and Elgart saw Judy Gerowitz painting abstractly and ambitiously on Masonite panels, as large as four by eight feet. Perhaps they were puzzled by her abstract yet biomorphic imagery, which came directly out of the emotional turmoil of a young widow who had lost her husband suddenly and violently. Painting in a colorful, hard-edged style, she began making recognizable references to what she has described as "phalluses, vaginas, testicles, wombs, hearts, ovaries, and other body parts. The first one, *Bigamy,* held a double vagina/heart form, with a broken heart below and a frozen phallus above." "The subject matter," she explained, "was the double death of my father and husband, and the phallus was stopped in flight and prevented from uniting with the vaginal form by an inert space."[6]

Another panel in this series was called *Flight.* It included a butterfly below and an upper image with a double cross, referring to the deaths of both her father and her husband. She called a third large panel painting *Birth* (Figure 4), echoing the title and theme of an abstract composition painted by Jackson Pollock around 1938–41 and reproduced in Frank O'Hara's monograph published in 1959, coinciding with her time in New York and her developing interest in abstract expressionism.[7] Hers showed pelvic, ovarian, womb, and heart shapes in bright, hard-edged patterns. Despite the fact that men like Pollock had previously painted such anatomical motifs, her work met with dismay from her instructors, who gave her B's, not a positive grade for graduate work. She later recounted how her "male instructors felt uncomfortable with my 'female' images, and made me feel that there was something wrong with me. They even threatened to throw me out of graduate school."[8] About her *Mother Superette*, an acrylic abstraction on paper, one professor remarked disdainfully, "It looks like breasts and wombs."[9] These negative comments led her to try to suppress personal content in her work.

Although these events took place in the early 1960s, her male instructors responded to a powerful residue from the 1950s, when the link between the twin dangers of women's uncontrolled sexuality and atomic power became established and marked popular culture: from the use of *bombshell* as the slang term for a sexy woman to the abbreviated two-piece swimsuits, named for the Bikini atoll, where the bomb, dropped in 1946 just after the Second World War, was said to have been decorated with a photo of the Hollywood sex symbol Rita Hayworth.[10]

But since the 1950s the old double standard that required premarital chastity for women only was giving way to sexual liberalism. *Playboy* magazine published a round-table discussion in 1962 in which Alexander King, an editor at *Life,* argued, "The assumption that a woman is supposed to get something out of her sexual contact, something joyful and satisfactory, is a very recent idea. But this idea has been carried too far, too. It's become so that women are sitting like district attorneys, to see what the man can or cannot perform and this has put men tremendously on the defensive. . . . It is a mistake because democracy is all right politically, but it's no good in the home."[11]

In 1963 Betty Friedan's *The Feminine Mystique* appeared, igniting a renewed interest in feminism that would come to be called the second wave, taking up where the suffrage campaigns of the previous century had left off.[12] She brought attention to the limited career prospects that women then had and to the myth that the suburban housewife had found fulfillment. But Judy never needed *The Feminine Mystique.* She had never even imagined herself as a suburban housewife. One topic might have caught her eye: "In the past fifteen years, the sexual frontier has been forced to expand perhaps beyond the limits of possibility, to fill the time available, to fill the vacuum created by denial of larger goals and purposes for American women."[13] Judy certainly did not agree with Friedan that "the mounting sex-hunger of American women" or the "voracious female appetite for sex phantasy" was evidence that something had gone wrong, reducing American women to "sex-seekers."[14]

Years later *Penthouse* magazine would report that "because the imagery in many of Chicago's early paintings and sculptures was so overtly vaginal and feminine, her male colleagues began referring to them as 'Judy's cunts.' Such remarks horrified Judy then, and for several years she deliberately cooled down her directly genital imagery, producing abstracts."[15] Until the late 1960s female sexuality remained shrouded, but she believed that such imagery was evident in the work of other women painters, such as Georgia O'Keeffe and Emily Carr. Eventually Judy would adopt her male colleagues' derisive term and make it a term of female pride.

Such images were the reason, recalls Lloyd Hamrol, that Judy's professor, Sam Amato, insisted that he could not bring his family to Judy's graduate show. Lloyd explained: "Her feelings were finding their way to the surface. We all knew that there were fewer women in graduate school. This was the first poke in the eye that she could claim as an artist."[16] Joan D'Angelo recalls that Judy hung out with fellow student Susan Titelman, who was then involved with the sculpture professor Oliver Andrews, and says that "Judy drew herself into a kind of combative stance."[17]

Interviewed today, Amato admits that he misunderstood Gerowitz's direction and adds that she was "multitalented" and "wanted the freedom to examine new possibilities."[18] He sees now that she was "breaking away from more traditional concerns and recognizing new developments in art." On the other hand, Elliot Elgard, who was then married to a woman artist, viewed Judy as very intelligent and inquisitive but not *that* talented. He recalls her as making figurative painting and looking around to find a mode of work that looked right to her. He sees her success as resulting from her strong intellect and thinks that successful students are "driven by a strong internal need that leads to their stylistic discoveries."[19]

Other women then at UCLA—for example Vija Celmins, who was a graduate student from the fall of 1962 until 1965, and Judith Von Euer, who from 1959 to 1963 did both undergraduate and graduate studies—appear to have functioned much more successfully with their male painting teachers than Judy Cohen Gerowitz did. Celmins nonetheless recalls a group of "old-fashioned" men teaching there, who were into Cézanne, Matisse, and Bonnard, while she was more interested in figures like Willem de Kooning, Giorgio Morandi, and

Jasper Johns. Since the studio where she did her work was not on campus and no studio classes were required of her, Celmins was not much bothered by faculty, but she remembers that the male professors were eager to sleep with their female students and that many obliged them.[20]

In view of Judy's childhood with her doting father and his progressive attitude toward women, one wonders how little she was willing to tolerate what other women simply accepted without questioning. Then too her unconscious effort may have been to subvert the conventional outlook of her professors, who did not appear to be going anywhere with their own work. Her own vision of her future as an important artist was clearly fixed before she arrived at UCLA, and no authority was going to convince her otherwise.

By the time she entered graduate school, Judy had undoubtedly heard of the notorious arrest of the artist Wallace Berman by the Los Angeles police at the Ferus ("wild man" in Latin) Gallery on June 7, 1957, for exhibiting "lewd and lascivious pornographic art." Hoping to provoke his audience, he had suspended a tiny photograph of two people engaged in sexual intercourse from a large wooden piece called *Cross*.[21] To an outside observer, it might seem that Judy also wanted to provoke—in her case, her stodgy professors—with transgressive imagery. She, however, insists, "I had no idea it would be provocative because I was not thinking about how others might respond but rather about my own pain and grief and how to express that."[22]

On the other hand, the faculty at UCLA surely knew not only about this incident but also about recent trends in contemporary art in Los Angeles. *A Tableau at the Ferus,* Edward Kienholz's one-man show at the gallery in 1962, had featured an installation of a brothel called *Roxy's* that included a figure of a prostitute that would gyrate when a viewer stepped on a foot pedal. This time city authorities ignored the provocation.[23]

Despite the painting faculty's initial rejection of her imagery, Judy received her master's degree in both painting and sculpture in the spring of 1964. She had obtained special permission for an atypical but ambitious program.[24] Her mother observed how hard her daughter worked, remarking, "She drives and drives and wears herself out."[25] But Judy was doing exactly what she wanted.

Preparing for her master's thesis show, at which she showed painted sculpture, she recounted working "15–18 hours a day, just painting—sleeping 2 or 3 hours a night—the rest of the time filled up with the incredible trivia of the profession of being an artist."[26] She confided in Janice that she managed to stay up working by taking "quantities of Dex" (the drug dextroamphetamine, a central nervous system stimulant) that, although now known to be addictive, was often routinely distributed by college health services during the 1960s to soothe menstrual cramps and was also used by college students as a study aid.[27] This was not a practice that she continued but part of a determined effort to finish the work for her master's show.

She described being present at the show at UCLA on June 4, 5, and 6, 1964, the few days that it took place, watching people coming and going and trying to "ignore them emotionally." She noted "how the whole relationship of objects in a room is altered everytime something is put in or taken out."[28] She was rewarded when the artist Bob Irwin came: "It was a gift to watch him look. I could see him looking at every choice I made, analyzing it, examining all the other possibilities, seeing why I made every choice I did. He is really beautiful." After he looked at the work, she was thrilled that he came over and shook her hand, commenting, "It's a damn fine show." They talked a little, but he had already given her all he could. Of all the people in L.A. who mattered to her, she said, he was probably the most important.[29] She was grateful that Rolf Nelson had installed her show so well.

She reported to her friend Janice about how thrilled she was with Rolf: "We are great & very honest friends. Our professional relationship is resolved, & as a dealer he is really too much. He believes in me as an artist & loves me as a person which is a rather remarkable feeling when it is accomplished by the detachment of friendship."[30] At the time Nelson showed mostly male artists, including Joe Goode, Jess (Collins), Irving Petlin, Llyn Foulkes, George Herms, and Alfred Jensen, although he did show Georgia O'Keeffe's large canvas from her series *Above the Clouds* in 1964. With Rolf, Lloyd Hamrol, and others, Judy would visit the L.A. artists' bar, Barney's Beanery, later immortalized by Edward Kienholz in a sculpture installation by that name. Hanging out with male artists, whose ambition she shared, she longed to be "one of the boys," so she tried to act tough by wearing boots and smoking cigars, a degree of posing that caused at least one of her friends—the less secure Lloyd—to cringe with embarrassment.[31] She later noted, "It's no accident that it was during this whole period when I was least overt about my womanliness—1965—that I made my reputation as an artist. It was a period in L.A. when no women artists were taken seriously. The men sat around Barney's and talked about cars, motorcycles, and their joints. I knew nothing about cars, less about motorcycles, and certainly didn't have a joint."[32]

Ed Bereal recalls that he met Judy at Barney's just at this time, right after she lost her husband. Bereal was already famous as the African-American component of the notorious poster *War Babies*, a photograph by Jerry McMillan, who would later take Judy's name-change photo in the boxing ring.[33] *War Babies* was a response by Henry Hopkins to a *New York Times* article by UCLA art department chair Lester Longman, who had called in 1960 for a retreat from postwar art and a return to American values. "Judy has to be given a lot of respect," Bereal says. "I watched her be the first woman. It was very tough. Men were very mean at the time. It was a boys' game. A lot of arrows were shot in her direction. I really respected her."[34] He considers her "a straight talker" and says, "Judy is a character . . . hilarious . . . always upbeat."[35]

"My level of encounter and struggle was more than any man would ever have to endure," Judy recalled of her years just after art school. "It was a struggle of not only wanting to be myself, but to be accepted in the male art community."[36] She did have valuable male friends, including her art dealer. Judy noted that Rolf was about to move his gallery, which would probably mean that he would move out of the house that they shared and that his artist, Joe Goode, whom she also really liked, would move in. Rolf's stable, according to Judy, then included besides her, Lloyd Hamrol, Joe Goode, with Paul and Ed Ruscha "kind of periferally [*sic*] involved." She described a kind of "marvelous cohesion taking place" in the gallery and predicted that before long it would be "giving the Ferus boys a good run for their money. Not just because there'll be another group of artists but also because there will be another group of ideas, & the more alternatives there are, the better art will be made."[37] Looking back, the artist June Wayne also objects to the emphasis of critics (then and now) on the guys showing at the Ferus Gallery, as if they were the only scene in Los Angeles.[38]

After the most intense period of working that Judy had ever known, she was ready for a break, so in early June she sublet her apartment for six weeks and took off for New York. She had initially planned to go with Nancy Gowans, the classmate who had married and then left Lloyd Hamrol. But Judy sensed that Nancy, then dating artist Ed Bereal, wanted to force her to choose between being friends with her or with Lloyd. Judy told her friend Janice that if that happened, only Nancy would be hurt. In the meantime she valued her longtime friendship with Lloyd and made an effort to comfort him, whom she perceived as having suffered from the recent breakup with Nancy. She tried to spend time with him to keep him from being alone and seemed relieved when he began to work again and was going out a lot.[39] "It's really terrifying," she reflected, "how very little we can do for other people—love them, believe in them. But, it seems so meager in the face of profound pain."[40]

Judy, then twenty-four, had been having a brief affair with the artist and art critic John Coplans, who at the time was forty-three and twice divorced. Born in London, he grew up in South Africa and came from England to the West Coast in 1960. He was working as an artist when he became one of the founders of and an editor and writer for the new magazine *Artforum,* moving with it from

San Francisco to Los Angeles in 1963. Like Judy, he had a grandfather who had been a rabbi who immigrated from the Pale of Settlement in the Russian Empire, in his case to England. John and Judy shared a concern with social issues, and both were strong verbally and visually. Their intimate relationship took place shortly after he showed his work in an exhibition of Southern California art and decided "to pack it in" as an artist. "It was a conscious choice on my part but painful," he recalled.[41] He then became a curator at the Pasadena Art Museum, located in a wealthy town connected to downtown L.A. by one of the first freeways built in America.

In her memoir (published just over a decade later) Judy described this affair without identifying Coplans by name, categorizing him as among the men "who were very supportive, but not without reservations. One man, an art critic, used to bring me paint and canvas, mention my work occasionally in his articles, and take me out to dinner. But then he would say, in the middle of a discussion, 'You know, Judy, you have to decide whether you're going to be a woman or an artist.' "[42]

John was attracted to Judy's drive and energy and to her work; he later organized a show of her work for the Pasadena Art Museum, during the period he served as curator from 1967 to 1970, and he proved helpful to her in other ways. She, however, was ultimately disappointed in him as a lover. She wrote and told Janice at this time that "John & I are through. Nothing much happened—it just kind of dissipated & his inability to really function as an adult. Like everyone else, he's a cop-out. Besides, I am getting tired of talking about Art. He said something to Lloyd about how he guessed he wanted either a 'real' relationship or none at all, whatever that means—probably 'real' can be equated with possession, dependence, etc." She was philosophical, saying it had to end sooner or later and resolving to "learn sometime to be alone & not dependent."[43]

Years later Judy made a comment that may refer to Coplans. "Until the development of the women's movement," she explained, "my feelings about criticism were very hostile, because even though I had been written about, and even though I had been taken seriously as an artist, the critics refused to confront what was very important to me at this point: the relationship of my life as a woman with my life as an artist. It was taboo to bring that up in the 1960s. One did not even discuss it. When I tried to bring it up, the critics were very resistant to it."[44] She elaborated: "For some women artists, it's not an issue, but for me it was, because I was trying to introduce something of my experience as a woman into my art, and communicate that through my art, and to break a kind of historical silence that has existed about what the world looks like through a woman's eyes."[45]

John's comment to Lloyd about the relationship that Judy and John had been having raises the question of what possible effect (conscious or not) Lloyd's subsequent relationship with Judy might have had on the way Coplans viewed and wrote about Lloyd's work. Just about this time, in June 1964, Coplans had included Hamrol as one of "a whole wave of very young painters"—including, among others, Larry Bell, Llyn Foulkes, Joe Goode, and Ed Ruscha—in his article "Circles of Styles on the West Coast," published prominently in *Art in America*. Coplans was a very valuable advocate for an emerging artist. He was not the first or the last to become intimately involved with the subjects of his professional attention.

By May 1964 Judy had already made it into *Artforum* reviews. Critic Clair Wolfe discussed Gerowitz's work in the context of a show called *Painted Sculpture*, which included artists such as H. C. Westermann and Hamrol. Shown at Mount St. Mary's College, a Catholic women's college in Los Angeles, the show prompted Wolfe to point out the "increasing interest on the part of many sculptors in utilizing the gestural and expressive connotations of color as it is used by painters. Foremost of these painterly techniques applied to three-dimensional mass are the works of Lloyd Hamrol and Judy Gerowitz." Wolfe then contrasted Hamrol's use of primary colors and primary shapes, which "achieved an almost altar-like monumentality," with Gerowitz's concern "with an organic sexuality rendered in painted plaster. Like the 'colorform' idea, the color also assists in defining the shapes, which are sometimes used as a bas-relief protruding from the three-dimensional surface. Her color-sense is astounding, and one senses an almost spontaneous abandon in selection." But, Wolfe warned, pointing out one of Gerowitz's not-so-subtle titles: "For the most part, they create fascinating tensions; but they can become burdensome unless one is willing to accept a considerable amount of whimsy, if not wit. A case in point is *Fetish V*, which has some truly weird, sometimes banal colorations painted over spiraling, undulating forms topped by greenish-yellow feathers."[46]

Several works from this series, produced in 1963–64, are now known only from photographs. One has feathers on top of polychrome and patterned acrylic paint on plaster and is entitled *Sculpture with Pink Feathers*. The aesthetic appears to be an original spin on abstract expressionist painting, now made three-dimensional, although the size was small, just fourteen by eight by four inches, mounted on a wood slab for a base. *Artforum* reproduced in black and white Gerowitz's painted clay sculpture *In My Mother's House* (Figure 5) alongside a color reproduction of Hamrol's sculpture in polychromed wood entitled *T.F.*, in the summer issue of 1964 as part of a feature on contemporary Los Angeles art. It is clear in hindsight that the vaginal iconography for which she would become well known was already well developed in this piece, which is unfortunately lost and known only from the black and white reproduction in *Artforum.*

At this moment of achievement Judy understood that she paid a price for the position that she was achieving as an artist. "It is that I cannot afford the pure pleasure of being appreciated as or related to as a woman, simply wanted on that level by a man, if that man happens to be an artist who in any way represents anything of worth," she explained to Janice. "He must accept me & relate to me on my terms, which usually negates the possibility of any simple sexual pleasure, as too many levels become involved. This is a loss that I feel with pain, but a loss that I am, nonetheless, accepting."[47] This complex situation had troubled women artists in earlier generations. Some, like Sonia Delaunay and Lee Krasner, had managed to accept the terms of a relationship in which their own career took second place to that of their more famous husbands, who at least accepted their identity as artists. Others, such as Jo Hopper, who had suffered her husband's active disdain for her willful insistence on continuing her art career after their marriage, had responded with anger and growing resentment.[48]

The past year had given Judy some insight into the depth of her need to make art. She found that it went deeper than she had realized before. She was happy working those nineteen-hour stretches, she said, "as I've never felt before. Happy is a curious word—real might be more apt." She reflected, "It has been a long year since Jerry's death, & I have finally made my peace with him & our past. The last piece I finished is a 7-ft. high gravestone—in which I buried my husband, my childhood, & my innocence. And I am ready to go away & play in order to start again."[49] She anticipated coming back to her studio to start solving problems with craft in order to get just the look she wanted. To her, it was only incidental, if "kind of grim," that she had suffered lacquer poisoning from spraying Kandy Apple Lacquer on her newest piece.[50] She did plan to buy a respirator when she returned.

Just after her master's show, Judy was pleased to have her work at Rolf's in a group show of the gallery's artists, who included, besides her, H. C. Westermann, Nicholas Krushenick, Jess (Collins), Alfred Jensen, Charles Mattox, and Hamrol. She described Krushenick as "competent"; Jensen's painting as "very mystic thick paint that's very difficult for the Los Angeles sensibility to cope with—but all right"; Mattox as "a machine-maker from Frisco—a marvelous man, very scientifically oriented. Kind of makes Flash Gordon, 1930s machines"; and about Jess she commented "semi-pop art montages & landscapes—the less said the better."[51]

In the end Judy traveled alone to New York, where she stayed with Lanny,

Tippy, and their new baby boy, who completely absorbed her hosts. She wrote to her friends Janice and Louie, "I've finally given up dexedrine, after several months. I've felt very knocked out, but I'm slowly recuperating. It isn't exactly that I got physically addicted to it—more like as I got more & more exhausted, I wanted more & more to feel energetic. But, I've finally decided to get myself back together. So, I've been kind of dragging my tail this week, but I'm getting rested."[52]

While in New York, Judy got together with the sculptor John Chamberlain, whom she knew from L.A. and who was in the process of moving to New York. He came over to Judy's with a friend, telling her how he had gotten drunk in the Village and "into a scene with some cops, resulting in a big gash in the head, a clubbing on his back, arms, and legs, a night in jail, etc. However, the cops were rather disconcerted by the hundreds of people who flocked to the jail to get him out. When asked for his name, he kept insisting he was Jackson Pollack [*sic*]."[53] When they took off in Chamberlain's car, which lost its axle after only three blocks, she reflected, "John really has to keep himself on that cross at any cost. It's amazing how he structures his life in a way that will create situation after situation . . . his salvation is that he can take it."[54]

While in New York, she had an appointment to meet the major New York critic Harold Rosenberg, which her friend John Coplans had set up. Although the two powerful critics are not identified by name, she described this encounter in her memoir, telling how as soon as she arrived in New York, she called Rosenberg, who, having been alerted by Coplans, responded warmly and invited her over. "As I climbed the stairs to his upstairs loft," she wrote, "I was very excited at the idea of meeting a man who was so well-known. I imagined him writing an article on my work, introducing me to artists in New York, taking me to galleries and museums."[55]

The encounter proved to be other than what she had imagined. "When I walked into his place," she continued, "I saw a large man, who limped toward me on what appeared to be a wooden leg. He shook my hand and invited me to sit down. We began to talk, and I asked him if he'd like to see slides of my work. He nodded, but as I reached into my purse for a box of slides, I saw him look me up and down, and I suddenly felt very anxious."[56] Rosenberg, who was then fifty-eight, married, and a womanizer, barely looked at her slides and ignored her attempts to discuss her work.[57] To her dismay, he "began to try to caress me and push me down on the couch. I moved away from him and suggested that we go to dinner. He agreed, but I knew that the evening was ruined and that I had been totally deluded into thinking that this man was interested in anything but a sexual encounter."[58] She reflected that she never found out whether Coplans had given Rosenberg the idea that he was sending her "so that he could get laid or so he could see my work."[59]

Her rejection of Rosenberg's crass behavior did not reflect any aversion for sex. She wrote to Janice, "Men here really faint over me. Eventually, it will all pay off, but it's still all future investment: An actor who's coming to L.A. in the Fall for 6 wks; a lawyer who's moving there; an art critic doing an LA show, etc."[60] What she wanted was "the ability to let myself open up again . . . just a female. That part of me was really closed up as a result of Jerry's death, & it took a year & a trip here to let me feel it again. It's not a question of getting married again."[61]

At times when she felt lonely, Judy admitted to thinking about the possibility of remarriage. She felt the need for a man: "I'm finally ready. I'm still scared, but at least, that part of me is coming alive again. And it was this painter, Luther, who gave me this. What else we have is really unimportant—whatever it will be, coffee, a drink, a fuck, is just giving each other pleasure & something of what we each are. The important things have been exchanged—and we feel more alive for it."[62] She felt that Luther, an African-American painter, was ahead of her "in his head" but that she was "ahead of him in my art & he needed what I had learned about making things—and I need what he knows about what matters & what doesn't—i.e., Nothing matters really, & it is only that realization that enables one to be free enough to make things matter."[63]

Judy spent the rest of her time in New York, going to museums and galleries, to a James Baldwin play, and to the movies. *The Servant,* with its screenplay by Harold Pinter and starring Dirk Bogarde, seemed a "very curious, compelling drama of the manipulation of a spoiled young English aristocrat by his servant, until the relationship is totally reversed, and the servant controls the master completely. It's a fascinating and altogether believable interplay, owing a lot to *Les Enfants Terribles,* or at least it couldn't have been made without Cocteau." She kept returning in her mind to the film, remarking, "It's fantastic, I think, the way we keep making the same room and the same complex, intertwined relationships over and over again. It gives me shudders, and I am determined not to get trapped."[64] This was surely a rare but clear reference to her problematic relationship with Jerry. *The Guest,* the movie of Pinter's play *The Caretaker,* elicited the comment: "Wow! It's really too much—like that's the way it is—with no lies."[65] In the end, though she had enjoyed New York, she said she found "there is something old about it—like the new world really is the West Coast."[66]

She left for home on July 5, having found a ride as far as Chicago, where she arranged to meet her old flame, Allen Podet, by now a rabbi. The two of them planned to spend two weeks together, driving across the country. She wrote to Janice Johnson, "I'm very nervous about the whole thing and don't know what will happen or how I'll feel about him, or anything—but it has to happen . . . I knew the day would come when Allen & I confronted each other across the myth of all these years."[67] They visited Yellowstone National Park in Wyoming before going on to Portland, where they separated, he going on to a new post in Seattle and she to Los Angeles. As Judy put it, "He to his world; I to mine." Though they had already corresponded, she remarked, "It's difficult to sustain our level of contact without physical proximity, but we'll do what we can."[68]

"For a while I thought I might be in love with him," she confided to Janice. "I'm not, but perhaps I could be. He's an extraordinary man—the only man I know who's really enough for me. But I have my life & he has his. I'm farther away from the thought of a marriage or even an intense & constant relationship than I've ever been. I know now, Jan, what you always anticipated my knowing—that I have to make Art—& I don't know what else can fit into my life."[69] She admitted that her relationship with Allen was nowhere near marriage, but she saw him as "truly an adult & as much, maybe more of a person than I am . . . I can't even conceive of sharing my life, my bed, my mornings with anyone."[70] She could not then imagine entering his world or he hers but did not rule that out for the future. He represented possibility.

At this time Judy concentrated on making herself into an artist, insisting, "It is the only thing that really concerns me. I am lonely, of course—tho there are countless men anxious to screw me, befriend me, etc. I miss Jerry still, but that is passing, too. How can I say? I'm just more me, as a singular entity, than I've ever been—& this is where I have to be for a while."[71] Her friends, then, were her colleagues in the world of art. She observed that John Coplans, who had just returned from the Saõ Paulo Bienale, was becoming so powerful that she hoped that "the day doesn't come when he can no longer relate to my work, as it will probably fuck up our now marvelous friendship."[72] Other current friends at the time included Larry Bell, Billy Al Bengston, and still Lloyd Hamrol. They, along with Robert Irwin, Kenneth Price, Ed Ruscha, Joe Goode, and Llyn Foulkes, had been included that summer in Philip Leider's *Artforum* article on the Los Angeles avant-garde, which he dubbed the "Cool School."[73] Judy was not yet included, but she was circling the wagons, planning her next move.

It was around this time, at a party given by Larry Bell, that Judy met Stanley and Elyse Grinstein, the prominent Los Angeles art collectors who had founded the print studio Gemini G.E.L. They have remained lifelong friends and supporters. "We're Jewish. Ideas are an aphrodisiac; creative people were very crucial to us," Stanley commented. He recalls watching Judy appear on television with two well-known male artists and that she was "mind-boggling . . . so brilliant about what the art world was about. She was so clear."[74]

Influenced by the clean and shiny "finish fetish" style that then dominated the L.A. art scene, she attended auto-body school later that summer after graduating from UCLA. Her goal was to learn to spray-paint so as to fuse color and surface. The result was that she also gained a greater appreciation of the role of craft.[75] With Lloyd Judy enrolled in the auto-body school, where she was the only female out of 250 students.[76] She described the experience as "a pretty funny scene—the school. They made me wear a Mother Hubbard type smock—you know 'Be a dyke & the world is yours'—gave me my own private bathroom (I was the only chick) there were a lot of hassles & bad scenes, but I learned a lot. The first day I was there (we went 8 wks) nobody swore. It was awful—I really had to watch my tongue. I had a swinging, but short affair with the Painting Instructor (We'd run into the back room & neck)."[77] Even today she recalls that the instructor, Percy Jeffries, an African-American show-car painter, drove a lavender candy-apple convertible.[78]

An immediate result of the session at auto-body school was her painting *Carhood* (Figure 6, 1964), featuring precisely delineated abstract geometrical forms rendered in acrylic lacquer directly on the metal of an actual car hood. "The vaginal form, penetrated by a phallic arrow, was mounted on the 'masculine' hood of a car, a very clear symbol of my state of mind at this time," she later wrote.[79] She also said, "I put my very sexually feminine images on this car hood, which is in itself quite a symbol. Over the next few years, I retreated from that kind of subject matter because it had met with great ridicule. . . . There was no radical departure, just a slow moving away from a content-oriented work to a more formalist stance; then, much later, a slow moving back."[80] She showed *Carhood* in *Some Aspects of California Painting and Sculpture,* a group show at the La Jolla Museum of Art in 1965. Among the sixty-five artists in the show were Hamrol, Llyn Foulkes, John Baldessari, Wayne Thiebaud, and six other women, including Joyce Treiman and Deborah Remington.[81]

She was also beginning to cast in fiberglass, anticipating a show of her work, perhaps the following spring. She predicted that her fiberglass pieces would be "clean, simpler, sprayed, and look like me."[82] But she was so broke that she was faced with finding a job for a month or two so that she could afford to buy a spray gun and a compressor. She was hoping that John Coplans, who was no longer actively making art, would keep his promise to move and give her his loft, since he had become established as "*the* West Coast Art Critic."[83] If not, she would have to scout around for some other space adequate enough for her work.

Gerowitz was included in an important group show at Rolf Nelson's new gallery on La Cienega in Los Angeles in the fall of 1964, which also included, among others, Hamrol, John Chamberlain, George Herms, Nicholas Krushenick, H. C. Westermann, Llyn Foulkes, Alfred Jensen, and Jess (Collins). The West Coast critic Clair Wolfe wrote that Gerowitz and Hamrol "have achieved an astounding development during the past year—in an essentially 'formal' environment."[84]

With her own life undergoing dramatic changes, Judy was surprised in the autumn of 1964 by news of friends, past and present. She learned that Jerry's friend Frank Mecoli, whom she had briefly dated, had broken up with his wife; that Julie Ross, her former roommate, had left her husband and moved back to L.A. with her baby; and that her own former lover, Leslie Lacy, had run into her friends Janice Johnson and Louis Lunetta in Légon, Ghana, where they were living. She wrote Jan that she was happy to hear about Leslie and inquired, "What's he like now?"[85]

The news of her first lover made her even more aware of what her life now lacked. Awaiting impatiently a promised visit from Allen, from whom she had not heard, she wrote to Janice that if Allen "doesn't come soon, I'm going to try & find something else for a while, as I really need an affair—but have been trying to hold out till he gets here."[86] She admitted, "I've been in a really bad depression for some time. It's almost as if I warded off this 'low' by the constant work of the last year & a half & now that I'm not working (due mainly to financial problems, but also in part because I just don't feel well)—I'm finally feeling the profound emptiness & loss in my life. This is probably a stage in my recovery that was accelerated by the possibility of Allen's arrival next month."[87] Not one to give up, she said that she was determined to ride "the funk" out.

Judy's depression was not evident to her neighbor, Joe Goode, a painter from Oklahoma City who had had a solo show at the Rolf Nelson Gallery in 1963. They became friends when they were next-door neighbors at 2322 Miramar Street in downtown Los Angeles. He recalls her at that time as "very outgoing" and remembers that she was throwing a big party, for which he agreed to open up his side of the house. The event stuck in his mind because it was around the time in December 1964 when the singer Sam Cooke died. He remembers Billy Al Bengston arriving at the party with Cooke's sister.[88] About a hundred people turned out, "all of whom got really smashed & just danced," Judy reported at the time. She had Lloyd paint her eyes "in a kind of hard-edge, abstract, butterfly pattern" and wore her hair "high up with a huge fan comb & a to-the-floor shift gown," no shoes, and pink toenails.[89] She was pleased that she saw the beginnings of "a breakdown in the Ferus boys' alienation," reporting that both Bengston and Bell showed up. By giving such a party, Judy was already working hard at networking and securing her place in the Los Angeles art scene.

Allen finally did arrive to spend a week with Judy in December, only to make her realize that what they had was "profound friendship."[90] She wrote to Jan, "You're right in one thing, I need a relationship. But the kind I'm interested in is one that allows me the mobility I need. I have that with Allen, & surprisingly, I now have it with Lloyd. . . . He has become a man—& in the process we've been able to fulfill our relationship on levels we previously had been unable to do, while still maintaining the separateness so necessary to what each of us is."[91] For the moment she did not need "a consuming exclusive relationship," she claimed, because "the gap in my life left by Jerry was filled in great part by me in discovering myself as an artist. My need to relate to a man is filled by my relationship with Lloyd (as it always was, in part)."[92] She did not see the need to give up either her relationship with Allen, who was so involved with "something so far away from me," or with Lloyd, whose "adulthood & understanding of me feel very right."[93] This was quite a leap forward with Lloyd, with whom she had been planning to share equipment during the next year, but it was not exactly clear how that would work out.[94]

By early January 1965 Judy had moved to downtown Pasadena with Lloyd, whom she had known since undergraduate days at UCLA.[95] Through the help of the artist Paul Sarkisian, they had found a loft (of five thousand square feet) on the second floor of a commercial building at 12 North Raymond Avenue that they rented for $75 a month from James Plotkin, who had taken over his grandfather's vacuum cleaner business on the ground floor. Plotkin, who is Jewish and Judy's exact contemporary, became a friend and eventually a patron, buying one of her sculptures. He describes her as "charismatic" and "determined to be an outsider," commenting, "This was a volcano exploding . . . that burning light, that energy, was always part of Judy."[96] Not eligible to join the Pasadena Athletic Club because he was Jewish, Plotkin joined the Chamber of Commerce as a part of his effort to promote old Pasadena.

At that moment downtown Pasadena was in a state of economic decline: buildings had decayed, and the large minority population that had moved in coped with de facto segregated schools. Thus Pasadena was perfect for artists with scant resources. Gerowitz and Hamrol, now a couple, were sharing their loft with Llyn Foulkes, who had a studio space but did not live there. Foulkes, who was five years older than Gerowitz and Hamrol, was more established in the local art scene. He had begun showing with the Ferus Gallery in 1959 and had his first solo show there in 1961. But in 1963 he showed with Rolf Nelson, less than two years before he took the studio space adjacent to Judy and Lloyd. Foulkes also had a show at the Pasadena Art Museum in 1962.

Though Judy and Lloyd could watch the annual Rose Bowl Parade passing on the street just beneath them, their new place had plumbing problems and represented anything but easy domesticity. They had taken a two-year lease and were sinking in their own money and sweat equity to fix it up.[97] Judy planned to make it "pretty," painting it white with black trim.[98] Her mother had treated her to a compressor and a spray gun, as well as to a drafting table, prompting her to comment, "She's gotten very generous."[99] The primitive nature of the loft's plumbing prompted her to comment, "It means living without a shower (as the hot water pipes are fucked up) & with a hot plate—but it's worth it to have a really right place to work in."[100]

Their block on Raymond Avenue became the setting for a participatory collaborative piece known as *The Raymond Rose Ritual Environment.* With the support of Jim Plotkin, their landlord, Judy, Lloyd, and a woman named Barbara Turner from Caltech arranged in 1968 to close down the block on New Year's Eve and organize a "huge multimedia environment for all the people lined up on Colorado Boulevard waiting for the Rose Parade." Lloyd recalls that they brought in fog machines used in theatrical productions. "It was fabulous," Judy recalls, "color wheels, smoke, road flares, films projected on the facades of buildings. When I saw the smoke rise up in front of the color wheels (on klieg lights) I got the idea for my *Atmospheres.*"[101]

When the Grinsteins visited Judy and Lloyd in their new Pasadena studio home, they noticed that the couple, who paid little attention to domesticity, lacked proper dishes. To Judy's amazement, they soon sent over a set of white porcelain. This was her first real experience with patrons who could afford to support her work and the lifestyle required to make it. It was their first gesture of support. Elyse, who became an architect, says that Judy's feminism greatly influenced her as well as her two daughters. At the time she first met Judy, Elyse recalls, she (Elyse) was so conventional that she still wore "a girdle and matching shoes and bags."[102]

After Judy settled in Pasadena, her personal life seemed to settle down. The several brief affairs that occurred after her return from New York had discouraged her: "The men with whom I became involved either used me sexually, expected me to 'take care' of them, were threatened by my work, or, if they could relate to my work, were unable to relate to me personally. Lloyd seemed to be the only man I knew who cared about *me,* who could relate to my work, and who wanted to be involved with me in other ways as well."[103] She wrote to Janice, "I kept wanting to surprise people by telling them about me & Lloyd, but no one was surprised—except maybe me. I guess I had taken loving him for granted for so long that I didn't realize its implications consciously. It's so good—it's almost like I've never loved anyone before—It's old & new all at once. Like it's taken us 7 years to grow up to the point where we can handle a relationship this profound."[104]

Judy could not believe how well she and Lloyd knew each other and yet how surprised she still was at their relationship. She was amazed that he seemed to support her drive and relentlessness instead of asking her to suppress it.[105] She saw Lloyd as "Male to my Femaleness, & yet, at core, the same."[106] Most anyone who ever knew Lloyd has described him as "nice"; Clare Loeb, who asked "What man could cope with Judy?" also labeled him "passive."[107]

As Judy saw it, the situation of her own career and Lloyd's seemed "really absurd." Neither one of them had any work available, but suddenly both were being shown and written about. She was excited when Lloyd got a call from the Los Angeles County Museum of Art (LACMA), requesting a piece for the March opening of its new building. His career seemed poised to take off, she figured, imagining that he had probably sold his next five pieces at about $1,000 each. Thus she felt it appropriate that he planned to quit teaching the next fall. At the time they each taught two classes in UCLA's Extension Division. Since she too had been selling work, they had more money than she had ever known.[108]

Lloyd was doing extremely well in 1965, the year that he, along with four other men—Melvin Edwards, Tony Berlant, Llyn Foulkes, and Philip Rich—won the New Talent Purchase Award of $1,200 at the Los Angeles County Museum. The museum bought his large yellow corner sculpture, made of painted canvas on wood, that he called *Goodboy.* Don Factor, writing a rather contentious review in *Artforum,* pointed out that the work related intellectually "to the recent work of Judd and Morris in New York" and carped that giving this honor to Hamrol, who only showed the one work, was "premature."

A photograph (Figure 9) that documents the award ceremony suggests what a dynamo Lloyd had in his companion. Lloyd stands on the right, while Llyn Foulkes, another of the honorees, stands on the left, a bit aloof and holding a cigarette. Between them is Judy, standing immediately next to Lloyd, and on her other side Maurice Tuchman, the museum's contemporary curator. Maurice looks down and grins lasciviously at Judy, who, having turned her head toward him so that we see only her profile, gives him a big smile. She, clearly dressed up for the occasion, wears a fashionable dress, elegant heels, a long string of pearls, and a number of large rings on her visible right hand, which holds a cigarette.

The Los Angeles County Museum had a long tradition of not including sufficient numbers of women in its exhibitions, and Tuchman, one of the most stubborn male chauvinists, could only have regarded Judy as a sex object. As late as 1981 organizations called Double X and Arts Coalition for Equality demonstrated against LACMA and Tuchman specifically by showing up at the opening of a show called *Seventeen Artists of the Sixties* wearing Tuchman masks as a protest against the failure to include any women or minority artists. Tuchman looked foolish as he defended his position to Suzanne Muchnic of the *Los Angeles Times:* "In the last half of the 1970s, many young art historians became involved with revisionism. They dredged up minor artists of the nineteenth century—people of little importance. I don't think they have shed much new light. I think this activity is a cover for anti-modern sentiment . . . I don't want to be just another trendy curator. You have to do what you believe in."[109]

Rolf Nelson believed in Judy and had promised both her and Lloyd solo shows in the coming year. Unfortunately he was having money problems and had gone to New York to find a backer. Judy noted that "Nick Wilder, who's the Eastman Kodak heir," had opened a competing gallery in Los Angeles and was offering his young artists a monthly salary, an arrangement that sounded very attractive to her.[110] It was Rolf, however, who knew well Judy's energy and talent, having first put her work in group shows.

Between the completion of auto-body school and the move to Pasadena, she had been "hung up" by not having enough money and a place to work, but she took advantage of the interval to work out new pieces in her head: "I really discovered the problems & broke through a lot of space things & image hangups. My new pieces are going to be a whole new kind of thing."[111] She was working in this period on some "silk" (actually steel) screens. Her efforts were recognized when the Museum of Modern Art in New York purchased the first one, *Flashback,* a serigraph of a circular composition, printed in black, red, yellow-green, and blue that she wrote to her regular correspondent, her friend Janice, "really looks bitching."[112]

In March 1965 she spent two weeks making a series of small paintings, since Nelson had sold everything that she had sent him. Several pieces out of her next series were sold before she had even made them. "This has been the longest I've ever gone without a lot of pieces—& yet I've been working harder than I've ever worked. I've been turning myself into a professional—teaching myself to be an artist. I feel as if I've completed what I've been working for during the last 7 years—& that includes working out my relationship with Lloyd," she reported to Janice.[113]

"You know we're living together—or did I tell you that? I don't think things were so resolved as they are now when I wrote to you last. Sometime we'll have a baby—but not for some time, as there are many things to be done in the next few years."[114] At the time of this moment of unprecedented optimism, Judy was twenty-five. Her hopefulness contrasts to the feelings she had while with Jerry, when all she had wanted was two abortions. She changed the subject rapidly to the show that she was preparing for that fall and told how her work kept her in the studio for days: "It was scary at first—to be so committed to being in one place—me, who's always kept so many escape clauses—but once I faced the fact that there's really no way out, it started getting better."[115]

Judy admitted to Janice that if she had understood then where her track was headed, she would have gotten off quickly "'cause it sure is hard—but for the first time in my life I am facing challenges that are not only *enough,* but often too much, & I feel the limitations & boundaries of this all-too human frame."[116] Evidently, at just twenty-five, those limitations did not yet include the biological clock limiting when a woman can bear a child.

In early 1965 Judy had a conversation with her friend Billy Al Bengston, one of the Ferus Gallery crowd, at Barney's Beanery, about which she reflected: "God bless him—despite himself he taught me so much about being an artist—I had to get smashed one night in order to thank him." Bengston had quipped, "Oh, you're just a flash in the pan," to which she replied, "No, Billy, you're wrong. I've got staying power." He then rejoined, "Then you're a bigger fool than I thought," to which she responded, "May be true!" She told Janice, "He's been at it longer than I have—but I'm slowly beginning to understand many things about him, as they become true of me."[117] Bengston, who is five years her senior, refers to feminism as "horseshit"; he recalls Judy Gerowitz as "overweight, pushy, complaining, whining that she wasn't taken seriously. All the boys I knew were interested in girls that were really girls—not girls that wanted to act like boys."[118] He adds that Gerowitz "had stepped onto my turf—the car hoods," adding that he was the first to paint with a spray gun in 1957.[119]

Rolf Nelson opened her first solo show at his gallery in January 1966. Judy wore a backless tuxedo (that she herself had transformed) to the opening. Allen Podet arrived for the occasion but, in Judy's eyes, appeared threatened by the event.[120] The show, referred to as "this young artist's first one-man show," earned positive reviews in both *Artforum* and *ARTnews.* It was presented in two installations, the first of which was a four-part room-sized sculpture called *Sunset Squares.* Each of the free-standing squares in graduating sizes contained a square hole at its center. Judy enlisted the help of Jerry McMillan to photograph her, marking this historic moment in her career. McMillan, whose paintings done on top of photographs had been in Rolf Nelson's show of up-and-coming artists in 1965, recorded Judy posing amid the four parts of her monumental sculpture, looking out with a serious gaze at the camera. She chose to pose in skin-tight black pants, a baggy top, sandals, and a close-fitting hair band or cap. The look is casual but confident. What is striking is how small she appears next to her own sculpture. That discrepancy seems to comment on her great ambition.

Judy's second installation included a work called *Rainbow Pickett* (Figure 8), which was composed of a series of six volumnar trapezoids of different lengths and colors, made from monochrome-painted canvas stretched over plywood frames. The six trapezoids leaned against a wall at forty-five-degree angles in decreasing order of size. Gerowitz named *Rainbow Pickett* after the popular African-American soul singer Wilson Pickett, but the reference was lost when the work was repeatedly exhibited and reviewed misspelled as "Picket."

She had begun this work the previous May, describing it as her "first big piece . . . 11 feet long & about 7 feet high—Canvas stretcher across a wooden frame—very warped space—very simple—My ideas are growing quickly now. I'm looking for a way to make sculpture as direct as a Frank Stella painting. I'm finished with the kind of surface & craft preoccupation of the Ferus boys. It's a dead end that leads to preciousness, & they're really fucked up by it."[121] Her shift of interest to Stella suggests that she had taken on a larger perspective, looking beyond the Los Angeles scene to New York. Her use of pastel colors actually anticipated those in Stella's "protractor series" of 1967.[122] But the monumental scale she chose for *Rainbow Pickett* does relate to Stella's large paintings.

The critic Peter Plagens remarked that "Gerowitz's work is another step along a path recently manifested in American sculpture: simple geometric volumes imposing in size, static quality and physical presence. *Sunset Squares* is no outright imitation; it is, so to speak, its own man, but a man who has freely ingested the groundings of the work of say, Robert Morris and Donald Judd, who in turn owe a great deal to the later sculpture of David Smith and a few painters." But he found fault with what he called "a touch of elegance in the assignment of its floor positions," when, he insisted, it should "just—plunk—be there."[123]

The next month Plagens weighed in on *Rainbow Pickett,* noting that the piece was more engaging but claiming that it lost "some of the vulgar power of *Squares*" and that "the sweet flatness of color has usurped the effectiveness of physical form."[124] He went so far as to suggest, "Perhaps real primary and secondary colors instead of mint green, aqua, heliotrope, rose, persimmon and ochre could have jarred the viewer into involvement with sculptural elements."[125] Yet this highly original and sensuous choice of colors was a new direction, one that led Gerowitz to reconsider painting. Later some would declare her colors characteristic of Southern California, as opposed to the sober tones of New Yorkers like Morris, Smith, or LeWitt.[126]

Plagens also praised the smaller three-part work entitled *Lilith* (Figure 7) as "charming but overwhelmed," ignoring completely the significance of the artist's choice of naming her sculpture after Lilith, an aspect of the great goddess, who was demonized for being an independent female.[127] There are many aspects of Lilith, from the Sumerian goddess of more than two thousand years B.C.E. to the "consort of God" in Kabbalism as late as the eighteenth century.[128] Having experienced negative stereotypes of women far too often, Gerowitz may have found attractive the subversive image of "the beautiful seductress who joined lonely men in their nocturnal unrest, enjoyed sex with them, and bore them demonic offspring."[129] A medieval reference to Lilith as the first wife of Adam portrays her as refusing to assume a subservient role to Adam during sexual intercourse and deserting him, going on to mate with other demons. God, answering Adam's plea to bring Lilith back, sent *three* angels in pursuit of her. This led to the practice of protecting a mother and her newborn child from Lilith with the help of *three* angels.[130] This is the link to the name that Gerowitz chose for her sculpture with its three forms.

The review in *ARTnews* was the work of Fidel Danieli, another graduate of the UCLA art program. He called Gerowitz's debut "ambitious," and though he admitted that he had so far viewed the forthcoming work, *Rainbow Pickett,* only in a photograph, he wrote about both installations: "Given the *dernier cri* stance, they are lyric and elusive and suggest a theme of atmospheric change and open-ended or elliptical movement."[131]

Gerowitz's work during this period can best be described as adhering to a formalist aesthetic concentrating on color and form without overtly addressing content. She began to create her *Colorbook,* in which she drew abstract studies with Prismacolor colored pencils. By changing colors, she eventually achieved the illusion of shapes turning, expanding, or constricting. She also produced large minimalist geometric forms and small domes from innovative techniques and materials including fiberglass and lacquered acrylic. Seen in retrospect, she was a pioneer of Minimalism, which would not be canonized as a movement until 1967.[132] Minimalist art investigated structure, form, material, and the relationship of the object to the space in which the spectator viewed it. Although Gerowitz tried to leave personal content unstated in these abstract sculptures, her developing feminist ideas were expressed indirectly in her choices of soft, feminine colors and in her title, *Lilith.*

By now, John Coplans's article "The New Abstraction on the West Coast U.S.A." had appeared in *Studio International.* He wrote with understanding about two young artists whose work he associated: "Both Lloyd Hamrol and Judith Gerowitz work in a polychrome frontal sculpture with overt biomorphic references—sprayed color is used to deny the bulk and weight of sculpture."[133] Nelson had to be pleased with the attention the press paid to his young female star. Taking note of her pronounced midwestern accent, he began calling her "Judy Chicago." Soon she even listed herself that way in the phone book.[134] Rolf, after all, was a kind of father figure to his artists.

Judy had become a friend of Rolf's brother-in-law, the innovative architect Frank Gehry, her former landlord. When, to help support herself, she taught a summer school class in sculpture at the University of California at Irvine in 1966, Gehry, in town to show the area to a city planner from New Zealand, paid her a visit and spent nearly two hours talking to her students.[135] Short on funds, Judy had taken a three-week teaching gig and was living alone in a hotel room, shocked at having traded their huge loft for six square feet. She complained to her mother that she missed Lloyd, her studio, the cats, and being able to call either her or Janice. She was teaching a morning class in painting and an experimental workshop in the afternoon to "a combination of teachers, housewives, & amateur painters" but was concerned that the latter group of students did not seem motivated or especially creative.[136]

Though she was not earning a living, honors kept coming her way. The curator Kynaston McShine selected *Rainbow Pickett* for his show *Primary Structures,* which opened at New York's Jewish Museum on April 26, 1966.[137] (At the time the museum's exhibition program featured contemporary art, not Jewish themes or artists in particular.) Gerowitz was one of forty-two artists from the United States and Britain to be included. McShine had developed the idea for this show in 1965 in speaking with Lucy Lippard, then his colleague at the Museum of Modern Art.[138]

Entering the lobby of the museum, viewers immediately encountered *Rainbow Pickett* juxtaposed with Robert Smithson's *Cryosphere,* a row of hexagonal shapes on an adjacent wall. Her work stood out in the company of Smithson and other strong sculptors in the show, including Robert Morris, Robert Grosvenor, Walter de Maria, Carl Andre, and Ronald Bladen, as well as what McShine referred to as "a number of young sculptors from California," including, besides Gerowitz, Larry Bell and John McCracken.[139] *Rainbow Pickett* was also featured, albeit cropped, in a photograph accompanying a *Time* magazine review of the show.[140] The magnitude of this singular honor was at the time lost on Gerowitz, who did not go to New York for the opening because she lacked the money. Certainly she would have encountered detractors too. The critic Corinne Robbins, who appears to have reacted to the soft colors as both feminine and foreign, as in California, dismissed Gerowitz's color as "pure Disneyland," claiming that such brilliant color undermined the perception of the work's shape.[141]

An immediate reaction to *Primary Structures* was the July 1966 issue of the fashion magazine *Harper's Bazaar,* which promoted a "minimal look" and featured Francesco Scavullo's photographs of male artists posed with women—their wives or gallery assistants—wearing the latest couture. One can only imagine the result if Gerowitz had been featured as one of the artists, wearing the latest colorful minimal fashion herself, but it did not happen: the artists selected for the fashion feature were all male.[142]

The art historian and curator William Seitz later noted Gerowitz's presence in *Primary Structures,* comparing *Rainbow Pickett* with John McCracken's less complex lacquered planks. As for Gerowitz's beams, he liked the way the "smallest at the right . . . postulated the disappearance of the series into the corner, whereas the large left side of the arrangement seemed capable of infinite additive expansion according to a prearranged increment. The containment of the work was therefore threatened by its potential for infinite conceptual extension." He related this work to the term "systemic," which was also used for a show of painting at the Guggenheim Museum in 1966. But the system, he noted, was "not just modular redundancy, as in Judd's repeated boxes, but a successive, ordered enlargement from element to element with no change of form."[143]

During this same period Gerowitz produced temporary collaborative works, for which she sought public patronage. Lloyd recalled that he and Judy had "both worked in a street piece that Oldenburg did in L.A. called *Autobodys.* . . . I loved it, but the whole idea of temporary events just didn't jibe with what I had learned Art was supposed to be about."[144] That "drive-in" happening, which took place in December 9–10, 1963, in the parking lot of the American Institute of Aeronautics and Astronautics, included spectators who sat in their cars with their headlights illuminating the action of the performance. But Judy and Lloyd were among the people who donned white suits and participated in the action illuminated by the headlights. Planned with the theme of the sterility of the automobile, it morphed after President Kennedy's assassination on November 22, 1963, into a piece concerned with death and violence.[145]

Despite the reservations he expressed, Lloyd and Judy worked together in 1966 on a collaborative "environment" shown at "the old Rolf Nelson Gallery." The installation received an enthusiastic review in the *Los Angeles Times* from

William Wilson, who wrote, "Young L.A. vanguard artists Judy Gerowitz and Lloyd Hamrol have finally made something that this reporter can subscribe to wholeheartedly," going on to add: "By controlling the entire environment they clarify their aims and bring them to peak effect. The environment inclines one to total unselfconsciousness. It induces a sense of dreamy floating."[146]

A Pasadena newspaper published a feature with a photograph of Judy in the room of feathers with the punning caption "Girl with Pluck—Pasadena artist Judy Gerowitz surveys her plastic-walled 'chicken feather room.'"[147] The reporter, Ray Duncan, described Judy as "a tiny young woman who thinks large . . . her proudest achievement so far is her founder-membership in a group which calls itself the Rooms Company [including herself, Hamrol, Eric Orr (a Kentucky-born sculptor of Judy's age who died in 1998), and Roger Zimmerman], because it makes rooms as a form of art."[148] The group's interest was said to be "the 'environment' movement in art. It seeks to create an environment which envelops and involves the spectator, rather than letting him passively and intellectually 'appreciate' a work."[149]

This article, which itself demonstrates Judy's knack for getting publicity, noted that the chicken feather room became so controversial that "it is being visited and recorded by television, and a French magazine has just sent its correspondent to discover what the fuss and feathers are all about."[150] The reporter was also early to single out an important aspect of Judy's art: "Scale is an attribute of art which interests her intensely. A work of art, she feels, has most impact when it is miniature and makes a little world of its own—or is so vast in scale that it won't comfortably fit into a man-sized world. Art that is comfortably scaled to man-sized proportions can be easily accommodated, 'appreciated'—and ignored."[151]

All this public attention prompted Judy's mother, the former dancer, to describe this show with gusto to a friend:

> They built walls of inflated plastic in the old gallery, with 300 lbs. of chicken feathers on the floor. Sure it stinks somewhat, although they are constantly spraying it and dusting it with talcum, but when the room is entered it is truly an experience. Suddenly you are in a sense of timelessness, the walls seem distant . . . there is an eeriness about it which threatens some people, who won't enter, but once inside—all I felt like doing was arabesques.[152]

A few months later she described her daughter as "always dreaming up something new," noting that she was "the most self-disciplined person."[153]

Political activism motivated Chicago to take part in another group endeavor to make a temporary work of art. The Artists Protest Committee, a group organized by Irving Petlin, met at the Dwan Gallery in Los Angeles to begin to protest the Vietnam War. The group organized demonstrators who picketed at various museums and galleries, as well as at the RAND Corporation because of its involvement with American foreign policy in Vietnam. But when the press failed to cover their activities, the group decided to make an art object that could not be ignored.[154]

Judy and Lloyd worked together with sculptor Mark di Suvero and others on a Peace Tower (built of tubular welded steel) set on a vacant lot at the corner of La Cienega and Sunset boulevards in Hollywood.[155] Di Suvero and Mel Edwards collaborated on the design of the scaffold for the Peace Tower. Some four hundred artists made paintings on panels (each two feet square) to go on the sixty-five-foot steel tower.[156] American artists who were among the 418 participants to contribute panels, and whom the organizers called "illustrious" in a fund-raising letter, included Gerowitz and Hamrol as well as Robert Motherwell, Jim Rosenquist, Sam Francis, Elaine de Kooning, Herbert Ferber, Roy Lichtenstein, Ad Reinhardt, Claes Oldenburg, Frank Stella, Mark Rothko, George Segal, and Philip Evergood.[157] Other participants included Philip Pearlstein, Wallace Berman, Arnold Mesches, and Gerowitz's former instructor from her brief sojourn in New York City, Raphael Soyer.[158] Filmmaker Johanna Demetrakas recalls briefly meeting Judy, who was working with a pneumatic drill on the Peace Tower.[159]

From conception to completion the tower took about five months and remained on view for about four months after its opening on February 26, 1966. A photograph was published of di Suvero preparing "to start welding base of tower on Sunset Strip that will feature panels of paintings protesting Vietnam war. In the background, sculptors Judy Gerowitz and Lloyd Hamrol study plans."[160] It was through their friendship with Mark that Judy and Lloyd became part of the project's inner circle, since she had helped Mark find his loft, next door to her and Lloyd in Pasadena.

After relying on men to promote her work—from Mark di Suvero to Rolf Nelson to John Coplans—Judy finally met a woman who could champion it. Dextra Frankel visited her studio in 1967 to select a work for a show called *Recorded Images/Dimensional Media* for the gallery at Cal State Fullerton, where she was the curator.[161] At the time she was also active as a sculptor.[162] The two energetic women hit it off and became lifelong friends.

In 1967 both Judy and Lloyd were chosen by curator Maurice Tuchman to participate in the large survey, *Sculpture of the Sixties,* at the Los Angeles County Museum of Art. Their work was shown along with sculpture by Joseph Cornell, Anthony Caro, Edward Kienholz, Claes Oldenburg, Robert Rauschenberg, and others of renown. Chryssa, Marisol, Louise Nevelson, Anne Truitt, and Gerowitz were the only women among the eighty artists in the show. Gerowitz showed just one work, *Ten Part Cylinder,* which she produced at the San Pedro boatyards.[163] It appeared in the exhibition catalog, photographed in her studio, with the couple's black cat, Lamont Cranston (named for the character on the radio program *The Shadow* that she used to listen to with her father), climbing on one of the nine fiberglass units, which ranged in height from 36 to 108 inches.[164]

Gerowitz's use of fiberglass was the result of a course she had recently taken at a boat-building school in Long Beach. Like auto-body school, the boat-building course represented her attempt to level the playing field by mastering nontraditional processes and techniques usually associated with men. "In the fiberglass cylinders," she commented, "the color was right *in* the surface. I couldn't have a lot of colors because it was too expensive, so I tried to make a color which, when light hit it, would seem to change."[165]

For his part, Hamrol showed a group of small works in Formica on wood called *Five by Nine;* the largest dimension was only thirty inches. The large catalog contained essays by ten leading critics, including Greenberg, Coplans, and Lucy Lippard, but only Coplans gave Gerowitz a brief mention, calling her one of the "fabricators" along with "Larry Bell, Tony DeLap, John McCracken, Ronald Bladen, and Anthony Caro—in contrast to the assemblagists," but he did not even mention Hamrol.[166] In his introduction, however, Tuchman cited Hamrol as an example of someone making sculpture that "denies the role of a base or plinth," but he ignored Gerowitz.[167]

Further recognition for Gerowitz and Hamrol came through the Aesthetic Research Center, a new form of cooperative begun in 1966 by twenty artists in Southern California who intended to move out of their studios and "into the industrial environment." The exhibition, which opened around Christmas in 1967, included Judy, Lloyd, Eric Orr, Oliver Andrews (who had been their professor only a few years earlier), DeWain Valentine, and others. In coverage of their work in the *Los Angeles Times,* Judy managed to make herself sound like the most interesting figure: "Rambunctious iconoclast Judy Gerowitz came up with the idea of creating a dry ice sculptural happening for the opening of the current Aesthetic Research Center exhibition at Century City. The vanishing construction not only symbolized her rejection of permanence as a valid artistic goal but also projected her conviction that 'art if privately possessed somehow loses its power.' "[168]

Dry Ice Environment (Figure 10) involved working together with both Lloyd and Eric Orr; the trio worked with thirty-seven tons of dry ice donated by the Union Carbide Company. The work was also called *Disappearing Environments, Part I and II.* The first installation featured dry ice, arranged in low walls, through which viewers could walk, enveloped in the icy fog and what might be perceived as a stage-fantasy of heaven. The second part was a series of ziggurats that changed form as they melted. *Time* magazine featured the trio at work with the caption "From Ziggurat to Marshmallows" and told how visitors delighted in walking through the vapor with their feet invisible.[169] These pieces turned out to point to a new direction for Hamrol, who soon pursued site-specific work, taking into account the architectural surroundings in creating each of his sculptural installations.[170]

Judy stressed in her interview with the press that technology interested her not as a means to an end but for its implications, asserting, "To retain creative freedom artists must aim to become the manipulators rather than the victims of technology. Only by moving art out of the studio into the factory and ultimately into all suitable public places can the artist hope to affect society."[171] This expressed commitment to "affect society," following her earlier work in the civil rights movement and study of George Herbert Mead, suggests that she was consciously following her father's teachings, just as she had promised as a teenager reciting the Yizkor prayer in his memory.

Lloyd was featured in the same newspaper article, as "Seeking to Make the World His Studio. . . ." He predicted presciently, "Eventually it will become necessary for the artist to involve himself not only in sophisticated crafts and technologies but in the methods of science, evolving new aesthetic concepts from an understanding of electronics, optics and optical physics. Such an approach would end the isolation of the artist from society and destroy artificial barriers between art and technology."[172] Some years later Lloyd discussed his work with Judy, including *Feather Room* and *Dry Ice Environments,* which were more abstract and formalized but still public and accessible: "The fact of being that exposed put me uptight, you know . . . I couldn't take that much constant exposure, so I would have to run back to my studio and work on something that was entirely in my control."[173] Judy, who thrived on the attention, did not suffer the same insecurity. Although Lloyd and Judy managed to collaborate successfully, the transition from longtime friends to live-in lovers was not as easy as she had anticipated. They continually struggled to make their relationship work in the face of unresolved issues concerning self-esteem, ambition, sexuality, and equality.[174]

Without a dealer to represent her after Rolf closed his gallery, Judy began to make smaller pieces, which she sold herself out of her studio. Her public, collaborative works served to keep her name current.[175] She took Rolf's decision to close his gallery in stride and boldly claimed that she did not want another gallery. An *Art in America* piece on Los Angeles artists maintained, "Sculptor Judy Gerowitz has avoided gallery representation since 1966. 'The old system is irrelevant,' said Gerowitz. 'You go with a gallery only if it helps. I'm happy this way for the moment. I like the freedom and control over my own destiny.'"[176] The magazine concurred, explaining that "some of the foremost Los Angeles artists—Sam Francis, Richard Diebenkorn, [Robert] Irwin, Gerowitz, Peter Alexander and a great many others—prefer to have no gallery affiliations and show an indifference to gallery exhibitions. This attitude is . . . new and surprising. . . ."[177]

When a Los Angeles radio station featured Judy in May 1968, an interviewer asked why she was not represented in the Lytton Center's show *California Women in the Arts.* She responded, "I won't show in any group defined as women, Jewish or California. Someday when we all grow up there will be no labels. And we give the professional categorizers pads and pencils and binoculars and birds to divide into groups."[178] Clare Loeb, who then hosted an arts-oriented interview show on Pacifica radio, recalls that "Sam Francis spoke highly of Judy Gerowitz," whom she viewed as "very attuned to publicity, very political. She quickly emerged as a leader—a very impressive person, though she could be strident, aggressive."[179]

That fall when she showed in a group show at Cal State Fullerton called *Transparency/Reflection,* she attracted the attention of critic William Wilson in the *Los Angeles Times.* He wrote that her work was "nominally formal and minimal but her tray of tubular plastic objects becomes funny and expressive as we slowly understand the human inspiration behind their icy purity."[180] Here Wilson came close to recognizing the underlying concern with sexuality that Gerowitz had begun to develop in her work after her previous effort to suppress it.

In 1967 Judy gave a lecture at Southwestern College in San Diego, where she knew Allan Kaprow and Miriam "Mimi" Schapiro. Judy recalled that she had stayed overnight at Mimi's and that the two had a lot to say to each other.[181] Mimi, who is almost sixteen years older than Judy, had moved with her husband, artist Paul Brach, and their son to California from her native New York, where she had established herself as a prominent woman artist. She essentially abandoned her New York career to follow her husband to La Jolla, where he had found a new job teaching at University of California at San Diego—which, contrary to her expectations, initially gave her only a part-time teaching position. Brach's next appointment was in 1969 as the first dean of California Institute of the Arts (CalArts), a newly expanded art school in Valencia founded and funded by Walt and Roy Disney, soon to be located on sixty acres in the hills about thirty miles north of Los Angeles. He was able to hire Schapiro the following year, since the old nepotism rules preventing couples from teaching in the same department no longer applied at the newly founded school.

Not only were nepotism rules falling away by the late 1960s, but the women's liberation movement was exploding all around. Gerowitz, who had long been unhappy and frustrated with the sexism that she had encountered at UCLA and in the art world, was more than ready. She now felt free to explore openly the nexus of sexual expression and gender in her work. With a vocabulary, an analysis, and a movement to bolster her, she now moved quickly toward overtly feminist art. During this period she continued to create works of performance that were outdoors, public, and temporary. She called these performances *Atmospheres* or "smoke pieces." She later described them as "flares of colored smoke out doors and in the landscape. They're all about the releasing of energy."[182] She also stated that her aim was "to transform and soften (i.e. feminize) the environment."[183]

Gerowitz produced the first *Atmospheres* in January, February, and March 1969 at Brookside Park in Pasadena, later describing them as reflecting "the release that I felt as a result of making these paintings," referring to the first of her series called *Pasadena Lifesavers.* Some have viewed these *Atmospheres* as a link to the Southern California Light and Space movement, which includes the work of Robert Irwin, Larry Bell, and Jim Turrell, all of whom she knew in this period. More of her *Atmospheres* followed in May on the beach in Santa Barbara and in June in the desert near Palm Springs. The artists Keith Sonnier, Jackie Winsor, and Tina Girouard, who had met Judy at a party at the home of her patrons Stanley and Elyse Grinstein, recall traveling to San Diego with her when she was training to become a licensed pyrotechnician. Sonnier also remembers being present for one of Judy's *Atmospheres* and says that he "loved it." He thought that Gerowitz was a very committed artist but "hell on wheels."[184] In fact, she had begun working with a fireworks company to produce the required smoke devices but was studying to become a pyrotechnician. She had to abandon this work when the man running the only suitable fireworks company in the area became insistent on having sexual relations with her.[185]

Ironically, at the same moment that she had to fend off unwanted sexual overtures, Gerowitz was dealing with the expression of her own sexuality through her work: "I was also discovering that I was multiorgasmic, that I could act aggressively on my own sexual needs. The forms became rounded like domes or breasts or bellies and then they opened up and became like donuts, and then the donuts began to be grasping and assertive. I went from three forms to four and started the *Pasadena Lifesavers* (Figure 11)."[186] Another time, she explained wanting to spray-paint in order to "make forms feel as if they were dissolving. I was trying to invent a format for expressing what it was like to be female and to have a multiorgasmic sexuality (this is before Masters and Johnson studies were published)."[187] Based on her own experience, Judy's assumptions about female sexuality would never allow her to accept that women were "less sexually driven than men," an idea that became part of the feminism defined as cultural rather than radical.[188]

For this series of abstract paintings on acrylic Plexiglas surfaces, produced during 1969 and 1970, she developed color systems in which she tried to create the illusion of forms that "turn, dissolve, open, close, vibrate, gesture, wiggle; all those sensations were emotional and body sensations translated into form and color. I called them lifesavers because in a way they did save my life by confronting head-on that issue of what it was to be a woman."[189] She later commented that she had been "attempting to deal with issues of female identity and content, though their form belied their real content."[190] One critic has observed: "The personal, referential qualities of her *Pasadena Lifesavers* give them an iconographic dimension seen in no other artist's work during this period."[191]

Gerowitz had a solo show at the Pasadena Art Museum, described in *Art in America* as "a group of medium-size tripled plastic domes spray-painted with washes of romantic, pearlescent color"; the review was illustrated by a reproduction of her *Large Domes I.*[192] What she showed was a series of sculptural domes and a related series of paintings that she described in the accompanying catalog brochure as "diagrams of the color systems used in the sculpture."[193] The domes were intimate in scale and shown in small groups on acrylic or mirrored Parsons table tops or other surfaces. She later explained, "With the domes I was trying to explore my own subject matter and still embed it in a form which would make it acceptable to the male art world—that 1960s idea of formalism. It was so frustrating in the art world."[194]

In her attraction to plastics for the domes and other work in this period, Gerowitz fit into her Southern California environment. For some of her sculpture, she experimented with vacuum-forming and blow-molding techniques, as did her contemporaries such as Craig Kauffman. She was searching for a means to merge form and color. Plastic had become as acceptable a medium as stone or wood and seemed appropriate in a region that emphasized modernity and not tradition.[195]

Curated by John Coplans, the Pasadena show, held from April 28 through June 1, 1969, included a small brochure catalog, but with Judy's own notes printed in her own longhand script instead of an essay by the curator, who declined to write anything. That probably had more to do with the contentious internal politics of the already-disintegrating museum than with his feelings about the artist, his onetime lover. William Wilson wrote about Gerowitz in the *Los Angeles Times* as "one of the few female artists who has managed to flourish in the local vanguard" and described her sculpture and drawings at Pasadena as "variations on three acrylic domes impregnated with bright shadings of sprayed color. . . . I did not experience this art as tough, theoretical New York type art. It rather blushes with ample hedonism." What he saw instead was "spreading Baroqueness" and noted, "Shaded colors . . . finally have the innocent lyricism of a bag of marbles, a pretty lady's beads, or a '36 Ford."[196] *Art in America* declared that Gerowitz's show was "consistent with previous work though new in form, the domes initially appear reductive and systematic, but soon prove lush, emotive and human."[197]

But *Art in America* emphasized her role outside the gallery structure: "Gerowitz has spent progressively more time as a rallying point for artists concerned with transient events in outdoor environments. Since 1966 a changing roster of artists has made art of ice, smoke, balloons, skywritings, feathers and other such tangibles/intangibles."[198] She did another *Atmosphere* at Cal State Fresno in June 1969 and two more that August in Trancas Beach, California, and at the Santa Barbara Museum of Art. At the height of the Vietnam War and antiwar protests, *Art in America* also reported a planned event that few recall, including the participants: "Sam Francis, together with Judy Gerowitz and James Turrell, recently planned to stage a spectacular antiwar demonstration on land, sea and air at Santa Monica Beach, until it was stifled by two thousand police officers."[199] Although that protest never happened, Francis and Turrell did create a series of airborne works with clouds and airplanes over Pasadena in 1969.[200]

Judy and Lloyd got married on June 28, 1969, in Santa Barbara. It was a marriage of two longtime friends, collaborators, and equals: two artists who, having attained the first signs of success, were working toward further recognition. They held their wedding in a wooded glen, telling the invited guests to meet them in a park at a certain crossroads, and from there a four-wheel drive vehicle picked up the guests and transported them to the ceremony. The guests, besides family, included Judy's close friends Janice Johnson and Louis Lunetta and the couple's friends and patrons Stanley and Elyse Grinstein.[201] Their friend Mark di Suvero gave them a small metal sculpture, telling them that they were free to sell it if they ever needed money.[202]

7 Feminist Class

A new twist in a typical old-boy network transplanted the urban activist, idealist, and budding feminist—Judy Gerowitz—from the sprawling, restless conurbation of Los Angeles to the more compact and centered Fresno. Isolated amid the densely cultivated fields, orchards, and monster dairies of the Central Valley, Fresno was a stark contrast to Los Angeles. Calibrated to georgic and bucolic industry, Fresno State College had grown from its origin in 1911 as a normal school—training mostly women as teachers for the prosperous farming region—chartered to include agricultural education. Early photos feature women wielding rakes and hoes (Fresno Farmerettes with victory gardens during World War I). It became successively Teachers then State College (University in 1972),

▲
Judy Chicago and the California Girls, 1970.

including a Division of Agricultural Sciences and Technology created by vigorous local initiative to offer hands-on farm experience. Liberal arts and sciences rounded out the curriculum. The department of fine arts was favored by a local philanthropist and trustee who worked in ceramics herself and had facilitated a new edifice for the arts building that was under construction when Judy came on the scene. The art department's men—both traditionalist and more vanguard—could hardly have foreseen that her ambitious drive would transform their classrooms and campus so dramatically.

Some of the art faculty were "Fresno cowboy types"—Dal Henderson, Allen Bertoldi, and Gene Thompson—in the eyes of a former student, who remembered also, with less provocative brand names, "Chuck Chesnut, a printmaker; Stan Hui, a Chinese painter; Charles Gaines, an African-American painter."[1] Another teacher from the time, Frank Laury, recalls Judy as "a woman of great energy and ideas who expressed them without hesitation."[2]

Dal Henderson might have found common ground with Gerowitz beyond their obvious clash of styles. His favorite grandmother had been a Jewish immigrant, a leftist, and a feminist who worked in L.A. as a writer for the IWW (Industrial Workers of the World). His older sister is both a feminist and an artist. His new colleague, though, he recalls, did not have a lot of respect for him, since the content of his work often exploited stereotypes of commercial advertising and his parlance still styled young women "chicks"—anathema from a feminist point of view, which struck him as "strong-willed, dominating, and aggressive."[3]

The two never penetrated surfaces to intertwine shared roots, but something must have come across, for Henderson took the trouble to photograph performances by Gerowitz with her students, including an *Atmosphere* that she recalls doing "on the construction site of the new art building that was going up—wanted to try and 'disappear' that masculine looking structure."[4] The *FSC Staff Bulletin* for October 26, 1970, introducing an exhibit of her paintings, sculptures, and drawings in the old college bookstore, reported her changed name and its motivation, continuing, "Miss Chicago also made points soon after she arrived on campus for the spring semester. On February 17 she held an art demonstration on the site of the new Art Building, at the time only a hole in the ground. The demonstration was called a smoke *Atmosphere.* It employed chemical smoke, thick and multihued, which could be sculpted in the air. Unfortunately, an unseemly wind somewhat ruined the effect."

Henderson also remembers "speculation [among the men] as to whether Judy was bisexual or a lesbian," since she "didn't seem that interested in Lloyd," whom they met when he came up briefly as one of the many occasional artists in residence.[5] Clearly the men did not get wind of an incident that made an indelible impression on a student, Vanalyne Green: "I'm sure someone has mentioned the time Judy talked about her eighteen (or was it sixteen?) orgasms the night of her marriage to Lloyd Hamrol. We were talking in a pizza parlor. That cleared it out."[6]

Decidedly not the cowboy type and rather fresh to the situation, Heinz Kusel had chaired the art department only since 1967, just three years after it granted him the master's degree with an outsider topic for his thesis—Joaquín Torres-García, the Uruguayan painter, then not well known in the United States.[7] The previous summer, he had sought out a course at UCLA with Rico Lebrun—a modernist, often apocalyptic painter and sculptor of themes like *Genesis, Crucifixion,* and *Buchenwald*—who also attracted that summer John Baldessari, the future conceptual artist.[8] Kusel also showed his modernist sympathies by basing a class on the color theories Josef Albers, who left the Bauhaus in Germany to teach at the experimental Black Mountain College and then Yale University.[9]

Kusel's taste for novelty stemmed from his unique Hispano-Germanic background: born in 1916 of German parents in Lima, Peru, his mother had taken him to Germany in 1925, only to return in 1933 to join his father, still an engineer in Peru, leaving Heinz in school in Germany, where he was forced to join the Hitler Youth.[10] In 1935, now nineteen, he fled Germany for Peru, first Lima but then seeking out, by 1944, the jungle near the Amazon's head, where he experimented with *ayahuasca,* a very potent psychedelic drug that, along with Allen Ginsberg and William Burroughs, he was one of the few white men ever to try.

Kusel adventured too as department chair. He imported such talents as Wayne Thiebaud and Vija Celmins, only to see them move on, leaving him with two vacancies to fill. When the department organized a group show in July 1969, it included an unconventional sculptor from UCLA, Oliver Andrews. Though invited to give a talk, Andrews delivered a demonstration, flying one of his "sky fountains" made from Mylar and balloons. The spectacle so impressed the faculty that they asked him to recommend any students of his to fill their vacant positions. He had been a favorite teacher of Gerowitz, whom he suggested, along with her classmate and friend Susan Titelman. Both received and accepted offers, Gerowitz beginning in the 1970 spring term.[11]

It says a lot about the influence of Andrews and Kusel's principled daring that Kusel would hire someone who came across as "a very aggressive, very hostile feminist," acting on his judgment very specifically that "she was nonetheless interesting and dynamic." Indeed, he used his power as chair to overrule his colleagues' objections and give his new hire free rein in her teaching. He also prided himself on the result: "Despite severe opposition, I decided she would be good for the department and I hired her. I allowed her to create a strictly Women's Art Program. It became the first of its kind in any university and a key contribution to the beginnings of the whole feminist movement in America."[12]

One day when Judy had been teaching for a while, she and Kusel got together for lunch: "During the meal she leaned over the table and said, 'You know what I like about you, Heinz? You have a strong feminine quality about you.' "[13] She must have meant it as the ultimate accolade for his innovative and open mind, but it left him "quite upset," as he let her know, without going so far as to explain what he would reveal in his autobiography: that after his mother entrusted him—age thirteen in 1929—to a Berlin boardinghouse, the man who became his legal guardian sexually molested him. The abuse left him feeling "worthless at the core of my being" so that he lost his "capacity to be active and fully engaged in life."[14]

Why Gerowitz would accept Kusel's initiative and trade L.A. for Fresno intrigued filmmaker Judith Dancoff, who elicited a response at once retrospective and programmatic, interpreting the move as a further logical step in building a life understood as unfolding through successive stages. First came "values and attitudes, my sense of what I could and what I couldn't do [that] were developed in the 50s when I was a teenager." On top of that came "the whole advent of the hippies and the revolution and the Left . . . the Panthers, the Blacks," which she saw "had really changed the nature of our society and our values"—change that dictated change, also for her: "I felt that I had built my identity and my art-making as a person—as an artist—on the framework of reality that I had been brought up in, and now that framework had changed, so I wanted some time out, to look around and find out what was appropriate now. I sensed that what I could do now differed from what could be done twenty years ago."[15]

Judy had responded strongly to the early writings of the women's movement, which confirmed and seemed to valorize her own feelings. She described how she "shuddered with terror reading Valerie Solanas's book and some of the early journals. . . ." She admitted that she found Solanas "extreme" but "recognized the truth of many of her observations. . . ."[16] " 'Great Art' is great because male authorities have told us so," wrote Solanas in 1968 with satirical hyperbole, having just referred to " 'Great Art,' almost all of which, as the anti-feminists are fond of reminding us, was created by men."[17]

Judy's quest for a new "framework of reality" began with a critique of the old: "it has been the male experience that has always stood for the human condition . . . like Hamlet or Godot." A different premise and goal would shape her quest: "In terms of my aspirations as an artist, I needed to find a way to embody the human condition in terms of female experience, and that required that I study women's art. I wanted to find out if other women had left clues in their work that could help me. I wanted to explore my experiences as a woman openly and somehow wed those to the sophisticated techniques and skills I had as an artist."[18]

As a first step this new aim "required moving away from the male-dominated art scene and being in an all-female environment where we could study *our* history separate from men's and see ourselves in terms of our own needs and desires, not in terms of male stereotypes of women."[19] On another occasion, to an intimate supporter, she described her new mission in bluntly personal terms: "I lived away from Lloyd for a year and tried to begin to undo the damage I'd done myself competing in the male art world. I wanted to make my paintings much more vulnerable, much more open."[20] The Fresno cowboys were not entirely wrong to sniff a lack of focus on Lloyd.

The move to Fresno looked less feminist to the mother conveniently distanced back in L.A., whose topics arguably echo what her daughter reported about her conversations with Kusel as he sought to persuade her to trade the hot art scene in L.A. for Fresno. She saw only tremendous opportunity, good pay, and that Judy would have sufficient freedom to carry on her own work. "They are trying to build up a more exciting program to attract art students there, and Judy has a reputation already," May Cohen informed a friend.[21] She also noted that both Judy and Lloyd were planning to move to Fresno and that he had been offered a teaching position [at CalArts in Valencia] midway between Fresno and L.A., so he could commute. But at first it was Judy who shuttled back and forth from Fresno to the outskirts of L.A.—their place downtown in Pasadena, where in January 1970 she staged more of her signature *Atmospheres* at the museum of art; followed on February 17 by the windblown try at the Fresno construction site; then, back near Pasadena on February 22, by a *Snow Atmosphere,* which Pomona College sponsored at neighboring Mount Baldy.[22] The sculptor Guy Dill recalls that it was with considerable persuasive skills that Judy recruited him and other artists to pitch in and carry out her plans on Mount Baldy.[23]

Her feminist agenda and her outspoken manner did not escape the men who perceived her as hostile and aggressive when she began teaching at Fresno in early 1970. Her first lectures, one eyewitness recalls, were booed by some of the guys: "People hated Judy; they were so threatened."[24] One of her students who would succeed as a professional artist, Suzanne Lacy, recalls that "Judy was a lightning rod for people's projections."[25] Her developing feminism shaped both her art and her teaching. In her mixed classes that first term, she tried saying, "Okay now, none of the men talk; only the women talk."[26] From this she would move to the next stage in her quest and create "a year-long class for girls who wished to be artists."[27]

One of her male students in that first sculpture class found it unforgettable: "When I first met Judy in class, she was such a breath of fresh air in Fresno," Jack Rhyne recalls, "she was dressed sort of like Jimi Hendrix: colorful shirt and pants, scarf and boots. Her hair was Afro-style." He remembers her as "very open and friendly and supportive to whatever level you were on."[28] Rhyne was "knocked out" when she started speaking about "earth sculptures" and "smoke pieces"; it was new enough to interest even the nonartists.

For Earth Day, Judy got permission to stage an environmental show on campus and had students haul in dirt, grass, and other such materials, intriguing most of them but disturbing the dominant culture of future farmers and homemakers, for whom moving dirt was work—pure, simple, and hard—not art.

A woman in that first class—only nine credits short of graduating as a psychology major—was taking art just for fun: Vanalyne Green, a Fresno native. "The first class of Judy's, she said that she moved two thousand miles for college to get away from her mother," she recalled. "At that time I wasn't getting along with mine, and I remember thinking, here is the teacher for me. I had the sense that I would learn more about psychology from her art class than all the psychology classes I had taken."[29] Less generic, more expressly feminist attitudes followed: "Judy asked us what images we wanted to make work out of. I had an image of a female manikin on a circular track, going around and around. She asked if I knew that was a woman's image, and I lied and said yes, I did. Of course at that stage I didn't have a clue what feminism was. I was mesmerized by Judy. Later I asked to be part of the Feminist Art Program she was starting. She accepted me but warned that we would have conflicts,"[30] which they did. Green rebelled, says a fellow student, Laurel Klick, when really challenged by her teacher, who retorted: "Don't be mad at me. I'm not your mother."[31] Klick recalls too how that first class suffered attrition, as students one by one dropped out because the teacher demanded so much: "She took us seriously and made us accountable."[32] Klick compares other sculpture classes, where students made boxes all semester out of different materials, while in Judy's they made earthworks and participated in her "smoke piece."

Laurel, Vanalyne, Jack, and the rest of Judy's students got help with some of the earthworks when Lloyd came up and pitched in.[33] By late spring her mother could report that "Judy is practically moved to Fresno," and the buzz was good: "She seems to be somewhat recharged in her role as professor, especially as she feels that she can make a contribution to women who are trying to become 'liberated.' " May was also proud to report that Lloyd had just had an "environment show," which had received a positive reception and reviews.[34]

Tired of driving the monotonous flats between Fresno and Pasadena, Judy finally rented a space twenty miles south on Route 99—the main drag bisecting the valley—at 1399 Marion Street in Kingsburg (population about 3,000), a recently closed meat market. For the summer of 1970 she hired Jack Rhyne as her apprentice, paying him $100 weekly plus room and board.[35] He built the studio interior and installed an old claw-foot bathtub in the kitchen, the only place it would fit. He also found himself recruited to share her vegetarian diet and abstinence from alcohol. She would listen to music while drawing and once suspended her pen to ask why all the songs seemed to be about love.[36]

Allowing themselves a break, Judy and Lloyd drove up the coast to visit their old friend and former Pasadena neighbor, Mark di Suvero, who was living by then on a houseboat in west Vancouver, near the quaint fishing village of Ucluelet. Opposing the Vietnam War, he moved to British Columbia and would soon decamp for Europe. A snapshot by Lloyd records how he took them out in a small aluminum skiff through the fjords to an area known for dolphins. Suddenly six-footers were all around them, jumping virtually straight into the air. Not dolphins—"Killer whales!" Mark misnamed the Pacific grays, triggering panic. "I can't swim," Judy virtually screamed. Mark shepherded them back to the dock, admiring her courage as an artist and activist, if not in the water.[37]

Meanwhile, early in the summer, Gerowitz legally adopted the name Judy Chicago "as an act of identifying myself as an independent woman."[38] Her mother spread the news to her friend Pearl, expressing amazement that her daughter had not only legally changed her name to Judy Chicago but had spent money to do so. She was also impressed that Judy had taken out an ad in *Artforum* announcing why she had done it.[39]

The *Artforum* ad in October 1970—a full page placed by the Jack Glenn Gallery for her show at the still relatively new California State College at Fullerton, Orange County, in metropolitan L.A.—featured a head shot (shown twice, once reversed) of Chicago wearing a headband and dark glasses with a companion text: "Judy Gerowitz hereby divests herself of all names imposed upon her through male social dominance and freely chooses her own name: Judy Chicago."[40] Beneath this box another one reads: "Judy Gerowitz One Man Show Cal State Fullerton October 23 THRU November 25." The name "Gerowitz," was crossed out and the name "Chicago" was written above it in script. Likewise, "Man" was crossed out and "Woman" written above it in script.

A second ad in *Artforum*—run without charge by the editors—followed in the December 1970 issue.[41] This one used the photograph of her posed in the boxing ring, her dealer listed as "Manager, Jack Glenn." Five years later Chicago recalled the boxing pose with what her male interviewer called a "vehement giggle": "It was a joke, but it took on mythic proportions."[42] "I had a new dealer, and he thought up the idea. I thought it was going to be a crack-up—I knew all these male artists who were into macho, and they knew I was just like a flower. I was sure they'd get a kick out of seeing me as superstud. Then the editor of *Artforum* saw the photograph—at a time when the women's movement in art was just beginning, and we were all coming on like Black Panthers—and suddenly it's a full-page ad in *Artforum.*"[43] She continued: "It was like, 'Hold on, guys, here they come!' I thought it was amusing, but it freaked out the art world." She laughed also that "years later male artists would come up and say, 'You know I used to box too.' "[44] The poster had meant to spoof the macho announcements, posters, and ads typical of some of the "wild men" who showed at the notorious Ferus Gallery.

The new name and the Fullerton show unhinged *Los Angeles Times* critic William Wilson, who earlier had had appreciative things to say about works by Judy Gerowitz. He led with the changed name, quoted the bit about "divesting" herself of "all names imposed upon her through male social dominance," then indulged himself in the first of what would swell in the years ahead into a chain of petulant sneers: "It is a nice gesture of liberation. I hope its seriousness is not diluted when she is introduced socially as Miss Chicago. How awful if some dolt asked what year she was Miss Chicago. Well, it's not as touchy as if she had picked Judy America."[45] With bad conscience perhaps for his own bathos, he tried getting back on track: "Enough of that. Despite feminist statements in the catalogue, Judy Chicago's art bears no relationship to names or Women's Lib. Its exhibition has been installed with economy and brilliance by Cal State Fullerton gallery director Dextra Frankel."[46]

Maintaining this workmanlike style, Wilson divided the works shown into three categories: "geometric-abstract spray paintings in spectral hues, five sets of triple-domed table sculptures set on mirrors, and photos of her *Atmospheres* moving and still. (*Atmospheres* are made by spewing pretty colored smoke over various real landscapes.)"[47] The large paintings (the five feet square *Pasadena Lifesavers,* which made their debut in this show), though "painted with great precision and planned with elaborate variations," nonetheless rarely worked. Better the dome sculptures, but the atmospheres he found "poetic," although he was quick to point out that Chicago had not herself taken the photos.[48]

Judy's mother saw through his screed: "The critic was quite critical about the name change, and I somewhat suspect that it colored some of his feelings about her work. I'm sure that he would protest that he's objective." Judy too got the point and firmly captioned her copy of the review "perceptual sexism."[49]

The name change was right in your face, an unmistakable target, but the catalog, though ignored by Wilson, provided plenty of further feminist content. Frankel described Chicago as "a leader in the vanguard West Coast art scene" and underscored her feminist quest. Chicago furnished a "Dedication to the Grinsteins" (Stanley and Elyse, her devoted patrons in Los Angeles), followed by the first of many compendious honor rolls—compiled from her reading in women's history and reaching their fullest form nine years later in *The Dinner Party*—of both contemporary and historical women with ties to feminist thought: "Abigail Adams [First Lady interested in the rights of women], Susan B. Anthony [abolitionist and crusader for women's rights], Ti-Grace Atkinson [contemporary feminist writer], Simone de Beauvoir [French writer], Lee Bontecou [sculptor], Shirley Clarke [avant-garde filmmaker], Colette [French writer], Roxanne Dunbar [-Ortiz, founding member of the early women's liberation movement who worked on the journal *No More Fun and Games*], George Eliot [novelist], Jay DeFeo [contemporary painter], Angelina Grimké and Sarah Grimké [two sisters from South Carolina who were the first women to argue against slavery and insist on equality for both blacks and women], Georgia O'Keefe [*sic,* painter], Doris Lessing [novelist], Lucretia Mott [abolitionist and early crusader for women's rights], Anaïs Nin [writer], Rochelle Owen[s] [playwright], Margaret Sanger [birth control advocate], Elizabeth Cady Stanton [leader of the women's rights movement], Lucy Stone [abolitionist and reformer who campaigned for women's rights and kept her maiden name after marriage], Sojourner Truth [abolitionist], Harriet Tubman [former slave who ran the underground railroad], Agnès Varda [Belgian filmmaker], Virginia Woolf [novelist], and Mai Zetterling [Swedish filmmaker]."

Although the list was still in formation, Chicago clearly had already focused on women who struggled to abolish slavery: Anthony, Mott, Stanton, Stone, Truth, and Tubman but also the Grimkés, who asserted their rights as women to be able to continue denouncing slavery: they called female slaves their "sisters" and affirmed, "Women ought to feel a peculiar sympathy in the colored man's wrong, for like him, she has been accused of mental inferiority, and then denied the privileges of a liberal education."[50] Chicago herself, imbued with her father's values, had started with civil rights and the NAACP, before broadening her concern to include equal rights not only for African-Americans but for women as well. Her own background and experience prepared her to absorb Shulamith Firestone's argument in *The Dialectic of Sex: The Case for Feminist*

Revolution, which declared women's need to "face their own oppression." For Firestone, white women's involvement with the movement for black civil rights represented their "closest attempt since 1920 to face their own oppression: to champion the cause of a more conspicuous underdog is a euphemistic way of saying you yourself are the underdog. So just as the issue of slavery spurred on the radical feminism of the nineteenth century, the issue of racism now stimulated the new feminism; the analogy between racism and sexism had to be made eventually. . . . And if racism was expungable, why not sexism?"[51] Chicago was ready to take up the challenge.

At the same time this first list also reveals her concern with women artists, such as contemporary painters DeFeo and O'Keeffe and filmmakers Clarke, Varda, and Zetterling. She would expand the lists into a virtual canon as she kept reading classic and contemporary fiction by women along with feminist texts.

To her tentative canon Chicago appended three quotations intended as emblematic—Simone de Beauvoir on "the situation of woman . . . where men compel her to assume the status of the other" (1953); George Eliot in *Daniel Deronda* on "what it is to have a man's force of genius in you, and yet suffer the slavery of being a girl" (1876); Sojourner Truth on slavery's brutality: "And ain't I a woman?"[52] (1851)—and her own declaration of equal rights: "Until the egos of both male and female are valued equally throughout all levels of society, the work of a female artist cannot be clearly perceived or accurately judged. For our standards of judgment and modes of perception arise from a history which is primarily the record of the male, the imagery of the male, and the perceptions of the male."

The new name and emphatic agenda riled not only Wilson but an *Artforum* reviewer, Thomas H. Garver, who declared that Chicago had "taken advantage of a California law which permits anyone to have one alias without complex court approval."[53] Turning to the display—"The paintings, fifteen in all, dominate the exhibition although they are not her best work. Installed in a darkened room and individually lighted by framing projectors, the effect is holy indeed." With a manner condescending at best, he pontificated, "One tends to regard Judy Chicago as more an intuitive than intellectual artist, and the other works in the exhibition demonstrate this quality more adequately."[54] He compared her domes on tabletops to a male artist—"suggestive of the pearlescent lacquered plastic forms of Craig Kauffman"—using the comparison to put her down: "but Chicago has not controlled the spray so that it is not opaque"; like William Wilson, Garver judged the *Atmospheres* "her most intuitive productions, and perhaps her best, for they are perceptual and spatial experiences of momentary nature but powerful impact."[55]

To protest Garver's inaccuracies, Chicago wrote to editor Phil Leider: "It is important to note that I changed my name legally. I did not use an alias. I elected to use the legal process because married women are nonpersons legally and I wanted a name of my own."[56] As for the women cataloged, "The list of women's names included painters, writers, political activists and women who have distinguished themselves by struggling for the rights, dignity, and identity of women in and out of the arts. I consider these women as representatives of my history and was proposing in the catalog that my work must be understood within the context of this struggle."[57] She also protested the reviewer's dismissal of her paintings as "demonstration pieces for her theories," a charge, she said, that he left "unexplained."[58] Never slack to explain where others erred or traduced, Chicago brought her unfolding creed as a woman and artist up to date:

> These misperceptions and omissions arise from a misunderstanding of my art and of the way my femaleness relates to my art. In my work, my name change and my catalogue I make explicit my commitment to an Art that is emotional, direct, sensate and derives from my psychic and emotional struggle to realize myself as a female. I believe that *Pasadena Lifesavers,* the fifteen paintings included in my show, fully fulfill my commitment. To understand these paintings, one must approach them with a willingness to experience reality through the physical and emotional framework of a female.[59]

Chicago wrapped up her point by quoting Anaïs Nin's diary of 1934–39: "I do not delude myself, as Man does, that I create in proud isolation . . . woman's creation, far from being like man's, must be exactly like her creation of children, that is it must come out of her own blood, englobed by her womb, nourished with her own milk. It must be a human creation, of flesh, it must be different from man's abstractions."[60]

While male reviewers seemed to operate by the rule "If you don't like the message, shoot the messenger," a woman and artist, Miriam Schapiro—already an acquaintance and by now moved from La Jolla to Valencia to teach at CalArts—"brought her class to my show," Chicago later recalled, welcoming an evident rapport: "it was obvious that she could 'read' my work, identify with it, and affirm it"[61]—not a simple accomplishment, since Chicago saw the *Pasadena Lifesavers* as "reflecting the range of my own sexuality and identity, as symbolized through form and color, albeit in a neutralized format." Although in fact they were opaque to male viewers, she herself had felt "frightened by the images, by their strength, their aggressiveness."[62]

Schapiro had arrived at her feminist insight and outlook by a circuitous route. After the birth of her son and only child in 1955, she struggled to reconcile her dual desires to be both mother and artist. She gradually overcame this crisis of identity, although she never completely conquered her guilt at what she perceives as failure to fulfill her duty as a nurturer.[63] After her son's infancy, resuming work in 1957, Schapiro took part in the *New Talent Exhibition* at the Museum of Modern Art, showing canvases painted in a gestural abstract expressionist style. The following year she had the first of several solo exhibitions at the prestigious André Emmerich Gallery in New York. Yet because her work in the abstract expressionist mode left her discontented, she began searching for a more personal style, experimenting in the early 1960s with a series of hard-edged shrine paintings that embody female forms such as the egg.

Schapiro was ready, then, to penetrate the surface finish of *Pasadena Lifesavers,* from a feminist viewpoint not shared by Chicago's friend and erstwhile neighbor di Suvero. "Judy, I could look at these paintings for twenty years," he had told her, "and it would never occur to me that they were cunts."[64] Today di Suvero insists that he would not have described the paintings in that way: the C-word was hers. He sees Chicago is a "trailblazer" who "has brought a complete social consciousness to a lot of people" and "given an image to everybody in the feminist movement."[65]

The five *Lifesavers*—with their five-foot squares spray-painted in three different color series on the back of clear acrylic sheets, mostly in the Pasadena studio—came to represent for Chicago her " 'masculine' aggressive side," her " 'feminine' receptive side," and the self-concealment in which she then engaged.[66] The daring and exacting technique took on an allegorical—self-exploratory—dimension: "It's very difficult to work intuitively with a spray gun if you're dealing with forms, especially balancing a carefully sprayed and rigid surface against a soft overlay, which I could do later. There's something fantastic, though, about that process, about playing on that edge; you can just push it and lose it. It's so tempting, because it's trying to pursue perfection, like the perfect orgasm, perfect pleasure, and you know you always have to stop just before it's perfect."[67]

The hidden significance quite eluded Santa Barbara Museum of Art director Paul C. Mills, when he borrowed one of the series for a show called *Spray* in spring 1971: "these clear, pastel candy colors, handled with great reserve and delicacy, radiate from perfect patterns of precision lines and circles and suggest the candy lifesaver forms her title for the work included here, *Pasadena Lifesaver,* also indicates."[68]

Meanwhile the 1970 fall semester opened at Fresno State, and Chicago launched her pioneering art program for women. Her growing sense that dominant male structures and attitudes inhibited women from expressing their female perspective in art had led her to get Kusel's permission to conduct full-time a separate course of study open to women alone. She and fifteen recruits would eventually seek and renovate an old off-campus site—"a space of our own," as she called it after Virginia Woolf's *A Room of Her Own*—so as to escape "the presence and hence the expectations of men" and to explore connections between women's history and visual work.[69]

For recruits, Chicago sought women determined to become artists who were "aware of themselves as women" and "able to be emotionally honest with themselves & others."[70] One who met the criteria was Nancy Youdelman, who had been at Fresno since the fall of 1966 but kept changing majors. She had studied drawing and painting but not sculpture, when she saw a notice posted by Chicago in 1970, offering interviews for a sculpture class for women only. At the interview, on a day that also saw a bomb scare, Chicago asked if Youdelman wanted to be a "professional artist," to which the candidate, who "drew all the time," replied that she already was one. "No, you're not," shot back Chicago, laying down one of her rules, that an artist has to have a dedicated studio space: "You can't make an eight foot painting in your bedroom."[71] That convinced Youdelman: "I really liked her manner; she was so straightforward and clear."[72]

For the first two months Chicago focused on helping her students deal with "the ways in which their conditioning as 'women' prevented them from setting real life goals, from achieving, from acting on their own needs."[73] The approach left Nancy Youdelman remembering a lot of talk about sex, bad experiences, and how men took advantage of women. Other students, Chris Rush and Doris Bigger (aka Dori Atlantis), who describe themselves as "hicks from Fresno," remember that Chicago "was pretty confrontational with everybody."[74] At the term's first meeting, which was held off campus in the basement of a student's home, everybody was just chit-chatting when Judy "blew up" and rebuked them: "If you were a group of men artists, you'd be discussing your work. You'll have to change."[75] Rush describes the year in the program as "like a whirlwind—the most exciting of my life."[76]

From her own perspective as one who became a successful artist and teacher, Suzanne Lacy observes, "You know, in the sixties in California we were always mucking around in each other's psyches—experimenting in psychology. Mostly it didn't hurt anybody . . . it was a tremendously affirming experience to be with all women, to have such a charismatic woman role model in Judy. We talked a lot about role models. I think it organized people's psyches in a different way and allowed them to move forward with a lot more courage."[77]

"Faith [Wilding] and I, who were older," says Lacy, "were privy to conversations with Judy, who is very open about her process. Judy's a very, very fine teacher. She's incredibly demanding, and she knows how to push through to the tenderest parts of your psyche, and she goes right for the jugular in her criticism, which I think is good. Not in a humiliating manner, as it is in some art schools, but in a very direct and compassionate way"; and Lacy adds, "She's also tremendously supportive of her students. I remember many times over the years when I had trouble with money, she'd just quietly hand me twenty-five dollars. And I would never have to pay her back. I mean, it was just an issue of supporting me."[78]

By contrast, Vanalyne Green reports that "in some ways Judy was a bit of a fascist. She called the one-year program 'personality reconstruction.' "[79] Green reflects, "As with some of the other women in the group, I believe that I suffered from post-traumatic shock syndrome for several years afterward. This is not to negate the great parts of the experience of working with Judy. I have often wondered if I would have found my way out of a provincial life in Fresno, California, without the experience of being in a year and a half of classes with Judy."[80]

Chicago's experimental pedagogy kept inviting comparisons with the consciousness-raising practiced in the women's movement—a group activity in which each participant "shares and bears witness to her own experience in a non-judgmental atmosphere. It is a political tool because it teaches women the commonality of their oppression and leads them to analyze its causes and effects."[81] Chicago "didn't know about classical consciousness raising then or we would have done it."[82]

She prefers to describe her own practice as "going around the circle and including everyone, which is something I started doing when I first started teaching in the sixties, prior to the women's movement."[83] For her, this carefully controlled activity is "connected to content search in terms of art-making," while it also enables each participant to be heard uninterrupted and to have her say. It became central to the work produced in the Fresno program.

Although the phrase "consciousness raising" keeps recurring in interviews with Fresno veterans, Chicago viewed consciousness-raising as "something closer to 'healing ourselves' than the goal-oriented technique it is in my usage."[84] "I was really pushing those girls. I was really demanding of them that they make rapid changes in personality. . . . I gave the girls an environment in which they could grow."[85]

By no means everyone took to the method. According to Vanalyne Green, "I want to think that such aggressive tactics wouldn't have been necessary—the phrase 'personality reconstruction,' for example, that Judy used to describe her pedagogy, resonates with my experience. I called in sick once, and Judy asked me what was wrong. I wasn't actually sick at all; I was lying," as she had when asked if she understood that her mechanical manikin was female. "I didn't want to go because I was so uncomfortable with the class. She suggested that either one or the other students could bring some food for me or that one of them could come and get me. Such tactics terrified me, although now I see the reasoning. She was suggesting that we be accountable, that we communicate rather than withdraw."[86]

Chicago devoted the third and fourth months of the school year to finding and equipping a studio so that the students could literally isolate themselves from the men and work in a female environment. "We had to make a major commitment of time and (for us) money," Lacy explains. "That is, we could take anywhere between three and twelve units of school credit. For many of us, over fifty percent of our schooling was this program. The first thing she [Chicago] did was ask us to buy work boots. Then she taught us how to deal with realtors, as we canvassed Fresno to look for an abandoned space to make into our studio."[87] Once they settled on a cavernous old theater at the intersection of Maple and Butler on the edge of town, the students—dressed in their boots—began to transform it. "Judy taught us carpentry," Lacy recalls. "I was certainly familiar with tools and stuff, but I'd never learned how to Sheetrock. We made flawless walls. We completely renovated this whole place. And in order to do that we had to pay money; I think at that time it was twenty-five dollars a month, which was, given that I think my total income was two hundred, a rather major commitment. I was freaked out."[88] Chicago stressed, "You just can't cheap out when it comes to your art."[89]

During the week students were expected to work in the studio from four to eight hours each day, besides having individual conferences with Chicago. A group met on Mondays to read novels by women as well as the "works of Ti-Grace Atkinson, Roxanne Dunbar, Simone de Beauvoir, Anaïs Nin, and other women writers."[90] Chicago was "also brilliant about historical context," recalls Lacy. "The woman reads incessantly. Whenever she wants to know about something, she sits down and plows through scores of books."[91] In the reading group they focused on how the novels served them in terms not only of literature but of their "personal struggle for identity" and "an understanding of our history as women."[92]

The students' reading that year also reflected the emphasis in the women's movement on the need for both knowledge and pride in women's anatomy, sexuality, and health. A group of women who called themselves the Boston Women's Health Book Collective published *Our Bodies, Ourselves: A Book by and for Women* in 1971.[93] Chicago assigned this book, which was to become a classic.[94] Its matter-of-fact illustrations of the vulva and details of its parts surely inspired more explicit "cunt" imagery among both Chicago and her students.

The studio space—some five to six thousand square feet, Karen LeCocq remembers—included a big kitchen where Wednesday-night dinners took place and what they called the "rap room," with carpet samples glued to the floor and varicolored pillows, where discussion kept on after meals.[95] The rap room could make you feel both uneasy and at ease, reports LeCocq, who did not join the new program immediately, since she had already established herself in the art department: "I felt real alien. I wasn't used to it at all."[96] She recalled the experience as "soul searching, gut wrenching, tumultuous, cleansing, exhausting, exhilarating" and the space as "suffocating and uncomfortable one moment and nurturing and comforting just a short time later."[97]

"Judy spilled her guts one day," recalls LeCocq, and described her first husband's death. "For the first time I felt that she was a vulnerable person instead of an adult over us. We felt like children. She could manipulate us . . . She didn't have it all together but put on a tough front. She had boots, short hair, a dykey look."[98] LeCocq viewed Judy as threatening, like a female "Che Guevara," who was intent on turning her students into "great artists."[99] On the other hand, LeCocq confirms that Chicago was correct about male attitudes toward female art students: "Every male professor in the art department hit on me . . . I did kiss a few of them, but I'd stop and say: 'You're married.' "[100] She later specified that Kusel, "who was already old," in this regard had not been one of the boys.

Chris Rush also felt intimidated by Judy, whom she recalls stressing both a "commitment to art" and "pressure not to be too feminine, not to shave your legs."[101] Another student, Jan Lester, agrees that the students in the Fresno program dressed in work boots and coveralls and refrained from wearing makeup, shaving their legs, or plucking their eyebrows. The situation was "something almost cultlike . . . We had this sense that we were doing something important," adding, "Judy made everyone in the program believe that they could do whatever they wanted to do."[102]

One conversation focused on the long blond hair of Cheryl Zurilgen, whom Chicago rebuked for using her looks to get things from men, only to have Zurilgen cut it all off that same night. Shawnee Wollenman, who helped Zurilgen trim what was left of her hair, then cut off her own dark tresses. When Nancy Youdelman followed suit, Zurilgen felt as if her own martyrdom had been cheapened. Too "fragile," unable to stand the pressure, she would soon withdraw from the program, drop her artistic ambition, marry, and become instead a devoted full-time mother of three artistically gifted children and, eventually, a member of the Jehovah's Witnesses.[103]

The cut-hair story disturbed Chicago so much that she shared her concern with Schapiro, who took it less to heart: hair, after all, unlike an arm or a leg, would grow back. Chicago herself felt "great empathy" for Zurilgen, remarking that she too had been traumatized when she stopped wearing eye makeup and cut off her own hair. "I experienced the sheer terror of facing the world with my plain face," she reflected. "Oh, what they do to us with these notions of 'pretty' & 'ugly' & how hard it is to let go of all of that & just be human."[104] Youdelman confirms Rhyne's memory of Chicago in jeans and shirts, no makeup, her naturally curly hair in an Afro.[105]

On another dramatic occasion, Vanalyne Green brought in a painting and placed it on the wall at an angle: "Judy yelled, 'It doesn't go that way.' This was the paradox: to foster autonomy but under a particular set of terms. I was bewildered: if we were being allowed the freedom to learn in a progressive environment, why was Judy telling me how to hang my painting?"[106] At a group dinner "Judy once threw a bottle of wine across the room when I said something that angered her," Green also remembers.

"Every week—on a Wednesday night, perhaps?—we had a type of confrontational scene, with a different person chosen for group criticism. How I dreaded those evenings."[107] "Judy thought that I was anti-Semitic because I hadn't been exposed to Jewish culture and history," she recalls, "growing up in the vacuum of working-class West Coast culture."[108] "Her remark," recalls Green, "which was never addressed to me directly but to the other students, was deeply traumatic, and there were many discussions with friends about what this meant and how to interpret it. That was the thing about the program: it encouraged a Darwinian fight for life among the women students, and we often abandoned each other to gain her approval. We behaved very badly."[109]

On one occasion Green telephoned Lacy: " 'You know, you're gonna present your work in crit tomorrow, and I heard some people saying they don't trust you and they're gonna use this as an opportunity to get you.' Apparently there was some rumor going around," notes Lacy, "that at one point I was a CIA agent."[110]

In the months before they got the studio ready, nobody made much art, a student recalled, but then they were encouraged to write autobiographies and derive images, using any medium they wished—drawing, painting, sculpture, mime, dance, performance—from their own experience, "e.g. being used sexually, walking down the street & being accosted, etc."[111] The experiment produced results that astonished its designer: when the women "talked about feeling invaded by men," Chicago reported, she had them "make images of those feelings. They brought this work to the class, and I nearly fainted. Everything was so direct. It was imagery that had to do with a whole area of female experience we had never talked about . . . like really feeling raped and violated and used and all that."[112]

That fall Chicago assigned a research project in art history. Each student was told to select a woman artist from history whom she would research and then act out in a performance. Shawnee Wollenman recalls that she chose Emily Carr, Nancy Youdelman chose Rosa Bonheur, and Chris Rush chose Leonor Fini.[113] Eight students led by Faith Wilding, who like Suzanne Lacy was already a graduate student, pursued work on an art history of women. The students began their research in the fall, several months before January 1971, when art historian Linda Nochlin's now classic article "Why Have There Been No Great Women Artists?" appeared in *ARTnews*, which some of the students recall reading.[114] The project took students to Los Angeles libraries, including the Glendale Public Library, in search of material on women artists.[115]

All in all the program was "transformative" for Lacy, who was already in her second year as a graduate student in psychology. Chicago had hesitated to admit her, doubting she would become an artist, but Lacy warmed to the increasing emphasis on performance, in which she would later distinguish herself.[116] Already in December 1970 a few of Chicago's students performed for a graduate art seminar at the University of California at Berkeley. By then some of them were progressing, while others lagged.

The occasion prompted Chicago to articulate a programmatic point: "That night after the seminar I told them I wasn't going to relate to them on an emotional level anymore," she recounted to an interviewer. "I had begun to understand that it's very easy for girls to continually be involved with their feelings, and it's much harder for them to move over to a work ground."[117] She intended for the students to transfer their dependency from her to "the structure of the group itself," wanting "to build an environment for women to function in—not a hierarchy with me as leader. In fact, the whole point was to move away from that kind of structure.[118] If the group environment worked, it would benefit and sustain not only the students but her own artistic growth. "I wanted to do what no woman has ever done," Chicago wrote, "& that is to transcend my femaleness—to ascend to a level of *human* identity that women have been unable to reach because they are frozen into the roles of women as enumerated by a patriarchal social structure."[119]

Her ties to her own mother, prompting a letter in mid-November, gave Chicago a chance to stand back from her creation for a moment and report the bright side: "I'm finding it marvelous to teach girls, & next semester I will have only sixteen students, all girls. They have a studio away from the campus, so I hardly ever have to be at school. It's a good thing—college campuses are so dehumanizing & depressing these days."[120] She did not expect to get back to L.A. till after Christmas: "Lloyd will be doing a piece in the gallery here in December, so he'll be here most of the time." She missed him but was getting a lot accomplished in the two renovated spaces—not only the theater with her students' dramas but down in Kingsburg at the old meat market. She was completing a series of five large paintings, five by ten feet, which she called *Fresno Fans.* Each of the fans was composed of a system of squares, sprayed with gradated color so that the image appeared "to breathe, open and close, expand and contract"; she related these images to "a body gesture."[121]

The students' dramas spilled over from the theater into their lives. The experiment with transferring responsibilities from teacher to students triggered insecurity, and Chicago found herself faced with unexpected and seemingly uncontrollable "crying jags, depressions, and self-deprecating remarks." When the laboratory seemed to spin out of control, Chicago turned to Schapiro as an experienced teacher of feminist faith. Memories vary and waver as to how the exchanges developed. Chicago told an interviewer of visiting Schapiro at her home in L.A. and mentioning her desire to teach a class of all women. "Since Mimi had once put me down for having approached her on that subject, I had not brought it up again; but somehow it came up in our conversation and she told me, much to my surprise, that she thought what I was doing was wonderful. That was the extent of our contact when I called her up."[122]

The call to Schapiro, caused by rising turmoil in the Fresno experiment, was desperate: " 'I have to talk to you. I can't tell you how much I need to talk to you. You are the only woman I can talk to. All of these things are happening in my class, and if I don't talk to you, I won't be able to handle them. You've just got to let me.' She [Schapiro] took this big breath, sat down, and said, 'Okay.' And I just laid it all on her, everything that had happened that day and how terrible and how scary it was."[123] The resulting talk really helped, Chicago felt, and laid the groundwork for the ensuing "partnership" of the pair.

Still in November, then, Schapiro made a well-documented visit to Fresno, where she spoke to Chicago's students and observed the new program for herself, as both recounted in separate interviews not long after. "I gave a talk there and visited with her group of women afterward, in a studio they rented off campus," related Schapiro. "I was teaching at CalArts, and Judy and I spent a lot of time together talking about the problems of teaching. She was involved in restructuring the school situation and breaking down the role barriers between teacher and student." Schapiro was impressed by the students' performance pieces expressing their feelings, "their environmental works made out of autobiographical material," and their development of "new definitions of female iconography."[124]

"We really had a wonderful night when Mimi came up," Chicago told her interviewer. "It was terrific and I think that she had, for the first time in her life, a vision of what another kind of teaching situation could be. I think she was really comfortable for the first time. There was no resistance; there was no defensiveness; everybody really responded to her. They were eager to hear what she had to say; and she had the experience of what I was talking about—being released from the double bind in the male culture."[125]

For Schapiro the students put on a "rivalry play," written by Nancy Youdelman, in which "a glamorous hooker and the fat matron" confront each other violently at a bus stop, when the hooker drops cigarette ash in the matron's popcorn. They end by stabbing and strangling each other. "We just did things without thinking of the consequences," says Jan Lester, who played the matron, dressed sloppily with hot pink stockings rolled under her knees. Chris Rush played the hooker, dressed in a swish fur coat and hat with a veil.[126]

The players dressed fit-to-kill thanks to Nancy Youdelman's fascination with costumes—ever since high school she had collected Victorian clothes. She and Jan Lester had dressed up and posed for photographs, which won Chicago's encouragement, no doubt aware of the value of make-believe in exploring identity. Chris's clothes were made to come apart, says Youdelman, and she was wearing a "merry widow corset dyed hot pink."[127]

For another occasion LeCocq remembers being "dressed up as a Victorian whore. This was fun for me. It felt like playing dress up as a child. I enjoyed being made up, having my hair piled high on my head and wearing the delicate antique clothing. The corset, however, was not enjoyable. I could barely breathe."[128] Part of the Fresno program's big studio became the costume area, and costumed performances became routine. The students' photographs of themselves costumed as fictional archetypes were conceptually close to those that Cindy Sherman would title *Untitled Film Stills* and produce from 1977 onward to lasting acclaim.

Schapiro wanted the students to costume her too, although Youdelman recalls that she did not like being photographed. They dressed Schapiro as a Victorian lady, in an exercise that examined female identity, "imposed behavior," and sexual roles.[129] Doris Bigger, who had constructed a darkroom in the studio, photographed Schapiro in her Victorian guise, producing images that so pleased Schapiro that she has repeatedly reused them to represent herself both in various artworks and on the catalog cover for a show of her work in 1975 (all without credit to Youdelman and the other dressers or Bigger).[130]

Schapiro was at her most charming—Chris Rush recalls her as "very positive, warm and nurturing, not confrontational."[131] The visit was clearly positive for both Schapiro and Chicago, for it prepared them to join very soon in an effort to move the Fresno program to CalArts.

Besides recourse to Schapiro and the dramatic therapy of the visit, Chicago addressed her students' tension with five assignments: "evaluate in writing the course and one's own growth in it; read Simone de Beauvoir's *The Second Sex* and relate this to one's own struggle; formulate goals for personal growth for the remainder of the year; decide on a work project for the coming month; and make a calendar of daily activities for that month."[132] Chicago then met with each student individually to discuss the assignments and repeated the meetings each month.

Reading *The Second Sex,* the students might have focused on de Beauvoir's chapter on "Sexual Initiation," where she discussed women's eroticism as much more complex than men's and dubbed "the female the prey of the species."[133] When she wrote, "We speak of 'taking' a girl's virginity, her flower, or 'breaking' her maidenhead . . . as an abrupt rupture with the past," she emphasized a familiar metaphor that Chicago would soon adapt as a theme for her series of paintings *Through the Flower.*[134]

Other books also inspired the group. Lacy remembers when "Nancy Youdelman came to class one time with the book of the 1893 Chicago World's Fair and the first Woman's Building. This was revolutionary to us. We pored over this and other books and found photographs in esoteric places. I emphasized feminist literature and tried to get the group more cognizant of the major themes, like racism, lesbianism, violence against women, etc., that were under discussion in the feminist movement (which Faith and I were more connected to than the others)."[135]

Field trips also proliferated, including a visit to the Los Angeles home of the art collectors and Chicago's patrons Stanley and Elyse Grinstein.[136] Vanalyne Green recalls "an experience that completely opened me to becoming an artist. Judy took us on a field trip to the then Pasadena Museum of Art. I knew zilch about contemporary art, and stood in front of a Kenneth Noland painting, stymied and intimidated. I asked her to help me understand the painting. She told me to stand there and see how the painting made me feel. It was the beginning of my life as an artist and art lover (though the artist part took a long while to develop)."[137] Chicago's impact on her student's development was much greater than she realized at the time, as Green says: "Suddenly I realized that I didn't need critics or interpreters to comprehend art: I had my own sensate responses to form and color, and I could have a direct relationship with a work of art. This was a staggering realization. Pure liberation. You could hear the doors opening, and I was stone sober."[138]

Among the most memorable destinations was Miriam Schapiro's studio in Santa Monica. Faith Wilding drove her VW bus down from Fresno, packed with students. That night Jan Lester remembers that they visited the charming Spanish house where Schapiro and Brach lived. One of the students asked: "'What's that wonderful smell?' It was the scent of orange blossoms, but Schapiro replied: 'money.'" This, Lester recalls, was "the moment when Schapiro suggested that Chicago bring the Feminist Art Program to CalArts."[139]

The story was not so simple. Chicago's husband had already been teaching at CalArts when Schapiro's husband, Paul Brach, the dean, asked her if she would like to teach there too. Her reply—"Yes, but I would teach only women"—provoked his immediate refusal and the query, was she out of her mind? His wife's reports from Fresno and further reflection changed his mind. Chicago recalls that they decided to bring her program to CalArts, and "Mimi began preparing the way, talking to the deans and getting it accepted as an idea."[140] At some point, Chicago's initiative got the name that would prove historic: Feminist Art Program.

The ferment of the experiment in Fresno inspired Chicago, who with characteristic self-awareness determined to start her first journal—precisely on March 8, 1971—its first page headed in firm script, *"This book belongs to Judy Chicago,"* along with the Kingsburg address. A second thought betrays itself in capitals printed above "Judy Chicago"—"COHEN*"—the asterix referring down to a note: "**who changed her name but not her fundamental identity.*"[141] By then—little over a year after starting the new curriculum at Fresno—she was growing ever more aware that she had created a radical new departure that needed to be recorded and merited a place in history rather than women's usual fate of getting erased: "I want to begin to establish regular contact with the growth of the first Feminist Art ever attempted," she wrote in what could be the first documented use of the phrase.[142] Historians have so far failed to discuss who named the movement now known as "feminist art," but Chicago's journal entry at a moment of historical consciousness soon found public resonance in a new name for her Fresno experiment—Feminist Art Program."[143]

Chicago framed the experiment at Fresno and her own development in the wider cultural context, realizing that "the Women's Liberation Movement represented (for me) support to make overt all the feelings, beliefs, and ideas I had lived with covertly since the day I had begun to consciously make art and consciously to struggle with my conditioning as a woman in order to make art."[144] In that moment "it finally occurred to me that I could say what had been unsayable and do what had been undoable. I was going to try to come out of hiding into the bright light of the day and expose what it *really* was to be female in a society that held the female in contempt."[145]

In these inaugural entries—aimed both at developing her own identity and self-knowledge and at addressing the future readers that a journal's creation implies—Chicago recasts and recounts her experience in the form of a quest or journey that progressed through successive steps, like any traditional tale about origin; and she adapts other traditional metaphors about origin, such as primal motivation or causal desire, which prompts successive acts of making or building, followed by acts of getting and keeping by means of struggle, combat—all of which get described in retrospect as derring-do, hence consolidated and confirmed. In the journal, thus, the action stems from Chicago's primal desire "to build an environment *based* on my needs as a woman and as an artist." This leads to a decisive initial demarche and its segues: "My first step was to change my name—thereby seizing control of my identity and making it my own. My second step was to give several lectures in which I told of my struggle as an artist and the difficulties I had encountered because I am a woman." In one of these, delivered at California State College (Los Angeles) in early 1969, she had introduced metaphoric comparison with male combat, declaring that she was "preparing to go to war against the culture."[146]

The historic change would create further tensions. Not every student in the Fresno program would be able to make the move to CalArts. Each woman had to submit a portfolio of her work. On March 9, in the second day of the journal, Chicago wrote that she worked in her own studio and then went to see the students who had spent the day preparing their portfolios with Schapiro. The sight of them made her feel threatened, as she admitted to herself and to future historians: "I had thought I'd gotten over those feelings, but they came back when I saw her with the girls." Chicago also felt that the students hadn't given her enough credit in their personal statements for CalArts: "I sometimes feel that I'm going to be pushed out of the picture. But then Mimi sometimes feels (she says) that she'll go under because of me."[147] At the request of *Artforum* editor Phil Leider, the two began to work on a critical article about "artists from O'Keefe [sic] to Frankenthaler, from a feminist point of view."[148] They also met with CalArts women who "want to participate or extend our program."[149]

The very success of the experiment with her students also created a dilemma that Chicago would feel ever more acutely in varying forms in the following years: the imperative to be in her studio making her own art and yet the want, commitment, and need to be with her students in the supportive environment of their collaborative work. She began to wonder where her primary loyalty was. "I keep feeling like I *should* be working. The idea that one's *whole life* is one's work is very difficult to come to terms with."[150] Yet at the moment even her work owed something to the collective, for she was producing a series of collages based on "cunt" images that she felt were influenced by her student Faith Wilding's drawings. These eventually became a series of twenty-six alphabet collages, one for each letter, using the cunt form—entered as a landmark in the journal: "It's a breakthrough for me to move from cunt as subject to cunt as formal device."[151] Wilding has recalled that "cunt art" began when they tried to "analyze, confront, and articulate our common social experiences; it was not a set of predetermined images based on essentialist notions about women's sexuality."[152]

Moving in the direction of still greater engagement with the collective, Chicago began to collaborate with Jan Lester, Nancy Youdelman, and Shawnee Wollenman on a *Bathtub* movie. She concluded that she had "made a real personal breakthrough in terms of emerging from the psychological isolation women who achieve live in. But, oh boy, it's scary!"[153]

Another collaboration took place when Tom Marioni invited Chicago to participate in a group show of women artists, called *California Girls* held at the Richmond Art Center in the spring of 1971. Although she thought the title was condescending, Chicago invited her students to think of a collaborative piece, and Jan Lester suggested a beauty pageant spoof—complete with their work boots and hairy legs.[154] They each picked names of cities and made banners to wear across their chests, Chicago becoming "Miss Windy City," flanked on her left by Nancy Youdelman as "Miss San Francisco." Jan Lester stands in front of Judy as "Miss North Hollywood." Doris Bigger, who took the photo with a timed exposure, is seen reclining on the bottom left across from Faith Wilding. There were twelve original copies, each autographed and adorned with lipstick kisses.

All this devotion to the women in Fresno had caused her colleagues to wonder about the importance in her life of Hamrol, her onetime collaborator. That she herself monitored their relationship from the viewpoint of her crusade may be inferred from a journal entry: "Now Lloyd is growing more and more toward active involvement in the Revolution," she registered, only to posit a question that would haunt her and keep coming back more acutely in varying terms at each stage of the quest through the coming decade: *"Is it really a Revolution*? If I'm right, if there really is a revolution occurring, then *everything I'm doing is productive. If I'm wrong then everything's a waste of time.* That is my *agony.* I struggle with it every day. Only time will release me from the uncertainty. But that's what exhausts me, frightens me, & then alternatively exhilarates me. Is it real? Or will it prove to have been a monumental delusion, & worse, a waste of time?"[155]

Both Chicago and the collective took encouragement from the other artists and feminist writers who came to Fresno to speak or perform. Roxanne Dunbar, who came on March 22, was touring college campuses, speaking about "women's liberation, capitalist exploitation, racism, the Vietnam War, other national liberation movements, and the necessity for revolution."[156] She impressed Chicago as "articulate, but too quiet for all of us," although the occasion did allow for a rapprochement between Chicago's students and women from Fresno State who were "in the Movement" but suspicious of the program because of its location off campus.[157]

Among the most memorable visitors was the feminist writer Ti-Grace Atkinson, who followed Dunbar by just two days. Lacy recalls that she had to tell the other students in the program, who had not yet done their assigned reading about Atkinson, and convince them to greet her at the airport. She recruited four women (Doris Bigger, Cay Lang, Vanalyne Green, and Susan Boud), who decided to let Atkinson know what their program was all about. They met dressed as cheerleaders in pink, as in one of their earlier performances spoofing themselves, with letters across their chests spelling "C-U-N-T."[158] "Off the plane came forty or so Shriners as we were screaming, 'Give us a C, give us a U,'" recalls Lacy. "Right behind them came this giant leggy woman wearing sunglasses at six o'clock in the evening and carrying a cigarette holder. She had buckskin pants and a giant fur coat. That was Ti-Grace Atkinson, who stood there sort of bemused while we were performing madly for her. It was quite a night."[159]

At the all-women party after the talk, the feisty, diminutive hostess took issue with the statuesque guest, in a clash of proportions epic enough to merit space in the new journal—"a ferocious argument which ended in my telling her to fuck off. I do, of course, deeply respect her. She is a strong, courageous woman. . . . Nonetheless she made me furious. She put us all down & came on with a holier-than-thou number."[160] Core dissent in regard to men contributed to the tiff. Lacy, who labeled Atkinson "the only woman in America now who might be assassinated," remembers that Atkinson was "very down on men," while "Judy has never been down on men; she has seen feminism as a two-gendered activity. Most of us had made choices to live with a man."[161]

The journal allowed Chicago to spell out her take on the matter. Atkinson was "greatly dehumanized & does not realize that her feelings about consciousness raising, marriage, etc. are based on her own fear of the personal," recorded

Chicago, who concluded that Ti-Grace was "a great woman, altho I disagree vehemently with her. But what a delight to see women standing up & saying it like it is."[162] Atkinson had written that "female oppression was essentially a class confrontation,"[163] with a much more provocative corollary: "The price of clinging to the enemy is your life. To enter into a relationship with a man who has divested himself as completely and publicly from the male role as possible would still be a risk. But to relate to a man who has done any less is suicide."[164] Only later did it get back to Chicago and into the journal that their bout had made the visitor burst into tears: "I feel terrible that I couldn't have been there when she cried & held her because she *really* is my sister. But she intimidated me."[165] In the end, Chicago had to conclude that she preferred Roxanne Dunbar's quiet style.

If variety were not enough, Chicago programmed sharp contrast when she invited an old friend to visit—one of the wild men of the Ferus Gallery—Larry Bell, who happened to be her exact contemporary and to share her Eastern European Jewish heritage. He drove up from L.A. in his little "macho jeep," with which he liked to go "plinking—shooting at targets—thinking that he would practice while in Fresno." Upon arrival, he pulled out his guns, prompting Judy to tell him to bring them in and add them to the performance planned.

"I was the perfect foil—that's why I brought all this macho shit with me," he chuckles. "It brought some of the ladies to tears."[166] Bell submitted to having the students dress him in costume and raise his consciousness in the rap room. While thirteen women danced around him, he took out his gun and showed it to everyone. "I am pretty sure that he was having fantasies of having sex with all of us," Jan Lester recalls, "but that didn't happen."[167] Both Chris Rush and Nancy Youdelman remember being quite frightened. So was Vanalyne Green, who recalls a group performance for which Bell "needed three of us to participate. I guess I volunteered; I don't remember, actually, but I was going to be one of the ones. But when I found out that we were to prance around the foothills of the San Joaquin Valley with no clothes on, I once again dissembled and said that I couldn't do it."[168]

Bell's visit was recorded by Judith Dancoff, then a film student at UCLA who, with an all-woman crew, spent nearly three months making her film *Judy Chicago and the Fresno Girls*. At about this time too Chicago completed her *Cock and Cunt Play*, in which two women wear outlandish costumes designed to personify a giant Cunt and a colossal Cock, both sewn in pink vinyl by Shawnee Wollenman.[169] In the film Faith Wilding dons the Cock costume and Jan Lester the Cunt. Chicago continued work on her *Cunt Alphabet* collages and some abstract paintings on plastic, even though Lloyd told her that he thought abstract art was "counterrevolutionary." She was not yet dissuaded, not yet able, in her own words, to " 'transcend' the cunt."[170]

Chicago used this same language in a letter to the admissions committee at CalArts, justifying the need for the school to accept a critical mass of her students from Fresno: "We all have to begin together—me, and Miriam Schapiro and Faith Wilding and Jan Lester and Nancy Youdelman and Shawnee Wollenman and Chris Rush and Cheryl Zurilgen—because we're all we have and we have a big job before us. We must unearth the buried and half-hidden treasures of our cunts and bring them into the light and let them shine and dazzle and become Art."[171] She went on: "With Miriam Schapiro as my partner, I am going to bring down the program for women that I began this year at Fresno State College. I went away from Los Angeles to start this program because I was afraid that no one in Los Angeles would give me a chance to do what I wanted to do, i.e., to begin to build an environment in which women could feel free to make the art that derives from their beings."[172]

To justify bringing her students from Fresno into the program at CalArts, Chicago documented some of her results: "To go on with what we have begun, we have to bring all of our beginnings with us. We cannot afford to let go of anything we have begun—not of our work in the studio, not of our films, or our tapes, not of our studies of women writers, nor of the starting of a Female Art History, and most of all we cannot let go of each other. For we are the beginning of a new world, a world in which women can be together and be themselves and let themselves be seen in the world."[173]

The next day Chicago drove with Hamrol and some other couples to San Francisco to see a retrospective Georgia O'Keeffe exhibition at the Museum of Modern Art. The paintings struck her as beautiful but achieved at the "price of almost total isolation" because O'Keeffe "could not transcend the cunt. She stay[ed] immersed in it. She made great paintings, but I want to liberate myself from the context of the cunt and become a *complete* human being, neither cunt nor cock, but *me.*"[174] This was her goal, despite the trouble she had reaching it.

A second day off from work was precious: she relished the time with Lloyd, whom she perceived as "getting more beautiful every day now. I can let down when he's around & know that he'll take care of me."[175] "Lloyd is really becoming a very giving person, & our relationship is beginning to have a consistent closeness & tenderness, without constant struggling," she wrote in her journal. "I love him more than ever. Since he's been integrating the meaning of what I'm doing into *his* life, he's becoming happier with himself, in as much as he's standing for what he believes in, a condition of humanness all people need."[176]

Back in her studio, Chicago took another day off from teaching to begin some large eight-feet-square paintings, which she had to stand on a scaffold and try to paint. She produced this series of five, titled *Flesh Gardens,* by spraying acrylic lacquer on big pieces of Plexiglas. To move them around required two heavy-duty dollies, which Rhyne built, but also the help of a big Swede named Charlie, who worked as a car painter at Don's Auto Body, a couple of blocks over on the other side of the tracks. Charlie was big enough to reach across the surface, eight feet square, and spray on a beautiful top coat.[177] The format of repeated squares with colors fading in and out achieved a sense of physical vibration, making them seem almost visceral.

On April 6, after a party in Los Angeles at the Grinsteins with Schapiro among the guests, Chicago recorded how Mimi got a male artist "uptight" and later Lloyd asked the man about his feelings. The tense response caused a "little confrontation [that] totally freaked Lloyd out. He's terrified at the idea that anyone might dislike him. I can't understand it at all. Anyway, I've decided (again) to stop struggling with the men. I can't stand it. They really are cowardly about standing up for what they believe. . . . The only ones speaking their minds these days are women. The men seem completely paralyzed."[178]

With Schapiro she scheduled a joint lecture for the Contemporary Arts Council in Los Angeles, which led to anxiety: "I'm afraid everybody will put me down & make me feel bad. I feel afraid to be exposed & like I'd like to stay up here in hiding, safe. It really scares me, the prospect of coming out in the open—in the big, cruel nitty gritty L.A. Art World, where feelings don't count, & I'll have to be tough."[179] Adding to her sense of vulnerability, she registered again that recurrent impulse to retreat to her own studio, recalling her own ambitions as a child student of art: "I feel it necessary to keep that part of me alive that got on the old #53 Bus in Chicago every Saturday & went off to the Art Institute."[180]

As the first year of what had come to be called the Feminist Art Program was winding down, Judith Dancoff continued to film. She, together with Chicago, Schapiro, and the students, worked up a special issue of the newspaper, *Everywoman.* Chicago explained her willingness to experiment in so many areas: she credited "the women's movement—new options were opened so that I could actually think about using my talent in a variety of ways which had simply not been possible before."[181] To the movement she had already given credit as a supportive context in which to realize herself, and about the Fresno experiment, she would reflect, "I became aware of the women's liberation movement, and I immediately understood what that meant . . . I realized that I could actually begin to put out all this information I had about my own struggle, my own perceptions, and I also understood that the structure as it existed in the art world and the world as a whole had no provisions for that kind of information."[182]

In mid-April the program staged a Rap Weekend, inviting visitors to observe the work produced. Chicago expressed anxiety lest the women who came might think less than well of what had been achieved in the course of a year. In the end Chicago judged the Rap Weekend very stimulating but "exhausting." Schapiro brought two women: Sherry Brody and Barbara Smith. About forty women attended on Saturday, mostly from L.A. and San Francisco, and twenty others, mostly from Fresno, came on Sunday. Saturday started with lunch, then a program. On display was Faith Wilding's environment, which she had made by "creating a life sized figure of herself dressed as a bride with her midsection cut open with cow guts spilling out. With each showing of the piece, she had to go back to the slaughterhouse and obtain fresh cow guts. Another feature of her environment were the bloody Kotexes that trimmed the walls at ceiling height."[183] Anything else might seem anticlimactic: Chicago gave an introductory talk, a student read "Daddy" by Sylvia Plath, which addresses the poet's feelings of abandonment at the age of ten when her father died and once again as her husband leaves her. There followed plays, films, slides, and art history testimony that "resurrected women artists from the past & let them tell their stories," along with a history lecture on women artists.

Afterward came informal raps—brief discussions—then dinner, followed by a performance by Vicki Hall, who had recently received her B.A. and M.A. in sculpture from UCLA and was teaching introductory sculpture at Fresno. In her performance piece, *Ominous Operation,* she turned five "women into hermaphrodites by transplanting penises to their groin."[184] Hall played a satyr doctor and a student in Chicago's program, Susan Boud, her assistant. Chicago recalls that Hall "cast penises and applied them to the women performers, then had them all lift their operating gowns (it involved medical procedures). I thought the audience was going to have a collective heart attack."[185] About two hundred people were there. The performance came to a climax with a pseudophallic prance.

"At the time I was in Fresno I didn't know much about feminism," says Hall, "but the idea of protesting my treatment at UCLA really appealed to me, and from there I came up with various performances and installations that explored, among other things, women's victimization. So I got into feminism through art. I guess my process was more intuitive because I was not involved in CR [consciousness raising] and I was not reading the literature at the time."[186] "I am sure," she adds, "the question about women's position, which was something that had always bothered me, was more on my mind because of Judy and the Feminist Art Program. . . . I didn't usually give it much thought at the time. Now and then someone would complain about something going on at the studio." Hall also helped various students in Chicago's program "cast their face, which we were doing in my sculpture classes. I cast Faith Wilding's face screaming for the piece she installed at the studio with the entrails."

On balance, the enthusiasm of the spectators—mainly other women artists—and the aesthetic accomplishments of the students pleased Chicago, who understood that the theatrics were not meant to be formal theater but rather a mingling of "live action & performance with films, slides, voices, taped voices, sounds, music, light."[187] The results reaffirmed her program to "recreate women from the Past whose lives have been distorted by men's history books. I want women from all ages to mingle on the stage, telling their stories, comforting each other."[188]

Drawing up accounts and closing her books on the year, she concluded that "the really exciting part of this is over for me. I have done what I set out to do. I have begun the structure whereby women's work will finally be able to reveal itself & women will be able to assume their rightful place. It's real now—I don't doubt it any more. From now on, I hope that it will grow quickly. Several women at the weekend were turned on to starting classes for women. I was only 1 person in the Fall, there are probably 12 or 15 of us now."[189]

Moving some of the students to CalArts while leaving others behind was proving problematic. Although Chicago considered some of those left behind less serious about their work, she made an effort to train her successor at Fresno, Rita Yokoi. While meeting with those who would remain, Chicago admitted to being tired of dealing with everyone's emotional problems. One student had become intimately involved with at least two of the male professors in the art department—exactly the kind of behavior that Chicago had hoped to prevent when she created the program.[190] She wanted her students to become artists themselves instead of falling into the more typical roles of wives or mistresses for the male artists. Schapiro advised her to "de-escalate," and she told herself that she had to do so now. She wrote in her journal: "GRRRRRRRR! It is both a privilege & a pain in the ass to have been born a woman at this time in History—a privilege because we may change History—a pain in the ass because I'd like to be *FREE!*"

After working with Schapiro, helping her prepare for the Contemporary Arts Council talk in L.A., Chicago reported that it had gone very well since the audience was very enthusiastic (with the exception of Allan Kaprow, for whom the level of emotion was frightening). Chicago spoke first; then Schapiro gave a testimony about her life. Next they gave an art history lecture about feminist art, focusing on the nature of female identity.[191] The evening pleased not just Chicago and Schapiro but their hostess, Elyse Grinstein, who let Judy know.

A letdown followed as April closed. Chicago was finding it hard to do her own work, and Lloyd was "coming apart at the seams." They were house-hunting pending her move to CalArts, which was his turf, and she figured that he must be feeling "threatened by the level of demand on him now due to our involvement with CalArts, Paul & Mimi, & the implications of my work." Her programmatic rigor with herself made her judge very sternly: "I find myself losing respect for him as he wallows in a kind of self-indulgent misery, not really making any changes towards greater self-fulfillment but rather sinking into self-pity."[192] Their relationship remained in flux.

Even before entering the new stage, Chicago had already begun to plan with some of her students the "structure for artmaking next year" and "begun to implement it. I & the girls have begun the creation of 25–30 female characters, either from history or representative of fantasy images of women. We *will* prepare costumes, characterizations, & testimony for each one, & then let them mingle in an environment of high level emotional intensity." She had in mind to stage "the trial of Joan of Arc with a jury of her peers—i.e. women from all times in history."[193] She saw this leading "not only to theater but to films, books, slide images, photo pieces, etc. That part of my work is going well. I love it. I've found myself."[194]

But she lacked confidence in her own studio, even starting to question "the very nature of painting."[195] The positive feedback from her feminist pedagogy made it harder still to go back to the isolated, internalized studio world. The new life—so much more engaged with people—made her doubt: "I'm beginning not to know who I am independent of my public existence."[196]

Beset with confusion herself, Chicago tried to deal also with Lloyd's, including his contradictory need to achieve greater recognition and yet "remain protected."[197] She got word that he was involved with some collaborative video pieces that "dealt directly with masculine issues—i.e., castration & control" but were poorly received by Lloyd's student seminar, unlike the enthusiastic reception for her lecture with Schapiro: "Of course, the only time you really have a chance of strong recognition is when you risk disapproval. The men seem terrified of that level of risk & exposure, desiring instead to go on being protected, as they have always been."[198]

Fissures between them loomed. "Lloyd's been trying to run back into his neurosis & his failure patterns," she judged. "But this time, there is nothing I can do for him. He will have to look the world in the face & decide for himself how he'll deal with it. Until then, I guess we'll just bumble along, holding on to our friendship, if not our love affair. If he were really to decide to run away rather than risk losing the approval of the male world, I guess that would be that. He hasn't failed me in his humanity yet—I hope he won't this time."[199]

In the meantime Chicago planned a trip to New York, where she would meet Schapiro and they would spend time together with "the radical women" and go see a show of women artists organized by Lucy Lippard, now an established critic, whom Chicago had known since her stay in New York in 1959. She also hoped to "get all the information I can about Eva Hesse so as to reincarnate her."[200] Chicago's interest in the sculptor Hesse, who as a Jewish child fled Nazi Germany, grew out of her own friendship with Lippard, who had included Hesse's work in a show called *Eccentric Abstraction* at New York's Fischbach Gallery in 1966. Chicago perceived sexual suggestiveness in Hesse's abstract sculptures and saw her as a kindred spirit, mourning her death in 1970 from a brain tumor at the age of thirty-four.[201]

Arriving in New York on May Day, Chicago promptly encouraged revolution in the home of her hosts. Irving Petlin had shown his work with Chicago's old dealer, Rolf Nelson, and was a founder of Artists and Writers Against the War in Vietnam, which had organized the L.A. Peace Tower. His wife Sarah—rebelling against her roles as "wife & mother"—was striving to recover her identity as the dancer she once was, a move seconded by Chicago "like mad."[202] Sarah identified with her friend Joyce Kozloff in a struggle with her husband, Max, prompting Chicago to note: "The real meaning of Wom. Lib. is that women are identifying with women for the first time in History."[203] Sarah, who later became known as a poet, recalls that "it was a 360 struggle getting back to dancing, and Judy was enormously encouraging."[204]

Chicago and her hosts joined artists demonstrating against the Guggenheim Museum for closing a show of Hans Haacke, whose work—*Shapolsky et al. Manhattan Real Estate Holdings, a Real-Time Social System, as of May 1, 1971*—exposed a corrupt slumlord, and for firing the show's curator, Edward F. Fry, who refused to be censored. At the demonstration the dancer Yvonne Rainer was making loud wailing sounds and Chicago and her hosts chimed in: "soon the whole inside of the museum was resounding with sounds, cries & chants. Paper floated down from all levels. It was really lovely for a few minutes."[205]

The trio went on to an opening of Schapiro's at André Emmerich Gallery and to a dinner that followed, after which Chicago with Paul Brach and Don Lewellen, a painter she knew from UCLA, continued on to a party at Bob Rauschenberg's, where she danced and got "really stoned."[206] The next day Hannah Wilke brought slides to show to Chicago, who found it "very interesting.

She makes cunt-shaped pieces from clay & latex. We talked for a while. She has a lot of confusion about her loyalties & still wears makeup & sexy clothes. Whether she really wants to be seen as a 'woman' or as an artist & person. We'll see how she resolves it."[207]

Chicago and Schapiro continued to campaign the next day, paying a visit to the sculptor Louise Nevelson, a successful woman artist whom they admired. They thought her very responsive, since she promised to visit CalArts in the fall and to do an interview with them. Yet later, when they ran into the artist June Wayne, a mutual acquaintance who had seen Nevelson later that same evening, they were disappointed to hear that she had not mentioned their visit.

Collecting further "Art History testimony," Chicago went alone to visit Lucy Lippard and made a tape of her talking about Eva Hesse. Hesse's remarkable early success, including the purchase of a major sculpture by the Museum of Modern Art in 1969, was a point of pride for women and made her particularly interesting for anyone concerned with the fate of women artists. Chicago also interviewed a close friend of Hesse's, the artist Sol LeWitt.

After a long talk with Marcia Tucker, then a curator at the Whitney Museum of American Art, Chicago "ended up crying and telling Marcia about my needs for recognition & my fears that I would do all this work & end up with nothing for myself. Marcia reassured me that this wouldn't happen & made me feel better. I must say, tho, that I ended up feeling a little manipulated, altho I couldn't quite understand why."[208] Tucker pointed out that Chicago seemed to be playing a role with her—"the woman who knew everything"—rather than just being herself, which hit home: "I get into that role often because I feel it forced upon me by other people. As Mimi says, right now I am a leader. But I felt good that Marcia was releasing me from that role."[209]

The New York excursion looked like a military campaign to Chicago's mother, who wrote to a friend about her daughter's work in a show at the Whitney and queried: "How do you feel about the women's lib movement? I think I told you that Judy is very involved in it; she is already beginning to feel some of the scars of battle, but this is one movement that she actually feels strongly about and is willing to do battle. Nothing before really moved her; she did her bit for peace, but this thing really has meaning for her on a very basic, almost elemental level."[210] Yet, May Cohen added, "She is tired, my daughter, but understands that everything worthwhile that had been won had been won by hard struggle."[211]

The pace did not slacken. Next day Chicago spoke at Douglass College, then the undergraduate school for women at Rutgers University in New Brunswick, New Jersey. She invited her friend the sculptor Jackie Winsor to come with her—to her later regret, because she felt that Jackie, just two years younger, "doesn't understand the mechanics of resistance" and the day went badly.[212] For Winsor, who had just taken her master's degree from Rutgers in 1967, this was "not a neutral space"; she felt that she was "walking on eggs" and considered Chicago "outspoken."[213] Chicago found the faculty "apathetic" and was surprised when the male students walked out after she said that she would talk to the women and that the men should listen. She was "upset by the abysmally low consciousness of the women," which forced her to speak on a very "primary level."

What Chicago found most depressing was that although Douglass was a women's college, men from Rutgers took courses there. Painfully aware of the history of women's struggles, she protested in her journal: "These women's colleges were created by my forebears (the suffragettes & feminists) to educate & illuminate women. They trudged across the country on foot, in carriages, in rain & snow collecting nickels, dimes, & quarters to get those schools started, and now it seems like the women's colleges have become a major force in the repression of women. A more depressing scene I have never been involved in."[214]

Facing a second day at Douglass, which had so depressed her, she bribed Schapiro to join her, offering half her fee. They began the day meeting with about twelve people, mostly women, trying "to get them to do something about their situation in that school." The evening activity was a panel discussion with Chicago, Schapiro, Lippard, the art critic Jill Johnston, "who expresses the Lesbian position in the Movement; Faith Ringgold, who speaks for black women," and Barbara Garson, author of the play *Macbird,* whom Chicago did not find helpful. It added to Chicago's disgust when her attempt to provoke the audience to speak out was foiled by a female member of the Douglass faculty. She concluded that the panel's "interminable discussion" was a waste of time: "Women seem to be able to talk & talk, but it's difficult to get them to dare anything. The success of the Movement will hinge on that."[215] Chicago was so disheartened by the response at Douglass that she told herself not to accept any more speaking engagements unless they were really special. She would consider workshops with women, where she might have a chance to effect change.

The next day Chicago and Schapiro met for brunch with the sculptor Lee Bontecou, whose work Chicago had admired while still a student. During the 1960s Bontecou had produced a series of evocative wall-mounted sculptures made of fabric stretched over welded steel armatures centered on dark, gaping apertures that conveyed a threatening mood, leading critics to compare them to an archetypal *vagina dentata* (toothed vagina), although Bontecou stressed connections to war and science, expressing her desire "to glimpse some of the fear, hope, ugliness, beauty, and mystery that exists in all of us."[216]

Bontecou, who from 1960 was the only woman showing with the prestigious Leo Castelli Gallery, along with star artists such as Jasper Johns, Robert Rauschenberg, Don Judd, and Andy Warhol, would choose in 1972 to stop showing, drop out of the art scene, and spend time raising her child, exploring, and finding herself. Chicago described her as "in hiding with her husband & son" and claimed that she reminded her a lot of a San Francisco artist named Jay DeFeo, "who is also very much in 'hiding.'" To Chicago's by turns analytical and synthetic way of processing information in her search for women's art history, a pattern emerged: "What seems to have happened to a number of women artists is that after their initial drive & push, they do not understand the nature of the pressure upon them—they simply seem to lose the strength that first drove them. I believe that this comes from not having understood &, in fact resisted coming to terms with, the implication of their femaleness. Thus they become wiped out by something they didn't even perceive acting upon them."[217] Chicago was delighted that Bontecou was planning to go to a consciousness raising session with Marcia Tucker and thrilled when Bontecou "admitted to the implications of her imagery, when she was making the pieces that established her reputation. It is certainly feminist imagery, i.e. imagery that deals with the nature of female identity."[218]

That evening Chicago and Schapiro entertained thirty women—critics, curators, and art historians—to tell them about the Feminist Art Program and to show slides from the art history file. When the usual attacks began, Chicago spoke up and said that she thought that she "deserved some appreciation & support" for what she was trying to accomplish.[219] That enabled those who responded positively to express their feelings. Next Marcia Tucker led a women's liberation technique in which each woman expressed her feelings, leaving Chicago at once pleased and relieved.

On their last day in New York, Chicago, Schapiro, Lippard, and Winsor went with Grace Glueck, an art reporter for *The New York Times,* to see a show—organized by Lippard at the Aldrich Museum of Contemporary Art in Ridgefield, Connecticut—of twenty-six New York women who had never been shown before. Chicago pronounced the work "terrific," very fresh and lively.[220] Glueck wrote up their visit in *The New York Times,* with a tone that appears to poke fun at feminism: "One of the most telling works, according to a pair of visiting specialists from California, artists Miriam Schapiro and Judy Chicago (we'll get back to them in minute), is a huge, corrugated paper construction of concentric circles enclosed by claustrophobic space, by Mary Miss (honest!). It expresses, claim the two Californians, the compressed, centralized imagery that women tend to favor."[221] As for Chicago, she liked Lippard's catalog essay, in which she recognized her own ideas, but she was anxious because the mention of her was so minor. She shared her uneasiness with Schapiro, who labeled Lippard "very ambitious." Chicago nonetheless wrote of Lippard, "But I like her a lot."[222]

After her write-up of the Aldrich show, Glueck, who claimed that she saw "unmistakable gynecological references" in some of the "biomorphic abstractions," gave the Feminist Art Program its first mainstream publicity in the East: "Meanwhile, back to the Misses Schapiro and Chicago (a show of work by the former has just closed at the André Emmerich Gallery here). Both teach at the big Disney-backed California Institute of the Arts in Valencia; both are pioneering in a brand-new art endeavor titled—brace yourself—Feminist Art Program." One wonders why she chose to interject "brace yourself," but she no longer remembers. Glueck did say that no editor imposed this language upon her and suggested that perhaps she wanted to sensationalize the topic for her readers.[223] Her article continued: "The program, which *has* to be the world's first, deals with women artists' 'reality as women,' says Miss Schapiro, who is married to Paul Brach, painter and dean of the art school. Designed to provide a framework for the understanding of women's art, it will involve such disciplines as art history, art criticism, art making and art education." Glueck went on to highlight issues raised by the new program: " 'We've been asked why we want to start a ghetto,' says Judy Chicago, a sculptor married to a sculptor, Lloyd Hamrol. 'But we're not interested in "high" art, built on male tradition. It's the beginning of education for women, by women, about women. We'd like, in fact, to take over women's colleges and blast their male structures.' "[224] Glueck went on to describe how the two artists worked with students on research for women's art history, quoting Schapiro that she and Chicago had gotten so far into it that they would have opened up an office someplace else had CalArts not come through with funding for their program.

The day and entire sojourn closed with a cocktail party at Marcia Tucker's loft, where Chicago was pleased to learn Tucker would be starting a small program for women artists at the School of Visual Arts in New York the next fall. She was hopeful that such programs would "pop up everywhere."[225] There were already other links between Chicago's feminist activities and those taking place in New York. With Lippard she had organized the W.E.B. (West-East Bag), "an information network for women in the art world," with branches in a number of cities and slide registries on the work of women artists in New York, L.A., and San Francisco.[226]

While she was in New York, Chicago shared with Schapiro her anxieties about her relationship with Lloyd, even admitting "to some Lesbian stirrings as a result of seeing Jill Johns[t]on, who is certainly one fantastic woman."[227] Judy and Mimi were met at the airport in L.A. by Lloyd and Paul, who arrived with their arms full of flowers. "It was really fantastic," Chicago reported in her journal. "Many of my fears about Lloyd were allayed by the realization that he had really come to terms with some things in himself . . . he's finally allowing himself to realize his need for me & for some stable homelife." She was thrilled to learn that he had found and rented for them a great house and planned to work at getting it ready while she completed her work in Fresno. She spent such a happy day with him before she had to go back there that she looked forward to seeing him the following Saturday.[228] She was eager for Lloyd's move from Pasadena into the new place and happy that they would once again be living together despite a residue of anxieties about the change.

Chicago's absence from Fresno had fomented new insecurities among the students, forcing her once again to address individuals' problems and feel as if she were "becoming nothing but a therapist."[229] The students needed to earn money to pay for their move south to CalArts, but they also had to prepare for the final show of their work at the end of May. She also had them working on costumes for the characters they were creating for the theater that she planned for CalArts. Even the issue of the newspaper on which they had worked so hard no longer excited them; it was out and impressive, but it was behind them now.

Chicago needed time to finish her own collage series as well as a film that she had been working on with Lloyd. She felt discouraged in part because there was no time to think about new work and prepare for the next year. Continuing with the cunt imagery of the collages seemed increasingly difficult "after seeing all that work of women in the art history slides which go over & over the ground of female identity."[230] In fact, she never finished this series, discarding those she had finished and the idea.

Perhaps it was age, but Chicago was growing ever more aware of "the limits of existence": "My femaleness is every day being revealed to me as a scar on my humanity in the sense that until the ideas of 'masculine' & 'feminine' are wiped out of our consciousness there is no possibility to be free. The constant resistance, antipathy, hostility, which erupts against every action of ours sometimes becomes overwhelming. It is as if the whole society is bent upon preventing women from gaining their rightful place in the world."[231]

Uneasy insight fueled resolve to renew her quest for a path of her own forged by experimenting with her female collaborators and not dictated by men in advance, at whatever risk: "I understand that for women to be truly free would mean the total restructuring of the society so as to enfranchise the half of the world that remains disenfranchised. I guess I am becoming aware of my limits & I do not like the feeling of entrapment. If I make art like I used to I will be merely going around & around about the nature of female identity. If I ignore that issue or put it aside I could make Art qua Art as men have defined it, e.g. dealing w/ ideas, the nature of materials, etc. & that really is not interesting to me."[232] As a way out, she saw that she needed to "pursue the path I have begun this year—to make Art out of it. In doing that, we will at least feel at peace while we work, but we will alienate many people who, at first, supported us, for ideas about women reach to the deepest level of the psyche & produce irrational responses. There is no where to go but on, but I am afraid."[233]

As before, Chicago gave combat to fear by way of intellectual growth. She was reading deeper into the work of Simone de Beauvoir, whose work she initially had not liked. Now she found *Memories of a Dutiful Daughter, The Woman Destroyed,* and *A Very Easy Death* all very moving. She identified with de Beauvoir's preoccupation with death: "I felt, with her, the terrible fear of life ending & the terror that lies within us, under the surface of everyday life. And, somehow, the path I'm on puts me in constant contact with the void, with that terror. Life becomes unbearable at moments, but the alternative of Death is even worse—and there it lurks, always there!"[234]

Reflecting on *The Woman Destroyed,* Chicago realized that it had been "overlooked & rendered invisible." She concluded: "the battle to become visible is indeed what it's all about. We seem to attract attention when we dispute our role, because then we're in dialogue tacitly with men, but we're invisible when we deal with our own reality & address other women. Oh, to be free of the implications of my body form!"[235]

Chicago resumed work on the *Bathtub* film with her students Wollenman and Youdelman and felt good about their collaboration. Themes raised in the Rap Room had given her a glimmer of what she wanted to do in her own future paintings: "images that would be angry, painful, speaking of brutalization & invasion & destruction of self." She expected to draw upon those feelings in the next year's female collective and then make images out of them. She was not sure whether she would continue to make paintings, but she knew that she was finished "dealing with the nature of female identity" in paintings.[236]

Back in L.A. she would hold interviews for the coming CalArts Feminist Art Program with Schapiro, but first on the weekend with Hamrol she would visit their families and attend a party at the Kaprows, which she dreaded because she expected Allan to "hassle" her: "I really don't like dealing with resistant or uneducated men. It's such a drain on my energy."[237] Chicago and Hamrol called on the Grinsteins, then took her mother to the Los Angeles County Museum for its *Art and Technology* show, which Chicago declared a "disgrace," since it included no women. At the Kaprows, Judy and Allan "had a big scene, which worked itself out & now everyone feels much better. He, like a lot of other people, became frightened by my intensity & rage, & react, if they're men, to these feelings with the male response which is to think of killing. In other words, because men are conditioned to back up their anger with their fists or guns, they become frightened by female anger & assume it will lead to bloodshed."[238]

The understanding they reached was that Kaprow was not to feel threatened by Chicago's "personal confrontational style" and was to admit their right to disagree with each other's point of view. Kaprow recalled that he and Chicago first met through the Pasadena Art Museum and that she had been making "quite good" abstract paintings. He saw her as "attractive, but more strident than Mimi [Schapiro]; she tended to be adversarial very often. I found it annoying."[239] Kaprow, according to Suzanne Lacy, did not have the worst attitude of the men at CalArts: "It turned out that the feminists who were conceptually oriented gravitated toward Kaprow, because he was infinitely more receptive to that than Baldessari, who used to discuss such things as how rape might be considered an artform. . . . John didn't bring it up; it was one of his students that brought it up. Such topics were common, however."[240]

Monday morning after the scene at the Kaprows', Chicago and Schapiro found themselves overwhelmed when some sixty women out of the total two hundred on campus turned up to apply for the Feminist Art Program at CalArts in the fall. Later Brach telephoned and screamed at Chicago, under pressure from other faculty who felt threatened by women wanting power at the school. What the women wanted was control of admissions to their own program and some help learning to use some of the available equipment "without being put down." They also requested a female film crew in the film department, "a couple of workshops in critical studies" to accompany their program, and a sector directed by Sheila de Bretteville in the design department.[241] CalArts was divided about the new program, with some faculty and students supporting it and others hating the very idea, but everyone was talking about it. "I guess that it's getting to Paul," Chicago mused, "'cause it's on his head, & when his male peers turn on him, he'll really be caught between the frying pan & the fire, so to speak."[242]

After this tussle Chicago returned to the Fresno studio for the students' final program. They had felt tremendous pressure because people from CalArts would attend. At dinner with the core group that was going on to CalArts, they faced the fact that the following fall they would no longer be able to function independently and do whatever they wanted as they had in Fresno: acting, film-making, painting, sculpture, art history, literary criticism, polemics, talks, discussions, and the like. Now, with the program expanded, there would be a professional art historian, a designer, and others to deal with. As Chicago looked ahead, she sighed and told herself: "But we'll never have this year again, unfortunately."[243]

The final program, held on a Saturday night, drew about 150 men and women, including Allan Kaprow, John Baldessari, and others from CalArts. They sold all fifty copies of *Everywoman* newspaper.[244] The students placed their art on exhibit, with environments by Wilding and LeCocq. Jan Lester recalls that she made a "very outré soft sculpture of a woman in a horrible shade of pink. Her vagina was red velvet. Her face was an oval mirror, meant to suggest that men wanted sex as a reflection of themselves. It was rude, crude and sexually graceless. Baldessari came up and stuck his cowboy boot into her vagina."[245]

Also in the audience was Paula Harper, then a graduate student in art history at Stanford, who would eventually be hired as the art historian for their program at CalArts. The students' performances included the "C-U-N-T" cheerleading, which Harper recalls as "so hilarious, so bold, so funny . . . to me it was irresistible."[246] The students then handed out "Friend of the Cunt Kisses" to those men "who had supported us at Fresno State & at CalArts."

The planned showing of films fell victim to projector trouble. The *Bathtub* film could not be shown. They could and did stage performance pieces, including Chicago's *Cock and Cunt Play* and the *Rivalry Play,* now amplified with a longer fight sequence before the final mutual murder. More mayhem ensued with a *Slaughterhouse* piece that "ended with Faith being strung up like a cow & covered with blood, then the last image was a slide superimposed on her body," with accompaniment by Chicago's voice, which became "the instrument of my rage."[247] The audience clapped and cheered, perhaps egged on by the program claque.

Chicago was amazed at how rapt the audience was throughout the forty-five-minute art history lecture. She had previously received criticism that their art history of women had errors and was unprofessional. But having relied upon the information collected by the students in just a few months, she was proud that they finally had a "female art history" and confident that it could be perfected later on.

A performance piece by Vicki Hall was last and the most provocative, eliciting both praise and criticism from the audience and participants. Judy and

Lloyd were in it, but Mimi and Paul had declined to take part. Hall's idea was to have six males and six females of authority who would, for the duration of the piece, relinquish their authority. Participants were tied up and blindfolded and had their mouths taped. They were then touched, kissed, or pinched. The idea was evidently to break down the barriers of the theater and give sensuous pleasure to the participants, but some of the gestures, perhaps inflected by latent hostility, began to look like sadism to the disturbed audience.[248] Hall says that this was not her intention and that her basic concept was about "initiation and the barriers or prohibitions to touch, to experience and to act."[249]

Chicago was glad in the end that the piece really "struck nerve endings" that the other pieces did not. Although she at first felt guilty for the controversy caused by the piece, Lloyd, who was not made uptight, helped her come to terms with its positive aspects: "Even tho I trust Mimi, I know that she's very uptight about her body & therefore her responses are not altogether reliable."[250]

After the event Chicago stayed up until five in the morning talking in the studio with Paula Harper. Later that Sunday morning she, Paula, Lloyd, Mimi, and Paul went for breakfast and discussed Paula's coming to work in the Feminist Art Program at CalArts the next year. The group went to the Underground Gardens, which Chicago describes as "an incredible labyrinth underground environment tunneled over a period of four decades" by Baldasare Forestiere, who had worked on the New York City subways.[251] Afterward Paula and Judy met with the students in the studio. Snapshots taken with Harper's camera record the excursion (Figure 12). In one Chicago is seen leaning toward Schapiro, whose plump figure, emphasized by her drooping posture, contrasts with her younger colleague's petite, svelte frame. Brach, who appears quite thin, sports long hair and his trademark cowboy boots, hat, and cigar, while Hamrol appears bearded and balding. Harper appears carefully coiffed and smartly dressed.

Harper also joined the Fresno students for their final dinner of the year. Afterward a group went dancing at a gay bar. Chicago remarked that Paula was a good dancer and noted, "It was nice to see women & women dancing, men & men, & men & women. All my attitudes about homosexuality are changing & I don't feel at all uptight about it. I still haven't tried making love with a woman & I feel a little nervous about that, but I'm sure I'll come to terms with that sooner or later."[252]

But when Paula stayed with Judy and Lloyd until Monday morning, Judy noticed that Paula "makes the whole makeup, pincurlers, nailpolish trip & that turned me off. I guess she needs her consciousness raised." But, she concluded, "As Faith says: We need her, & I hope we can work out the 'female' trip she's on."[253]

Harper recalls that she especially liked Chicago, appreciated her directness—"you never wondered what was really on her mind. She was brilliant, funny, fast, good-humored, temperamental, warm." She describes Schapiro as "a darker, heavier presence" and says that she "didn't take to her as immediately," finding her to be "older, heavier, mean, lacking in Chicago's spontaneity." She felt that Schapiro was "energized" by Chicago, who looked to Schapiro as having "made it in the art world."[254]

Chicago recorded a strange thought that had come to her the previous night, "how Mimi is older than I, & Mimi sounds much like Mommy, & I had a best friend named Paula when I was young & if Paula comes to L.A., I will again have a Paula in my life, & Lloyd is like my father & my brother inasmuch as he is really my male companion, source of comfort & friendship. It's like I'm getting back all the people I lost when I was young." She sorted the history out: "Paula, my first friend died, my father died, & I lost my mother & was alienated from my brother. I guess I've searched a long time for my family & maybe now I'm going to have it again plus *sisters.* We'll see. Paula Harper is the same age Paula Levine would have been."[255] Hints of deeper and contrary currents would be set aside, deferred, so high were the expectations and hopes.

▲
Mark di Suvero and Judy in Ucluelet, British Columbia, 1970. Photograph by Lloyd Hamrol.

Beyond the Abstract: *Womanhouse* 8

The summer of 1971 Chicago lingered for two months in the Kingsburg studio—closing out the abstract phase of her career and starting a quest for new ways to make art. She would read women writers, especially Americans, especially women's life stories. An essay on Simone de Beauvoir was in the works and maybe another on Doris Lessing, whom she found "strange." She exchanged essays with Faith Wilding, who was "studying the Amazons & doing research on matriarchy & mother cults. Really fascinating."[1] The house just rented at 4120 Van Nuys Boulevard in Pacoima would have less studio space for Judy and needed repairs. Lloyd set to work.

▲

Judy Chicago and Anaïs Nin at the Woman's Building.
Photograph by Maria Karras.

CalArts opened the summer with a three-day faculty retreat, including a seminar on the new Feminist Art Program given by Chicago and Schapiro. Her new institution was radical, Chicago inferred—"institutionalized avant-garde," quipped the dean, Paul Brach.[2] "Always before I've had to hedge a little on how radical some of my ideas seem to other people," Chicago mused, "not really expose all my feelings. At the retreat I went to a couple of meetings, where I found a great desire for a new kind of school but, often, not too much understanding about how to achieve it."[3] She was particularly encouraged by meeting the dean for dance, Bella Lewitzky, and looked forward to working with her.

Those who took part in the feminist seminar were mostly men. For the ensuing discussion they formed their own groups, led by Lloyd and others, leaving the women to go to another room. The men quickly moved on, reported Lloyd, to talk about their own issues and being men. Chicago was cheered, however, when she heard that Paula Harper had accepted an appointment to teach history of art.

In her own work Chicago had come to a turning point. Not only would she have to deal with diminished space, but she asked whether painting was still relevant, and if not, what kind of art would she make. Clues might emerge from the coming year's planned collaboration: "I am going to start preparing myself for the next stage in my artistic life, & it's going to take some time, some studying, some observing. I'll work out of & with the group next year, allowing my work to grow naturally."[4]

Her transition stood to benefit from the new venue. The School of Art was superior to others, Chicago judged, and its faculty was ambitious, eager to be "the Bauhaus of the 70s" (a nod to the famed Weimar-era German faculty of art, architecture, and design that the Nazis eventually closed) and wanting to create more than a school—a real community of artists. "Lloyd, I, Paul, Allan Kaprow, & Mimi have been working thru a lot of things this year," she told herself, "& we provide a strong bloc of ideas & support for those ideas. So within the Art School, it seems likely that I may have a lot of effect on what takes place . . . I'm sure that there's a lot of frustration in store for me, but right now I'm feeling very positively towards the whole framework of the school & my life there."[5]

In the old studio Chicago finished painting *With Death & Cunt & Self*—the last of the abstract, sprayed series begun in 1968—and took stock: "I seem to have gone past any cunt issues, & I was thinking only of landscape, the sky, the light, & then sometime flesh—& myself in the nothingness that I've lived in this year & the emptiness & the feeling of openness in the grape fields & the sky & the hot sun & no sound & no contact & it's almost over & I'm glad."[6]

The works took her back to the Indiana dunes she had visited as a teenager, and she realized that her "senses of connection with earth, sky, water were manifesting themselves in the paintings."[7] She later described the series—*Flesh Gardens*—as "a new space—one that is both emanating from the surface & relating to the surface. The gesture in the paintings is of looking out from the body, arms & legs spread, center exposed & looking at the structure of the painting—i.e., both in & out simultaneously or both perceiver & perceived, subject & object, male & female—an integration of the opposites."[8] Ordinary viewers might see just variously schemed geometries of color and light with a centering, even spiritual, role, but no specific ideology. Chicago judged that she had "said what I had to say & now it's time to move on."[9]

At the end of June Chicago made time for the curator Dextra Frankel, who sought advice for a show of women artists for the Long Beach Museum. (Chicago herself was planning for CalArts to show her own *Boxes & Domes.*) She and Frankel began jointly visiting studios of women in L.A., then San Francisco and San Diego. The first two days for Chicago were "fascinating, elating, & painful. There seem to be unknown women working in nooks & crannies all over the city. Some of them are really good artists; some simply the equal of their male peers, & unrecognized; some really wiped out."[10] Women would begin making art that seemed to be "very female, cunt imagery or other feminine or feminist imagery," Chicago saw. "Then, they move away . . . towards a more neutral image—or they do 2 types of work, 1 public & neutral, the other private & feminine."[11] She reflected, "In comparison to the situation of most women, I've done pretty well. But pretty well's not enough."[12]

Personal issues impinged. She would go with Lloyd for his vasectomy, "about which he was nervous," and visit Schapiro in the hospital after gallbladder surgery. Herself thirty-two, she no longer wanted to have a child. She began describing her life "primarily in terms of death & sex, & what happened to me that affected &/or shaped me." She conceived the idea of recording the entire story for an art piece. "It's very difficult for me to face the humiliating sexual experiences I had," she wrote. "Somehow my self-image rested in my life as an artist & I simply blocked out a lot of what went on, & what it meant. Anyway, I've written to the point of Jerry's death."[13]

In August Chicago and Frankel went with Schapiro to San Francisco to look at more art by women. Chicago and Schapiro met with "the art historian Linda Nochlin from Vassar, doing pioneer work in feminist art history." They found "a totally underground repository" of "Feminist Funk," as Schapiro dubbed it. Chicago inferred "that the S.F. Funk movement gave permission to the women to deal with images that are distinctly female in content. They're all small, intimate, & compulsive, but they have real clues towards the building of a female art." She especially liked the work of Joan Brown, whose paintings she found "strong & feminine, but still timid in content."[14] Brown had rejected abstraction and invested five painstaking years to teach herself realistic painting. That Brown was giving most of her compassion and sympathy to men angered Chicago, but she welcomed a pledge of help. Brown's hard-learned realism might aid her own move from abstraction to "develop a female imagery."[15]

The next day the visitors met with Nancy Graves. Chicago found the rather successful sculptor "uptight, closed off, unwomanly, patronizing—everything her male colleagues are."[16] They got a better impression of Ann Shapiro: "terrific girl & well on her way towards a female expression."[17] An evening went well with Joyce Kozloff, who had "become truly militant & strong." Chicago also met a graduate student in political science, Isabel Welsh, whom she admired so much so that she considered working with her on *Joan of Arc*—the ambitious theater piece Chicago had in mind for the fall.

Finally at Stanford University they spent the day with Nochlin and Paula Harper. Nochlin planned to visit them in L.A. to consult Chicago's art history slides and slides of student work from the Fresno program.[18] Attending Nochlin's seminar, they sat through student papers like Carol Ockman's "'Women Sculptors of Rome' (Harriet Hosmer & Co.)" and then encouraged the women to organize against the repressive all-male faculty. A few months later, when Ockman realized that the two visitors had created *Womanhouse,* she wrote, "Freak. If I had known who you were beforehand, I would have done some condensing."[19]

At this time, Chicago also records discovering another kindred spirit. "I found my new ideas reflected in Shulamith Firestone's book, in which she talks about the birth of a true female art. I guess that's what we're doing, inventing a female art, a female art education, a female method of dealing with Reality, & the S.F. women artists have the clues for that art."[20] Firestone, a founder of the radical feminist groups Redstockings and New York Radical Feminists, had published *The Dialectic of Sex: The Case for Feminist Revolution.*[21] She described "Female Art" as a "new development" that might "signify the beginnings of a new consciousness"; and she envisioned the new art "arising in conjunction with the feminist political movement or at its inspiration—that will, for the first time, authentically grapple with the reality that women live in."[22]

Characteristically, Chicago took stock: "The 10 years in which I worked abstractly have distanced me from those skills & now I have to retrain myself in order to make the pictures of the reality I see. Even my autobiography means something different to me—I want to draw pictures of my sexual experiences. I want to show the world the way it looks to me, a woman."[23]

Finding her way, Chicago began to "develop a personal, symbollic [*sic*] iconography" with butterflies, rainbows, and lipsticks. She would "reject all heavy technology or material orientation—no films or plastics or complex indirect processes. Only direct straightforward painting & drawing on paper or canvas or whatever."[24] She wanted to draw realistically "objects that derive from the cultural experience of women . . . I just know that I wish to base my artmaking entirely on female reality—using objects, items, references that relate to beauty parlors, makeup, menstruation, victimization."[25]

In mid-August the school year loomed. Chicago and Schapiro met with the head of design, Sheila de Bretteville, who had designed the special issue of *Everywoman* that featured the Fresno program. The trio plotted to develop "a mass Feminist art, using mass communications techniques."[26] Their shared interests and resolve cheered Chicago. Sheila—born in Brooklyn to Jewish immigrant parents—was just a year younger than Judy and likewise came from working-class roots.

Chicago and Schapiro also sketched out the first quarter's activities and met with students who had chosen to enroll in what the catalog described as "an experimental project, in which a group of young women work with Judy Chicago and Miriam Schapiro. It is aimed at the development of subject matter, history and criticism of art rooted in feminist identity. It is open to a limited number of women who are struggling to realize themselves as artist[s] within the context of their femaleness."[27]

For the experimental part Chicago and Schapiro adapted an idea of Paula Harper's—"making a house. We'll rent a house for a couple of months & 'do' it—i.e. paint, plant, decorate, etc. doing it in the most 'feminine' way possible, incorporating work by Calif. women artists where it's appropriate—buying handpainted china, crocheted, embroidered, etc. pieces—everything that is 'feminine i.e. trivial' in the eyes of society. Then we'll show it."[28]

Harper had imagined "soft, enveloping womb-like shapes—like a garden of paradise."[29] She maintains that her idea was "to honor the house as traditionally the art of women, while Judy turned it into a place of imprisonment of women." In fact, Chicago and Schapiro meant to challenge gender stereotypes and raise consciousness of ways in which women's creativity was marginalized and repressed. The gender disparities that animated feminist discourse had brought the two together, but they also shared an underlying cultural bond. Like Chicago, Schapiro was formed by a Jewish heritage that had been rabbinical in the old world only to turn secular and radical in the new, and that included not only an ideological commitment but a strong component of traditional women's crafts, although Schapiro's father, unlike Chicago's, lived to a ripe old age.[30]

The similarities in background masked differences that gradually would obtrude. At CalArts Schapiro was clearly in a position of privilege: she had joined the faculty earlier and was the dean's wife. Chicago's position was new and tentative, her program's prospects uncertain; she worried about "Mimi & her relationship with Paul." During the planning sessions one of the Fresno students, Cheryl [Zurilgen], had become "a destructive force, dividing the girls & talking about how fanatic we were last year & how she doesn't want that to happen this year, etc. She's been filling Chris's ears with this, setting up tension with the other girls, & now she wants to move over into Mimi's 'camp' so to speak. I have no objection to her becoming involved with Mimi & working closely with her. I just don't want hostility to divide the group."[31] Chicago began to suspect that "Mimi has large pockets of uptightness & protectiveness toward Paul that make her reluctant to let down her authority position & reveal herself to the group."[32] Chicago was discomfited too by another visit to women's studios—this time in San Diego. It left her divided between an urge to barricade herself in a new work space to chart a new course and her commitment to "a year of letting go & experimenting."[33]

Making matters worse, Chicago got into a dispute one evening with Brach. It began as one of those theoretical arguments about the position of women in society. He would never move anywhere, he said, on the basis of his wife getting a job. Even if she earned his $25,000 salary, "he wouldn't be a *woman,* he wouldn't work at a second-rate job or teach adult education as Mimi had had to when he was the dean in San Diego. He didn't care enough about her or his marriage to be a woman. Moreover, he insisted, he was a better teacher than Mimi, he was a professional—he didn't get flustered or upset, etc."[34]

But Brach was not a good teacher, thought Chicago, but rather was "oppressive—he always has to be in control—carrying on & telling stories. His self-image is really distorted & he has a real unwillingness to change."[35] More ominous still, Chicago was finding that Mimi "has to walk a tightrope between her commitment to Feminism & her commitment to Paul."[36] Chicago did not see how Mimi would be able to carry it off. She worried that the program would be in jeopardy very soon—"dependent upon Paul's whims, & the school itself shudders & shakes every day at the pleasure or displeasure of Roy Disney."[37] Some days Chicago admitted that "my faith in Mimi is very shaky. She has large pockets of conservatism in her."[38] Already Chicago wondered about going somewhere else after a year. "I guess I can always get a studio," she thought, "& go back to work alone & try to get a job at a girls' school."[39]

Though wary, Chicago continued to work and socialize with Schapiro, who organized a party for Joyce and Max Kozloff that would give Chicago a crucial ally in her quest. The co-hostess, Clare Spark Loeb, produced art programs on Pacifica Radio, including her own show, *The Sour Apple Tree*, where she had interviewed the writer Anaïs Nin. Now at the party, Loeb introduced Nin to Chicago.[40] Then more than three decades older than Chicago, Nin seemed to radiate warmth. Chicago, whom Loeb remembers as "incredibly articulate," recalls Nin as "tall, slender, and elegant," with a "delicate voice."[41] Chicago was thrilled to hear that Nin had read, enjoyed, and approved of her article on "Woman as Artist" in *Everywoman.* Chicago immediately began to imagine doing a large performance to celebrate Nin.[42] Admiring her for denouncing constraints imposed by society on women, Chicago made time to visit her in L.A.

Nin's "eternal feminine" image could not have differed more radically from the external trappings of Chicago, who by her own admission had "rejected everything about my behavior that smacked of femininity. This dilemma is what I had gone to Fresno to resolve, and it was this that I discussed with Anaïs the first time I visited her. In a rush—no a torrent—of words I told her everything I was thinking about and grappling with."[43]

Nin saw through surfaces to the heart of the matter: "Our first meeting was very interesting. I was intimidated by [Judy's] powerful personality. She was intimidated by the lady of the *Diaries* . . . But what happened is that we immediately felt tenderness and recognized that we needed each other.[44] They shared firm belief in "a female-centered art."[45]

To an inquiring biographer of Nin, Chicago explained, "When I read the scene in *A Spy in the House of Love* in which the man uses her sexually and she runs after him trying to give him back his anger . . . it was breathtaking. I will never forget it."[46] Chicago later wrote that this was the only one of Nin's novels that she did not find "difficult": "The main character, Sabrina, seemed to reflect many of my own conflicts. In fact, the novel dazzled me with its description of the heroine's quest for the kind of sexual freedom that men enjoyed: The freedom to couple, achieve physical release, then disconnect from the moment of love without a backward glance."[47]

While Chicago welcomed Nin's support, she was wary of Marcia Tucker, then curator at the Whitney Museum of American Art in New York. Tucker had just included a large piece from Chicago's *Pasadena Lifesavers* in a group show called *The Structure of Color,* which featured thirty-nine artists, from Josef Albers to Clyfford Still, only four of them women.[48] For the catalog, Chicago wrote:

> I have developed three systems of color. The first system is based on color opposites, primarily red/blue-green; the second system uses spectral color and changes from warm to cool; the third system relies upon consecutive colors of

> close value, such as blue/green/chartreuse and is essentially cool. All of these serve as a framework for the transmission of esthetic or emotive information. They allow me to deal with three different feeling states, to establish and then break down form, and to manifest a wide range of direct sensations based on a central or female core image.[49]

Despite Tucker's interest in her work, a dinner together with Schapiro and Harper convinced Chicago that Tucker was a "popularizer" and that some New York women had been right to label her an "Aunt Tabby."[50] Another evening Tucker "admitted that she had grossly misunderstood Mimi's & my notion of central imagery," wrote Chicago, "which didn't help us, as she's been reinforcing attitudes that are negative in a number of women, who thought we were taste-making & didn't understand that we were simply naming something that had existed."[51] Tucker, Chicago concluded, could not stand rejection. "So I represent a conflict for her," Chicago inferred, "because she likes me, but my ideas often alienate people or frighten them—& Marcia is thus caught in a bind . . . Rejection is the price for introducing unfamiliar ideas into the culture."[52]

Earlier the same day, however, meeting with Nin, Chicago felt such intense rapport that she could barely contain her excitement: "We got along wonderfully & she didn't want me to leave. She walked me all the way to my car & we kissed. She said that I was the only woman in the women's movement to whom she felt she could relate—because I was an artist."[53] They spoke about the "implications for art making of the [feminist] movement," and Chicago confided her dilemma about what to do next—"this drastic opening up that had taken place in me & how I didn't know which road to take."[54] Nin encouraged her to do more than one thing and suggested that she write a book "outlining all the directions" that she saw. Figuring that she could work for two hours daily every morning before the day at CalArts got under way, Chicago calculated that she could do it, but she still lacked confidence. "Anaïs says that I can write," Chicago told herself. "I know that she would advise me & criticize the work as it went along; & I think I'd like to do it. She said that when one cannot act out all of one's ideas, one can write about them, thereby carrying them to their logical extreme theoretically, & letting someone else enact the theory."[55] The outcome would be her first memoir—*Through the Flower: My Struggle as a Woman Artist.*

Chicago intended nothing less than "to outline a whole Feminist Program in the Arts—Theatre, Film, Art, Dance, Etc. plus History & Criticism." She wrote, "Along with this, I'd outline Feminist Education in the Arts plus deal with a new relationship between Artist & Public. I know that I could do it, but I'm afraid to take on such a big project. But I'm trying to work up to it. I'll think about it for a while & see if my initial excitement maintains itself."[56] She also discussed with Nin her "ideas about theater—the notion of bringing back women in history & letting them engage in dialogue with each other."[57] She explored the idea of a collaboration, only to have Nin explain that, nearing seventy, she had to limit herself to editing her diaries.

Chicago had hoped to begin a major work of her own in the fall, perhaps the Joan of Arc theater piece, but Nin pointed out that Joan had worked for a king, which "would make a problem for a Feminist premise." The quest still inspired intensive reading, especially biographies like those of Lucy Stone (feminist, abolitionist) and Carrie Nation (a leader of the Women's Christian Temperance Union). "I don't know what I'll do with all this information," she admitted, "but I feel strongly about reading all this week."[58]

Chicago planned to travel to San Francisco the next week to "do rape tapes." Convinced that she ought to replace Joan of Arc with a "better symbol of victimization & sacrifice of the female for wishing to transcend her role—perhaps one of the witches,"[59] she planned to see Isabel Welsh again. To prepare, she read the autobiography of Emma Goldman, who brought sexual politics to bear on anarchist thought.[60] Goldman believed that it would take more than a political solution to change the unequal and repressive relations between the sexes and argued for a substantial transformation of values, starting with those of women themselves.[61]

No anarchist, Chicago did want her art to redress the sexes' inequality. On September 15 she drove down to the lithography shop of her friend Sam Francis to investigate doing what she variously referred to as the "Tampax print" or the "menstruation print," which eventually became known as *Red Flag* (Figure 13). She had arranged for Hamrol to take a picture of her pulling out a bloody Tampax and print a photograph from which the lithographers would make a working negative. The significance of *Red Flag,* according to Arlene Raven, was that "the title, hidden language for menstruation and revolution, would also be 'hidden' information to most men and even some women. Nevertheless, the directness and strength of the visual image elicit immediate, powerful reactions."[62]

Amid contrary signs—supportive women such as Nin, but men, such as Brach, whom she viewed as challenging or threatening—Chicago approached the new school year. To the students who transferred from Fresno, she explained how this one would differ from the previous, when she had demanded a lot from them and they had "survived a trial by fire." At CalArts they were joining very sophisticated students; there would be somewhat fewer demands, she implied, and she sought to reassure them, especially Cheryl and Chris, who seemed anxious. Other faculty members saw her "as a sort of evangelist; she had a missionary zeal . . . like a little general—forceful, a good organizer."[63] Once, decrying the old saw "that women should not be selfish, she pounded on the table and said: 'You have to think what you want.' "[64]

From herself Chicago demanded more, determined to develop her autobiographical project, make weekly drawings for a new series (some of which might become prints), finish her films, keep reading women's biographies, create a series of laminated figures of women, and furnish an image to accompany a text of Nin's and get it printed—a lithography project to raise money.

The situation at school preoccupied. Chicago wanted to "try to build liaisons between the strongest women there, so that if something happens to the school, we can go on";[65] she had in mind a loosely organized group of purposeful women artists who met every other week. CalArts might pretend to be home to the avant-garde, but it remained "a very sexist place." Her life when not with women or at home with Lloyd was becoming "more & more agonizing,"[66] so much so that she thought that she ought to stop going to movies unless she knew in advance that they were free of sexist content.

One of Chicago's strong women was the printmaker June Wayne: "how impressed I was at her organization and how it taught me something in terms of what was necessary" to found something. Wayne too had attended the Art Institute of Chicago's Junior School, although she was born in 1918 and thus was a generation older than Judy.[67] Winning a grant from the Ford Foundation in 1959, Wayne had founded the Tamarind Lithography Workshop in L.A. to spur a revival of printmaking in the United States. (In 1969 she transferred the workshop to the University of New Mexico in Albuquerque, creating the Tamarind Institute there.) That fall Wayne organized "Joan of Art" seminars in her Los Angeles studio to teach women how to function in the art world, where she had demonstrated her own savvy.

Although Chicago did not attend the seminars, Wayne considers her "a force of nature" and admires the "absolutely brilliant" way she has managed her career, doing "what she had to do."[68] For her part, Chicago once described Wayne as "difficult," noting that "Mimi can't stand her." But more recently Chicago reflected that she prized Wayne's strong will: about her "men spoke very disrespectfully"; they "referred to her as a 'ballbuster' and all that sexist language of the time, but I found her absolutely terrific."[69]

Chicago's vision for strong women looked beyond the L.A. Council of Women Artists, which Joyce Kozloff, Schapiro, and others had started in protest a year earlier, in the fall of 1970, when the Los Angeles County Museum left all women out of its *Art and Technology* show. The council struck Chicago as too big. She wanted to create a smaller group of stronger women who were "being alienated by the passivity of the large group" and who could grow into "a coherent female community."[70] Her quest for a new direction would unfold through collaborative work in a "Feminist Art School."[71]

Any hope for a radical and productive future at CalArts shrank when the Disneys, alarmed at the radical bent of their creation, abruptly fired the provost and dean of the theater school, Herb Blau. The entire faculty felt that their positions were now jeopardized. Very stressed, Chicago resolved to go "underground" and not show any of the students' work until late in the school year. She decided that she wanted "nothing more to do with full-time institutional jobs—it's just not possible to do any thing significant for women & stay involved with institutions which are at best chauvinistic & at worst fascist."[72]

Returning to San Francisco, Chicago with Harper and a friend went to see Carol Doda, a topless dancer "who got silicone injections in her breasts to make them larger and started the who[le] topless rage in S.F." The spectacle for Chicago was "really depressing . . . the men's faces were like infants waiting to be suckled—so needy, so empty. I wondered what kind of dehumanized existences they led to need such a pitiful substitute for human contact as that show was. Also, I was very angry with the women who worked there for contributing to their own victimization."[73] Doda, however, rationalized her work: "Sex is a part of life and we can't hide it."[74] She had been performing topless since 1964, a period when erotic entertainment seemed liberating or progressive. But the politics of sexuality had become a central concern of the women's movement; thus Chicago and Harper chose in 1971 to explore the lives of sex workers by witnessing an oppressive spectacle aimed at heterosexual men.[75]

Sensitized by her interviews with victims, Chicago had seen even the men on the Stanford campus "as potential rapists"; women had told her again and again of going, after being raped, to seek comfort from other men. Both men and women were victims of the same values, Chicago reflected, but men had the power in the society, and thus, themselves oppressed, they oppressed women even more. After dining nearby, when the group met Doda on the street, they chatted, then on impulse embraced her, saying "we're your sisters."[76]

Meanwhile Chicago had continued to get up at five in the morning and devote two hours to her writing. She hoped to be finished by the end of the year, despite the envisioned scope: "It will deal with the development of a Female Culture, complete w/ heritage (our word for history), criticism, a new relationship between artist & society, everything that I've been concerned with." At a loss after getting under way, she read a part to Faith Wilding, who "made some perceptive comments & got me back onto the track."[77] She decided to show it to Anaïs when she returned, but to no one else, not even Mimi.

When Nin's fourth diary got censured by Gore Vidal in the *Los Angeles*

Times, Chicago wrote to express outrage, considering his piece "unjust to a woman whose contributions to women, & indeed to literature, are profound." She found the review "full of the sexism that greets every woman's attempt to tell the truth." Particularly offensive was his failure to grasp Nin's "ideas about direct, human response, which does not at all preclude one's intellect, but rather demands a synthesis between emotion & intellect that the male culture obviously cannot comprehend, if Vidal's remarks are indicative of masculine sensibility."[78]

Meanwhile Chicago and Schapiro had been planning to coauthor an article on "central imagery." But Schapiro was off to New York, leaving Chicago to complain that "the load is too heavy for me alone."[79] Hearing that Mimi had arranged a retrospective of her work and would get back by the weekend, Chicago wrote: "Good for her—she certainly deserves it."[80] Schapiro appeared to be getting some perspective on how their activities related to women elsewhere and returned "feeling really good about herself."

The Feminist Art Program lacked space of its own because the school was in temporary quarters and construction of its new building was behind schedule. Thus the women advanced their experimental project from the term's end to its start, setting out to "rent a house and furnish it, make different rooms, etc.", wrote Chicago, "using all the things that women have always done: needlework, embroidered pillowcases, quilts, crocheting, painted plates, collected knickknacks, artificial flowers, fantasy rooms, etc., & call the whole thing *Her House.* After it's done we'll show it."[81] A catalog, to be designed by de Bretteville, would be a foldout version of the house, with a photograph on the cover of Chicago and Schapiro, which later provoked anger from students who thought that they too deserved coverage.[82]

They would find a site off campus on Mariposa Street in L.A.—a borrowed dwelling slated for demolition. Chicago was optimistic again: "The ideas for rooms are phenomenal & it seems like it will work out well. Everyone's very excited & ideas range from a quilted bedroom to the bedroom for Léa, from Colette's *Chéri.*" It did not hurt that in Spanish *mariposa* means "butterfly"—one of Chicago's chosen symbolic motifs.

At a group meeting of women artists in L.A., Chicago and Schapiro discussed opening a women's center. Chicago envisioned a center that would have exhibition space, performance space, facilities for painting posters and newspapers, space for running workshops for other women in art, music, and literature, showing films by women, and having talks. She even imagined Nin talking and sharing her knowledge—"a real structure that will satisfy our needs as women & provide a new model for artists & for the world."[83] Yet she could also reflect:

"All that is ever discussed is Feminism, & it gets wearing. The only alternative is when I'm home alone with Lloyd. I really love living with him. It's terrific!"[84] For the moment, she also wrote, "my relationship with Mimi is quite good; we seem to have moved into a time of comfort with each other. We're working on an article & it's going pretty well."[85]

A drop in energy began cutting into Chicago's furious pace, creating anxiety, even fantasies that she was dying.[86] Forced to reflect, she realized that she was scheduled to be on five radio shows, send out an issue of *W.E.B.* (*West-East Bag*, the newsletter of the National Coalition of Women Artists), continue work with Schapiro on their article, meet with other women artists about organizing a center, work on a historical theater piece with Isabel Welsh, plan a West Coast Conference of Women Artists for January, and finish the Tampax litho as well as a silkscreen collaboration with Lloyd.

Although convinced that her abstract phase was behind her, she also wanted her dealer Jack Glenn to keep his promise to exhibit in January her abstract paintings from Fresno, so she could take stock of her achievement. Dextra Frankel's show of women artists was on for the Long Beach museum; the two of them planned to produce a catalog in December. "Periodically I get waves of excitement & fear about what I'm doing," Chicago confessed to herself. "I so want to be a success & well known. I'm hoping that my book will do that for me. I know that I'm really doing good work, & I hope that I won't go unrecognized. A lot of the time it stops mattering, when I get really into the work itself. But one doesn't get up at 5 AM & push past one's limits & really put oneself on the line without wanting some reward."[87]

Life at school took an unexpected turn, after a woman student of dance was raped in her dorm. Chicago and Schapiro joined the dance school dean, Bella Lewitzky, to organize a meeting about rape. Women students gave testimony, and all were very affected by the chance to discuss a subject that had been taboo: "We talked openly about our terror of men & of the constant onslaught of remarks."[88] Women from the antirape squad at the women's center spoke, as did a policewoman. The three leaders also instituted an antirape squad on campus.

With feelings of vulnerability so palpable among her students, Chicago saw the need to develop her performance ideas with those who were "prepared to deal with high-intensity emotion."[89] The students conducted consciousness-raising sessions and performance pieces that "dealt with mother/child relationships." To create ideas to perform, Chicago collaborated with Schapiro, Wilding, and others, with results that she judged very satisfying: "Turns out that Mimi & I have the same ability to act directly out of our feelings & we really get it on together. Yesterday afternoon, we did drawings out of the performance pieces about birth, shelter, & mothering. I thought it was terrific & as I was drawing, I felt like I had when I was 9 years old in art classes at the Art Institute—like I was working out of myself in a way that professional artmaking somehow prohibits."[90]

Birth pieces also provided ideas for theater: "One consisted of all twenty women lining up, standing both legs spread, arms around each other's waists, their legs creating a birth passage, which one woman after another entered & moved through in a simulated birth. The whole line of women bent & stood, pushing down in the birth/motion, crying 'Push, Push,' in the grunting sounds of childbirth. It was really fantastic. Then we lay on our backs, legs open, knees bent & all panted & labored together."[91]

Several performance exercises involved repeating the words "Mommy," "Mother," and "Mama" in different voices and postures and with varying emotions. Another dealt with "the body as shelter: We began with pairs of two, & one woman sheltered the other with her body. Then we changed. We rocked each other and hummed to each other, comforting, protecting, & shielding with our bodies. Then 4 women made a group, 3 sheltering, 1 being sheltered. I discovered in this piece that if I curled up in a fetal position, I began to get prenatal memories when rocked by three women whose bodies provided comfort, warmth, & softness."[92] Yet "informal performance, while extremely valid for some women in terms of search for subject matter," Chicago admitted, "is not the appropriate method for others, who are probably better reached thru drawing & painting exercises also aimed at reaching female subject matter."[93]

All the intensity made some students protest, which showed that the "subject matter of female experience is still frightening."[94] Students, many of them nonplussed by the nontraditional activities, demanded to know more about what they were doing and why. They seemed unable, Chicago realized, to accept women, that is Schapiro and herself, as authorities "without associating us with their mothers, which caused them to start heaping on us the hatred & anger they felt towards their mothers." They had "no basis in experience to see women as authorities based on expertise & achievement, but rather saw women as authorities only in the mother role."[95]

While working on a radio program with Chicago, Schapiro told her that although her views of female art were right, her methods were all wrong. Schapiro told her, Chicago wrote, that "my anxiety about getting recognition causes me to escalate into a hysteria that drives people away. . . . She is, I know, absolutely right & I don't even like myself when I get like that. She promised to try & tell me to Relax when I start getting anxious & I hope that I could respond to it. It is true about my anxiety for recognition. I want so much to be famous & successful & have my work honored & appreciated & I've lived so long without my due."[96]

Chicago would have her place, Schapiro told her, and did not have to keep reminding people that she was a leader, since people already knew it. "Maybe if I can really finish my book & if it is published, maybe it will become popular & my dreams of being well known will come true," Chicago concluded. "I know I have a lot to give, & if the world will let me give it & acknowledge my gift, I'll become more relaxed & probably even be able to contribute more. I hope so."[97]

In the context of these exchanges, Chicago initiated drawings (some of them intended for sculptures and some for paintings) that she called *Egg Cartons:* "They're sixteen boxes with eggs in them,"[98] a concept that recalled a favorite format of Schapiro's paintings—a rectangular canvas divided into sixteen boxes, as in *Empire* (1965). The egg motif, as a metaphor for herself as a female, also recurs in a series of Schapiro's paintings and drawings from 1961 to 1963, including *The House* and *Shrine: Homage to Cézanne.* Chicago inscribed at least two of the new drawings with homage to Schapiro, acknowledging her impact at the moment. On one of these (Figure 14) she wrote: "If sculpture: white plex box/shelves of trans[parent]/refl.[ective] Mirror-Back pieces sprayed w/fade—Eggs cast resin w/ color."

When in company with Schapiro around CalArts, men such as the "shop guy" treated her differently, Chicago observed, inferring that because Schapiro was married to a dean, she represented his power to other men. Unaware of the men's true attitudes, Schapiro nurtured "a fantasy that she'll be able to educate the men to gratuitously equalize the school."[99] Another ambition also occupied their conversations: "We talked the other day about her need for recognition & I encouraged her to write a book on Art Education & Art History. I feel funny that I can't do anything that she doesn't want to do, but I also support her desire to contribute something significant. This is a really brilliant woman & she owes it to herself to do more with her abilities."[100]

Schapiro also took a very different approach to conflict. After Chicago interviewed Nin on local radio, she, Schapiro, and Nin over lunch got into "an intensive argument about making art out of anger. Both Mimi and Anaïs felt uneasy about this idea," Chicago noted, "particularly Mimi, with whom I'm having an ongoing fight about putting out what she considers 'unacceptable' material, inasmuch as it could make men, particularly those at CalArts, uptight, & cause a backlash."[101] The next day Nin called Chicago and told her that she was her "radical daughter" and that she loved her. She also commented on the inappropriate way that Schapiro tried to threaten Chicago to rein her in.[102] But Chicago had no intention of allowing Schapiro to censor work by herself or by their students: "Mimi tries to make it seem that it's a personality quirk of mine & that women who express 'rage,' etc. do it because they're working with me—really peculiar! Anyway, I guess this reveals her fear of her own rage & her continually moving into areas of expression that are 'more loving & gracious.' "[103]

Tension arose between the two colleagues over the article they planned to submit to the new magazine *Ms.* "We got into a thing right away because she kept subtly putting me down & referring to Anaïs, & sort of rationalizing why Anaïs liked *me* so much. It's true that Anaïs didn't respond to Mimi like she did to me, but that's hardly my fault. Anyway, I began to realize what Mimi was doing & I called her on it."[104] They discussed why Schapiro had so much "anxiety about herself—which erupts whenever someone doesn't see her as she sees herself . . . I'm beginning to see that Mimi lives, to a great extent, in fantasy. Lloyd suggested that in her lengthy analysis (Schapiro had seen a therapist), she learned to replace a self-image of incompetence with one of super-competence."[105]

Chicago and Hamrol held a Thanksgiving dinner marked by notable discord among their guests: Mimi with Paul and their sixteen-year-old son, Peter, the two of whom "got into a struggle for control & Peter lapsed into a sullen withdrawal for most of the day. Paul was very nasty to Rita [Yokoi]. Faith had a terrible reaction to Mimi's whole family scene. Paul didn't like Roger & got pissed off at Everett. Isabel & Roger didn't like Paul & Isabel questioned me about my relationship with Mimi, who seemed very conservative to her."[106]

Her insight growing, Chicago began to reckon that Schapiro's "age & conservatism prevents her but not me, from going certain places. She does try to be supportive of me even in those areas which are difficult for her. Right now, everything's OK, but I'll have to be aware of her limitations & of her strengths. I have the tendency to want complete unity, altho I know that that isn't possible."[107]

While Chicago and Schapiro tussled, their students scheduled a meeting in their absence, which Chicago described as "a monster-making session." She identified the ringleaders as an activist lesbian named Marcia, Mira Schor, and Vicki Hodgetts. Chicago found this effort fascinating in terms of female psychology: "The women were feeling pressured in the House project. They felt that a lot was expected of them, that they had to achieve. They are struggling to work in a scale beyond them & many of them are feeling somewhat overwhelmed. The most significant fact in all this has to do I'm beginning to see, with expectation." She concluded, "Society expects very little from women. It asks them to be 'good' & to get good grades in school, but there is little social expectation to achieve. One of the real struggles in female education rests in how women react who have never *really* struggled, when they are asked to struggle, push beyond their limits, both physical & mental. This is making them angry. The angrier they feel, the more they strike out."[108]

Chicago's own interpretation of the students' anger was that they were projecting their own senses of inadequacy onto Mimi and herself, but mostly onto her. She was a bit surprised that even some of "the Fresno girls . . . got into the act, notably Shawnee & Nancy."[109] Despite the turmoil, Chicago was pleased that "all the issues we struggled with last year are occurring within the process of working—but very intensified because we're in L.A. & because the girls are so much more sophisticated than in Fresno."[110] Chicago also faced student resistance to devoting their time to her theater projects. Most of the students clearly preferred working in the *visual* arts, which was why they enrolled in an art school and took classes with two visual artists. Chicago too felt the pull of the visual, writing in her journal, "I don't really want to altogether give up my art. I really thought, when I was in Fresno, that I could cut off my Past, but now I'm not sure of that."[111] She had given herself the entire year to make an "esthetic voyage"; on a practical note, "If I want to paint again, Lloyd suggested that we build me a small spray studio on the property."[112]

A disappointment came from Jack Glenn, who postponed her show again.[113] He blamed the delay on the women's movement after some women attacked him at a panel discussion, demanding to know why he did not show more women artists. "He got very uptight, especially because all of his collectors were there & they ragged him about it," she wrote. "He didn't want to have my show because he thought it would make him look as if he were succumbing to pressure. He was very irrational & I felt very upset, because of all my beautiful pictures from last year are sitting around, unseen & it's really awful."[114]

Pained at the "art world" and feeling that she could get nowhere, Chicago meditated again on whether to make "a clean break & really make Feminist Art. I'm at a real crossroads & I don't know what to do," only to answer herself at once: "That's bullshit! I do know & I'm anxious about it. I can't go back. I can only go on—& on is into the Feminist ideas that are occurring to me. I really don't want to do the egg drawings."[115] She also knew at the same moment that she wanted to "deal with the issue of Death," but she had no idea how that fit in.

For the house project, she had elected to make *Menstruation Bathroom.* Although she did not feel deeply invested in this installation, she thought it should be an included theme. She missed the time that she used to have to daydream and think and the freedom to create work, but she questioned who the audience was: "The more we study female art history, the more we see the obscured heritage of women artists. They've been wiped out of the history books. I can't even count on the idea that, if I don't receive recognition in my lifetime, it'll happen when I die. Famous women painters have been completely swallowed up w/ no remains."[116] After so much study, she knew what she was talking about: "There was a woman's building in the Chicago Exposition of 1893—designed by a woman architect, run by women, filled with paintings by women. Mary Cassatt did a mural for it—very strange from the small reproductions we've seen. The mural is lost."[117]

Nostalgia for the contemplative quiet and sense of control in her studio, making abstract art alone, yielded to fear of erasure. She recognized the need for "contact, recognition, understanding" and renewed her view of feminism as an aid to her venture.[118]

Despite the discordant Thanksgiving, Chicago continued to work with Isabel Welsh on their women's history play. They also outlined a play about menstruation, which they hoped to have performed in Berkeley the following April. The two got along extremely well. "Our ideas really coincide & we're making plans to paint together," Chicago wrote. "If she were to move down here, we'd start a theatre together, but she doesn't know which way to go now, either."[119] In the meantime, Isabel had taken the entrance exam for law school, was trying to complete her dissertation, and considered having children with Roger. "When she's here," Chicago reflected, "I just want to merge with her—when she leaves, I sort of forget about it, but our communication is really astounding."[120] The two were discussing getting together to paint female images over the summer for four to six weeks.

As to whether Chicago should produce feminist imagery, Schapiro pointed out to her that she already had: the Tampax lithograph, the book that she was writing, and the play on which she'd been working. Chicago, however, felt that she lacked "reference points" and someone "to bounce off of. That's why Isabel is so important to me—she has a head full of imagery & I have the skills to realize the images."[121]

Chicago and Schapiro postponed the opening of the house project until the end of January 1972. They saw its potential as twofold, both as an educational experience and as an artistic creation. As 1971 came to a close, Chicago felt that some aspects of the house were realized, while others were not, due to a lack of clarity. She described what they ultimately called *Womanhouse* in her journal:

> As one enters the House, one steps into a spider-web like room full of hanging strings, made by Judy Huddleston. The living room is the theatre & we plan to perform on the weekends. We don't know how the performances will turn out. The pieces themselves are very good. Then there's Mimi's doll-house, a womb-like encircling room painted by Ann Mills, a very gifted young woman who

> used to live with Lloyd's first wife. The dining room will be worked on communally, the kitchen is a nurturant room, painted flesh-colored, covered with eggs transmuting into breasts. I'm doing the menstruation bathroom in the back of the house—all white and clean save for a garbage can full of bloody Kotex & Tampax. Faith is making a kind of woven Bontecou environment.
>
> Down the stairway is a bridal scene. There's a bright red bathroom, walls, floor ceiling, fixtures, etc. Jan Lester is doing a secret room within a room, Karen and Nancy are making Léa's room from Colette's novel, "Chéri." Robin Mitchell is doing a muslin-lined room that I don't understand. Mira, a strange Leonor Fini–type girl from the East, is making a painting inside a closet, Shawnee doing a nursery, & Beth Bachenheimer is making a shoe closet & a laundry room.[122]

Chicago anticipated having to improve some of the rooms that looked amateurish. But she and Schapiro meant the project not only to help their students acquire the means to become art professionals but also fundamentally to alter the ways of art history, which then neglected and even erased women artists. After the fact she elaborated on the goal: "The premise of *Womanhouse* is that women have embedded a lot of creative energy in the house for centuries; they've quilted and embroidered and sewed and made the home nice but all that was considered unimportant. We were interested in the idea of the home, not as a nest but as a creative environment."[123] Queried another time about the artistic goals of *Womanhouse,* Chicago commented that it "synthesized all female activities and the invisible achievements of women," adding, "I want to change the world." Schapiro responded to the same reporter: "I want every woman strengthened."[124]

The expressed rationale for *Womanhouse* appears in the essay for the catalog by Chicago and Schapiro: "Female art students often approach artmaking with a personality structure conditioned by an unwillingness to push themselves beyond their limits; a lack of familiarity with tools and artmaking processes: an inability to see themselves as working people, and a general lack of assertiveness and ambition."[125] They clearly state: "The aim of the Feminist Art Program is to help women restructure their personalities to be more consistent with their desires to be artists and to help them build their artmaking out of their experiences as women. WOMANHOUSE seemed to offer the perfect context for this educational process."[126] By now Chicago had realized that starting the program "changed my life & being in it changes the lives of the women."[127]

"If you have a real drive or a desire to be somebody or do something with your life," Chicago told an interviewer, "I think that up till now the only permissible way for a woman to achieve that was to see herself as somehow different, a breed apart, a third gender. And of course that's very destructive because what happens at a certain point is that you *can't* go any farther. After a while, if you're drawing on yourself as an artist and you're not *anybody*, neither a man nor a woman, there comes a limit to where you can go."[128]

The participants on *Womanhouse* acknowledged changes, not always for the better. Those who entered the Feminist Art Program at CalArts had rather different perceptions from those who started out with Chicago at Fresno. More of them resented the emotional intensity. They sensed and resented too Chicago's loyalty to those who had begun the experiment with her. As a result, new students who worked on *Womanhouse* gave the experience and the faculty mixed reviews.

Faith Wilding, who had been a graduate student in Fresno, acted as teaching assistant for the program, both faculty and student at once. She was "Judy's girl, more vicious than Judy," according to Robin Mitchell, who had joined the program at CalArts.[129] Wilding in turn describes Schapiro as "both a bad mother and a good mother" and says that she had to mediate between Schapiro and Chicago, both of whom she considered "authoritarian and narcissistic." Yet she was close to and learned a lot from Chicago, including "how to critique my own work."[130] Wilding is featured on film in Chicago's *Cock and Cunt Play*, performing together with Jan Lester. She is also the performer of *Waiting*, which traces a woman's lifespan from childhood to old age; Wilding herself wrote it, as Chicago acknowledged when she promoted the piece by including it in the appendix to her memoir.[131] *Waiting* emerged from the collaborative process of Chicago's performance workshop, recalls Wilding. She recognizes Chicago as "very smart, an incredible craftsperson," who, like Diego Rivera, "wanted to make art for the people." Wilding herself has since become a successful performance artist.[132]

Robin Mitchell first learned of Chicago when her artist mother heard Clare Loeb's show on KPFK radio interviewing Chicago about the program at Fresno. They got in touch with an art-world acquaintance, Larry Bell, who suggested that Mitchell write Chicago, who invited her to Fresno for a session of the program—a slide show of women's art history and a performance of Vicki Hall's *Ominous Operation*, depicting surgery on a woman to attach a penis. Mitchell found the performance both "scary and moving."[133] By that time she had been accepted at CalArts to which she transferred for her senior year, joining the Feminist Art Program. But she disliked the program's exercise of control over their lives, working them too many hours a day. Mitchell also found inappropriate the "psychodramas" about mothers, since she loved hers—supportive and loving as well as an artist.

All the talk about mothers also disturbed Mira Schor, who was extremely attached to her mother. The consciousness-raising sessions got "out of control," thought Schor, who had reached CalArts from New York City, where she grew up the daughter of two Polish-born Jewish artists, who had met at the Warsaw Academy of Fine Arts and fled the Nazis. Schor was twenty-one and had studied art history at New York University, when she decided to produce art and enrolled at CalArts. She began in the Feminist Art Program but left before the end of the year to pursue other options at the school. She considered Chicago aggressive but simple to deal with, although Schor was not interested in studying performance and pursued painting, which Schapiro taught; Schor found her more "seductive" but "very complicated." Schor lived in the CalArts dormitory and recalls getting a ride to the house with Shawnee Wollenman or Chris Rush and that the students were stuck there with "no functioning plumbing," while they toiled on renovating. She hid out and avoided learning construction skills: for her, *Womanhouse* was "challenging" and "physically stressful."[134]

Robin Weltsch, who grew up in Los Angeles and arrived at CalArts for her senior year, says that she was then "a bit of a hippy." She saw Judy as "idealistic and committed, outspoken, very political," and more present than Schapiro, who was "softer, less confrontational." Though intimidated by Chicago, Weltsch says that the consciousness raising "helped her shyness."[135] She worked with two other students coloring pink the *Nurturant Kitchen.*

Robbin Schiff arrived as a seventeen-year-old freshman from a broken home in New York City and found *Womanhouse* a "political boot camp. It had nothing to do with my development." Among the male faculty Schiff sized up Brach with his "cigar that never left his mouth" as "his own male chauvinist" and Alan Hacklin as "the cock of the walk," whose talk was "tough and macho." She preferred the Feminist Art Program. For the first three months she found herself glazing windows, sanding floors, and otherwise fixing up the derelict house, "working ten to twelve hours a day." She felt very oppressed and points out that she did not drive, had no car, and was stuck at the house from nine in the morning until someone gave her a ride home around seven in the evening.[136]

Schor's, Schiff's, and other students' complaints are the source of false rumors that Chicago later "enslaved" the workers on *The Dinner Party.*[137] Such stories dogged Chicago's collaborative work throughout her career. It is true, however, that Chicago projected her own intense dedication and drive onto those around her, pushing others to go beyond their usual capacity for work. Few could match her energy and zeal; many resented having her expectations thrust upon them. Some would later look back and credit Chicago with changing their lives, but at the time it was often a stressful process.

At the house, Schiff produced the *Nightmare Bathroom* with a body in the bathtub, choosing that room "because it was small." She recalls being tongue-tied when Anaïs Nin visited and came to her bathroom. Although she found both Chicago and Schapiro intimidating, she became and remains a feminist. She nonetheless considered that Chicago was "overbearing" and talked too much about her sex life ("demanding her orgasms"), while Schapiro was "passive-aggressive" and "motherly in a way that I couldn't trust quite."[138] Her observation recalls that of Betty Liddick, a reporter for the *Los Angeles Times,* who contrasted Schapiro, as "a dark, tousle-haired warm grandma of a woman," with Chicago, who "is all energy and nerve endings."[139]

Schiff gave Grace Glueck of *The New York Times* the impression that she was pleased with the program: "I felt if I didn't join, I'd miss something," she confessed, adding, "I hadn't been much involved in the feminist thing before, but when we talked about it, I felt that a lot of the things I'd done were very applicable, and it seemed to click."[140]

Jan Oxenberg transferred to CalArts from Barnard, where she had felt "constrained by academia." A "newly minted lesbian" without any background in visual art, she discovered the Feminist Art Program only after she arrived. She worked on *Womanhouse* part-time, while enrolled in the department of critical studies and the film program at the school. She views Chicago as a passionate revolutionary who inspired her own career as an independent filmmaker, but she declined to get involved in constructing the house, although she did pitch in and help with the painting. Oxenberg appeared as "Sparkyl, the hippy chick" in one of the performances, whose memorable line she recalls: "My stars are on my boobs, not in my eyes."[141]

All the performance exercises about mothers had their effect on Chicago herself, who tried to improve her relationship with her mother, not wanting her to die with things as estranged as they had been as a result of her complete refusal to communicate with her children about their father's death. Despite the letters that she wrote to her mother, Chicago had not stopped resenting her failure to deal with their mutual loss and maintained an emotional distance.

Chicago's spiritual mother, Anaïs Nin, continued to nurture her creativity, not only reading the book manuscript when it was finally finished but taking it to New York to find a publisher. Yet Chicago criticized Nin for focusing on men during a celebration at Berkeley, and the two argued. Nonetheless they planned a joint radio show the following February to discuss the "physical aspects of female reality in art—e.g. menstruation & other aspects of our biology." Chicago noted, "She thinks the emphasis should be on feeling—I that first we must make the hidden visible & acceptable."[142] Afterward Chicago regretted arguing with Nin and attributed her aggression to anxiety about exposing her book. She feared that no one would publish it or, if it did get published, that no one would like it and it would not make her well known. "This book represents my bid for leadership & fame," she wrote.[143] "I deserve the kind of recognition that Steinem, Millet, Greer, & Firestone have gotten," she added, confessing, "I want it so badly, I won't really relax until I get it. . . . I do so hope that I can 'be a lion' as Gertrude Stein called it."[144]

At the end of December 1971 Chicago starting drawing "a flower image with the inside of the flower opening up to a sky vista. The image deals w/ going through or breaking through the flower or the cunt. I really love the image, but now I've starting work on it. I've laid out another drawing that's more abstract & transformed than the first. I'm going back to the tools I've built—symmetry & color changes."[145] Discounting her "eggs" influenced by Schapiro, she felt she had lacked good ideas since the previous summer when she finished *Flesh Gardens.*

While she awaited news from Nin's trip to New York, she had been reading a newly published book by her first lover, Leslie Lacy. "I was in it & it really threw me," she wrote. "I responded incredibly to the book & wrote to him. He's written back & he'll be in L.A. in several weeks, so I'm going to see him."[146] His conduct around the autobiography influenced her eventual handling of her own manuscript: "He talked about the period when we went together. He filled in a lot of gaps for me & made me remember all sorts of things. He's become quite radical & the honesty in his book really moved me. I can't wait to see him, if only to replace my insane fantasies with some degree of reality."[147] She was disturbed that she suddenly felt "like going on a wild tear—like having a mad romance. The feelings really frighten me."[148]

Torn between a return to painting and plans for the theater, Chicago imagined falling madly in love with Leslie and painting all summer with Isabel, only to realize that if none of that happened, she had no choice but to work in her studio. "Am I perhaps in the grip of destiny," she asked, "& it is going to carry me somewhere I'm not aware of?"[149]

An invitation for her and Schapiro to speak in Washington at a national conference on women in the arts struck her as "even more exciting" because that was where Lacy lived: "I had continual fantasies about him. On Sunday I told Lloyd that I was having lots of desires for a romance or an adventure. He was, of course, very understanding, & we sort of tacitly agreed that a small adventure would really not hurt anything. The fact that he recently told me that he had slept with 4 or 5 women during our relationship had a big effect on me. As long as I don't know what he does, I suppose it doesn't really matter & vice-versa."[150] Lloyd's tacit support for the women's movement may have been like that of many men who were not hostile to the movement because they thought it would help their girlfriends "get over being so uptight about their sleeping with other women."[151] She had not told him about Leslie, but she had discussed the matter with Faith as something that she had to explore in order to "come to terms with both my fantasies & my feelings."[152]

She continued to work on the her new image "through the flower"; and she agreed when Brach told her that her next task would be to pull together her feminist point of view and her formalist aesthetic. She was having a lot of trouble making "an image of a cunt/flower/formal structure, which is opening up onto a vista of blue sky & open space."[153]

The week before *Womanhouse* opened to the public, it served as the venue for a conference of women artists. In two hours 180 women went through the house, and eighty crammed into the performance space. Grace Glueck in *The New York Times* called the conference "a sort of mammoth consciousness-raising bee believed to be a first," where participants, who included women from the East Coast, heard talks on feminist art history, the concept of female imagery, and the professional and economic problems of women artists.[154]

For the women's conference weekend, Saturday morning featured Paula Harper lecturing women in art history, which Chicago liked. (Since Schapiro and Harper did not get along, they were searching for a replacement for next year's program, although Harper maintains that she never planned to take more than a year off from her graduate work at Stanford.) Jan Lester also gave a talk—on the Woman's Building in the Chicago Exposition of 1893 and Mary Cassatt's mural. Then Chicago and Schapiro gave their "central imagery" talk. That afternoon women from San Francisco, Los Angeles, and Fresno gave slide presentations. After a dinner there were film showings. Discussions and more slides followed on Sunday.

The *Los Angeles Times* ran a big article on the house, and its creators were then besieged by other press, including the magazines *Ramparts, Life,* and *New Woman,* as well as CBS and NBC news. Schapiro worked at organizing the house interior, while Chicago rehearsed the performances. They included one about four masochistic women (later reduced to three), one about female passivity, a birth and mothering piece, two maintenance pieces—one ironing and one scrubbing floors—and for comic relief, the *Cock and Cunt Play.* The all-women audiences at the conference had cried and cheered and laughed through the performances, but the subsequent mixed audiences were more reserved.

After a week of rehearsals Chicago concluded that she did not want to pursue repertory theater. She did confirm her theories about men coming into "a female environment," being forced to relate to "our" subject matter in our framework.[155] She was still interested in performance but more as workshop pieces with single or onetime showings as "a work of art rather than theatre." She decided that she did not enjoy the repetitive aspect of theater, only the conception, preparation, and initial performance.

Time magazine, which featured *Womanhouse* in an article called "Bad Dream House," reported that "some 4,000 traipsed through the 17-room creation" and described "an exhibit that proved to be a mausoleum, in which the images and illusions of generations of women were embalmed along with their old nylons and spike-heeded shoes."[156] The article stated, "Womanhouse interiors were not designed to please," and quoted Chicago: "These are very clear images of women's situation expressed as works of art. . . . In essence you walk into female reality and are forced to identify with women."[157]

Womanhouse turned out to be more important than Chicago and Schapiro ever imagined. The spectacle provoked wide media attention and controversy, attracting, it was said, more than ten thousand visitors during the month it remained open to the public from January 30 through February 28, 1972. Chicago sensed that the students felt very good about the success of *Womanhouse* and that they had "completely forgotten about the major struggle" to create it.[158] Clare Loeb, who helped to publicize feminist activities with her interviews on Pacifica Radio, recalls *Womanhouse* as "fantastic, incredibly ingenious," and that it "made a huge impression."[159]

Large crowds continued to come to *Womanhouse,* including men and women from the art world. Chicago was especially pleased that the audiences seemed to like the performances. Among the visitors was art historian Linda Nochlin, who spoke about the project at an "open meeting for women members of the College Art Association" at the group's annual meeting, held in San Francisco that year.[160] She came with Carol Ockman, then a student, who had been in her seminar the previous summer at Stanford. Ockman, now an art historian, recalls that they stayed with Schapiro, who was friendly with Nochlin. But it was Chicago's *Menstruation Bathroom* that stands out in her memory: "I was shocked and I loved it . . . the irony in this piece—pristine and messy—the fact that the female body can't be contained."[161]

Chicago noted the presence of "Maurice Tuchman, the curator of the L.A. County & a sexist from way back. He is one of the 3 men in the U.S. art scene that I hate & so it was with great pleasure that I watched him watch the *Cock & Cunt Play.* He followed me around telling me how great everything was & kissing up to me. I felt exalted because I've waited a long time to see those 'macho' guys have to acknowledge me & who I am & what I've done."[162] She mentioned that another of her evil three was Walter Hopps, the former gallerist then working at the Corcoran Museum in Washington, D.C., where she was invited to speak at the women's conference that was to be held there in April. Based on his coercive behavior when she met him in New York, the third man was probably the art critic Harold Rosenberg.

By now Chicago was clearer on where to direct her quest: through recovery and transformation of her own achievements in painting. She gave up the idea of doing either theater or painting with Isabel Welsh. Instead she wanted "to use the form language I built so carefully to make some new images. Images that are more explicit in what they say—that are simply made & exactly what I want."[163] She anticipated not showing the new work before the fall of 1973. The women's movement had given her new choices over the last two years, but now that she had established a new educational program, experimented with the theater and filmmaking, written a book manuscript, and tried being a public spokeswoman, she could see that she had made good choices in her painting and sculpture.

Chicago took account of herself at thirty-two: "I'm a painter, I teach at a good school for $14,000 a year (next yr's salary), I have a good marriage, some degree of fame—now I want to make simple, unadorned paintings. No complex techniques or sophisticated materials. Just me & canvas & my spray gun & airbrush. I have discovered that my visual language is viable—I have only just built it and freed it from doing service to prove that it's ok to be a woman."[164] She wanted only to make "beautiful pictures & go on where O'Keeffe left off."[165]

A phone call from Leslie Lacy left Chicago at once excited and confused, uncertain of whether the whole thing was insane or whether she would fall "head over heels in love with him." She reflected in her journal, "Contact with him is making me feel a part of myself that's been covered up since Jerry's death. I felt a lot of attraction for Jerry & there was a lot of electric current between us. I had felt the same way about Leslie. When Jerry died, I couldn't find another man I could get on with & when Lloyd & I got together, I was very lonely & needy. It took us a long time to work things out & now everything's pretty good except—here it is—Lloyd often bores me."[166] She lamented that Lloyd, while bright, did not read and was not intellectually challenging to her. She felt that he was conservative and naïve politically, "altho his good heart makes him entirely sympathetic to the women's movement. I love him dearly," she wrote, "but there are no sparks between us & I figured that was the way it was & then along comes Leslie & I have butterflies in my stomach."[167]

By the end of February Chicago had spoken twice more to Leslie and concluded she was suffering "from trying to live within the constraints of monogamy. While I have multiple relationships with women, I only have one relationship with a man."[168] That, she concluded, was why she had never gone to bed with her friend the artist Sam Francis, despite intense feelings between them and his support for her work. Her last conversation with Leslie had brought out their mutual fantasizing, as if they were teenagers together once again rather than adults with real lives.

Chicago got at least some of her privacy back with the closing of *Womanhouse.* Overflow crowds turned out over the last weekend, and people implored them to keep it open, but worn out, they were glad to see it close. Chicago noted, "It really marks the beginning of female art. There will be a period of very overt imagery & then, in a few years, things will be more open & women will be able to be more subtle & sophisticated & then my work, I hope, will be appreciated."[169]

They held a sale of objects from the house and a gigantic feast for the students and the camera crew of filmmaker Johanna Demetrakas, who was making a documentary about the project, to be distributed on the college circuit with that of Judith Dancoff about the Fresno program. Schapiro tried to get herself included in that film, but Dancoff refused. Schapiro then worked on Demetrakas, who originally planned to focus more on her than on Chicago, to avoid duplication with the Fresno film. At Schapiro's urging, CalArts even provided a grant of three hundred dollars.[170] Her continual interference managed to alienate Demetrakas.

As Chicago reflected on how Schapiro had usurped half credit for initiatives of hers, including the women artists' conference, which Chicago conceived and organized alone, and especially starting the Feminist Art Program in Fresno, her difficulties grew: "I often feel pushed out of the way & as if Mimi's taking over."[171] Chicago told herself that she had trouble sharing. She recalled how her father doted on her as "a special little girl" and she was considered extraordinary in her family. She relished being "in the spotlight and always getting all of the attention."[172] It was difficult to break that old habit. She condemned herself but could not feel otherwise.

At a rap session with the students from the Performance Workshop, Faith was talking about getting the rhythm right in the *Waiting* piece but neglected to mention that Chicago had created it with her: "In the *Everywoman* last year all the girls talked about me. I liked that. Now they're becoming independent. They claim credit themselves, often to things I helped them with. I don't like it. I want the focus to be on me—all the time. It's really awful. I either like to be alone or the star of the show."[173]

On March 4 Chicago attended a meeting of an Ad Hoc Women Artists' Group at Bea Cooper's about creating an exhibition space for women called

Womanspace. Their goal was to raise thirty thousand dollars by the end of March in order to apply for a matching grant from the government. Chicago reported that she alone was confident of reaching their goal, yet reflected, "It's really happening that women are beginning to act in our own behalf. It's terrific."[174] The founding board of Womanspace included Wanda Westcoast, chairwoman; Max Cole, vice chair; and Chicago, Schapiro, Judy's patron Elyse Grinstein, Betye Saar, Faith Wilding, and many others.

That a woman's gallery was needed is made clear by a "Situation Report" in *Time* magazine for March 20, 1972. Of the galleries showing modern art in Manhattan, only 20 percent were reported to belong to women. In museums, women were alleged to represent 9 percent of the collection of the Museum of Modern Art (MoMA) and only 6 percent of the Corcoran Gallery. As for exhibitions, MoMA had held a thousand one-artist shows but only five of art made by women.[175]

Chicago reported having "a big fight" with Schapiro that, ever optimistic, she told herself clarified some issues between them: "I was really able to come through for her yesterday, which made me feel good, & I think made her feel more trusting of our friendship. I feel that our relationship will now move onto firmer ground."[176] At the same time she realized that she was ready to get on alone with the next stage of her artistic life: "I thought it was all over, but now I know my psyche was just resting & refueling, all the work by women that I've seen has really been important."[177]

Chicago continued to put energy into teaching at CalArts and devoted herself to students whom she perceived as having real potential. One of them was Laurel Klick, whom she had taught in her first sculpture class at Fresno. Klick did not participate in the Fresno Feminist Art Program because she spent her junior year in Sweden. When she returned, Chicago had moved on to CalArts but was still in touch with Rita Yokoi, who was teaching Laurel. Having seen some of Klick's work, Chicago took the trouble to write a letter to her parents, who were reluctant to pay for their daughter's continued education: "I saw several of her works, and I was impressed with the talent, the energy, the ability Laurel has . . . she is an enormously gifted young woman. She has been accepted by the California Institute of the Arts, which is probably the most distinguished art school in America. I would really be proud of Laurel if she were my daughter."[178]

Klick arrived to join the Feminist Art Program for the spring term, just before *Womanhouse* opened to the public. She studied graphics with de Bretteville and participated in Chicago's performance art workshop, then located in E60, a basement room. She recalls the division of students on the first day of class; traditional painting students went to work with Schapiro. She thought it strange that students from the two classes did not mix and that there was "no group energy."[179] She had money enough for just one term's tuition, so she was quite happy, at the end of that term, to move with Chicago to the Woman's Building.

Chicago "gave far beyond what anyone could expect from a mentor," Klick reflected. "I look back, amazed at her insight and drive to build a better, more equal art world for both her and other women. We, her students, were starved for direction and motivation, and Judy gave us that and more. Much of which we all wished our own mother had been capable of giving. We were little angry half-broken birds being told we could fly (or at least I was)."[180] She recalled that Chicago "was the first and only teacher that told us to draw from our experience, and that our experiences are valid subject matter. Up until that time I was trying to figure out the secret of knowing what my subject matter should be."[181]

Among the other new students that term was Susan Mogul, who had arrived from New York at the age of twenty-three. She found Chicago, her assigned mentor, "positive and exhilarating."[182] Chicago recognized at once that Mogul, who had recently earned a degree from the Museum School in Boston, was talented. Soon Chicago put her together with Suzanne Lacy and Laurel Klick to perform at Womanspace Gallery. When Mogul tried to take a class with Schapiro, the older professor heard that she had been working with Chicago and "wanted nothing to do with her."[183] Mogul recalled Chicago's empathy when she told her how she "identified" with Mogul's suffering from the loss of her boyfriend through a fatal automobile accident. "She touched me very deeply," Mogul says, attributing Chicago's abrasiveness to her impatience with other, less committed people.[184]

Nancy Youdelman, a veteran of Fresno, managed to study with both Chicago and Schapiro at once: "Mimi was angry that I took performance class with Judy. Judy was always the motivating force to open up new ways to do things. That was exciting. . . . I felt inspired."[185] Schapiro looked more at what students actually did, recalls Youdelman, so that when another student, her sister Rachel, was making large drawings in oil pastel that Schapiro did not like, she insisted that Rachel switch to paint. Rachel switched instead to making artist books and photographs, never drawing again.[186]

But for Chicago, Schapiro was not the only stumbling block. Lloyd suffered "fantasies about losing me because of my growing success," she complained, and "still brings his father's relationship to his mother into our relationship."[187] Tired of dealing with what she considered Lloyd's neurosis, Chicago also continued her own fantasies about Leslie, about getting out of CalArts and L.A. and getting time once again to focus on painting. She wanted others to take over Womanspace. What she envisioned for herself was work and travel, and she admitted, "I'm even thinking about whether I might like to have a baby (if I find another man, that is)."[188] In a room in the San Francisco Hilton Hotel, as she awaited her reunion with Leslie, she fantasized another life: "I really don't like many of the things about being a public figure & if I don't pull back now, it is likely that I will be consumed."[189]

The reality of the reunion squelched all her dreams; she described the twenty-four-hour encounter as "horrendous." "He alternatively carried on about [why] we couldn't have a relationship because I was white; discussed the extraordinary similarities between his struggle & mine; told me about the symbolic place I've held in his life; discussed feminism; & pranced back & forth in front of the mirror admiring himself. He is still a very beautiful looking man."[190] When he made it perfectly clear that only a black woman could fit into his life, she rejected his overtures to have sex and retreated to her own hotel room. Finding him full of hate, anger, and black rhetoric, she felt "a little sick."[191]

Returning home to find Lloyd cooking chicken soup and kissing her on the cheek, however, she was completely deflated. She concluded that "the only place to go now is back into my studio, where I can try to make images of my deep longing to transcend the limits of my culture, my sex, my skin, to be free, & to make *real* contact with another human being & the seeming impossibility of that dream."[192]

She channeled the despair into art: "I still don't understand all of it. I know that when I went back to work, I felt again the eternal & childlike 'want' that spurs creative effort."[193] She had made a "terrific drawing out of the anguish I felt after the encounter"[194]—*Heaven Is for White Men Only* would eventually become the basis for a major canvas (Figure 15). It was neither the first nor the last time that she rallied in the face of rejection and turned anguish into art.

For all her personal turmoil, Chicago was still able to hold a crowd of college students spellbound in a three-hour lecture on March 24 at Southwestern College in Chula Vista, California, or so reported a student, who described her as "a fiery artist" and quoted her narrative about her struggle: "Every day I would have to return to my studio alone, since I had no woman to relate to, and I'd say to myself, I'm not a castrator because I'm strong! I can make forms that have to do with me! And that is the struggle that men don't know anything about."[195] Chicago also told the students: "The only thing that justifies your existence is work," and, "Men can't provide what we need. We have to do it ourselves."[196]

A visit with Isabel at the end of March helped to clarify what had taken place with Leslie: "My father's death, my discovery that he was a Communist, the breakdown of my family life & security, due to his death, plus the repeat performance of Jerry's death, left me with a terror of trusting life or a life framework."[197] All this accounted for the sudden impulse to run away with Leslie, quit CalArts, leave Lloyd. She was comfortable with struggle, she reckoned, but the struggle would have to take place in her studio.

The entire experience with Leslie clarified her quest: "I intend to focus on the eternal wanting of the human being & the agony of never having all one wants, due to limitations out of one's control / with otherness & alienation/ longing for more/limitation /containment of self/mortality & death—all within a female language structure in which my femaleness will reveal a common humanness."[198]

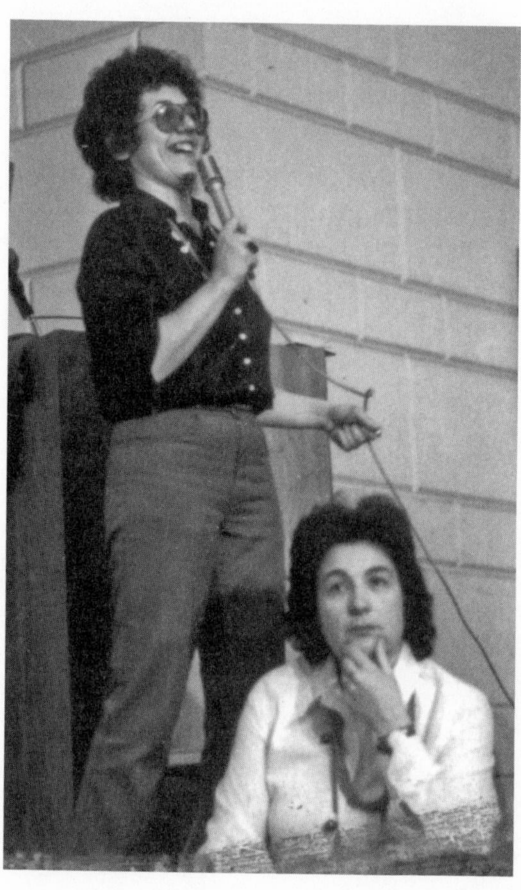

Working Through Feminism 9

Fallout from *Womanhouse* kept coming: in April 1972 Schapiro telephoned that someone at Doubleday had seen the *Time* article about the project (which quoted Chicago extensively and Schapiro only once) and wanted them to develop their ideas into a book.[1] Eager for the chance, Schapiro urged Chicago to clear the way by cutting all *Womanhouse* photos from and otherwise revising her recently completed manuscript.[2] But Chicago had begun to write before going to CalArts and was counting on this book to get her "personal visibility," a dream she would not so lightly give up. They could write another book to-

▲

Judy Chicago and Miriam Schapiro at the Corcoran Conference of Women in the Arts, Corcoran Gallery, Washington, D.C., April 1972. Photograph by Susie Fitzhugh.

gether. That was not enough for Schapiro: her "ambitions had no bounds," fumed Chicago.[3]

The exhibition put together by Chicago and Dextra Frankel for the Long Beach Museum finally opened. *Invisible/Visible* addressed the issue of differences between male and female art and included twenty-one women, among them Schapiro and Chicago, the latter showing two large (five by ten feet) acrylic paintings from 1971, *Evening Fan* and *Morning Fan,* concerned "with the nature of female identity. The central image in the paintings refers to the center or core of the female. The paintings speak of flesh and landscape, of softness and delicacy, while at the same time asserting strength."[4] They provoked from William Wilson in the *Los Angeles Times* an instance of the jaundiced, virulent streak that would recur whenever women gave him a chance to sound off. He styled the feminist art movement political, not aesthetic: "It might save us remembering 1972 as the year of the local art Rip-off. The year has already manifested more overt buddy-system carpetbagging than has happened within memory. . . . What is not OK is that this politicking has justified itself, pompously, under the aegis of crucial social issues. At the very least it lacks a quality artists are supposed to possess. It has no style."[5]

Notoriety is the handmaiden of fame. Oberlin College and Cornell University invited Chicago for workshops and talks. But the fame she had fantasized about for so long did not turn out as expected. It came in the form of further hard work. On the road she felt that she missed Lloyd, with whom her relations had greatly improved as she put behind the fantasy of Leslie. When she called Leslie from New York and arranged to see him in Washington, her idea was to purge the romantic dream and salvage a friendship.

A brief stopover with her cousins Howard and Corinne Rosen in Chicago brought home to her how her father's death had shattered security for young Judy Cohen. Worn out with travel and sick with a bad cold in a New York hotel, she wrote: "Last night I thought about taking sleeping pills & ending the struggle. I don't even know why I'm thinking about that." She found herself unable to say why she should want to meet Leslie again when there in the room were beautiful roses sent by Lloyd.[6]

Seeing work in a retrospective show by Lee Bontecou occasioned awe that gave rise to brief insecurity. Recharged at a party given by Lucy Lippard, her mood took a further turn upward the next day, meeting the painter Nancy Spero and hearing interest expressed in her book by editors at Doubleday and Beacon Press.

On April 19 both Chicago and Schapiro spoke at the University of Maryland, then went on to the Conference of Women in the Arts at the Corcoran

Gallery in Washington. Attended by more than 350 professional women in the visual arts, including artists, museum curators, critics, and art historians, it had been organized by seven artists and historians out of disgust that the Corcoran Biennial for 1971 had excluded women.[7] The artists' statements, distributed in advance, included Chicago's account of her personal and communitarian quest:

> I have been involved in a long search . . . first in my studio for almost ten years, searching for my identity as a woman and as an artist in a society which said those two aspects of myself were incompatible. Once I found my identity as woman/artist, I began a search for my community and my tradition. . . . I believe that I have contributed something to the formation of a female art community and the visibility of a female art.[8]

True to the session's avowed purpose, various forums addressed discrimination against women's art and against their hiring and promoting in museums and art schools. Linda Nochlin described her Vassar classes in women's art history, which attempted to "provide a total cultural conception of women in the society of their age."[9] Elaine de Kooning and Alice Neel testified to their own search for identity as women artists. When Neel showed slides of her painting of pregnant women and suggested that "women should retreat during pregnancy," according to *The New York Times,* she provoked a vocal sculptor, Lila Katzen, to shout back, "I've done my best work during pregnancies."[10]

In the opening session Chicago and Schapiro spoke about *Womanhouse,* triggering "one of the principal disagreements [which] centered on whether a 'feminine' art exists," as reported in the *Times* by a male journalist. Chicago and Schapiro held that feminine art "was based on a 'state of emotional reality and a focus on the nature of female identity,' " he wrote. "Other artists said that an imagery of 'repeated circular forms' and preoccupation with 'inner space' could be seen in works by women. Some advocated a movement of 'feminine' art."[11] Chicago called her talk "Female Imagery/Female Sensitivity" and Schapiro hers "The Possibility of Female Imagery in Art," further suggesting that she and Chicago had created a nurturing structure for their women students that was more "womblike."[12]

"It was important for women to be part of a group that supported each other," Chicago stressed, "and to come out with things the way they really are." She showed slides and described what emerged from *Womanhouse* as "shocking, volatile—dynamite—the symbolic images of women's fears."[13] Cindy Nemser, who was distributing the first issue of her new *Feminist Art Journal,* also reported in *Art in America* that Chicago showed the *Nurturant Kitchen* (which

Nemser misidentified as the *Nutrient Kitchen*), the *Lipstick Dressing Room,* and her *Menstruation Bathroom,* noting "a woman uses approximately ten thousand Tampax in her lifetime—which, of course, you couldn't walk into."[14] "Most of the audience was delighted with this imagery," Nemser added. "But there were dissenters. Chicago remarked that she was glad the students had brought the taboo topic of menstruation out into the open since she could never discuss it before with anyone. At that point, Lila Katzen, a sculptor, shouted out, 'That's your problem.' Katzen voiced the sentiments of many who resented having the old stereotypes of women's bondage resurrected and laid on them again."[15] Although older artists harbored reservations, according to Nemser, "many of the younger women in the group loved the funky displays so characteristic of the West Coast."[16]

Facing down the combative Katzen, Chicago looked instinctively for support to the audience, which responded with overwhelming sympathy and enthusiasm, making her momentarily the focus of all eyes. But the appeal that stole the show appears to have kindled jealousy in her shier, senior colleague.[17] In a photograph by Susie Fitzhugh, an ebullient Chicago stands and works the mike, while Schapiro is seated glumly below in the lower-right corner, one hand gripping her chin.

Cutouts of Chicago and Schapiro from this photograph would make their way to the left-hand border of a poster, *Some Living American Artists/Last Supper,* produced soon after by Mary Beth Edelson, one of the organizers of the Corcoran conference, who thus had access to press photos of the event.[18] Cutting out photographs of eighty-two women artists, she pasted them onto a reproduction of Leonardo's *Last Supper.* She sent copies to each of the artists enshrined, exposing Chicago to the conceit, which Edelson later interpreted as "a challenge . . . to the established assumption that because of their gender women do not have direct access to the sacred."[19] Over the face of Christ she pasted a photograph of Georgia O'Keeffe, who already for Chicago was an example and a feminist icon.[20] O'Keeffe did not appear at the Corcoran conference; nor, unlike Alice Neel or Elaine de Kooning, who did, was she then active in the feminist movement.

At workshops the following day Chicago suffered through one entitled "The Education of Women Artists," where the vocal Lila Katzen "tried to overpower me & compete with me."[21] Oblivious to Schapiro's festering pique, Chicago felt much better about a session where she and Schapiro worked together. Debate centered on whether to educate women artists with men in coed programs. Budding female talent, before it has a chance to mature, risks being overwhelmed in typical male-dominated situations, Chicago and Schapiro agreed:

they wanted women students to become artists, not just wives or virtual concubines for male faculty and students, which was the all-too-usual female fate.

Chicago welcomed the chance to hear the array of brilliant women, although several artists spoke out against her concept of central core imagery. Agnes Denes, a conceptual artist, argued against "vaginal sensibility," averring that "the only inner space I recognize is where my brain is—and my soul."[22] "Art has no gender," asserted a New York artist, Pat Sloane. "When the women's movement is quite properly committed to the proposition that biology is not destiny, how can we as women artists be so stupid as to propose that biology might be the determinant of one's artistic destiny?"[23]

The dialogue would eventually escalate into the great "essentialism" controversy: whether a woman's being resides in differences from men that are inborn or rather socially and culturally conditioned.[24] Just months later Shirley Kassman Rickert, who had heard Chicago at Cornell, wrote that she "came away realizing that I had been dealing unconsciously with female imagery in my work for almost twenty years."[25] Rickert supposed that many women disliked Chicago's idea of a woman's art because "past psychological conditioning is so strong; women's art has been by definition *inferior* art."[26] She recounted Chicago's belief "that there is a definite and pervasive women's imagery based on women's biological and social experience, and that prevalent images are: a central focus (or void), spheres, domes, circles, boxes, ovals, overlapping flower forms and webs," only to add, "There are others who point to the many women not working with these elements and to the many men who are, and there are still others queasy at the prospect of having to think about women's experience in aesthetic terms at all."[27] Rickert doubted "if any conclusions can be drawn at the moment, since there are still women who consider it a compliment to be told that they 'paint like a man,' and since art is inevitably influenced by other art publicly made visible, which now means primarily art by men."[28]

Pursuing the issue of central imagery as "female imagery," Lucy Lippard would get Chicago to explain: "I never meant all women made art like me. I meant that some of us had made art dealing with our sexual experiences as women. I looked at O'Keeffe and Bontecou and Hepworth and I don't care what anybody says, I identified with that work. I knew from my own work what those women were doing. A lot of us used central format, and forms we identified with as if they were our own bodies."[29] A centralized target painting by Kenneth Noland differed from her *Pasadena Lifesavers,* said Chicago, because he could not experience the same body identification with the form that she did. Chicago further reminded Lippard, "It's important to remember what the climate was when I said women made art different from men. That was a real tabu. Everybody flipped out."[30] "What often differentiates men's and women's art is not style, but *content,*" Chicago would tell another interviewer, "which is frequently embedded in a style that is similar to men's, but whose intent is not the same."[31]

A different dissident at the Corcoran was Linda Frommer, an art historian and spokeswoman for the National Caucus of Labor Committees, who blamed the women "for not utilizing their art in the struggle to free the working class." She "called Georgia O'Keeffe a bourgeoisie [*sic*] who had isolated herself from the people and accused Judy Chicago of 'wearing the symbols of her oppression like diamonds.'" The class issue got little traction for Frommer, who appears to have been totally unaware of Chicago's own class as the daughter of a union organizer hounded by the FBI.[32]

On the plane back Chicago reflected that many women had said a lot of nice things to her: she had been a big hit. But Schapiro was miffed and they had quarreled, nominally about a joint television interview that never took place. Schapiro had forced herself to get up at seven to wash her hair and get ready, only to be told that the taping was off. Since Chicago had heard from one of the conference organizers, Barbara Frank, that "the TV guy was an asshole," the cancellation meant little to her.[33] In fact, she was getting tired of the media, which was hard for Schapiro to grasp. Chicago was also tired of dealing with Schapiro: "her rage & her paranoia & ambivalence & all the rest of it."[34] She felt that Schapiro had just about taken over the program at CalArts, except that she could not handle all thirty students alone.

Back home, when Chicago telephoned Schapiro, she was busy and did not call back, though she did return another call the next day. When Chicago informed her that a German TV crew wanted to do a program about *Womanhouse,* Schapiro curtly declared her intention to commit "herself to her painting and teaching & dropping all her activities—W.E.B., Womanspace, etc.—except the Program and her own work. Then she hung up." When Chicago invited her to the postponed opening of her show at Jack Glenn's gallery, Schapiro said that she and Paul would be "out of town," which later turned out to be false.[35]

Although Schapiro was also making other women at CalArts—Wilding, de Bretteville, Harper—feel alienated, Chicago felt devastated. She had tried to share everything, only to find Schapiro increasingly suspicious, accusing her of "'manipulating' people's responses. It apparently enrages her that response to me is generally more positive than to her." Evidently when her younger, thinner, more charismatic colleague seized the Corcoran conference limelight, something had snapped. It dawned on Chicago that Schapiro "never really trusted me or treated me like a friend—rather like a wayward daughter, whom she had to keep in line."[36] Chicago blamed herself: "my need for a mother figure, for stability, outweighed my judgment."[37] The maternal matrix—an age-old stereotype—trumped the newer ideals of sister and woman.

But the Corcoran conference also engendered a constructive and long-range sequel. A graduate student in art history, from nearby Johns Hopkins University in Baltimore, expressed admiration for Chicago, eliciting a warm response. Arlene Rubin Corkery would divorce and change her name, taking Chicago's advice to become "Arlene Raven."[38] In May she spent an intense week with Chicago, understood her painting, and "bought one of the *Pasadena Lifesavers.*"[39] She wrote Chicago, "The department at the Hopkins was so freaked out by the fact that I was raped that they didn't seem disturbed that I was traveling to LA to do further dissertation research in the feminist archives . . . I haven't been able to reflect enough on what has happened to me through and with you to be able to write you a letter."[40] In the fall she would replace Paula Harper for art history in the Feminist Art Program at CalArts. Chicago hoped to find with her a "fair exchange" of ideas and feelings, but was cautious, burned by her failure with Schapiro.

To the Feminist Art Program Chicago also welcomed an artist, Sherry Brody, who had worked with Schapiro on the dollhouse in *Womanhouse.* Now a mother of thirty-five, Brody was about to enter CalArts as a graduate student and staff assistant to the program. Schapiro needed "a supportive woman," opined Chicago, to deal with her own "anxieties and insecurities."[41]

For the summer Chicago and Hamrol, whose relationship was back on a harmonious track, planned to go to Albuquerque, where she would work on lithographs at the Tamarind Institute founded by June Wayne, whom Chicago had perceived as "strong" and "difficult" but exemplary for her ability to organize collaborative work. Before leaving, she led the students in a performance called *Ablutions* (meaning literally "washing away") that took place off campus in June at the studio of Guy Dill in Venice, the bohemian beach town south of Santa Monica.[42]

The performance of *Ablutions*—by Suzanne Lacy, Sandra Orgel, Aviva Rahmani, and Jan Oxenberg and utilizing the rape stories recorded in San Francisco—took place in a space covered with skeins of weblike ropes on a floor strewn with broken eggshells, amid three large aluminum washtubs. At issue were not only rape but binding (as in Chinese foot-binding), brutalization, body anxiety, and entrapment. An accompanying tape concluded with a woman's voice repeating over and over again, "I felt so helpless, so powerless, there was nothing I could do but lie there and cry softly."[43] Oxenberg was one of three nude women who immersed "ourselves in a tub of cow's blood, then eggs, then clay. We were breaded with blood, which was crusted to our eyelids, then wrapped in a sheet from head to toe and tied with a rope." "It was claustrophobic," she recalls, still hoping that "it was a powerful artistic experience for the audience."[44] Shawnee Wollenman, another of the performers, recalls the distress of the unpleasant experience—"having no way to get cleaned off, shivering . . . being driven by my friends to one of their homes where I could take a warm shower."[45] A witness seated with the audience on the floor, Clare Loeb, confirms that "three naked women came out and sat down pouring blood, and a tape was playing describing their rape experiences; then they were bandaged so that they looked like mummies." She describes the effect: "It was one of the most scandalous events ever. There was no heckling, the audience was rapt. It was unforgettable."[46]

When the new CalArts campus finally opened in Valencia, Chicago hated it as "too sterile and institutional," which "together with the rift that had developed between me and Mimi caused me to decide that—despite the job security—I would work out my two-year contract and leave"—this though Schapiro pressured her to invest more in the school.[47] Defusing the issue of job security, Chicago made it known in early June that she would stay for only one more year. Her trust in herself had been shaken by her interaction with Schapiro, yet it was from self-confidence that she derived whatever personal power she had.[48]

With publishing contacts still not materializing, Chicago determined to rewrite the book. The phase of anger and rage about the status of women needed to give way to "something more real, more solid. It must be the culmination of my looking, searching, thinking, teaching women, reading women's lit, my own experience, etc."[49] At this transitional moment she attracted the attention of Susan Stocking, a feature writer at the *Los Angeles Times,* who was reacting to the strictures of William Wilson: "Judy Chicago . . . is an aggressive woman, a natural leader, and as an artist she has been deeply affected by the fact that she is a woman."[50] Stocking quoted Chicago about her own developing artistic goal: "It's about doing what women have not been doing—coming to terms with our femaleness and transcending it."[51]

In Albuquerque, as Chicago and Hamrol settled into their tiny student apartment, she recalled her "mad idea" of buying a tiny, derelict house on a piece of property in L.A.: "What a fantasy that was. Part of my little girl dream about 'happy ever after.'"[52] Hamrol had vetoed the notion, preferring a more rootless life and a trip to Europe in the early fall. In the provisional quarters, the claustrophobic atmosphere impinged on the need for private workspace and challenged their relationship. Chicago put in long hours trying to make prints at Tamarind and making time to revise the book. Disappointed with the narrow range of gray tones she could obtain with lithographic crayons, she tried to create lithographs by spraying tusche (the dense black liquid used most often with brush or pen to paint a design on lithographic stones instead of drawing with crayon, which was the usual way). Unable to produce fully what she could imagine, she was nonetheless pleased by her lithographs. She achieved "a delicate overlay of transparency," recalls Judith Solodkin, then a trainee at Tamarind, who was quite taken with Chicago's "clarity of purpose" and describes her as "forceful, directed, and charismatic."[53]

In the midst of experimenting and revising, Chicago began to conceptualize her next step: a series of paintings to be named for famous women, drawn from her tireless study of biographies: "Recently I've been reading about women during the period of the French Revolution—Marie Antoinette, Madame du Barry, Pompadour, Roland, Lafayette, & de Staël. They're fascinating & had an enormous amount of power. I want to name all my new images after great women in History & the whole series 'Great Ladies' or 'Great Women,' thus honoring them & also again affirming women & my womanhood."[54] The images, she thought, would be white or very pale.

Meanwhile, at the University of New Mexico Hamrol transformed an abandoned fishpond, which Chicago's mother described: after "dripping adobe mud on all the inner sides, [he] covered the bottom with tar and lay Plexiglas on top of the whole area . . . When clouds drift by, or when the sun shines on it, it is all reflected in the tar below. Judy says it is a thing of beauty."[55]

Chicago could admire Hamrol's invention, but the work of a male painter whom she met at Tamarind made her reflect that "men are not raised to confront or even 'see' the content of their actions, their paintings, or their fantasies. Thus men can kill without ever really thinking about what they're doing, they can exploit people, use women, paint paintings that reveal clearly their whole exploitative mentality & still see themselves as 'nice guys.' " She differentiated women from men because they " 'see' content & men do not. Why? Because women are allowed to stay close to their feeling & not alienated from them? Biological? Cultural?"[56] She did not see the way clear to answers but instinctively knew they would emerge only through work.

Provoked to work with renewed urgency, Chicago reached for threads leading back to *Womanhouse,* where she celebrated embroidery and hand-painted china among women's traditional arts.[57] The previous summer too she had received a strong impression in an Oregon antiquary. Her eye caught "in a locked cabinet, sitting on velvet . . . a beautiful hand-painted plate . . . [Its] gentle color fades and soft hues of the roses, which seemed to be part of the porcelain on which they were painted."[58] The inkling of an idea would jell, vary, and stretch to transform painting on china into a new aesthetic: "A technique usually associated with old ladies & not taken seriously. I want to push it into 'art.' "[59] She later explained her decision: "For me, there has to be a fusion of surface and color and form, and the only technique available to me that would allow those things to happen seemed to be china painting."[60] She added: "I was looking for a way to be very specific. I wanted specific abstract images that were content-oriented. I have always used color pencil, which is terrific, but it is not permanent enough. Oil painting seemed to be the only other painting technique. I knew I wanted something that delicate. But I don't like the color on top."[61] Much as she had wanted when she went to autobody school in the early 1960s, she continued her efforts "to fuse the surface and the image."[62] She longed for a few years to pursue nothing but this new departure in art: "I just wish someone would take care of me. I'm probably facing another 5 yr. struggle in my work before I produce another body of work."[63] Seven years would be more like it—the actual outcome would be beyond even fantasy then, not to mention books to read, rewrite, or write.

During the six weeks at Tamarind some of the men acted up. "I know that Clinton [Adams] gave you a hard time," Judith Solodkin would write Chicago. "He's not to be taken seriously. He reminds me of Richard Nixon."[64] Even though one didn't take them seriously, Chicago reflected, the men were still there, and Adams kept up his "anti-women's lib" barrage. Where Solodkin could ironize, Chicago felt discouraged to find eternal sexism in such a ideal place to work. "I think often of Virginia Woolf," she recorded. "I know in my heart she killed herself because she just couldn't stand it anymore. I feel like that sometimes—often in fact. It used to be difficult, but my anguish seems greater now."[65] Solodkin says that Adams could be counted on for "lascivious looks and remarks."[66] June Wayne confirms that he was "deeply sexist: a sexist pig."[67]

Another bout with a recurrent dilemma also merited note: "my idiotic ego—as if no amount of recognition will ever satisfy me. Of course everyone says I'm famous. I still can't sell my work & I don't have enough opportunities to show."[68] Likewise familiar was the dilemma felt when, back in L.A., she discussed with Sheila de Bretteville setting up an independent school, only to feel divided between the contrary desires "to keep struggling in the movement" and to withdraw into her art.[69] With Lloyd she discussed leaving L.A., maybe even living in Europe.

Bidding the journal "Bye," she hinted at a "lot going on in my head" that she would discuss "maybe later."[70] Not till mid-November would she get around to transcribing her notes from their early September trip to Europe. In London she was "knocked out" by the Egyptian collection at the British Museum and "the late Turners at the Tate," likewise by "a fantastic Magritte painting and a late Giacometti painting of a seated female figure. Only the head was alive, the body was just sketched in. The head was like the last shred of consciousness left in a dying body. I knew he had painted it near the end of his life, & it really broke me up."[71] Madame Tussaud's Wax Museum fascinated with "the original work by her . . . particularly the heads she cast from the actual decapitated heads of people guillotined . . . Marie Antoinette, Louis XVI."[72] At the Louvre it was a "*fantastic* Berthe Morisot pastel, 3 Rosalba Carrieras, & some very interesting paintings showing the plans for the Grand Gallery of the Louvre—crammed full of paintings, with artists working, & the artists were both men & women . . . [It] really underlined [Élisabeth] Vigée-Lebrun's contention (in her memoirs) that the eighteenth century in France was a good time for women."

They rented a car and drove to Versailles, where the luxury of the palace seemed to explain the wrath of the French Revolution. A room with paintings by Adélaïde Labille-Guiard and Élisabeth Vigée-Lebrun fleshed out memoirs Chicago had read. Then their route across hamlets and fields led them to Chartres—"the stained-glass windows . . . colored shadow patterns all over the floor." Chicago developed nightmares from "learning to drive a shift car . . . a short while each day," but as with china painting, "although it was difficult, I kept working at it." With the china painting in mind, she took in a porcelain exhibit at Limoges.

Charmed but wary of the " 'petit bourgeois' mentality . . . 'niceness', 'beauty,' & 'pastoral contentment,' " Chicago contrasted it with "CalArts & Mimi . . . a big struggle, but I guess there's no getting out of it yet—at least not till next spring." Used to long periods working apart, being together twenty-four hours every day was proving a strain, but they worked on getting Hamrol to match her in expressing his innermost thoughts.

It came as a revelation at the Léger Museum in Biot that Ferdinand's wife Nadia had also been an artist, "maybe as good as Ben Nicholson of England—but not as good as Léger." Chicago then began to worry about women artists' visibility and about keeping her identity separate from Hamrol's. Did marriages between female and male artists work for or against the women? Take Georgia O'Keeffe and Alfred Stieglitz, Sonia and Robert Delaunay, Barbara Hepworth and Ben Nicholson, Helen Frankenthaler and Robert Motherwell. In her "generation," she predicts, "some women will gain power to influence taste without having their power exist because of men's support."[73]

Deploring women's relative invisibility, Chicago drew an inference that would authorize and reinforce her artistic ambition: "seeing all this work makes me realize that I haven't *begun* to assert my ego. Artists like Matisse, Léger,

Picasso, Miró, Braque, Chagall, etc., moved into sculpture, pottery, mosaic, stained glass—all sorts of enormous projects, which demanded fantastic ego projection. I am learning so much here about the limits of my personality, my confidence, my ability to do what I want & the world be damned."[74] The great men of art set standards for daring and pointed a way that a woman would have to travel to become great in her own right.

Two "very wild days" later they celebrated in Milan with "a *fantastic* pizza," a "marvelous Mantegna painting, a beautiful Rembrandt, & Da Vinci's *Last Supper.*"[75] Steady rain beset them all the way from Nice to Florence, where all they managed to see was the Duomo looming white and wet in the dark. Unable to find a room, in the city center or outside, and not wanting to sleep in the car, they drove the whole way back north to Milan. Still fearful, Judy left most of the driving to Lloyd but felt guilty, because "Mimi lets Paul do all the driving & is very dependent in that place & I never liked it & now I see that I'm the same."[76]

While transcribing the travelogue, Chicago noted a change in her attitude toward sexuality. She had expected her husband, as a man, to be "aggressive." But now she realized that he was "acting in accord with his own autobiography & I decided to act on my sexual impulses when I want to & forget about who does what when, which is based on sex role-expectation on my part."[77]

Chicago left the steep Alpine curves to Hamrol, remembering her "feelings of guilt and being responsible for my father's & Jerry's death." Around Frankfurt they strolled for a few hours, "fighting our many bad feelings about being in Germany," but they spent a day and a half walking and visiting museums in Brussels.[78]

In Amsterdam they "looked at the famous street . . . where the prostitutes sit in lighted windows. It was pretty awful, but not as awful as my fantasies." Thinking of living in Amsterdam, they went to visit an artist they knew from L.A.: Doug Edge was living with his wife and children in a tiny rented house—enough to explode any dreamlet and make Chicago realize that she really wanted nothing so much as getting home and back to making her art. Still she savored the Rijksmuseum, especially the Vermeers and the *Nightwatch* of Rembrandt. Next day the Anne Frank house made an impression that would shape her future work: it "unexpectedly moved me to tears."[79] As a whole, the venture deepened and confirmed her developing analysis of an art world and tradition ripe for revolutionary revision: "Seeing all that old art confirmed my alienation from the contemporary male art scene, which seems to me to produce art that is unreal & unrelated to human issues."[80]

"Poor Lloyd. I got immediately swallowed up by the women, who all came over when got home. We talked all night."[81] Ideas that had been fermenting along the road poured out: a new form of journal, with drawings; many small paintings on paper, with acrylic; china painting to learn; a butterfly book and "painted plates, called 'Papillons', which is French for butterflies. I want to make cunt images from butterflies, using the central body form as the cunt, the wings will be symbollic [*sic*] of movement. It's a step, I think, from the flower, which tho lovely too often seems passive, whereas the butterfly is active."[82]

Here Chicago has conceptualized the plate designs that would appear most frequently in *The Dinner Party*, although she had not yet conceived of the piece itself. Her idea of making symbolically active—rather than passive—female images is central to that piece and to much of her other work. Hostile critics, however, have often ignored her intention, focusing instead on the fact of the female form itself and declaring it inherently offensive.

In October one of the Corcoran conference organizers, Barbara Frank, came for a brief stay that cut into "psychic privacy" but shed unexpected light. Chicago recorded that when Frank and Hamrol discussed some works on paper—two drawings of the *Great Ladies* that stemmed from reading women's biographies and two extending an older series of grids and doorways—"they made me see that the grids related to my struggle with Mimi & that I was 'holding on' to her & hence to my mother. This was very apparent in the fact that in the *Great Ladies* I've really let go & am more myself than I've ever been."[83] She would abandon her obsessive concern with the doorway images, which by now she had made into prints, drawings, and paintings, but expand the *Great Ladies* into six square canvases, forty by forty inches. She had also started her first butterfly plate, "very reminiscent of my early work." With this she returned to the more overt erotic imagery that she had repressed because it scandalized her professors in graduate school in the early 1960s. It would be almost a quarter of a century before Eve Ensler made such subject matter acceptable with her 1996 play *The Vagina Monologues,* which by now has gained the status of a classic.[84]

Chicago found a more sympathetic audience in Arlene Raven, the art historian and critic who arrived from Johns Hopkins. Raven established herself in the CalArts community, took hold in the Feminist Art Program, and declared her intention to write about Chicago's work, also helping Chicago interpret her relationship with Schapiro as doomed to failure because it did not allow "us to be ourselves."[85] Optimistically Chicago wondered, "Perhaps sometime we will even be able to reapproach each other on a better footing. I remember how I was unable to stand up to her & how frightened her rages made me & how I had to manipulate situations because of I was afraid to say no to her."[86]

Although Chicago and Schapiro kept their discord out of sight, tension made itself felt. Even physical differences could feed the tension. Older by sixteen years, Schapiro was furious when a reporter from the *Los Angeles Times* called her "grandmotherly."[87] She was "a motherly type, who dyed her hair to look younger," according to Karen LeCocq.[88] Nancy Youdelman remembers Schapiro grappling with being overweight, always dieting. Chicago, who recalled Schapiro at the time as "zaftig, middle-aged, dark-haired, attractive," strongly disapproved of the students' obsession with appearance, even discouraging shaving legs and plucking eyebrows with tweezers. Weight, however, remained an issue, even among budding feminists.

Tension fed too on contrasts in personality. The younger woman was direct, while the older was "manipulative," "much more diplomatic," and "would try to make you see things in her way."[89] Their fathers' characters and beliefs help to account for their differences in dealing with others. As a Communist and union organizer, Arthur Cohen favored direct action and revolutionary change, while Teddy Schapiro, after sitting out the First World War with his wife's family in Canada, became a lifelong Socialist, opting not for revolution but for trying to effect change from within the system, even running without success for New York State Assembly from Brooklyn during the late 1920s.

The two fathers differed not only in politics but in the ways they treated their daughters and in the legacies they left. Arthur made Judy the apple of his eye, endowing her with a keen sense of her own worth. His death when Judy was just thirteen left her with a permanent longing. In contrast, Miriam's father, Teddy, did not nurture her but placed demands on her and continued to do so until his death at the age of ninety-nine, when she was in her mid-seventies. His commitment to politics and his professional difficulties had left him with little time to devote to his only child. She recalled somewhat bitterly: "I knew this as a little girl and asked him why he did that, since he never was elected. He told me that someone had to bring the news of Capitalism to the workers. He used to take his wooden 'soap' box (and like many other speakers) walk to the nearest park and set up for his speech."[90] He also took on the role of mentoring his daughter in art, imposing a weekly ritual of drawing assignments that she dreaded but diligently prepared. "I was a loner kid," she remembers. "My parents were making this artist out of me."[91] Teddy recalled that "Miriam would get mad when he corrected her drawings, but she was an excellent draughtsman."[92]

Despite the tensions between herself and Schapiro at CalArts, Chicago felt that her work in creating a female community was paying off in "*real* feedback" about herself. She cited women of her own age—Arlene Raven, Barbara Frank,

Suzanne Lacy—as seeing her more "realistically," which helped her to become a "new person . . . the one that has always made my art."[93]

It was in this context that she produced the drawings for her *Great Ladies* series and prepared to prime the canvases. She also started to carry out her plan to paint on china—a butterfly plate, which she would fire, reaching back to develop the previous summer's metaphoric linkage between "female reality" and forms of butterflies with wings distended in flight. Styled a "butterfly/cunt image," it was meant to imply that "the butterflies are really liberated images. I was thinking about 1964—after I had my masters. I was working on my house on Mirimar & had locked myself up for a month, pacing the floor, working & struggling. I made images of a cock & a cunt; the images of the cock were gorgeous—plumed, feathered, flying, but the only cunt image I could make was passive & stationary."[94] She recalled one titled *In My Mother's House* (Figure 5). "It's taken almost 10 yrs. to reach a point, both personal & historical where I could make a liberated cunt image," she reflected. The results disappointed her. Vision outstripped skill in a medium that for her was still new but that she was determined to bring by hook or by crook from the status of craft to the realm of art.

Her "10 yrs work" was already, thanks to Raven's assessment, beginning to look like "a coherent decade's struggle & achievement . . . as if something has happened, without my really realizing it & now it's there. For 10 yrs I've been struggling consistently—to shape my life, to make my art, to deal with my femaleness, to make symbollic [*sic*] images of my struggle, my femaleness, my humanness."[95]

Chicago's estimate of her own work was not exaggerated. Since she entered graduate school, she had worked with a ferocious intensity, turning out art that caught critical attention, and in the last several years she had created a new feminist pedagogy. Museums had begun to show and even to purchase her abstract work. At this point she had achieved the beginnings of a strong career. But she was ready to risk it all to venture into unknown territory. She resumed trying to deal with images that more directly expressed sexuality from the female point of view, taking up the very themes and forms that had so offended her professors in graduate school.

Chicago's new consciousness of her achievements brought renewed anxiety about death and losing it all. Nearly ten years had gone by since the summer of 1963, when Jerry died, and twenty years since her father's death in the summer of 1953. Would it be her turn in the summer of 1973? Awareness of mortality was a "psychic state" that Chicago felt that she and Raven shared, once she learned that Arlene suffered from "incipient leukemia and could die at any time"; yet she counted on Raven's "energy force in the community" to give her "psychic space," to allow her to "see a way to go on from CalArts, which is sure to blow up soon."[96] They might even ask her to teach men, which she would never do. She thought of renting a studio space and taking in three groups of "10 women each for year @ $500 each": women needed "to be in a space of their own—not part of another, larger institution."[97] Meanwhile the Womanspace project continued, but a new location had to be found.

More than two weeks later, the day before Thanksgiving, Chicago found another moment for the journal. She had painted her first plate ten times, only to have it come out "lousy in the firing." She still couldn't get the hang of china painting. She had finished the first of her *Great Ladies,* which left her feeling "caught between the accepted, but male, art standards & the new, emerging, not yet defined, female art standards"; but a new series begins to take shape, in a first drawing, "Crowded Ladies," "named after women who have been crowded out of history & the recognition they deserve."[98]

Almost casually she appends, "A lot is going on. I sent in my letter of resignation."[99] Rather than continue at CalArts, Chicago would form a "partnership" with Raven, who was complementary and supportive, rather than competitive and threatened. Since Schapiro had abruptly ended their relations after the Corcoran conference the previous spring, things had further deteriorated between them. In the fall she had seemed "warm and friendly" but complained to Raven that Chicago was ripping her off. Ironically, she may have been referring to some of Chicago's paintings, the drawings for which are labeled *Homage to Miriam Schapiro.*

After Raven tried to mediate between Chicago and Schapiro, Schapiro put pressure on her to stop relating to Chicago and to "trust her," to help rebuild the program if Chicago decided to leave. "Arlene had to make a stand & she did," wrote Chicago, "telling Mimi that she was committed to the beliefs that I held & that she was going to be involved with me."[100] Tension had come to a head when Schapiro pressured Faith Wilding to remove from a graduate show one of her "cunt" paintings because Brach and one of her professors, Alan Hacklin, did not like the imagery. Although Brach had been familiar with such images in Chicago's work and those of students in the art program at Fresno, he caved in to pressure from his male colleagues and chose to put pressure on a powerless student. Schapiro also suggested that Wilding consider changing her work so that the men would grant her master's degree. Incensed that the program's first graduate student had to suffer the same censorship of female imagery that she herself had faced in graduate school—the very reason that she had begun the program—Chicago had handed in her long meditated letter of resignation, effective at the end of the spring term.[101] To her, the values at CalArts were "in direct opposition to those of the Program" as she had begun it in Fresno.[102] Paul Brach wrote to Chicago that her resignation did not come as a surprise but she would be missed, and he held her in high regard as a woman, an artist, and as "a truly inovated [*sic*] educator."[103] Schapiro then offered Chicago's position to Raven, who replied that she planned to work with Chicago the next year.

Alan Hacklin's behavior was a key factor in Chicago and Raven's decision to leave CalArts. According to Robin Mitchell, Hacklin favored male students and subjected females to vicious critiques; she remembers him telling a young woman with very tentative paintings, "They're the inside of a baby's pants: they're just poop," then demanding, "Why are you an artist?"[104] She also heard Hacklin and Brach chortling over lunch that art schools were great hunting grounds for mistresses and second wives. Mitchell remembers too that Schapiro told her, "It's not that Judy takes power, it's that people give it to her."[105]

Relations between Chicago and Schapiro had effectively ended after the Corcoran conference, despite Chicago's efforts to reconcile. Schapiro complained that Johanna Demetrakas, the filmmaker of *Womanhouse,* was usurping credit for her work, but Chicago refused her demands to intervene with Demetrakas. Chicago herself, fed up with trying to work with Schapiro, decided to concede her complete credit, rights, and profits for the *Womanhouse* book, should a contract come though. This was more than Schapiro had bargained for, prompting the inference that she had intended to get Chicago to do a lot of the work while getting the credit herself.[106]

Chicago and Schapiro's participation in the Corcoran conference had prompted a query from the New York–based critic Cindy Nemser, who also edited the *Feminist Art Journal.* She had reported the dissent at the conference between older East Coast artists and younger women who "loved the funky displays so characteristic of the West Coast."[107] Now she was preparing a panel for the January (1973) College Art Association meeting. She wrote to ask Chicago how the Feminist Art Program started, how it developed the themes of women's life that provoked controversy at the Corcoran, and how it handled responsibility, work sharing, and group recognition for individual achievement. Chicago found the questions "sort of general" and so urged Nemser to come out and experience Southern California's female community for herself. To this inquiring, potentially hostile eye from the East, Chicago gave no hint of the tensions then at CalArts but postulated "a geographical difference which influences the quality of the female communities in L.A. and New York."[108] She emphasized that her involvement with the women's movement grew out of her own needs as an artist and told how she had dealt "with the nature of my own identity as a woman in my work."[109] She went on to explain: "Once I had acknowledged my own identity and asserted it, I had to face the fact that this assertion was going unheeded in the culture. I recognized that my situation as a woman artist was tied up with the entire situation of women in the society and that unless that changed, my situation and the misunderstanding and lack of honor accorded to my work would not change."[110] She recognized her own need for "a female support group and environment in order to grow as an artist and as a woman. I didn't want to simply make art the way men did, as I felt that their language form was not sufficient for what I wanted to say. I thought perhaps other women had the same needs I had and decided to find out by starting a women's class. I wanted to be in an all-female environment, and in order to do that I had to create one."[111]

Qualifying her aim with "perhaps" and "find out," she signaled a strong commitment to women, which implied sharing a cause with Nemser too, while avoiding postures that might seem reductive and essentialist, still less dominating and aggressive. Chicago sought acceptance for her ideas among East Coast feminist artists. She anticipated other criticism and thus specified "that the program started, not as a consciousness-raising group, altho we did CR, but rather as an educational program, of which I was the leader. But I didn't want a rigid hieratic structure in which I was frozen into a leadership role, as that would not allow me the growth potential that I was looking for. So I tried to build the group in such a way that, as they become stronger, they took over more and more of the responsibilities of the group."[112]

Chicago took pride that the group had "reached a point where the women took over the critiques, with me functioning as a member of the group . . . and they will structure the program for the next quarter, with me in an advisory role."[113] She saw the problem as how "to reconcile leadership and democracy" and determined that "the key to this is power. Men, who have power, wish to keep it, and thus tend to prevent growth which will threaten their dominance, while I am not invested in power, as I think many women are not . . . and my inclination is to share, not to hoard . . . it is sharing of leadership, sharing of responsibility, sharing of power that we are after, it seems to me, not the abdication of it."[114] She wanted to create more and more strong women who could act as leaders, "when the time comes to share responsibility."[115]

Despite or perhaps because of her experience with Schapiro, she went on to assert an ideal—that "the tenets of the women's movement, e.g., consciousness raising, teach us to share, to make space for each other, to listen to each other, and if these tenets are carried into all aspects of our lives, sharing will result."[116] Then she justified the thematic focus that had drawn flak at the Corcoran:

"Once I had established an all women group, and given permission for the women to work out of their *real* concerns, e.g., abortions and parents and boyfriends and menstruation and violation and all the rest (I never directed them toward these things, I just never prevented them from dealing with them) . . . the class just took off. The easiest thing in the world is to educate . . . just don't stop the natural growth process."[117]

"Once one helps people to plug into themselves, they take off, but that is irreconcilable with controlling people or dominating them and that's the rub . . . you have to be able to relinquish control and power in order to allow natural and organic growth . . . and that is what the development of the group was based upon . . . organic growth."[118] "Group recognition of individual accomplishment . . . this is not a problem in our groups," asserted Chicago in response to Nemser's query.[119]

Since Nemser not only wrote but edited her own journal, Chicago closed by recommending Raven as a contributor, who she described as "doing incredible work here . . . building up theory for feminist art criticism."[120] Then for the first time she described their future partnership, saying that she was quitting CalArts as of this year and that she and Arlene would open up an independent program to be called the Feminist Studio Workshop. They planned to start with thirty women, who would "pay $750 each, cash on the barrelhead, and they will have a studio space, a female support group, me and Arlene to work with, consciousness raising, readings in literature and history, investigation of work of women of the past, etc." She further explained that they had developed the entire program "*in our space,* without the contradictions that grow out of being in a male institution, without high tuition, etc. It really is an attempt to establish an alternative institution, based entirely on feminist principles. I figure it is going to be hard to get going . . . I am very scared and anxious about leaving the security of institutions."[121] But she added, "If Arlene and I can make this work, it would mean that women all over the country could rent spaces, start programs to train young women, make enough money to survive, have control over our own educational programs, determine our own values, not have to beg for crumbs from men."[122]

With all these plans for the new program, Chicago was also working on her own paintings. By the end of 1972, she extended the *Great Ladies* to include *Catherine the Great* and *Christina of Sweden;* also in the works was *Marie Antoinette*—seen at Madame Tussaud's. Chicago posited metaphorical relations between her abstracted, stylized images and the historical lives. She viewed *Christina* as a blocked image, which she tried to convey by overlaying a square. She felt that Christina's life was just like that since she was unable to fit into any of the available roles in her society. Chicago's idea was "to let each picture stand for an emotional state." She had struggled with *Catherine* because she could not formulate a clear image of her and felt anxious about this latest one, "it's so clear & plain & naked. I hope I'll have the courage to let it hang out."[123]

Chicago still harbored thoughts of rendering in paint the image she drew the previous year after her awkward reunion with Leslie Lacy. Out of the blue he telephoned to apologize, saying how much he wanted to have contact with her. They spent "a really wonderful day together," prompting her to reflect how long and how profoundly she desired a relationship with a man who could match her own intellectual and radical traits. She fantasized that Leslie was that man, seeing his struggle as identical to her own. She was constantly amazed that they shared so many feelings and admired his plans to start his own school, publish his own books (if necessary), and his struggle "to let go of seeing white male authoritarian structures as necessary for his validation."[124]

This better reunion inspired her to transfer the old drawing and enlarge it on canvas as *Heaven Is for White Men Only* (Fig. 15), which Lucy Lippard saw and praised. Pressing on with her large, new metaphoric abstractions, Chicago repainted *Catherine the Great* and *Marie Antoinette* and laid plans for a large *Through the Flower* once she got back from an impending trip to New York.

Her mixed success with her first china painting led to a switch in teachers so she could learn more about color and firing. Blending practical engagement with theoretical awareness, as ever, Chicago reported: "It's the first time in my life being female was a distinct advantage in the art world," observing that "the classes were role reversed; male students weren't taken seriously. Women teach other women in a way that's traditionally feminine: nonlinear, informal, non-authoritarian. China painting is complicated. I had to unlearn a lot of things. Colors must be fired consecutively, and there are no books detailing what to do or how to do it."[125]

The trip east took her to Buffalo for a lecture and workshop but also to New York City, where she arranged to meet Leslie—still uncertain about her future with Lloyd and trying to develop a positive working relationship with Raven for their new independent program. Chicago told herself to be open to Arlene's ideas, but she felt burned from her experience with Schapiro: "I just trusted, like a child with a mother—and she just sold me & the Program right down the river."[126]

The New York reunion with Leslie left Chicago judging herself very severely: "Oy, am I an idiot! I wonder when I'll give up these fantasies about LOVE & ROMANCE & all that JAZZ & accept life in its own terms & in particular, accept *my* life & its richness & its limits."[127] Safely ensconced at the Waldorf-

Astoria, she called it a "bummer meeting," like the San Francisco debacle in March, except that this time she got herself out of it right away. She had been impatient with his eagerness to have sex without paying her attention, and then he became impotent, citing as an excuse thoughts of his girlfriend in Washington. She concluded that they were not ready to "physicalize the relationship," but he seemed "flipped out by it."[128] She left him there and went out on her own, taking in a show of photographs by Diane Arbus and two films—one of which, Ingmar Bergman's *Cries and Whispers,* dealt with her familiar fear of death. Back at the Waldorf she found Leslie gone, together with *Heaven Is for White Men Only* (not the new painting but the old drawing made after their troubled San Francisco round). This closed the relationship for good, she thought. Fantasizing that the small plane to wintry Buffalo would crash, she got Arlene Raven on the phone.

Once she began her talk in Buffalo at the State University of New York, she recovered her equilibrium. "The reason many women are not able to realize themselves as artists," Chicago told her Buffalo audience, amplifying what she inferred in Europe about heroic egoism in male-dominant art, is that women do not feel free "to act aggressively. They do not feel that they have the right to act out their own needs and wants. . . . The personality structure of a woman, as dictated by the society in which we live, is inconsistent with the personality structure that is necessary to make art . . . I think we need a support climate."[129] She urged students to understand their own history as women artists, and she argued that women needed their own art criticism, which would deal with "our own ideas and issues, and in what ways they are different from men's ideas and issues in their work." She posited that perhaps we would find existent forms of art suited "for the ideas that men have had, but . . . inadequate for the ideas women have."

Chicago's invitation to Buffalo had come from its women's studies board, which by then had a growing number of counterparts on campuses all over the country. The first courses in women's studies were being offered, most of them in English departments. SUNY Buffalo itself offered a thirteen-course major with the Women's Studies Center. One of the earliest such programs had been created back in California at San Diego State, in the spring of 1970, when twenty women formed a committee and pressured the college into allowing a ten-course major within the Arts and Letters Division,[130] about the time when Chicago herself was planning her Feminist Art Program at Fresno. Chicago was not then aware of these programs, although she certainly felt supported by the larger women's movement.

In Buffalo, Chicago not only lectured but conducted a workshop in which she organized several consciousness-raising groups and a group of women artists. As students began to flock to women's studies, they searched for the chance to gain a sense of their own identity as people rather than as baby-makers and housewives. For the first time it became routine to study historical contributions by women in the arts and sciences, which had once been passed over and forgotten. The idea was to restore the identity and the sense of worth that too many women had suppressed in a male-dominated society.[131]

Back in New York City, Chicago met with the writer Alix Kates Shulman and with Lucy Lippard and Paula Harper, who were in town for the annual meeting of the College Art Association, which Chicago attended for a day. She had agreed to accept an award from the magazine *Mademoiselle,* only to find she was being exploited for a publicity event, where Mayor John V. Lindsay spoke, and that her TV interviewer was sexist.[132]

With her habitual frankness, Chicago told herself that the whole last year had been crazy. Her imagination had caused her to direct energy into romantic pursuits that had proved unrealistic and ultimately undesirable. She had dreamed too of abandoning public life for total seclusion in her studio, "copping out" of the new program with Sheila and Arlene. She had even considered signing a contract to continue at CalArts and work with Schapiro. Instead she resolved to settle down, accept her life, get a new loft with Lloyd, sign a five-year lease, and open the new independent women's program with the collaborators she could trust. She would put the wild flights of fancy into her work, not her life.[133]

She appreciated her relationship with Lloyd, her friendship with Arlene, and the female community. And of course there was always her work. She wrote how her sense of self as a special and darling person with all the answers had given way to an image of herself as a "complex woman with great energy & vision, with some rigidity & fear of embracing other ideas, with great difficulties living *in* my life & not always trying to run off to something else."[134] She felt that she nonetheless had a strong inner core.

Chicago had returned to L.A. in time to join the crowd that mobbed the opening of the cooperative gallery, Womanspace, over which Wanda Westcoast presided. The *Los Angeles Times* and other media paid significant attention.[135] For Chicago, it meant a space where she belonged, as she told *Womanspace* journal, echoed in the magazine *Ms.:* "Some years ago, at the height of my isolation, I dreamt of a time when women would come together, to affirm each other, to see each other's work, to provide support, comfort and criticism for each other, to see in each other a reflection of our womanhood, our humanhood. Now that time is come. We are opening a space; our work will hang in a context that we have established, one that is relevant to women's struggles, women's subject matter, women's values."[136]

Affirming other women and their art did not exclude pursuing their husbands, as Chicago had pursued Westcoast's earlier in the year, only to turn away when he became interested. It was the 1970s, when sexual freedom was in the air, and Chicago had long since read the ideas of erotic liberation of Norman O. Brown, who explored Freud's argument that civilization demands sexual repression.[137] In *Life Against Death: The Psychoanalytical Meaning of History,* Brown wrote, "Art, if its object is to undo repressions, and if civilization is essentially repressive, is in this sense subversive of civilization."[138]

Female sexuality was the subject of a show presented at Womanspace after its thronged first weeks. The organizers were disappointed when the opening attracted only a couple of hundred people. Chicago was pleased that the show included a new painting of hers, called *Let It All Hang Out* (eighty inches square, Figure 16). With a certain perverse bravado, she named this abstract picture with a vulgar phrase from male sexual lingo (referring to exposing the male genitalia) for a female form and audience.[139] She remarked how much this image had disturbed her when she finished it, causing her to become hysterical and feel that the painting was somehow wrong because it was so powerful and at the same time so feminine. She felt that she had taken a huge step, and it took her a while to internalize it.[140]

Chicago produced *Let It All Hang Out* in the context of the women's movement's stress on pride in women's anatomy and sexuality. The book *Our Bodies, Ourselves* had become so popular that it was reissued in 1973 (and many times thereafter, becoming a classic). Having already assigned this book to her students in the art program in Fresno, she found new inspiration for her own work. The theme of *Let It All Hang Out* concurred with a central message of this book: the need for women to become familiar with the appearance of their own sexual organs and to accept their own anatomy, moving from societal-induced "self-hate toward self-love." The book recommended that women use a mirror to examine their sexual organs so that they could conclude: "I am not obscene. It was good to realize that our vaginas are cleaner than the insides of our mouths. . . . We still had many bad feelings about our selves. . . . We have not been able to erase decades of social influence."[141]

To the uninformed viewer, *Let It All Hang Out* looks like a dynamic abstract painting in tones and tints of red. Its three concentric circles suggest movement, as do the lines that radiate outward from the center. These concentric circles—in tension with sinuous centripetal and centrifugal lines, the symmetrically alternating dynamics of color and tone—may not suggest the female form to all viewers, but to the artist, there at conception and birth, it constituted a major emotional and technical breakthrough. The symbol got through to at least one viewer, for Barbara Smith wrote in *Womanspace* magazine, "This seems to be a most ecstatic, orgasmic image, more expressive than any work I've yet seen of hers. It is not as obvious a cunt image as orgasmic . . . at once sensitive yet assertive."[142]

Also early in 1973 Chicago shared with Westcoast the space at 707, a new private gallery on La Cienega in L.A., run by a sculptor and painter, Anait, and devoted to showing women's art.[143] Westcoast, who had contributed to both *Womanhouse* and to the beginnings of Womanspace, showed a group of her trademark "vacuum-formed plastic and painted curtains."[144] Chicago showed six handmade works, in square formats that were illusionistic grids of squares. In each one central arches or repeated circles appear through the flat area of the square. She created the grids by making degrees of color appear to be three-dimensional; the arches or circles appear as doorways into a shaded though infinite space. The show also included colored drawings from the *Flesh Gates* series.[145] To Lucy Lippard, Chicago explained that "the grid in the *Flesh Gates* is built on Mimi Schapiro's paintings; I related to it as a kind of imprisonment. I wanted my work to be seen in relation to other women's work, historically, as men's work is seen."[146] Capturing a paradox of any claim to tradition, Chicago reads the grid as a metaphor of her problematic personal bond; yet in the next breath she interprets the grid as a bond with Schapiro's art that affirms art history and shows that women too can construct tradition—putting a complex spin on the tie to Schapiro intuited that evening at home when Barbara Frank and Lloyd both agreed that she should abandon Schapiro's form and move on. In the same show Chicago also showed lithographs representing her breakthrough to new directions the previous summer, including the group she called *Through the Flower* (Figure 18), which a reviewer described metaphorically as like seeing through "the diaphragm of a camera" and also as "obviously vaginal or visual."[147]

That spring, at a print workshop called Cirrus Editions, owned by Jean Milant, who had previously also been a printer-fellow at Tamarind, Chicago was working on new lithographs, including one called *Mary, Queen of Scots.* Larry Gagosian sold a lot of these prints, Milant recalled, in his print store, which was right next to a bookshop window that displayed Chicago's book when it finally appeared.[148]

During the spring break at CalArts Chicago lectured at the University of Kansas, which gave her a solo show, and at the University of North Dakota, where she found the women to be passive, repressed, apathetic, isolated, and ignorant. At the University of Minnesota she only lectured, but at St. Catherine's College, a women's school in St. Paul, she discussed helping them set up a women's program, to start with consciousness raising. While she was in town, the *Minneapolis Star* sought an interview, only to hear: "If they don't have a woman to interview me, it is an indication that they should hire more women." The journalist, Martha Rose, who reported this comment, recognized Chicago's stance as supportive and also recorded Chicago's remark, "Men need to put women down as an ego trip." Rose added, "She says she 'just doesn't want to have to put up with it.'"[149]

At a stop-over in her home city, Chicago stayed with her cousins but also visited with the artist Ellen Lanyon at the Art Institute. Lanyon, who knew Chicago from work on *W.E.B. (West-East Bag),* took her to see the Art Institute's Wabash Transit Gallery and then to the faculty room, where they encountered Emilio Cruz, an African-American artist of Cuban descent, who was a figurative painter and a performance artist. Lanyon recalled that Cruz "vociferously" attacked Chicago, shouting that white women had it so good and that black men were not getting the support they deserved. Chicago asked Cruz why he was not organizing to change the situation for blacks as she was working for the cause of women.[150] Chicago, who was well aware of the black power and black arts movements, believed that activism was the way to correct what was wrong with society. But his hostility disturbed her, and she wished that his female colleagues, Lanyon and Eileen Van Vlack, who happened to be there, had replied with like strength.[151]

Chicago then stayed as artist in residence for ten days at West Washington State University in Bellingham, where she made a boxed suite of lithographs called *Potent Pussy: Homage to Lamont,* in memory of a cat just dead after seven years and sorely lamented, now to be laid symbolically to rest by the box. Nine lithographs of three images, done three ways, referring to the nine lives of cats, were to be produced in seven editions, one for each of Lamont's seven years. The three images were to vary (one straight, one light, one dark) for the three aspects of life: birth, life, death. The frontispiece was a photo of Lamont, and the last page showed Chicago herself with her eyebrows shaved, an ancient Egyptian observance for the death of a household cat.[152] Only six prints got made, including a cover sheet, the colophon page, and a slip sheet with a quotation from Colette: "Since there can be no love without loss, I accept being, in the feline heart, a favorite who is led, through a narrow and burning strait, to the very heart of the cat." Chicago's once-thick eyebrows seem never to have grown back.

While in Bellingham, she looked forward to having some time alone and dreaded the pressure to socialize, noting that in college towns away from the big cities "everyone likes to sit around, get drunk & /or stoned, & talk—which is probably my least favorite activity."[153] She was busy reading a book about Virginia Woolf called *Feminism and Art* by Herbert Marder and was astounded to discover how many of her ideas were already in Woolf. "Virginia Woolf found evidence of barbarism in every aspect of modern life," wrote Marder. "It took many forms: paternal tyranny in the home, male supremacy in the state, intellectual rigidity within the mind. Excessive 'virility' was responsible, she maintained, for the rise of dictatorships and the horrors of war."[154]

Back in L.A., Chicago, Raven, and Sheila de Bretteville plotted the Feminist Studio Workshop, as they dubbed their "experimental program in female education in the arts," and advertised in recruitment brochures: "Our purpose is to develop a new concept of art, a new kind of artist and a new art community built from the lives, feelings and needs of women."[155]

Beyond their feminist values, Raven and de Bretteville shared with Chicago, and indeed Schapiro, their working-class Jewish backgrounds. Raven, younger than Chicago by eight years, grew up a bartender's daughter in Baltimore; de Bretteville, four years Chicago's junior, grew up in Brooklyn, the child of Polish Jewish immigrants.[156] She teamed up with Chicago and Raven as soon as Raven asked her to design their brochure. They differed inasmuch as Chicago was imbued with the tradition that apprentices learn skills from a master, who supplies overall vision and design. Raven was an art historian, not an artist, and de Bretteville, as a graphic designer, conceived of art more as collaborative work among equals.

De Bretteville's concept for the brochure was a tour de force: nine squares and three photographs of the three women founders. In each photo one of the women faces front, flanked by the other two. Each woman's three vertical squares contain examples of her work, quotations by historic and contemporary women, and information about the experimental program. Chicago included her favorite quotations by Sojourner Truth and George Eliot, but her influence also appears in Raven's section (quotations from Anaïs Nin and Simone de Beauvoir) as well as in de Bretteville's (Virginia Woolf, Margaret Fuller, and Emma Goldman).

All the while Chicago had continued her efforts to paint on china: now for the first time she envisioned as many as twenty plates, still with the butterfly motifs first attempted in 1971, but now each to be dedicated to a "famous woman" with "writing around the outside edge describing the accomplishment of each."[157] She would combine the famous women with the symbolic butterflies by working on "plates, porcelain, embroidery, vacuum-formed, large, small, etc. I want to work in a variety of media—some from male culture, some from female culture. I want the butterfly forms to allow me to express a variety of emotional stances & to be free, liberated forms."[158]

Building confidence after four years of effort in the women's movement, Chicago decided to join Hamrol in seeking financing to buy a building in North Inglewood for studio and living space. Once again she felt anxiety that she was taking a big risk for the sake of stability, twenty years after her father's death and ten years after Jerry's death. She told herself to put her fears aside and keep on trying: "I am just beginning to trust the possibility that I may have a normal life span, that I may have time to do the things I want to do."[159]

Meditating on death and struggle prompted another ambitious project. In her mind's eye she projected three paintings, which would materialize as five foot squares in sprayed acrylic. By the beginning of April, she knew "the structure, but not the color. It'll be a *Great Ladies* format with a square in the center. In the first one, the square will be in front of the form, blocking it; in the second one, the square & the image be locked in tension, neither one dominant; in the last one the image will be forward, the square behind, recessive, receding, but still there, a shadow of its former strength—only scar tissue."[160]

With her usual metaphoric flair, she assigned implication both personal and general to the successive forms: "First, imprisoned & blocked by a rigid system—my past, my conditioning as a woman, society, etc. The second image, of course, reflects the struggle between those two faces in stalemate. The last image is a reflection of my liberation, my emerging ability to be myself. I struggled for a while with whether the last image should be totally without the square—but I decided that would be dishonest, because the lingering square is there, the image of scars of my struggle."[161] *Reincarnation Triptych* (Figure 17), she called the project, and related it to three women: Madame de Staël, the novelist, philosopher, and political writer in postrevolutionary France; George Sand, the feminist novelist; and Lou Andreas-Salomé, one of the first female psychotherapists and a confidante of Nietzsche and Freud. Chicago felt that she "could have been any of those 3 women & that they represent different stages of the struggle to be oneself as a woman in a culture that despises everything womanly."[162] On a preparatory sketch for the triptych, she had written, "I have been thinking . . . about self-sabotage and why I consistently become involved with women who *cannot* go where I go. Am I afraid to be the Butterfly?"[163] In a state of self-transformation, she had not yet decided which woman's name she would give to each of the successive icons.

Writing to Lippard from Pacoima in the summer of 1973, Chicago elaborated on her identification with the triptych, explaining that she had named each one after one of the three women in history with whom she identified most closely. She told of writing on her painting: "Mme de Stael, philosopher and intellectual of the 19th century. She was flamboyant, eccentric, had a bright and showy facade. Arrogant and brilliant, she once said: 'if I don't understand it, it must be nothing.' "[164] Chicago went on: "Now anyone who knows me as well as you do will instantly see why I identify with her. I love the painting . . . it is bright and flamboyant and romantic and corny and 'retrograde' if that means what I think it means."[165] With her emphasis on the "flamboyant," Chicago had already begun to move away from modernism's formalist austerity to embrace the new aesthetic pigeonholed by the academic sobriquet "postmodernism."

Chicago confided in Lippard her concern about her own appearance, describing her attire in the summer weather as "a stretchy red t-shirt with no arms" and admitting, "I have actually dared to show my horrendously huge muscled arms whose biceps measure about 16 inches. For years I have hidden them in long sleeved shirts but it is too hot for vanity and besides, what's wrong with having big muscles, a husky, firm body and a cunt, she wondered as she shuddered from the momory [*sic*] of having gone to a nearby boutique and tried on little girl fashions, into which her big woman arms did not fit."[166] Despite her campaign to get her students to stop focusing on their appearance and the trappings of femininity, Chicago was even then not so unconcerned with her own appearance that she lacked an interest in feminine fashion or the painful awareness of its unfitness for her figure.

Even at a long distance her friendship with Lippard was such that Chicago tried to orchestrate a day in which she and Hamrol would get together with Lippard and her partner, the artist Charles Simmonds, and Ethan, Lucy's son by the painter Robert Ryman. By the time Chicago got back from Bellingham, Hamrol had ditched the idea of buying the place in North Inglewood, not wanting to be tied down when his work required travel around the country. They found a large loft building in Santa Monica to lease for $450 a month, which they would share with a designer.[167] Chicago was excited that her side would have two stories since the ceilings were so high. They planned to do a lot of work on the loft themselves and create a "teeny" living space, with most of the area devoted to their studios. She considered this move an affirmation of her life as an artist, especially because the past two years their rented house had offered such inadequate space for work.

Despite the forward-looking plans, Chicago could not get over her fear that if she had security again, she would die. She constantly fantasized about dying in plane crashes. She described "a real freak-out with Lloyd," who "was wonderful," made love to her, and comforted her: "I cried with relief because I needed to be taken care of so badly. I was so overwhelmed that I couldn't talk & could communicate only by writing. I made contact with some very deep feelings inside me. I felt like I was a little girl & Lloyd was my daddy & I felt loved & protected. It was a wonderful feeling & I felt that I had back the security I had lost when my father died & my family life fell apart."[168]

Thus again she documents the complex relationship with men and the strong need for them in her life that goes back to her closeness to her doting father and the shock of his early death. Her strong commitment to women and women's rights (and to civil rights for all) was part of the values that she had internalized from and identified with her father. It was thus difficult for any man to measure up to the ideal that her father represented in her memory. The anger toward men that Chicago sometimes expressed reflects her disappointment with some men's behavior, not a dismissal of all men. As for Hamrol, he was only rarely able to rise to the occasion and represent the strong male protector that she longed for. It did not help that he constantly vetoed any nesting instincts that his wife expressed.

Feeling ready again to throw herself into her work, Chicago cast a slightly different light on one of the dilemmas that always seemed to obtrude at pivotal times: it would be a "struggle to turn away from the ego gratification available to me in public life." Yet she did withdraw from Womanspace gallery on grounds that it had gotten so large and she no longer wanted to devote time to being an organizer.[169] Originally she had expected to find "a real alternative structure—a challenge to the values of the art world. Instead, it is turning into an exhibition space for women who don't really have a chance in the art world. . . . I'll support it because women need a place to show. Perhaps if it gets a grant, it will, sooner or later, become the place I hoped it would be."[170] Most people don't want radical change, she opined, just a piece of the existing pie.

In fact, Chicago's idealism often met with disappointment. The reality of other artists who were not willing to embrace her vision, make sacrifices, or fight for necessary goals too often meant having to compromise her standards. The real lack of ambition and dedication among some of her students, Schapiro's eagerness to make concessions to her male colleagues at CalArts, and Womanspace gallery's marketplace values all chafed upon her deeply ingrained values.

She was now feeling more confident about herself and her point of view, a far cry from the crises of doubt in Fresno that prompted the turn to Schapiro for guidance. She had learned an immense amount during the last three years "about my position as a woman, about women, about men. I knew so little when I began & I was so afraid—afraid to be myself, afraid of my own power, afraid of men & their reactions. I hope I live to be 80. Wouldn't that be incredible! I'd have time to do so many things."[171]

As for her art, she knew that she wanted to make it "emotional, romantic, embarrassing, free, generous—like I am."[172] The new confidence also let her resolve "to struggle to not feel competitive & not do things because I'm afraid someone will get ahead of me, to not be jealous if other people get attention, etc.; in other words, to stop being a little girl."[173] She joined various sparks from her recent thinking into a creed at once ethical and aesthetic: "I feel real strongly about being a part of life, rather than separate from it. I have a feeling that, at this moment of history, artists have been narrowed into a remote position—outside of life & thus able to only make art about art about art—out of contact with themselves or their community. Maybe artists have to be like congress people—representatives of the needs, feelings, & aspirations of a group of people. At least that's what I want to be—to speak of the longings & yearnings & aspirations of women."[174]

Two of the projected canvases for *Reincarnation Triptych* were finished—*Mme. de Staël* and *George Sand*—leaving the third unresolved. Her friend Isabel Welsh reminded her about Virginia Woolf's "brooding English quality" and set her to rereading Woolf: her essays on Austin, Brontë, Eliot, and Wollstonecraft; her book *3 Guineas,* "a Feminist tract," wrote Chicago; "& I re-read *To the Lighthouse,* an extraordinary book."[175] She recalled in Bellingham reading Marder's book on Woolf, "which analyzed the relationship between her feminism & her work. It gave me a lot of new insight into Woolf & my day's reading today. Showed me how her feminism pervaded *To the Lighthouse.* Mr. Ramsey is certainly the unfeminized male—the male whose masculinity, out of contact with his humanity, has led culture to its present madness. When Mr. Ramsey loses Mrs. Ramsey, his final connection with the feminine is cut off. Anyway, her novel never is simple polemic, but is a series of transformed levels of reality, beautiful in themselves, themselves & symbolic simultaneously."[176]

To the Lighthouse (1927) takes place on two days ten years apart, looking forward to and meditating upon the Ramsay family's jaunt to the island beacon and the emotions entailed. The motif of the painter Lily Briscoe's struggle with the creative process enabled Woolf to address gender stereotypes: "Charles Tansley used to say that, she remembered, women can't paint, can't write."[177] Chicago could identify with such a struggle, having herself encountered plenty of men who were as insecure and condescending as the young philosopher Tansley. If only she could address these issues in her art.

The elusive and brilliant Lou Andreas-Salomé had to make way for lucid, tragic Woolf on the third piece of *Reincarnation Triptych* in order "to make her symbolic of a woman who had broken thru into a female form language, one typified by light & transparency, like O'Keefe [*sic*] & Nin & me. There would be a trace of the square left, remnant of damage done to her (to me) in the struggle to be herself (myself)."[178] Around the squared borders of the delicately spray-painted canvas, she inscribed: "*Virginia Woolf*—first woman to forge a female form language in literature. Conscious to the point of agony, she controlled her anger, yet did not emerge undamaged from her struggle to balance the excesses of masculine culture with feminine values."

By July 4 *Virginia Woolf* was finished and the triptych complete. Chicago sought again to capture in words the drama she tried to embody—damage imaged—in pictorial form: "both the intensity & integration with the brooding and damage. The center square is there, but receding, leaving damage, but the image is integrated & almost whole; combining areas of pure transparency with grayer, more opaque areas . . . the mark of the struggle still there. I cried when I finished the last painting—it's such a strange image of where I am right now—the parts are coming together. I'm becoming integrated & whole, but the mark of my autobiography will be there, perhaps forever."[179]

Intensifying her quest to express women's aspirations in ways both "beautiful in themselves, and themselves symbolic," Chicago picked up yet another thread from the project sketched back in March, when she first envisioned painting her vaginal butterflies on plates, but also looked to using embroidery and other traditional media.[180] At a dinner party given by a collector in L.A., she met Murray Pepper, who owned fabric stores and said that embroidery machines cost thousands of dollars, but that she could use the one he intended to purchase. Before exploring the offer, she finished a fourth queen painting in the *Great Ladies* series—*Queen Victoria,* which she described as "both steely & repressed." She would extend the series by two: *The Liberation of the Great Ladies* and *The Transformation.*[181]

Chicago allowed Raven to persuade her to rejoin Womanspace, which was supposed, then, to join with their projected Feminist Studio Workshop in a new Woman's Building, to be located in the old edifice of the Chouinard Art School, which had evolved into CalArts. The new space would also feature a women's bookstore and a restaurant. The name was meant to reclaim the historical precedent of the Woman's Building, the pavilion at the 1893 World's Columbian Exposition that Nancy Youdelman had first brought to Chicago's attention in class in Fresno. Chicago imagined organizing a show of china painting at Womanspace. In the meantime she tried "a little consciousness-raising" at the meeting of the China Painting Association, getting the women to vote to give a scholarship to women only.[182]

When Womanspace, led by Westcoast, pulled back from its commitment to join them, Chicago, Raven, and de Bretteville decided to rent the old

Chouinard building themselves and sublet some of the space. Their need was urgent since the Feminist Studio Workshop opened in September, holding classes with thirty women in de Bretteville's living room. With the Woman's Building clearly on her mind, Chicago considered getting one of her more established friends, the collector Stanley Grinstein or the artist Sam Francis, to sign for them. She recorded in her journal that the women in Womanspace had anxiety about being connected with her. "It's too bad how deep social conditioning is—that a powerful woman is by definition a bad woman & must be avoided at all costs."[183]

Chicago heard that Johanna Demetrakas had completed her film on *Womanhouse* and that her colleague's hassling had caused its maker to leave Schapiro on the cutting-room floor. "Mimi could never learn to trust women & so always tried to dominate them," Chicago reflected. "In return, they turned on her. Johanna & I would both have honored her, but she couldn't trust either of us." Ambivalent, Chicago could be variously sad for Schapiro or amused by her antics, but at other times the motherly image would induce her to write how she thought of and missed "Mimi."[184]

Still meditating on the damage inflicted by male mores on women's creative potential, Chicago plotted another new series—each work on "a woman in history who was trapped in her circumstances and though she achieved, could never really transcend."[185] Although she anticipated a "madhouse" in the fall, what with moving into the new studio, starting the workshop, and the Woman's Building, and getting her own book going, she now felt that she was about to make her major contribution. She had the sense that the next five years would represent a big struggle but that the goals, when reached, would be very worthwhile.[186] Almost exactly one year earlier she had been less confident about what five years would mean as she ventured into china painting. Now with the insights and mastery from two sets of heroic canvases and themes, she could be less worried about taking on the further challenge of embroidery. She was dreaming anxious dreams that stemmed, not from her studio, but from the perennial challenges posed by her commitment to artistic community for women's art: "I had a lot of feelings this week about not wanting this whole new struggle to begin—about wanting to die &/or cop-out. It's really hard to keep on struggling—to push oneself forward—farther & farther—& yet, there's no going back & no standing still."[187]

Besides her china plates, to which she dedicated Saturdays, Chicago had a vague idea of exploring embroidery through her core content of eroticism, using the proffered embroidery machine. To free herself to explore, she inquired about going to Minneapolis in January to teach for a month "in order to make enough money for the rest of the year."[188] Even if money were no object, getting her book published and getting the workshop and the Woman's Building organized as "a public center for Women's culture" would still take time from her new project.[189]

The first cohort of the Feminist Studio Workshop (FSW) who gathered in de Bretteville's living room came mostly from California but some from as far away as New York, where Maria Karras had heard Chicago's presentation at SUNY Buffalo in January: "She spoke to our experience—the idea of connecting art to personal experience was revolutionary—and about using content."[190] Karras recalls that Chicago engaged the undergraduates in a conscious-raising exercise, where each student had to say "something personal." When Karras told of moving out of the coed house where she had been living and not being allowed to remove her own telephone because a male student aggressively insisted she leave it behind, Chicago organized a group of women to accompany Karras, and they went and retrieved her phone. This represented an "empowering experience" so compelling that Karras, who was graduating, began working as a waitress to save enough money to move to L.A. and enroll in the FSW. The workshop arranged for another student, Ginger Canzoneri, to meet Karras at the airport and provide lodging until she found a place to rent.

Another arrival, Cheryl Swannack, came after taking part in a three-day workshop with Chicago at New Mexico State University at Las Cruces, traveling from her MFA program at the University of Tulsa.[191] Two graduate students at Las Cruces, Christe Kruse and Susan E. King, who had been teaching a course on women artists, invited Chicago. Kruse had come to New Mexico from the Maryland Institute of Art in Baltimore, where she encountered "men sitting around the studio drinking beer." Already married, separated, and the mother of a small child, Kruse had heard about the CalArts program at the Corcoran conference. She wanted to go there but found the tuition too expensive and felt she could afford the $750 at FSW.[192]

The shock for Karras, Swannack, and others was that the FSW had no facility of its own. From Sheila de Bretteville's living room in the Silver Lake neighborhood of L.A., they moved to the old Chouinard building, which needed major renovation, from sanding floors to painting bathrooms. Karras, now a portrait photographer, recalls that this was an "incredible experience" and that as a result she can now easily handle remodeling projects and work with contractors. "Judy Chicago," she says, "played a pivotal role in the way that my life unfolded."[193]

Laurel Klick, whom Judy first taught at Fresno, then helped come to CalArts, also joined that first cohort, as did another CalArts veteran, Susan

Mogul, now a video artist. She recalls that Chicago would say, "'Okay, I'll do this speaking engagement if two of my students can present their work too.' . . . We were encouraged to be very public. There wasn't this concept of waiting until you were ready and your work was polished. Being in the Feminist Studio Workshop was all about moving out into the world."[194]

After reading about Chicago in an issue of *Ms.* while doing her laundry, Linda Yaven decided to enroll in the workshop, having already graduated from the California College of Arts and Crafts in San Francisco. She recalls that at first she stayed in de Bretteville's house. For her, Chicago was "visionary, tenacious, committed, and intuitive."[195] She also remembers that Chicago invited her to bring her drawings to her studio for a monthly critique and asked her, "How do you want me to critique your work? Tough or gentle?" "Judy was great to me. She gave me a way to articulate my vision," says Yaven, whose efforts were rewarded by a show at the year's end at the 707 Gallery on La Cienega, where Chicago herself had shown.[196]

What students got from the Feminist Studio Workshop probably depended on what they brought by way of background and expectations, how open they were to new experience. At least two, Yaven and Karras, managed to get MFA degrees for their work in the FSW from Goddard College's satellite campus in Los Angeles. To Laurel Klick, the workshop was "truly amazing"; she found that the building, set around a courtyard, "invited interaction."[197] She took to heart Judy's lesson to "go for it" and became one of the first two women in her field of "visual effects" in the film industry, winning an Emmy award for her work.

But by October 7, with all the tensions of getting the new program going, Chicago had taken to staying in bed. Exhausted and crying, she thought that she was having a "nervous breakdown." The doctor, who prescribed bedrest, did not know if she had a low-grade infection or nervous exhaustion or both. "I'm afraid I'm suffering from a profound failure of nerve," she wrote. "I keep wishing I were *really* sick—dying, in fact—I want out something terrible—Out, away, enough, over—I've had it. I can't take it anymore. I feel compressed, overloaded, overwhelmed—I don't know where to start—there's so much to do."[198] She felt paralyzed and unable to work, yet she realized, "The more I grow as a person, the larger my ideas become, & the larger the framework I have to build to accommodate those ideas."[199]

Rebellious at the continual challenge of having to create her own avenues for her art to enter society, Chicago no longer wanted to have to organize her own gallery in order "to show in it, to have to organize a building of women's art so that that gallery will have a context, train other women artists to do the same thing—write a book, then have to start a publishing company to get it published, raise money to do that, then have to deal with starting a distribution system in order to get it distributed. It's too much—it's not fair."[200] She noted that men "who are far less visionary, far less talented, who do far less work, of far less quality—are supported, helped, promoted by the various mechanisms of the social structure."[201] Chicago realized that for the past four years she had "made her own job bigger & bigger," her needs expanding until she felt "crushed by the weight of what I've made for myself."[202] She wrote in her journal that she was feeling "DESPAIR, ANGER, ANGUISH."[203]

Two weeks later, in both body and mind, she had picked herself up. Postponing her venture into erotic embroidery, she was working on the projected homage to women who, though accomplished, "could never really transcend." It would grow into the six drawings forming the series *Compressed Women Who Yearned to Be Butterflies.* The first she named after Margaret Fuller, the nineteenth-century American journalist who helped inspire the movement for women's rights: "The reason I chose the theme was because I realized that it is *not only women* whose lives are compressed, but *most people.* However, the society resists dealing with women's experience . . . recognizing it, even though *most* people have lives that are closer to those described in my drawings than like the macho, heroic lives described in popular culture. But, the society is invested in fantasy . . . and to deal with women and women's feelings and experiences in a real way is to confront the real circumstances of human lives."[204] This, she believed, would "break through mythology to plainness, fear, frustration, struggle, terror . . . all the real things that inform our real lives. To identify with a woman is to recognize her humanity and through that recognition, one's own."[205]

From the drawings she opted to make a suite of lithographs at a Fresno shop, where Faith Wilding had apprenticed herself to Chuck Chesnut, who had been a colleague at Fresno. After tinkering with the conception of some of the drawings, Chicago spent most of the month of December working on their lithographic stones.

As the opening of the Woman's Building neared, Chicago remained of more than one mind. She was glad that one of its first shows would include her, yet she felt alienated, longing just to retreat to her studio to work all day. She blamed her discontent on "that 3 yr. old Judy-Pudy, craving the limelight"[206]; yet beyond that, as she put in some last touches helping to ready the building, she recognized that part of her still was committed to freeing the "Art Scene" from pervasive male dominance.[207]

She also longed to get her book published and felt dismay when Georgia O'Keeffe refused permission to reproduce any of her art, claiming that she did not consider herself to be a "woman artist."[208] Chicago had wanted to reproduce three canvases by O'Keeffe: *Black Iris I* (1926), *Grey Line with Black, Blue and Yellow* (c. 1923), and *Jimson Weed* (1932).

On another trip to her home city, where Lloyd had a show of his work, Judy found a gallery to handle her prints and give them a show the following spring. Through Ellen Lanyon, she also arranged a show of her paintings at Walter Kelly's gallery. She was suddenly selling her work with regularity. One of her queens, *Catherine the Great,* appealed to two new friends and patrons: Susan Rennie, a political scientist in love with history, and Kirsten Grimstad, a writer with a background in German literature. They sought out Chicago on the advice of their mutual friend, Isabel Welsh, by then a political scientist and activist in feminist circles. Rennie and Grimstad produced *The Women's Survival Catalog,* a compendium of alternative women's institutions; and its royalties made it possible for them to purchase *Catherine*—a painting that Lloyd had wanted himself.

When the future patrons first tried to contact her, Chicago had not responded, so they dropped by the Pacoima house, which stood in a dusty farming area in rapid transition to working-class suburb, and knocked on the door. Both recall that an unassuming woman came to the door wearing a T-shirt emblazoned JUDY CHICAGO; beyond they glimpsed some of the *Great Ladies.* A strong friendship sprang up on the spot, and the visitors determined right then that one of the *Ladies* would be theirs.[209]

The Woman's Building opened to a crowd of five thousand people on November 28, 1973. It housed the Feminist Studio Workshop, the Sisterhood Bookstore, the Associated Women's Press, the Los Angeles Feminist Theater, Women's Improvisation, and several political groups, including the National Organization for Women (NOW) and the Women's Liberation Union. The exhibition spaces included Grandview I and II (cooperative galleries, both named for the boulevard on which the building was located), Gallery 707 (which had been private), and Womanspace, which did in the end make the move from its old location in a former laundromat, though it lasted only eighteen more months. The Woman's Building also eventually housed Arlene Raven and Ruth Iskin's Center for Feminist Art Historical Studies and Sheila de Bretteville's Women's Graphic Center.

Linda Yaven, who lived nearby in Santa Monica, recalls that Chicago and Hamrol gave her a ride to the opening. She arrived at their house in time to see Lloyd connecting the clasp of Judy's necklace, which she wore with a dress for the occasion, abandoning her combat boots. But boots it had been when she pitched in and helped lead the campaign to renovate the building. She had even sanded floors in the Grandview Gallery, where her own show would open, and elsewhere around the building.

When Chicago installed her show, she had planned to use wooden letters, but Raven suggested writing directly on the walls. Thus this show of her *Great Ladies* and *Reincarnation Triptych* (Figure 17) became her first "installation." It took her two full days, working with help from Faith Wilding and a few others in the workshop. The text began: "*The Great Ladies,* begun in the fall of 1972, completed in the summer of 1973; these women represent themselves, aspects of myself, and various ways in which women have accommodated themselves to the constraints of their circumstances."[210] She went on to supply some of the cultural context in which she worked:

> Some years ago I began to read women's literature, study women's art and examine the lives of women who lived before me. I wanted to find role models, to discover how my predecessors had dealt with their oppression as women. I was also searching for clues in their work, clues that could aid me in my art. I wanted to speak out of my femaleness; to make art out of the very thing that made me the "other" in male society. I developed an increasing identification with other women, both those who lived before me and those who, like me, felt the need for a female support community. Together we build an alternative institution—the Woman's Building. My paintings can only be fully understood in this new context we have made. I want to thank all those who helped me install my show. This was the first time I've received such remarkable support, and I feel honored to be a part of the reappearance of the Woman's Building, 80 years after it was first established in my home town.[211]

The concepts of the Woman's Building "were all there in microcosm in that funky community theater [in Fresno]—& now we're here—& I say *we* advisedly—because somewhere during those years the I became a we—& I'm a part of a We now—& I can't believe I've done it. I mean that I've realized my dream to be a part of a We—in the sense of a social, not a personal context."[212]

Ladies and *Reincarnation* garnered many enthusiastic comments. An exception was Paul Brach, who disapproved of her show, confirming her view that he represented all that she was against.[213] The reviewer for the feminist newspaper *Sister* pronounced her "one of the foremost artists of our day."[214] Melinda Terbell praised *Great Ladies* in *ARTnews* for its "intense impact" and considered *Reincarnation Triptych* even more successful.[215] Afterward Chicago admitted to some journalists that she had been apprehensive about showing *Great Ladies:* "Everybody was going to find out that what I really thought about, what I was really interested in and what I really concerned myself with was what other women had done—women's biographies, women's histories and my life as a woman—and there was no place in art for that. I thought everybody would put me down; everybody thought it was terrific."[216]

A breath of approval encouraged Chicago to think that maybe she might take things a little more slowly: "I want to enjoy this process I'm in now—as it is the PRIME OF MY LIFE and I'M GOING TO RISK ALL."[217] In fact, three of her projects had been on hold: she was still not set to fire porcelain, had not yet tried to use an embroidery machine, and had not returned to the Fresno lithography shop. She thought of giving herself a "few months to dream."[218] Weeks later her new literary agent, Peri Winkler, telephoned that she thought she had sold the book to Doubleday and wanted to sell it to the movies. The editor who bought it, Betty Prashker, recalls her reasons: "I thought it was an honest, straightforward memoir that pointed up the difficulties of being an artist and a woman in a man's world. I liked her no-nonsense approach to art and life. I had read about Judy in various publications before I read the manuscript, therefore I was aware of her and of her art. I had published a number of books during that time on women's issues, and some of them—*Sexual Politics* [Kate Millet] and *Women and Madness* [Phyllis Chesler]—were quite successful"[219] She also came to enjoy "working with Judy. I think she is brave, talented and full of energy. Loretta Barrett was running Anchor Books at the time, and she agreed to do the paperback."[220]

The book news, which at first seemed only tentative, arrived just after the dealer Walter Kelly brutally rejected her work, telling her that he could not respond to her paintings. Kelly had scheduled a show and had her ship two paintings to his Chicago gallery after she showed him some drawings during a stopover on her way back from the College Art meeting, this year in Detroit, where she had appeared with de Bretteville on a panel organized by Raven. Kelly's rejection particularly hurt because she greatly wanted the show so that her family and old friends could catch up with her work.

Not till the end of January 1974 did Chicago get back to Fresno to work in Chesnut's shop on the *Compressed Women* lithographs, which she explained as derived from her reading of women's biographies and fiction: each was "named after a woman of the past, and each represents one of the limited choices available to women."[221] In addition to her first subject, *Margaret Fuller,* she chose to represent *Mary Lamb,* an English writer whose brother took credit for her work; *Mme. Deronda* (Figure 20), who grapples with her genius in George Eliot's *Daniel Deronda* and who "felt compelled to make a choice between her life as a woman and as an artist"; *Lily Bart,* the young woman in Edith Wharton's novel *The House of Mirth* who is sacrificed to the false ideals of New York social life or, as Chicago said, "couldn't conceive of surviving except by being dependent on a man. When she couldn't find a man, she killed herself"; *Elisabet Ney,* the German sculptor who, before immigrating to the United States, became the first woman to attend the Munich Art Academy; and *Paula Modersohn-Becker,* the German painter who died in childbirth at age thirty-one, "her life and accomplishments," in Chicago's view, "cut short by her conflicts as a woman."[222] Chicago considered that Ney worked "twice as hard as any man would ever have to" and "managed to make a very successful career," only to stop "working for twenty years."[223]

The process of moving her studies from drawings to stone did not go smoothly. "Chuck, who bragged to me about his expertise, lost one of the stones—meaning that he destroyed one of the drawn images, which happens in lithography & has happened to me before. I was relaxed about it but he wasn't."[224] Taking somewhat of a master-apprentice approach, he objected to Chicago's collaborating directly with the young people who worked in the shop. He wanted her to discuss everything directly with him. They argued over their contract, and a shouting match ensued. Chicago turned off the heat in his studio, opened the door, and spoke directly to his employees, Chesnut complains.[225] Although she badly wanted to make these prints, she found him "overbearing, domineering," and unresponsive to her attempts to get over their conflict. Completely crushed, she felt that she had no choice but to leave. Tears followed, but she told herself, "Ten years ago in similar circumstances, a man whom I needed to help me made me feel humiliated as a woman—I allowed him to do it so that I could finish my prints. This time, I felt I couldn't—particularly since it seems to me that he was trying to force me to leave by being horrible. I thought that maybe he felt inadequate because he lost that stone after bragging so much, but who knows?"[226] She concluded the series "in a fit of feeling," by writing on the drawings for the prints, on which she had already written notes about the women and technical notes for the execution of the prints. She now drew "analogies between the lives of the women who the images are named after, their inability to be realized within male society, & the stopping of the project of the prints."[227] Lucy Lippard observed that these emotional eruptions "ironically enhance their effect."[228] The abstract images draw power from the pain expressed by the written texts.

Between bruises and blessings, Chicago recalled Rose Kennedy's dictum: "When you get a lot, you pay a lot."[229] In February she addressed Doubleday's request that she expand her book and discuss her marriages. She was willing to compromise but suspected that they might be using her book "to buttress heterosexuality."[230] At the same time she poured the pain from the rejected show and abortive try at lithography into a new series on a large scale, which she called *Rejection Drawings* and counted as a further, fundamental breakthrough in her laborious quest, getting beyond even the achievements of *Reincarnation Triptych* and *Let It All Hang Out*.

At last in these drawings Chicago, freeing herself of rigid structures and grids, felt able to work directly. She hailed a break with the past (including the constrictive matrix of her homage to Schapiro) that would allow her to press on with her suspended projects in stitchery and painted china. For the first time, she wrote, "I was able to *clearly draw the content* I've been involved with. The Butterfly plates will be done like that."[231] In order to operate at this deep level, she had had to virtually shut herself up in her studio doing nothing but work. The imposed isolation was facilitated by Lloyd's absence since the end of March, when he had gone to work on a piece in Bellingham. Yet the sense of achievement made her feel more than ever "alienated—even from the female community as I felt that they couldn't actually comprehend the place I had reached—& I still believe that. Arlene was threatened by my abrupt withdrawal from our relationship, but a withdrawal that was made imperative by the intensity of the inner necessity I felt—a necessity stronger than anything I had ever felt before."[232]

The way to the breakthrough had not been easy or straight. The first *Rejection Drawing* provoked a critique from Lucy Lippard, who "brought up her feeling that there was a gap between my rhetoric & my imagery. I got upset but was also glad she said it. It forced me to examine the structure in my work & I began to try & work through it. In so doing, I had to struggle with my fear that I would be rejected if I exposed my real feeling."[233] To get at those feelings, Chicago wrote on the drawings about her emotional struggle. On a print that she made from the central drawing she explained that the series had been originally inspired by several experiences in Chicago, "one with a male dealer, the other with a male collector, both of whom made me feel rejected and diminished as a woman."[234] She continued: "I decided to deal with my feelings of rejection and in so doing confronted the fact that I was still hiding the real subject matter of my art behind a geometric structure as I was afraid that if I revealed my true self, I would be rejected. In the first drawing, I asked: 'How does it feel to be rejected?' and answered: 'It's like having your flower split open.' In the last drawing I asked: 'How does it feel to expose your real identity?' and answered: 'It's like opening your flower and no longer being afraid it will be rejected.' "[235] Pointing to the central piece in what had grown into the *Rejection Quintet*, Chicago added, "In this the transitional image, I 'peeled back' the structure to reveal the formerly hidden form. What a relief to finally say: 'Here I am, a woman, with a woman's body and a woman's point of view.' "[236] She was describing "the

Butterfly Vagina," which she asserted "is what my real content is."[237] "The statement is a vaginal form." she persisted. "In its development, the vagina becomes a cave and then a butterfly. It goes from being passive to active. It is probably the first time in history that there is a feminine image that is active, a feminine self that is active. If you think about Georgia O'Keeffe's flowers for example, they are strong and powerful, but they are not active. They cannot get off that canvas and fly away."[238] She also admitted that "I could never have made that breakthrough if I had not been able to experience myself in an environment that was not male-dominated," by which she meant the Fresno program, the L.A. female community, and now the Woman's Building, despite her need to work in isolation and her ambivalence toward the group.[239]

As spring came on in 1974 Chicago resumed her migrations, giving talks about her work at campuses around Seattle, so that she could get a free trip to see Lloyd in Bellingham, dropping by to visit family before heading for Philadelphia to speak at a conference advertised as Focus on Women in the Visual Arts and see a show of her six *Compressed Women* at the Kenmore Gallery, whose dealer, though male, had given a very positive response.

Held up at the airport on her way to Philadelphia, she reopened the journal neglected since February. She told herself that she had made the stop in her home city, despite her recent hurt there, to "retreat into my childhood—to escape the loneliness that my consciousness, my talent, & my recent breakthrough have thrust on me," but she found that impossible.[240] Her mother and brother had long since moved to L.A., but she still had cousins whom she wanted to see.

She totted up sums from a difficult year—"the Workshop, the Building, the print project, the hassles, the book, my struggle in my studio"—yet found herself "physically, psychically, emotionally, & personally free to be & to make the Butterfly." So she sensed she was "on the brink of my major work. I can feel it. I'm ready now—& I feel weak & tired & unable & unwilling & frightened & like I DON'T WANT TO BE SO GODDAMN LONELY—& yet I must or everything I've been doing will have been an illusion."[241]

Her first solo show on the East Coast opened without her because of the flight delay. Next day she went with Arlene Raven to a large exhibition of women's art at the Museum of the Philadelphia Civic Center titled "Women's Work," where she registered a recurrent distress, feeling "quite alienated from the sensibility expressed by most of the women—whose orientation was clearly to get *into* the male system by making mainstream art. Mimi was in the show & I wasn't—which pretty much sums up the whole problem between us."[242]

As ever, she found shocking the number of people in the women's art movement who were only invested in "'making it' & not in changing values." "I felt a bit sick that all the work I had done had been predicated on the idea of altering consciousness & making a space for women to work out of their own experience—& a lot of women are rejecting that space, preferring instead the cramped, dehumanized, victimized, powerless, hierarchical & tyrannical structure of the male art world—Unbelievable!"[243] Despite her expressed beliefs, Chicago herself still yearned and tried to show at art galleries that were owned by men. When they rejected her work, she felt the sting and responded with bitterness. In order to show her own work, she bridged the gap between what she said she wanted and what she felt she had to do. Thus her judgmental attitude toward women artists who made necessary compromises to show their work seems insensitive.

At a Focus conference session, she "made a big fuss at a panel of women gallery directors, who were spouting the biggest bunch of bullshit I'd ever heard," but they responded positively, and she was happy to be "able to challenge them & then ease the situation with humor"; she let an art magazine editor, Betsy Baker, sleep over in her hotel room, and they went to the Barnes foundation next day: "fantastic collection, but too many Renoirs & too many asses for my taste"; she cited Baker's behavior—on her panel and having seen her show but saying nothing to her, only later confiding what she thought to Lucy Lippard (a known supporter, so presumably a positive judgment)—as typical of "East Coast women in the art establishment—they are still not out-front like we are on the West Coast."[244]

As for her own Philadelphia presence, *Art in America* published Judith Stein's praise for her "masterful control of a variety of mediums," "sophisticated language of color-fades and rainbows," as well as her expansion of the idea of the use of writing as a "visual component of the work itself, compelling us to spend time 'reading' the image in several ways."[245] Stein found the six drawings for *Compressed Women* "powerful," especially *Lily Bart,* about which she wrote: "Here the impact of the very formal pictorial language is heightened by Wharton's writing. Wharton's paragraphs which cross the circle image in neat rows calmly describe Bart's suicide; the additional word 'DEAD' violates this space three times, serving both as a strike mark for the aborted project and as an emblem of Bart's decision."[246]

From Philadelphia, Susan Rennie and Kirsten Grimstad picked up Chicago and drove her to New York, where they gave a party in her honor, attended by about 150 people. Among them were New York feminists she had met before and was happy to catch up with, like the writers Ti-Grace Atkinson and Alix Kates Shulman, but also new contacts—Barbara Seaman, Susan Brownmiller,

Kate Stimpson, Rita Mae Brown.[247] Chicago wrote on the wall around her *Catherine the Great.* They set up a continuous show of Chicago's work and had her give a talk, which was so well received that many women "felt *compelled* to buy a picture—even though they had never bought art before."[248] She sold two more of the paintings of queens: *Christina of Sweden,* to Janet Bajan, a New York stockbroker and a lesbian member of New York Radical Feminists, who had never before owned art but even took out a loan to pay,[249] and *Queen Victoria* to Barbara Seaman. Rita Mae Brown would also buy a drawing.[250]

In New York, Chicago handed in the final manuscript of *Through the Flower,* newly revised but minus a work by Schapiro, who refused to send a photo without first reading the text.[251] Their exchanges during the spring led Chicago to express disgust: "I tried to honor her & she wouldn't let me do what I could. Lucy mentioned that people would think that I deliberately excluded her, but I don't care. I put myself out there & she consistently rejected me."[252]

Although sisterhood had failed with Schapiro, Chicago had found common ground with other women. All but one picture from her show at the Woman's Building had now been purchased and almost all by women. It made her realize that she had connected with a new audience and created a new market by the very nature of her work: "an audience & a market that values my work *because* it expresses my womanhood . . . I must say the level of affirmation I received in the East was *fantastic* & for my ART."[253]

When Chicago had begun to show her work more than a decade earlier, she had done so within the confines of the art establishment's galleries that promoted vanguard work. She had been quick to attract serious critical attention both in California and in New York, when *Primary Structures* at the Jewish Museum featured her minimal sculpture and the Museum of Modern Art purchased one of her abstract prints for its permanent collection. After repeatedly coming up against sexism in the art establishment, however, she had taken a cue from the burgeoning women's movement and retreated to Fresno to reconsider both the kind of art she made and the nature of the art community in which she functioned.

Chicago's solutions to the problems she perceived were radical, but they were now working. Her art was no longer unreadable; in fact, she had added many clearly legible texts with feminist messages. Once-supportive male critics such as William Wilson had bristled at her overt politics, but many women responded profoundly to this new explicit work. She had sold $8,000 worth of art since 1974 began and recognized a turning point in her life: "My work is now wanted by women who are outside of the art world & the whole of my ideas are going out into the world. This means that I, as a woman artist, am escaping the constraints of the male art world & in so doing am moving to a new place. . . . I am satisfied with what I've done in this last decade & am now eager to produce the work that my struggle has given me the right to make."[254]

Unable to change the art establishment and eradicate its sexism, Chicago found a way around it. The feminist network in New York embraced her new women-centered art, finding in her work bold icons with which women in the movement could identify. On the other hand, despite much agreement about the need to rid the art establishment of sexism, local feminist artists were ambivalent. Some saw her as an important leader, while others viewed her as cutting into their territory and their market. Some women artists had rejected Chicago as a result of the essentialism controversy, which was already emerging as a significant issue by the time of the Corcoran conference. Others made common cause. Miriam Schapiro's move back to New York in 1975 would further exacerbate these tensions.

▲
Sheila de Bretteville, Judy Chicago, and Arlene Raven in the Woman's Building, 1974. Photograph by Maria Karras.

To *The Dinner Party* and History 10

The visions, trials, breakthroughs, bonding, setbacks, and paranoia of Chicago's journey from Fresno, through CalArts, and back to L.A. lofted her toward her most ambitious production, *The Dinner Party* (Figure 22). She originally conceived of a theater piece with historic women conversing. Then she shifted her vision and planned to employ one hundred painted china plates to tell heroic women's stories. As the project developed, Chicago incorporated new styles of abstraction. By the spring of 1974 she had determined "to work on smaller projects—the first one will be called *Dinner Party* or twenty-five women who were eaten alive & will consist of twenty-five painted plates presented in the context

▲

Judy Chicago working in *The Dinner Party* china-painting studio, April 1972.

of a table setting—either a long or a round table—cloth, napkins, silver, water glasses, etc. I don't know about chairs yet. In fact, there are a few aspects of the idea that are still unresolved. I'm struggling with them."[1]

Four years later Chicago would tell a newspaper reporter that she had been "at an academic dinner party when it all jelled: the men at the table were all professors, and the women all had doctorates but weren't professors. The women had all this talent, and they sat there silent while the men held forth. I started thinking that women have never had a *Last Supper*, but they have had dinner parties where they facilitated conversation and nourished the people."[2]

Chicago's connecting *The Dinner Party* to the *Last Supper* suggests the theme of reunion in the piece, not just recognition for the individual woman. The Christian Last Supper reenacts the Jewish Passover seder, which Chicago grew up celebrating at the home of one of her paternal aunts. This same aunt is present in the treasured photograph of the Cohen family seder in 1922, taken when Chicago's father was just thirteen. During the interwar years, American Jews transformed the seder "from a sacred, highly ritualistic event into a Jewish exercise in domesticity," a kind of family reunion.[3] The seder not only symbolized reunion to Chicago but also emancipation, since a main focus of the seder is the annual recitation of the story of the Jews' passage from slavery in Egypt to freedom. As Chicago conceived of her monumental chronicle of women's achievements, this theme took on increasing importance: "I decided that I would like the plate images to physically rise up as a symbol of women's struggle for freedom."[4]

At first she considered putting images on the front of the plates with writing on the back, but displaying the plates so that people could read the essential information about the women was a stumbling block. She imagined a wide range, from very famous, accomplished women forgotten by recent history to wives of famous men who sacrificed their careers, to obscure women who failed to win recognition.[5]

"Feminist art is that art which illuminates women's life experiences. You know a woman did it," she explained to a journalist.[6] Thus her thinking had evolved to combining ordinary women china painters, "who worked within the definition & sphere of women," with more famous women in political history, "who moved out of & challenged the female role, but somehow the larger condition of women contained them all & allowed their contribution, big or small, to be swallowed up."[7] She destined Susan B. Anthony and Elizabeth Cady Stanton for the head of the table because their joint efforts helped overturn an array of laws severely restrictive of women. Other less well-known women would join them, introduced by historical essays on the backs of the plates, but "all will be ultimately offered up in the dinner party metaphor—contained within domesticity, served up to be consumed. . . . The plates will be sitting up on plate racks—*rising up*, so to speak from their confinement—but not off the table yet."[8]

Chicago projected that she would make drawings for the plates when she went to stay with Lloyd in Bellingham, Washington, in June 1974; then back in L.A. she would start painting the china and finish by the end of the summer. As for the embroidery, which she envisaged for a tablecloth, she knew that she would need to take some classes. She resolved to give herself whatever time would be needed and think about the ideas, letting them "lead me where they will."[9]

"I'm very excited about this piece," she wrote. "I feel it's a big step & allows me the full range of my talents, ideas, & knowledge."[10] She continued to research the different women china painters in libraries in the Philadelphia Museum and again in L.A. She allotted just three hours to make each drawing for a plate, hoping to give her intuition more play and to work more loosely than she usually did, without the restrictive, geometrical systems she had used. She hoped to "make butterfly images that are hard, strong, soft, passive, opaque, transparent—all different states—& I want them to all have cunts so they'll be female butterflies & at the same time be shells, flowers, flesh, forest—all kinds of things simultaneously."[11]

This early decision to deploy what she called "the butterfly/cunt" motif would cause enormous controversy. Images of female genitalia have existed for centuries in many non-Western cultures, particularly at fertility shrines, where together with phalluses they serve as symbols for the perpetuation of life. Standards for public display in the United States, however, reflect the legacy of the Puritans, along with the Christian story of the Virgin birth. At the same time some of the same art critics who reject images of female genitalia as shameful have deemed acceptable corresponding images of phalluses (sometimes thinly veiled or metaphoric, such as Brancusi's *Princess X*) as well as renditions of female genitalia produced by men from their perspective—from Courbet in the nineteenth century to Duchamp in the twentieth.

The "butterfly/cunt" motif was still on Chicago's agenda when she joined Hamrol in Bellingham in May, planning to produce the drawings for the plates. She had purchased plates of white porcelain, which she planned to paint from the drawings on her return to L.A. She had given up the idea of writing text on the plates' backs; nor did she want to write over the designs on the front. Her china-painting teacher, Mim (Miriam Halpern), whom she met through the sculptor Bruria, suggested making a menu to describe the women, and this seemed to the best solution so far. Chicago credited Halpern with helping her to break down the basic components of china painting so that she was able to adapt this process for her own work.[12]

In Bellingham Chicago found Hamrol to be "CRAZY." She asked herself, "Why are men such big babies? I'm beginning to think it's biological."[13] She had expected to pass a good time together, even bringing with her an adorable new kitten, which she had named Orlando, after the character in Virginia Woolf's novel about a young English nobleman who mysteriously falls asleep and changes into a woman.[14]

The work schedule she had laid out soon proved arbitrary and unreal. Even working in monochrome, she could not complete a drawing in the allotted three hours, although sometimes four or five were enough. One took two full days. Still, by June 14, though due to go back to L.A. in six days, she had done ten and was working on five more, with results that by turns satisfied and displeased. She would focus and set clearer problems to get at "specific feeling states—making the images grow out of a feeling." Otherwise, the images went "flat & decorative. The only way they work is if they're infused with emotion, & that means I have to be 'inside' and not wandering off thinking about something else."[15]

Hamrol turned "alternately nasty, withdrawn, hostile, angry, self-preoccupied etc."[16] She sent him off to a motel until he finally opened to tell her what was on his mind. Away from Chicago, he said, he felt more important in the world and liked it. He had felt the need for relations with less forceful women every year of the ten they had shared. His inability to express his needs to her hurt Chicago, who still considered his admission a breakthrough: they made love for several days and affirmed their need for each other, although she regretted his habit of holding in his feelings, leaving her unaware.[17]

Hamrol's new demands coincided with a renewed desire to put aside feminist politics for work and personal life: "I think I'm ready to try to integrate the fact that I'm a woman & its implications into the entire range of my life—I have faced the fact that the world will never apprehend me—because of my sex & *because of my genius,* apart from my sex. I am struggling now to face the alienation, isolation, loneliness, misunderstanding, distortion, etc. & to try to go about my life & my work."[18] For the moment Chicago had had enough of the women's movement and told herself to give more to Hamrol, whom she loved, to "slowly disengage myself from the world. Over the next few years I'm going to increase my art life & decrease my political life. I have a level of commitment that I will maintain, but I will not extend it."[19] She feared that if she did not pull back, she would ruin her health, deplete her energy, and fragment her talent. She hoped to have the strength to put the "aching need for recognition behind me & get on with the important things."[20]

Arlene Raven arrived in Bellingham, both to see Hamrol's new sculpture and to go with him and Chicago to Vancouver see work by Emily Carr, whose journal Chicago had been reading. Raven already knew about Hamrol's extramarital affairs, both because Schapiro and Brach had told her about his reputation and also because he had propositioned her once at the Grinsteins' home.[21] But she could not have imagined that all this suppressed conflict had come out just before their meeting and trip together.

On their return from Canada, Chicago and Hamrol discussed and agreed how she would schedule her time so that he would be able to feel satisfied. She would have five and half days in her studio and three nights a week for meetings, classes, and friends. It was less than she wanted, but she was trying to meet his needs.[22]

In her studio she pressed on with *The Dinner Party.* Painting the first ten plates wasn't easy: "horrendous & frustrating. It's slow, tedious, & I was having a lot of technical difficulties," she wrote in her journal.[23] Wanting to do some of them over, she now estimated that the work might stretch to eight if not eighteen months. Until the first ten were painted, she would not do studies for the rest. Working out in the gym at the end of a day relieved some of the tension and tedium of the china painting. Basically the freedom to go deeply into her art was a thrill. Through the art—rather than through political organizing—she now hoped to give to the women's movement.

In an interview with Ruth Iskin, Chicago spoke out about politics and art:

> The issue of politics for me arises at the point where my work interfaces with culture; it does not arise at the point of origin in my studio. I never think about politics when I make my art; rather I think about being true to my own impulses, and for a woman to be true to her own impulses is, at this point in history, a political act. . . . What I challenge is the idea that masculinity is inherently better than femininity; that hardness is better than softness, that defensiveness is better than vulnerability, and that violence is better than sharing. The assertion of womanhood is a challenge to all those values that allow war, dehumanization, rape, and art that lacks relationship with reality to continue.[24]

Chicago learned that the owners of the structure that housed the Woman's Building had sold it, displacing all the organizations that rented space there, including the Feminist Studio Workshop. She felt relief, since she had decided that she wanted to put her energies into her own work. She and Lloyd now had enough money to get along on, so she had already decided to derive no income from the Feminist Studio Workshop during the next year. She would discontinue her weekly meetings, just visit sessions to rap biweekly, and make herself available one day a month. Meanwhile at the Woman's Building she was showing *Rejection Drawings* in the exhibition called *Open Wall* because any female artist could show there, along with photographs by Edie Gross, Lita Albuquerque,

Vaughan Rachel, Beverly Parker, and Diane Gelon. Gelon's images of partial views of her face struck a reviewer as "the best photographs here, [which] serve as feminist soulmates to Chicago's drawings. There is an ambivalence in these photographs, a simultaneous concealing and revealing of the artist as woman."[25] The *Rejection Drawings* themselves won praise: "Because of Chicago's exquisite draftsmanship and hypnotic storytelling ability, the images are mesmerizing."[26]

The five *Rejection Drawings* so moved Tracy O'Kates, who hailed from Chicago, that she bought them for $8,000 and offered to donate them to the museum of Judy's choice. Rejected by the Art Institute where she had first studied, *Rejection* found acceptance in her adopted state at the San Francisco Museum of Modern Art. Also in the Bay Area, the Oakland Museum sought to commission another of Chicago's *Atmospheres*—her first in four years. Initially reluctant, she warmed to the idea of adapting one of her new butterfly designs, to be outlined with road flares.

By the end of August 1974 Chicago had made good on her resolve to resign from the Feminist Studio Workshop and the Woman's Building (but not from the corporation).[27] After all she had struggled to achieve, she intentionally turned away in order to focus on her own artwork. "There's no room for that in the structure we have built in L.A., because everybody has to be equal in leadership," she complained.[28] She would have liked to remain involved and do much, much less.

Arlene Raven saw the situation somewhat differently. She observed that Chicago had broken with the sense, instilled by her father, "that making art was not enough." "So now—I've *been* my father," she reflected, "—acted out his/my organizational leadership abilities, affected the social structure, taught, spoken, discussed, etc.—& outgrown it—as I couldn't years ago—because he died & I couldn't automatically & normally grow past my identification with him."[29] She lamented that this society discouraged women from identification with their fathers, tainting those who tried with the "fear of becoming unfeminine. Perhaps that's what the whole Movement is about—allowing women to find out that they can be their fathers as well as their mothers."[30] Having tried social activism, she now found that the devotion and focus it required conflicted with her intense ambition to make art in her own studio.

Even as she loosened her public ties, Chicago took comfort from the fact that she could count on the alternative art community that, it might be said, she had both mothered and fathered. She no longer had to "dissemble" in her art in order to be taken seriously. She had found "some alternative to having to be denied & diminished as a woman—some alternative to the stereotypical assumptions & misperceptions that were continually being laid on me."[31] Now she wanted to take advantage of the increased mobility, opportunities, financial freedom, and ability to be herself that she had helped to create through the women's movement. She only regretted that she had not been more honest with herself and feared that she had given some of the women in the workshop the impression "that they would have to give, give, give all the time."[32]

The end of August 1974 found Chicago thinking about *The Dinner Party* in yet another way: "not as twenty-five women who were devoured—but rather as a female version of the *Last Supper*—a panoply of the greatest female figures, mythological, historical, fictional—all of whom were crucified by the fact of their sex." She further believed that each of the women she chose "could have been Christ's disciples, i.e. the 'shapers' of the world, of culture, had it not been for the fact that they were women—all of whom did, however, have an affect & exist now as the positive basis of a new concept of womanhood—one based on strength, achievement, power, & scope."[33] Tempered by experience, she would now let the piece evolve over time.

Despite the Art Institute's snub, Chicago at last showed her work in her home city: September 6–29, 1974, at Artemisia Gallery, a women's cooperative founded in 1973 by twenty-one women, among them Joy Poe and Hollis Sigler.[34] The support the women gave during installation touched Chicago. Hamrol came for the opening, and her extended family turned out. Afterward at dinner Susan Rennie and Kirsten Grimstad told Chicago's cousin Corinne that she was "the first real genius that they had ever known."[35] At this her cousin gave a quizzical look, then rose to declare that if Judy was a genius, she was "the culmination of all the various traits in the family—they had all somehow come together," meaning the intelligence of her father, the directness of her cousins, and the sensitivity and expressiveness of other family members.[36] Chicago felt that this was the most significant recognition that she could ever receive: to be acknowledged by her family, in the city where she was born, as a part of her whole life and history. To add to her sense of achievement, Emanuel Jacobson, her old teacher from the Art Institute Junior School, pronounced her work "lyrical."[37]

Chicago was relieved to have worked out her differences with Rennie and Grimstad. She had been "horrified by the kind of hateful anti-male rhetoric Susan was using";[38] now she looked forward to their moving to California the next summer to found a feminist art journal, *Chrysalis.*

Even in her hometown Chicago received reminders that not all professional women bought into feminism or feminist art. "Apart from the whole issue of propaganda art, Ms. Chicago's images cut across the ideology of equality into a form of separatism and the danger of stereotyping the female from the other side," wrote Nory Miller in the *Chicago Daily News.* "The attitude is prevalent in the women's movement, but it gives me the uneasy feeling that I'm hearing the Rev. Jesse Jackson extolling the virtues of natural rhythm."[39] Not very far from home, however, Linda Korenak reported for *Amazon (A Feminist Journal)* in Milwaukee: "Here was an artist I could really understand, and who understands me. I left energized by the experience, grateful for the release of being able to say with Judy Chicago: 'What a relief to finally say, "Here I am, a woman with a woman's body and a woman's point of view." ' "[40]

Also writing in *Amazon,* Jennie Orvino described her experience of the Artemisia show as "sensual delight and woman-centeredness, the like of which I had never known." She praised Chicago as "a woman of great talent and a pioneer of the development of the feminist point of view in art. My first exposure to her was . . . *Red Flag* . . . an extreme close-up of a woman removing a Tampax, executed with such drama and assertiveness that it seems to be 'a warrior's act.' "[41] *Red Flag* had in fact elicited heated dialogue among men and women. Arlene Raven wrote that it "revealed the woman-hating attitudes which caused viewers to be repulsed at the sight of a woman handling menstruation, an experience which most women have each and every month. It exposed sexist ignorance which resulted in misreading the tampax as a penis. . . . It explosively pointed to a subject which had been taboo, eliciting shock and rage at the audacity of the artist to bring up the embarrassing, despised topic of her, women's menstruation."[42]

After the Artemisia show Chicago and Hamrol went on to the Twin Cities, where she spent two days preparing for a workshop and show at the College of St. Catherine in St. Paul. She also planned to do a suite of prints at a new shop run by a woman who had attended the conference she had organized in 1971 at CalArts. The couple then took a much-anticipated vacation, driving through the Badlands and Black Hills of South Dakota, Yellowstone National Park in Wyoming, and southern Utah, where she found a place to get her "tablecloth for the Dinner Party."[43]

In South Dakota they inquired about purchasing property with an outdoor and indoor space and "complete psychic privacy."[44] Already looking beyond *The Dinner Party,* Chicago envisioned turning to erotic embroideries, work with porcelain, and fusing painting with sculpture. She wanted to be far away from the nuclear war that threatened to materialize in the coming decade: "I can't believe men will give up their dominance & the way things are going in this country, they may have to. At the beginning of this century, the Feminist Revolution was stopped by war, & I'm afraid it will happen again."[45] Even if there would be no war, she hoped to find some place away from the city to live at least part of the time and have her main studio. Lloyd would have a smaller studio there, but she also wanted them to buy a small industrial building in L.A., where Lloyd would have his main studio and she would have a smaller work space. Things seemed to be working out between them.

Things weren't so smooth between Chicago and the Woman's Building. She had not realized that she owed them 20 percent of the sale of the *Rejection Quintet* and had therefore not paid them. Michele Kort, then the Woman's Building manager, recalls that since Chicago had not delivered the work herself, she had failed to sign the usual contract, which stated that the building would take a 20 percent commission for any sale.[46] After the unexpected sale and upon Chicago's return, the building's women went to her studio and demanded a pledge in writing. This convinced Chicago that she despised all institutions. She felt that she had battled "the male world to learn the tools of that world & to make a place for myself; then battling in the female world to explore the nature of my femaleness & to find a way to use it in my art. Both worlds were filled with mistrust, distortion, neurotic, uninformed people who couldn't apprehend me." Although she saw many differences between the two, she felt that "underneath, they're really alike."[47] She told herself that she was "alienated from everyone who is not self-generated, mature, creative, responsible, gifted, & sensitive, & there aren't too many people like that around."[48] In the end, however, she paid what was due, in addition to the prints and cash she had already donated.

Rededicating herself to her art, Chicago anxiously worked out details for her *Atmosphere* in Oakland. The piece depended upon a male crew, since she had had to dismiss the only female pyrotechnician she could find because she turned out to be irresponsible. Entitled *A Butterfly for Oakland* (Figure 19), it consisted of an image of a butterfly, Chicago's metaphor for female form and identity, which lit up at sunset and lasted for seventeen minutes, until its bright red color, created by two hundred road flares, dissipated into smoke. It took place on October 12, 1974, as part of a show of public sculpture. Chicago said that this *Atmosphere* configured the form of "a female butterfly" who is "gentle and generous, like a woman."[49] It was visible mainly from the opposite shore of Lake Merritt. Technical difficulties kept Chicago from getting a good view of her own piece, which she witnessed only from her place with the crew and afterward in photographs. She wept at her inability to view the piece from afar and worried that it had failed, only to hear that people liked it. At the time she said she had learned a lot from this, her most complex piece to date.[50] "Can I kiss you even tho I'm a man?" the curator asked her. "And there were the usual jokes that revealed that several of the men thought I was a dyke—& it goes on & on."[51]

Given Chicago's strong attraction to men and her constant need for a man in her life, it is ironic that some who did not know her well imagined that she preferred women. She has always been relaxed about her sexuality and not particularly uptight about others' perceptions. Among her closest friends have long been a number of lesbians, including Arlene Raven. From time to time she expressed curiosity in her journals about what sex with another woman would be like. She was not afraid to experiment, but the opportunity had to be right. There was speculation at the Woman's Building as to whether Chicago had had a relationship with a woman.

Deena Metzger, who taught writing in the Woman's Building, responded to Chicago's idea of making explicit the underlying metaphor of the "Last Supper" for her *Dinner Party,* asking her who would be Judas. Not wanting to get that literal, preferring more "multilayered" meaning, Chicago returned to the idea of a menu explaining each of the figures, all of whom would be role models for the "development of a whole new woman. Perhaps," she reflected, "I need to outline what facets a truly independent woman would have & then choose women who represent all those facets."[52] She asked her friends Rennie and Grimstad to help her compile a list of the twenty-five most important women in history. She was looking forward to two whole months of work on the *Dinner Party* plates.

During this period Chicago was undergoing Rolfing, a process invented by Dr. Ida P. Rolf that claims to manipulate soft tissue to align the body and thereby reduce chronic stress.[53] Chicago felt the need to be more self-protective and not expose her thoughts to others to the same degree that she had been. She felt that she now understood why artists conceal and transform their subject matter into a personal language: to protect oneself "from the brutality of the world."[54]

She also reflected on her own teaching in relationship to the years she "spent learning to draw, to paint, to turn form in space, etc. Yet when I taught, all I taught was making art out of experience—forgetting about art training. Why? That's why we produced so few painters or sculptors—only video performance, photo people—how do you train an artist? All my ideas are up in the air now."[55] For Chicago, experience then trumped formal issues because the times merited investigating the nature of women's relationship to society. For the moment it appeared as if real change would be possible. If there was to be a revolution in women's roles, Chicago wanted her students to take part in it.

After Oakland, Chicago had to fly to Cedar Rapids, Iowa, to set up a show of her work at Coe College and give a talk, but her old anxieties about plane crashes came back to haunt her. She wanted to stay in her studio and resolve the issues around *The Dinner Party,* but she needed the money. She wondered what to say: "I'm sick to death of talking about 'My struggle as a Woman Artist.' I'll be awfully glad when my book is out & people can read it & perhaps approach me at another level."[56] Her mother, however, felt the trip was "rather meaningful," since Judy's father had been born there and his father's name was "carved in the temple there."[57] In the end, she basked in the Iowans' hospitality and enthusiasm for her work.

Increasingly she was getting annoyed with Hamrol: "Mimi once said that husbands are, by definition, boring. Maybe that's true," she told herself.[58] Then she met an artist named Bruce (at twenty-five, a decade younger than she was), who came over to purchase one of her photo offset posters called *Peeling Back*. He evidently liked what he saw because he returned a couple of times, provoking Chicago's interest. When they ran into each other at an art opening, Chicago was there with Hamrol, who "was being very draggy—complaining, & miserable," talking to a man who was constantly nasty to her and refusing to leave. So she left with Bruce and stayed out till three the next morning. Hamrol was usually the one to act this way, sometimes not coming back all night. Now it was Chicago's turn, and Bruce was willing and ready: she "felt sexually alive," she recorded, in a way she had not "for a long time."[59] On balance, she was happy to see that she could be herself with a man "even in that most vulnerable place of all—the bed."[60] It might have helped that Bruce had hung her *Peeling Back* poster, with its vaginal image, right above the bed.

She was open with Hamrol, telling him that she needed "to have some space & time" with someone else. She was beginning to empathize with male artists' sexual cravings: "it's like an insatiable urge for 'pure pleasure' after having given so much energy into work & feeling empty & used up & depleted. So I'm happy for this experience what ever happens from here."[61] Bruce (a friend of Linda Benglis) wrote to Judy from New York that he hoped his letter would find her and Lloyd "well and happy," adding: "I think I'm going to go crazy not being able to have sex (coming to you) with anyone for months. . . . I get into this sort of existential delima [*sic*] when I find myself in bed with you for some reason. You know, I think you are a very important person to me."[62] But what she called "an interesting experience" seemed to energize both her and Lloyd, whom she observed approvingly was now becoming "much more aggressive about his work."[63] This reverberated in a better relationship between them but also seemed to draw her closer to Arlene Raven, with whom, she felt, any differences were behind them, replaced now by "closeness & trust & it's terrific. Maybe we'll even physicalize the relationship when we are in Minn. It doesn't matter a lot, tho."[64]

Chicago was putting in marathon workdays, eight to ten hours, trying to finish the first set of plates. Seven had been finished a month earlier, but the rest were not coming out as well as she hoped. Frustrated, she feared not knowing enough to produce what she wanted: "I've never taken on as much as this Dinner Party. All I ever do is think about it."[65] She kept asking for lists of important women, and even considered making each plate double, with a past and a present woman—for example, a goddess with Margaret Sanger, the visionary feminist theoretician who promoted birth control. She discovered the "blood-red butterfly called *Sangaris*" and envisioned the Sanger plate "all red . . . a sacrificial figure & herself simultaneously (or a goddess connected to blood sacrifice)." She wanted to layer each image "so that it compresses history & unites present-day feminist struggle (the last four centuries, that is) with matriarchal times."[66] But getting her vision onto the plates remained hard.

Obsessed with *The Dinner Party,* Chicago heeded advice from Dextra Frankel, who warned from her curatorial experience that the plates would have to be shielded from spectators tempted to touch. The whole thing could be enclosed "within a viewing area—4 white walls—waist high, with wood tops—which people can walk around to see the piece—which will be just out of arm's reach but readily visible."[67] By this time Chicago had changed from a menu to a catalog to caption the piece.

The public sphere obtruded from another direction. Lucy Lippard wrote of "her desire to *do* something that would shake things up a bit as the movement is kind of quiet these days" and suggested that it was the time for a traveling show of feminist art. Chicago allowed that this would "launch the feminist art movement—the goal of all these many years of my work—a woman's art movement that would affect the culture in a way that would change it & thus the work would become part of history—that's my goal—either personally or thru a group movement—to *enter* history."[68] But she returned to her view that her best shot at changing history would have to emerge from her studio, and she redoubled her work on the plates—ten down, still the recalcitrant four to go.

Despite Chicago's drive and purpose, she had to cope with her own doubts: "I've hit some huge pocket of fear, insecurity, terror, something. It started after I told Lloyd that I was trying to create a masterpiece. I thought that he would scoff at me—he didn't—but it made him uncomfortable—my own discomfort with my level of ambition seen in his eyes."[69] "Admitting my ambition to Lloyd freaked me, but—admitting it to a man, even him, made me feel dumb & foolish—& made me hate him too—I hate men—Yes, I do—at least right this minute—because they have made me feel so stupid & so evil for my ambitiousness."[70]

Some believe that such ambition creates great leaders. In Chicago's case, her unambiguous focus on her dream of success enabled her to channel her own energy and, at the same time, to engage and inspire others to join her effort to make her dream a reality.[71] Sometimes, however, she rallied others only to face resentment. At the Woman's Building that she helped to found, "the women there hate me & talk about me . . . they say I ripped off the women's movement—I'm bad—I'm a bitch—Why do people lay this all on me? They've gotten to me."[72]

Abruptly the journal verifies steely resolve, its usual calligraphic script giving way to block letters: "TOMORROW—I WILL START MY SCHEDULE AGAIN—I WILL PUT ONE FOOT IN FRONT OF THE OTHER & GO FORWARD."[73]

In her colleagues at the Woman's Building, she created emotions that ranged from disappointment to ill will by abandoning her original commitment to their joint project. In fact, her participation and vision had been key to their complex endeavor. Neither Raven nor de Bretteville, however, required the same individual focus in their own studios to realize their ultimate goals. Chicago's commitment came into conflict with her own needs. Since she had to have this time to make her own art, this setback did not still her for long. She rallied, and in scarcely more than two weeks she capped months of effort and polished off the last four plates of the first fourteen, only to lose four when she opened the kiln early during the tenth firing. She found time too to make four miniatures on ivory, *Clitoral Secrets*—intimate in scale, utilizing the "butterfly vagina" format from the *Goddess* series. They were meant as studies for a suite of prints, *Butterfly Vagina Erotica,* with four takes—*The Descent, The Approach, The Contact, The Climax* (eventually called *The Throb*): "I have succeeded in creating a new image of female sexuality as an assertive force," her journal very specifically claimed, "& simultaneously been able to make images that are tender & humane, something not too prevalent in male erotica."[74] By now she considered her earlier set of porcelain miniatures, *Sex from the Inside Out,* to be "somewhat passive, frozen images."[75]

Images of female anatomy are often read as merely erotic. But to a feminist in the early 1970s the political issue of female identity trumped all other meanings. "Much of feminist art that has been labeled 'erotic' because it depicts or alludes to genital images is nothing of the sort," wrote Barbara Rose in a 1974 article, "Vaginal Iconology." "It is designed to arouse women, but not sexually. . . . Judy Chicago's yoni-lifesavers [*Pasadena Lifesavers*] are all vaginal or womb images. What is interesting about them is the manner in which they worshipfully allude to female genitalia as icons—as strong, clean, well made, and whole as the masculine totems to which we are accustomed."[76] Rose understood that women's images that "glorify vaginas . . . attack one of the most fundamental ideas of male supremacy—that a penis, because it is visible, is superior." In her imagery, as in her life, Chicago was determined to place women's pleasure ahead of the usual situation where men called the shots.

Chicago had originally intended to show her new erotic images in the Woman's Building during the publication party for her book. But the hostile feelings there led her to yield her space in the building's Grandview Gallery to Cheryl Swannack, a participant in the Feminist Studio Workshop who had publicly accused Chicago of taking too much from her during the three sessions that they had worked together on drawings the previous spring. Swannack recalls that she had also been making "cunt" images, even in ceramics, while a student at the University of Tulsa. She maintains that Chicago saw her drawing a cunt "peeling back" and making three-dimensional constructions of the same image in cigar boxes, when she asked, "Do you mind if I use that?" Swannack recalls responding that she did not mind and that "few artists would bother to ask."[77] Chicago commented in her journal: "I got some permission that the Workshop women had gotten from me, but I had been unable to give myself."[78] Other women were asking if Chicago had "copped out to the male establishment," and some wanted to know if she was "deserting the Women's Movement for the art world." She called all of this "craziness—real craziness, mythology, misunderstanding, anger, etc. all not handled well by the FSW staff, which probably had its own unexpressed feelings."[79]

Chicago was disappointed that the staff allowed Cheryl's outburst in the workshop because, she wrote in her journal, "the main growth step in female education comes when undeveloped women are disallowed the possibility for shitting on women of achievement as a way of rationalizing their own basic lack of achievement—BASIC—FUNDAMENTAL rule of the programs I've been involved with is to help women break out of their oppression by stopping the chain of oppressing other women as a way of not taking responsibility for one's own inadequacy."[80] She concluded that the staff had allowed it because they had felt the same feelings and could not admit them. In her view, Cheryl had become the means for the staff to vent their anger at Chicago's decision to leave the FSW behind.

Yet despite her public accusation, for Swannack the workshop was a "life-changing experience" and de Bretteville, Chicago, and Raven "magnificent teachers."[81] She remembers Chicago as "a tireless worker" from whom she learned two major lessons that remain important to her: "With women, you always have to consider the nature of the damage and overlook it," and "Just because I'm a woman and older and stronger, doesn't mean I'm your mother."[82] She appears to have realized that Chicago had acted fairly when she had asked if Swannack would mind if she too worked with the idea of "peeling back." Perhaps Swannack saw that, at the time, she felt wounded that she had not yet received the credit that she thought her work merited. She did see Chicago as devoted to her own achievements, which inspired her to focus on her own work. In the mid-1980s Swannack became associate producer for the Broadway play *The Search for Signs of Intelligent Life in the Universe,* which includes a piece about the dynamics of three feminist artists.

Painting in miniature on china reclaimed Chicago's attention, including twenty-nine in a series—*Butterfly Goddesses and Other Specimens*—for a show called *Metamorphosis* at the College of St. Catherine from January 5 to 31, 1975. In a lecture at the show, she explained what she had been after in these porcelains: "The female artist's obsession with vaginas represents her attempt to get in touch with who she is."[83] She titled one of the porcelains *Fecundity as an Image of Creativity (or the female artist producing ideas in the form of eggs)*.[84] She seems to have gotten over her earlier association of egg imagery with the misplaced and contentious mothering of Schapiro as well as her fantasy of a romantic binge to produce a child.

In *The Butterfly Goddess* she said that she envisioned one "who can fly and be free, who can lift us and inspire us."[85] Another time she explained, "Porcelain has had a magic about it since Marco Polo brought it from the Orient. . . . There's something about the surface, its fragility. It's a metaphor for human life. It can withstand high temperatures and yet is so fragile."[86] She averred that she no longer wanted to paint on plastic: "I wanted more detail, and I wanted paint to be part of the surface, not on top of it. I see the surface as my body."[87] The *Metamorphosis* concept at St. Catherine's had been a joint venture, solidifying her bond with Raven, who wrote the catalog essay and took part in the college workshop, which was intended to sow "the seeds for an ongoing feminist program."[88] *Metamorphosis* served Chicago as a metaphor identifying herself as an artist with the butterfly motif in her work.[89] The show recapitulated her recent progression over a varied range of media and scale, including *The Queens, The Reincarnation Triptych, Compressed Women Who Yearned to Be Butterflies,* and *The Rejection Quintet.*

The Rejection Quintet, with its reflection of five low points in the artist's own experience, moved a woman journalist to report, "One male viewer was overheard commenting: 'No one could feel *that* rejected.' Try being a woman in a patriarchal society, Mister," retorted the writer.[90] This series and *The Reincarnation Triptych* incorporated cursive writing, which Chicago said she did to express ideas that she could not convey visually and "to make the images more accessible to women outside the art world."[91]

Another reviewer, Don Morrison, wrote in the *Minneapolis Star:* "To a man, inevitably there is a somewhat shrill and querulous tone to her annotations, but I cannot pretend to know what frustrations a high female talent endures in an obviously masculine art autocracy." More sympathetically he concluded: "Even allowing for a measure of self-pity or intemperate anger lashing out, however, the most obtuse male cannot but recognize the supreme discipline and lapidary perfection with which Judy Chicago's hand beautifully expresses whatever depths of outrage or passion [are] in her soul."[92] The reviewer for the student paper wrote, "Her show has so obsessed me that I find myself going back. I can sit for hours, staring at her work. . . . Perhaps I have never seen the inside of an artist before. Perhaps I feel no struggle to be free, but rather, an airy freedom from struggle."[93]

Chicago spent an entire month in Minnesota, joined by Raven and Hamrol, whom she "missed terribly" at first, counting the days before his week's stay.[94] Her first chore had been the all-too-familiar experience of readying space. Like a veteran trouper, she pitched in once more with the mixed crew of volunteers and "professional construction guys" who worked seventeen hours a day to get ready in time. Chicago had insisted that she had to have Sheetrock walls constructed over the brick walls of the gallery or she would not hang her work.[95]

The opening on a Sunday evening was well attended by local standards, but Chicago was disappointed that no one showed up from the Walker, the local museum for contemporary art: "I wonder how long it will be before I realize that the male establishment just does not want to acknowledge the importance of my work."[96] She told herself that she made art because she wanted to and had to just keep "putting it out there. That's all that counts. And there is no reward for it other than the act & the accomplishment itself."[97]

Chicago ran the workshop with Carol Fisher, an artist on the faculty, and "a young radical nun named Ann Jennings."[98] She found "a group of passive, apathetic women—with some exceptions." Of the initial 37, a dozen dropped out, "really freaked out by the level of demand."[99] As Chicago led consciousness raising and an art workshop among the group, which she viewed as afflicted by "low energy," she anxiously hoped not to lose any more participants. But even as she was focused on training the two faculty women to run a feminist program, she was disconcerted to see the women in the workshop sitting in corners on the floor, working "small—like little girls in kindergarten—which is probably where their growth stopped."[100] She saw her role not as teaching art but as the "undoing of role conditioning, which comes unraveled in the same pattern it was knitted by social pressure."[101] If they could find themselves as women, they might then learn to make art.

Still teaching at St. Cate's but no longer a sister, Ann Jennings recalls Chicago as "charismatic, dynamic, intellectually interesting, someone who lit a spark. She was inspiring, an entrepreneur and a visionary." Sandra Taylor, a then thirty-year-old student at the Minneapolis College of Art and Design, signed up for the workshop, tired of having all male professors who did not take seriously either women or art that dealt with women's lives. She got what she wanted, although she found Chicago pretty "abrasive" and showing "little patience for traditional women's ways."[102] Chicago loved traditional women's crafts but demanded a serious professional attitude that many women she encountered lacked.

Besides the workshop and show, the college sponsored an evening discussion of the artist's work, a lecture on feminist education, and a seminar on china painting. Chicago also provided a reading list: Virginia Woolf's *A Room of One's Own,* Robin Morgan's *Sisterhood Is Powerful,* Mary McCarthy's *Memories of a Catholic Girlhood,* Doris Lessing's *Golden Notebook,* and Anaïs Nin's *First Diary.* Chicago also suggested Eleanor Flexner's *Century of Struggle,* Eleanor Tufts's *Five Centuries of Women Artists,* and *Art and Sexual Politics* edited by Linda Nochlin and Thomas Hess.[103]

After ten days Raven arrived with her partner, the art historian Ruth Iskin, and took over the workshop, freeing Chicago to devote most of her time to making her own art in the print shop at the Minneapolis College of Art and Design—a substitute since the Flat Stone Studio, where she had expected to work, had failed. She also kept up her research for *The Dinner Party,* which kept on "fermenting" in her head. Now she focused on religion and women, although her work was punctuated by the separate arrivals of Lucy Lippard and Hamrol. Lloyd had arranged to build a snow structure at the University of Minnesota, in which the women from the workshop performed. He then went on alone to New York, making contacts, which Chicago felt would help him to realize his strength and talent.[104]

Chicago managed to produce a suite of prints, *Butterfly Vagina Erotica,* "complete with a sweet, rainbow-rolled folio tied with satin ribbon—very dainty and sweet (wonderful how adjectives like those would have been taboo for a serious artist a decade ago)."[105] She thought that she had learned something useful about positive and negative shapes that would affect the embroidered series she had in mind, perhaps with a new boldness that could be read from afar. She designed a folder for the prints to open from the left "to show they're from a different point of view," not consciously aware that the Hebrew prayer books in her grandmother's house opened this way too.[106] While at the college, she did a rap, a panel, and had a discussion at a potluck with a group of women.

Having weathered the "terrible scene" with Raven and others over the Woman's Building the previous month, Chicago now came to believe that "the whole experience caused something to snap inside me—some change to take place—Now I think I've made another step into aloneness and separation. Like the female community—which I support but can never be one with again because I need my aloneness to do my work—I need my differentness & my energy."[107] She also had begun to acknowledge to herself that her friend and mentor, Anaïs Nin, then hospitalized in great pain from a malignant tumor, was dying. Chicago had gone to see her before leaving for Minnesota and was upset about the impending loss.

The stay at St. Catherine's had given her a new interest in "the rise of Christianity and the idea that all persons were the same in the eyes of Christ . . . which had enormous implications for the position of women. Women flocked to the convents, or rather to the orders, as there weren't many convents before."[108] After the workshop (then Sister) Ann Jennings wrote, "Today women, together with all oppressed peoples, 'groan inwardly because we are still anticipating our adoption as children and the full liberation of our human existence' (Rom. 8:22–23). But we have experienced solidarity in our groaning for freedom; we call it 'Sisterhood,' and . . . we have made art out of it."[109] That this opened a rich vein for research, Chicago instinctively grasped: "After all, why should women leave the society in the numbers they did unless they got something in the monasteries they didn't get in the culture?"[110]

Carol Fisher too had responded to Chicago. She wrote, "I miss you! Very much. . . . You are confronting (honest, open) and make me confront myself."[111] She sent Chicago a pair of "cow socks." It was at this time that Ruth Iskin convinced Chicago to compile a bibliography, which she now began, having already lost some of the obscure materials that she had used for the project early on.

Back in Los Angeles with Hamrol, Chicago observed, "He's his usual up, down, & backwards—but I don't react to it like I used to—I'm so obsessed."[112] Between *The Dinner Party* and the book about to appear, her husband's problems paled. Her motifs and message attracted ever more media interest, and requests for interviews flowed.

The book's publication at last thrilled its author, who no longer saw it, however, as her means to acquire fame; the only road there lay, she was now convinced, through heroic studio work, as her journal very shortly affirmed: "I have a real certainty these days that if I live & am healthy—I will become a great artist—the 3rd woman of this century—Hepworth, O'Keeffe—& me—but I will increasingly feel alienated from my present name—what name will I use? My original? *Judith Sylvia Cohen*—probably! But, not yet."[113] She had to work out promotion plans with Doubleday and submit to interviewers and photographers, including one sent over from *Playgirl.* Her thoughts about returning to her original name reflect her constant conflict between her public and private identities. "Judy Chicago" seemed to her like too much of a role that she had to play without time off for good behavior.

She kept up her research on *The Dinner Party* and settled on a number of figures to honor: "What I'm doing is a sort of *Genesis*—starting with early Mother Goddess figures—& working thru the change from matriarchy to patriarchy—then on thru the centuries, trying to make a link-up between women & their efforts, aspirations, & situations that can bring me to the 20th cent—where I've decided to end with Woolf & O'Keeffe & the first steps in reestablishing the feminine thru imagery."[114] She sought female figures whose lives and deeds would permit them to stand for a larger history of women and of the feminine. She wanted "an historical curve" from the beginnings of human society to the development of matriarchy and its concomitant woman-worship. She focused on the shift from mother-right to father-right and the ongoing struggle of women to take back some power or self-respect, the chronological stages of women's condition, the growth of the women's rights movement, the reemergence of the female creator, and hence "the development of the notion of re-introducing the feminine into male-dominated & destructive society."[115] She began with the Primordial and Fertile Goddesses, then Ishtar, Kali, and the Snake Goddess. Sophia, Amazon, Hatshepsut, Judith (Figure 23), Sappho, Aspasia, Boadaceia, and Hypatia completed the first and earliest wing.

Her research had reached the sixteenth century, but Chicago still lacked a powerful religious woman of the Middle Ages and a Renaissance woman. For the rest of the plates she decided that "the later images will require a more active, struggling form—for Mary Wollstonecraft (for example) struggled against her circumstances a lot more than earlier women."[116] She determined to produce "a feminine history which would explicate the symbolism & the women of the Dinner Party." She was amazed at how her art life was now "infinitely more real than anything else."[117] She had no idea of where she would show such a work or how she could pay for the catalog, but she was going to continue.

The publication of *Through the Flower: My Struggle as a Woman Artist* in March 1975 made Chicago even more of a public figure, in part through the publicity the book received, but mostly through the many who actually read it. On the official publication day she opened a show, *Some Erotic Images,* at Re-Vision Gallery in L.A. She underscored her feminist vision by bathing the works in pink light to suggest "the zone of female sexuality—translated into a soft, warm, inviting & human space"[118]: *Butterfly Goddess and Other Porcelain Miniatures, Some Erotic Images Entitled Giving and Taking,* and *Sex from the Inside Out.* Chicago believed that these images were important historically because they represented "an active, generous, tender female sexuality & an eroticism that is at once lusty & connected."[119]

The day after the opening Chicago signed books at the Woman's Building, where she had been forgiven, and the Grinsteins gave her an evening party. Then she and Lloyd left for five days in San Francisco, where she gave a lecture at the Museum of Modern Art. Afterward her classmate from UCLA, Ellie

Neil, and her husband, the film director Francis Ford Coppola, gave a party in her honor at their splendid Victorian home. Coppola told her that he had been at the airport with nothing to read so had bought eleven books, including several on Hitler, who fascinated him. Back in L.A., Chicago purchased eleven feminist books, including her own, and sent them to him, hoping that he would be inspired to make a film that "could illuminate women's cultural history."[120] He never acknowledged the gift. More satisfying was the time she and Hamrol spent with artists Christo and Sol LeWitt.[121]

Meanwhile, Doubleday's promotional flyer featured comments by writers Adrienne Rich ("I want to see it in the hands of 15-year-old women imagining their futures"), Marge Piercy ("it has changed my perceptions, it has even changed my own past for me"), and Eve Merriam ("a significant autobiographical document extending the frontiers of the women's movement"), as well as the anonymous *Kirkus* review that stated: "She writes very well, simply, directly, assertively—about sexual relations, work, her role as a leader and a cultural catalyst . . . she is . . . about as passive as dynamite."

Writing the book had released her, Chicago told some interviewers: "I rewrote the book eight times, and each time I peeled away more. I had first hidden behind a lot of rhetoric. I would get feedback from my friends that the best parts were when I was being exactly myself."[122] She admitted to fear at the book's publication because "in our culture we've been made to feel very ashamed of who we really are and what we really feel."[123]

The book was widely reviewed and was excerpted in *Playgirl,* which reproduced *Clitoral Secrets.*[124] Another piece of hers—described as "genital art [that] carries political messages about women's power and their spiritual strength"—appeared in *Penthouse (The International Magazine for Men).*[125] To a British woman journalist asking about a work's appearing in *Playgirl,* Chicago responded, "They bought an excerpt from my book from the publishers. I felt very ambivalent about it . . . very hostile to it until I spoke to the editor. She was telling me how many letters they get of absolute rage. For example, men seeing themselves displayed in the way that we, as women, have been seeing ourselves for so many centuries."[126]

Some reviewers took issue with *Through the Flower* from points of view more conservative or more radical. In the daily *New York Times* editors assigned Chicago to a resolute antifeminist, Christopher Lehmann-Haupt. He must have relied on influences other than the text, since he referred to development "from youth to maturity—from Judy *Gerowitz* [italics mine], the bright troubled child who felt herself different," erasing Cohen, father and daughter, in favor of the ill-starred Jerry. The review eschewed comment on "her program," maintaining that if positive, "it will amount to nothing more than patronization," and if disapproving, "Well, what did you expect, anyway?" He sniped at the prose, critiquing it as "unappealing jargon" and the person as "befuddled."[127]

In contrast, Karla Jay in *Lesbian Tide* noted that Chicago's was "an exciting autobiography, one that should finally bury the notion that artists can't write. I found myself caught up in Judy's struggle and often couldn't put the book down."[128] Jay did object that in the discussion of so many women artists and writers, Chicago never mentioned that "Rosa Bonheur, Romaine Brooks, Willa Cather, and so on—were lesbians. She thus obliterates lesbian presences and contributes to art and literature in the same way she complains men have done to women! I also felt that in these sections and elsewhere the author glossed over the issue of class."[129] Chicago focused neither on sexual preference nor on class, although she certainly made clear her working-class roots, describing her father's work as a "union organizer" and "victim of the anti-Communists sentiments."[130]

"There are still people who are shocked to find a woman with such a superior image of herself," wrote Lucy Lippard in *Ms.*, "and the art world is probably the last place this book will be welcomed." Lippard agreed that the writing occasionally interfered with the content but observed that Chicago "ebulliently chronicles her beginnings as Judy Cohen," adding that although "*Through the Flower* may embarrass those who are not ready to take the trip themselves, it will enthrall those who have, and encourage others to do so."[131]

Others lodged vociferous dissent. Writing for the feminist journal *off our backs,* after an interview with Chicago, Frances Chapman carped: "What I miss in Judy's views and comments is the recognition that women oppression is a conscious political act on the part of the ruling class, a recognition which is essential to feminism as a political philosophy. Women oppression appears in Judy's book as merely the neglect of female values by men. Her feminism tends to be cultural and psychological rather than political. There is little hard-core political activism."[132] She quoted Chicago on individualism: "Art at its finest is dissent. Society moves ahead through individuals that dissent. The strength of the women's movement is in individual women who dissented from social expectations."[133] She criticized Chicago because she had identified society as the enemy, instead of patriarchy and men, and because Chicago had said that she found "the 'Black Panther' stance of some feminists 'ludicrous' and rejects Amazon nation à la Jill Johnston. 'Militant pluralism,' a phrase borrowed from Susan Rennie and Kirsten Grimstad, is the key, she said."[134]

More welcoming, Vera Goodman, in *New Directions for Women,* described *Through the Flower* as the work of "an immensely talented writer" who "can verbalize her emotional artistic intensity, an ability not many visual artists possess."[135] But a male journalist who misunderstood Chicago described her as speaking with "an ironic Jewish-princess whine." He asserted: "*Through the Flower* seems to have been written on the barricades, but Judy Chicago has turned inward on herself and her art. She and Lloyd have renounced children." He quoted her as saying: "There's some peculiar idea that because 50 percent of the population can spread their legs and pop out a baby, everyone should. But I don't like children: they're noisy, and I require a great deal of privacy and silence. Going to work is entering silence."[136]

An interviewer, Vicky Chen Haider, reported with particular care Judy's vigorous style: "Her sentences are punctuated by strong, positive verbs—build, create, change, revolutionize. At 36, she is a woman with an enormous amount of energy and an infectious spirit that makes her a natural teacher. When she speaks, she expresses herself with her whole body. When she is enthusiastic, her hands literally paint her thoughts in the air. When she talks about pain, rejection and the difficulties of being a woman and an artist, her hands are protective, close to her body."

Promoting the book in her home city, the artist described herself as "a nice Jewish girl from Chicago," only to add what was sure to provoke: "My vagina is a metaphysical question."[137] She had been rejected, she said, "as a woman because I am aggressive, outspoken. I've been rejected as an artist because my subject matter has been considered nonessential. We've had to deal with rejection much too much, especially women. I want to affirm the female experience, to tell women that their point of view is vital and all-important in this society, whether in art or in everyday life."[138]

Her imagery was meant to convey an active female role: "We've always been imaged by males as a passive hole. What I've wanted to create is a new, active sense of womanhood."[139] Haider understood Chicago's invention of "the butterfly vagina . . . as an early primitive form of femaleness. In this series, this image metamorphoses into a butterfly goddess—an active, positive, female force."[140] Chicago elaborated: "To me, the butterfly is a symbol of freedom, and liberation. And when I was in Minnesota at the College of St. Catherine, I was told by the nuns there, who were absolutely stunned and wildly enthusiastic about my work, that the butterfly has traditionally been a symbol of resurrection in the church."[141]

Working with the "butterfly/cunt" metaphor, Chicago needed more silent time to further conceptualize *The Dinner Party*. By mid-March 1975 she realized that she wanted to alter the number of settings and relate it to the thirteen of the witches' covens. Twenty-six seemed too few and the next multiple was thirty-nine, which prompted a thought: "Maybe I'll use a triangular table—3 sides of 13, which would allow me to use the fact that the triangle is one of the basic forms associated with work from matriarchal cultures."[142] The metaphoric connection with the triangular Greek letter delta D, which was widely employed to symbolize the female pubes, also connected Chicago's concept with the work of her mentor Anaïs Nin, who had written a series of connected erotic stories that she named *The Delta of Venus*.[143]

The geometrical increment and a projected complement of names beneath the table drew applause from a recent friend, the poet Adrienne Rich, on a studio visit. Rich wrote to Chicago that she found her concept "staggering" and that she loved the history floor with the names of women erased by time. But as she departed, she was not sure if Chicago had intended the table to be round or triangular, which she preferred, noting that the "Aurignacian caves" always had a "triangle (yoni)," to show where to enter the sacred space.[144]

Chicago wanted "the nature of the forms and the rhythm of the language to be feminine," but the content to be universal, which prompted a further comment from Rich, as they discussed a planned collaboration—a poster for the San Fernando Valley Chapter of NOW. Rich reflected that she had realized the universality of "the female body," noting that the female was the locus where all people, both women and men, had been "nourished," connecting woman with cosmic rhythms. She discouraged Chicago from concluding that issues such as menstruation or the link between mother and daughter had been treated in any but the most obvious ways. She argued that Chicago had brought vulvate imagery to metaphysical implications it had never before enjoyed and gave Chicago credit for freeing female imagery from being thought " 'merely' female, mere physicality or biology."[145]

The prompt enthusiasm of Rich and others encouraged Chicago, who wrote to Lippard, "All I really want to do is work on *The Dinner Party*. You know when I started it, I had this idea that I would do some research, enough to base an imaginary mythology on a small amount of historical fact. However, I have found so much material that I now have to completely reorder the piece so that it can grow out of the material, instead of vice versa . . . I am expanding the scope of the piece so that it will be a virtual female history, and I am not sure how many plates that will require."[146]

To Lippard, Chicago confessed that she now could see no way to complete *The Dinner Party* before 1977: "What I've done in the last 5 years encourages me to think large and have faith in the ultimate end of my projections. The other goal I have is to make another step in making feminist culture visible in the society in such a way that it can't be erased . . . and I'm thinking a lot about that . . . how to use my book as the base of some kind of film or TV special, which would allow a personal base, from which material, historical, documentary, etc., could be brought in."[147]

In L.A., Chicago continued a very minimal involvement with the Feminist Studio Workshop, keeping up her friendships with Raven, de Bretteville, and Iskin. But burgeoning aims in the studio demanded all and more than she had to give. Chicago described her rigorous work schedule to an interviewer in early 1975: "Amateurs work only if they feel like it. When you're a professional, you work whether you feel like it or not."[148] She claimed to start at 9 A.M. and go for seven hours a day, seven days a week: "Grown-ups work," she said. "Women have been infantalized, and not working is part of this."[149]

By the middle of April, Chicago had decided on most of her thirty-nine emblematic women, moving on from the goddesses and including such figures as Judith (Figure 23), Eleanor of Aquitaine, Emily Dickinson, Natalie Barney, and Margaret Sanger. She had further "expanded the piece to make it an environment that one enters—a kind of newly opened tomb—a triangular room—about 55' on a side. Inside a triangular table 39' on a side, 13 plates per side—the whole thing on a triangular dais slightly larger than the table which will be called the History Floor & covered with 441 triangular porcelain tiles, which will have a lustre surface & will contain hundreds of names of women from all over the world—women who have been buried in history."[150] She ventured to roll back her schedule for completion from 1977 to the end of 1976.

In the face of this ambition, Chicago felt her confidence shaken when the book on which she had worked so long did not bring her "instant fame" or much else except for some articles and other media attention.[151] She was both disappointed and embarrassed that it generated no shows in galleries or even lectures. She felt that men who had achieved a similar level of recognition would have no trouble in this area. Discarding her dreams of stardom, she felt lonely and financially insecure and realized that all she had were her energy, her ideas, and her fantasy that she was "perhaps potentially a great artist."[152] Unsure how long the energy would hold up, she felt that no one cared about her ideas. A recent visit with Hamrol to the sculptor Bob Graham's studio had brought the stunning revelation that "he thinks he's a great artist too—Perhaps *all* of us harbor that as a fantasy that keeps us going—& perhaps, *some* of us make it come true, thru chance, luck, the timing, & history all coming together."[153]

Encouragement came from her patron Tracy O'Kates, who flew Chicago to London on May 4 to promote the book, lecture at the Institute of Contemporary Art (ICA), and hold a show at the JPL Gallery, run by Patricia Fisher at 23 Grafton Street, of the six drawings (originally made for prints) *Compressed*

Women Who Yearn to Be Butterflies. The opening attracted Paula Harper, the art historian who had taught art history Chicago's first year at CalArts. Chicago managed to get back to the British Museum and added to her rounds the Victoria and Albert's collection of porcelain, to which she returned several times. To tour the Royal Worcester Porcelain factory, she traveled alone on a train for two hours. Fisher took her to visit Stonehenge and Bath, which Chicago recalled "Jane Austen described so well in her novels."[154] Seeking contact with local women's groups, she found them "definitely 5 years behind the states."[155] A Women's Video Day confirmed her impression that their "art comes out of a really passive ego development."[156]

The JPL Gallery was near to important Bond Street galleries, and the show caught media eyes. One reporter described Chicago as "a rather jolly chunky lady who works hard at her job," as "shrewd with questions," and as free from "qualms about making bread in the smart halls of male chauvinism."[157] Another reviewer, Margaret Richards, writing in the *Socialist Tribune,* appreciated the references to women such as George Eliot, Mary Lamb, and George Sand: "The prints [actually drawings for prints] suggest, by shape, colour and word-surround, how feminine physical-emotion experience can expand into creative achievement and then find itself stopped in full flight by the rigid framework of men's assumptions."[158]

Chicago responded to a female journalist in London who asked about her ivories in *Playgirl,* the issue of erotica and the feminist movement: "I hope to have a different definition of eroticism . . . not dehumanized images. They are images of contact, feelings, and tenderness—which is what I think is erotic. And women by and large find them enormously erotic—which says something about the fact that women have been accused of not responding to erotic images. . . . I think we have very little material from women about what their experience is."[159]

On the plane to London Chicago had written in her journal: "Other people will have to find the wherewithal to deal with the fact that I am a brilliant, talented, accomplished, generous, difficult woman. And if they can't, too bad!" Perhaps this was why she had written to Lippard that she had "very mixed feelings" about going to London.[160] She reflected on the intense feelings expressed in the art shown in the Woman's Building, observing that few of the women really "knew how to make art," while in the art world "very few of the artists know how to express anything real with the art they know how to make. And I, of course, want to do both!"[161] She was happy that the ICA lecture had been to "an absolutely packed room," especially since her publisher's publicist had been undemonstrative and slack.[162]

On return, she tarried five days in New York, having written to Lippard:

"I plan to divide my sleeping time among my various friends, so prepare for the descent of the Butterfly Vagina."[163] She spent time with Lippard as well as Susan Rennie and Kirsten Grimstad, and Adrienne Rich. She met Kate Millet and Robin Morgan, both well known as feminist writers. She also saw her former lover Bruce. Her futile efforts to find a woman dealer left her no choice but to peddle her slides around and face a slur from Nancy Hoffman that her gallery could not show such explicit content in work—an attitude like that of Chicago's professors in graduate school long ago. She compared her cold reception to the more productive one that Hamrol as a male sculptor had recently found.

The day after Chicago's return to L.A. the director of the San Francisco Museum of Modern Art, Henry Hopkins (whom she knew from graduate school days, when he taught extension courses at UCLA), visited and expressed his desire to show *The Dinner Party.* She busily prepared a proposal and made a model to send to him for what she realized was "another high risk situation."[164] She planned to audit a ceramics class the following fall, since she now wanted the plates in "the last section of images (from the eighteenth century forward) to begin to rise up from the surface" and knew that she needed to learn quite a lot to achieve that.[165]

The Dinner Party was proving a challenge, and her book had left her dissatisfied. Eager to promote herself on her home turf, Judy set out with Lloyd for a book party in Chicago, going by car with Jack Rhyne, who had begun as her studio assistant in Fresno and was by now like a member of the family. En route for five days, in Colorado they visited Mesa Verde, the ruined cliff dwellings of Native Americans. She found the idea of an entire community nestled into the rocks very moving and tried to imagine what it must have been like to live like that. The concept of time must have been quite different then, she concluded, aware of how labor intensive just getting water to the stone dwellings must have been. She saw the place as a tribute to the human spirit.[166]

Attendance at the book party suffered from rain and the failure of two scheduled feature articles to appear beforehand, further discouraging her publisher, Doubleday. Stripped of illusions that the book might be a best-seller, Chicago had to come to terms with the reality that she was strapped for cash. Though she was fed up with lecturing, she had no choice but to accept an invitation from a speakers' bureau.

On a positive note, by late July Chicago reflected that she and Hamrol had "definitely gotten closer & our relationship is, I suppose, better than it's ever been. . . . I became aware of the price Lloyd was paying for my involvement in the Women's Movement. I was giving more of myself to women I didn't care that much about than to Lloyd, whom I really love dearly."[167] Now she felt that she could just be happy working in her studio, though she was anxious about being able to finish *The Dinner Party* because of the technical and economic hurdles that it entailed. She had to risk living without financial security, "pouring 4 years of my life, all my energy, every bit of money I can muster into a piece that could be a masterpiece or could be the biggest white elephant that ever was."[168]

"I am entirely at the service of this piece," she wrote to her pal Lucy Lippard. "I don't even know why or how it happened . . . but I know that it is truly a major historical and esthetic step. The curator from the Long Beach Museum really understood it . . . and asked me if it didn't sometimes seem to be a burden. He also wrote in his confirmation letter that they felt privileged to show it."[169] She was pleased that the curator had referred to Michelangelo and the Sistine Chapel, telling her that people had also thought that he would never finish the project. She added, "Henry Hopkins doesn't entirely understand it, but he does understand something else as a result of my lecture at the museum in March and also the response that is happening to the *Rejection Quintet,* which is on loan up there. There were hundreds of women who came to my talk who never came to the museum before, and Henry, who is a responsible museum person, realized that I brought something that some parts of the community wanted."[170]

Money problems multiplied. No longer teaching full-time, Hamrol barely earned his own keep. Chicago earned $700 plus expenses for flying to South Carolina to tape a segment for a television program about artists but could not force herself to fly from L.A. all the way to Buffalo for just $150. She had lost the *Sophia* plate for the second time, since on the seventh fire the paint chipped. She was considering redoing various plates and thought of a luncheon party with some of her rejects, thinking that she would show it only in Europe.

Amid these technical troubles her brother, Ben, arrived from Japan. Back when she had been planning to study ceramics, he had been drawn there by an interest in martial arts. For a while he gave lessons in tai chi, then English. "I was a painter in the U.S. and I came to Japan to get away from the debris of my life," he recalled. "For a couple of years I couldn't paint. It was like writer's block. But I had this terrible hunger to make things."[171] In the interim, he took up aikido (a martial art), studied Japanese, and tried *zazen* (a kind of Zen meditation). Really eager to make something, however, he moved to Kyoto and took a pottery class. Feeling a vocation, he moved to Miyazaki in Fukui Prefecture, near Echizen, an ancient pottery center with a distinctive style,[172] apprenticing himself to a renowned potter, Shichizaemon Kitano, and learning to make Echizen ware, which he described as "strong, sculptural and very pure."[173] At the show that marks a potter's passage to professional status, his master pressed a wad of yen into his hand—a traditional token that the erstwhile apprentice qualifies as a master in his own right.

Chicago found the newly minted potter less threatened and intimidated by her than she remembered: "I was the favored child & it was hard on him," she reflected. "He grew up resenting me. Before this time the resentment grew so large that we couldn't be close, but we seem to have made a step!"[174]

By September, Chicago was upset with Hamrol again. She felt that he was immature and in some ways controlling. Whenever she made demands on him that he did not want to meet or did anything that made him uncomfortable, she felt that he began to behave badly toward her and that this was his strategy to keep her in line. She knew by now that when she went away, she felt like a different person. At home she was quiet and withdrawn, in contrast to the funny and gregarious person she became while away.[175] The couple had in common their devotion to their careers, but Chicago found herself thinking a lot about her first husband, Jerry, and longing for "a rich life—friends, activities."[176] She promised herself that she would reexamine her life after she finished *The Dinner Party.*

By now she had clarified her aesthetic direction, rejected all formalist tendencies, and announced her concern with "that impulse by the human being to make an image of his or her reality," noting, "It's valid to work out of any part of oneself one wishes. However, it hasn't been valid to work out of any part of oneself that one wishes. Impersonal art has been supported against personal art."[177] She blamed societal conditioning for what she perceived as women artists' tendency to feature the personal: "Women are very good at the personal and men are very good at the abstract. . . . Women have moved into the abstract and left the personal, hidden it away. That's how you did it if you wanted to make it as a woman in the world."[178]

To an interviewer, Chicago complained, "Now people want to diminish my art by saying, 'Well, it's only a bunch of vaginas,' which it is not. I'm not involved in that. I'm involved in metaphysical art. I think O'Keeffe must have experienced a similar thing when people were doing all this Freudian analysis on her work and she said, 'I'm a painter; I'm an artist.' "[179] Chicago argued that "we live in a period in which an historic silence is being broken. We've never been able to see the world through women's eyes. It's really an opportunity for women to give a tremendous gift to the culture."[180]

Chicago finally realized that she could not make herself into a potter, that she needed a skilled assistant to help her with the plates. She obsessed with other needs—someone to publish a companion book; cooperation from Henry Hopkins in San Francisco and other museums dominated by males; her agent

Peri's promise to manage her affairs so that she could concentrate on making art; above all, money enough to finish the piece.

Little by little Chicago found the needed help. In October 1975 a lecture tour took her to Indiana, Chicago, and Carbondale, Illinois. At the last a ceramics student then just twenty-one, Judye Keyes, asked to become her apprentice. Since Keyes could also sew, Chicago figured that she would be able to help work on the tablecloth as well. Although Keyes did not arrive until June 1977 and had planned to apprentice herself to a ceramicist, she spent most of her time on the project, noting that "it's hard work, pushing yourself, doing the same things over and over. But it's a way of expressing social change through art, visually instead of through the rhetoric you get all the time. I feel very important here."[181] By the end of the project, she was the head of ceramics.

Keyes recalls doing some "minimal" work on the runners and painting a little china, but her main contribution was working on the ceramic flatwear, floor tiles, and plates. Three times she quit work on the project, wanting to do her own work and needing money. She also took a job at the same time working for Shari Lewis, the television personality and ventriloquist, who made famous a sock puppet named Lamb Chop. Keyes describes both Chicago and Lewis as "workaholics" but says that Lewis was "less abrasive" and caused her employees less angst. No doubt Lewis could offer more money too, although Chicago stretched to pay Keyes enough to survive so that she would stay with the project.[182] Keyes was critical of other workers, feeling that they were often not "the strongest of entities" and "looking for a leader."[183] As technical assistant for making the plates, Chicago hired a graduate student in ceramics at UCLA, Leonard Skuro.

After hearing Chicago lecture in San Diego about the *Dinner Party* project, a 1965 graduate of Wellesley College, Susan Hill, then studying photography, had written to ask if she could help. After taking her on, Chicago soon decided that she was not skilled enough at research so tried to involve her with producing the envisioned embroidered cloth. Chicago had purchased a new Bernina sewing machine and intended to teach herself embroidery. With typical ambition, she had thought she could do ceramics in the morning, needlework in the afternoon, and research at night. Susan Hill suggested that, instead of the planned large cloth, Chicago substitute runners, "based on the fairlinens used in communion." Hill's idea that replicating "cloth like that used during the metaphorical meal in the church made it a very nice link," Chicago later observed.[184] Becoming the head of needlework, Hill took Chicago to the Episcopal Church Guild to see ecclesiastical embroidery and to the Skirball Museum's Hebraic textile collection.[185] There she found Nancy Berman, another Wellesley graduate, who showed them Torah covers, chuppahs (wedding canopies), and similar items.

▲ Figure 1. Judy at age three with family friend Millie Jordani, c. 1942. From Judy Chicago scrapbook.

▼ Figure 2. Judy Cohen, *Bittersweet,* c. 1948. Oil on canvasboard, 16″ × 11″. When she was nine years old, she painted this view from her apartment building. Collection of the artist.

▲ Figure 3. Judy Cohen, untitled drawing done at age eleven, 1950. Mixed media on colored paper, 18″ × 24″. Collection of the artist.

◂ Figure 4. Judy Gerowitz, *Birth,* 1963. Acrylic on masonite, 8′ × 4′. Destroyed.

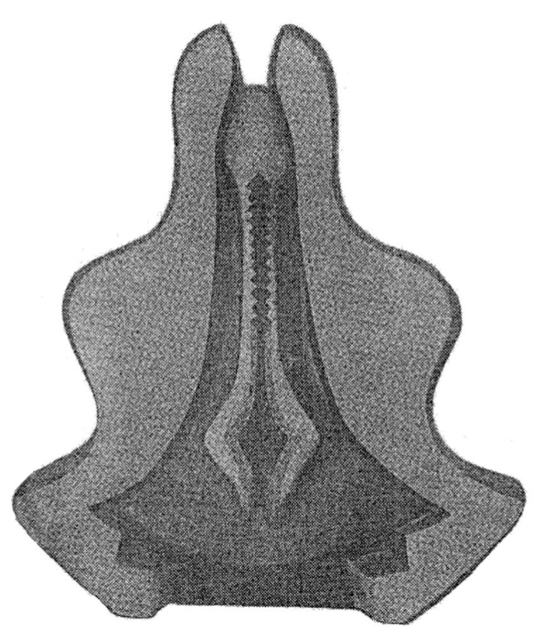

◂ Figure 5. Judy Gerowitz, *In My Mother's House,* 1963 or 1964. Painted clay, approximately 16″ × 24″ × 10″. Lost or destroyed; reproduced in *Artforum* magazine, summer 1964.

▾ Figure 6. Judy Gerowitz, *Carhood,* 1964. Sprayed acrylic lacquer on car hood, 4′ × 6′. Collection of Elaine and Rad Sutnar, Los Angeles.

▲ Figure 7. Judy Gerowitz with *Zig Zag* (destroyed) and *Lilith (Trinity)*, 1965. Canvas, plywood, and sprayed lacquer. Base: 60″ × 128″ × 63″. Collection of Glenn Schaffer.

▼ Figure 8. Judy Gerowitz, *Rainbow Pickett*, 1966. Plywood, canvas, latex, 126″ × 110″, as shown in "Primary Structures" exhibition. Jewish Museum, New York.

▸ Figure 9. Judy Gerowitz with Llyn Foulkes, Maurice Tuchman, and Lloyd Hamrol at the Los Angeles County Museum, 1965.

◂ Figure 10. Judy Gerowitz and Lloyd Hamrol (with Eric Orr, not shown), *Dry Ice Environment,* 1967. Century City Mall, Los Angeles.

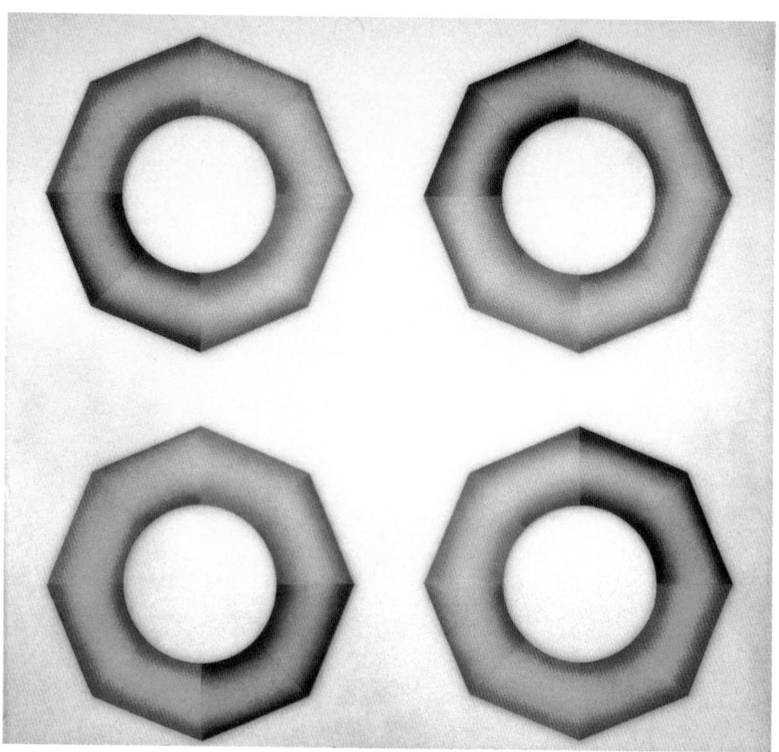

▲ Figure 11. Judy Gerowitz, *Pasadena Lifesavers—Red Series #4*, 1969–70. Sprayed acrylic lacquer on acrylic, 5′ × 5′. Collection of Mary Ross Taylor, Houston.

▼ Figure 12. Judy Chicago with Miriam Schapiro, Paul Brach, and Lloyd Hamrol, taken by Paula Harper in the spring of 1971, Fresno.

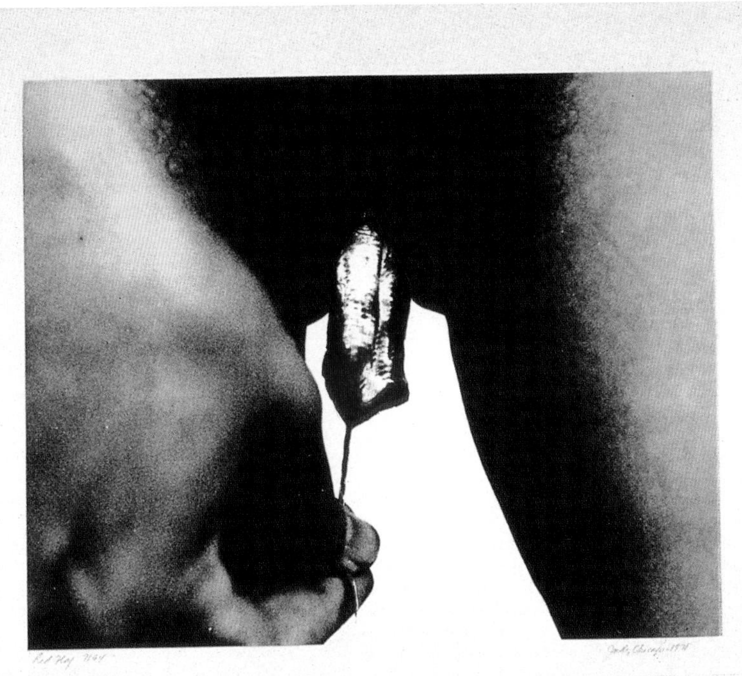

▲ Figure 13. Judy Chicago, *Red Flag*, 1971. Photolithograph, 20″ × 24″.

◂ Figure 14. Judy Chicago, *Homage to Miriam Schapiro*, 1972. Graphite on paper, from sketchbook, 6″ × 8″. Inscribed "If sculpture: white plex box/shelves of trans[parent]/refl.[ective] Mirror-Back pieces sprayed w/ fade—Eggs cast resin w/ color." Collection of the artist; courtesy Lew Allen Contemporary.

◂ Figure 15. Judy Chicago, *Heaven Is for White Men Only,* 1973. Sprayed acrylic on canvas, 80″ × 80″. Collection of the New Orleans Museum of Art.

◂ Figure 16. Judy Chicago, *Let It All Hang Out,* 1973. Sprayed acrylic on canvas, 80″ × 80″. Collection of the New Orleans Museum of Art.

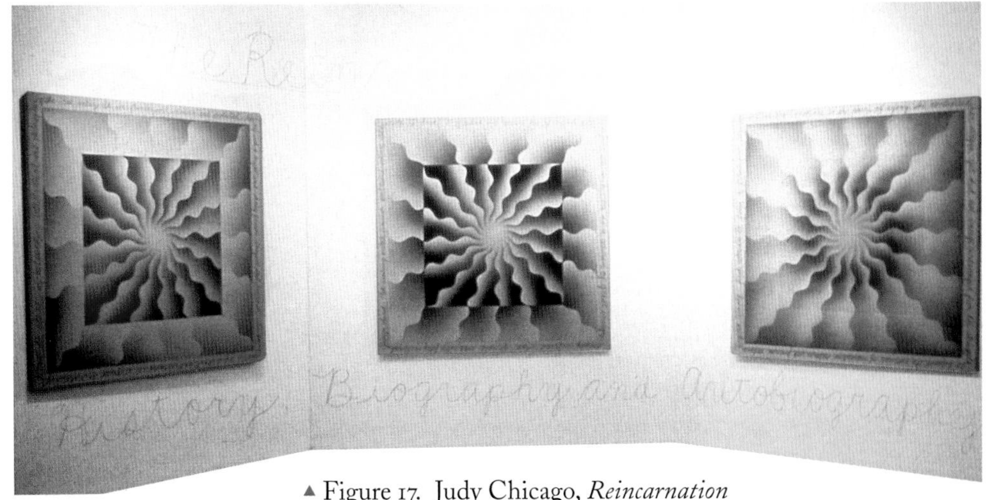

▲ Figure 17. Judy Chicago, *Reincarnation Triptych* (installation view), 1973. Sprayed acrylic on canvas, each 5′ × 5′. Private collections.

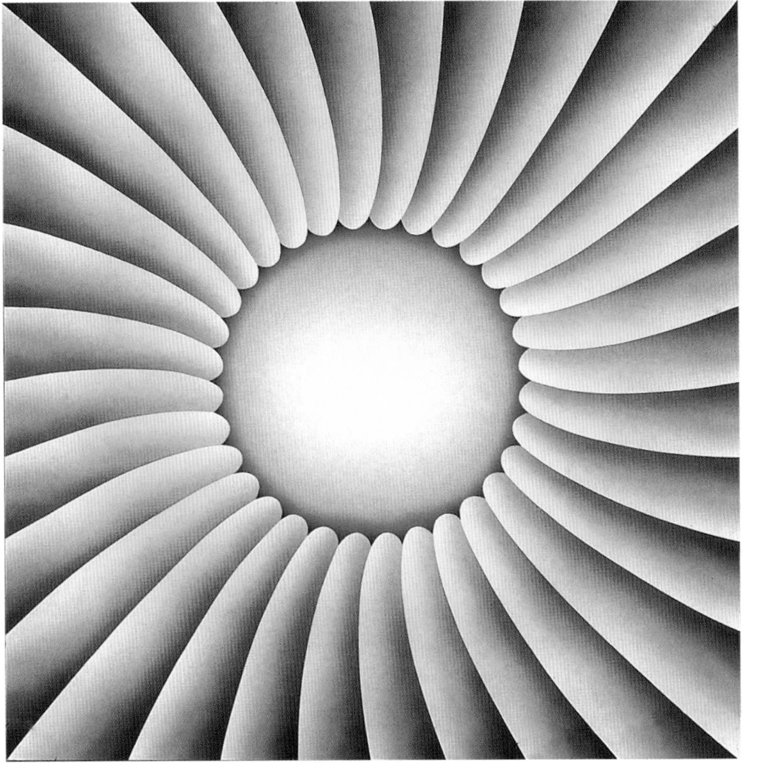

◂ Figure 18. Judy Chicago, *Through the Flower,* 1973. Sprayed acrylic on canvas, 5′ × 5′. Collection of Elizabeth A. Sackler.

▲ Figure 19. Judy Gerowitz, *A Butterfly for Oakland,* 1974. Fireworks, road flares, and magnesium flares. Oakland Museum of Art, Oakland.

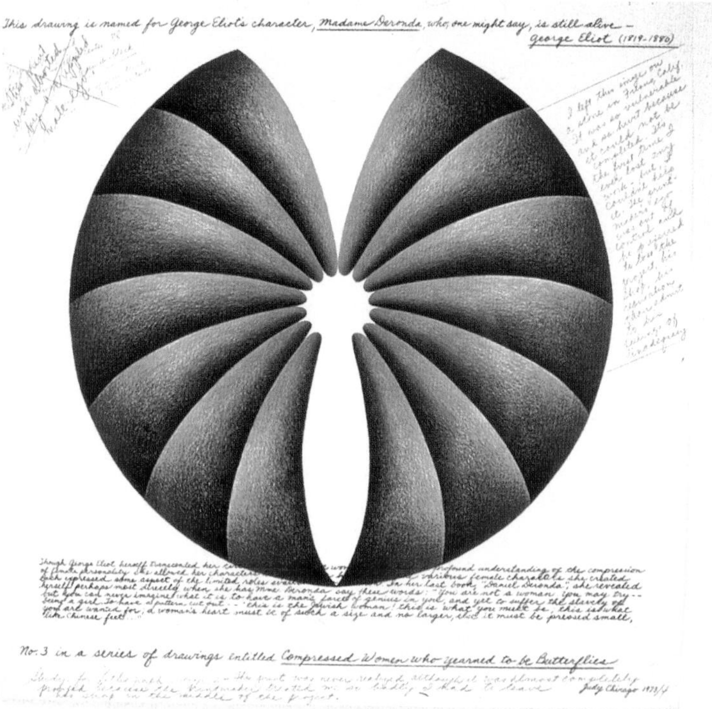

◄ Figure 20. Judy Chicago, *Compressed Women Who Yearn to Be Butterflies #3—Mme. Deronda,* 1974. Prismacolor on rag paper, 24″ × 24″. Collection of Arkansas Art Center, Little Rock.

▲ Figure 21. Judy Chicago's thirty-ninth birthday party in the *Dinner Party* studio, July 1978.

▼ Figure 22. Judy Chicago, *The Dinner Party,* 1979, looking from Wing Three. Installation at the Brooklyn Museum. Collection of the Brooklyn Museum.

◂ Figure 23. Judy Chicago, Judith place setting from *The Dinner Party,* 1979.

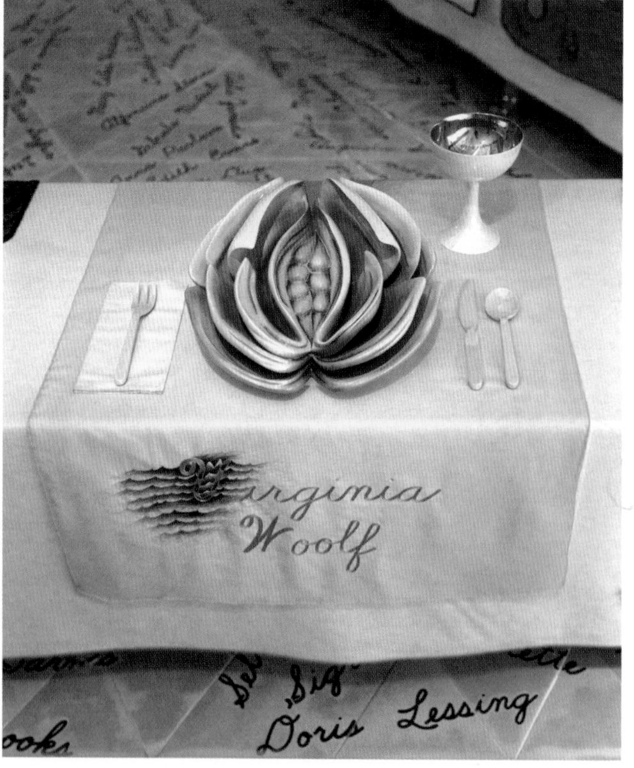

◂ Figure 24. Judy Chicago, Virginia Woolf place setting from *The Dinner Party,* 1979.

▲ Figure 25. Judy Chicago, *Earth Birth* from the *Birth Project,* 1983. Sprayed acrylic on fabric, quilting by Jacquelyn Moore, 5′3″ × 11′4″. Collection of Through the Flower Corporation.

▲ Figure 26. Judy Chicago, *The Creation* from the *Birth Project,* 1984. Modified Aubusson tapestry, woven by Audrey Cowan from Judy Chicago's cartoon, 43″ × 163″. Collection of Audrey and Bob Cowan.

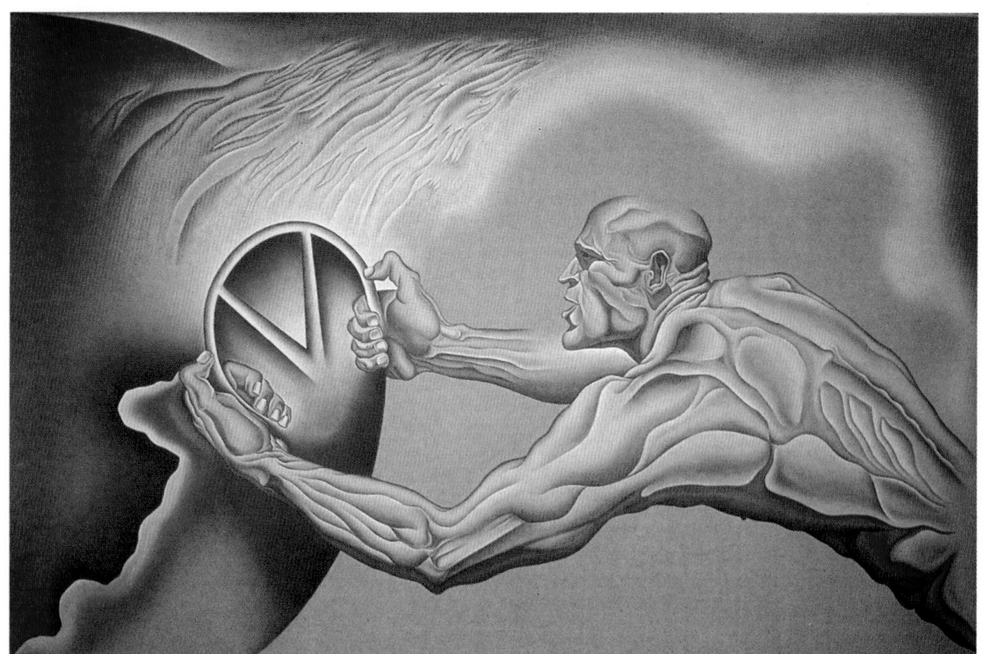

▲ Figure 27. Judy Chicago, *Driving the World to Destruction*, from *Powerplay*, 1985. Sprayed acrylic and oil on linen, 9′ × 14′. Courtesy Lew Allen Contemporary.

◄ Figure 28. Judy Chicago and Donald Woodman, *Treblinka/Genocide* from the *Holocaust Project* (detail), 1989. Sprayed acrylic, oil, and photography on photolinen, 48.5″ × 7′10.5″. Collection of the artists and Through the Flower Corporation.

◂ Figure 29. Judy Chicago and Donald Woodman, *Double Jeopardy* from the *Holocaust Project* (detail, panel 1), 1990. Sprayed acrylic, oil, and photography on photolinen, 3′7″ × 22′5″. Collection of the artists and Through the Flower Corporation.

▴ Figure 30. Judy Chicago, *Rainbow Shabbat* from the *Holocaust Project* (detail of center panel), 1992. Stained glass, fabricated by Bob Gomez, hand-painted by Dorothy Maddy from Judy Chicago's full-scale cartoon, 4′6″ × 16′. Collection of the artists and Through the Flower Corporation.

◂ Figure 31. Judy Chicago, *Bury the Hatchet* from *Resolutions: A Stitch in Time,* 1999. Painting, needlepoint, appliqué, and embroidery, needlework by Lynda Patterson, assisted by Jane Thompson and Mary Ewanoski, 24″ × 18″. Collection of the artists.

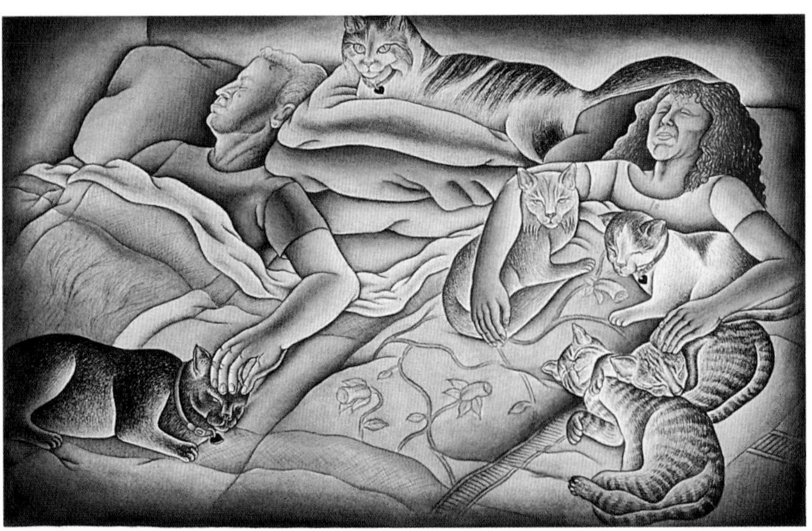

▴ Figure 32. Judy Chicago, *11 PM: Bedtime* from *Kitty City,* 2003. Watercolor on Arches paper, 22″ × 30″. Collection of Keith and Jim Straw.

Another key worker, Diane Gelon, was a young graduate student in art history when she first met Chicago in 1973 at the opening of the Woman's Building, where she had exhibited photographs alongside works by Chicago. Now she came to the project as a result of running into Chicago at a poster preview party for the National Organization for Women (NOW) in November 1977, for which Chicago had designed a poster. Chicago asked Gelon if she would be willing to help with the research for *The Dinner Party.* Chicago had already chosen the thirty-nine women at the table but needed more help to choose women for the Heritage floor, by now set to number 999. After briefly thinking about it, Gelon phoned to say that she would help, though at first she worked only a two days a week.

Gelon, who had graduated from UCLA in art history in 1970 and begun graduate studies there a year later, had taken a class in 1972 on women artists with Ruth Iskin, when she was active in the Woman's Building. It was there that Gelon recalls being "blown away" by Chicago's show of *Great Ladies*—so much so that despite her student status, she purchased the drawing "To Jay DeFeo," for $300.

Gelon had helped to found the Jewish Feminist Organization and organized a large feminist seder in 1973 (in the L.A. home of her parents, who were then away), to which Chicago, Raven, and "all the key women from the Woman's Building" came.[186] Gelon wrote an article entitled "Defining Jewish Feminism" for the *UCLA Daily Bruin* supplement in November 1974, in which she explained, "The Jewish feminist movement evolved out of a shared sense of identification and a shared series of problems. In a time when women are exploring their identities, Jewish women often discover a conflict of identity. The women's movement can give them a positive self-image as women but not as Jews. Jewish organizations affirm their Jewishness but seem to restrict the quality of their involvement because they are women."[187] She described the April 1974 meeting in New York City of Jewish women from all over North America that led to the founding of the Jewish Feminist Organization. She also promoted the Jewish Women's Organizing Project at UCLA, which reflected the philosophy of the larger organization and encouraged "the creation of consciousness-raising groups, study groups on Jewish women's history, organizing a women's Seder and Shabbat service, and other programs" for which she was the contact person.

Gelon, a lesbian who had already come out by the time she first met Chicago and who identified herself as a "religious school teacher and Jewish day camp director," had organized a Woman's Day program, sponsored by the Jewish Feminist Coalition, in May 1973. It featured panel discussions about Jewish women in history and their participation in contemporary Judaism, a bag lunch, and workshops dealing with topics such as "the Jewish American Princess; single, gay, and married women; the Jewish mother; Israeli women; professionals; alternative lifestyles; and feminist consciousness."[188]

Gelon maintains that only about 10 percent of the workers on *The Dinner Party* were lesbian. No one's sexuality mattered in the studio, she insists; people "left their lives at the door."[189] When an interviewer asked Chicago, "Do you ever get pressure from lesbian women to do work using your same symbols in a nonheterosexual context?" she replied, "I get pressure from everybody," and elaborated, "I'm not a lesbian. Therefore my art is not universal. I think that to some extent the feelings that my art gives are universal to women, even though the forms are not. I certainly support the idea of a strong lesbian art—I think it's very important. Lesbians have so far created very little open art that speaks out of the lesbian experience. I've done a lot of work on the whole history of lesbianism for *The Dinner Party.*"[190] She added: "I'm amazed at the hush—and it's understandable in many ways—but it's unbelievable how shrouded the whole area of (lesbian) experience is. I think it presents a rich potential for subject matter, but it's hard subject matter to use and not fall into rhetoric. And I don't think I'm the right one to do it."[191]

Lesbians were no different from other women who felt that their needs would be served by working on *The Dinner Party.* In this period Chicago remarked that she must be "sending out a lot of messages about being accessible & needy 'cause people just keep cropping up."[192] Her plans for the project had crystallized. She even imagined permanent housing inside of a "porcelain room."[193] Chicago applied to the National Endowment for the Arts for a travel grant to Europe, where she planned to study porcelain housing. Lucy Lippard wrote in her behalf: "It is extremely important that this piece, which may well be the culminating glory of the 'first phase' of art-feminism, be preserved as a female monument for future generations. So much energy has been expended on archaeology in the field of women's culture. It would be nice if something were simply out there in the public domain all along."[194] Lippard also wrote, "Not only is Judy the most brilliant and committed of the feminist artists working today, but *The Dinner Party* transcends individual style by its collective process. It will stand as a record of how much many women cared to have our history re-emerge, and how vigorous this tradition is and can be."[195]

To Lippard, Chicago reported that Cindy Nemser (whom she referred to as "Cindy the Nemesis") had told a woman in Canada, who was planning to invite her to open the feminist show there, "not to have me as I would cause trouble. Now that is going too far. . . . At any rate, they invited me anyway . . . but I couldn't go. Faith Wilding went instead and they loved her. She was dynamite.

So that's nice."[196] In a subsequent letter Chicago told Lippard, "Cindy Nemser is coming out here to promote her book, and I am, in the spirit of solidarity and sisterhood, giving her a party or reception or something. If, after I do that, the woman continues to put me down, the only thing to do is put out a contract on her."[197] Nemser recalls forming a negative opinion because she rejected Chicago's notion of "central core imagery," which she found "limiting and denigrating."[198] She still has the "nice letter" that Chicago wrote congratulating her before she traveled to California on her book tour, mentioning Nemser's talk at the Woman's Building: "Interesting that our books are coming out so close together . . . perhaps it is an omen, foretelling a coming together of the East and West in unity and sisterhood. In that spirit, I should like to have some sort of small party or evening for you at my studio. . . . Is there anyone you would particularly like to meet?"[199]

Not even the most politic letter could reconcile the feminist artists from the two coasts. Hostility to Chicago's ideas multiplied in the East, even as major New York feminists embraced her work. Vera Goodman's feature article, "Judy Chicago, Trendsetter," discussed a number of the issues that divided Nemser and Chicago: "California is a microcosm of America, only more so. People here seem to practice with emotional intensity the various movements developed in this country whether far to the right or the left. Hence it is not surprising that the feminist art movement has evolved on the west coast as one of the most exciting in the country. Its innovator and outstanding exponent is Judy Chicago."[200] She explained that Chicago "does not make feminist art consciously" but had "stopped censoring herself. She goes with her impulses now, which in her early period seemed too bizarre. Instead of conforming she challenges market-place values. Because of her independence the east coast has been deprived of viewing her work in full. Dealers in New York, including female gallery directors, fear her art is too explicit in its intensity."[201] She quoted Chicago: "I think New York women artists are unquestionably more tied to mainstream art values than women are anywhere else in the country. The best of them are painting within a context that is evaporating rapidly. It is very interesting because you take the art and hang it in a gallery in SoHo and it looks terrific. If you take that same art and hang it in a women's building it looks neutralized, it looks contentless. It looks emotionally dead."[202]

Although unable to budge Nemser or other women in the New York art world, Chicago reflected that things were fine at home in California. She was even content with Hamrol, although they spent little time together. He was busy working with Jack Rhyne to expand their living space, which, though in a huge warehouse, was tiny. They had no living room and a bedroom only about six by ten feet, a trailer-sized cooking space, and a small eating space. Their equal but separate studios were both large. Gelon viewed the couple as having "a very solid relationship"—like Jean (Hans) and Sophie Taeuber Arp, on whom she planned to write her dissertation.[203]

Chicago and Hamrol took a ten-day vacation on the beach in San Felipe, Mexico, over Christmas. She was reading more texts to include in *The Dinner Party*'s projected companion book, and she summed up what she wanted the work to do: "break through all the categories between fine arts, decorative art, painting, sculpture, male skills, female skills, etc. & present a wholistic [*sic*] vision which has substantial content."[204] Toward the end of the trip, which had gone smoothly enough, Hamrol confronted and challenged her about their relationship, making her begin to feel "strained": "Not so much the demands—tho it turns out that his needs for me are quite larger & they scare me some—but he still gets so angry when he's upset & so it's not only necessary to deal with the feelings, but this anger too & that's very tiring."[205]

Chicago traveled to San Francisco in early January 1976 in order to install her show of twenty-nine porcelain miniatures at the gallery, Quay Ceramics. Henry Hopkins made a speech at the opening, and the Oakland Museum bought the only piece that sold. Her longtime friend, the artist Manuel Neri, whom she had first met through Hamrol, took her to visit studios of some well-regarded Bay Area artists who worked in clay: Richard Shaw, Robert Hudson, and Peter Voulkos. That evening she walked around her show with Voulkos, which she said was "particularly pleasing as he started the whole West Coast clay movement."[206]

A female reviewer described Chicago's show as "exotic erotica" and noted that the use of words, including the show's long title, which Chicago had written in pencil around the gallery walls, was her "means of demystifying the art process and the meaning of her work."[207] She wrote on the wall the names of the three series being shown: *Butterfly Goddesses and Other Specimens* as well as *Six Views from the Womantree* and *Broken Butterflies/Shattered Dreams.* But the male reviewer for the *San Francisco Chronicle* dismissed the work for what he identified as "cartoonish eroticism" with an "essentially decorative prettiness" and a "total lack of artistic consequence."[208] Chicago wrote to her gallery: "I heard I got a heavenly review in the San Francisco paper. It has been a long time since anybody said that what I did wasn't art. I am thrilled." She also told them: "Send any sales money as quickly as possible. I am BROKE."[209]

Chicago had arranged in advance to meet in San Francisco a young man with whom she had worked on the television program in South Carolina. She had sent him a postcard mentioning that she regretted not taking him to bed, and he had responded with avidity. She viewed him as "a lonely, love-starved guy."[210] But by the time of her trip she felt guilty and wondered why she had done this, only to realize that what she really wanted was a television program featuring *The Dinner Party*. She quickly discovered his lack of consciousness about feminism and realized that she had no desire either to take on his education or to have an affair with him, although he was "a sweet young guy." She hoped that after Diane Gelon arrived she might take him off her hands. (The three of them were staying at the same apartment.)

Spending the day with Neri, to whom she had long been attracted (he had always been married in the past), Chicago decided to go to his place and get him to bed: "I finally felt attracted to someone & acted on it & it was a good choice—someone with whom I actually could make a human connection with."[211] Years later Neri would say of his longtime friend, "Judy is tough to say the least. She knows how to survive. I stayed out of her way."[212] Chicago told herself that she had had a terrific time and that "it's awful to admit but, tho I love Lloyd & probably have more satisfying sex with him than I'll *ever* have with anyone, I still get turned on to other people & now I intend to act on it whenever I feel like it."[213] When she could spare the money, she planned to get her tubes tied. She may also have been responding to what Lloyd admitted about liberties of his own while they were in Bellingham.

In San Francisco, Chicago realized too that her own project was getting to her: "In a way all these people with all their ideas about the piece & their raving about *it* & all that made me sort of intimidated—I'm afraid of its importance now instead of being connected to it."[214] She returned to work on the companion book and on raising funds, asking herself why she had taken on an art project that so often took her away from making art in the studio.

Chicago traveled to Portland, Oregon, for a show (March 3–27, 1976) of her china work at the Ann Hughes Gallery. (The show would later travel to Seattle.) She gave a very well-attended lecture at the art museum, and a local paper interviewed her. The reporter, Ellen McCormick, called Chicago's work "vibrant" and noted that the artist had worked with other men and women to install the show "to Judy's specifications," explaining: "Working with her required a lack of ego involvement, since her strong ideas and personality dominated the project, appropriately, but absolutely."[215]

In Portland, Chicago was thrilled to meet Rosemarie Radmaker, the vice president of the International China Painting Teachers Association, who came to her opening. She and Diane Gelon lunched with Radmaker, who responded positively to the lecture's feminist ideas. She saw Chicago as making a bridge from their craft world to the world of art and wanted to set up a demonstration by Chicago at the international show in New Orleans the following summer.

The fresh overture prompted Chicago to reflect on her ability to work with people: "Sometimes I'll be doing a workshop or a rap session . . . I'll be sitting there in the center of a group of people & suddenly, I'll flash on my father & I will feel as if I've become him. It scares me when I get that feeling & I want to run away from it."[216] She described a workshop on feminist education in which she was trying "to get the audience to see thru the eyes of a young female college student. At first they weren't relating to what I was saying, & then I began to tell a story, which I made up out of my need to get them to understand. Halfway through the story, I realized that I had done something I had seen my father do, both with me & with other people."[217]

Chicago remarked on the large crowds she attracted everywhere but New York, "which is still very rejecting of me." She wondered if her efforts to build a national audience were in vain, "if ultimately, it only matters if one makes one's mark in New York. Of course, if it really happens that changes take place that render the old art system obsolete, then all my work will be valuable."[218] At a lecture in Pocatello, Idaho, Chicago met Kathleen Schneider, a young woman who had just finished her master's degree and wanted to come and work on *The Dinner Party.*

Her trip also included lectures in Pullman, Washington; Kansas City, Chicago, and Minnesota, although they still left her conflicted—tired of talking about her work but needing the money to keep working. Not wanting to talk about *The Dinner Party* as yet, she had to focus on past work. Eventually the ideas that she wanted to convey in her lectures came together. She hoped to "directly influence art values. . . . I want to start talking about how I feel when I read magazines, go to galleries—my response to most art—what I'm trying to do both in terms of art/history/mythology (building a female version) & in terms of art becoming a vital force."[219]

When her show traveled to Seattle in May, the "and/or gallery's" space was too large, so she invited Hamrol to share. Once again she felt their relationship was going well. He was working very hard on his art, which was positive for them as a couple. The joint flyer featured a heart-shaped photograph of them both at their kitchen table and an inscription—"Best Wishes Lloyd Hamrol Judy Chicago"—around the heart. The day after the opening they held a joint discussion where the audience wrote out questions, which they took turns answering: "It was very educational for the audience to see an equalized relationship, & we both got a lot of good feed-back. I was really pleased that Lloyd got rewarded for all the work he's done in building our marriage. I get a lot of feedback & support from the Women's Movement—for my art, my relationship, etc. But L. gets less—so it was wonderful."[220] She felt good that they had come so far since the Bellingham trauma two years earlier. When they made a taped interview of each other for the journal *Criteria,* Chicago said to Hamrol, "You benefited me not only as a woman but as an artist, and I've benefited you as an artist and a man." He responded, "I love you," at which point, she rejoined, "You do? I love you too."[221]

For his show, Hamrol built a sandbag wall, which Chicago found "beautiful," and he showed photographs of other pieces, while she used pink paint with a butterfly image on the walls in her part of the gallery for an installation that took three days to set up. She involved about a dozen or so women volunteers—a complicated process that she had begun in the Woman's Building. Volunteers, for example, worked to thicken the letters that she had written with pencil on the walls; she was "demanding and precise about how it was to be done." Chicago was not surprised when a woman got upset at being told again and again that it wasn't right; she had pointed out in her book that she wanted to push women to learn to go beyond their limits.[222]

To a journalist, she reflected upon making art that could be seen outside museums: "Now art is made for a very small portion of society—and even if you were to take most art out of the context of museums, it has so little to do with anybody's life that nobody would look at it. So it might as well be in museums. The nature of art would have to change in order to have relevance to people's lives."[223] This brought her back to her concept of women's art: "That's why I think women's art would have such an incredible potential in doing that, taking art out of museums and putting it into a wider audience if their art is clearly addressed to a women's audience and dealt with women's experience in a way that women could really identify with. That's what's important about women's art—not 'Right on, sister!' not polemic political art that does not aspire to the highest level of excellence."[224]

A group of Seattle women, including Mary Avery, Judy Kleinberg, and Susan Macleod, had raised money through an auction to have Chicago give two lectures, so she stayed on after Hamrol left. Chicago then donated one of her paintings for the women to raffle off so that they could use the money to begin organizing a women's center.[225] Chicago told them that she "wanted to show the female principle acting upon the male, acting on her own behalf instead of being acted upon."[226] She elaborated: "Our cunt is a metaphor for us. I mean you act through your cunt; you act sexually. All this stuff comes in and goes out. How you see it is a real mirror of how you see yourself. That's why the whole idea of being affirmed by art. I think that's what art has been for men."[227]

Another interviewer in Seattle drew Chicago out concerning her decision not to have children: "There is a fundamental terror programmed into us very early that leaves us with a terror of being alone. There is a will to retreat in women, a terror of going out into the world alone and making it." Chicago questioned whether women used children to escape the world's pressures but said that this had not been worked out yet.[228] This probing set Chicago's mind to work: "It was easy to see how women often protect themselves from taking responsibility for their lives by having children, & I began to get interested in the whole area of motherhood in terms of images. I don't know when or if I'll get to it, but if I can, today when I think I'll have some time before my talk, I'd like to go to the library. When I was about 12, I did a lot of drawings of pregnant women & also, about that time, became interested in the praying mantis."[229]

When she returned to L.A., Chicago signed a contract with Ruth Schaffner as her Southern California dealer. Ruth loaned Judy her home in Santa Barbara for two weeks in June so that she could be alone and concentrate on finishing her book manuscript about *The Dinner Party*—she was still working on a feminist version of Genesis, a section on the Apocalypse, and a "witch tale."[230] For the Apocalypse she had found a printshop eager to do a limited illustrated edition. At least one publisher responded to doing a book on *The Dinner Party* but wanted only reproductions of the plates and a short statement about each, not the grand narration that she had imagined.[231] She reflected, "The writing is very hard for me—I really think I'm not really a writer—but rather an artist who feels compelled to write in order to establish a context for my art."[232]

During her retreat in Schaffner's house, Chicago had an angry exchange with de Bretteville, Raven, and Iskin about activities at the Woman's Building and in the Feminist Studio Workshop. Despite her repeated resolutions to withdraw into her private space, she felt deeply wounded at being left out of a meeting at Susan Rennie and Kirsten Grimstad's home, since the meeting regarded the relationship between their magazine, *Chrysalis,* and the building that she had first proposed.[233] Grimstad recalls their doubting that Chicago really wanted to be involved.[234] Chicago also still harbored ideas about how the Woman's Building should be run. Michele Kort recalls that Chicago thought that the building should pay for Michele to take a grantsmanship course and told her colleagues that they should all donate a certain amount of money to that end, to which they agreed.[235]

When Chicago, together with Raven and de Bretteville, founded the Feminist Studio Workshop, she sought to implement her vision of how to teach feminist art. She emphasized that women should "go from content—to subject matter—to form . . . to develop form that is most consistent with the content."[236] She welcomed expression through film, video, performance, books, painting, or sculpture but noted that the last two media required "enormous skill" and training and thus other media that "can reach people more quickly, and have greater impact have been gaining in popularity."[237] She questioned whether painting and sculpture "aren't antiquated. . . . There have been so many other ways developed in the twentieth century to make art . . . very direct ways to deal with subject matter."[238] This point of view disappointed some participants in both the Feminist Studio Workshop and the Feminist Art Program at CalArts, who arrived with more traditional notions and goals about art.

De Bretteville felt that her design work for Chicago's projects, including the catalog for *Womanhouse,* which she had done as a favor, had not been appreciated. De Bretteville expressed pain that Chicago had disparaged her in letters to others: "Perhaps it is a problem as I am sometimes honored as in your painting at the Museum in San Francisco and in Deens's [Deena Metzger's] book where the fictional character's name is derived from mine . . . and in your book which as a documenting of your experience with little transformation you fairly and warmly checked with me. I do not deny that some of my comments about these issues might have had some 'bite' to them. I was in pain too!"[239] More recently De Bretteville commented, "Judy likes to run things. She has an incredible sense of agency—energetic entrepreneurship. It's part of her makeup." She described Chicago as an "incredibly healthy terrific model for other people."[240] At the same time de Bretteville did not approve of what she described as "Chicago's use of confrontation in her teaching style."[241] More than once she accused Chicago of thinking only of herself.

Chicago might have agreed with de Bretteville. They had squabbled at one of those recurrent moments when Chicago was not sure that she cared so much about relationships. In an unflinching critique of herself she admitted, "I guess I'm sort of opportunistic & interested in relationships benefiting me & my work mostly—except for Lloyd, of course, whom I genuinely love. As for other people in my life, by & large, if they aren't useful to me I lose interest."[242] She reflected, "I wonder what a reader of these words would think of me—I seem so warm & human & I am, while at the same time, I'm cold & uncaring & interested only in reaching my goals. That's true, you know—I want to be a great artist (or creator) & that's about all I care about, except for Lloyd & my cats & even the cats are symbolic, for though I missed Lamont when he died, I replaced him with Orlando."[243] The magnetism that attracted disciples could seem a curse. De Bretteville also describes her as "incredibly charismatic."[244]

Among the most devoted was Gelon, who remembers visiting Chicago in that Santa Barbara retreat and hearing for the first time her vision of a major traveling art ensemble, too vast to erase. It would present women's history on three levels: as art, as a book, and as a film. Gelon felt that the project was "a fantastic dream" and that there was no way that "it could happen without Judy in her studio. . . . I bought into the dream. I felt that I had the skills to do it."[245] Soon she dropped out of graduate school and began working full-time on *The Dinner Party,* earning her living by driving a schoolbus for the Stephen S. Wise Temple in L.A.

For the last two days of her retreat Hamrol joined Chicago. He was about to depart on what she described as almost a year of "nonstop activity for him around the country. It's really quite amazing that we've managed things so that both of us make a surge forward at the same time. . . . It's a good thing our relationship is strong—strong enough to survive the periods of separation & probably to flourish as a result of our independent growth."[246] After Hamrol left, Chicago noted though that she didn't miss him: "he drains my energy, tho I care about him. He's still difficult emotionally."[247] She saw herself as so overwhelmed by work that she had little time or energy for him.

They reunited for four days in July in New Orleans, where Chicago went to attend a show of china painting. After Hamrol left, she received her assistant Gelon, the china painter Rosemarie Radmaker, and the filmmaker Johanna Demetrakas, who was planning to document *The Dinner Party.* Bereft at not being able to paint, she was puzzled that, despite her success so far, she felt so "fragmented."[248]

By the time Chicago returned to L.A., Kathleen Schneider and Judye Keyes had built a mockup of a corner of *The Dinner Party* so that they could work out all the problems of proportion, construction, and design. They set the piece up with six full table settings and invited about forty people in to see it. Buoyed by the demonstration of craft and the harbinger of success, Chicago wrote that "working on this piece is wonderful & I have to really fight off the terrors that I will lose it all."[249]

By June 1976 the National Endowment for the Arts had awarded Judy Chicago a fellowship grant of $5,000. Chicago and Susan Hill, who now was supporting herself by part-time employment with a dentist, were actively recruiting helpers for the work, spreading the appeal through Chicago's lectures and through ads in craft and art magazines. The master artist's use of studio assistants goes back at least to the Renaissance, but Chicago had observed the idea early in her own development, watching the story of the painter Gulley Jimson in the film *The Horse's Mouth.* As this fictional character struggled to realize his exalted vision, he convinced others to come to work on his masterpiece, even to pay him for the privilege.

Besides those who actually worked in Chicago's studio, groups from Hawaii to Maine helped to gather data for three thousand women, from whom were chosen the final 999 represented on the Heritage floor.[250] A research team for the floor met weekly all summer to share findings. Hill had assembled a team of needleworkers who prepared samplers for Chicago to use when she designed the runners. "We are designing these absolutely beautiful runners for the plates," Chicago wrote, "but they will require enormous work to be translated into needle-work & right now, we do not have anywhere near enough needleworkers."[251]

Among the volunteers who responded to an ad was Audrey Cowan, who saw the notice in *Artweek.* Cleveland-born, Cowan had attended art school but had not made a living from her art, although she continued to produce it, even while putting her energies into marriage and supporting and raising children. She began at *The Dinner Party* around 1975, at first doing research and then doing stitchery for the *Hildegarde of Bingen* runner. One day Chicago called to say that a weaver needed help on the runner for *Eleanor of Aquitaine.* On a second call, she reported that the weaver could not do it at all, and she implored Audrey to take over the task, despite the fact that Cowan had never woven a tapestry. Chicago arranged to pay for training, and Cowan mastered the technique, acquiring a skill that she still practices and develops.[252] She considers Chicago a "good role model" who expects more from you than you expect from yourself.

Another needleworker was Marjorie Biggs, who taught ecclesiastical embroidery for the Episcopal diocese of Los Angeles and began work as a consultant. Talking after she had been working "two years in it 'hip-deep,'" Biggs said: "They've taken on such an enormous project of lasting beauty that you just want to be part of it."[253] When Biggs showed Chicago and the other workers "her first piece of handwork, a millennium runner stitched in white silk," they "oohed and aahed," recalls Cowan, causing Biggs to burst into tears. She was crying, she told them, because "through thirty-eight years of embroidering altar cloths and vestments, no one had ever before said anything about her work."[254] Other volunteers included Chicago's aunt Dorothy Polin, who also embroidered. Although the average age of the workers was said to be about thirty, there was Betty Van Atta, "a grandmother from Sun City who . . . originally came here because of the stitchery but got involved in both feminism and consciousness-raising."[255] Van Atta's daughter Jeanne had suggested the project to her mother after hearing Chicago lecture in Cleveland.[256]

Among the volunteers who arrived in 1976 was Kathy Erteman, who had graduated with a degree in ceramics from Cal State Long Beach and taken courses at UCLA. She worked part-time and lasted until work on *The Dinner Party* was finished. In her own studio she produced for each place setting the ceramic chalices that Ken Gilliam had designed. Erteman, whose teachers had all been men, says that she volunteered so that she could see a woman artist at work. She reports that the experience demonstrated to her "how to make it as a woman artist." She gained confidence and felt affirmed, but she notes that though Chicago was "nurturing in her own abrasive way," she was more attentive to women whom Erteman considered "wounded birds."[257]

Another volunteer, Sharon Kagan, was about to graduate from UCLA when she heard Chicago talk at the Woman's Building—"an amazing lecture that spoke my language."[258] Kagan had studied at UCLA with Oliver Andrews, who had been Chicago's own professor for sculpture. But at the Otis Institute of Art, where Kagan went for graduate work, she felt that there was a backlash among her male professors, including Emerson Wolfer, because they did not approve of her working on *The Dinner Party*. Though women faculty members—Wanda Westcoast and Betye Saar—did not express the same contempt, they refused to get involved in the matter.[259] At the *Dinner Party* studio Kagan worked on various tasks such as carving and painting the plates, doing needlepoint, helping to design runners, and embroidering part of the *Hatshepsut* runner. She also used to run with Chicago in the mornings. She recalls that "Judy had a temper, but we figured out how to deal with her. She wasn't controlling, but was under a lot of stress."[260] By the second year of Kagan's graduate study, after working for a year and a half, she felt that she had to devote full-time to her graduate program but says that Chicago felt abandoned and made her feel like a "persona non grata." Nonetheless, says Kagan, she would choose to work on the project again, since she "learned a lot, had an amazing time—it completely formed who I am."[261] She considers *The Dinner Party* an important work of art, "nothing like that exists today."[262]

One of the other artists who volunteered, Ann Isolde, arrived in Los Angeles from Colorado, where she had received her MFA at Boulder. After reading *Through the Flower*, she was attracted by the promotional material on the Feminist Studio Workshop. On her arrival in 1976 she found that Judy Chicago was off working on some special project. After taking Ruth Iskin's feminist art history class at the Woman's Building, she came to realize that she "wasn't crazy and that there was something wrong with the educational system."[263] She soon joined the workers on *The Dinner Party*, becoming the head of research. She later expressed how significant and timely she and others considered *The Dinner Party* and its message to be and that they believed this made cooperative work the fastest means to get that message out: " 'I've always looked at a piece of paper on which I made *my* mark,' says Isolde, 'but I'm willing here to express myself cooperatively because women's history is so fragmented that if we also fragment it stylistically, it would further contribute to the confusion.' "[264]

Isolde described the creation of the runners: "Maybe a team of about four or six people would do research and come in; then there would be a brainstorming of ideas and they would start working on it together. . . . It's clear walking into the room that no one person made *The Dinner Party.* It's clear that one person's aesthetic vision shaped it, but no one person could have come up with that many ideas in that period of time." She explained that "a lot of times Judy's ideas were the most in tune with what the image was trying to say, but other times other people's ideas were more in tune and some of her ideas would be set aside. She was very flexible that way. . . . Judy did not pull power trips when it was clear that people had things to offer which would make the image better."[265]

Many who worked on *The Dinner Party* report gaining invaluable experience that they put to use later. Dorothy K. Goodwill, for example, a married woman with three daughters from South Euclid, Ohio, volunteered for a summer and was asked to work on the design of the runner for *Hildegarde of Bingen.* Goodwill not only went on to design and make liturgical vestments and altar hangings for Episcopal churches in northern Ohio; she had her own show of wearable art at a gallery in 1981.[266]

By August 1976 Diane Gelon had moved into Lloyd's loft for the summer, while he was away. Chicago did not know how he could work there when he returned, since, as she noted in her journal, "we *occupy* the studio psychologically." Most days there were then eight workers. Although they numbered about twenty-six in total, most worked part-time. Chicago considered the women on the project to be "involved in the process of feminist education. They're in CR [consciousness raising], & we have weekly open evenings in which we discuss various subjects. It's nice, tho sometimes tedious for me. I try & remind myself that all these people are working for me for nothing, & I try & be responsible to their growth & needs."[267]

Despite the evidence of cooperative energy and creativity in her cohorts, doubts kept haunting Chicago about completing the project: "it is in forcing the powerful people to accept one's ideas as significant, important etc. that ultimately one is assured of having those ideas act in the world."[268] She feared "a growing gulf between my own belief in myself & how I present myself to the world—a crack in the wall, as they say—one that could perhaps lead to despair, madness, suicide—I am not immune though I have thought myself to be. It is getting harder, not easier."[269] But then she took comfort from reflecting that if her faith faltered now, she had brought up others whose faith would hold: "I am pretending I will accomplish this. If I do, it's only because of others' investment in the project—because I, who don't believe, have made them believe, & it will be their belief that will pull us through."[270]

That autumn Juliet Myers, a teacher in Kansas City who had heard that acquaintances were working on an incredible project, moved to Los Angeles, hoping to take part, only to be turned down. A few weeks later someone from the project called to say that they needed a "researcher in women's history." Myers, who had earned a master's degree in printmaking at the University of Missouri in 1973, signed on. Very social, she recalls that Ann Isolde and others "took odds on how long she would last."[271] In the end, however, Myers became part of the paid staff and worked for Chicago for six years in L.A., took two years off, and worked six more in New Mexico. Myers says, "Judy is the greatest teacher I've ever had. She always demanded more from me than I thought I was capable of doing."[272] Today she is the director of education and public affairs for SITE Santa Fe, a private not-for-profit contemporary arts organization that organizes exhibitions and interdisciplinary programs.

Myers recalls the time that Susan Hill was looking for a long measure that she shared with the graphics studio, asking, "Has anyone see the big ruler?" "I think Judy went to the post office," Myers quipped.[273] A photograph in the first book on *The Dinner Party* documents that Chicago set Myers at a table in the middle of the studio so she could focus and placed a sign by her that said, "Don't talk to me—I'm working & if I stop Chicago will kill me!!!"[274] Myers considers this an important lesson. She viewed Chicago as "the artistic director—woman of vision—she was the leader and some saw leadership in the negative and wanted to have more input. There was collaboration, but, in the end of the day, it was Judy's vision."[275]

Not everyone who worked on *The Dinner Party* was so collegial. Two women who traveled all the way from Australia on a grant from their government to work on the project both did ribbon work for the *Emily Dickinson* runner. "They were quite discontented with the *Dinner Party* structure," Chicago later recalled. "They were radical Marxist feminists, which was OK, people have a right to their opinions. But they wanted it to be a collective and it was not a collective. It was a community only inasmuch as people worked together on one idea, my idea."[276]

By the end of September 1976 Chicago had designed eleven of the thirty-nine runners. Through Leonard Skuro, she met Ken Gilliam, an industrial designer who was then twenty-four. When he began doing some work on *The Dinner Party,* she responded to what she felt was a lot of energy between them and perceived that he had begun "wooing" her.[277] They arranged to meet for a few days in San Francisco, where Chicago had to go to see Henry Hopkins about showing *The Dinner Party* at the museum. The trip marked the beginning of a passionate relationship with Gilliam and signaled the end of her long involvement with and marriage to Hamrol, who, she felt, had rarely opened up to her. At thirty-seven Chicago felt that men of her generation could be neither open nor vulnerable, as Gilliam could. She felt affirmed by Gilliam and that Hamrol came into contact with his need for her only when he felt like he was losing her.[278]

Gilliam grew up in Anaheim in Southern California and graduated from Cal State Fullerton in 1974. He was in his first term when Chicago presented a show in Fullerton's gallery and announced her name change, but no wind of it reached him. Although he majored in psychology, he pursued a strong minor in design and went to UCLA for a master's degree in industrial design. For Gilliam, who still admires Chicago, working on *The Dinner Party* represented an opportunity for "great personal growth."[279] He had set up his own industrial design office adjacent to Chicago's studio, so he worked on *The Dinner Party* mostly at night. Asked whether that was "a labor of love," he responded, "Yes, on two fronts!"

Still, romance with Gilliam took second place to the project. In October Chicago went on the road to raise money by lecturing and to visit publishers in New York. In her absence, as well as that of Diane Gelon, who was also off fund-raising, the energy level in the studio was low and several people dropped out. Chicago and Gilliam, who had arranged to meet in Colorado, then decided to come out into the open with their relationship. Upon her return she told Hamrol about Gilliam and learned that he too was involved with another relationship. They made plans to separate for a year, as neither was prepared to end the marriage for good. At the time she and Gilliam were discussing living together.[280]

Chicago finally confided in Lucy Lippard about this new romance: "I just couldn't tell you what was then still in my mind a fantasy. But now that it has become more real, I am going to tell you that what has happened to me is something I thought was only a fairy tale. Even as I write the words, I am sure the experience is going to dissolve. I have fallen in love . . . it is almost the first time in my life I just wanted to 'be' with someone . . . it doesn't matter what we do."[281] Caught up in the moment, she told Lippard that Gilliam was "barely 25, absolutely wonderful, at least now. I don't even care how long it lasts . . . it is divine. We started getting together at the end of the summer and by October it was hot and heavy. We both had this sense that we wanted to build a life together. So, now we're going to try."[282] She described Gilliam to Lippard as "a designer . . . with natural building and mechanical skills, a very keen esthetic sensibility."[283]

Chicago rationalized to herself and to Lippard that this was the perfect time: "Lloyd and I need a separation. I can no longer tolerate his limitations and if he is ever to change them, he needs some time to do it. I don't know how I feel about him . . . in a year, after we get together to evaluate things, I am sure I will know. At that time, things will either have built into something solid with

Ken and me or I will know that it was a lovely fantasy. Lloyd and I will be able to know if we wish to resume our life together."[284]

There were days when she felt sad, Chicago admitted to Lippard, "about the demise or at least temporary end" of the marriage: "It is strange. On the one hand I feel sad, but on the other hand, I feel that Lloyd had twelve years to make a go of this relationship with me and he never could really step over the wall that keeps him separate . . . and now, someone else is trying and I'm going to go with it."[285] When Chicago and Hamrol began their official separation on January 1, 1977, they had been married seven and a half years, but since they had been together for so much longer, their separation represented a major turning point for both.

In the midst of her personal drama, Chicago made a commitment of $13,000 to a company to fabricate the floor tiles for *The Dinner Party.* The needlework runners were progressing slowly, but the plates kept chipping. With Hamrol still around getting ready to move out, Gelon decided that Chicago would do better elsewhere and moved her into her own place in Van Nuys so that she could concentrate on drawings for the projected book.[286]

During all the confusion Chicago's cat Goldfinger was hospitalized and died. Despite her romance, she again shaved off her eyebrows (now much thinner) in commemoration, as she had done years earlier for Lamont. She and Lloyd shared anguish at separating after so long, even getting together occasionally to make love.[287] She considered their sexual relations satisfying but always longed for him to be more open. She told herself that she had never gotten over the devastating disclosure in Bellingham of his serial infidelities. Although she welcomed the change in her life, it left her exhausted and numb.

Meanwhile Chicago prepared to push to finish *The Dinner Party* the next year. She envisioned seventeen-hour days and felt that she was rearranging her life to accommodate her work. "I need a man who can be part of my work now, even tho it hurts me to be separate from Lloyd. Perhaps in 1 year or a few years, we'll resume our relationship. In the meantime, as hard as this all is, it is essential. I am going to have a full year—an integrated year, [in] which work & play, personal & professional, inside & outside will be merged."[288]

After Judy told her mother that she and Lloyd were "separating," May Cohen wrote to her friends that "Judy says that I am suffering more than they. . . . She assures me that at present she has enough emotional support from all the people surrounding her, and she is too busy working to worry about how it will be 20 years hence."[289] Judy's mother reflected that "Lloyd is just now beginning to feel that pressure within him to forge his talent"; after having him alone for dinner, she noted that he was "approaching 40 and I think he is frightened."[290] As for Chicago, her feelings of guilt at Hamrol's pain were assuaged only when he admitted to her that their separation was the right decision.[291] But she had already replaced Hamrol with Gilliam, who made plans to rent the space of Hamrol's old studio for his own industrial design firm. He would work in the space adjacent to Chicago's own, where work on *The Dinner Party* continued despite her domestic drama. The rent would cover her own, easing some of her financial woes.

Gilliam and some of the *Dinner Party* workers helped Chicago with the installation of her show of china painting that took place in January 1977 at the Ruth S. Schaffner Gallery in Los Angeles. She had wanted to create a sense of the sacred in a "nonintimidating" environment. The show was planned to coincide with the large exhibition on women artists at the Los Angeles County Museum (organized by Linda Nochlin and Ann Sutherland Harris), which itself coincided with the annual meeting of the College Art Association. The opening was mobbed. Chicago showed a series of works from 1976 of painted porcelain china surrounded by pastel satin that she said depicted six stages of women's aspiration, the first of which was called *Broken Butterflies/Shattered Dreams* (*Nearly Free and Almost Flying*). Also included was a porcelain triptych (1976) entitled *Did You Know Your Mother Had a Sacred Heart?* which relates both to the Virgin Mary and to the idea of motherhood. It included six lit blue candles and a red silk cloth embroidered by Susan Hill and Arla Hesterman, celebrating female spirituality.

Ruth Askey, who reviewed the show, wrote of her "curiosity and delight in china-painted images on porcelain seen out of their usual context (i.e., tea roses painted on dinner plates) and a positive impact from the thematic celebration/affirmation of women's values."[292] She reported that Chicago had acknowledged her concern with "levels of leaving that (confined) space, of liberation; nonetheless, all the sheets (spaces) are brutally shattered—a metaphor of women's aspirations as well as her own."[293]

But William Wilson, writing in the *Los Angeles Times,* was clearly tone deaf to the subject of female spirituality. He went out of his way to pan the show: "The funeral-parlor ambiance of this wretchedly overinstalled exercise might be funny if it weren't so painful, forgivable if its lugubrious redundancy ceased at the works themselves. It does not. A series titled *Broken Butterfly/Shattered Dreams* comes in a row of casketlike boxes lined with satin. . . . This art has the symbolic delicacy of a swinging sledgehammer."[294] His review did not help generate sales, which were few but were needed to finance continuing work on *The Dinner Party.* Chicago realized that "my audience is still primarily people without a lot of money. But I'm still engaged in validating female experience as the subject matter for high art, which this show makes a big step in doing."[295]

By the new year Hamrol had moved out and Gilliam had moved in, and Chicago felt better than she had in years. She remarked on the various men who were now around the studio: not only Leonard Skuro but also Ken, his business partner John, and Jack Rhyne, the next-door neighbor and Judy's former studio assistant who had also constructed all her studios. She noted, "Hearing their voices & feeling that male energy fill the studio is fascinating. Had it happened some months ago, I think it would have broken the fabric of the atmosphere here—but not now."[296] Despite their old problems, Chicago could not completely dismiss her deep feelings for Hamrol. Still, Gilliam was present and pitching in to help.

By the middle of January 1977, Gilliam's friend Skuro had nearly solved the technical problem of the plates with reliefed surfaces. Chicago began to work on the plates, but the process was extremely frustrating; an air bubble could cause a carved plate to blow up in the kiln. In March she realized that she had only ten plates finished, since some had cracked in the kiln; she dropped a light on one by accident, and paint occasionally chipped.

Anxieties about losing the plates combined with those about finding enough money. Chicago and Susan Hill went east to study embroidery in museums in New York and Washington, so that she could increase her visual and technical knowledge. It remained for Chicago to design the runners for the second and third wings, but she was still anxious about those of the first wing, now approaching completion. But Diane Gelon continued to find solutions to Chicago's needs, raising money and organizing the studio so that she could do her artwork.

Encouragement too came from the many new volunteers and from the visitors who interrupted the routine in the studio. Adrienne Rich arrived, having read Chicago's manuscript on *The Apocalypse,* which, however, remains unpublished. Betty Prashker, her editor from Doubleday, came with Chicago's agent. Henry Hopkins also arrived to take a look at the state of progress in the studio, as he would continue to do in the months ahead. Chicago's aunt Dorothy worked on needlework, and her mother helped out by typing.

By March 1977 Chicago realized that she needed the volunteers to take on greater responsibility, overseeing the work of others, if they wanted to see the project through to completion. Now needleworkers also took part in doing the research and the design for the runners.

Not until May did Chicago succeed in successfully making a painted, carved plate. Even then another plate broke in the kiln for the second time, leaving her frustrated with the lengthy, difficult process.[297] In July the NEA awarded Chicago another grant, this time for $4,000, called a Service to the Field Grant. The NEA simultaneously gave another grant for *The Dinner Party* to the San Francisco Museum of Modern Art, making a total (so far) of $21,000 in government support. Although the grants helped ease the financial strain, the project definitely took a toll on Chicago's personal life. She wrote to Lucy Lippard in May that her life was "work . . . work—progress on the plates (at least)—designing a new round of runners (Wing 2)—Almost certainly going to try and develop a traveling structure (breakdown) to travel the piece in. Ken's designing it. Might as well go all the way. Things are great between Ken & me. Ah, love."[298]

Despite her romance with a younger man, Chicago concluded that she would not have children and decided to have her tubes tied. Ken was present during the outpatient procedure, which took place that June. She was in bed, frightened after bleeding from the navel. She wrote in her journal: "On some level I knew it had symbolic meaning . . . my body was telling me that this project was bleeding me of all my strength and that somehow I had to be relieved of that part which was not essential for me to do."[299]

Besides working on *The Dinner Party,* Chicago had begun training some of the workers to lecture and others to be facilitators, keeping up her commitment to feminist art education. But it was all too much for her to handle. She decided that she had to "get another space where I can be alone and apart from the mythic 'Judy Chicago.' "[300]

Frustration was also a problem while working on the plates. Both she and Skuro continued to face a high percentage of breakage. At the end of July 1977 they tried switching from porcelain to clay bodies and slowing down the firing.[301] But a crucial challenge was for Chicago to find enough "psychic privacy" to be able to concentrate in her own studio, now shared with increasing numbers of volunteers. And she needed to get "deep in" despite the distractions in order to be in touch with her creative juices.[302]

Chicago's immediate crisis in the studio was helped when a ceramicist from San Francisco, Daphne Ahlenious, whom Chicago had met while she was on a lecture tour, agreed to come down and help finish the plates. With her help Chicago was ready to begin "making the last five plates—Blackwell, Anthony, Smyth, Woolf (Figure 24), and O'Keeffe, the women I most identify with. My goal is to individuate them. . . . Each of them is me, and I am all of them."[303] By the end of November, Skuro left the project, bowing to "internal pressures."[304] At least one worker on the ceramics team, Kathy Erteman, considered him to be "sexist."[305] Judye Keyes had to mediate to convince him to remain responsible for the few specialized things that he alone could do, but ultimately the women who remained to work on the last plates felt inspired as "an all-female team."[306]

Gilliam stayed on, however, working among the women. He designed the ceramic chalices and plastic molds for the flatware at each place setting. He began to conceptualize how to modularize the floor, the table, and the lighting, so that the piece could travel. He eventually contributed to the carving of the Ethel Smyth plate, shaped like a piano to commemorate the English composer and suffragist. He also worked on creating the jigger machine, which squeezed out the clay into a specific shape with a consistent thickness suitable for carving.

This consistency of the clay was essential for the more complex plates of the last wing. As Chicago faced having to redesign some of the runners that did not work well, she felt frightened about what was coming out of her for the last wing: "my rage against woman's condition—and the absolute out-front images that only needlework techniques will make into art. There will be images that have simply not been seen: Mary Wollstonecraft dying in childbirth, her strength trivialized by flowers and butterflies and scenes from life done in a technique called stump work."[307]

One of the project's administrators, Lynn Dale, an urban planner, explained to a reporter that "Chicago's stamp is on everything"; "the bottom line is that her ideas go."[308] A journalist reported that, according to Chicago, the exhibition would include "photodocumentation of work and workers, while names are embroidered on the back of each runner and all research cards signed. Any profits that might come of the book or other sales, she says, will be divided. 'If it goes well, it will help a lot of people,' says Chicago. 'But I'm the one whose reputation will stand or fall on the project.' "[309] Since the San Francisco Museum did not want to deal with their fund-raising efforts, which resulted in many small donations of even five or ten dollars, Chicago had set up Through the Flower, a 501(c)(3) nonprofit organization through which to funnel support for *The Dinner Party.*

Fortunately Chicago could rely on Gelon, who stepped up fund-raising efforts at this time. She "worked Washington" together with Juliet Myers, whose "outgoing" personality, Gelon recalls, worked well.[310] They decided to go public and rented a booth in Houston in November 1977 at the National Women's Conference, which attempted to assess the status of women in the United States. Attended by three thousand, including former First Lady Betty Ford, this conference offered access to important potential supporters of *The Dinner Party.* Gilliam designed a booth with rear-screen slide projection, and they distributed a leaflet, "Support *The Dinner Party.*" Gelon met Lael Stegall of the National Women's Political Caucus, who gave her various helpful introductions into the world of politics. Gelon eventually got to meet with Joan Mondale, the vice president's wife, and organized her visit to *The Dinner Party.* Supporters of the work now extended outside the art establishment into the political sphere of the women's movement.

Influenced by Chicago, Dextra Frankel, the supportive gallery director at Cal State Fullerton, organized a show in December 1977, called *Overglaze Imagery: Cone 019–016,* which was actually a history of china painting. This survey included work from the thirteenth to the twentieth century. Chicago's own work, along with artists such as Viola Frey and Bruria, was included in the contemporary section, which featured only women who are credited as "the keepers of this flame" of this traditional craft. William Wilson, reviewing for the *Los Angeles Times,* called Chicago "a born-again china painter" who "emphasizes the feminist aspect of what we might call underground china painting," and he carped that "Ms. Chicago's own work is less impressive than her organizational skills."[311] Elaine Levin wrote in *Artweek:* "Judy Chicago forgoes structure for a painterly approach to clay surface with her personal, feminist iconography as subject matter. In a triptych of tiles titled *Did You Know Your Mother Had a Sacred Heart?* she joins the feminine with its religious image, placing wood-framed tiles on a cloth-covered altarlike pedestal."[312]

By early 1978 publicity for *The Dinner Party* had begun. Diane Gelon, who was in San Francisco when Chicago lectured, wrote in her journal: "Well they love her in San Francisco. Judy lectured to a packed, overflowing house at the Art Institute. She is wonderful."[313] One woman who interviewed Chicago there remarked that "unlike many who are committed to a cause, Chicago has a sense of humor. Tension creeps into her voice only once, when she is reminded that her work has often been classified as 'vaginal art,' focusing on the private parts of the female anatomy and going so far, at times, as to incorporate used sanitary napkins [a reference to *Menstruation Bathroom* in *Womanhouse*]."[314] The writer reported Chicago's reply: "That was 'my earlier work,' she said with some annoyance."[315]

Since the early 1970s, when her paintings began earning recognition, Chicago said, "I've gotten way from the physiological aspects of being a woman." The only connection with what she is doing today—"flowers, fruits, butterflies, rocks, a million other things"—is that "all the images have a center opening just like we have."[316] The same reporter noted that Chicago was twice married and now separated from her husband after knowing him for twenty years: "we're not sure what will happen next."[317] She then quoted Chicago: "To say these are only vaginas . . . you know what that is . . . it's like someone looking at you or me and saying, 'She's only a c—.' "[318] Chicago then made a prescient comment: "People say to me, 'What will happen to you after the times change and social conditions change?' I say that I just hope people will look at my work and see how beautiful it is."[319] Another time she said, "When confronted with the plates in my *Dinner Party,* many people think that they have 'seen' them when they have merely 'identified' them as vaginas. They have not even begun to comprehend the images, but rather only named the outline of the form. It is like saying that Albers's paintings are 'squares' and thinking that that is properly understanding the complexity of his work. The vaginal form in my work is simply the framework for a series of ideas."[320]

The *Fresno Bee,* noting that Chicago was one of the founders of women's studies at Fresno State University, ran a caption that read: "The tradition of the old-fashioned sewing bee, with volunteers pitching in under the direction of one craftsman, is reborn with the needleworkers of *The Dinner Party* Project in Santa Monica. The scene is Judy Chicago's studio."[321] The reporter quoted Chicago: "For years I had a dream—yes, like Martin Luther King—of some kind of work which would bring women's needs and women's achievements to the attention of the world at large. . . . More and more I began to think that we have been deprived of the information we needed to survive as a species. I even thought (with a small chuckle) of filing a class action suit against the schools for not teaching us."[322] Chicago told the reporter: "Then I became interested in medieval art, the way it taught and shared with people. Our culture is illiterate about women; what better way to teach than through art?"[323] Another newspaper feature quoted Chicago on her high hopes for *The Dinner Party:* "I hope it will change consciousness, demonstrate another way for art to enter society, open up more ideas for art making and provide a new base for an artist to work from."[324]

In May 1978 Chicago lectured at the University of California at Davis and encouraged those present to break art gallery controls and survive by working together to create alternative markets for their work. She said: "you have the opportunity not to be powerless. You can break the hold that the art gallery world has by bringing back values associated with humanism, by making expressive, accessible art, by making situations responsive to needs by creating alternative markets."[325]

Newspapers also reported that Chicago had received a matching grant for *The Dinner Party* from the National Endowment for the Arts for $17,500 and had raised $70,000 by lecturing, jurying, and selling posters and art.[326] Another paper reported that the project would end up costing $125,000 and that she would need to raise another $100,000 to $150,000 to finance its national tour.[327] She was trying to recruit workers who would pay $175 each to help complete the project that last summer.[328] In February 1978 Chicago announced that there were a dozen men among the approximately fifty people who were helping with *The Dinner Party,* three of whom had "integrated the needlework department."[329] By April she estimated that there had been two hundred people moving in and out of the work and that "maybe" twenty-five of these were men.[330] Chicago told one reporter that she spent about $2,000 a month on studio rental, utilities, phone, and five $200-a-month salaries.[331] In July 1978 they learned that the NEA had awarded *The Dinner Party* a grant through the Museum Program, cause to celebrate at a party for her thirty-ninth birthday, held in the studio (Figure 21).

In September 1978 Chicago wrote to Lucy Lippard, telling her how her own studio felt "like an occupied zone & every time I went in there I felt resentful." She admitted that she had resolved the situation by "deciding to *give* my studio to the people who are working in it—so it no longer belongs to me—it is theirs & if it's dirty, I say to myself as I feel the upset rising in me—'it's not my studio, at least not now.' "[332] She was proud at how well the crew functioned without her, which she found a testament "to how feminist values work. I go in for consultations, discussions, support (for me as well as them) & to kibbitz [gab]."[333] Meanwhile Chicago was holed up in her home writing the accompanying book. She was discouraged when Doubleday informed her that they did not want to put the Susan B. Anthony plate on the cover because it was too explicit and they were afraid of losing half their audience. Ann Isolde wrote to Judy to support her, explaining that Katie Amend had quipped: "Which half?" Isolde consoled Chicago:

> And that plate isn't even as challenging as Sanger. All over the country, every day and every night men are ogling *Playboy, Penthouse, Hustler, Clit, Beaver.* Woman as object, woman as victim. Finally, we women are taking control of our own bodies, claiming them for ourselves, celebrating our sexuality and all the symbolic expression of openness, vulnerability, enclosure, folding and revealing, mystery softness. And STRENGTH. And Doubleday is scared. They are scared to present a strong, overt image of female sexuality. It is because they see it in the old way. I finally understand what Georgia O'Keeffe meant when she said, "You look at my flower and you think you see what I see and you don't."[334]

Rather than writing the book on *The Dinner Party,* Chicago would have preferred to be making art. She felt exhausted and admitted that "it's hardest now—now that I know the piece will probably appear in the world—not knowing what will happen—whether this five-year effort will be worth it—whether I will personally survive it in the sense of being able to go on. I am very scared, more scared than I've ever been. This was too much this time, too much even for me."[335]

Meanwhile Chicago's personal life suffered. She confided in Lippard that she and Gilliam were having trouble. The project had taken a toll on Gilliam and their relationship. He had started therapy and felt weighed down by the demands of their relationship and the pressures to complete *The Dinner Party.* Chicago was concerned and anxious, hoping that things would work out between them. She told Lippard that they loved each other but that Gilliam had taken on too much without really understanding the consequences.[336] Chicago knew that it was her vision for which he struggled, and so she was at once conflicted and filled with remorse at the thought of losing him.

By November 1978 Diane Gelon was back in New York making a last stab at fund-raising. She had by then raised about $80,000, but they needed to raise another $35,000 in order to open in March 1979. She noted in her journal: "every single dollar takes so much work."[337] Over the last year Gelon had traveled around the country, meeting with museum directors and curators and potential funders. She had lectured to groups and collected the admission tickets as donations for *The Dinner Party.* Often either the museum space available was too small to accommodate the piece or the director was too conservative to show it, but Gelon did not give up.

By early December 1978 Chicago, perhaps taking note of the early publicity, wrote: "It's possible that there will be a huge to-do, then a pulling back, which we'll have to survive—I suspect that fear will set in after the initial enthusiasm & the audience will not be ready to move forward until they've had a chance for the information—& the permission the piece implies" to set in.[338] Her relationship with Gilliam ended by the end of the year, although he continued to work on *The Dinner Party* and worked with her on lighting the piece. His design for the table for the project had failed and had to be reconceived at the last minute. Susan and Diane took over and redirected the process, but Chicago saw that he had to save face by withdrawing personally, bringing their intimate relationship to an awkward halt.[339]

Chicago faced the intense disappointment that yet another man had let her down, although she had been aware from the start of the problematic disparity in their ages. She had not gone after a mature man who was ready to settle down and could give her the stability and emotional commitment that she needed and craved. She faced the fact that she had focused so intensely on her work. Desperately alone, she longed for a man to love who would love her for herself: "Not because I am *Judy Chicago.* But I am Judy Chicago—I invented her & now I want to abdicate because the price is too high."[340]

Unexpectedly one of the female workers on *The Dinner Party* professed her love for Chicago. Although she always welcomed gay women working on the project, she had never been involved intimately with any of them. Chicago was touched by this woman's expression of love and felt real affection for her, but she also recognized how vulnerable her authority made her friend and coworker. The two spent the night together, but Chicago noted in her journal that she felt no sexual drive toward this, the first woman she was ever with.[341] She realized how little she had to give in any relationship at this time. All her energy and emotion had to go into in her work.

The ambitious scale of the piece, its employment of traditional female crafts, and its audacious rewriting of history to foreground women would have provoked controversy even without her chosen metaphoric ground, but not at the visceral level it did. Yet without the resultant notoriety, *The Dinner Party* could not have achieved its revolutionary impact and might well have met the fate of so much past art made by women: impotent to counter male hegemony, ultimately irrelevant—just voided, sterile, erased.

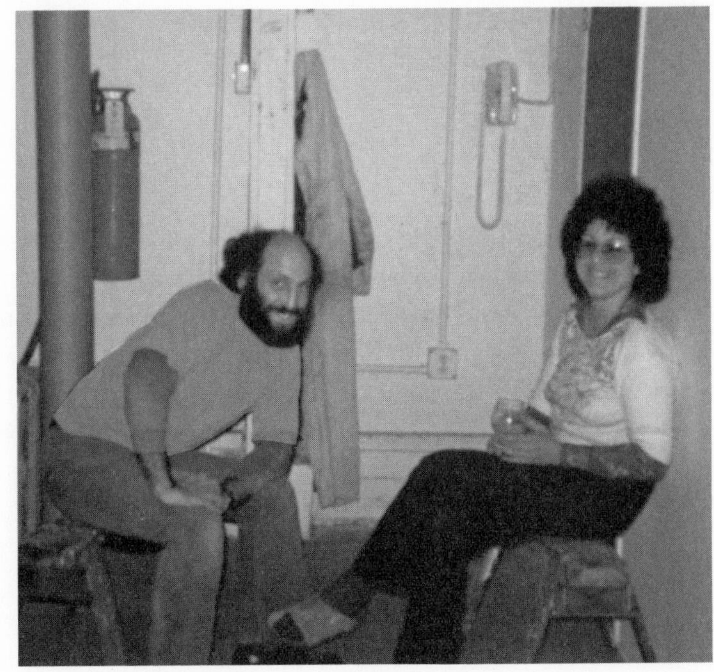

▸ Judy and Lloyd Hamrol in Judy's Santa Monica studio, November 1974. Photograph by Jack Rhyne.

The Dinner Party Makes Waves 11

When asked in 1977 what museum would show *The Dinner Party,* Chicago complained that few had expressed interest: apart from the Museum of Modern Art in San Francisco, "every other major museum in the country has turned it down . . . There are problems that have nothing to do with sexism. Just the sheer scope and scale of the piece itself go beyond the capacity of the art system, as it exists now, to handle it easily. It requires a large investment on the part of the art system, and as we know, they have not exactly had a good record on investing in women."[1] As the debut neared, Chicago was relieved that the work would tour beyond the Modern in San Francisco to the Art Museum in Seattle and the Memorial Art Gallery of Rochester, New York.

▲

Judy Chicago with *The Dinner Party,* 1979.

The Dinner Party opened on the Ides of March (15) 1979. Attuned to the liberal cultural nexus of San Francisco, Henry Hopkins could write that Chicago "with deliberate irony . . . has utilized 'women's techniques' . . . in a 'women's context' . . . to create a major feminist statement," adding that "the overall context is universal in its impact with no sexual or historical limitations," in sum, "an idea of consequence."[2] Fulfilling its role of cultural leadership, the museum was showing in *The Dinner Party* not just art but a work that communicated the idea—ahead of the times—that women had played a significant role in the history of Western civilization.

The version that finally reached the public consisted of a great triangle, each of its three arms or wings with thirteen settings for female figures from myth, legendary lore, and history.[3] The first wing features five divinities, including the abstract primordial and fertility goddesses, Mesopotamian Ishtar, Indian Kali, and the tantalizingly elusive Serpent Mistress of Crete; two legends—Sophia (personified "wisdom" of the early Gnostics) and the Amazon female warrior; and six historical figures—Egyptian queen Hatshepsut; Hebrew Judith, who beheaded her people's foe; Greek Sappho, from Lesbos island, who sang of love; Greek Aspasia, the brilliant companion of Pericles, who led democratic Athens; Boadaceia (Boudicca), warrior queen of the Britons; and Greek pagan Hypatia, who emulated her learned father and was brutally martyred by a Christian mob.

The second arm stretches from the beginnings of Christianity through its turbulent reform, including Marcella, Christian teacher and organizer of women; Saint Bridget of Ireland, who founded convents and comforted the poor; the Byzantine empress Theodora; Hrosvitha, early German poet and dramatist; Trotula, physician of the Salerno school; the queen Eleanor of Aquitaine, known for her feisty independence; Hildegarde of Bingen, abbess and scientist who composed music; Petronilla de Meath, executed as a witch; Christine de Pisan, author of *The Book of the City of Women;* the Renaissance noblewoman Isabella d'Este; England's first Queen Elizabeth; the Italian Artemisia Gentileschi, the painter daughter of a painter; and Anna van Schurman, a seventeenth-century Dutch scholar.

The third wing reaches from the American Revolution to the women's revolution of modern times and features Anne Hutchinson, nonconformist daughter of a father who dared denounce a corrupt church; Native American Sacajawea; German astronomer Caroline Herschel; English feminist Mary Wollstonecraft; abolitionist Sojourner Truth; feminist Susan B. Anthony; physician Elizabeth Blackwell; poet Emily Dickinson; composer and suffragist Ethel Smyth; birth control advocate Margaret Sanger; lesbian writer Natalie

Barney; and two particular emblems for Chicago: writer Virginia Woolf and painter Georgia O'Keeffe.

Clustered with each of the thirty-nine place-holders in roughly chronological order come the 999 women's names inscribed in gold on the porcelain-tiled Heritage floor. These names were chosen based on whether the woman made "a mark on (male) history" and "a contribution to her own sex."[4] Like pilgrims approaching through a passage hung with banners woven by hand with apothegms and emblems from Chicago's manuscript *Revelations of the Goddess*, which she composed in the tradition of William Blake's prophetic books and which remains to be published, visitors suddenly saw open before them the spectacle of the great triangle, dramatized by light, so that it seemed to float above the tiles and sparkle in the shadowy hall.[5]

For the Thursday-night opening Suzanne Lacy, who began as Chicago's student at Fresno and was now a performance artist, orchestrated an International Dinner Party. She and Linda Preuss organized women all over the world to hold dinner parties to honor living women and by extension the aims of Chicago's work. Lacy read aloud their telegrams of congratulation and posted inverted red triangles marking these events on a large map of the world that was displayed in the museum.[6]

Among the worldwide parties was one in Ota, a village in the outlying prefecture of Fukui in Japan, where the hosts were Chicago's brother, Ben Cohen, by now an acknowledged master potter in an old Japanese tradition, and his wife Reiko Kakiuchi. Ben told Judy that he wished they could be with her at the opening in San Francisco, but would come to the planned reception in Seattle.[7]

The Thursday-night opening also occasioned local panels, workshops, and poetry readings, followed on Saturday by an all-day conference, A Celebration of Women's Heritage, held at a Holiday Inn to accommodate the crowds.[8] Panelists were Jan Butterfield (an art critic who was then the wife of Henry Hopkins), Ruth Iskin, Suzanne Lacy, and Lucy Lippard, with Diane Gelon as moderator. Talks followed about various figures commemorated: on witches and Amazons by Susan Rennie; on Sojourner Truth by Raye Richardson; and "Natalie Barney and Her Circle: Feminist Lesbian Tradition" by Arlene Raven. Three classical scholars from Stanford—Harrianne Mills, Marilyn Skinner, and Bella Zweig—discussed "Women in the Ancient World."

On Friday, between the opening and the conference, Chicago lectured to a sellout crowd. It was a chaotic moment, when several mishaps took place. Ira Kamin, a reporter for a San Francisco paper, was assigned to cover the extraordinary event and overflowing crowd from Chicago's perspective, tracking her behind the scene. He reported that someone handed Chicago a note backstage from "Julie and Giovanna," who requested to meet her afterward to say hello. She responded that she had no idea who they were, then reflected that maybe they were childhood friends from her hometown, remarking: "Oh, my God. They're coming out of the walls."[9] This was duly reported in the paper, only to insult her two old friends from UCLA, Julie Ross and Joan d'Angelo; Joan had created the confusion by switching to the Italian version of her name since Chicago had known her in the early 1960s. Spurned friends, embarrassed in print, do not repay the insult kindly.

At the same lecture Chicago was stunned when some women spectators alleged that she had exploited those who worked on the project without pay. Even more damaging, the San Francisco reporter quoted a colleague from Los Angeles: "Some of the people who worked on the piece are upset. They say, 'Why does she (Chicago) get all the credit when so many worked on it? Some of them feel used, taken advantage of.' "[10] At the lecture some of the actual volunteers spoke up at once to testify that the experience had been "empowering and growth-producing" for them.[11] Later Chicago regretted not responding right there and then to the charge, which she considered quite unjust, since no participant had ever complained to her of feeling exploited. She had taken pains to credit the participants both in wall charts for the exhibition and in the books that described the piece and its production process. These credits were far fuller and more explicit than anything artists historically gave to assistants, apprentices, and artisans (whose contributions were anonymous and remuneration notoriously slim). Work with a master might prove to have great worth for those able to absorb and use the experience to their own advantage, as so many of the workers testified that they had in the present case.

The influx of apprentices from across the nation who mastered traditional women's crafts to embody a women's message, and often discovered and developed artistic gifts in themselves, challenged modernist notions of the aesthetic object as sacrosanct and apolitical, produced and practiced by heroic males in the hieratic roles of prophets or quasi-priests of "high art." The project's very scale challenged norms, requiring the egotistical force that the dominant culture repressed in women but heroized in men, as Chicago had reflected during her first sojourn in Europe. To redress Western culture's inveterate neglect and insouciant erasure of contributions by women topped Chicago's agenda; and she guaranteed getting attention by casting her emblematic figures as metaphorical butterflies based on female anatomy. These images were meant to astonish with their visual invention and technical expertise, as well as illuminate important thematic points. Threatening the status quo in so many (dis)respects, *The Dinner Party* was designed and destined to engender media commotion and incessant controversy.

An initial report from San Francisco in *The New York Times* appeared without a byline and noted that the piece "is dominated by Miss Chicago's feminine imagery, or what she calls a 'butterfly symbol,' which can be seen on most of the fourteen-inch plates. Although the image suggests the vagina, Miss Chicago has in numerous interviews rejected that as simplistic and reductive. She said the imagery was symbolic of liberation and resurrection."[12]

"An ambitious paean to feminism" that will "be wonderfully controversial on all counts: as art, as message, and for combining the two," said an early review by Mark Stevens for *Newsweek.*[13] "The needlework is the glory of *Dinner Party,*" he argued, while "the plates don't bear sustained looking; you don't see more the more you look." He quibbled too that "there's not much suggestion that evil can occupy the heart of women as well as men," apparently without conning closely the contrary signs of a grim goddess like Gaia (who contrived to castrate her son-husband) or vengeful Furies, or of Lilith, Jezebel, even Eve, or Clytemnestra (but not the likewise ferocious Medea—powerful in love, furious when wronged). Averring in oracular style that visionary art is difficult and had best be made by geniuses, he limply allowed that visitors admire the art and women "take palpable pride in the work."[14]

"The emphasis throughout the show is primarily biological . . . women's reproductive functions . . . women as a source of nutrition," insisted Alfred Frankenstein, then in his early seventies, in the *San Francisco Chronicle.* "If any man were to put on a show like this, the feminists would burn it down."[15] His failure to comprehend provoked Beverly Terwoman to complain that he had "abandoned his responsibility as an art critic . . . in a revealing fit of fear, fantasy and projection,"[16] arguing herself instead that "the vulval or butterfly imagery is also there to get the viewer to experience women's powers of creation and transformation on multiple levels. This power has been feared and attacked by some men, appropriated in fact by means as varied as the Inquisition, patriarchal religions, and modern day gynecology and obstetrics. Disguised envy of women's power to create life actually and symbolically is at the heart of difference between the sexes."[17] She could have cited the poignant examples, among so many, of Hypatia martyred by brutal Christians envious of the power of her Platonistic school; or Anne Hutchinson and Mary Dyer, hounded to death for independent conscience by the fanatical Puritans Winthrop, Endicott, and their ilk, worthy of the worst that Pharisees, Holy Roman Inquisitors, and Star Chambers could inflict.

A society reporter covered the preview for the *San Francisco Examiner,* prompting a corrective from Stephanie von Buchau: "I urge everybody who takes delight in visual arts to see *The Dinner Party.* It is so beautifully executed, the needlework so exquisite, the china painting so bold and assured, the concept so unified and vivid, that it offers pure aesthetic pleasure whatever your sexual politics. Men especially should not be deterred by rhetoric about 'the movement' or by the puerile banalities of the movement's opposition."[18]

Chicago's message was recognized as revolutionary in the section called "Women Today" of the *Durham Morning Herald,* where the critic Blue Greenberg told readers that even if they never got to see *The Dinner Party,* "the ripples this will make are like those that appear on the surface of a pool of water after a pebble has been thrown in. One circle will make another and then another larger than the last, repeating the message that there is a new way to look at history and that process has begun."[19]

The *Los Angeles Times Book Review,* however, published a condescending feature by Charlotte Harmon, who made much of the "vaginal imagery" on the plates: "The plate is an ironic symbol, says Chicago, symbolizing how women's aspirations were limited. 'It's a celebration of all our achievement and a terrible shriek about the containment of all our power.' "[20] On the same page Suzanne Muchnic, true to her history of hostility to any and every work by Chicago, mustered a volley of alliterative jibes, viciously styling *The Dinner Party* "a sophomoric sham," "a soggy spectacle, and a grotesque embarrassment: on aesthetic grounds the project is a near disaster—a lumbering mishmash of sleaze and cheese. As education, the piece falls flat, succeeding only as Chicago self-aggrandizement."[21]

In the dynamics of public opinion, Muchnic's fervid rhetorical fireworks could not be left to fizzle, discredited by their own patent commitment to self-display. They hardly deserved the reasoned rejoinders they sparked, as from L.A. critic Ruth Askey: "Is it Muchnic's own lack of feminist consciousness that prevents her from dealing with the piece fairly?"[22] From La Jolla, the artist and professor Robert Nelson chimed in: "Not only was her article on *The Dinner Party* biased, it failed on all levels to convince me of anything but Muchnic's puritanical repression. As a man, I enjoyed—along with thousands of other men and women—the experience of seeing beautiful art produced by women about women in a major museum."[23] Another art critic, Sandy Ballatore, remarked that Muchnic's incantatory and repetitious style smacked of ritual or cult, constituting almost an "-ism": "Muchnicism is exactly what *The Dinner Party* transcends. Her pitiful review gives the art real rather than idealized meaning for me. History *will* decide which work is valuable and why. Thousands of us, however, already know."[24]

Despite the turbulent eddies and conflicting currents, Chicago felt as if she were in "a dream" for the first few months: "People I didn't know would come up to me in restaurants and tell me the piece changed their lives; the media in the Bay Area and even some of the national media like NPR *All Things Considered, Newsweek, Life,* and *People* was mostly positive—it was only later in the show that I even knew there was a backlash—like the *LA Times* review—but it seemed like a tiny negative ripple in a tide of positive response."[25]

In April, Grace Glueck interviewed Chicago for a feature in *The New York Times* that focused on the difficulty encountered to get the piece shown, and she downplayed the positive critics: "Though it's caught the attention of the public, *The Dinner Party* has not received rave notices from critics, some of whom have perceived in it more message than esthetics. But Miss Chicago, in New York last week on a promotion tour, insists that she seeks a wider audience than the 'elitist' art world, that hers is an art that is meant to 'encourage social change.'"[26] Glueck reported that the Seattle Art Museum had dropped out of the tour, claiming that the space had been preempted by another project; and she quoted Chicago's description of the work as a metaphor "for the way women's achievements are regarded in our society," remarking the "crusading light in her eye" when Chicago asked: "Do you realize that the site in Seneca Falls, New York, where the first feminist convention was held in 1848, is now a laundromat?"[27]

The controversy took on political overtones that Clare B. Fischer, among others, sought to address, asking whether art should convey political meaning and replying that "most of western 'high' art has been commissioned by the rich and powerful and *that* is political art."[28] To the suggestion that the "imagery is too explicitly vaginal," she countered that this view comes from those "concerned with the truth of the phrase 'anatomy is destiny,'" arguing that she "found the imagery sensual but diversified . . . rich in variation in line and color."[29] Refuting directly the charge that Chicago "gets all the credit for the work which was performed by apprentices," she recommended the detailed credits presented in the exhibit's accompanying photo documentation and in the companion volume, where the presence of long lists of names suggests that she may have conceded too much to rumor when she wrote that "the collaborative process is a tough one which feminists have not perfected."[30]

To an overheard "complaint that the notion of the dinner party itself was middle-class," Lippard countered, calling the conception "elegant" in a substantial article for the New York weekly *Seven Days:* "The richness of color and texture, the gold and the glitter of *The Dinner Party* itself refers not to ruling-class splendor but to the rightful creative heritage of all the women to whom *The Dinner Party* is dedicated."[31]

Any New York chorus in those days would have been incomplete without the *Village Voice,* where Diane Ketchum called the work an "awesome undertaking" and caught the significance of Chicago's command of widespread popular response: "her audience is what is forcing the art world to take Judy Chicago seriously," adding, "the fact is that what she has done works." Ketchum even quoted an older woman at the show who told her, "I felt I was in church. It was like visiting the cathedrals of France. She made these women into something holy."[32]

The *Voice* rarely spoke with one mind. In the same issue Kay Larson insinuated that Chicago was "heavily into goddess-worship" and claimed, inconsequentially, as even a superficial look confirms, that Chicago "hopes to reach a broad public but keeps the central metaphor—communion via female genitals—under, not on, the table. She invites women to acknowledge a common heritage but gives us forms that are aggressive, willful, and offputting."[33] Larson's rejective stance surprised, since she had been both art critic and editor in charge of recruiting feminist articles for the *Real Paper* in Cambridge, Massachusetts, during the early 1970s and considers herself to have been "deep into the feminist movement."[34] A mitigating factor may be that she was in her first year at the *Voice,* when she took issue with Chicago's way of paying homage to great women. Looking back, Larson suggests that writers for the old *Voice* were very casual in their tone, as if they were "writing letters to each other," and that today she would "express it differently . . . be less harsh."[35] Her reaction may have owed something to other contacts too, for when she wrote about *The Dinner Party,* Larson had come to know members of the Heresies collective, a feminist group founded in New York in 1976 that published the journal *Heresies* and included Miriam Schapiro and Mary Beth Edelson, both of whom had longstanding personal gripes with Chicago. Larson had interviewed Schapiro and written positive reviews of several of her shows.

In *Ms.* magazine a reviewer whose byline identified her as "art critic for the *Village Voice,*" April Kingsley, wrote that Chicago "has created the most ambitious exhibit ever undertaken by a woman artist. *The Dinner Party,* which was 'intended to challenge the values of society,' will probably succeed because it is so beautiful and profound that it leaps beyond art to life—and art *can* change the world when that happens."[36]

Kingsley intuited an intention that Chicago herself had articulated before any public showing, when she shared with two interviewers a vision that in retrospect resonates with a certain irony, given the blizzard of contradictory judgments the piece evoked when finally unveiled: "I wanted to make a piece that was beyond judgment. For example, if you go and you see the Sistine Chapel, you don't say, 'Oh, I don't like it.' It's irrelevant whether you like it or not. Whether it's good or bad is irrelevant, it simply stands as a testament to human achievement. When I was in Europe traveling around, I went to see the Léger

Museum and the Matisse Chapel and Picasso's house. And I so longed to see that kind of achievement having been made by a woman."[37]

Responding to *The Dinner Party* affirmatively, the California Academy of Sciences included Chicago in an exhibition called *Creativity—The Human Resource,* which opened on April 29 in San Francisco before touring the country. The show focused on nineteen creative individuals, including in the arts, besides Chicago, Romare Bearden, John Cage, Merce Cunningham, R. Buckminster Fuller, Jasper Johns, and Roman Vishniac, and in the sciences Linus Pauling and Jonas Salk, among others. One newspaper feature reported reasons for choosing Chicago, including that "she constantly challenges the assumptions of the male art world" and "advocates that art include the audience and a number of participants—as shown by the cooperative effort of nearly three hundred people for her place settings in *The Dinner Party.*"[38]

The mixed fallout from the debut was not what Chicago had dreamed of during her years of single-minded sacrifice, but several months passed before the reality sank in "like a shock wave."[39] The ups and downs of the reviews that kept coming found Chicago struggling with loneliness and despair. She was getting ready to leave behind the studio where she had outgrown her longest personal bond and seen her tentative vision solidify and mushroom into the collective bustle and creative fervor of so many women and men. She would seek harbor in the Bay Area, all the while also looking for a lasting relationship, seeing several men at the same time. Most were younger, and all proved either intimidated, plagued by sexual problems and fear of intimacy, or afflicted by some combination of the above. One, for whom she cared a great deal, proved to prefer men.

At least amid, if not on the rebound from, these tentative liaisons, Chicago went to New York, where she had her first significant affair with a woman. It began when she responded to what she perceived as neediness in a friend. The two knew each other well and were near contemporaries, and both were powerful professional women. Chicago initially concluded that sex with a woman was really not so different, but that a woman could be more supportive and comforting. In this instance, both had just emerged from relationships with men that lasted long and came to a bad end. Both felt the need for emotional sustenance. Both agreed to keep their relationship secret.[40] Given its premises, the intimacy lasted longer than it might have, because the partners remained apart on opposite coasts and saw each other only occasionally, though frequently speaking by phone. As with all of her lovers, what Chicago insisted upon was respect for her intense need for quiet and psychic space. Chicago soon realized, however, that although she loved her friend, she did not feel sexually drawn to women. Though the relationship ultimately ended, Chicago's friendship with this particular woman has lasted far beyond its physical phase; this was less common in her affairs with men.

During the highly successful show in San Francisco, where news articles remarked that museum-goers waited in line as long as five hours to get in to see *The Dinner Party,* Chicago had been counting on the promised tour to the Memorial Art Gallery in Rochester and the Seattle Art Museum, but both reneged. Seattle's curator of modern art, Charles Cowles, finally spoke out against the piece: "I do not consider it fine art, but an interesting project by a group of women of whom the leader was an artist. I saw it more as a political statement than art."[41] He had tried to move the project to a space at a science center and was amazed that Chicago insisted on a museum-type space and climate control.

Rochester balked at the shipping costs, which had increased $4,000 from the earlier estimate of $8,000, and cited only "irreconcilable differences."[42] Rochester, thought Chicago, was afraid.[43] After the work closed in mid-June, news stories featured an upset artist who spoke of "an antifeminist backlash." "What is art?" she asked. "That is debated all the time. I have a right to be thrown into the debate, but that can only happen if my work is visible."[44] The sudden change of fortune and the collapse of the planned tour devastated her all the more because they were unforeseen and ran so counter to the public success—the throngs at the San Francisco Modern and even a visit from Joan Mondale, the wife of the vice president, an advocate for the arts, and a ceramicist herself.

The cancellations brought out an aggressive streak in Kay Larson: "An exhibition with a gay-woman theme has no connection to the beautiful people, therefore it's easier to get someone miffed. Even the nonestablishment press—the *Voice,* for instance—attacks you for duplicity in not being more open about the gay theme: sitting down to 'dinner' before plates depicting women's labia. You reply that you never intended to hush it up. Was the museum being coy? If not, then who? The straight press? Who creates public image?" Snidely she jeered, "But how do you create a major art event that speaks for all women yet derives mainly from your personal involvement with the goddess cult?"[45]

One wonders if Larson had been reading the *Lesbian Tide* for her research, since a few months earlier Jan Adams had praised the work, only to remark, "Yet though a charge that lesbians are treated as tokens seems justified, I feel a lesbian sensibility in the imagery of the art," adding that "as a lesbian, I feel conflicted about our presence in *The Dinner Party.* We are there, highlighted by Sappho's green and lavender floral plate and an exquisite lily motif portraying Natalie Barney." But Adams objected to the fact that some of the other 999 women on the Heritage floor—"Jane Harrison, the early twentieth-century

English student of Greek mythology, and Jane Addams, pacifist recipient of the Nobel Peace Prize"—were not identified as lesbians.[46]

To the proliferation of metaphor spawned by the piece, Thomas Albright in *ARTnews* added a culinary fillip, declaring *The Dinner Party* "as overdone as a Russian Easter egg. And it requires a similarly elaborate framework of conceptualization to convert what the naked eye perceives as simply a display of gay, rather gaudy and sometimes downright shlocky ceramic ware and stitchery into something of more consequence than the contents of a 'counter-culture' gift shop or an 'alternative' school project." He skirted the potential art world effect when he remarked, "The anarchic state of the contemporary, or 'post-modern' art world could hardly have had a more dramatic demonstration . . . *The Dinner Party* seems to epitomize the atavistic 'post-modern' esthetic."[47] Chicago's work was to have enormous impact on subsequent postmodernist art by both women and men.

Allowing that the work was "a substantial accomplishment," Hal Fisher in *Artforum* took a different theoretical tack: "Chicago's conception originates in her own interpretation of medieval art: just as art taught the Bible to illiterates, so should *The Dinner Party* instruct us. To this end, the presentation is obsessively literal and cloyingly ecclesiastic. . . . The piece is underscored . . . by proselytizing self-righteousness that replaces art with cultism and offers literalism under the guise of education. Chicago not only underestimates the viewer's intellectual capacities, but unsuccessfully tries to sidestep the modernist tradition."[48] He went on to pick fault with the "spectacle" and decry the incompleteness of scholarship—at a time when feminist scholarship was still in its infancy. Yet he offered no hint where a more complete story would lie.

A less theoretical, more reality-grounded report from the museum floor came from Henry Hopkins himself: "The audience was overwhelmingly favorable and patient. Some raise the question: but is it art? *The Dinner Party*'s appeal to me became even stronger as I watched during the twelve weeks the power it held. It remained in pristine condition; no one tried to touch it. The audience found it a real experience. That's art."[49]

"I was not upset by the sexual symbolism theme—if you want to call it that," Hopkins added. "This museum has no problem with that, although there are pockets in the country that do. We are more open in attitude than some institutions and people. That is good for us and sad for other areas."[50] The piece's popularity in San Francisco could not be gainsaid. Some ninety thousand people saw it during twelve weeks. It more than repaid all costs to the museum and broke all the records for attendance set during the five and a half years that

Hopkins had been director. He reported that most of the hundred or so reviews were positive.

Producing *The Dinner Party* had cost $250,000 in hard cash, of which $85,000 came from Chicago herself, $17,500 from the National Endowment for the Arts, $30,000 was outstanding from the Los Angeles Women's Bank, and the rest came in small donations. The NEA suggested tabulating the cost of the volunteer labor force at $3 to $4 an hour, which totaled about $11,000 to $15,000.[51] The Ford Foundation awarded *The Dinner Party* $10,000 in 1979. Now, with the work dismantled and crated, storage in a warehouse was costing Chicago $1,000 a month, and the work's future was uncertain.[52]

"After the show closed," Diane Gelon recalls, "Judy and I had a fight. She was truly devastated and had no energy. She had poured everything into this work. And then the reviews and the canceled tour."[53] Gelon had not invested herself so long and so much for nothing. Sharing Chicago's anxiety about its being erased from history, she rebelled at the thought of leaving *The Dinner Party* to molder in storage. So she went on the road and followed all leads, drumming up support and venues, even working with community groups. Chicago too set out to raise money—selling posters after her lectures and even passing the hat.[54]

The Art Institute of Chicago, among other general art museums, and at least ten major contemporary museums rejected the chance. But grassroots groups began organizing to bring the work to their communities. At least some of the museums approached did not have adequate space to accommodate the work's large size. In Chicago itself John Neff, the director of the Museum of Contemporary Art, said, "Artistically, I have absolutely no reservations about the piece. It's a moving installation with a great deal of historical interest and an impressive anthology of approaches."[55] But he lacked a suitable space. The *Chicago Tribune* published one woman's letter reporting that she was "incensed and appalled—though not surprised—at the Art Institute of Chicago's refusal to show it."[56]

The artist, who realized that dialogue was important, was not shy about telling the press how "devastated" she felt. "I have never been suicidal. I have never before been close to despair," she said. "But I have gone through a long and terrible black period asking myself what is going to happen now . . . do I now have to pay storage on this piece for the rest of my days?"[57]

Succor, however, was on the way, from a source so often ambivalent toward Chicago: New York. For her campaign to get the work out of storage and into new venues, Gelon found an ally and mentor in Sarah Kovner, through the good offices of Lael Stegall from the National Women's Political Caucus (NWPC). Kovner and Bobbie Handman ran Arts, Letters, and Politics, a New York public affairs firm that worked for the NWPC to build a constituency by organizing a regular lunch meeting, Second Tuesday, where they charged ten dollars and invited women to speak who were "on the cusp of something." Chicago fit the bill perfectly. Kovner had read about *The Dinner Party* in San Francisco and would go to see it in Houston. Now with Gelon she arranged for Chicago to deliver one of the luncheon talks. Moreover, as later reported in *Ms.* magazine, "Kovner, also chair of the First Women's Bank, huddled with Nanette Rainone, who managed communications for Howard Goldin, the Brooklyn Borough President, and they agreed that *The Dinner Party* must come to New York."[58]

To the cause Kovner also recruited Ann Rockefeller Roberts, a daughter of former governor and vice president Nelson Rockefeller. Active as a feminist, Roberts served on the board of *Ms.* and invested in the First Women's Bank. Now to help bring *The Dinner Party* east she hosted a fund-raiser at her elegant Fifth Avenue penthouse.[59] The gesture brought not only financial but telling moral support, since her grandmother, Abby Aldrich Rockefeller, had been a founder of the Museum of Modern Art (MoMA). In the late 1920s Abby (Mrs. John D. Rockefeller, Jr.) and two friends, Lillie P. Bliss and Mrs. Cornelius J. Sullivan, all "progressive and influential patrons of the arts," joined forces because they "perceived a need to challenge the conservative policies of traditional museums and to establish an institution devoted exclusively to modern art."[60] Extending the line, Roberts's daughter, Clare Pierson, just out of college, also signed on as an enthusiastic and active supporter of *The Dinner Party.* Starting to work at Arts, Letters, & Politics, she helped to arrange *Dinner Party* tours—both in Boston and in Brooklyn.

But although the spirit of a principal founder of MoMA was alive and well in her descendants down to the third generation and the fourth, who were campaigning for *The Dinner Party,* the museum itself had succumbed to institutionalization and become rear guard—frozen into a stereotype that stripped modernism down from its full diversity to a mummified masculinism, to a mere five solo shows for women out of a thousand overall by 1972.[61] Since then the pattern has persisted to this day: MoMA has consistently snubbed most women artists and completely ignored feminist art.[62]

When Roberts met with Kovner, Gelon, Rainone, Lippard, architect Susan Torre, and others on May 31, 1979, at a luncheon in Doubleday's suite to strategize which local museum might show the work, MoMA was not a likely candidate.[63] Rainone, however, convinced her boss Howard Goldin as borough president to write the Brooklyn Museum's director, Michael Botwinick, promoting the idea that *The Dinner Party* would be good for Brooklyn. But in the teeth of a budget deficit and rumored hostility by a top female curator, months dragged on, and it took intense lobbying before the museum signed. Not until November 30, 1979, could the exhibition be scheduled, and that for the following fall. Director Botwinick told the press: "I know it seemed like a long time before we made up our mind. But this is a costly installation—and it's controversial. . . . We are showing this piece as an event of our time; we recognize that people very much want to see *The Dinner Party.*"[64]

Another breakthrough followed at once. On December 2, 1979, the Sarah Institute, a not-for-profit organization "established to give recognition to women in the arts and humanities who have been denied equal access and support of their talent," opened a Second Floor Salon at 45 East 65th Street in New York as a benefit exhibition for *The Dinner Party.* The invitation was issued by "Alice Neel, Gloria Steinem, The Sarah Institute, and the Through the Flower Corporation."[65] Patrons paid $35 for the cocktail reception and $75 for an autographed copy of Chicago's new book on *The Dinner Party.* Among those on the benefit committee's long list were David Rockefeller, Jr., Honor Moore, Elinor Guggenheimer, and Lucy Lippard. Seventeen examples of Chicago's work, mostly borrowed from New York City collections, were on display, including three of the *Great Ladies,* studies for *The Dinner Party,* and *The Butterfly Vagina as a Shell Goddess* (1974).

Lucy Lippard introduced the artist: "Judy Chicago needs no introduction—but she's going to get one anyway. Little did I suspect when I met Judy Cohen twenty years ago in New York that this woman would change my life, change the lives of endless other women, and conceive of a *Dinner Party* with a then unimagined scope and power. I'll spare you the details. I'll spare you my second encounter, thirteen years ago—the *Primary Structures* phase—with Judy Gerowitz, whom I met again at a California wedding. And I'll spare you the productive and continuing transcontinental relationship with Judy Chicago, except to say that she has been one of the great influences on my life. I'll just skip to the core. You know the hole in the center? Judy has filled it for many women. She's filled it not with herself but with *our* selves . . . in a way so new, so impressive, so revolutionary that I am—you'll be happy to hear—speechless.[66]

Meanwhile, feeding on Chicago's new celebrity status, *Los Angeles* magazine declared her "one of the 78 most interesting people" in the city (responding to a joke made by Neil Simon in *Playboy* magazine, about the mild temperature in L.A. compared to New York City, versus the number of interesting people in each).[67] The compliment, such as it was, called to mind the familiar curse, "May you live in interesting times."

Looking back on the tumultuous year from slightly beyond and above the fray, a Montreal journalist, Adele Freedman, lauded Chicago's agenda in general, agreeing that "female artists fall into two camps . . . women artists and feminist artists. Women artists are women who make art which could be mistaken for men's art. Their politics are confined to fighting discrimination. Feminist artists, however, address themselves to wider issues, like the nature of art. In other words, feminist art has content—female experience."[68]

In early 1980, more herself again and unbowed, Chicago reiterated and redoubled her claim that "American Formalism is toppling. We are definitely seeing a new humanism, which is attributable to the women's movement though we're not getting the recognition."[69] Even when most discouraged the previous summer, when walking down a street a strange woman had approached her to say, "I work in a drugstore. You're an inspiration to women. I'm glad you're alive."[70] A few years later Chicago looked back on 1979: "That summer after *The Dinner Party,* when everything collapsed, I was working. I was in bad shape and I didn't know what else to do. But every day there was another person, another friend on the end of the phone, pulling me out."[71]

Meanwhile, by the spring of 1979 Chicago had already left the Santa Monica studio with its indelible memories and moved north to Benicia, California, where her friend the artist Manuel Neri lived. A lush, green town east of Berkeley on the Bay Area's outskirts, Benicia's population was then about sixteen thousand. Neri helped her find a small apartment, and she got a studio space in a nineteenth-century blacksmith's shop, part of an industrial complex she shared with other artists and artisans. Through Neri she soon met the artist Sandy Shannonhouse and her husband, the sculptor Robert Arneson.

Chicago's original goal was to start work on a porcelain room to house *The Dinner Party.* To help her with ceramics, Judye Keyes also moved there. Plans had to be tabled when much of the project's press was so negative that the tour fell apart. Chicago was so discouraged that she did not send out her invitation for new work/new building until September 1981, for an open house she held in her new Benicia studio on October 4, 1981.

The cancellation of the planned *Dinner Party* tour coincided with the moment when her divorce from Lloyd Hamrol became final. The divorce reinforced the impression that "the male art world didn't want my art and men didn't want me."[72] Chicago faced the contradiction between the popular success of *The Dinner Party* and the art establishment's resistance. "I was so lonely and in debt from *The Dinner Party*—that summer of '79," she recalls, "I had to exercise two to three hours a day in order to even begin to combat the depression that threatened to overtake me. But I went back to work on the drawings for the needlework book—that's all I knew how to do; keep working."[73] She still exercises daily.

Reacting to *The Dinner Party*'s rejection by so much of the art world, Chicago defined her own program: "Generally, I'm antimodernist, which means that my art differs in content, intent, meaning and purpose—not only from West Coast art—but from contemporary art in general. Most of the art I've seen lately looks like wallpaper. It seems so devoid of meaning . . . I am so committed to the idea that art can operate in a larger sphere that I feel like an alien in an art community where artists accept the assumption that art is powerless."[74]

This statement demonstrates the distance between Chicago's philosophy and that of her onetime colleague Miriam Schapiro, who, back in New York, took part in a movement called Pattern and Decoration. Its stylistic emphasis on the decorative was precisely the "art that looks like wallpaper" that Chicago denounced. She saw the artist's role as "visionary, rebel and outsider" but viewed most artists as "court jesters in an art scene that would be ludicrous if it did not represent the only viable distribution system for art at this time."[75] She told of working on an image base that would be understandable beyond the art community, since she wanted to reach a wider audience. Reaching that audience was limited by the general presence of male bias in the culture. Chicago reflected: "I had set out to test the system—to find out how deep the prejudice, discrimination & hatred of women goes—and I found out."[76]

Even critics friendly to Chicago could not escape the dominant attitudes. A profile of her in *New York* magazine suffered a "heavy edit" that added snide "editorialisms" and innuendos, provoking the writer, Marta Hallowell, to write Chicago to apologize: the issue was "what do you pay when you work in the mainstream," and she was sorry that she had to learn at Chicago's expense.[77] A similar complaint was later lodged by Eva S. Jungermann. Clearly some editors wanted Chicago to appear less positively than writers and interviewers intended.[78]

By the summer after the debut of *The Dinner Party,* Chicago reflected: "I really miscalculated. I thought the force of the work would carry it right past the bigotry of the art system. On the basis of scale, audience & most of all, profit—but even profit isn't enough. That means that the war is on the level of symbols and values. Women have never been the symbolmakers of the culture—they've participated in symbolmaking but they have not created the symbols from their own perspective."[79]

Chicago remained $30,000 in debt for finishing touches to her masterpiece that continued to cost her $1,000 a month to store. Nor had any sales resulted from a show of the project's test plates that spring in L.A. Her only source of income continued to be the fees from lectures (of which she was weary) and advances and royalties (always intermittent at best) from books. For the first extended period too in her adult life, she had no companionable male. She complained that although she tried to meet men, the encounters were unsatisfying and transitory. "Judy Chicago the feminist" was simply too threatening for most men. She was "desperately lonely."[80]

Word about *The Dinner Party* spread, however, to Houston when a Doubleday sales representative, Evelyn Hubbard, with two Chicago items—the autobiographical *Through the Flower* and *The Dinner Party: A Symbol of Our Heritage*—to peddle, dropped by a feminist center, the Bookstore, run between 1973 and 1983 by an Arkansas native, Mary Ross Taylor. She, when local museums refused, determined to find a suitable venue and formed the Texas Arts and Cultural Organization (TACO). She got in touch with Chicago, who told her about Calvin Cannon, a dean at the University of Houston's suburban campus, located at Clear Lake City (near Galveston). Approached earlier by the local chapter of the American Association of University Women, he had proposed showing the piece in a black box theater on campus. Now he and Taylor got together, spurred by Cannon's fervor after meeting Chicago and Gelon in California, where both impressed him with their energy. "We haven't seen anything like this in America for a long time," he said. "It had the same kind of feeling of human solidarity for me as the civil rights movement in the '60s."[81]

Although not thrilled with the locale, which lacked both the prestige and the lighting of a museum setting, Chicago was glad to see the work come out of storage and reach a new audience. She came up with a community participation event, called the International Quilting Bee, to respond to criticism about her choice of the women represented. Now those interested could submit triangular quilts, two feet on a side, honoring women of their own choice.

The university location would also prove to have other advantages over a museum. It allowed Deborah Lipton, an assistant professor of art history, to organize extensive educational programs, including lectures and panel discussions. Feminist art historians and artists were invited from around the country, including Arlene Raven, Suzanne Lacy, and Ann Sutherland Harris, who saw the piece "in the flesh" for the first time.[82] Another faculty member, Jean Quataert, created an entire history seminar entitled "Women in Europe," which she called "a semester-long *Dinner Party.*"

Sixty thousand people would see *The Dinner Party* in Houston. Among them was Elizabeth Stevens, the art critic for the *Baltimore Sun,* who sent a note and the payment of $100 that she had received from her newspaper, explaining that she was turning it over as a donation to Judy Chicago "for future works."[83] Johanna Demetrakas's film about the piece, *Right Out of History,* was also screened and judged very supportively by the *Houston Chronicle*'s Donna Tennant: "No matter how many superlatives are used, no matter how many mind-boggling statistics are quoted, mere words cannot prepare one for the impact and beauty of this monumental work of art."[84] She also liked the film, which she called "top-notch entertainment," "powerful and poignant," and "a remarkable story."[85]

The Houston showing brought renewed national notice: in a cover story for *Art in America,* Lucy Lippard went to bat for *The Dinner Party,* describing herself as "dazzled" by the "awesome" work: "One of the most ambitious works of art made in the postwar period, it succeeds as few others have in integrating a strong esthetic with political content. . . . For all its didactic content, *The Dinner Party* is first and foremost a work of visual art. . . . One perceives the major form, the major symbol—a shimmering white triangle looming in the darkness."[86]

A sidebar called "*The Dinner Party:* Dollars and Cents" refigured the financing, demonstrating the complexity of realizing the project, the kind of support that it had elicited, and the sacrifice that Chicago had herself made: $35,500 from the National Endowment for the Arts (not including a $5,000 grant to Chicago early in the project); $10,000 from the Ford Foundation; $6,000 from the Women's Fund Joint Foundation Support; $1,800 from the NOW Legal Defense and Educational Fund, courtesy Bo-Tree Productions; $1,000 from the Eastman Foundation; $1,000 from Philip Morris; $900 from the Washington, D.C., Women's Art Conference; $35,000 from individual donations over $1,000; $30,000 from individual donations under $1,000, the majority of which were under $50; and more than $100,000 from Chicago's earnings over six years and from the personal loans she took out.[87]

Meanwhile the Museum of Fine Arts and the rest of the art establishment in Boston had turned down *The Dinner Party.* To redeem Boston's revolutionary heritage, Virginia Boegli, April Hankins, and Libby Wendt determined to bring *The Dinner Party* to Boston and founded the Boston Women's Art Alliance. They raised about $100,000 to cover shipping, insurance, advertising, and a $5,000 rental of a dilapidated space, the Cyclorama. The alliance raised the last $50,000 by a loan from the alternative newspaper the *Phoenix.*[88]

Hankins, then in her mid-twenties, had read Chicago's memoir *Through the Flower,* which inspired her to get in touch with the support group of the same name: "I saw a woman who focused her frustrations of being a female artist in a male-dominated art world and used the obstacles she encountered to the advantage of her art. She had guts and she inspired me, and my primary motivation to 'bring *The Dinner Party* to Boston' was to give her something back in return for what I felt she had given me."[89] Hankins was then married to a TV news producer and used her contacts to advance the cause. Through the Flower put Hankins in touch with Boegli and Cate Bradley, an enthusiastic young feminist, both of whom had made similar inquiries. Bradley and Hankins traveled to Houston to see *The Dinner Party* for themselves, where Hankins was impressed and viewed Chicago as "a vocal and fearless personality. She was fascinating, a woman who highly valued her own work and importance as an artist—and conducted herself accordingly," differing in this regard from Chicago's Houston supporters, since "many women in the community weren't ready to enshrine Judy for the creation of *The Dinner Party,* but pulled out all the stops for her heralding the near forgotten achievements of so many women."[90]

To rehabilitate the decrepit Cyclorama, Cate Bradley took charge. Volunteers built new walls, resurfaced the floor, cleaned and repaired the bathrooms, built ramps and railings to afford access for wheelchairs, and constructed an office and shop. Bradley found an architect to donate a geodesic structure to be tarped and hung within the dome, both to protect the art and to control the light. A security system was rigged. Bradley managed to employ women-owned businesses whenever possible and attracted many contributions.

As for Hankins, she says that although neither Chicago's art nor women's issues ever affected her artwork, "Judy had influenced me by giving me courage to find my voice, and for that I will always be thankful."[91] Hankins says that Chicago acknowledged Cate, Virginia, Libby, and herself and that they "felt warmly appreciated," but others remained disappointed, feeling insufficiently recognized.

Running for July and August 1980, the exhibition was linked to the city's 350th anniversary celebrations through the efforts of Katherine Kane, a member of the city's planning committee. Fifteen hundred people attended the opening party.[92]

Despite the exceptional efforts of so many citizens, the *Boston Globe* bristled. Robert Taylor delivered a tongue lashing, decrying "Judy Chicago's monumentally grotesque agitprop installation" with "the lunatic, obsessive vulgarity of a full-scale model of a Gothic cathedral built from toothpicks." Taylor faulted the style—calling the entire project "valueless" as a work of art—the sale items at the exhibition, and the choice of women represented at the table.[93]

In the *Globe* Betty Kaufman, who identified herself as "not a member of the Women's Art Alliance" but "a lover of art," "the spouse of an artist," and "a proud attendee" of the project's opening, commented that Taylor's review "expressed in totality the defensive and threatened response that the male establishment has used throughout history in an attempt to repress and suppress expressions of loving and humanism."[94]

Taylor also provoked Diane Gelon, as the project's longtime coordinator, to write in the newspaper *Sojourner* that Chicago challenged the kind of contemporary art void of content that Taylor admired: "She is trying to expand the role of the artist, to share the art-making process with others—artists and non-artists—and in so doing to redefine the relationship of art and society, to break down barriers between fine art and the crafts traditionally practiced by women."[95]

Despite the *Globe,* forty thousand people saw *The Dinner Party* in Boston.[96] They came from as far away as Maine, where one reviewer, Darah Cole, complained of standing in line for two hours: but "it was well worth the trip to Boston and the wait," going on to argue that "the work attempts to redefine the role of women for themselves and provide the world with a new image of women and their history. Simultaneously, it challenges the accepted role of art and the rules under which art is made. By acting beyond the boundaries of these rules it is successful in what it attempts."[97]

"As an immediate visual experience, *The Dinner Party* is dazzling," wrote Art Jahnke in the *Boston Phoenix;* but he complained about the expressly metaphoric program: "Chicago's web of metaphor weighs down the work so that it ultimately hangs in limbo somewhere between fine art and illustration," while "the modern art establishment has a predelection [*sic*] for the abstract."[98] He did not perceive that the departure from modernism presaged the postmodern aesthetic, within which *The Dinner Party* would eventually be grasped and enshrined.

Such a transition had already been heralded by Chicago in the summer of 1973 writing to Lippard: "I am about to come up with a very convincing argument for a 'retrograde' movement. . . . Because, it seems that we have gotten very out of kilter in our world between our ability to conceptualize at the very outer limits of abstraction and the basic, down to earth, unfulfilled needs of millions of people and maybe we have to go backwards a bit and catch up at the point of difference between abstract concept and real need."[99]

Already pushing on to the next stage in such a program, while struggles over the *The Dinner Party* still raged, Chicago began using her interviews and lectures to advertise for needlework artists to join a further endeavor, the *Birth Project.*[100] She asserted in a lecture at Harvard in 1980: "I share Virginia Woolf's belief that one of the basic differences between art and propaganda is that art addresses a deeper level of reality—for I have been particularly concerned with the meaning of the female life as part of the human experience."[101]

After the nontraditional locations in Houston and Boston, *The Dinner Party* returned to museum status. The Brooklyn Museum showed the piece from October 18, 1980, through January 18, 1981. Five thousand people thronged the members preview alone.[102] For the first time, the museum had to institute a ticket system to accommodate crowds. The press also turned out in force. A few powerful New York critics went on the attack. Years later Chicago attributed their focus on the center of the plates to "a very deep seated attitude that women's sexuality is obscene."[103]

Among the first to weigh in was Hilton Kramer in *The New York Times*, a neoconservative, whose "turn to the right first came in the mid-1970s with mutterings about sinister connections between homosexuality and radicalism."[104] From that time forward Kramer bemoaned what he identified as "an insistence and vulgarity more appropriate, perhaps, to an advertising campaign than to a work of art. Yet what ad campaign, even in these liberated times, would dare to vulgarize and exploit imagery of female sexuality on this scale and with such abysmal taste?" He went on to criticize the variations of the "genital organs of the female body," claiming that they were "not without a certain ingenuity, to be sure, but it is the kind of ingenuity we associate with kitsch."[105] Kramer had long demeaned any art with a discernible political content and held consistently to an antifeminist and antipopulist creed. He asked: "Is *The Dinner Party* art? Well, I suppose so. After all, what isn't nowadays?" And he bounced from facile rhetorical query onto repetitive rungs of anaphorical climax: "But it is very bad art, it is failed art, it is art so mired in the pieties of a political cause that it quite fails to acquire any independent life of its own."[106] Nonetheless, he confessed to admiring some of the runners, where he found "some details of real artistic interest."[107]

Labeling him a "Neanderthal," Ellen Willis answered Kramer in *The Village Voice:* "Cunt phobia rides again. In a culture where female genitals are still widely regarded as ugly and/or dangerous—a deficiency no self-respecting women would voluntarily call attention to, a mysterious, dank morass in which the unwary penis gets lost, or perhaps bitten off—it is inherently tasteless to presume to consider the vulva as legitimate a subject for formal and metaphorical elaboration as any other."[108] As a radical feminist, however, Willis had trouble with what she viewed as Chicago's equation of "femaleness with femininity." She accused Chicago of subscribing to "matriarchalist politics," of wanting to reestablish the feminine rather than "breaking down the masculine-feminine polarity." She regretted that there were "no cracks or chips in the dinner plates, no overturned goblets, no real recognition of the devastating human cost of a feminine domesticity," claiming that she wanted to see "women's rage and violence."[109] No one, it seems, could view *The Dinner Party,* except through the prism of personal politics and psychology.

Joanne Materra declared the plates "breathtaking" and elaborated: "Chicago's symmetrical butterfly/vulva imagery is soft, floral, delicate, yet hard, powerful, and strong, suggesting flight and resistance and generation by turns and . . . with their deep core, the images are hypnotic and meditative."[110]

Equally enthusiastic, John Perreault, in *The SoHo News,* stated that he found *The Dinner Party* "magnificent," "a key work," and emphatically declared: "Certain conservative critics may call it kitsch to their dying day, may puritanically rage against its sexual imagery, may imply over and over again that it can't be good art because it is too popular; but I know it's great. I was profoundly moved."[111] He, like others of theoretical bent, perceived that the work challenged stereotypes and demanded reformulations of critical thought: "Whether *The Dinner Party* is modern or post modern or beyond category will take some time to figure out. I hope that a public, permanent home can be found for it." He went on to augur the piece would not be "like so much other work by women artists, shoved under the table," but optimistically closed: "I don't see how it can be; it has already proven too influential to be avoided, too powerful to be forgotten."

In the liberal *Nation* Lawrence Alloway found the piece "flawed," though he allowed that Chicago had "made a brilliant use" of feminism "for public statement."[112] But Sheryn Goldenhersh for the *St. Louis Jewish Light,* which had already featured Chicago, intuited a more complex cultural matrix for the work. She identified Chicago as a fighter who "feels the need to speak out and participate where she finds injustice. Descended on her father's side from a long line of rabbis, although not emerging from a traditional background within her own household, her sense of community responsibility and respect for the intellect, continued by her father's activities as a union leader and political civil rights activist, is long and strong." Goldenhersh found relevant, too, themes emphasized in Chicago's lecture at the Brooklyn Museum: "I start from the assumption that I'm okay. I've a certain pride in my body, my sexuality, my intelligence. I believe that the female form can be as much of a base to build on in terms of universal language as the male form. There is no visual language that shows women as being active, dynamic, and thrusting. This is now unfamiliar to us."[113]

The cultural matrix hailed by Goldenhersh also elicited reactions to *The Dinner Party* of a different stripe, as Diane Gelon reported overhearing to Letty Cottin Pogrebin, who was doing research on anti-Semitism in the women's movement: "It must have been done by Jewish women; it's so blatantly sexual."[114] In effect, Jewish tradition places few limits on "the free expression of woman's sexuality" to her husband, as exemplified in the Song of Songs, where a woman's words directly convey her pleasure in lovemaking.[115]

Women's sexuality also figured in lectures in four cities of western Canada, which were arranged by Doris Larson of the Shoestring Gallery in Saskatoon. Chicago traveled there as well as to Banff, Edmonton, and Calgary, where her lectures drew large supportive crowds.[116] Unable, however, merely to bask in the positive, Chicago dwelt on the sting of the seemingly endless barbs from hostile critics, all the while feeling bereft at the lack of a partner in life. When asked about the breakup of her marriage, she winced, reported an interviewer at Edmonton, Alberta, in November 1980: she let pass a long silent moment before she replied: "It was very painful. But I guess you can't have everything."[117] Most poignant of all, to another interviewer, she revealed: "I had this fantasy when we were finishing *The Dinner Party* that I would be there on opening night, very pregnant, to say, 'See. You can be a woman and an artist, too.' "[118] Chicago imagined a world in which there would be no barriers whatsoever for women as artists, but in her generation, few women managed to achieve both fame and stable families.

The San Francisco opening had also set off another chain reaction that would bring *The Dinner Party* next to Cleveland, Ohio, not of course to the Museum of Art, which rejected it as "craft," but to a former (Jewish) Temple in Cleveland Heights, where it was shown from May 10 through August 16, 1981.[119] "It is true that I understood the irony of using women's crafts to express women's history, but *The Dinner Party* actually *crosses* crafts. Nobody ever talks about the industrial design of the table, the technological structure of the floor, the way it's engineered," Chicago later asserted. "It's as if the plates and the runners exist off the structure, out there in some space!"[120]

The Cleveland project actually began when a student at the University of Akron, Tina Bronako, returned from seeing the San Francisco opening.[121] One of her teachers, Robert Zangrando, a professor of history and women's studies, had heard Chicago lecture in 1977.[122] He joined with his colleague, Faye Dambrot, a professor of psychology, and other men and women from Akron, Kent, and Cleveland, who worked together to find a venue and raise the funds, calling their organization the Ohio-Chicago Art Project, Inc. Thirty-three thousand people attended the Cleveland showing, buying three-dollar tickets and raising $58,000 beyond the costs. All of these surplus funds were then distributed as charitable contributions to northeastern Ohio women's groups, including a rape crisis center and battered women's shelter.[123]

The Ohio committee, though untrained, worked with Chicago's staff (Diane Gelon, Susan Hill, and Peter Bunzick) to install *The Dinner Party*. Zangrando recalls the moment when one of Judy's staff dropped one of her early test plates, which were included among three dozen in the accompanying china-painting exhibition. It shattered to bits, while Chicago herself stood not ten feet away. The fact that "Judy never flinched" impressed Zangrando, as did her reaction: "I'm glad that it wasn't one of your volunteers, because they would have felt so bad."[124]

Already by the summer of 1979 Cleveland's leading newspaper, the *Plain Dealer,* had been carrying Associated Press coverage on *The Dinner Party,* quoting Chicago: "I'm interested in images that change consciousness. I believe in the artist as a visionary."[125] To a Cleveland reporter interviewing Chicago for the *Plain Dealer*'s fashion section and wanting her to distinguish between art and craft, Chicago replied: "I now am doing for needlework what Peter Voulkos [a noted California ceramic sculptor] did for ceramics. People think that the difference between art and craft is that art has personal content; that craft is not a service of personal vision. I would use bubble gum if it did what I wanted it to say."[126]

Chicago told a *Cleveland Jewish News* reporter: "Being Jewish has had a profound effect on me. I come out of a humanist-intellectual Jewish tradition." She referred to her father's descent from twenty-three generations of rabbis and called him "a natural teacher" and a " 'Theoretical Marxist' during the McCarthy era," explaining that she was "brought up with (unpopular) radical causes."[127]

Perhaps the perceived radical nature of Chicago's feminism was what motivated one woman journalist in Ohio to write disparaging and cranky pieces. Dorothy Shinn, of Akron, insisted: "*The Dinner Party* doesn't belong in any art niche. It isn't primarily a work of art. Chicago's work is, first and foremost, an indoctrination. It is the religiofication of the feminist cause."[128] If Shinn was reactionary and conservative, Lolette Kuby, a freelancer who wrote in *Cleveland Magazine,* claimed to be a feminist and that she had "no trouble accepting female genitalia as an artistic design" before going on to attack the plates. She claimed: "*Playboy* and *Penthouse* (offensive as they are to feminists) have done more to promote the beauty of female parts than *The Dinner Party* ever could.... Yet *Playboy* and the like are curiously less reprehensible than *The Dinner Party.* They are what they are."[129] Her article elicited a number of letters that were published, including one from Liz Lincoln, the director of counseling and training for Women's Health Services in Pittsburgh, who wrote that she saw the piece as "a tremendous validation and celebration of being female and left feeling good deep inside. It was not a reduction of women to the reproductive function but a statement that women are effective and powerful in their own right."[130]

Some Ohioans expressed pride that the embroiderer of the runner for Hildegarde was Dorothy Goodwill of South Euclid, Ohio.[131] Goodwill, after attending a lecture by Chicago, had arranged with her husband and three daughters to leave them and spend two summer months working on *The Dinner Party.* She was one of those who testified, "It changed my life."[132]

The Cleveland women's newspaper, *What She Wants,* featured an interview with Diane Gelon, describing her evolution from art history graduate student to crucial apostle for Chicago, to her impending entry into law school that fall. When asked what she sacrificed, Gelon replied, "I didn't give up anything. I got. . . . She challenges me all the time. You have to keep growing. You can't stagnate working with her. She is very demanding in a real wonderful way that pushes other women to work and pushes me. She is a wonderful example and inspiration."[133]

Due in part to Gelon's hard work and persistence, *The Dinner Party* finally made it to Chicago in the fall of 1981. Although none of the local museums was either able or willing to show it, more than three hundred people, mostly women, volunteered to realize the exhibition. One of the organizers, Diann DeWeese Smith, director of marketing of the South Shore Bank, had not even seen the work, but she was proud of "guaranteeing" her "right to see it."[134] A women's group incorporated itself as the Roslyn Group for Arts and Letters, the name of a local women's literary salon that had read Chicago's *Through the Flower.* They raised money and found a space.[135] Marilyn D. Clancy, former special assistant to U.S. senators Adlai Stevenson and Alan Dixon, chaired the Roslyn Group's steering committee. She commented that "the old girls' network has grown up a lot. . . . We know where the money is, and we're much better at getting it . . . our access isn't as good as men's. The day they have to have a bake sale to raise cash, then we'll know we're equal."[136]

The Dinner Party was finally shown in a donated space in the thirteen-story Franklin Building on Printer's Row, at 720 South Dearborn, where it was booked from September 11, 1981, through January 3, 1982. The organizers had to cover a massive skylight and deal with a leaky roof. Despite a contentious and conservative press, the show was so successful in Chicago that it drew forty-seven thousand visitors in the first three months and was extended to February 7. Judy even gave a personal tour to the female mayor, Jane Byrne, who then pronounced the piece "very beautiful."[137]

When reporter Neil Tesser attacked *The Dinner Party* for having a gift shop, it was too much for John Grod, who wrote in to defend the work and the artist: "*The Dinner Party* speaks the fact that we're still stumbling out of the dark ages when it comes to our history as a race. *Hypatia,* whose flesh was torn from her alive on the steps of the Alexandrian Library by Christian reformers, sits at *The Dinner Party*."[138] He demanded, "How many people know she was the greatest scientist of her time and had mapped the globe before Galileo or Columbus were twinkles in anyone's eye? As a man, artist, and father I find it not only unfair, but boring that every school kid knows what Beethoven looks like, yet may never know that Hypatia even lived."[139]

Alan G. Artner, writing several times about *The Dinner Party* in the *Chicago Tribune*, was totally closed-minded: "Our interest is in the entire process by which one shrewd person has convinced countless others that an inane idea, foolishly developed and poorly executed, deserves their time, money, approbation. In that, and only that, lies the art."[140]

While publicizing *The Dinner Party* in her hometown, Chicago landed an appearance on Irv Kupcinet's local television program, *The Kup's Show*, only to find herself on stage with Roy M. Cohn, there to promote a book of his own. Cohn had served as chief counsel when Senator Joseph McCarthy was investigating Communism in the U.S. government and had worked earlier for the United States Attorney on high-profile anti-Communist cases, including the 1951 espionage trial of Julius and Ethel Rosenberg. When Cohn claimed that he came from a liberal Jewish family in New York but that McCarthy had been "quite right" to say that the "free world was threatened by the Soviet Union and Communism," Chicago spoke up: "I remember the hearings. I'm also from a liberal Jewish family, from Chicago. My family and my family's friends were victims of the McCarthy persecution. . . . It was a shameful period in the history of America, a shameful period in the history of ideas. Artists were silenced; writers were silenced. It was a period of fear and terror that I personally lived through. People's lives were ruined; friends of my family's lives were ruined unfairly."[141] Cohn attempted to shift the blame from McCarthy to the House Committee on Un-American Activities, but he was no match for Chicago.

Her response to Cohn came at a moment of family pride. She had brought her mother from California for the opening. She visited her father's grave for the first time, taking her mother, her aunt Enid Rosen, and her cousin Howard. Chicago had to insist on her mother's coming, but at the cemetery May stayed in the car. "I broke down crying and talked to my father," Chicago remembered, "saying that he had deceived me by telling me that I could be myself and be loved. And I had just had it clearly demonstrated that by being myself, I had lost everything—my career, my studio, my staff, my marriage, what little support I had been able to put together, everything."[142]

Despite the grassroots organizers and the record crowds that turned out to see *The Dinner Party,* Chicago felt crushed by the rejection of most of the American art establishment and the two museums who withdrew from the original tour. She had invested so much in making the piece and had believed that it would earn her a place in art history. Instead, she found the vicious attacks by much of the art press difficult to bear. But the loss of both her marriage and her lover had left her lonely and despondent.

In Canada, museums were more amenable to showing *The Dinner Party.* No legacy of the Puritan tradition overshadowed the work's reception there. When the work next traveled to Montreal, where it was shown at the Museum of Contemporary Art (Musée d'art contemporain) from March 11 through May 7, 1982, it drew record crowds, seventy-five thousand, more than usually come in an entire year, an attendance record comparable only to those who turned out for King Tut.[143] In the francophone press, at least once critic pronounced the work "audacious," praising the work's "rigor, sensuality, passion, and tenderness," and noted: "Thousands of visitors gathered to file by in an almost religious manner before the three tables forming an equilateral triangle—the symbol of woman."[144] In the anglophone press, Lawrence Sabbath expressed a "sense of awe" and noted: "Message art is always controversial, although unlike politicized art which relates to a specific time period and can lose contemporaneity, women's fight for equality goes on forever."[145]

Booked at the last minute, the show then traveled to the Art Gallery of Ontario in Toronto, brought, not by curatorial enthusiasm, but "because the Volunteer Committee wanted a fund-raiser."[146] Because of the initial success in Montreal, the committee expected that huge crowds would turn out to see the work before it closed on July 4, and they were correct, when they drew fifty thousand, limited only by the time visitors took to file through the exhibition—only 125 per hour as opposed to 400 per hour for their recent show of Van Gogh. The show was sold out by its second week.[147] They cleared $65,000 for their art purchase fund.[148]

Natalie Veiner Freeman, in *Macleans* magazine, showed a rare appreciation of the controversial plates: "More important than the awesome scale, however, is Chicago's inventiveness. Her plate images are startling in their directness and sometimes terrifying in their revelations of a private female world; in them, Chicago has created a new visual language for emotional experience. Butterfly, vaginal and flower imagery all flow together to speak of the symbolic duality that has been central to Chicago's struggle as a woman and as an artist."[149] Freeman, the wife of Canadian senator Jack Austin, was so enthusiastic that she organized a private tour of *The Dinner Party* and held a dinner at her home, where Chicago met with Prime Minister Pierre Trudeau and his wife Margaret, as well as Canada's preeminent novelist and poet, Margaret Atwood, who is Chicago's exact contemporary.

John Bently Mays, the critic for the *Globe and Mail,* thoughtfully addressed Chicago's strange success with the popular public and failure to win support of most of the major critics across the United States, concluding: "The object itself has been executed with immense devotion to the least detail and with brilliant contemporary hand-craftsmanship. Yet all this labor has not been directed to the making of just one more self-enclosed museum piece. *The Dinner Party* reaches out to embrace women of every time and every vocation, and does so with great strength and compassion."[150] He further explained: "Miss Chicago committed her first blasphemy by deciding to make a very large statement that was not about art, but about the world—and not merely about the world in general, but about the history and contribution of women to it. In an art world still dominated by formalist criticism, and narrowly materialistic art historians and museum curators, a vast narrative, eloquently personal work such as *The Dinner Party* had the chips stacked against it from the start."[151] Mays also thought that "she promoted the idea of collective creation in opposition to the art world's male-oriented theory of heroic artistic individualism. She made nothing to sell. She made nothing *collectible.*"[152] He referred here to the appetites of art collectors, not to the small souvenirs sold to the public as part of fund-raising.

The reviewer for a feminist paper concurred, claiming that the work's "most daring feature is the challenge to the art world, not its feminist politics."[153] "The audiences are participating in one of the most stirring events in the recent history of public art," pronounced Robert Fulford in the *Toronto Star.*[154] Most of the Canadian press would be positive, especially in comparison to the mixed reception in the United States.

Following Toronto, *The Dinner Party* left for Atlanta, where it was on view from July 23 through October 3, 1982. Since the High Museum had already refused to show the piece when it was first offered in 1978, the show took place in the Egyptian Ballroom of the Fox Theatre on Peachtree Street, one of the grand theaters from the golden age of movie palaces.[155] Mayor Andrew Young and his wife Jean came to the opening; she was the honorary chairperson for "*The Dinner Party* in Atlanta," which the Sculptural Arts Museum, then billed as "Georgia's newest and Atlanta's second-largest art museum," sponsored.[156] The Georgia Council for the Arts and Humanities helped to fund the showing. The day after the opening Jean Young took Chicago out for soul food. In August the Atlanta Lesbian Feminist Alliance, which had been enthusiastic and supportive of bringing the work to Atlanta, held a benefit evening with a private showing.

At a press conference, however, Chicago's lack of southern-style charm rather than her work became the topic of discussion for a male reporter. He gleefully included her comment upon learning that *Women's Wear Daily* would have photographers at the opening: "I'm dressing Southern; ruffles and gardenias."[157] He appears to have viewed Chicago as a pretender to style familiar on his home turf, oblivious to the fact that she actually loves such feminine attire and usually wore a flower behind her ear at openings, reminiscent of her childhood enchantment with Carmen Miranda. But no style of dress could transform what southerners perceived as her harsh Chicago accent and northern manners. Even the chief local art critic, a woman, described Chicago as "abrasive," speculating that "a lifetime of fighting has resulted in a direct, uncompromising and sometimes antagonistic personality."[158] She nonetheless acknowledged that though *The Dinner Party* "may not be timeless . . . it's message and the process by which it was made have earned it a place in history."[159]

New Ventures

12

While the controversy over *The Dinner Party* swirled, Chicago began to focus on her new project. She had also begun thinking about how she could "introduce images into the culture so they *can't* be blocked by the institutions" and she was also thinking about myth and "how myths are the underpinnings of a culture."[1] She had begun the new project in 1980, asking "Why are there no images of birth in Western history?" She had first become interested in the idea of birth when her friend, the radical nun at St. Catherine's, asked her to write a feminist version of the Book of Genesis.[2] Thus she explored themes of creation and birth, drawing from myth and from women's realities.

▲

Judy Chicago and Mary Ross Taylor at the *Birth Project* book signing, April 1985. Photograph by Michele Maier.

During the summer of 1980, as a part of her research, Chicago arranged to witness a birth, which she described in her journal as "really quite incredible."[3] On September 22, 1980, she reflected in the journal upon "the fact that the birth process, so central to human existence, is virtually a 'taboo' area for open human expression. Little attests to or explains or symbolizes or honors or renders this primary experience, so I'm practically starting from scratch."[4] What came to be called the *Birth Project* takes birth as a metaphor for creation itself, for female production rather than just reproduction.

Artists and needleworkers who had either worked on *The Dinner Party* or just admired it volunteered to work on the *Birth Project.* Audrey Cowan, who had learned to weave a modified form of traditional Aubusson tapestry technique for *The Dinner Party,* had told Chicago of her interest in collaborating on another project. They discussed Chicago designing a tapestry cartoon for Cowan to weave, which eventually became *The Creation* (1984, Figure 26), measuring three and a half by fourteen feet. Chicago's abstract vision of creation includes recognizable sea creatures and birds in black silhouettes, as well as the pinkish leg, arm, and hand of a human being emerging from the landscape. The hand grasps an emblematic representation of the sun. Georgia O'Keeffe's New Mexican landscapes that seem like metaphors for female anatomical forms were an important influence on this monumental work.

Similar allusions to landscape are evident in *Earth Birth* (1983, Figure 25), produced by Chicago spraying acrylic paint on fabric, which Jacqueline Moore then quilted. A monumental female figure is shown reclining and interacting with the landscape. The lyrical tones are shades of blue, gray, and black animated by white and yellow highlights. One male critic recently compared this work to its antecedents in the work of sculptors Henry Moore and Michelangelo.[5]

Some *Birth Project* images evoke the supernatural, including the pregnant *Shiva* in *Mother India* (1985), *Birth Goddess* (1984), or *Guided by the Goddess* (1983). Some, such as *The Creation* (1984), woven by Cowan, are immense in scale, while another, *The Creation of the World* (1981), delicately embroidered by Pamella Nesbit, measures only fifteen by twenty-two inches. In this latter work, nature is shown in tiny, elegant detail. Chicago designed the *Birth Project* pieces to be shown separately in a variety of different nontraditional venues, although quite a few are now in museum collections.

Chicago was able to take on such a further large-scale project only because she found a capable administrator who could organize the needleworkers and a rather complicated exhibition tour. She later recounted: "Mary Ross Taylor, who had helped organize the Houston exhibition of *The Dinner Party,* came to visit me. We discovered that we had a mutual interest in empowering women and that we both had the feeling of wanting to work together."[6] Taylor represented intelligence, charm, and wealth to Chicago, who was then struggling and lonely.

More than five years younger than Chicago, Taylor had grown up in Pine Bluff, Arkansas, and married her college boyfriend, a computer scientist in Houston, whom she divorced after eight years. A bright, attractive, even elegant woman, she describes herself as a "product of the 1960s," pointing to "sex, drugs, and rock n' roll."[7] Having helped bring *The Dinner Party* to Houston, she continued to support Chicago's work, eventually becoming an important patron. Since her divorce, she had had female partners, but she insists that she was only interested in Chicago's work, when "Judy announced that she was interested in me."[8] Taylor's response to a postcard from Chicago hints at Chicago's interest: "You write such wonderful postcards that I *cant* [*sic*] help responding. Your most recent was read to me by The Bookstore staff (they're all literary voyeurs & love reading my mail). In answer to your questions, I have for the moment given up on love, but none of the *other* elements. And please keep it to yourself. Love MR." Taylor added a postscript in reference to her choice of postcard of a woman dressed as a butterfly, holding a placard that said "in a world full of Caterpillars it takes Balls to be a Butterfly": "I'd have said brains not balls, wouldn't you?"[9] She clearly knew that the butterfly motif would resonate with Chicago.

In her journal Chicago recorded a visit by Mary Ross to Benicia on Sunday, September 21, 1980: "Mary Ross and I have been having a great time. She arrived Wednesday, and that day was tough on me (re-entry into intense communication after quiet weeks in the studio). We made a lot of contact, which we continued on Friday, when we drove to Napa Valley, discussed plans for *Birth Project* workshop in Houston . . . and our mutual interest in empowering women generally and our intuitive attraction toward working together and the need for the permanent housing of *The Dinner Party*."[10] In Taylor, Chicago had found someone who shared her mission and had the intellectual and financial means to help her realize her goals. Working as the administrator for the *Birth Project* was a meaningful task for Taylor, at once enlisting her managerial experience and opening new horizons.

Taylor and Chicago began living together in Benicia, although Taylor, who maintained her Houston bookstore until 1983, was often traveling. Taylor worked with a staff in Benicia, eventually setting up an eleven-thousand-square-foot building to house Through the Flower. The staff included Sally Babson, the needlework supervisor, whom Judy had hired when she first began the *Birth Project;* Patricia Reilly, the curator; Michele Maier, the photographer; and

Hazel Kiley, the office manager. Judy came and went as *The Dinner Party* was touring and she attended the various openings. Taylor and Chicago were a couple, yet maintained somewhat separate lives, in a sense repeating the pattern that life with Lloyd had established.

On March 20, 1981, Taylor wrote to Chicago, noting "*Gaywyck* has affected my style. I hope it's a transient influence."[11] She was referring to Vincent Virga's 1980 novel, *Gaywyck*, the first gay gothic romance, which substituted the young and handsome Robert Whyte for the traditional damsel in distress. Extant letters from Taylor to Chicago document their closeness, as she refers to Chicago as "Sweetie" and "dear one." In July 1982 Taylor wrote to Chicago from Atlanta, where she was working to help install *The Dinner Party* for its showing at the Fox Theatre.[12] Chicago would arrive only in time to participate in interviews before the opening. In August 1982, Taylor wrote, imagining a possible trip that they might take together the following summer. She described their connection as feeling like "a psychic oasis," noting with relief that it was not a "mirage."[13]

Yet despite her assertive role in beginning their intimacy, Chicago remained at best ambivalent about being involved with another woman. Her waffling may have brought out Taylor's jealousy, at least as perceived by Sally Babson, who was working closely with Chicago.[14] And Chicago continued to see the occasional man. One of these was Stephen Hamilton, the exhibition designer for the *Birth Project.* Chicago recalls: "We loved each other very much, but he was gay. Nevertheless, early in the 80s, we went to bed once. He was a great guy and we spent a LOT of time together working on the *Birth Project*—he designed all of the 85 exhibition units which traveled around in a kind of mix and match at various venues."[15]

Taylor observed that "Judy is never as emotionally engaged with women as with men. I think that Judy is straight. If her response is that 'I didn't inhale,' that's not true. She has led a very lively sex life."[16] Chicago and Taylor also spent time together at the latter's vacation home in Santa Fe, first for Christmas 1981, after the emotionally exhausting experience of the opening of *The Dinner Party* at the Brooklyn Museum. Chicago began spending time alone in the Santa Fe house in 1982, seeking the solitude she needed to develop another new project, in which she would consider masculinity. Inspiration for this work came from a trip that fall through Italy with Taylor that included Rome, Naples, Florence, Venice, and Ravenna. Chicago recalled that she had been "greatly influenced by actually seeing the major Renaissance paintings. Looking at their monumental scale and clarity led me to decide to cast my examination of masculinity in the classical tradition of the heroic nude and to do so in a series of large-scale oil paintings."[17]

Despite her relationship with Taylor, Chicago told an inquisitive reporter in April 1982, "I live alone. I think if you are a serious artist you make that choice first of all," referring to her lack of family life. "My life is not an easy life. . . . But I feel so affirmed by what has happened that it renews my spirit," referring to record-breaking crowds at *The Dinner Party* in Montreal.[18] Chicago never publicly acknowledged her intimate relationship with Taylor; nor she did fully conceal it.[19] In August 1983 the journalist Raymond Sokolov wrote from Santa Fe: "While waiting to go to the evening's opera, local artists and art dealers gathered at the home of Mary Ross Taylor and her friend, the feminist artist Judy Chicago, for a New Mexico meal."[20] Taylor does appear in Chicago's second memoir, *Beyond the Flower,* but the intimate dimension of their relationship does not. Taylor has insisted that the sexual part of her friendship with Chicago was the least significant aspect of their complex relationship and was "over in a New York minute."[21] She has remained a close friend who is committed to Chicago's artistic vision.

The importance of Taylor's support for Chicago and, especially, for the *Birth Project* cannot be underestimated. Even Chicago's longtime friend, the critic Lucy Lippard, had her anxieties about this new project: "any idealization of motherhood is dangerous at a time when the Reagan administration is cheering on abortion clinic bombers and threatening to ban abortions altogether, when thousands of women will bring unwanted babies into the world because some 'religious' men get off on 'morality' more than they care about women's lives."[22]

Lippard acknowledged Taylor when she wrote that Chicago's *Birth Project* represents "a brilliant, unprecedented organizing and administrative achievement, but it wasn't all fun and games for anyone concerned. Labor/management relations were not perfect, and some disaffected would-be mothers will blame the miscarriage on the Mother of It All. Chicago, who habitually works 10 to 12 hours a day, had to come to terms with the fragmentation and lack of concentration that is reality for most women."[23] Lippard nonetheless recognized the project's "visual and technical glories" and that Chicago had succeeded in showing "that you can make 'fine art' with 'minor art' and that you can paint with thread."[24]

Michele Maier, who worked two and a half years as the *Birth Project* photographer, describes the experience as "incredible, inspiring, life-changing."[25] This despite the fact that her pay was only five dollars an hour. Mary Ross Taylor first found Maier to photograph *The Dinner Party,* while it was in on view in

Houston. Maier recalls traveling around the country in 1982 to *Birth Project* reviews together with Chicago and Sally Babson. "We were somewhere in the Carolinas at a needleworker's home one morning when Judy barked at me about something concerning our schedule or not getting enough done, and I, rather uncharacteristically, just burst into tears. She later apologized and told me it shocked her to see my reaction. . . . She thought I was a hard-nosed pro, but clearly I had a long way to go."[26] Maier views this as "the day Judy gave me a valuable gift. It was the first of many lessons to learning a tremendous work ethic. She taught me to 'work to the work.' And that has served me extremely well for these many years in all my endeavors. People speak of how demanding Judy is, how hard to work with, etc. Well, of course she is difficult, she knows what she wants! There is no greatness in 'whatever'!"[27]

Among the participants in the *Birth Project* were two artists, a mother-and-daughter team in Houston, Lee Jacobs and her daughter, Gerry Melot. They worked on similar needlepoint designs, having learned about Chicago from Lee's husband, who saw *The Dinner Party* while on a business trip to San Francisco. When asked why they would work on someone else's project without pay, Jacobs responded: "I believe in the whole idea behind it, and my name is going to be on my piece. I feel that when I'm long gone, something of me will be left behind so I won't be one of the vast unknown."[28] Melot answered: "Look, I think it's a fabulous experience to be apprenticed to a famous artist. You can learn so much and believe me, I am. . . . The fun thing to me is to meet a famous living artist and to find out that she is as exciting in person as she is on paper. . . . It will be something for me to have set such a high goal and achieved it. It will increase my stature as a person and as an artist."[29] Chicago also chose to mention to the press workers such as Dolly Kaminsky of Bethlehem, Pennsylvania, "a gray-haired mother of four children, who is claiming a new life"; and Franny Lyons, "a pretty, plumpish housewife raising two kids in Belle Mead, New Jersey."[30]

Pamella Nesbit, another participant, had studied art during the late 1960s at San Jose State College in California, where she found it difficult to relate to her male art teachers and eventually dropped out. She taught herself embroidery that she called "free stitching" and was at home taking care of her new baby in Sebastopol, California, when she saw a newspaper article about the *Birth Project* and wrote to Chicago, sending photos of her needlework.[31] Chicago's response was an invitation to attend an organizational meeting in Benicia, about which Nesbit recalled: "When showing her my needlework and discussing my art past, I was excited as well as intimidated, for she knew far more than I did about color, design, texture, craft, art and the business of art. I had hit a ceiling in my work so I let Judy know my desire to learn more about art and to develop my skills. I wanted to move it from craft to art but didn't know how to do that with my limited art training. Judy was more than willing to teach those who would learn."[32]

Nesbit worked at least ten hours each week on the project and put her "ego on the shelf so as to learn everything I could."[33] When she needed to attend weekly Friday meetings in Benicia to work with Chicago and other *Birth Project* members, her husband, Bud, took care of their young son. Chicago included his comments and a photo of Pam, Bud, and their son, Christopher, in her book *The Birth Project:* "Initially, my only concern was that Pam would be unpaid, working on a piece designed by another artist. Later when it became clear that Judy had structured the project to give appropriate credit to the stitchers, and as I came to appreciate the education Pam was receiving by being a part of the project (both technically and in terms of her perception of art), I supported her participation completely (as she had supported me through graduate school)."[34]

Nesbit embroidered the small but elegant *Creation of the World* that is now in the collection of the Pennsylvania Academy of the Fine Arts in Philadelphia, and worked on about ten other pieces. She is proud that Chicago chose her version of the project's logo for the book cover from those submitted in a contest held among the participants. She summed up her experience: "Judy is a powerful and perceptive teacher, and although she can sometimes be brusque and emotional while I am shy and restrained, I refused to allow Judy's explosions to interfere with the work we were doing together or the harmony of our relationship."[35]

Sally Babson, who traveled from Benicia with Chicago on an extensive trip across country to review work for the *Birth Project,* observed what a hard worker Chicago was and recalled that although she was very sweet with her, she could be very abrasive: "She wanted people to do what they said and demanded a high level of performance."[36] Babson added that she herself learned from this aspect of Chicago's character; she also learned about "art, working with people and meeting deadlines."

Some volunteers on the *Birth Project* turned out less happily than these. Ida Aber, who identifies herself an early supporter of *The Dinner Party,* volunteered to work on the *Birth Project.* She said that she put in many tedious hours "because of the belief in how important it was."[37] Aber made feminist art as early as 1969–70 and specializes in needlework, though she has also produced scholarship on Jewish decorative arts. She recalls that she made a donation to support Chicago's work.[38] But she relates that her work came to an end when "visiting a gallery in Manhattan, where Chicago had experimented with oversize prints—the likes of which had never been done before. She had gone on to bigger and better things while those of us who believed in what she was doing worked away. She got lots of grant funding which she did not share with the women she exploited." (Chicago says that she actually won only $6,000 in grants for the *Birth Project.*)[39] Annoyed, Aber called Chicago's studio and reached only someone on her staff. "In being turned off," she stated, "I never completed my assignment but returned everything to her."[40] She recalls that Chicago paid a visit to her in New York and arrived for lunch, bringing a bouquet of flowers, when Aber returned her unfinished piece.[41] Asked about Aber, Chicago says that she was forced to drop her from the project because her work was not up to the level of quality that she required: "She was a good stitcher, but did not understand how to put her technical abilities in the service of the image and therefore, her work was very decorative, on TOP of the image rather than serving the image."[42] She nonetheless thanked Aber, whose name appears in the book on the *Birth Project* under the heading: "Many people wanted to become involved in the project and tried very hard. We appreciated their efforts."[43] Aber was not aware that her name appears in the *Birth Project* book.[44]

The *Birth Project* eventually comprised about eighty-five separate exhibition units, each including documentation about the ninety-five unpaid women who worked at least ten hours a week to produce the needlework. Multiple simultaneous shows brought Chicago's designs to a wider, more diverse audience, without making her dependent on institutional support in the art world. Exhibition venues included banks, libraries, and other nontraditional sites, as well as museums, universities, and commercial galleries—more than a hundred exhibitions in total, mainly between 1985 and 1987, all managed by Mary Ross Taylor. At the conclusion of the tour Through the Flower donated various portions of the *Birth Project* to museums, schools, and other sites.

Once again Chicago's imagery managed to be provocative. As for the female images of creation, Chicago told an interviewer who asked about her goddess imagery and her religious beliefs: "I myself am not really into any of the goddess-worship rituals. The issue for me has to do with iconography. That is, when I was looking for ways to counteract the contempt for the feminine that is all around us in every culture, all over the world, I began to look at other kinds of images of the female and, of course, one of the things I, like a lot of women artists, found were all of those early goddess images . . . those images come from a time when there was reverence for women."[45]

Another time, when asked, "Does God or the idea of God fit into your life?" Chicago responded: "Yes. But believe me, I don't believe in some white guy with a white beard somewhere up there. I believe in God. I believe that I'm sitting here in my kitchen and the sun is on my arm and the leaves are trembling and the light is shimmering and I hear birds singing and my cats are roaming around and I'm part of this whole, large fabric of life and it's a miracle and that's God for me."[46] She explained that she sometimes used "the birth process as a metaphor for the creation of life in the largest and most metaphorical sense—that is the female as the source of life and the feminine as the affirming life principle."[47]

Some critics who dealt with the *Birth Project* lined up in predictable ways. Muchnic carped, claiming that Chicago had "switched from gynecology to obstetrics, with a predictable lack of subtlety," and argued: "The saddest aspect of both collaborations is that very talented women who are probably capable of making art far superior to Chicago's have contented themselves with copying her designs, getting fulfillment from her 'constructive criticism,' and professing adoration for their task-mistress."[48] Here Muchnic failed to recognize that needleworkers usually interpret art designed by others, and few are trained in art. Chicago herself addressed Muchnic's accusation that women are capable of making better art: "There are 30 million needleworkers in America. Traditionally, they work from kits; they are not encouraged to create on their own. You know what patterns you get in those kits? Sunflowers, snails, mushrooms, cartoon characters for the kid's room. They are cutesy and kitschy . . . I wanted to challenge women more, and also have them work with images that have to do with women's lives."[49] The opportunity to use their skills on meaningful designs is one of the reasons that workers chose to work with Chicago. Muchnic also accused Chicago of turning women into "flaming vaginas, erupting breasts, spurting mouths and tortured bodies. She may mean to extol the naturalness of birth and to apply the authentic power of primitive art to her vision, but her art doesn't read that way. Once again, she has taken a good idea and bullied it into a freak show."[50]

Chicago's goals were lost on Paul Richard, who reviewed the *Birth Project* (then on view in five venues in the greater Washington area, thanks to the efforts of art historian Mary Jo Aagerstoun) in the *Washington Post.* Richard claimed that it "embarrasses and drains," calling it "political," comparing her images to crotch shots in *Hustler* magazine and claiming that Chicago evokes "disgust, disquiet, shame . . . of privacy invaded," turning "viewers into voyeurs."[51] Clearly discomfited by her imagery, Richard labeled Chicago "the Werner Erhard of the art world" and attempted to debunk the many needleworkers' positive testimonials that accompanied the show, comparing Chicago's influence on women to the Scientologists' leader, L. Ron Hubbard. Letters by two of the women who wrote to protest Richard's review were printed in the *Post.* One was by Linda Monk, who wrote that she was "stunned and disgusted" by Richard's reaction and argued: "The images of pain and glory of childbirth gave me a sense of my power as a woman beside which my Harvard law degree pales in comparison. That 'The Birth Project' affirms women does not mean it degrades men. In fact men should have a profound interest in seeing . . . how the power of their own lives was begun—and how their mothers brought it into being."[52]

Among many satisfied workers on the *Birth Project,* some of whom were interviewed just after Muchnic's attack, was Audrey Cowan, who recalls that their process consisted of "talking a lot, and I really tried to understand what she was driving at. She doesn't weave, but she's an incredible colorist, and she was very interested in my input. In fact, I'm often asked, 'When are you going to do your own work?' And I say, 'This is my own work.' I would not be interested in working with her if I were a machine."[53] Another woman, L. A. Hassing, a schoolteacher from Claremont, California, who learned needlework as a young woman by working on *The Dinner Party,* reported: "People say, 'You're being abused!' But I feel I've gotten a tremendous amount of credit as a result of working with Judy. There's a book published (*The Dinner Party*), my work is in it. And she really trusts me to make choices in the stitches. She trusts that I will make that kind of choice correctly. . . . I've learned a tremendous amount about color from her."[54] "She's inspiring to people. Judy inspires people to do better than they knew they could do," said Janis Wicke, a Walnut Creek housewife and cooking teacher "who had her share of disagreements with Chicago."[55] Others, like Ann Stafford, a student at the University of California at Berkeley, claimed that she learned to sew for the project, which changed her life, making her politically aware.[56]

Various press articles also reported that some workers considered Judy "a tyrant, a slavedriver," who "doesn't accept less than perfection in herself."[57] "If it's not right, you do it over—and over and over," said Jacqueline Moore, a suburban wife, feminist, and mother of three, and a project worker from Hopedale, Massachusetts, who happily worked for four years on quilting various pieces, including *The Crowning* and *Earth Birth* (Figure 25).[58] Another worker, Mary Burke, said, "I didn't feel I had made that significant a contribution. I was very surprised to see that I was given a whole page in the book."[59]

In 1984 ten women in Houston, spoke to *Dallas Times Herald* reporter Anita Creamer, telling her that working on the *Birth Project* changed their lives. Jane Gaddie Thompson, a local housewife who embroidered one version of *Birth Tear,* depicting pain that radiates in waves and ripples from a woman in the throes of giving birth, admitted that the image was not a pretty one but emphasized "that's life."[60] Rhonda Gerson, another participant, described the project's images as "shocking, but that's what birth is like. For centuries, we've seen pictures of wars and blood—that's a thing that men do, not women, but is it less shocking?"[61]

Some women, such as a retired General Motors worker named Lois Golightly, had been inspired to help Chicago after seeing *The Dinner Party,* in her case, in Cleveland, which she had heard about while attending a Quaker gathering. Ever since then Golightly, who had raised three children, wanted to take the time to help support Chicago's work because she felt it spoke to her and encouraged her "to make time in my own life to write."[62] After several years of trying to find a permanent home in the Midwest for *The Dinner Party,* she decided to bring the *Birth Project* tour to northern Michigan.

As it toured, the *Birth Project* continued to provoke. In Philadelphia the local art critic, Edward Sozanski, wrote that Chicago, "as if intoxicated with hubris, took on a truly cosmic subject. If she were the female reincarnation of Michelangelo she might have had a chance."[63] Robin Rice responded in another paper, expressing her surprise at the hostile response to Chicago's work, which she found "a unique collaborative achievement in contemporary art": "The unnecessary introduction of femaleness into his comment is the real clue to Sozanski's problem with the *Birth Project.*"[64]

By 1984 Chicago was spending more of her time in Santa Fe, living in Taylor's vacation home.[65] That summer *The Dinner Party* had made its way to Europe, stopping first at the Edinburgh Fringe Festival, which hosts cultural events in nontraditional spaces during the Edinburgh International Summer Festival. Its presence there was the result of Diehard Productions, a one-woman organization formed by Diane Robson, who had a background in theater production.[66]

Before the opening on August 11, Chicago wrote to Bill Harpe, her friend from Blackie, the Great Georges Community Culture Project in Liverpool, England, where she had spoken in "A Tribute to Virginia Woolf" in October 1982, telling him, "I will not be able to attend the opening, but my partner, Mary Ross Taylor, will be there and I hope that you will greet her with all the warmth you showed to me."[67]

Since Woolf's work had long inspired Chicago and merited one of the thirty-nine plates in *The Dinner Party,* she had readily participated in the Blackie conference, quoting Woolf, who spoke of "a language that weds idea to feeling" and said that women had to find a "new style appropriate to new subject matter," that is, subject matter that related to women's experience.[68] *The Dinner Party* earned praise in Scotland, even from male critics. "This brilliant and moving installation," wrote Edward Gage, ". . . is a ritualistic and revelatory work of art celebrating the historic and life-affirming genious of the female principle—which so often has been ignored, denied or trivialised."[69]

The Dinner Party still needed to find a permanent home. By the end of the 1984 publicity for the search was coordinated by Susan Grode, an attorney, who served as cochair with Susan Loewenberg of "Chicago in L.A.," a group that had been searching for a site for the last three years. She told the press, "I think its controversy has lessened. We have not been *told* (by a museum) the piece is too controversial. . . . That may be a hidden agenda."[70] Grode pointed out that three thousand square feet would be required, but that the piece had earned $115,000 for the Glenbow Museum in Calgary, Canada, and $70,000 for the group that sponsored the showing of the work in a Cleveland warehouse.[71]

In London *The Dinner Party* was shown in the Warehouse in the spring of 1985. Richard Cork praised the work's "strong theatrical presence," its "awesome" execution, and the history that the work illuminates, but he noted the work's "sacramental overtones . . . fused with feminist polemic."[72] Michael Shepherd found the piece "underresearched" and felt that "the genital imagery overpowers the individual characters," but he called *The Dinner Party* "unique, powerful, perhaps seminal. It comes at a time when women's traditional amateur artforms are neglected. And its message is, mercifully, a transcendent one: 'the belief and hope that once reverence for the feminine is re-established on Earth, a balance will be restored to human existence and everywhere will be Eden again.' Most of us," he quipped, "have a list of people we'd like to employ as domestic servants at *that* party."[73]

Another British interviewer confronted Chicago, in London for the opening, with the notion that "some left wing critics" find her work "uncomfortably religious. . . . Her exhibition has a holy quality to it: she uses the religious symbol of *The Last Supper* and pushes it in a new dimension, making womankind the figure on the cross. Such a daring artistic journey twists recognisable religious symbolism to cast light on a sexual struggle which transcends class analysis."[74] Chicago astutely told this interviewer that her own religious background is Jewish and that her family was "intellectual, left wing. . . . My father's family were extremely matriarchal. Grandfather was a rabbi and made no money, grandmother had nine kids and ran a store. Men weren't macho in my family: the emphasis was on intellectual rigour not physical strength. For women there was no taboo about being assertive and aggressive."[75]

Another woman journalist, Jane Lott, who remarked that "Chicago is an artist strong minded enough to do without husband, family, conventional support structures, because they would have got in the way of her concentration on her work," quoted her: "Men just don't know how to support the way wives do.

Of course I'm lonely. I often wish I were lesbian: it would make things easier."[76] By this time Mary Ross Taylor was involved with another female lover but remained very supportive of Chicago and her work.

From 1985 to 1990 Taylor served as executive director of Chicago's nonprofit corporation, Through the Flower, which was then described as "dedicated to art that honors women's experience." Taylor has continued to donate to and work for this organization, of which Chicago is "artistic director." At the time, the mission of Through the Flower evolved to "housing *The Dinner Party,* exhibiting and placing the *Birth Project,* and sponsoring the *Holocaust Project."* Taylor, who remained "a great friend and patron," arranged to rent Chicago her Santa Fe home for a "pittance in terms of money," accepting instead her artwork as compensation.[77] (Taylor, who has continued her support, assumed the presidency of the board of Through the Flower in 2006.)

Chicago had in the meantime escalated her search for the right man in her life, hoping to contain her enthusiasm for younger men and find someone who might be able to sustain long-term intimacy. At her new gallery in New York, ACA, Judy met the Native American painter Fritz Scholder, who introduced her to his wife, Romona, who was a therapist in Galisteo, New Mexico, not far from Santa Fe. Romona became a friend but also served as Judy's therapist, when she sought counseling to overcome the panic she had begun to feel when making public appearances. Scholder, who describes herself as a "Neo-Freudian psychodynamic psychotherapist," was evidently successful in helping Chicago, who now appears quite comfortable speaking before large groups.[78]

Romona Scholder also introduced Chicago to a mutual friend in Galisteo, a psychiatrist named David Burke who was close to her in age. They had been dating for several months when Chicago left to go on the road during the spring of 1985 for six weeks, lecturing on the occasion of the *Birth Project* book and exhibition tour. Burke threw a rodeo party for Chicago's forty-sixth birthday in July 1985, but by then she was no longer very engaged by him. Since she had been trying to get over her habit of having transient affairs with younger men, she had postponed having sex with him for a couple of months, only to find herself disappointed, inevitably comparing him to some of the younger men with whom she had been having quick "flings."[79]

The birthday party was her first visit to a rodeo, a type of spectacle that she deplored: "Grown men lassoing little calves, how appalling."[80] While there, she met the photographer Donald Woodman, a tall, attractive, rugged man six years her junior. Not quite forty, Woodman seemed even younger than his years, a plus for Chicago, who recalled that "he turned me off by asking me if I would like to 'see the bulls' with him (he was photographing them), a comment that seemed too much like the old cliché about seeing 'my etchings.'" Sexual prowess would not be enough; she required a seduction savvy as well.

Chicago's standards had left her high and dry. Men often concluded that she was too demanding, too self-involved, or just too intimidating for a long-term relationship. This was clearly a result of her strong personality and fierce intelligence, not her unprepossessing physical presence. The press frequently commented about her appearance; reporting about her art was often relegated to the style or women's sections of newspapers. Reporters took note of her "trademark tinted aviator glasses" and her "mass of graying curls bobbing furiously." She characteristically dressed with a certain amount of panache and flash, evoking comments such as "resplendent in red and black."[81] Most often journalists described her as "a diminutive woman."[82]

Chicago's small stature became a plus when, just after Labor Day, she once again ran into Donald Woodman. He turned up with Romona Scholder and Patrick Mehaffy, another of her male artist friends, at a picnic organized by David Burke at Fort Marcy Park in Santa Fe for the local fiesta known as "the burning of Zozobra" or "Old Man Gloom." The ritual destruction by fire of a fifty-foot papier-mâché figure symbolizes getting rid of the last year's anxieties. Crowds gather hours before the fire for plenty of drinking, eating, music, and dancing. Judy had taken the trouble to buy a special fiesta dress with flowers embroidered in bright colors, which she had shortened to well above her knees.

After sundown, when Zozobra had been consumed by fire, the crowd surged toward the plaza in the center of the town for more celebration. Having vied with David for Judy's attention over several hours, Donald saw his opportunity. Judy was so short that she could not see above the surging crowd, which was crushing against her, so he hoisted her onto his shoulders and carried her all the way to the plaza. He first recounted that he told her, "Your cunt is burning red hot against the back of my neck."[83] Asked to confirm, he added, "I may not have made the comment that night, but I like the story."[84] While such drama might not have succeeded with just anyone, Donald had finally figured out how to get through to Judy.

Like any good foundation myth, erotic violence lurks at its heart. Romans grabbed the Sabine women and hauled them up the hill. Hades snatched Persephone from her girlfriends and took her for a ride. Zeus enticed Europa to mount the sturdy taurine neck that Titian limned, her bare legs exposed and red scarf flying. When Donald tried to get Judy to come watch bulls, he failed. But then some atavistic instinct prompted him to place her on his neck. To be sure, their little group of friends was still around them, engulfed in the intoxicating rhythms of the crowd, yet he took her to himself, above, apart. Quick to temper bravado with tenderness, he bought ten purple balloons that Judy had admired and tied them to her wrist before he set her down. She was still floating. "I saw Judy fall in love," Romona recalls.[85]

Donald got Judy's phone number from Romona and immediately followed up with a phone call, inviting her to go out for dinner. For that dinner he planned his strategy, carefully orchestrating the evening in what he considered Santa Fe's most elegant restaurant, which happened to be owned by a friend of his. He arranged for a good, quiet table, a bottle of champagne, the best waiter, and no bill, preferring to settle it later. He recalls proudly that theirs was "a mutual seduction" and recounts that after their third date or so, Judy gave him the key to her house and wrote David a "Dear John" letter.[86] She recalls that he told her that he believed that they were uniquely "destined for each other."[87]

After that first weekend with Woodman and another dinner on Monday night, Chicago, then in the midst of painting *Driving the World to Destruction* (Figure 27), made a list of the twelve qualities that she sought in a man: "1) tall, slender & well built; 2) sensitive & non-sexist; 3) visually acute; 4) mechanically adept; 5) good in bed; 6) fun; 7) creative; 8) dissents from the culture, as in refusing to go to war; 9) funny; 10) emotionally reliable; 11) able to cook; 12) supportive." "Guess what?" she wrote in her journal, "Donald is all the above—things moved *very* quickly between us—we have made plans to meet in LA, when I'm there, go to NY together at the end of October, etc. etc. I can hardly stop thinking about him. . . . I'm trying to slow down as I'm not sure if it's the 'real thing' or just one of those fantasy trips I've been into before—like . . . years ago, when I was going to run away with Leslie Lacy (after we hadn't seen each other for years)."[88]

"On Sunday afternoon," she recorded, "I burst into tears upon realizing that I hadn't felt like I did with Donald since I was married to Jerry . . . he reminded me quite a lot of Jerry. In realizing this, I felt so much hurt & pain & knew how I had closed off one whole part of myself since Jerry died—& it scared me. I also got scared Sat. aft. & Donald went home & brought back a picture of himself for me so 'I could get used to having him around.' "[89] She was astonished to realize that she wanted to get married again and had "started fantasizing (or imagining) that Donald & I would get married & I would get out of this cramped, trapped life I've been in."[90]

But after a mutually pleasing week Chicago panicked. The day before Donald's fortieth birthday, which he had planned to celebrate with a big party complete with a band to be held at Romona's house, Judy "freaked out." She took back her key and told him that she never wanted to see him again. She later explained: "I just couldn't accept that I had met someone and fallen head over heels in love like a teenage girl." Donald was devastated, but Judy felt that she had done the right thing—at least for a day. Then she had some regrets; she recalls that she "was beside myself."[91] Meanwhile, Donald had turned for solace to alcohol and drugs.

Judy called Romona, who intervened calling Donald and telling him that Judy wanted to speak with him. She invited him to come over for lunch on her patio. He recalls that he knew very well that Judy, who works all day, did not "do lunch." He arrived with a big bouquet of flowers. She admitted that she was frightened by how fast things had gone between them. He insisted that he was not interested in a casual affair, demanding that either they get married or he would leave. He recalls that she turned white as a sheet and hesitated briefly before saying yes.[92]

"I am ecstatically happy about all this," she wrote in her journal. "Now I want a home life & someone to share with & build with. I can't believe this is all happening to me. I'm scared to death but I'm going for it with all my heart."[93] She even told Donald that she wanted to "live & work deeply & if I never gave another interview & answered another question, it was fine by me."[94]

Donald Woodman was finally the right man for Judy Chicago. Romona Scholder explains: "Donald's ego is not particularly large, but it's extremely strong. He doesn't need constant bolstering."[95] Donald grew up in Haverill, Massachusetts, and was born to first-generation American Jews. His grandparents, like Judy's, had emigrated from Eastern Europe, although his family was less intellectual than Judy's. His maternal grandfather had been a tinsmith on the Trans-Siberian Railroad but fled Russia in 1905 for political reasons. He remained an admirer of Trotsky, turning away from the Communist Party in the late 1930s.[96] Donald appears to have inherited his grandfather's manual dexterity.

Donald was always well coordinated. From the age of five until he was thirteen, he took classical ballet lessons. Then at the age of thirteen he auditioned for the New York City School of Ballet, which accepted him. But his mother was loath to send him to live with her elder sister in New York, so far from home, and his father was fearful that ballet would turn his younger son into a homosexual. In high school he played basketball for the local Jewish temple, since the coach at school was anti-Semitic. He ran track, played in the school band, and served as the photographer of the school's yearbook, advised by two brothers who ran a local portrait studio. He considers himself somewhat dyslexic and did not excel in school. Yet he won an award for a photograph of his high school at night, which appeared in the yearbook.

At his parents' insistence and hoping to avoid the draft during the Vietnam War, Woodman followed his older brother to the University of Cincinnati to study architecture. The school had a co-op program that enabled students to work alternating quarters. He took painting and drawing courses there and hung out with a lot of art students. He recalls that a lot of his life focused on "sex, drugs, and rock 'n roll," the same libertarian phrase that Mary Ross Taylor had used to characterize her life.

While at the University of Cincinnati, Woodman won a fellowship that allowed him to travel around Europe in 1965, photographing architecture, from East Germany to Basel to Corbusier's cathedral at Ronchamps, France, and Gaudi's in Barcelona, and to Italy. He returned to college in June 1966, when he ran out of money and the prospect of being drafted loomed.

At home his girlfriend, one of the only four women in his original class in architecture school, insisted upon getting married or ending their relationship. His new father-in-law happened to be a commercial and portrait photographer, who allowed Woodman to print his photographs in his studio. The couple were both still students, she having switched to art education, when they moved to New York City for the work of their next co-op term. Woodman, who feared that he would end up a draftsman, not a designer, tried to apprentice himself to Ezra Stoller, the architectural photographer whose views of the icons of modern architecture are highly regarded. Turned down, he got a job working as a draftsman and was put on a project for a school district in the Bronx. He sat in on the meetings, and when he commented that they were designing "a prison," he was told "to shut up."[97] He quit after the fourth week and returned to Ezra Stoller, who had already refused to employ him, this time offering to work for free. After the first month Stoller paid him fifty dollars a month to cover his costs for gasoline. At the time, he worked with Stoller's assistant, Jonathan Green, since Stoller was on assignment in Europe.

Woodman arranged to complete his last two terms consecutively so that he could return to work for Stoller, graduating in 1969. Stoller's assistant, Green, had just quit to teach at MIT. Stoller, who hired Woodman, taking him on the road as his assistant, was supportive of Woodman's activity in the antiwar movement, much more so than his own parents. Woodman recalls the photographer fondly: "One of the things I learned from Stoller was that to be a great artist's assistant one was not only to stay in the background, but the assistant had to be accomplished in as many areas as the principal to work well as a team."[98] Yet he was unable to get a raise or a credit line from Stoller, from whom he had learned how to photograph buildings and "everything I know technically about photography." Woodman decided to follow Green to MIT and applied to study there with Minor White, a highly regarded photographer and teacher who was a friend of Ansel Adams, Edward Weston, and Alfred Stieglitz.[99]

Before he could begin study in 1970, Woodman got a call from his draft board for his preinduction physical exam in Boston. For some time he had "connected with some very good draft counselors who had contact with people on the East Coast. . . . So when I started to work for Stoller I was advised to start seeing a shrink and to begin establishing a history of paranoid schizophrenia (I was counseled as to the patterns and how to act)."[100] Woodman already had a psychological history, since, when he was thirteen and insisted that he wanted to be a dancer, his mother had taken him to be examined at Children's Medical Center in Boston. His parents feared then that Donald was not "normal." With this history he put his psychiatric papers in order and hoped to get a 1Y deferment for six months. Instead, he managed to qualify as "mentally unstable," receiving the coveted 4F designation.

Having saved the money, found a sponsor, and prepared to go to Canada if he received the 1Y, Woodman suddenly felt free from the threat of being drafted. He took the money and his wife and left for six months bicycling and photographing across Europe. Finally able to focus on what he wanted for the future, he returned home, decided to separate from his wife, and went to study with White, who he says "taught me how to see photographically." This included White's interest in the metaphorical nature of photography.

At the end of his studies Woodman was visiting some of White's former students in New Mexico, who offered him a temporary position at the Sacramento Peak Solar Observatory at White Sands, where he ran the processing laboratory and the facility for making solar observation films. He describes an indulgent and carefree time. When that job was over, he eventually ended up selling his treasured antique car, an MGTC, which he had lovingly restored, and buying some land in Galisteo. He was not yet living there but in Albuquerque.

Woodman was earning a modest living photographing artists' work and assisting Jay Burkett, a cabinetmaker. In 1977 the Canadian-born abstract painter Agnes Martin (1912–2004), who had been in the United States since 1931, hired Burkett to produce props for a movie that she was making about Genghis Khan. It was to be her second film, following *Gabriel* (1976), about a young boy exploring the world on "a day of freedom." When Martin met Woodman, she offered him $400 to work on the film with her. Her offer was beguiling. She insisted that "photography has been neglected in motion pictures. People may think that's exaggerated, but, really, I think that photography is a very sensitive medium."[101] They then flew up to Vancouver for her to shoot at Bouchard Gardens, near where she grew up.

Later Martin, who at sixty-five was three years older than Ezra Stoller, offered Woodman, then thirty-two, $200 a month to live on his Galisteo property and do whatever she wanted there. He recalls that she was quite proud that her lifestyle was as stripped away as her Minimalist painting. At the time she had returned to extreme restraint in her paintings of graphite grids superimposed on monochrome gray grounds, which characterized her personal reductive aesthetic. An obituary reported that Martin "disavowed politics and any connection with the feminist movement. In 1967, when she was honored by *Harper's Bazaar* as one of 100 'Women of Achievement,' she came to the luncheon wearing moccasins and an unironed skirt and blouse."[102] But Woodman, who had relished Minor White's mysticism, also responded to what one interviewer has called "her compelling persona" and her "undeniably influential, creative force."[103]

Woodman had already had a well dug on his property by the time he and Martin moved into her camper on the back of a pickup truck and lived there together for three or four weeks. When she then "threw him out," he moved into a tent on the same property, continuing to work as her assistant. Woodman considered Martin to be asexual, although others have identified her as a lesbian.[104] Her instruction to Woodman about the art world was to give him Lee Seldes's 1978 book, *The Legacy of Mark Rothko: An Exposé of the Greatest Art Scandal of Our Century,* the story of the bilking of that artist's estate by his dealer in collusion with his close friends.[105] Martin, who saw Rothko's work as "pure devotion to reality," told an interviewer, "I don't believe for a minute that Rothko committed suicide. Nobody in that state of mind could. He was murdered, obviously . . . by the people who have profited or have *tried* to profit."[106]

Woodman traveled with Martin to Calgary, Alberta, near her birthplace in Maklin, Saskatchewan. She kept a sixteen-foot metal boat on the McKinsie River, where they camped out together in a tent in June 1978. "We had to wait for the ice to go out of the Great Slave Lake," he recalls, "so that we could go down the McKinsie River, one of Martin's longtime desires." Back in New Mexico, Woodman became involved with a younger woman from Houston whom he met when she worked in an architect's office in Santa Fe, where he maintained a darkroom. When she returned to Houston in 1980, Woodman visited her and looked into graduate study at the University of Houston. He continued to divide his time between Galisteo and Houston, where he enrolled in an MFA program in photography and worked as a preparator at the Blaffer Gallery at the University of Houston.

He remembers a presentation about *The Dinner Party* by a group of women who came to the class he was taking on art and law with Sharon Lorenzo. Woodman recalls that he suggested the Lawndale Annex, an alternative exhibition space that he and some other graduate students had begun with James Surls as the faculty adviser, but that its space was too small because of its columns. The Lawndale group volunteered to install *The Dinner Party,* but he remembers that the women's community said, "Men are not allowed to be involved in the project." As a result, he declined to go and hear Chicago when she came to give a lecture, and he never saw *The Dinner Party* there.

Although he built a simple house for Martin on his property, she often traveled for long periods of time. In 1983 she was missing when he returned to Galisteo. He learned where she was only when he received a call from a state mental hospital in Colorado Springs. Martin had been taken there after she had been picked up ranting on the street and had given them his phone number. Woodman went to pick her up and brought her back to New Mexico, where she was required to seek mental help.

Woodman tried to watch over Martin but observed that she was disturbed by visions of demons. He finally called Arnold Glimscher, her dealer at Pace Gallery, to report that she had started to destroy her drawings. Woodman was dismayed when Glimscher blamed him for Martin's condition. She moved to the psychiatric ward of St. Vincent's Hospital in Santa Fe, and Glimscher forbade Woodman to see Martin again, purchasing from Woodman his Galisteo property, where Martin had been living.

Woodman's friendship with Martin proved that he could deal with a demanding, even difficult woman. And having worked with both Stoller and White, he knew how to treat an art star. His profession as a photographer made him more attractive to Chicago, for it replicated at least one aspect of Georgia O'Keeffe's relationship with Alfred Stieglitz. As Stieglitz was for O'Keeffe, Woodman would prove to be supportive of her art work. Woodman did not have Stieglitz's fame, nor was he an art dealer, but he had trained in architecture and offered a mastery of many practical tasks, including building skills—somewhat reminiscent of Ken Gilliam, who had earlier attracted her. Though she also found Woodman young and attractive, their age difference was much less.

Woodman explains: "When I first met Judy I acted with a lot of bravado and not from much consciousness . . . I was raised by my great-grandmother, grandmother, and mother (three women) and I was raised with the idea that I should marry a Jewish girl and was only allowed to date Jewish girls while in high school (while I was under my parents' roof, at home). Judy was unlike any Jewish girl/woman I had known in the past or dated and unlike any woman I had ever dated."[107] He maintains that he struggled to overcome his shyness and the sense that he was not worthy. He considered Chicago "a real prize, since my family didn't think I would amount to much and for me to marry a Jew (neither my brother nor cousin married a Jew) and a famous artist was a vindication for me and changed the whole family dynamic."[108] He did not want Judy to meet his family, since he knew they would try to diminish him in her eyes, but she insisted on it. He recalls that he was so estranged from his family that they did not even have his phone number.

Chicago may have insisted that she meet Woodman's family because her Jewish heritage was becoming more important to her. By October 1985 she had become interested in her "history as a Jew, particularly in relation to the Holocaust," and on October 5 began keeping her "Jewish Journal" in a yellow looseleaf notebook. She intended to record her feelings, ideas, and thoughts not only about her investigation of the Holocaust but also about what it meant to her "as a woman, a Jew and a person of the late 20th Century."[109] She recalled a chance meeting at a Christmas party in Santa Fe with poet Harvey Mudd, whom she identified as "a goy [non-Jew]," reverting to the Yiddish that she had used in writing letters home to her mother from college. What had struck her was the subject of a poem that he had discussed with her, which she had thought at first that she might like to illuminate. After reading it, she gradually realized that he was dealing with the Holocaust "in a fatuous way." She even made suggestions to him about shortening his poem and making it clearer. But she had begun reading on the subject and realized that his poem "was too narrow a vehicle for this subject."[110]

The subject of the Holocaust continued to hold Chicago's attention. She and Woodman traveled together to New York in late October to see Claude Lanzmann's film *Shoah*, which takes its title from the name Israelis have given to the Holocaust and means "chaos" or "annihilation." Nine and a half hours long, the film reflects the six years Lanzmann spent looking for eyewitnesses. He found some Germans and Poles who either worked in the camps or observed what went on in them.

Chicago reflected this was one of the few times in her adult life when she had an experience of "otherness" that was not gender-based. She was relieved to share the feelings with Donald, noting, "Despite my radical political background, I cannot remember *any* discussion of the Holocaust during my childhood." She began to wonder why. While in New York, she visited the YIVO archive on Eastern European Jewish culture, where she had sought out a photograph of the tomb of her ancestor, the Vilna *gaon,* about whom her father used to tell her. She wondered why this figure and the twenty-three generations of rabbis in his family were so important to him, "an atheist, a Marxist, & a rebel against the tradition he was brought up in." She reflected that his father "used to beat him when he was a child of 10 because he wouldn't go to Hebrew school. He never did either. But I wonder why neither of his two older brothers became rabbis."[111]

But after witnessing all the filmed interviews with SS officers, Holocaust survivors, and Polish peasants—all men—Chicago also asked, "Where were the women?"[112] She would eventually address the "double jeopardy" of sexism and racism in the Holocaust. But at the time she noted that she had never before begun a project on which she wanted to work so slowly, "but the horrors of the material are such that I have to go slow or I shall go mad!"[113]

Around this time Chicago fell in a freak accident and broke the wrist of her drawing hand. She had prevailed upon her doctor to shape her cast so that she could grip a pen and document her situation. As her broken wrist was still healing, she found both writing and drawing difficult, but she did both, including a drawing that she captioned "Stopped by her arm from starting down the road to madness." The small pen and ink drawing features a nude woman wearing an armband with a Jewish star.[114] She began her investigation, reading widely, making a note to look into both Sholem Aleichem and Isaac Bashevis Singer, and she was fascinated by Yaffa Eliach's book called *Hasidic Tales of the Holocaust.*[115] The series of linear *Cast Drawings* that documented her pain and dilemma show that she responded positively and with humor to a frustrating situation and a loss of control, even adding a handwritten narrative and a photocopied "catalogue."

After their brief courtship Judy and Donald planned their wedding for December 31, 1985. They designed the wedding ceremony to reflect their Jewish heritage. Judy noted in her journal that Donald insisted that the ceremony be "meaningful," and she agreed with him.[116] Together they made the traditional chuppah, or ritual canopy, under which they were wed. They were married by Lynn Gottlieb, a female rabbi from Albuquerque, ordained by the Conservative Jewish movement, who was "trained (in part) by a Hasidic Jew" and an Orthodox rabbi, but who considers herself a Reform rabbi influenced by feminism. They also wrote their own vows in the *ketubah* (marriage contract) that they designed, and they incorporated Judy's "Merger" poem about "merging the masculine & feminine" (which the liturgical arts director of Hebrew Union College in Cincinnati had already set to music) into the ceremony.[117] They began their celebration with what they defined as a "contemporary version of a ritual cleansing or 'mikvah' "—but they did it together, rather than follow the tradition of the woman going alone for the ritual bath—in the sauna and hot tub at a small inn outside of Galisteo, where they were then married at the home of Romona Scholder.

For this, her third marriage, Judy was anxious. For Donald, it was his second marriage but his first to a Jewish woman and his first real wedding ceremony. Judy and Donald slept separately the night before the ceremony, and she awakened every hour, getting up at five-thirty in the morning.[118] Donald's mother, thrilled that her son had a Jewish bride, had sewn a veil and a blue garter for Judy and loaned her a handkerchief for something "borrowed." Judy was excited to participate in all the traditional rituals, which neither of her earlier marriages had involved. She rationalized in her Jewish journal why a feminist would participate "in a ceremony that included veiling, which is associated with some extremely oppressive customs—like purdah, dowries, etc." She had been reading a book about a Brooklyn Hasidic community that told how many of their customs had been misunderstood: "According to the book, some of the marriage & sexual rituals derive from a belief in the sacredness of the sexual bond & are intended to enhance the erotic bond."[119] Donald liked the theatricality of unveiling her before the ceremony in a quiet room and again under the chuppah. They arranged to have a traditional klezmer band play at the reception. Judy felt that the ceremony not only married them but affirmed their Jewishness "in a very spiritual way."[120]

"It was both my determination to marry Judy and my single-minded focus on staying married," Woodman has said, "that has been the bedrock of our relationship. It took her a while to realize that I was the calm steady current that created the space for her to exhibit all the emotion that her personality and art needed in the studio or in private (and it took me a long time to bring this to consciousness)."[121] He does not deny his own "fits of emotional explosions" and admits to impatience, but he insists that he tries "to keep my eye on the goal of Judy's desire to be recognized for her accomplishments (she is more ambitious than me)."[122]

Woodman got to know Chicago just as she was finishing her series of images, inspired by the classical tradition of the heroic nude male, which he named "Powerplay." Most of the images show men as destructive or angry, including *Pissing on Nature* (1983), *In the Shadow of the Handgun* (1983), *Trying to Kill the Woman Inside Him* (1983), *Crippled by the Need to Control* (1983), *Disfigured by Power 1* (1984), and *Driving the World to Destruction* (1985, Figure 27). He recalls, "I really responded to that work and was the one that suggested to her that she should do the Woe/Man image" so that men would have some idea of what "a woman really wanted. I was the model for Woe/Man."[123] Chicago responded to Woodman's suggestion and stated: "I came to understand how much men need images that support them in their vulnerability and sensitivity." She further explained that women really want "men to be as soft and vulnerable as women, we want men to be as human, we want them to let themselves be vulnerable and also to feel strong in their vulnerability, not powerless."[124]

With Woodman as her model, Chicago modeled *Woeman* (1986), a relief that she then had cast in patinated bronze. She made another version in hand-cast, hand-painted paper. Both the bronze editions and the painted-paper casts were published as multiples. She also showed her studies for these images, which she had executed in Prismacolor pencils on paper, a favorite medium. Her *Maleheads* show men with exaggerated emotional expressions—grimacing, growling, and exclaiming. She explained how she came to make these images: "I came to the point, somewhere in 1982, where I couldn't make images of women anymore. I realized that men depict women and women depict women—women are everybody's love (or hate) object, and I said to myself—women are not the problem. I've never been anti-male. I've had deep, profound connections with men. They're not the enemy. I wanted to show them as human, but acting in ways that are intolerable."[125]

Just three weeks after their marriage, in February 1986, Judy was hit by a truck while she was jogging alone on Upper Canyon Road in Santa Fe. Severely injured, she spent a week in the hospital, where she and Donald celebrated their one-month wedding anniversary. Recuperating at home, and in keeping with her interest in making art out of her own experience, she began a series of twenty-one drawings about the accident, which combined photographs taken by Donald. They began to work together, with Judy supplying the content and Donald coming up with the image, often using her as his model, his Stieglitz to her O'Keeffe. Chicago considered this an exercise in working together and already anticipated Donald's collaboration in the *Holocaust Project.* Making art out of loss was also by now a ritual for Chicago, who had tried to deal with the subject in graduate school and again in her suite of lithographs *Potent Pussy: Homage to Lamont,* inspired by the death of her beloved cat.

The Andrew Smith Gallery in Santa Fe showed the work resulting from this first collaboration as *Judy Chicago Accidents, Injuries and Other Calamities* in the summer of 1988 with the credit, "Photography: Donald Woodman." The show was at the gallery at the same time as a show of photographs by Annie Leibovitz. The two women posed affectionately as "friends" for a photograph by Neil Jacobs that appeared in *Journal North,* a local publication. Also included in Chicago's show was a series called *Coast to Coast Cancer,* which was her and Donald's collaborative response to dealing with the difficulty of simultaneous illnesses of his father on the East Coast and her mother on the West Coast, and the emotional and physical demands of this unfortunate circumstance.

Through these first collaborations Chicago's difficulty in relating to men evolved into a lasting marriage. Four years or so into the marriage, Chicago would quip: "This is my third marriage, I keep saying, 'Three is a charm.' Donald's not exactly the reward I expected to get, but he's the reward I got! I'm very happy to be married to him, and I think he feels the same way. Being intimate with another person is a wonderful antidote to despair, it's a way of making life in the present worth living."[126] A few years later she told another interviewer, "When I met Donald, I think we would have had a kid except it was too late in our lives. When I married Donald I was forty-six years old. Donald and I say it's probably a good thing, because we are enough for each other. We are full time jobs for each other, but if we could have, we probably would have done it anyway."[127]

Their progeny would be their work together. The *Holocaust Project* took shape slowly. On a trip to Washington, D.C., Chicago and Woodman met with Isaiah Kuperstein, then the education director of the Holocaust Museum Council. They learned from him "the fact that Jewish survival over the centuries is deeply rooted in the Jewish ability to organize. Given my own history, that was a *very* illuminating thought," wrote Chicago in her journal.[128] She had been reading a book of Holocaust stories introduced and annotated by Elie Wiesel but found that she disagreed with him. Although she felt that the Holocaust "stands out as singular in the history of the human race—it's true that it is singular in its systematic nature but to truly understand it, I think it's important to see it as an aberration in the history of human cruelty—in that they went too far, much too far. Anyway, my interest is in showing the relationship between Nazi philosophy & the general nature of patriarchy. I wonder if I can do it?"[129]

That same spring, while visiting Los Angeles, Judy and Donald went with Audrey Cowan to UCLA to listen to uncataloged interviews with female Holocaust survivors. In contrast to the men who spoke in the film *Shoah*, Chicago felt that there was "more emphasis on family connections, staying with &/or protecting other female family members."[130] She found that despite all the talk of Jews being "willing victims," the survivors told of "all levels of resistance." They also did research at the Los Angeles Museum of the Holocaust, founded in 1961 by a survivor, and at the Simon Wiesenthal Center. They found the latter's exhibition to be too "slick & high tech," preferring the former's straightforward and simple presentation.[131]

In many Holocaust museums that Chicago and Woodman visited, she found the "incredulous, shocked tone of 'How could this have happened in such a civilized world?'" annoying, especially in the audiovisual presentations. "I guess its the denial of what kind of world we really live in that bothers me.

I hope that the work we do can clarify the context in which the Holocaust took place—that understanding the Holocaust should lead one to a real understanding of the nature of human civilization."[132]

Research on the Holocaust was very much on Chicago's mind when, in June 1986, she and Donald traveled to Frankfurt, Germany, so that she could take part in the Dinner Party Festival. This invitation, which paid their way to Germany, was an opportunity for them to travel to Essen, to visit what was then the only Holocaust museum in Germany. Recommended by Isaiah Kuperstein, who was himself born in Essen, this museum was located in an old synagogue. Its exhibition moved them, since it emphasized visually what had transpired in that particular place. But the more they saw about the Holocaust in Europe, the more that they would be shocked at how differently it is presented in the United States.[133]

Chicago thought that this opportunity was ironic. But she was completely unaware of the direction that the festival would take. The festival organizer was Dagmar von Garnier, a woman in her mid-forties who describes herself as a "folkloristic dance expert" and a feminist.[134] She had first seen *The Dinner Party* in Edinburgh and determined that she would bring it to Germany. Chicago insisted that the work be shown in a museum space, and von Garnier had to figure out how to convince Christoph Vitali, the director of Frankfurt's newly opened Schirn Kunsthalle, who was reluctant to show the piece. With this in mind von Garnier threw her energies into organizing the festival, in which women were invited to pay an admission fee of 390 marks (then about $240) and come dressed in the costume of one of the 1,038 women named in *The Dinner Party*.[135] Each woman was to research the life of the woman she represented and be prepared to discuss or perform her character. Von Garnier has made clear that, in her opinion, Chicago sees *The Dinner Party* as her artwork, while for her the work is something to inspire women to "consider their own situation in life—to raise consciousness."[136]

Chicago felt that the hundreds of people in the audience were receptive to her feelings as a Jewish woman coming to Germany. She revised her lecture on *The Dinner Party* to begin "by discussing Judith of the Bible first & my Jewishness & the whole issue of 'openness.' It terrifies me but I did all the feminist stuff when I started & this is just another step in being who I am," she noted in her journal.[137] She also incorporated the witch hunts and Petronilla de Meath, who symbolizes the witches in *The Dinner Party*. But Chicago had a huge falling out with von Garnier, who would not allow her to speak about the Holocaust at a witch memorial on the third day of the festival. Chicago wanted to point out that there was a commonality between the hunting of witches for annihilation and, later, the Nazi persecution of the Jews. She spoke out about her discontent with von Garnier's decisions in *Der Spiegel,* pointing out that she felt hurt and did not like the program, and the "folklore made me sick." In fact, some journalists and participants found that the group dances and rituals were too reminiscent of those typical of the Nazi era.[138] Von Garnier, in turn, circulated a thirteen-page letter to fourteen hundred people, attacking Chicago and others.[139]

Chicago took it all in stride and continued to focus on her art then in progress, interrupting as usual to attend openings of completed work. In September 1986 the *Birth Project* was shown at the R.H. Love Galleries in Chicago, with the opening event a benefit for the new maternity center of the Michael Reese Hospital, the same charity hospital where she had been born. Then the next month ACA Galleries in New York showed *Powerplay,* about which Chicago asserted, "This show is about what people do with power and how people are controlled by power."[140]

Paula Harper wrote in the show's catalog: "Chicago's art alerts us to the danger of remaining fixed in sexual roles that no longer work in the modern era."[141] Harper admitted that she found the images of *Powerplay* both "memorable and disturbing. They alter our consciousness through the aesthetic gateway."[142] She suggested: "Chicago, in her new work, continues to do what she has done throughout her career—challenge taboos and break new ground. She treads dangerously close to what has been forbidden territory for women artists in these images of men: their faces are grotesque, distorted by anger or disfigured by power mania. They control women, disdain nature, equate guns and sexuality, risk nuclear destruction of the planet, all in the name of manhood."[143]

Chicago later commented that this was her first body of work that was greeted by silence: "It's too far ahead of its time. Of course, men don't want to hear what I have to say about them. They're not accustomed to looking at themselves operating as a class, they see themselves as individuals. In order to understand their behavior you have to understand how they have been shaped as men the way we say how we, our individual actions, were limited by our role-conditioning. Men have not gone through that yet."[144] By "role-conditioning," she referred to what is now known as the social construction of femininity, a nonessentialist point of view.[145]

But by the time *Powerplay* was shown, Chicago had long since given all her energy to researching the *Holocaust Project.* On a trip to Los Angeles that fall, Judy went with Audrey Cowan to speak with a Jewish caterer for a dinner that Audrey was giving in Judy's honor, where several of the guests kept kosher. Some of the guests were coming from the Jewish Federation. Audrey, who had a feeling that this woman was a survivor, insisted that Judy tell her about what she was working on. The woman opened up and told her story of being liberated at the age of nine from a concentration camp, with all of her family dead. This was the first time that Chicago had witnessed a survivor speak about "the madness, rage, hostility," and she wrote later that she could "*feel* the woman's hurt & realized how terrible it must be for these people—*to have to live with all that hurt inside for so long.*"[146]

Chicago also went to see her mother and taped a recording of the two of them discussing her feelings about being Jewish, her discovery of the Holocaust, and its effect on her and on her family. She was stunned to learn that despite her "parents' political activism, they did not mobilize around Jewish issues of any kind. They apparently did not 'like' Jewish organizations & as for Zionism, my father dismissed Israel as a 'potential powder keg.' Moreover, a prevalent attitude, my mother explained, was that Jews should remain silent. She went to a discussion at the temple about what was happening in Germany in 1939. At the end of the discussion, the rabbi put his fingers to his lips & said 'But we must say *nothing*!' "[147]

Chicago felt puzzled and deprived of her heritage. "I wish I had more of an understanding of my tradition as a Jew," she wrote in her Jewish journal.[148] It was at this time that she began to conceptualize the individual components of the *Holocaust Project.* Chicago wanted to find funding to make the project. She planned to sell a book and realized that she needed to bring it into some relationship with Through the Flower, the 501(c)(3) that had supported *The Dinner Party* and *Birth Project,* so that she could raise funds to create and tour the new work, which once again involved her working with Mary Ross Taylor.[149] Through the Flower always received all of the rental fees for tours of the *Holocaust Project;* Chicago kept only the proceeds from sales of her book, her studies for the project, and her lecture fees.

In April 1987 Chicago and Woodman again traveled to Germany, this time to install *The Dinner Party* at the new Schirn Kunsthalle in Frankfurt. *Art in America* reported that during the new facility's inaugural year, the "most popular presentation" was "*The Dinner Party,* which booked 43,000 paying guests."[150] Damaging reverberations of von Garnier's misguided festival a year earlier all but guaranteed that the German critics' would react negatively to *The Dinner Party;* they focused on biological determinism and "irrational spiritualism."[151] Even Gisels Brackert, who headed women's programming on a state radio station and was one of the speakers at the opening, cautioned women against the dangers of treating the piece as a "cult object," a warning repeated in the German catalog and in the press, where radical left-wing activist Ingrid Strob, writing in the feminist journal *Emma,* labeled Chicago "a born cult leader" and "perfect demagogue."[152] It did not help that news of the *Birth Project,* then circulating in the United States, fueled irrational fears among German feminists that Chicago was trying to reduce women to their biological functions. In Germany some feminists incorrectly came to view the *Birth Project* as having an antiabortion agenda, as Lucy Lippard had earlier feared.[153]

Focusing on the future and not looking back was a talent that Chicago had long since learned. After the installation she and Woodman traveled through Europe for ten weeks, visiting concentration camps and other sites of the Holocaust. They also met with dissident Jews in Latvia, Lithuania, and Russia. The couple were shocked to see that many sites had no monuments to the Jews murdered there. In what was East Germany the Holocaust had been presented as an antifascist struggle. In the former Soviet Union they also found the Holocaust presented only as "an antifascist struggle," with an absence of monuments to Jews, which had been illegal. Chicago recounted diverse aspects of the Holocaust about which they learned in Europe: "the slave labor campaign. We learned that homosexuals had been imprisoned and murdered. We learned that the Holocaust had touched, terrified, tortured and tormented the lives of millions of people, and that the scale and scope of it was way beyond what either of us had previously understood. And so our trip completely enlarged our perspective and changed our vision of what we wanted to do dramatically."[154]

The time of their research trip coincided with the publication, in the journal *Tikkun,* of an essay, "On Sanctifying the Holocaust: An Anti-Theological Treatise," in which the author, Adi Ophir, an Israeli scholar and cultural theorist, postulates "a religious consciousness built around the Holocaust."[155] He imagines that this new religion will have "four commandments," of which the first one is "Thou shall have no other holocaust." "There is no holocaust like the Holocaust of the Jews of Europe," he explains, and then elaborates upon this. The second commandment that Ophir imagines is "Thou shalt not make unto thee any graven image or likeness," which he follows with "It is possible to draw another *Guernica,* to sing the songs of the Partisans, to present *Ghetto,* but the Holocaust itself cannot be represented. Whoever tries to peek through the furnace of revelation and describe what he saw with his own eyes or in his mind's eye, is destined to fail."[156] He then argues persuasively that it is "dangerous" to create such a "Holocaust myth": "Because it blurs the humanness of the Holocaust; because it erases degrees and continuums and puts in their place an infinite distance between one type of atrocity and all other types of human atrocities . . . the Jewishness of the Holocaust (like its Germanness) is only one aspect of the horror . . . the overlooking of other aspects . . . is no less dangerous than the denial of the Holocaust by contemporary anti-Semites."[157] Among Ophir's conclusions is the necessity to "do everything that you can to concretize the horror. Honor its intricate details. Present as much as possible of its creeping before the explosion, its day-to-day occurrences, its uncountable human, all too human, faces."[158]

Chicago and Woodman appear to have taken Ophir's plea to heart. They worked full-time on the project, doing extensive research, which was both demanding and draining. Mary Ross Taylor had helped them considerably by renting them her house in Santa Fe at a very modest cost. Then, at the suggestion of Jeffrey Bergen and his brother Jonathan of the ACA Galleries, they applied to the Threshold Foundation for a grant to help finance work on the project. As a result, in 1988 Elizabeth A. Sackler traveled from New York to Santa Fe, in order to make a site visit for the foundation. She recommended the grant ($24,000), which was the foundation's first grant to any individual. Sackler followed up this recommendation with years of personal patronage in support of the *Holocaust Project.* Later that year Chicago accompanied Sackler on a visit to the National Museum of Women in the Arts, while her painting *Through the Flower* (1973) was on loan there. Sackler decided that she had to own that picture. It was the first of many works that she acquired for her unique collection of Chicago's work. Before long she sought out Chicago's four *Great Ladies* (1972–73) and was able to acquire three: *Christina of Sweden, Marie Antoinette,* and *Elizabeth in Honor of Elizabeth,* the latter renamed by Chicago in honor of her patron.

Elizabeth A. Sackler is the daughter of Arthur M. Sackler, a physician, art collector, and philanthropist who endowed galleries at the Metropolitan Museum of Art and Princeton University, a museum at Harvard University, and the Arthur M. Sackler Gallery, which is the national museum of Asian Art at the Smithsonian Institution in Washington, D.C. Now the head of the Arthur M. Sackler Foundation, Liz Sackler grew up a social activist. Even as a teen, as a student at the progressive New Lincoln High School in New York, she took part in the civil rights movement, demonstrating with SNCC and CORE. A cover story on the school in the African-American magazine *Ebony* featured a photograph of her at the FBI building in Manhattan with Lincoln classmates protesting voting restrictions in Selma, Alabama.[159] Among her diverse group of classmates was Adrienne Piper, an African-American who would become an artist known for her politically trenchant videos.[160] Sackler, like Chicago, adored her father, and she has kept in mind his words: "When we leave, we have to leave the world a better place than when we arrived."[161]

Sackler was privileged to grow up around her father and his friends, who included Linus Pauling, Isamu Noguchi, and Martha Graham. "I knew a lot of geniuses because they were hanging around," she says, "which is how I recognized Judy's genius immediately." Sackler recalls: "I loved her. We had a great time. . . . She took me into the studio and we talked about the *Holocaust Project.* She was clearly brilliant. We became fast friends. We'd have Passover together. I recognized her energy and temperament. She was a lot like my father. She had the same demand for accuracy. She didn't want to hear that something couldn't be done."[162]

It was part of that drive to be accurate, to master her subject, that motivated Chicago and Woodman to travel to Israel in November 1988. It was the first visit for both, and their purpose was to add to their understanding of the Holocaust. Ever the feminist, she was often dismayed at the "strict segregation of the sexes" required by Orthodox Jews, including at the Western Wall and in Meah Shearim, the Hasidic section of Jerusalem.[163] "What really got to me were the women with shaved heads," Chicago wrote. "As Donald remarked, it's a pretty direct way of depriving women of their identity."[164] Chicago kept a notebook recording this trip in which she both wrote and drew, often adding captions to her images. One drawing depicts her staring at the Orthodox women wearing their wigs and is captioned: "Underneath their seemingly happy faces, I couldn't believe they were bald." Her own hair she left exposed, causing a young man to stop Chicago to complain that she had not covered her head and was wearing jeans, which was "disrespectful." The next day, "in order to blend in," she wore a long dress and a scarf on her head.[165] Chicago concluded that "this 'Hasidic tradition' is totally tied up with the repression of women."[166]

They spent a day at Yad Vashem, the Holocaust memorial, and discussed "the trivialization of the Holocaust" with the museum's director. "It's an important point for Holocaust scholars," she reflected, "and I have to find a way to deal with it, although outside the Jewish community people make these types of comparisons all the time, sometimes quite inappropriately."[167] She recorded her fascination with micrography, the art of tiny writing that Jews had invented to produce texts for mezuzahs (small parchment scrolls inscribed with a biblical passage and affixed to the door posts in Jewish homes) and tefillin (little boxes with Old Testament texts, which are bound to the forehead and left arm by Orthodox men during the daily morning prayer). Before leaving Israel, Chicago and Woodman spent a day sightseeing in Tel Aviv and visited the Diaspora Museum. For her, this visit added to the pride she felt in her Jewish heritage and enabled her to view her experience in Israel as a positive one.

Despite the warning from the director of Yad Vashem, Chicago and Woodman concluded that they had to make links between the Jewish experience of the Holocaust and that of others, while they still sought to honor the uniqueness of the Jewish experience. She explained their effort "to be extremely precise in terms of our visual and verbal language. For example, in our visual language, we always present the Jewish experience of the Holocaust either on separate panels or in a separate visual space. This is a metaphor for the fact that we are not comparing separate experiences, but rather examining various historical experiences to see if there is anything that can be learned by looking at them side by side."[168]

What would be most controversial about the project finally begins to dawn on Chicago: "In short, we feel our work honors the memory of the Holocaust's victims, while examining the event in a way that demonstrates how much the Jewish experience can teach us all."[169] "I believe that my art grows out of the impulse to share and to educate," she says, emphasizing, "I believe that art should have a moral value. I am interested in shaping values, making the world a better place—that's the rabbinic tradition in my work."[170]

But it was not just didactic purpose that preoccupied Chicago. She also wanted to bring a feminist perspective to the *Holocaust Project,* since she felt that "we hear men's stories more than women's . . . my perspective as a feminist shaped my willingness to honor the suffering and the experience of all the people who were touched by the Holocaust."[171] Chicago emphasized that she and Woodman "feel very strongly that the Jewish experience can be opened, that there needs to be a really large dialogue about issues such as persecution and discrimination, and that this dialogue needs to cross over from the Jewish community into a broader audience."[172] After studying for three years, Chicago felt more strongly than ever that knowledge about the Holocaust was generally "fragmentary and the presentation biased; in many countries, it is presented in terms of nationalism or patriotism; in Eastern Europe and the Soviet Union, the 'anti-fascist struggle' is emphasized and throughout Europe, the Jewish experience is denied. In the United States, where the Jewish ordeal *is* emphasized, it is generally taken out of the context of the large-scale enslavement, suffering and death of millions; and the 'extermination' of gypsies, Jehovah's Witnesses and homosexuals is virtually ignored."[173] As for the exhibitions and most of the literature of the Holocaust, Chicago argued that "women's experience is omitted or minimized, despite the fact that it was women, children, and old people who were the most vulnerable victims of the Final Solution."[174] Chicago felt that art about the Holocaust failed to "illuminate the meaning of this contemporary human tragedy" and that most of the existing art was "confined to Jewish institutions and thus remains outside the subject matter of contemporary art."[175] She sought to make images that would communicate to a wide audience of viewers, both Jewish and non-Jewish.

To fabricate the project's triangular logo, Chicago called on Flo Perkins, Bob Gomez, and Michael Caudle, a stained-glass artisan in New Haven, Connecticut. The logo symbolizes the colored triangles that the Nazis forced inmates of concentration camps to wear. Chicago inverted the triangle to transform the form into an image of survival. Within a group of triangles within triangles, Chicago used yellow twice to suggest that the Holocaust began with the Jews but did not end with them.[176]

Chicago engaged Audrey Cowan to weave a monumental Aubusson tapestry called *The Fall* for the entryway piece for the *Holocaust Project.* Chicago took months to produce the cartoon from which Cowan would work. She employed a grand narrative structure intended to show " 'the battle of the sexes' as a metaphor for the historic defeat of matriarchy and the rise of patriarchy. The work will then visually chronicle the conquest of women and nature and the gradual development of male-dominated religion and society and then explore some of the tragic consequences of the Scientific and Industrial revolutions."[177] To do this Chicago depicted a male farmer plowing the land, which had the head of a female, "Mother Nature," abstractly embodied in the tilled soil. Christ on the cross is visible in the distance. In the center of the composition is Leonardo's Vitruvian Man, now holding a sword dripping with blood, emblematic of patriarchy.

On the right side of this tapestry Chicago attempted "to demonstrate visually how assembly-line techniques, originally used to 'process' animals, were eventually applied to human beings."[178] To accomplish this goal, she depicted male and female workers at a mechanized assembly line, urged on by a disembodied arm wearing a swastika on an armband. Above the machinery a rack holds human and porcine carcasses hanging from butchers' hooks.

Weaving the eighteen-foot tapestry took Cowan five years, so that the show had to open at the Spertus with the cartoon rather than the finished tapestry. She commented about Chicago: "She is an absolute perfectionist and highly disciplined. She expects it of herself and expects it of those she works with. That's why some people drop out. They can't or won't put forth what's necessary."[179]

Walking through the exhibition, one would next encounter the section called "Bearing Witness." An image called *Banality of Evil/Struthof* refers to Hannah Arendt's phrase and depicts the story of an inn where the SS and local people partied just three kilometers away from the concentration camp Natzweiler, in the Alsace-Lorraine region of France. There the Nazis turned a former bathhouse into a gas chamber. Chicago and Woodman worked together to combine her painting with his black and white photography, which was intended to "ground the image in reality."[180] Woodman took his photograph of the site and printed it, and then Chicago blocked out the areas where she would paint with white paint or gesso. He then rephotographed the altered image and printed it on photolinen, which she then sprayed with acrylic paint "to create visual ambiance, in which I would place the painted figures. I used sprayed paint because it has no texture or grain and hence, fuses with the photo surface and darks and lights to begin to fuse the painting with photography."[181] Chicago then painted carefully in the blocked-out areas, trying to match the level of detail in the photographs and sustain an emotional connection to the work. Another work in this section includes *Bones of Treblinka,* which attempts to restore Jewish identity to the blank stones that Chicago and Woodman encountered in this major death site in Eastern Poland.

Wall of Indifference depicts figures representing the United States, Britain, and the Soviet Union on the left and the Vatican and the International Red Cross on the right, while a train of Jewish refugees passes behind them on the way to death camps. In *Double Jeopardy* (Figure 29) Chicago and Woodman told " 'the story of the Holocaust' as it's generally told," using "standard photographs" as illustration. She then painted in what she considered "the untold story of women's experiences of those same events."[182] Male scholars did not appreciate her claim that she was contributing to the correction of what she viewed as the male bias in Holocaust history.

If this section was provocative, the one that followed upped the ante: "Power and Powerlessness: The Holocaust as Prism" included *Treblinka/Genocide* (Figure 28) that suggested parallels to the genocides of Armenians, Africans, Native Americans, and Gypsies. Then *Pink Triangle/Torture* and *Lesbian Triangle* raised the issue of Nazi torture of homosexuals and the persistence of such prejudice today. The final image in this section, *Im/Balance of Power* addressed the plight of children both during the Holocaust and in parts of the world today where they still suffer and perish.

Section three presented "Echoes and Reoccurrences: The Holocaust as Lesson," featuring *Arbeit Macht Frei/Work Makes Who Free?* an examination of race, class, and oppression in terms of Nazi slave labor and the history of African-American slavery in the United States. *See No Evil/Hear No Evil* examines denial of the Jews' plight in Europe, which was pervasive at the beginning of the Holocaust, and suggests the potential peril of nuclear programs, which are likewise being ignored. The last work in this section, *Four Questions: The Moral and Ethical Issues Raised by the Holocaust,* juxtaposes the Nazi sterilization program and other horrors with contemporary issues such as genetic engineering and reproductive technology, asking that the viewer consider the ethical implications. Technically complex, these works utilized photographs, collage, and drawing in various combinations, some of which were then colored by hand.

The final section, "Survival and Transformation: The Jewish Experience as Pathway to Action," begins with *Legacy,* which examines the survivor experience to ask what can be learned and includes a depiction of Jews in the "safe haven that Israel represents." The image that follows resulted from a suggestion from Caudle, who wanted Chicago to consider stained glass for the exhibition's final work, a proposal that she accepted. Her stained-glass painting teacher, Dorothy Maddy, brought her forty years of painting experience and painted most of *Rainbow Shabbat* (Figure 30) herself, working with Chicago's study and one assistant.[183] Chicago had envisioned "a final, transformative, redemptive image."[184] Bob Gomez, the primary stained-glass fabricator for the project, assembled the sections, including the side panels that incorporated both English and Hebrew, the latter text typeset in Tel Aviv.

Chicago's graphic designer for the project, Ginna Sloan, commented, "You have to be a hard worker, know how to work. You can't just fake your way through. I think that everyone has to have one big first disagreement with Judy. Survive that trial by fire, and you're fine. Because she's intense, has a strong personality, and has definite ideas about what she wants, it took me a while to realize that she truly wanted my input. Now we work together smoothly."[185]

In the meantime, as Chicago worked on the *Holocaust Project,* she was still receiving plenty of new criticism for work then being shown. Suzanne Muchnic kept up her attacks, panning Chicago's minisurvey show at the Jan Baum Gallery in Los Angeles in April 1988. Muchnic referred to *The Dinner Party* as her "most spectacular debacle" and to the artist this way: "As a politician, Chicago has asked important questions about the inequality of women and mobilized platoons of adoring minions. But as an artist, she is much less effective." Reversing herself, Muchnic did allow for the first time that in the *Birth Project,* Chicago viewed birth at times as "a tumultuous upheaval of the Earth—a more interesting concept that leads to a few relatively complex works that actually contain a streak of subtlety."[186]

But despite the negative feedback, Chicago kept working and touring her work. *The Dinner Party* made it to Melbourne, Australia, opening at the Exhibition Building in January 1988. One local journalist there recalled her own experience lining up to see the piece with her mother, sister-in-law, and hundreds of other women in the winter of 1980 in Boston. The younger woman was delighted by the work, the older one "miffed."[187]

Chicago celebrated her fiftieth birthday on July 20, 1989. Donald organized a party at their home, and more than fifty friends came, including Mary Ross Taylor and Audrey and Bob Cowan, who flew in from California. Bob read a long poem, called "To the Big Ruler," that he composed for the occasion, harkening back to the old joke about the long yardstick or ruler from *The Dinner Party* days. Everyone dressed up in outfits from the 1950s, while a band played 1950s songs.

The next day Judy's brother, Ben, called from Japan. He was not just calling for her birthday, but to break the news that he had been diagnosed with amyotrophic lateral sclerosis (known as Lou Gehrig's disease, the same illness that killed their uncle) and had been given less than three years to live. He and Reiko had two small sons by now, and Ben was just getting established as a potter. For Chicago, it seemed as if history was repeating itself, for her father had also died while still in his forties, leaving his wife to raise their two children. She and Donald arranged to pay for Ben to come and see an American doctor. They all conspired not to tell May that her son was dying, since she was already struggling with terminal cancer.[188]

▲
Ben Cohen, Judy's brother, in Japan.

Resolution: Finding a Home 13

On his swift trip to consult American specialists, Ben Cohen had been told that every available treatment was accessible in Japan. There, though, he learned that patients were generally confined to hospitals. Out of some three thousand known ALS sufferers in the entire country, only eleven were able to stay with their families. That would not do for Cohen. He intended to be with his wife Reiko and two young sons in Kadanji—high on a forested slope above rice fields in the lonely valley where he had built his kiln, about two hours north from Kyoto. From the spring of 1989, when he first began to grow weak, Cohen had determined that in the brief time allowed by the implacable disease, he

▲
Elizabeth Sackler and Judy Chicago.

would keep his pottery going. He arrived at his show in Tokyo that year in a wheelchair, still able to walk, but only with a cane.[1]

Cohen had named his pottery "Coh-en," using the Japanese characters for "joyous flame."[2] Friends dubbed it "Ben-yaki," using another Japanese word meaning "fire," as in the firing of clay.[3] He had begun working with pots thrown on the wheel, then reshaped by hand. Forgoing glazes, he relied instead on slow firing at lower-than-normal temperatures, burning local cedar, the ash of which fuses with the clay, bringing out its natural colors and creating a unique matte patina.

At first Cohen's potter friends pitched in to help make his basic shapes when he could no longer use his hands. Reiko began to intuit how to improve upon the shapes, and so began her apprenticeship.[4] She had worked in cloisonné some years before, but never pottery. He determined to teach her the craft that he had mastered in laborious years of apprenticeship to an austere traditional master. But by April 1990, with his illness progressing more rapidly than had been anticipated, Ben had become totally paralyzed. He had to travel to a hospital for a tracheotomy and learn to use a respirator to survive. Speech would be possible only by means of a voice machine, and a specialist would be required to help him learn its use. Friends and family raised money to import the specialist.[5]

Judy and Donald determined to visit Ben that spring before it was too late. He asked her not to come to Kadanji until he had recuperated from the tracheotomy and learned to use the voice machine.[6] Meanwhile, to help pay for their travel, she arranged to give lectures in Tokyo, Yokohama, Kyoto, and Hiroshima. Some Japanese women were already interested in her, since *Through the Flower* had been translated already in 1979.[7] Now her lectures made cultural waves of their own. After her talk in Kyoto, a number of women rose and testified to their own experiences of sexual harassment and rape, shocking the translator.[8] Journalists flocked to interview her; some of the notice in the press even reached Kadanji.

Chicago and Woodman found her brother totally paralyzed but spending many hours each day in the studio, instructing Reiko in his techniques, including the art of making new shapes from clay slabs. She learned to use the special oil-fired kiln he had built himself and became a true collaborator. "It's especially gratifying to be teaching Reiko and seeing unused talent come to life. I never thought I would enjoy teaching pottery. It's been a pleasant surprise," said Ben, even as he faced death.[9] He insisted that he be brought to the table in his wheelchair to be present and join the conversation. As much as Chicago admired her brother's courage, her heart ached, and she cried when she returned each day to the inn where they were staying.[10]

Ben and Reiko held two joint shows—first in Nagoya in October 1991, then in January 1992 in Tokyo, both of which sold out in an exacting market. He was unable to attend the last Tokyo show in January 1992, but he learned from Reiko that on the first night it had sold more than any other show. Reiko had found herself: "I am 45 years old and have found wonderful work to do."[11]

Ben Cohen passed away a month to the day after the opening in Tokyo. He was buried on the opposite slope across the narrow valley from the simple dwelling and stacks of split cedar by the kiln, under a boulder inscribed in English and Japanese—monument to a creative resolve as remarkable in its way as his sister's and carried on in Reiko and their eldest son, who went on to win admission to Tokyo University.[12]

With her brother's example in mind and inspired by her ongoing research, Chicago had told an interviewer, "One of the things the Holocaust has taught me is either you get up and keep going or you lie down and die; there aren't many alternatives. It's not in my nature to give up. I don't think it's in my lineage, either."[13] Still struggling to find a permanent home for *The Dinner Party*, she was counting on the board of Through the Flower, the nonprofit organization that she started in 1978 to raise funds for its support. Now the board was taking an active role in the search for permanent housing. In fact, this became their chief goal. It was through the board's efforts that the American Association of University Women had launched a nationwide campaign to find a college or university that would take up Chicago's offer to donate her major work. At the time when Elizabeth A. Sackler joined the board in 1989, some of the other members were Judith Sherman Asher, Audrey Cowan, Elyse Grinstein, Susan Grode, Holly Harp, Ruth Lambert, Mickey Stern, and Pat Mathis.

Mathis, a Washington businesswoman and former civil rights worker, first had the idea that *The Dinner Party* should go to the University of the District of Columbia (UDC), of which she was a trustee. She saw the gift as bringing together the struggles for freedom by both women and African-Americans, who were the university's primary population. This was a vision that coincided with Chicago's values and her history. It was in 1990 that Chicago decided to give *The Dinner Party* to UDC, where it would take its place as part of a growing collection of art that would focus on work by African-Americans but already included art by some of the local Washington "Color Field" painters and others who were Euro-Americans. The art collection, which was part of a plan to raise an endowment for UDC, was to be housed in the university's Carnegie Library, located at the foot of the Mall, across from Washington's Convention Center.

On June 19, when the UDC trustees accepted the gift of *The Dinner Party* by unanimous vote, Chicago thought that the planned multicultural art center that would house her work sounded "positive, future-looking."[14] When she and Woodman arrived in Washington on July 17, for the donation ceremony that was scheduled for July 20, 1990, she was unaware that opposition on campus was growing. Then on July 18 the conservative *Washington Times* reported that the University of the District of Columbia's Board of Trustees planned to "spend nearly $1.6 million to acquire and exhibit a piece of controversial art. 'The Dinner Party' by feminist artist Judy Chicago was banned in several art galleries around the country because it depicts women's genitalia on plates and has been characterized by some critics as obscene."[15] The *Washington Times* is a paper published by News World Communications (a subsidiary of the Unification Church), which the *Columbia Journalism Review* has identified as "the media arm of Reverend Sun Myung Moon's Unification Church."[16] It is hardly surprising that this paper took an activist stance and distorted the fact that Chicago was *giving* her artwork and that the university would pay only for transporting it there, insuring and exhibiting it. Though controversial for many, the work had never been banned.

Nor did everyone consider the work controversial. "It was controversial fifteen years ago," Patricia Mathis stated. "It is not controversial now."[17] The plan that the UDC board had approved was to renovate a wing of the school's Carnegie Library to show the piece. The City Council had already approved a $1.2 million bond bill from the university's capital budget to restore the library and prepare it to show *The Dinner Party,* but press reports gave various estimates, exaggerating the planned costs and hiding the fact that, even without the display of any artworks, the entire library (including the leaking roof) needed major repairs.[18] All of the funds (except for $80,000 to be replaced immediately from private sources) relating to the installation of *The Dinner Party* were to come from the capital, not the operating budget.[19]

But the press, especially the *Washington Times,* picked up on the story and began to distort the meaning of the gift, eventually provoking student demonstrations and a strike, congressional debates, and an amendment, introduced on July 26, by archconservative Representative Stan Parris of Virginia, sometimes called "Senator Jesse Helms's surrogate in the House," to the District of Columbia's appropriation bill that deleted $1.6 million from UDC's 1991 budget. This was exactly what the press had reported as being targeted for renovating the Carnegie Library before the gift of *The Dinner Party* had been announced. After an eighty-seven-minute debate, aired on C-Span television, the amendment passed in the House by a 2-to-1 margin.[20] The Senate Appropriations Committee met to consider the punitive bill passed by the House but eventually voted to restore the money. Senator Pete Domenici, a Republican from New

Mexico, spoke out: "I believe the cause of art and artists everywhere suffers when members of Congress seek to let their personal tastes determine funding levels for cities and programs that deserve funding."[21]

Meanwhile political discourse in both the House and the press had sunk to new levels. The editor in chief of the *Washington Times,* Wesley Pruden, quoted the owner of his local adult bookstore as saying that *The Dinner Party* was "a dyke's-eye view of some of the tough broads of the past."[22] In the televised House debate Representative Robert K. Dornan, a Republican from California, spoke out against "this disgusting dinner table . . . ceramic 3-d pornography."[23] Even the director of the Dallas Museum of Art, Richard Brettell, joined the fray and referred to *The Dinner Party* as "a slightly vulgar embodiment," saying, "The work itself neither moves me nor changes my mind about anything."[24] The definition of *vulgar* is in the eyes of the beholder; his diatribe came back to haunt him two years later when he was arrested for fondling a male undercover police officer in a Dallas park near the museum.[25] He "pleaded no contest to a misdemeanor charge of public lewdness."[26]

Once again the outrage over *The Dinner Party* focused only on the butterfly-vagina designs of most of the ceramic plates. The religious Right and the black religious Right weighed in, flooding Congress with propaganda. Even the Reverend Pat Robertson got into the act on his television show, bringing accusations of blasphemy into the discussion of Chicago's art.[27] In contrast, Representative Ron Dellums, an African-American from California, observed in the House debate: "We deal with pornography every day. I think that it is pornographic to see nuclear weapons standing erect . . . phallic symbols capable of doing nothing but destroying human life on this planet."[28]

Also defending Chicago were Wilhelmina Cole Holladay, president of the National Museum of Women in the Arts, who called *The Dinner Party* "a popular icon, a part of our modern world," and "a major monument of feminist art."[29] A few months later the author Riane Eisler would argue: "I am convinced that what the battle over *The Dinner Party* reflects is that we are living in a time when more women and men than ever before are questioning the inevitability of a dominator model—specifically of the domination of man over woman and nature, of race over race, and of nation over nation. But as long as this questioning remains a fringe phenomenon, it can simply be written out of what is 'significant' in both history and art."[30]

Assessments of *The Dinner Party* were beside the point. As two Democrats, Representative Mervyn M. Dymally of the District of Columbia and Representative Julian C. Dixon of California, had to point out, all renovation monies were covered by municipal bonds, not federal money, and that only the students' academic programs would suffer from punitively cutting the university's federal budget. "The issue is *not* the art, and *not* the reconstruction," said Dymally, "but the autonomy of the university and whether Congress has the right to punch the university if we disagree."[31]

But it was only after two hundred students took over two university buildings and listed, as one of their demands to end their strike, that UDC not expend funds to house *The Dinner Party*, that Chicago felt that she had no choice but to withdraw her gift, which she did on October 2: "I could not in conscience impose a gift on an institution that didn't want it. . . . On top of which, UDC wasn't capable of caring for the piece. *The Dinner Party* was obviously going to be endangered, it had become such a symbol. Imagine what might have happened on opening day. It was not going to be revered and protected, which was the goal of permanent housing in the first place."[32]

Chicago felt compelled to write to *ARTnews* in protest when it repeated "the torrent of misinformation launched first by the right-wing *Washington Times*." "*The Dinner Party* has triumphed over art world resistance, lack of support, misrepresentation and prejudice. It stimulated an unprecedented, worldwide grass-roots campaign which succeeded in exhibiting it more often than I'd intended and it entered art history," she wrote. "It could not triumph, however, over the ferocity of the assault mounted against it by the right-wing, the media and the Congress. Was it censorship? Absolutely."[33]

With so much distortion in the local and national press, it was left for Chicago's close friend, the art critic Lucy Lippard, to tell the true story of the UDC ordeal in an article she wrote for *Art in America*.[34] While the article was in progress, Betsy Baker, her editor, expressed her own annoyance with Chicago, whom she considered naïve and alienated from the anticensorship movement that had successfully galvanized the art establishment in the face of controversies provoked by other artists such as Robert Mapplethorpe, Karen Finley, Andres Serrano, and others.[35] Despite her editor's misgivings, Lippard's research into the matter so impressed New Mexico's representative Bill Richardson that he read a section of the article into the *Congressional Record*.[36]

Subjected to frequent attacks in the press, Chicago responded with anguish when Cathleen Rountree, about to publish an interview with Chicago for a book on women in their forties, submitted to her a draft of an unflattering introduction.[37] It referred to the apprehension that Rountree had felt upon arriving to interview Chicago as a result of "several warnings I'd received from women who each had 'a story about Judy.'" Chicago wrote to Rountree asking if her personality was at issue or her achievements and asking: "Why are people afraid of me if I'm a humanist & a woman of vision & impatient with people's cop-outs? Did Picasso have to be nice? Was he evaluated based on his personality? A woman is supposed to face what I've faced, keep going & be nice, too? Give me a break!"[38]

Aware that some of her most vicious critics have been women, Chicago acknowledges that the feminist movement is not united: "Why are women beating up on somebody who's devoted her life to empowering women, at great risk—personal, financial, everything—to herself?" she demands. "I think that that's something we have to ask ourselves."[39] Judith Lewis, a journalist, has suggested: "If women in the art world have been harder on Chicago than they have been on, say, Christo—an artist with whom she's been compared—they claim it's because she has set herself up as their representative."[40] A different reason struck retired museum administrator Tom Freudenheim. "Chicago's chutzpah [audacity] comes from being very Jewish. That's what people are put off by," concluded this veteran of the Jewish Museum in Berlin and the Smithsonian Institution. For him *The Dinner Party* is "a really seminal work."[41]

Another fan of Chicago's art, Janet Bajan, turned up in Albuquerque in 1991, when Chicago happened to go to see a stockbroker there. Bajan heard another broker in the same office exclaim: "Guess who's in Bob's office: Judy Chicago." Bajan recalls that she "threw all caution to the wind and hopped out of my chair and ran into that broker's office, grabbed Chicago by the shoulders and exclaimed, 'I own *Christina of Sweden.*' 'Where is that painting?' Chicago responded. 'I've been looking for it for years.' "[42] The painting had not changed hands since Bajan first purchased it as a result of Chicago's slide show at the feminist party given by Grimstad and Rennie in New York City after her show opened in Philadelphia in 1974.

Bajan is a lesbian who read Kate Millett's *Sexual Politics* as soon as it was published in 1970. She took to heart what Millett wrote: "One of the most efficient branches of patriarchal government lies in the agency of its economic hold over its female subjects. In traditional patriarchy, women, as non-persons without legal standing, were permitted no actual economic existence as they could neither own nor earn in their own right."[43] At the time Bajan had wanted to join NOW but felt that lesbians were not welcome. That was the year that Betty Friedan, the president of NOW, characterized advocates for the inclusion of lesbian issues in the organization's platform as a "lavender menace."

Bajan joined the New York Radical Feminists, which then had only about thirty members, including Kirsten Grimstad, Susan Rennie, and Susan Brownmiller, who recalls the excitement of those discovering their lesbian identity, while she and other heterosexual women just wanted "to change men, not our sexual orientation."[44] And thus Bajan turned up at Grimstad's and Rennie's party for Chicago. Although she says that she was "not much for art," she took out a bank loan to buy Chicago's painting. When she saw *The Dinner Party* at the Brooklyn Museum in 1982, she considered it "a sacred piece—the Notre Dame of, the Cathedral for Women. The women are our saints."[45] Its historical content and respect for women resonated for her, and she believed that *The Dinner Party* could change history.

Bajan had long since abandoned her previous positions teaching philosophy in a college and then working with delinquent children in New York State. Once she decided that she needed to have money in order to have freedom, she not only changed professions but also began to study biographies of the very rich. She had grown up poor but was quite observant of human behavior. Now in close proximity to Chicago herself, Bajan joined the board of Through the Flower about 1990, just a year after her move to New Mexico. She was determined to realize the goal shared by Chicago and the board of finding *The Dinner Party* a permanent home.

Through the board Bajan and Liz Sackler became friends. Bajan had joined the Committee to House *The Dinner Party,* which had found a piece of property south of Santa Fe. Sackler then told the board that she would match the $25,000 that they would need to raise. But the board seemed unable to act, leaving Bajan disappointed, frustrated, and impatient with the rest of the board. Sackler admitted that progress was too slow and agreed to go out and look at land with Bajan, Chicago, and the rest of the committee. Drawing a diagram to demonstrate her conclusion, Bajan says that she could see that Sackler was the "dot in the center" who could house *The Dinner Party.*[46] In her view of the board, Sackler, alone, had the money, the education, the good looks, the family, the motivation, the self-discipline, the experience, and the contacts to make it all happen.

Bajan was not unrealistic in her assessment. Sackler not only was a social activist with a doctorate in public history but also was experienced in doing daring and unlikely deeds. In college in Vermont, she won the title Miss Vermont in 1968 at the height of the Vietnam War. Motivating her to win was her desire to dance an antiwar parable in the Miss America Pageant. Having studied at the School of American Ballet for seven years, she performed a dance that she had choreographed to a tape she had made of the spoken text of James Thurber's *The Last Flower* (1938), which is a parable of man's destructive tendencies and repeated blindness about aggression.

While Sackler was in Atlantic City for the Miss America pageant winning the best talent award, Robin Morgan and other feminists were outside demonstrating and throwing bras, girdles, and curlers into a large Freedom Trash Can.

Sackler's sister, Carol, told her pageant chaperon: "if Liz weren't inside, she'd be outside demonstrating."[47] But Sackler, who first married in 1970 and was soon taking care of a new baby, has recalled that "when women were marching in the streets, I was at home, depressed, changing diapers."[48] Her immediate world, however, was not sexist: "It was assumed that I could do whatever I wanted to."[49] Yet even given the huge divergence in their paths and their families' circumstances and social class, Sackler's and Chicago's commitment to social activism dovetailed. "We became friends," she recalls, "and we remained in touch."[50] Another time she commented of Chicago: "We're soul sisters."[51]

Despite loyal support by Sackler and other close friends and patrons, Chicago was worn down by her brother's illness and death in February 1992, which must have brought back the pain of her earlier losses when her father and her first husband died prematurely. Tired of the art establishment's rejection and depressed by losing her brother, Chicago longed for both solitude and space to do her work. She was searching for permanent housing not only for *The Dinner Party* but also for herself and Woodman.

In the summer of 1992 the Committee to House *The Dinner Party* came up with another proposal. Chicago and Woodman went along with Bajan, Sackler, and Herb Beenhouwer to look at a former private school in Sante Fe. Beenhouwer's wife, Bernice, was active in local Santa Fe politics and wanted to see *The Dinner Party* find a home in the New Mexican capital. Although Sackler carried her family name, she had not yet inherited money enough to house *The Dinner Party* on her own. But she had the idea to have thirty-nine women of means contribute to provide the housing. That day in the car Sackler commented, "This board is never going to get *The Dinner Party* housed," inadvertently disparaging Chicago's long loyal supporters without whom her work might not have survived—Cowan, Grinstein, and Grode, for example. According to Bajan, Chicago felt insulted and reacted with anger, called her friend and patron "a rich bitch," and offered a few more caustic remarks.[52] As a result, the two women's friendship took a time-out for close to five years. Sackler devoted some of her resources and energy to the American Indian Ritual Object Repatriation Foundation, which she founded in 1992.

Chicago and Woodman announced in 1993 that they planned to move to Belen, New Mexico, just due south of Albuquerque, where they lived for three years in tiny quarters rented from friends. Before the move from Santa Fe to Albuquerque, Chicago had sent off most of the *Holocaust Project* for framing and crating. Now she had no studio space. Depressed, she began work on *Beyond the Flower: The Autobiography of a Feminist Artist* in the fall of 1993. She also began a series of small drawings, *Autobiography of a Year,* which eventually numbered

140, completed during 1994. She worked on them "whenever the urge to put marks on a page became overpowering. I would not draw for long hours—as had been my habit—but rather, in short bursts, sometimes doing the same image again and again until I located the desired aesthetic impulse, then expressed it as directly as I could."[53] She was interested in authentic feeling, unmediated by careful planning and revision. She decided to use colors to express her moods.[54] Her emotions are palpable in this powerful series of drawings.

Some describe Belen as "the anti-Santa Fe . . . without a hint of the sanitized tourist appeal found throughout New Mexico."[55] They paid $20,000 for an abandoned brick building that was once a railroad workers' hotel, first opened in 1907, and needed major renovation. Woodman planned to do the restoration himself, serving as both general contractor and designer (combining some of the twenty-two rooms), with financial support in the form of a loan from the National Trust for Historic Preservation and the New Mexico Historic Preservation Division. They would then have about seven thousand square feet, over half devoted to studio space, with plenty of room for their six cats.[56] Even with lots of professionals at work, they were not able to move in until 1996. Comfortable but not luxurious, this is the only home or studio that Chicago has ever owned. She had previously put all of her resources into making more art. As for Woodman, this was his third try at building a place of his own and his first success.

On her infrequent trips to Belen to see the restoration project, Chicago saw and admired the Los Lunas Hill that looms up on the west side of the highway. Used to spray-painting with an airbrush, she wanted something more direct. Under an assumed name, she signed up for a course in watercolor at the University of New Mexico's local branch in Valencia County. Though she had never before worked in the medium, she was, as usual, unafraid. At first she painted trees, and then she began to record these wider views. Mindful of approaching development, including an impending golf course, she said, "I hope that my watercolors will be like the early days of New Mexico. Once it was a sacred place. It gives out that feeling."[57]

Even more emotional intensity accompanied the opening of the *Holocaust Project: From Darkness Into Light* at the Spertus Museum of Judaica in Chicago, in the fall of 1993, eight years after Chicago and Woodman first began their investigation of the Holocaust and their own Jewish identity. The Spertus would be the first stop for the twelve-part, three-thousand-square-foot exhibition. The Spertus paid an exhibition fee and one dollar of the rental fee for each audio tour to Through the Flower, plus shipping, insurance, and installation costs.[58] Chicago and Woodman together received an honorarium of $4,000 plus modest travel expenses for overseeing the installation that they had designed, doing press interviews, docent training, and attending the opening. The couple spent four weeks in Chicago preparing for the show.[59]

This project, though guided by Chicago's vision, was collaborative, involving her husband's photography and intellectual input, as well as the weaving of Audrey Cowan, other needleworkers, stained-glass artisans, a graphic designer, and various scholars and consultants. Among those with whom she consulted was a board of advisors: Dr. David Bluemfeld, executive director of the New York Holocaust Memorial Commission; Dr. Konnilyn Feig, a professor at San Francisco State University; Elyse Grinstein, an architect and Chicago's longtime friend and patron; her husband, Stanley Grinstein, listed as a trustee of the Los Angeles County Museum of Art; Isaiah Kuperstein of the U.S. Holocaust Memorial Council; Betty Levinson, the director of the Learning Resource Centers at UCLA, with its Survivor Tape Archives; Dr. Gerald Margolis, director of the Simon Wiesenthal Center; and Dr. Michael Nutkiewicz of the Martyrs' Memorial and Museum of the Holocaust in Los Angeles.[60] "We work from consensus, not from a prevailing point of view," Woodman has asserted. "This work is not about ego, the art market or how it will play to the public."[61]

On the stationery produced for the *Holocaust Project/1990*, the following appeared: "Transforming the Jewish experience of the Holocaust into art that is understandable and accessible." Chicago wrote that this work "can probably best be summed up by Elie Wiesel's notion that Jews must act 'as watchpeople for the vulnerable,' a statement that we've tried to honor in our work. The *Holocaust Project* extends outward from the Jewish experience to explore victimization through the prism of the Holocaust. We are trying to commemorate the uniqueness of the Jewish experience of the Holocaust while examining its universal meanings for human existence today."[62] At the time of the opening Chicago defined the project's goal for the public, reflecting a distillation of years spent learning while conducting extensive research: "to stimulate dialogue that will contribute to the transformation of consciousness that may help to prevent the recurrence of another Holocaust."[63]

In Chicago's mind, the leap from feminism to the Holocaust was not that great. She was not only reconnecting with her own Jewish heritage but was also determined to look at the Holocaust in a contemporary context, working off Virginia Woolf's view in *Three Guineas* that Nazism was "patriarchy gone mad."[64] Thus she looked at the ways in which the "patriarchal paradigm was taken to its logical conclusion in the Holocaust, exploring the relationships between the Holocaust and other historic events from that perspective."[65]

"People think that I deliberately set out to attract controversy, but nothing could be further from the truth," Chicago told an interviewer. "No one's more surprised when it happens than I am."[66] Yet Chicago was early to break a taboo in attempting to examine the Jews' experience in the Holocaust in relation to other twentieth-century genocides. Not only that, she also found parallels to nuclear, environmental, and animal rights issues, causing some to fear that her efforts would trivialize the Holocaust. She also emphasized the experience of women and explored the plight of Gypsies and homosexuals, ensuring that still others would take offense.

Elie Wiesel, to take one notable example, has called the Holocaust a singular experience, asking in his compelling voice: "Why this determination to show 'everything' in pictures? A word, a glance, silence itself communicates more and better . . . the Holocaust is not a subject like all others. It imposes certain limits."[67] Although not referring to Chicago and Woodman's work in particular, he has made clear that he prefers abstract references to the Holocaust, such as those in the work of his niece, Mindy Wiesel. Fred Camper, who did criticize Chicago's efforts, attempted to apply, by extension, a quotation by the aesthetician T. W. Adorno to art about the Holocaust: "After Auschwitz, it is no longer possible to write poems."[68]

While Chicago understands this stance, she does not agree with it. She has pointed out that to those outside the Jewish community, "there is incomplete knowledge, indifference and ignorance about the subject of the Holocaust, a 'blame the victim' attitude, a lack of understanding about the importance of confronting this subject and/or the widespread attitude, 'What does the Holocaust have to do with me?' "[69] Her intent was to make not a memorial but rather an exhibition that would extend awareness of the Holocaust beyond the Jewish community. It's a sign of her success that an African-American male student told Chicago in the discussion following her classroom lecture at a college showing the *Holocaust Project:* "This is the first time that I can relate to the Jews."[70]

As for the critics, Chicago's message too often fell upon deaf ears. Even some who had identified with her as a feminist now resented her decision to investigate her Jewish heritage and the Holocaust. Elizabeth Hess, a close friend of Lucy Lippard and a critic at *The Village Voice,* made no effort to disguise her discomfort in an article subtitled "From Feminism to Judaism: Meet the New Judy Chicago." Hess clearly did not agree with fellow *Voice* art critic Arlene Raven, Chicago's longtime friend, who said: "I feel reborn as a Jew in the Women's Movement. What had been shushed out of me is now up front."[71] Had Hess read Woolf's *Three Guineas,* she might have understood what Chicago saw as the connection between her feminism and her Jewish heritage.

After using her tie to Lippard to gain access to Chicago's private party for supporters after the opening of the exhibition, Hess worked so hard to discredit Chicago that she unmasked herself, going so far as to write, "Jewish institutions always make me feel squeamish. Maybe it's guilt. . . . I confess that I've never had the desire to explore my Jewish identity, and yes, my family has always celebrated Christmas (with a tree)."[72]

Hess pressed on to protest the existence of the work's audio guide, the figures she claimed that Chicago painted over photographs by Woodman and others, her style, and her avoidance of Middle East politics. Hess asked, "Why does Chicago want us to identify with the victims?" and "What if she gave up the notion of identification with either the good or the bad guys? Maya Lin's Vietnam Veterans Memorial restores the dignity of every fallen soldier with just a name."[73]

By contrast, Michael Nutkiewicz, then the assistant dean of the Cleveland College of Jewish Studies, got over his initial fears, prompted when he first met Chicago in 1986, that she would trivialize or sensationalize the Holocaust: "I watched the evolution of a vivid and imaginative work that challenges us to think about genocide, the Holocaust, responsibility, Jewishness, and being part of humanity."[74]

But for some, such as author Philip Gourevitch, the child of two Holocaust survivors, even the U.S. Holocaust Memorial Museum in Washington, D.C., is an outrage: "There is something facile about opposing evil fifty years after the fact. Yet that is the price one pays for Americanizing the Holocaust; as soon as the Holocaust is set up as a metaphor for national ideology, it comes back to haunt us, making its utterance a constant potential embarrassment and tainting the otherwise irreproachable impulse to commemorate the dead."[75]

Gourevitch put his energies into his first book, *We Wish to Inform You That Tomorrow We Will Be Killed with Our Families: Stories from Rwanda,*[76] based on events, starting in April 1994, of "a program of massacres . . . in Rwanda that ended up claiming the lives of 800,000 in a hundred days. People were murdered at a rate that exceeded by three times the speed of the extermination of Jews during the Holocaust."[77] Gourevitch has also continued to speak out about the time when "they built the Holocaust Museum in Washington and *Schindler's List* was coming out and there was all of this very hyped-up Holocaust commemoration rhetoric going around that by standing tall against intolerance we would ensure that nothing like this would ever happen again. The Holocaust Museum was dedicated in Washington on the mall in 1993 with this idea that it somehow or other has a preventive function. And I thought that was rubbish . . . a fantasy."[78]

Others have affirmed the project's approach to the history of the Holocaust and the value of doing so. Raven wrote: "Abstract art about this piece of horrific history can remain so vague that the historical specificity of the generating events is lost. The nonnaturalistic nature, and light, clear colors of some of Chicago's figures and images when combined with stark historical photographs and contemporary photographs by Woodman are, in my opinion, simply, thoughtfully appropriate to their subject."[79]

Despite the objections raised by its harshest critics, the *Holocaust Project* remains valuable for those, especially younger generations, who remain unaware of the Holocaust and for whom a memorial such as that Maya Lin made for victims of the Vietnam War would have little impact. Contrast Rachel Whiteread's 1996 Holocaust Memorial in Vienna, which is in the form of a large white box; in fifty years it will still look to most like a white box, nothing more. It will not be able to instruct its audience either about the history of the Holocaust or about the lessons that it should teach us. Disregarding Chicago and Woodman's clear purpose, critics have often reviewed the *Holocaust Project* as a memorial, not as an art exhibition having an educational function. Critics fail to project into the future, when their work will still be able to instruct and contextualize what happened to the Jews in Europe during World War II. Raising awareness is Chicago's stated goal, although many of her critics cannot think beyond a memorial. She has argued, "I think that we are a long way from understanding the kind of world we have colluded in . . . and the effort to place the Holocaust in the past is dangerous."[80]

Chicago responded to an interviewer who asked why this exhibition struck such a nerve: "The unmarked stone markers at Treblinka are the most visual symbol of revisionist history in its most extreme. It's physical erasure that the Holocaust existed. Yet we shouldn't be surprised at this. We live in a world where revisionist history is the norm. We wiped out the Indians and presented our own historical perspective of that, and we've annihilated their memories. We've just about annihilated the memory of slavery and certainly women's history."[81] What some viewers reacted against was Chicago's presence in the narrative, which is framed as a self-discovery, and accompanied the images in the accompanying book, in the wall texts, and in the video. She attempted to share with the audience her own anguish dealing with this sensitive subject matter, when some have felt that she should have kept a lower profile.

Elizabeth Sackler, who had helped to fund the *Holocaust Project,* did not attend the opening at the Spertus, although she saw the exhibition there when she happened to be in Chicago. When the artist finally called her estranged friend to ask that she lend the studies for the *Holocaust Project* from her collection for a showing at the Laguna Gloria Art Museum in Austin, Texas, Sackler agreed, and some communication resumed. That presentation opened in the fall of 1994 to a more positive local reception. Rebecca Levy wrote that she had begun "to think of Chicago's *Holocaust Project* as a graphic metaphor for the process of recording history. . . . She makes no claim to have found answers, but she asks good questions. History, it seems, is never finished being written. Judy Chicago's art makes a provocative contribution to the process."[82]

But by now the *Holocaust Project* had attracted national attention and detractors began to single it out for criticism. Alvin H. Rosenfeld, writing in *Commentary* in June 1995 on "The Americanization of the Holocaust," characterized Chicago's and Woodman's work as embodying "a number of trends that inform the American culture and political mood today."[83] He accused the couple of narcissistic subjectivity, "increasingly intrusive political correctness," and the "cult of victimhood." He then accused them of the opposite tack: "the American tendency to downplay or deny the dark and brutal sides of life and to place a preponderant emphasis on the saving power of individual moral conduct and collective deeds of redemption."[84]

Rosenfeld traced the genesis of this tendency back to the 1950s stage and screen productions of Anne Frank's *The Diary of a Young Girl,* which, coincidently, Chicago had seen as an undergraduate in Los Angeles in 1958, when she wrote to her brother that she found it "wonderful." For Rosenfeld, the fault of the play was that one could "leave the theater feeling uplifted by Anne Frank's story rather than deeply disturbed."[85] Thus, he rejected Chicago's decision to close the exhibition with *Rainbow Shabbat,* which shows in stained glass a Jewish couple at opposite ends of a table giving the traditional blessings over bread and wine, while around the two sides of the table sit people symbolic of the world's population, including an Arab man in a kaffiyeh, a Christian clergyman, a Vietnamese woman, an African man, a Chinese man, and children. It is Chicago's vision of hope for all without limits imposed by race, gender, or class. "Shabbat ceremonies are traditionally begun with a prayer offered by a woman, and 'Rainbow Shabbat' suggests reverence for the feminine as an essential step toward the humanization of our world," Chicago said, explaining, "I'm uniting in this one image my values as a woman and a Jew."[86] And her hopeful vision is essential to her concept, subtitled *From Darkness Into Light.* This hope, as her friend Isaiah Kuperstein commented, is the alternative to writer and Holocaust survivor Primo Levi's decision to kill himself.[87]

Such a prominent attack as Rosenfeld's set the stage for more caustic remarks. A few months later, when the *Holocaust Project* reached the Rose Art Museum at Brandeis University in Waltham, Massachusetts, a suburb of

Boston, Christine Temin wrote in the *Boston Globe:* "it made me shudder—not at the horror of the subject itself, but at the horror of her exploitation of one of the world's great tragedies."[88] Temin's review was so disparaging that the paper assigned Renee Graham to interview the artist and called the feature, "Why Judy Chicago Is the Artist the Art World Loves to Hate."[89] Chicago made clear to Graham that she wanted to provoke: "If ideas make people comfortable, they say, 'That's nice.' If ideas have any power, they're going to make people uncomfortable because they're going to cause you to think about things you haven't thought about."[90] Graham interviewed and quoted others about their opinions of Chicago's work. Katy Kline, director of the List Visual Arts Center at the Massachusetts Institute of Technology, noted, "I think the reason people respond so strongly to her work is because it's completely in-your-face. It's unapologetic; it's deliberately highly colored. She plays deliberately to your viscera with the garish colors, even in the scale of the work. It's not subtle work."[91] Chicago was so grateful for this alternative voice in Boston that she wrote to Graham, "Words cannot express my gratitude to you for having forced into the open the art world attitudes that have—despite my disclaimer—hurt me terribly over the years. . . . My thanks also to the *Globe* for having been willing to devote so much space to a dialogue that is long overdue."[92]

The Cleveland Center for Contemporary Art joined the tour, only after Suzanne Tishkoff, director of the Cleveland College of Jewish Studies, saw the exhibition at the Spertus in Chicago. A committee to support bringing it to Cleveland was formed and included Marcia Levine and Mickey and Al Stern, who had been active supporters of *The Dinner Party* in Cleveland.[93] Yet a local critic in the *Plain Dealer* cynically panned the exhibition as Chicago's attempt to "exploit shocking material to stay in the public eye" and dismissed her style and her view of history as "based on an angry, militant feminism."[94]

During a May 2000 conference at the Philip and Muriel Berman Center for Jewish Studies that accompanied the showing of the *Holocaust Project* at Lehigh University in Pennsylvania, Chicago encountered Stephen Feinstein. A history professor at the University of Wisconsin, he served as co-organizer of the group show *Witness and Legacy: Contemporary Art about the Holocaust,* which was conceived by the Minnesota Museum of American Art and first exhibited in St. Paul in spring 1995, nearly two years after the opening of the *Holocaust Project.* By January 2002, Feinstein's show had traveled to a total of seventeen museums and galleries, inevitably competing with the *Holocaust Project* for venues, so he was hardly a disinterested party when he disparaged Chicago's work.

Feinstein subsequently raised what he viewed as problems with the *Holocaust Project* in a long letter he sent to Chicago. He disapproved of using figurative art as a basis for representing the Holocaust and noted that he found her artwork, combined with the audiotape, too literal, not leaving enough to the viewer's imagination.[95] He protested that her work lacked subtlety and questioned her conclusions about the link between the Holocaust and other types of repression. Though Chicago had conducted extensive research, Feinstein found fault with some of her assumptions. He argued against her attempt to "demonstrate visually how assembly-line techniques, originally used to 'process' animals, were applied to human beings" by the Nazis, claiming (incorrectly, according to some recent scholarship) that Hitler was a vegetarian and the Nazis had the strongest laws in the world for the protection of animals.[96]

Subsequently others have supported Chicago's point of view, particularly Charles Patterson in his much-translated book, *The Eternal Treblinka: Our Treatment of Animals,* which looks at the shared roots of animal and human oppression and the resemblance between how the Nazis treated their victims and how modern society treats the animals it slaughters for food.[97] Patterson dedicated his book to the Yiddish writer Isaac Bashevis Singer, from whom he took his title, which refers to the Nazi death camp north of Warsaw. Chicago too read Singer's description of the exploitation and slaughter of animals. "In relation to them, all people are Nazis," he wrote, "for animals it is an eternal Treblinka."[98]

In the face of the connections that Chicago made between anti-Semitism and antifeminism, Feinstein argued that the Nazi feminists were usually more anti-Semitic than the men; that women were in the SS and that camp memoirs detail their sadism; and that Jewish women could pass more easily than Jewish men, who were easy to identify since they were all circumcised. But he ignored Chicago's point that the architects of the Third Reich were almost all men. Jyl Lynn Felman, writing in the magazine *Lilith,* praises the links that Chicago made between women's oppression and Jewish oppression, especially "the burning of witches with the burning of Jews."[99]

Feinstein also objected to charging admission to see the *Holocaust Project* and to the sales of any related merchandise beyond the book that accompanied the exhibition. But in fact the *Holocaust Project* had taken Chicago and Woodman eight years from start to finish, during which time they needed to earn not only their living expenses but also enough to finance the cost of research and producing the elaborate exhibition itself.

Just as the *Holocaust Project* was on view in Cleveland in 1996, a large survey show called *Sexual Politics: Judy Chicago's* Dinner Party *in Feminist Art History,* opened at the Armand Hammer Museum at UCLA. Organized by art historian Amelia Jones, at the suggestion of Henry Hopkins, then director of the

Hammer and a longtime fan of Chicago's, this was the first time *The Dinner Party* had ever been seen in Southern California where it had been produced, and its first showing in the United States since 1983 in Atlanta.

A number of New York feminist artists, led by Chicago's old colleague Miriam Schapiro, became indignant that Chicago's work was to be featured in this survey of feminist art history and tried to organize a boycott of the show.[100] "I tried to convince [Miriam] that by refusing to have her work exhibited she was leaving the impression that Judy thought up all of this by herself," Jones reported somewhat naïvely, since that thought must have fueled Schapiro's refusal.[101] The catalog, with important essays by a distinguished group of writers, discusses Schapiro, but at her request her art was not in the exhibition.[102] Nancy Spero also kept out her work and wrote a "vitriolic" letter of protest to the museum, sending a copy to Jones, who experienced these artists' angry reactions as "traumatic."[103] Others who declined to have their work included were Mary Beth Edelson, Joyce Kozloff, and Joan Synder.[104] Jones wrote in her introductory essay in the catalog: "I had no idea that this exhibition, in spite of my efforts to work within a historical and theoretical (rather than aesthetic or monographic) framework, would prove as controversial as the piece itself."[105] She told a reporter, "It's so self-defeating, because it's viewing art history and the art world in this personal way. That's a mistake feminists make. That's not a mistake men make."[106]

As hurtful as it was to be the target of anger from other feminist artists, the experience of *Sexual Politics* was very positive for Chicago. Jones brought to *The Dinner Party* serious consideration and scholarship, now that it had emerged again from storage to sight. "Although (or perhaps because) the work has been controversial, both within feminist circles and in the broader context of the mainstream art world," Jones wrote, "it has also clearly informed the development of feminist art and theory."[107] Chicago's early work also received high-profile attention in an important essay by art historian Laura Meyer that examined Chicago within the larger California art scene.[108] A number of Chicago's former students from the Feminist Art Program—Suzanne Lacy, Karen LeCocq, Aviva Rahmani, Mira Schor, and Faith Wilding—were among the artists included in this show.

Predictably, Christopher Knight panned the show in the *Los Angeles Times,* calling it a "fiasco" and blaming its focus on Chicago's "notorious sculpture," which he dismissed as "agit-prop."[109] But Robin Abcarian, writing in the same paper, noted that Chicago's words and images provoke thought: "What, for instance, is the female equivalent of the Washington Monument, the Eiffel Tower or Seattle's Space Needle? Carlsbad Caverns? The Grand Canyon? The Grand

Tetons? But those are natural phenomena, not human ones. We live in a world where the phallic symbol is an aesthetic given. The feminine equivalent is controversial or dirty or repulsive."[110] Jennie Klein wrote in the *New Art Examiner*, "Unfortunately, Chicago as a personality tends to inspire either reverence or wrath, her historically populist appeal anathema to art critics and Poststructuralist feminists alike. . . . What all this fuss—fuss that most likely would not have occurred if Chicago were a man—obscures is the sheer power and beauty of this monument to women's history . . . [which] has stood the test of time much better than anyone could have imagined."[111]

By "Poststructuralist feminists," Klein referred to so-called "deconstructionist feminists" whose embrace of theory included their disapproval of the early California feminists' emphasis on the existence of a "female sensibility." To them, depicting female anatomical forms implies that "anatomy is destiny." Jones's exhibition and its catalog examined the reductive theory that assumed that women who preferred to depict their own bodies in their own way, rather than experience themselves in art as the objects of the male gaze, were guilty of "essentialism."

Chicago was dismayed that she had still not found permanent housing for *The Dinner Party*. "I had learned about this trajectory in art history," she explains, "of creation to exhibition to preservation. Okay, so I had encountered obstacles in being able to create the art I wanted to make, but I overcame them. And I encountered problems in the exhibition of my work. But miracle of miracles, they were overcome by this incredible outpouring of support that demonstrated to me that art could be far more powerful than even I had dreamed—and I had pretty big dreams."[112] The result of so many grass-roots efforts to show the piece had made her imagine that some institution would come forth to preserve it. She explained that she had not understood "that the cycle that *The Dinner Party* describes, the cycle of erasure, repeated erasure—I thought I was describing something in the past. It never crossed my mind that I was describing our circumstances today—that still, they threaten us."[113]

A brighter note occurred in June 1996, when the Arthur and Elizabeth Schlesinger Library on the History of Women at Radcliffe College (Harvard University) announced its acquisition of Chicago's archives, which she donated at their request.[114] "Women's rights movements past and present, feminism, health and sexuality, social reform, and the education of women and girls are core manuscript holdings."[115] Chicago's papers were the first of any living visual artist to enter this collection. This same year marked the publication of her second volume of autobiography, *Beyond the Flower: The Autobiography of a Feminist Artist*, which appeared that fall.[116]

As might have been predicted, reviews of Chicago's second memoir were mixed. Donna Seaman, writing in *Booklist,* pronounced it "admirably frank," noting that her "story is an unforgettable saga of passion, hard work, adversity, popular success, discord, and critical condemnation" that "deserves careful reading."[117] Liesl Schillinger, in *The New York Times,* commented that "there is something singularly impersonal and closed in this book. While it pretends to provide a life that can stand in for many women's lives, it reads more like the bated-breath rebuttal of a solipsistic genius who has been spurned one time too many." But she defended Chicago's art: "No one who has ever smirked appreciatively at a Jeff Koons piece or scratched her (or his) head thoughtfully at a [Jenny] Holzer has the right to question Judy Chicago's claim to art. In the face of the flouts and snubs she has endured, others would be stirred, as she has been, to self-defense. But in a sense, it is her very defensiveness, welded to overearnestness, that has made her such ready prey."[118] In Schillinger's opinion, Chicago undermined her artwork with the texts she produced to accompany them. But she viewed Chicago's art as having a larger cultural context, acknowledging that the *Holocaust Project* "makes fertile connections that remind the shocked observer of the links between torture of animals and of people, between genocide and nuclear war, between see-no-evil collaboration with Nazis and see-no-evil toleration of radioactive waste."[119]

Another mark of Chicago's growing impact on culture was Bella Lewitzky's choreography of *Four Women in Time,* the final creation for her thirty-year-old modern dance ensemble, "drawing her mythic and historical subjects" from Chicago's *Dinner Party.* Then already eighty, Lewitzky staged her piece around just four of the thirty-nine figures with place settings: the Primordial Goddess, Hypatia, Virginia Woolf, and Sophia. The first performance took place at Occidental College in September 1996 and then recurred as the company went on a national tour.[120] A reviewer remarked upon the portrayal of Virginia Woolf by the emotional and forceful dancer Heather Harrington, who "convincingly wrestles with internal demons; crawling, running in circles, slapping her face. After letting her hair down, literally, she experiences rapture, and eventual peace in a beautiful and moving display of floor work." This was at last a partial realization of Chicago's dream of seeing her vision of these historical women appear on the stage.

The collaboration was all the more remarkable in that it hearkened back to the brief time that Lewitzky and Chicago spent together on the faculty of CalArts. The two women were kindred spirits, for during the crises over funding from the National Endowment for the Arts and its right to exercise censorship, Lewitzky crossed out the prohibition in her NEA contract that forbade "obscene" art, refused to accept the grant, sued, and won the right not to have the federal agency impose creative restrictions on her work.

Meanwhile Chicago, with her usual energy and resolve, conceived of a new work that would build on the hopeful note expressed at the end of the *Holocaust Project* in *Rainbow Shabbat.* The message was to be global and optimistic in *Resolutions: A Stitch in Time* (Figure 31). After the deeply disturbing material of the *Holocaust Project,* she wanted to work with positive human values, following the Jewish mandate to "Choose Life."[121] Originally she planned to call the project *Resolutions for the Millennium.* She designed pieces for needleworkers to complete, each with an intentionally idealistic proverb expressing universal values. Chicago chose to feature seven themes necessary for human survival: Family, Responsibility, Conservation, Tolerance, Human Rights, Hope, and Change.

In the midst of working on *Resolutions,* which required a group effort, Chicago began a suite of prints to illustrate the *Song of Songs* from the Hebrew Bible. She had responded to a new translation by Marcia Falk, which emphasizes shared pleasure between man and woman, utilizing both voices, which Chicago placed side by side. She had these lithographs printed in Tampa, Florida, at Graphicstudio. Chicago may not have been aware, but already in 1928, at the time of Georgia O'Keeffe's show at the Intimate Gallery (run by her husband, Alfred Stieglitz), a critic saw a link between the theme of ecstasy in the *Song of Songs* and O'Keeffe's paintings: "It is enough to say that Miss O'Keeffe's paintings are as full of passion as the verses of Solomon's Song."[122]

When asked recently what she liked about sex, Chicago responded that the three activities she enjoyed most were "making art, making love, and working out" because she loves "being entirely in the moment."[123] More fully than ever before, Chicago had given her huge sexual energy and passion her own graphic form.

By the time of *Resolutions,* Chicago was working almost entirely with women with whom she had a history,[124] many of them with the *Birth Project* and several also with the *Holocaust Project.* Though designed by Chicago, 50 percent of each of the twenty finished works is owned by the seventeen women who made them over six years. The women decided among themselves how their share would be divided when more than one worker was involved. Often more than one woman worked on a single piece. They employed needlepoint, petit-point, embroidery, appliqué, smocking, macramé, and beadwork.

In designing *Resolutions,* Chicago reflected upon the mistakes of the feminist movement during the 1970s, pointing out that the movement confused "the issue of gender with the issue of values. We alienated some men who could have been our friends because we shared common values, and we promoted some women who were our enemies and don't share our values at all. Feminism is about working for a different world, not just for our own liberation."[125]

Among the resolutions, *Home Sweet Home,* which depicts various kinds of shelter, became the piece of Pamella Nesbit, who had worked with Chicago on the *Birth Project* and decided to take part again. She liked the overall subject matter, "a project based on values and fabricated in various forms of needlework to reflect the past and potentially affect change in the future."[126] *Home Sweet Home* involved the fusion of visible paint and thread: "The image of a globe, our world, with all the types of houses around it from igloo to skyscraper, log cabin to mobile home. Spending long periods of time stitching on a piece of linen with the imagery and words of 'home sweet home' offered me the opportunity to explore my own personal sense of home and family."[127]

But at the project's first meeting in Albuquerque, Nesbit also volunteered to work on a second piece, because, she later explained, "When I was younger, I longed to make art that inspired change, art that expressed my inner feelings and dissatisfaction with the way the world was heading, but I didn't know how to do this. *It's Always Darkest Before Dawn* answered that early longing."[128]

Nesbit described what she viewed as a collaborative project: designing a piece that is fully one-half Chicago's painting on the left, depicting "the depressing, darker aspects of our world." On the opposite side a rainbow spans the sky and people and animals frolic in sunny tranquillity. A woman wearing what looks like a crown and a blue strapless prom dress and long white gloves from the 1960s holds up a peace medallion. Different nationalities are evident through their stereotypical costumes. The concept is *Rainbow Shabbat* in the Garden of Eden, or something like the nineteenth-century painter Edward Hicks's repeated utopian images, all entitled *Peaceable Kingdom.* Nesbit recalled, "We decided that there would be no embroidery on the 'dark side,' that the embroidery would have to grow from the 'light side' into texture and richness, enhancing the happy harmonious scene. Judy took our rough sketches home and made a drawing using colored pencils. We mailed ideas back and forth until she finalized the drawing into a large and beautiful oil painting."[129] Chicago then shipped her painting to Nesbit, who also brought the piece back to Judy's studio so that she could work in quiet concentration and consult with her: "Once a painting is punctured with the needle, there *has* to be a stitch there, otherwise a hole is left in the painting."[130]

Jane Thompson, veteran of both the *Birth Project* and the *Holocaust Project,* found *Resolutions* much more participatory. Not only did she learn a lot, but she made lasting friendships. She did all of the needlework on *Turn over a New Leaf* and worked on part of another dozen pieces. "Things change when you go along working with Judy," she says. "What needs to be done next changes and is not set in stone from the beginning. It's not like a needlepoint kit."[131]

Jackie Moore, who had worked on the *Birth Project,* wrote to Chicago, who once contemplated a book about *Resolutions,* telling her that she thought the project was "your most spiritual and subtle creation" and encouraged her to articulate her political reasons for making this piece for her viewers.[132] Patricia Rudy-Base, who stitched *Hands that Rock the Cradle,* had also worked with Chicago on the *Birth Project.* By now she felt that "everyone, including Judy, had matured." Asked her opinion of Chicago, she responded, "She's a genius. And as such, her imperfections are magnified. As Jackie puts it, she's a feminist, a collaborator, supportive, etc. but at the global level, not the individual, personal level. She seems to put people into a hierarchy, based on what she needs at the time: inner circle, on deck if you have potential or just useful to her. Often this seems personal but it isn't. It's just how Judy is. . . . The bigness of her mind, art, intention and heart far outweigh her personal imperfections."[133]

The needlework images for *Resolutions* were accompanied by one carved wooden sculpture called *Find It in Your Heart.* While going to a local restaurant in Belen, Chicago's husband spotted a car custom painted by Reynaldo Gonzalez, whom Chicago subsequently commissioned to paint a five-foot, seven-inch androgynous figure carved from Chicago's small clay model by a professional woodcarver.[134] But for Chicago, the needleworkers were not just producers from whom she commissioned the fabrication of work. As Nesbit put it, they learned "about art, textiles design, framing, exhibitions and the business of art, not to mention collaboration. She in turn learned from us as we taught her more about needlework and about the challenges faced by creative women *fitting* art into our lives, as opposed to Judy whose art *is* her life."[135]

Paula Harper wrote for *Art in America* about *Resolutions,* when it was on view in New York at the American Craft Museum. Harper cites the fact that a unit on *The Dinner Party* is now a part of the fifth-grade curriculum in New Zealand, but that the New York art world still shows scant interest in Chicago's work.[136] In *The New York Times* Ken Johnson, known for his antifeminist reviews, declared that *Resolutions* dealt with clichés and was "aesthetically vacuous, conceptionally inane and morally disingenuous."[137] Carol K. Russell, writing in *Fiber Arts,* had a broader perspective, seeing potentially subversive or revolutionary themes couched in the clichés: "For example, the traditional folk-art motifs of Latvian textiles proved powerful statements of nationalism in the hands of Latvian tapestry weavers working subversively under Soviet occupation." Nancy Berman, curator at the Skirball Cultural Center in Los Angeles when *Resolutions* was on view there, explained that Judy was expressing that her secular upbringing was "imbued with Jewish values," but Berman also saw the project politically: "Judy's work has always had the elevated purpose of using art to teach and envision real social change."[138]

That art can teach and affect social change is a belief that Sackler and Chicago share. "Judy is a great humanitarian. It's one of her greatest gifts," Sackler allows, "one of the reasons that I love her."[139] Their mutual opposition to censorship would ultimately play a role in finding *The Dinner Party* its permanent home. Chicago recalls that Sackler came to a book signing that she did with the British art historian Edward Lucie-Smith at a Rizzoli bookstore in Manhattan, when his monograph *Judy Chicago: An American Vision* came out in 2000. "We just picked up as if nothing had ever happened."[140] This was just what Sackler's friend Janet Bajan had dreamed would occur.

Since the end of 1994, when the board of Through the Flower had still not gone to contract for any property, Bajan determined that she would encourage Sackler to house *The Dinner Party* herself, slowly coaxing her friend to take action. A decisive moment came when Sackler was introduced to an architect from New Mexico, Steven Robinson, in the spring of 1998. During the next year he inspired her interest in architecture so much that she envisioned building a museum to house *The Dinner Party* and began to imagine a Museum for Feminist Art, complete with other artists, a curator, and an educational program. In June 1999 she spent four days driving from New York to Santa Fe with her sister, Carol, and they talked about this project. Carol suggested that she could name it after herself and realized that giving it the Sackler name would "launch Feminist Art into the world of institutional, mainstream art."[141] She was thinking of the Sackler name on museums in Beijing, at the Smithsonian in Washington, D.C., at the Metropolitan Museum, at Harvard, and elsewhere.

Sackler began looking for land for the museum just south of Santa Fe. One property that appealed had once belonged to the Santo Domingo Pueblo that got her "repatriation antennae going—with much concern."[142] She and Robinson were discussing a structure "as stunning and important as the Dinner Party itself—a living jewel for the public." But upon reflection Sackler decided that it would be years before she could develop such a museum and get it up and running. Conversations with her friend, Wilhelmina "Billie" Cole Holladay, founder of the National Museum of Women in the Arts in Washington, confirmed her concerns. Instead, she began thinking of extant museums that might house *The Dinner Party.*

The Brooklyn Museum of Art, where *The Dinner Party* made its New York debut in 1981, had potential. Sackler had met Arnold L. Lehman shortly after he arrived as the museum's new director in September 1997. She liked the diverse audience that the museum attracted and admired Lehman's commitment to the community and to education. Her own parents had met in 1930 at Brooklyn's Erasmus Hall High School.

Thus when Mayor Rudolph Giuliani told the Brooklyn Museum of Art that it should cancel its show of contemporary art called *Sensation* before it opened in the fall of 1999 and threatened to withhold the annual $7 million municipal grant because he did not like its content, Sackler was outraged and rallied to the cause. *Newsweek* covered the story of the tug-of-war between the mayor and the museum and added a sidebar of "Ten Works of Art That Have Rocked the Ages." Among the ten were Michelangelo's mural *The Last Judgment,* Manet's *Le Déjeuner sur l'Herbe,* Duchamp's *Nude Descending a Staircase,* Diego Rivera's now-destroyed mural for Rockefeller Center with a portrait of Lenin, and *The Dinner Party.*[143] Sackler wrote to Lehman expressing her solidarity and to Giuliani protesting his political meddling with an art museum.

In March 2000 Sackler's mother died. Later that spring Lehman invited Sackler to several occasions and followed up with an invitation to join the board of the Brooklyn Museum, which she accepted. Then in early 2001 Sackler, now speaking often with Chicago, arranged to meet her in New Orleans, where the Museum of Art had a retrospective of her work on view. With the museum of feminist art in mind, Sackler made a list of important pieces that she planned to purchase. She continued to plan how to promote Chicago's work.

Sackler compiled a list of works by Chicago for an exhibition and put together a notebook of reproductions to illustrate her proposal for a show that she would fund at the National Museum of Women in the Arts. She then went to lunch with Billie Holladay, who was receptive to her idea. She had joined the museum's advisory board in 2000. Sackler edited a book that served as the catalog for the show that opened in 2002. Chicago's painting, *Through the Flower,* from Sackler's collection became the cover image.

Months after Sackler's meeting with Holladay, Lehman invited his new trustee to join the board's collections committee. She accepted, suggesting that they could lunch before the meeting on April 19. Before lunch she walked into the director's office and handed him Chicago's book on *The Dinner Party,* telling him, "I'd like to give you this."[144] He responded with alacrity, "Thanks, I don't own a copy. I'd love to have it." "No," she explained, "I mean the piece." Lehman had first seen *The Dinner Party* in Brooklyn in 1981 and thought it "fantastic, a fabulous work of art . . . one of the great icons of the twentieth century."[145] He recalls that he agreed immediately, cautioning, "We'd have to figure out where to put it." And of course, the board of trustees, of which Sackler was the newest member, had to approve of an acquisition that would take up a lot of space and require upkeep.

Months passed, and it was not until the end of 2001 that Lehman confirmed the museum's real interest. Complex negotiations began that Sackler says required experience navigating museum terrain. Initially she offered only to give *The Dinner Party*. The chair of the museum's collections committee, Michael DeHavenon, came back and said that this would be possible, but only if the museum could use her name on the gallery. She responded yes, but only if it would be the "Elizabeth A. Sackler Center for Feminist Art." Although some members found the work challenging or at least puzzling, the board responded positively and embraced both *The Dinner Party* and the proposed context. Sackler not only gave *The Dinner Party* but funded the center for the first five years.

At 8,300 square feet, the Elizabeth A. Sackler Center for Feminist Art will offer several other galleries in addition to the space for *The Dinner Party*, as well as extensive programming and a small auditorium. Its donor sees the center, due to open in March 2007, as a hub for women in the arts. Its mission is "to raise awareness of feminism's cultural contributions, to educate new generations about the meaning of feminist art; to maintain a dynamic and welcoming learning facility; and to present feminism in an approachable and relevant way."[146]

The Brooklyn Museum officially accepted *The Dinner Party* on April 18, 2002. After years of wandering, the 1,038 women had finally found a home. From the perspective of Lehman, one word sums up the story of how Judy Chicago, Elizabeth Sackler, and the Brooklyn Museum came together so that *The Dinner Party* could have a place to call its own: *beshert,* which in Yiddish means "inevitable, fated, destined, or meant to be."[147] Perhaps without even realizing it, Lehman touched upon Chicago's subliminal Yiddishkayt, what has been referred to in another context as "a generic old-fashioned Jewish manner of humane concern and complexity."[148]

When *The Dinner Party* went on temporary exhibition at the Brooklyn Museum in the fall of 2002, the New York press finally acknowledged Chicago's accomplishment. "Call it what you will: kitsch, pornography, artifact, feminist propaganda, or a major work of 20th-century art. It doesn't make much difference. 'The Dinner Party,' the extravagant ceramic and textile homage to women through history that Judy Chicago dreamed up and translated into reality in the 1970's, is important," wrote Roberta Smith in *The New York Times.*[149] She pointed out correctly that *The Dinner Party* was "almost as much a part of American culture as Norman Rockwell, Walt Disney, W.P.A. murals and the AIDS quilt."[150] Referring indirectly to Hilton Kramer's 1980 polemic in the same newspaper, she asked and answered her own question: "Is 'The Dinner

Party' good or bad art? So far, it's more than good enough, and it's getting better all the time."[151] She also pointed out that *The Dinner Party* led to the breakdown of the barrier between art and craft, and quipped, "Today, if you can look at Ms. Chicago's bright glazes, suggestive forms and handmade textiles without thinking at least for a second of, say, Jeff Koons and Mike Kelly, you're a better man than I."[152]

Others had already come to embrace Chicago's work. Art historian James Trilling, the son of the literary critics Diana and Lionel Trilling, took the trouble to write a letter about *The Dinner Party* to the Arts section of *The New York Times,* responding to a rather patronizing feature article that suggested that Chicago should expect "blunt scrutiny" when the piece went back on public view: "Of course the work is vulgar; as vulgar as a set of male emblems shaped like phallic knife-handles. It is also a beacon to our age, a real old-fashioned work of art with craft, style, iconography, social and cultural immediacy, and beauty that will survive when the polemics that inspired it have faded."[153] He asserted correctly that *The Dinner Party* would "eventually find its niche as a pioneering work of post-modernist decorative art. By this I mean no disparagement; scorn for decoration is one of modernism's excesses."[154]

In *The Village Voice* Leslie Camhi recalled: "When I was a baby intellectual . . . *The Dinner Party* occupied verboten territory. Judy Chicago's name, if it came up at all, was cited with the kind of embarrassment women in our feminist circles usually reserved for their mothers. Raised as we were on a steady diet of continental philosophy and deconstruction, we thought her West Coast populism smacked of biological determinism, an *Our Bodies, Ourselves* moment we had moved far beyond. We were wrong."[155]

John Perreault, an early critical supporter of *The Dinner Party,* wrote: "In retrospect it now seems that the Dinner Party came out of a social, feminist context as well as an art world one. That for the time was daring, to say the least. Whether you like the Dinner Party or not, it changed art . . . what really pleases me is that this is a really nervy, shocking artwork. It is still over-the-top."[156] Today Perreault sees the controversy around the piece as an "indication of the power of the work" and attributes the attacks by female critics such as Kay Larson and Suzanne Muchnic to "puritanism" and their "disgust with their own bodies."[157]

The Brooklyn Museum announced that the Elizabeth A. Sackler Foundation purchased *The Dinner Party* from "the Judy Chicago Remainder Trust, which will help support Through the Flower, a non-profit arts organization whose mission involves expanding the vision embodied in *The Dinner Party.*"[158] The value of the piece at the time of sale was reported to be $2 million, but the entire proceeds were invested. During their lifetimes Chicago and Woodman will benefit from the interest on the principal, which will eventually endow Through the Flower. Now that the organization does not have to expend resources to house and preserve *The Dinner Party,* it will focus entirely on education. This annual stipend has become the first financial security that either Chicago and Woodman has ever known. Since funds from Sackler's purchase will eventually go toward providing for Chicago's art and turning the Belen Hotel and Through the Flower's properties into a study center and art archive, she can now rest assured that she will not be erased from history.

Marking this inscription into the historical record is the inclusion of *The Dinner Party* into the seventh edition of *History of Art,* a college textbook originally edited by H. W. Janson and now edited by a team that includes women for the first time.[159] In the 1970s Janson's textbook had no women artists at all. Now a color reproduction of *The Dinner Party* appears as "the great monument to the women's movement" and as an influential work: "its gender politics, commentary on contemporary society, and use of so many different styles and periods announces the art of the 1980s, an art that still prevails today and has come to be called Post-Modernism."[160]

"What makes Judy important is not just the craft of art," observed Michael Botwinick, who was the director of the Brooklyn Museum when *The Dinner Party* first traveled to New York in 1980 and who served as the narrator of the audio tour for the *Holocaust Project.* Looking back, he characterizes most of Chicago's work as "intertwining with her humanity."[161] She has not forgotten her father's dream: to make the world a better place.

Postscript

In recent years Chicago, while concentrating on more personal artworks, has also returned to her early focus on education. Beginning in 1999 she resumed teaching, accepting appointments as artist in residence, usually on collaborative projects with her husband. After a twenty-five-year absence from academia, she wanted to reconnect with the pedagogic ideas that she had left behind in the 1970s. She was curious to discover what had transpired in university art education, especially for women, during her absence. She also wanted to see if she could apply her pedagogy to male students, and she planned to write a book about feminist art education.

▲
The Therapist 5/17/2000 from *The Therapist Series,* © Donald Woodman.

Just as she came back to teaching, the first overview exhibition of her oeuvre, *Trials and Tributes,* organized by Viki D. Thompson Wylder of Florida State University, was touring eight museums. A mini-retrospective with about seventy-five works, it included studies for *The Dinner Party,* the *Birth Project,* and the *Holocaust Project,* among others. It opened at the Indiana University Art Museum in the fall of 1999 while Chicago was there as an artist in residence and professor. The local newspaper quoted her on the subject of her critics: "I've been pretty beaten up critically. So a lot of my focus has been on how to keep going, how to keep working and keep growing in the face of this incredible critical assault."[1] She meant her story of perseverance and resolve to set an example for students, especially in the visual arts, where success is so chancy.

In 2000 Chicago taught at both Duke and the University of North Carolina at Chapel Hill; and in the fall of 2001 the Chicago-Woodman team went to Western Kentucky University in Bowling Green, where they "facilitated," working with male and female students and local artists to organize *At Home: A Kentucky Project,* which included both a *House Exhibition* and a *Photo/Documentation Exhibit* by Woodman's students, recording work on the house, which revisited the subject thirty years after *Womanhouse* and contained installations that explored themes such as marital conflict, childhood fears, aging, eating disorders, sibling rivalry, and rape.

On July 28, 2002, Chicago participated in *The Long March: A Walking Visual Display* in a remote corner of Yunan province in China. Invited to serve as guest curator for a part of a five-month traveling art show that followed the route of the original Long March by the Communist Red Army in 1934, Chicago chose the theme "If Women Ruled the World" for a feminist program that took place at Lugu Lake, a location well known to anthropologists for the matrilineal culture of the Mosuo, a Chinese minority group. Chicago, twelve invited artists, and twelve local Mosuo women were to meet and explore the history, myth, and reality of matriarchal society through an art exhibition. Things did not go as planned. A dialogue that ensued made clear that at least some of the Chinese women resented having the male chief curator of *The Long March* import a foreign feminist.[2]

At Pomona College in California in the fall of 2003, Chicago and Woodman facilitated a student exhibition called *Envisioning the Future.* The opening occasioned a reunion of such longtime friends as Mary Ross Taylor, Stanley and Elyse Grinstein, Manuel Neri, and Dextra Frankel.

In homage to another old friend and mentor, Chicago chose passages from Anaïs Nin's *Delta of Venus,* which she illustrated with a memoir of their close friendship. To mark the publication, Chicago scheduled a show in 2004 that surveyed thirty-five years of her erotic art, opening at the ACA Galleries in New York and touring both the United States and Canada. The show included, besides the new *Delta* watercolors, some of her earlier works: *Erotic Cookies* (1967), *Sex from the Inside Out* (1975), and *Voices from the Song of Songs* (1999).

Another volume of watercolors and an accompanying gallery show followed in 2005: *Kitty City: A Feline Book of Hours* (Figure 32). These playful watercolors reflect Chicago's devotion to a ménage that she and her husband of twenty years have shared with a fluctuating population of five or six cats, one named Romeo, that have long inspired occasional artworks and even memorials at their deaths. At the show's venues, she arranged to have the ASPCA make cats and kittens available for adoption.

In the fall of 2005 Chicago and Woodman became the first Chancellor's Artists in Residence at Vanderbilt University in Nashville. Meanwhile, as Chicago looked forward to the opening of the Elizabeth A. Sackler Center for Feminist Art, she realized that it would coincide with major feminist shows at the Museum of Contemporary Art in Los Angeles and at the Brooklyn Museum, as well as with the twentieth anniversary of the National Museum of Women in the Arts. Together with Arlene Raven, she cooked up a plan to acknowledge the importance of women's recent contributions to the visual arts and the international impact of the feminist art movement, which eventually became known as the Feminist Art Project.

Chicago and Raven[3] teamed up with Susan Sterling, the chief curator at the National Museum of Women in the Arts; Maura Reilly, the curator of the Sackler Center; Dena Muller of AIR Gallery (an early women's gallery in New York City); and Judy Brodsky and Ferris Olin of Rutgers University, which agreed to administer the project. The Feminist Art Project announced in early 2006 a call for participants and publicized its purpose "to bring public attention to the significant impact of feminist artists on contemporary art practice, highlighting their international influence, and guaranteeing their inclusion in the cultural record, past, present, and future."[4]

To launch the Feminist Art Project, Rutgers organized *How American Women Artists Invented Postmodernism, 1970–1975*. Invited to address the banquet audience at the opening (January 14, 2006), Chicago synthesized her own experience into a prophetic declaration that tied individual ambition and achievement to a broad community that must credit past struggle in order to avoid future erasure:

We must insist that cultural recognition extend to our historic antecedents as well as to ourselves, because it is only when our achievements are seen within the context of women's long struggle for first, education, then, art training; and finally, the right to be ourselves as women in our art, that what we have accomplished—often in the face of incredible obstacles—can be adequately evaluated.

▲
Judy Chicago and Donald Woodman with their cats in Belen, New Mexico, September 1, 2002. Photograph by John Babcock Van Sickle.

SELECTED BIBLIOGRAPHY

JCCSL = The Judy Chicago Papers, The Arthur and Elizabeth Schlesinger Library on the History of Women in America, Radcliffe, Harvard University, Cambridge, Mass.

BOOKS AND ARTICLES

Writings by and Interviews with Judy Chicago

[Chicago] Gerowitz, Judy. *Judy Gerowitz.* Pasadena, Calif.: Pasadena Art Museum, 1969.

Chicago, J. *Painting Sculpture Photographs of Atmospheres by Judy Chicago.* Fullerton: California State Gallery, 1970.

______. Interview by Judith Dancoff. *Everywoman* 2, no. 7, issue 18 (7 May 1971), 4.

______. *Personal Journals,* vols. 1–8, 8 March 1971 through 1980 as seen by the author, and selected fragments of subsequent volumes as provided by the author, and scrapbook. Collection of Judy Chicago, Belen, N.M.

______, and Miriam Schapiro. *Womanhouse.* Exhibition catalog. Los Angeles, 1972.

______. "Statements of Participants." Artists' statements. Conference for Women in the Visual Arts, Corcoran Gallery of Art, Washington, D.C., 1972.

______. Interview by Hazel Slawson. Typescript. 1972. JCCSL.

______, and Dextra Frankel. "Invisible Twenty-one Artists Visible." In *Twenty-one Artists—Invisible/Visible.* Long Beach, Calif.: Long Beach Museum of Art, 1972.

______. "Judy Chicago Talking to Lucy Lippard." *Artforum* 13, no. 1 (September 1974), 60–65.

______, and Lloyd Hamrol. "Two Artists, Two Attitudes: Judy Chicago and Lloyd Hamrol Interview Each Other. *Criteria A Review of the Arts* 1, no. 2 (November 1974), 8–14.

______. "Breaking the Silence." Interview by Su Braden. *Time Out Limited,* May 1975.

______. "Judy Chicago: The Artist Views Herself and a World of Love, Death and Longshots." *Playgirl* 2, no. 12 (May 1975), 80–81, 102.

______. "Interview with Judy Chicago by Jan Butterfield." *City of San Francisco,* 20 January 1976, 44–47.

______. "Judy Chicago Interviewed." *Northwest Passage* 14, no. 12 (May 1976), 14–15.

______. *Through the Flower: My Struggle as a Woman Artist.* New York: Doubleday, Anchor, 1975; rev. ed., 1982.

______. "Judy Chicago in Conversation with Ruth Iskin." *Visual Dialog* 2, no. 3 (May 1977), 14.

______. Arlene Raven and Susan Rennie. "The Dinner Party Project: An Interview with Judy Chicago," *Chrysalis,* no. 4 (1977), 96.

______. "Judy Chicago: World of the China Painter. *Ceramics Monthly* 26, no. 5 (May 1978), 40–45.

______. *The Dinner Party: A Symbol of Our Heritage.* New York: Doubleday/Anchor, 1979.

______. "A Date with Judy: A Dialogue with Judy Chicago, Suzanne Lacy, and Faith Wilding." Unpublished ms. intended for *Images and Issues,* 1980. JCCSL, Box 6, Folder 3.

______. "An Enquiry into the Relationship Between Art and Politics." Ms. for lecture at Harvard. 1980. JCCSL, Box 6, Folder 23.

______. *Embroidering Our Heritage: The Dinner Party Needlework.* New York: Doubleday/Anchor, 1980.

______. "A Tribute to Virginia Woolf." Blackie. 10 October, 1982. JCCSL, Box 6, Folder 27.

______. "Judy Chicago: The Second Decade, 1973–1983." *Women Artists News* 9, no. 5–6 (Summer 1984), 12–14.

______. *A Jewish Journal.* Unpublished handwritten manuscript. 1985–93. JCCSL, Box 72, Folders 23–38.

______. *The Birth Project.* New York: Doubleday/Anchor, 1985.

______. *Powerplay.* Catalog. Text by Paula Harper, ed. Sidney L. Bergen. New York: ACA Galleries, 1986.

______. "Judy Chicago: Artist's Statement." *Gallerie Women's Art* 1, no. 1 (Annual/June 1988), 37–40.

______. "Exploring the Significance of the Holocaust Through Art." *Holocaust Project Newsletter,* no. 6 (Winter 1991–92), 1–2.

______. Interview with Cathleen Rountree for *Coming into Fulness: On Women Turning Forty.* Typescript. 1991. JCCSL, Box 7, Folder 39.

______. *Holocaust Project: From Darkness Into Light.* New York: Viking/ Penguin, 1993.
______. "Being in the Presence of the Truth: An Interview with Judy Chicago." Interview by Nancy Jo Hoy. *From the Ear* (Spring 1994), 26–45.
______, and M. Spirn. "An Interview with Judy Chicago on the Holocaust Project." *NCJW Journal* 17, no. 1 (Fall 1994), 15–19.
______. "Merger Poem." In *In the Embrace of God: Feminist Approaches to Theological Anthropology,* ed. Ann O'Hara Graff. New York: Orbis Books, 1995. Bilson, Barbara, Rabbi Sue Levi Elwell, Betty Rosenfeld, Nancy Sogg, and Cantor William Sharlin. Leo Baeck Temple Shabbat Service, Los Angeles: Leo Baeck Temple, 1995. Berman, Donna. *Passover Haggadah.* New York: Port Jewish Center, 1995.
______. *Beyond the Flower: The Autobiography of a Feminist Artist.* New York: Viking Penguin, 1996.
______. *The Dinner Party: A Commemorative Volume Celebrating a Major Monument of Twentieth-Century Art.* New York: Viking/ Penguin, 1996.
______, and Edward Lucie-Smith. *Women and Art: Contested Territory.* New York: Watson-Guptill, 1999.
______. *Fragments From the Delta of Venus.* New York: PowerHouse Books, 2004.
______. "Judy Chicago: An Oral History." Interview by Jane Collings. Oral History Program. Transcript. UCLA, 2004.
______. *Kitty City: A Feline Book of Hours.* New York: Harper Design, 2005.

Writings by Others

Abbe, Mary. "Judy Chicago Says That Fame Doesn't Remove Sexist Obstacles to Art." *Minneapolis Star Tribune,* 14 January 1994, 4E.
Abcarian, Robin. "The Lesson of Judy Chicago: Fame Has Its Detractions." *Los Angeles Times,* 28 April 1996, E1, E2.
Aber, Ita. *The Art of Judaic Needlework.* London: Bell & Hyman, 1979.
Abrahams, Israel, comp. and ed. *Hebrew Ethical Wills.* Philadelphia: Jewish Publication Society of America, 1948.
Abramowicz, Hirsz. *Profiles of a Lost World.* Detroit: Wayne State University Press, 1999.
Adams, Henry. *Thomas Hart Benton: An American Original.* New York: Alfred A. Knopf, 1989.
Adams, Jan. "Chicago's Dinner Party A Feminist Feast." *Lesbian Tide,* May/June 1979, 4–5.
Albright, Thomas. "Judy Chicago." *San Francisco Chronicle,* 10 January 1976.
______. "Primarily Biological." *ARTnews* 78, no. 6 (Summer 1979): 156.
Aleichem, Sholem. "We Strike." In *The New Country,* trans. and ed. Henry Goodman. New York: YKUF, 1961.
Alloway, Lawrence. "Judy Chicago Philip Guston." *Nation,* 15 November 1980, 524–25.
Allyn, David. *Make Love Not War: The Sexual Revolution: An Unfettered History.* Boston: Little, Brown & Co., 2000.
Anderson, Judith. "The Ultimate in Female Art." *San Francisco Chronicle,* 13 February 1978, 21.
Andrews, Oliver. "Los Angeles Art Community: Group Portrait." Interview by George M. Goodwin. Oral History Program. Transcript. UCLA, 1977.
Anonymous. 1965. "New York's Avant-garde School Daring New Lincoln Strives for Student Self-assertiveness." *Ebony* (May), 34–44.
______. "Judy Gerowitz, Rolf Nelson Gallery." *Artforum* 4, no. 8 (April 1966), 14.
______. " 'Womanhouse' Opens." *Los Angeles Free Press,* 4 February 1972.
______. "Critic." *Neworld* 2, no. 1 (Fall 1975), 12–13.
______. "A Feminist Sculptures 'Dinner Party.' " *New York Times,* 1 April 1979, 52.
______. "Hot Type: The Dinner Party's Hosts." *Reader,* 11 September 1981, sec. 1, 4.
______. "Judy Chicago." In *Current Biography.* Bronx, N.Y.: H.W. Wilson Co., 1981, 62–65.
______. " 'The Dinner Party' une oeuvre colossale." *Le Céramiste* 1, no. 4 (July 1982), 10–11.
______. " 'Dinner Party' Draws 50,000 in Toronto." *Montreal Gazette,* 8 July 1982, 76–77.
______. "Dallas Museum Director Gets Probation." *Houston Chronicle,* 3 November 1992, 3.
______. *Feminist Directions: 1970/1996: Robin Mitchell, Mira Schor, Faith Wilding, Nancy Youdelman.* Riverside, Calif., 1996.
______. Obituary. "Dorothy K. Goodwill, 62, Church Embroidery Artist." *Cleveland Plain Dealer,* 2 November 2000, 9B.
Antler, Joyce. *The Journey Home: Jewish Women and the American Century.* New York: Free Press, 1997.
Artner, Alan G. "Inanity Outweighs the Controversy of 'Dinner Party.' " *Chicago Tribune,* 14 September 1981, B8.
Askey, Ruth. "Judy Chicago: Pride in Women and in Herself." *Artweek* (January 1977). JCCSL, Box 1, Folder 33.
______. "Letters: Chicago Vs. Muchnic." *Los Angeles Times Book Review,* 29 April 1979, 1, 2.
Atkinson, Ti-Grace. *Amazon Odyssey: The First Collection of Writing by the Political Pioneer of*

the Women's Movement. New York: Link Books, 1974.

Baarslag, Karl. *History of the National Federation of Post Office Clerks.* Washington, D.C.: National Federation of Post Office Clerks, 1945.

Balin, Carole B. *To Reveal Our Hearts: Jewish Women Writers in Tsarist Russia.* Cincinnati, Oh.: Hebrew Union College Press, 2000.

Ballatore, Sandy. "'Dinner Party' Needs a Host." *Albuquerque Journal,* 20 August 1989, G1, G2.

______. "Letters: Chicago Vs. Muchnic." *Los Angeles Times Book Review,* 29 April 1979, 1, 2.

Barnard, Rob. "Ben Cohen, 46, American Ceramist in Japan." *American Craft,* June/July 1992, 17.

Baron, Dvora. *The First Day.* Berkeley: University of California Press, 2001.

______. *The Thorny Path.* Jerusalem: Israel University Press, 1969.

Barras, Jonetta Rose. "UDC's $1.6 Million 'Dinner' Feminist Artwork Causes Some Indigestion." *Washington Times,* 18 July 1990, A1, A7.

Battis, Cindy. "Reviews." *The Wheel* (The College of St. Catherine) 42, no. 6 (17 February 1975).

Beals, Kathie. "'The Dinner Party': A Feminist Feast." *Gannett Westchester Newspapers,* 28 October 1980, B1.

Bee, Susan, and Mira Schor, eds. *M/E/A/N/I/N/G: Anthology of Artists' Writings, Theory, and Criticism.* Durham, N.C.: Duke University Press, 2000.

Bellow, Saul. "'Writers, Intellectuals, Politics: Mainly Reminiscence'" *National Interest* (Spring 1993).

Berman, Art. "Art Tower Started as Vietnam Protest." *Los Angeles Times* (1966): 3, 24.

Bernstein, Elizabeth. "Chicago View of Holocaust." *JUF [Jewish United Fund] News,* October 1993, 66–70.

Berry, S. L. "Art with Attitude." *Indianapolis Star,* 26 September 1999, 1, 2.

Bickelhaupt, Susan and Maureen Dezell. "Chicago Comes to Cambridge." *Boston Globe,* 5 June 1996, 34.

Bloom, Lisa. "Ethnic Notions and Feminist Strategies of the 1970s." In *Jewish Identity in Modern Art History,* ed. Catherine M. Soussloff. Berkeley: University of California Press, 1999.

Boime, Albert, and Paul Arden. *The Odyssey of Jan Stussy in Black and White: Anxious Visions and Uncharted Dreams.* Los Angeles: Jan Stussy Foundation, 1995.

Boston Women's Health Book Collective. *Our Bodies, Ourselves: A Book By and For Women.* New York: Simon & Schuster, 1971.

Broude, Norma, and Mary D. Garrard, eds. *The Power of Feminist Art.* New York: Harry N. Abrams, 1994.

Brown, Norman O. *Life Against Death: The Psychoanalytical Meaning of History.* Middletown, Conn.: Wesleyan University Press, 1959.

Brown, Ray, ed. *The Early Sixties at UCLA.* Los Angeles: Frederick S. Wight Gallery, 1977.

Brownmiller, Susan. *In Our Time: Memoir of a Revolution.* New York: Random House, 1999.

Buhle, Paul. *From the Lower East Side to Hollywood: Jews in American Popular Culture.* New York: Verso, 2004.

______, and Nicole Schulman. *Wobblies: A Graphic History of the Industrial Workers of the World.* New York: W. W. Norton & Co., 2005.

Butterfield, Jan. *Judy Chicago: The Second Decade 1973–1983.* New York: ACA Galleries, 1984.

Camhi, Leslie. "Dinner Is Served: Reassessing Judy Chicago and Other Feminist Avatars." *Village Voice,* 16–22 October 2002, 55.

Camper, Fred. "The Banality of Badness." *Chicago Reader,* sec. 1 (21 January 1994), 22–23.

Carrell, Steve. "The Birth Project." *American Medical News,* 24 September 1982, 9.

Cassim, Julia. "Friends Rally to Help Potter with Lou Gehrig's Disease." *Japan Times,* 24 September 1990.

______. "Stricken Ceramist in Fukui Shapes Skills of His Successor." *Japan Times,* 21 January 1992, 4.

Castro, Jan. "Jan Castro Interview with Kate Amend and Ann Isolde. The Dinner Party Talks." *River Styx* 9 (1981), 59–69.

Chapman, Frances. "Judy Chicago: Vaginal Iconographer." *off our backs,* July 1975, 16–17.

Charles, Nick. "Project's Not on Critics' List." *New York Daily News,* 22 April 1994.

Cheng, Scarlet. "A Future Defined by Needle and Thread." *Los Angeles Times,* 21 January 2001, 76.

Class of 1961 Yearbook Staff. *UCLA Southern Campus Yearbook,* vol. 42. Los Angeles: UCLA, 1961.

Cogburn, Laura E. "Plastics." In *Finish Fetish: LA's Cool School,* ed. Frances Colpitt. Los Angeles: Fisher Gallery, University of Southern California, 1991.

Cohen, Ben. "Joyous Flame." *Ceramics Monthly* 38, no. 6 (June–July–August 1990), 60–61.

Cohen, Israel. *Vilna.* Philadelphia: Jewish Publication Society of America, 1943.

Cohen, Tova. "Reality and Its Refraction in Descriptions of Women in Haskalah Fiction." In *New Perspectives on the Haskalah,* ed. Shmuel Feiner and David Sorkin. London: Littman Library of Jewish Civilization, 2001.

Cohn, Robert A. "Judy Chicago Describes Her Struggle as a Woman Artist." *St. Louis Jewish Light,* 9 April 1980, 7.

Colander, Pat. "Judy Chicago: Midwife to a Female Art Renaissance." *Chicago Tribune,* 16 June 1975, B2.

Cole, Darrah. "The Dinner Party: Judy Chicago." *Vision,* September/October/November 1980, 12.

Coplans, John. "The New Abstraction on the West Coast U.S.A." *Studio International* 169, no. 865 (May 1965), 192–99.

______. "The New Sculpture and Technology." In *American Sculpture of the Sixties,* ed. Maurice Tuchman. Los Angeles: Los Angeles County Museum of Art, 1967.

______. "Oral History." Interview by Paul Cummings. Archives of American Art. New York: Smithsonian Institution, 1975. Online at http://archivesofamericanart.si.edu/oralhist/coplan75.htm.

Corbett, Helen. "A Woman's Work: Rewriting History Through Her Art." *Edmonton Journal,* 29 November 1980, H1.

Cork, Richard. "Monumental." *Listener,* 21 March 1985.

Cottingham, Laura. *Seeing Through the Seventies: Essays on Feminism and Art.* Padstow, Cornwall, U.K.: G + B Arts International, 2000.

Creamer, Anita. "Celebrating Women's Creativity." *Dallas Times Herald,* 20 June 1984, 1F, 8F.

Crean, Susan. "The Dinner Party: Indigestion for the Establishment." *Broadside: A Feminist Review* 3, no. 10 (September 1982), 8.

Cross, Guy. "An Interview with Judy Chicago." *Santa Fe's Monthly,* September 1996, 42–43.

Crossley, Mimi. "The Men in the Kitchen of 'The Dinner Party.'" *Houston Post,* 25 March 1980, B1.

Cullinan, Helen. "Feminist Art Esprit Creates a Cleveland-Chicago Bond." *Cleveland Plain Dealer,* May 1979.

______. "Judy Chicago: 'The Dinner Party' Is in Keeping with Feminist Style." *Cleveland Plain Dealer,* 7 May 1981, E1, E4.

Cutler, Irving. *Chicago: Metropolis of the Mid-Continent.* Dubuque, Ia.: Kendall/Hunt, 1973.

______. *The Jews of Chicago.* Urbana: University of Illinois Press, 1996.

______. "West Side Story: Remembering the Days When Lawndale Was Where It, and We, Were At." *Jewish United Fund News,* May 1988, 12–17.

Dambrot, Faye, and Robert Zangrando. "The Dinner Party: A Reply." *Beacon: The Sunday Magazine of the Akron Beacon Journal,* 2 August 1981.

Danieli, Fidel. "Los Angeles: Judy Gerowitz." *ARTnews* 65, no. 1 (March 1966), 20.

Daniels, Sara, and Pamela Ruddick. *Working It Out: 23 Women Writers, Artists, Scientists, and Scholars Talk About Their Lives and Work.* New York: Pantheon Books, 1977.

Davis, Mike. *City of Quartz: Excavating the Future in Los Angeles.* New York: Verso, 1990.

de Beauvoir, Simone. *The Second Sex.* New York: Alfred A. Knopf, 1953.

Decker, Kiana. "Judy Chicago Visits Phoenix, Exhibits 'Birthing Project.'" *Arizona Women's Voice,* December 1985, 1, 5.

Dettebach, Cynthia. "'Dialogue, Controversy' Served at Dinner Party." *Cleveland Jewish News,* 8 May 1981, 31.

Diggs, Agnes. "Clue Offers New Hope for Solving 1977 Murder." *Los Angeles Times,* 9 March 1999, Metro News.

Dorsey, Candas Jane. "Women, Art, and Celebration." *Interface* (1980), 14–15.

Drew, Donald, and Stow Persons Egbert, eds. *Socialism and American Life.* Princeton, N.J.: Princeton University Press, 1952.

Drohojowska, Hunter. "Would You Eat Your Chef Boy-Ar-Dee Off of Plates like These?" *Los Angeles Weekly,* 29 August–4 September, 1980, 4–5.

______. "Prints of the City." *Los Angeles Times,* 15 October 1995, 62, 63.

Dunbar-Ortiz, Roxanne. *Outlaw Woman: A Memoir of the War Years, 1960–1975.* San Francisco: City Lights, 2001.

Eauclaire, Sally. "The Holocaust Project: A Controversial Artist's New Work Parallels Her Own Bittersweet Journey to Self-Discovery." *Chicago Tribune Magazine,* 17 October 1993, 17–20.

Echols, Alice. *Daring to Be Bad: Radical Feminism in America 1967–1975.* Minneapolis: University of Minnesota, 1989.

Edelson, Mary Beth. *The Art of Mary Beth Edelson.* New York: Distributed Art Publishers, 2002.

Ehrenreich, Barbara. *The Hearts of Men: American Dreams and the Flight from Commitment.* Garden City, N.Y.: Anchor/Doubleday, 1983.

Eisler, Riane. "Sex, Art and Archetypes." *Women's Review of Books* 8, no. 6 (March 1991).

Eliach, Yaffa. *Hasidic Tales of the Holocaust.* New York: Oxford University Press, 1982.

Eliot, George. *Daniel Deronda.* Hertfordshire, U.K.: Wordsworth Editions., 1877, reprinted 1996.

Elvenstar, Diane. "Into the Heart and Soul of Creativity." *Los Angeles Times,* 3 December 1979, Section IV, 1, 14–15.

English, Priscilla. "An Interview with Two Artists from Womanhouse." *New Woman,* April–May 1972, 36–43.

Epstein, Melech. *Jewish Labor in U.S.A. 1882–1914.* Miami Beach, Fla.: Ktav Publishing House, 1969.

Etkes, Immanuel. "The Gaon of Vilna and the Haskalah Movement: Image and Reality." In *BINAH Studies in Jewish History, Thought, and Culture,* ed. Joseph Dan, vol. 2. New York: Praeger, 1889.

______. *Rabbi Israel Salantner and the Mussar Movement: Seeking the Torah of Truth.* Philadelphia: Jewish Publication Society, 1993.

Evans, Sara. *Personal Politics: The Roots of Women's Liberation in the Civil Rights Movement and the New Left.* New York: Alfred A. Knopf, 1979.

Evans, Stan. "People, Places and Problems in the News." *UCLA Daily Bruin,* 1 October 1957, 3.

Evett, David. "Moveable Feast." *Northern Ohio Live* 1, no. 16 (4–17 May 1981), 26–29.

Fariello, Griffin. *Red Scare: Memoirs of the American Inquisition, An Oral History.* New York: W. W. Norton & Co., 1995.

Feingold, Henry L. *The Jewish People in America.* Baltimore: Johns Hopkins University Press, 1992.

Felman, Jyl Lynn. "Judy Chicago's Holocaust Project." *Lilith* 19, no. 2 (30 June 1994), 15–16.

Fetsher, Caroline. "Frauenkunst Soll aus Blut und Milch Sein." *Spiegel* 25 (16 June 1986), 166.

Fine, Morris, ed. *American Jewish Yearbook,* vol. 52. New York: American Jewish Committee, 1951.

Finkel, Susan. "The Art of Judy Chicago: Female and Feminist." JCCSL Unidentified Clipping Box 1, Folder 43 (21 May 1976), 7, 10.

Firestone, Shulamith. *The Dialectic of Sex: The Case for Feminist Revolution.* New York: William Morrow & Co., 1970.

Fischer, Clare B. "Reviewed: Judy Chicago's The Dinner Party." *Newsletter: The Center for Women and Religion of the Graduate Theological Union* Berkeley, Calif. 5, no. 3 (Spring 1979), 14–15.

Fischer, Hal. "San Francisco." *Artforum* 17, no. 10 (Summer 1979), 77–79.

Fitch, Noël Riley. *Anaïs: The Erotic Life of Anaïs Nin.* Boston, Mass.: Little, Brown & Co., 1993.

Flier, Elyse Katz. "Open Wall Show." *Artweek,* 13 July 1974, 8.

Fox, Catherine. "Guess Who's Coming to Dinner?" *Atlanta Constitution,* 27 July 1982, 1B, 3B.

Frascina, Francis. *Art, Politics and Dissent: Aspects of the Art Left in Sixties American.* Manchester, U.K.: Manchester University Press, 1999.

Freedman, Adele. "Dinner Party: Art or Exhumation?" *Toronto Globe & Mail,* 19 April 1982.

______. "Judy Chicago: The Artist as Full-Scale Feminist Myth." *Montreal Globe & Mail,* 23 February 1980, 5.

Freedman, Chaim. *Eliyahu's Branches: The Descendants of the Vilna Gaon and His Family.* Teaneck, N.J.: Avotaynu, 1997.

Freeman, Natalie Veiner. "Revelations of a Private Female World." *Maclean's,* 5 April 1982, 44.

Freligh, Rebecca. "The Feminist Artist—A Wizard Baffled in Oz." *Cleveland Plain Dealer,* 17 March 1990, C1, C4.

Fried, Albert, ed. "Communism in America." In *Communism in America: A History in Documents.* New York: Columbia University Press, 1997.

Fried, Richard M. *Nightmare in Red: The McCarthy Era in Perspective.* New York: Oxford University Press, 1990.

Friedan, Betty. *The Feminine Mystique.* New York: W. W. Norton & Co., 1963.

Fulford, Robert. "Dinner Party's Sweep is Breathtaking." *Toronto Star,* 12 June 1982.

Fuss, Diana. *Essentially Speaking: Feminism, Nature and Difference.* New York: Routledge, 1989.

Gage, Edward. "Impeccable 'Dinner Party.'" *Edinburgh Newspaper.* JCCSL, Box 2, Folder 15 (August 1984).

Galloway, David. "From Bankfurt to Frankfurt: A Cash and Carry Renaissance." *Art in America,* September 1987.

Garver, Thomas H. "Judy Chicago, Art Gallery, California State College, Fullerton." *Artforum* 9, no. 5 (January 1971), 92–93.

Gelon, Diane. "The Critic's Voice: Who Speaks for Us?" *Sojourner,* October 1980, 5, 29.

George-Geisser, Mary. "Judy Chicago: Artist and Feminist." *Gold Flower* 6, no. 7 (February 1975), 1, 3.

Gerber. "People." *Skyline Newspapers,* 7 January 1982, 2.

Gitlin, Todd. *The Sixties Years of Hope, Days of Rage.* New York: Bantam Books, 1987.

Glenn, Susan A. *Daughters of the Shtetl: Life and Labor in the Immigrant Generation.* Ithaca, N.Y.: Cornell University Press, 1990.

Glueck, Grace. "Judy Chicago and Trials of 'Dinner Party.'" *New York Times,* 30 April 1979, D10.

______. "The Ladies Flex Their Brushes." *New York Times,* 30 May 1971, D20.

______. "No More Raw Eggs at the Whitney?" *New York Times,* 13 February 1972, D21.

______. "Winning the West." *New York Times,* 16 April 1972, D19.

Goddard, Peter. "Southern Revival." *Toronto Star,* 29 January 2005, H1, H12.

Goldberg, Itche, and Max Rosenfeld, eds. *Morris Rosenfeld: Selections From His Poetry and Prose.* New York: Yiddisher Kultur Farband, 1964.

Goldenhersh, Sheryn. "Judy Chicago Hosts Her 'Dinner Party' at the Brooklyn Art Museum." *St. Louis Jewish Light,* 5 November 1980, 7.

Goldman, Emma. *Living My Life.* New York: Alfred A. Knopf, 1931.

Goldstein, Ann. *A Minimal Future? Art as Object 1958–1968.* Los Angeles: Museum of Contemporary Art/MIT Press, 2004.

Goodman, Henry, trans. and ed. *The New Country.* New York: YKUF, 1961.

Goodman, Vera. "Judy Chicago, Trendsetter." *New Directions for Women,* Spring 1976.

Goodwin, George M., interviewer. "Oliver Andrews Oral History." Los Angeles Art Community: Group Portrait. UCLA, 1977.

Gornick, Vivian. *The Romance of American Communism.* New York: Basic Books, 1977.

Gouma-Peterson, Thalia. *Miriam Schapiro.* New York: Harry N. Abrams, 1999.

Gourevitch, Philip. "Washington's Holocaust Theme Park." *Harper's,* July 1993, 55–62.

______. *We Wish to Inform You That Tomorrow We Will be Killed with Our Families: Stories from Rwanda.* New York: Farrar, Straus and Giroux, 1998.

Graham, Renee. "Why Judy Chicago Is the Artist the Art World Loves to Hate." *Boston Sunday Globe,* 24 September 1995, B27.

Green, Laura. "Finally, We're Invited to Judy Chicago's 'Dinner Party.'" *Chicago Sun-Times,* 6 September 1981, 6.

Green, Vanalyne. "The Feminist Art Program." In *Women of Vision: Histories in Feminist Film and Video,* ed. Alexandra Juhasz. Minneapolis: University of Minnesota Press, 2001.

Greenberg, Louis. *The Jews in Russia: The Struggle for Emancipation.* New Haven: Yale University Press, 1944.

Greenburg, Blue. "'The Dinner Party' Captures Essence of Women's History." *Durham Morning Herald,* 13 April 1979, 1B.

Grod, John. "Plastic Artist Under Attack?" *Chicago Reader,* 2 October 1981.

Grimstad, Kirsten, and Susan Rennie. *The New Woman's Survival Catalog.* New York: Alfred A. Knopf, 1973.

Gruen, John. *The Artist Observed: 28 Interviews with Contemporary Artists.* New York: A Cappella Books, 1991.

Haberer, Erich. *Jews and Revolution in Nineteenth-Century Russia.* Cambridge, U.K.: Cambridge University Press, 1995.

Hagberg, Karen A. "Dinner Party Cancelled: Women's Art Won't Be Shown." *New Women's Times,* 6 July 1979.

Haider, Vicky Chen. "Chicago's Butterfly." *Chicago Sun-Times,* 19 June 1975, 2, 81.

Hale, David. "Dinner Party Will Honor 1,038 'Significant' Women." *Fresno Bee,* 23 March 1978, D1. JCCSL, Box 1, Folder 45.

Halverson, Megan. "Bye-Bye Bella." *Houston Press,* 9 January 1997.

Hamilton, Mildred. "Judy Chicago's Dinner Party." *San Francisco Examiner and Chronicle,* 18 March 1979, Scene sec., 8.

______. "'The Dinner Party' Left Without a Second Sitting." *San Francisco Examiner & Chronicle,* 1 July 1979, Scene sec., 6.

Hammond, Harmony. *Lesbian Art in America: A Contemporary History.* New York: Rizzoli, 2000.

Hardy, Susan. "Judy Chicago—Artist, Woman." *Strait* 2, no. 8 (7 February 1973), 13.

Harmon, Charlotte. "A Generous Helping of Feminism on 'Dinner Party' Plates." *Los Angeles Times Book Review,* 15 April 1979, 3, 11.

Harper, Paula. *Powerplay.* Catalog, ed. Sidney L. Bergen. New York: ACA Galleries, 1986.

______. "The Chicago Resolutions." *Art in America,* June 2000, 112–15, 137–38.

Harris, Maxine. *The Loss That Is Forever: The Lifelong Impact of the Early Death of a Mother or Father.* New York: Penguin Books, 1996.

Heller, Fran. "Journey of Identity." *Cleveland Jewish News,* 3 May 1996, 14–16.

Hess, Elizabeth. "Planet Holocaust From Feminism to Judaism: Meet the New Judy Chicago." *Village Voice,* 2 November 1993, 43–44.

Hewitson, Michele. "Missing the BIG Picture." *Weekend Herald* Auckland, New Zealand, July 1999, J4.

Hickox, Katie. "Santa Fe Artist's Sculpture Gift Brings Controversy to University." *Santa Fe New Mexican,* 5 August 1990, B1, B3.

______. "Work by Santa Fe Artist Stirs Congressional Fray." *Santa Fe New Mexican,* 28 July 1990, A1, A2.

Hill, Carlene. "Dressing for 'Dinner': A Woman's Work is Never Done." *Boston Phoenix,* 1 July 1980, sec. 3, 2.

Hinson, Mark. "Retro Chicago." *Tallahassee Democrat,* 14 February 1999, Features sec. 1.

Hodgetts, Vicki. "Womanspace: Rezoning the L.A. Art Scene." *Ms.* 2, no. 1 (August 1973), 24–27.

Hopkins, Henry, with Evris Tsakirides. *Lloyd Hamrol: Works, Projects, Proposals.* Los Angeles: Los Angeles Municipal Art Gallery Associates, 1986.

Horowitz, Daniel. *Betty Friedan and the Making of the Feminine Mystique.* Amherst, Mass.: University of Massachusetts Press, 1998.

Houston Chronicle news briefs, "Dallas Museum Director Gets Probation," 3 November 1992, 3.

Hudson, Jean Barlow. "The Dinner Party." *Wimmin's Voices,* 2 July 1981.

Hyman, Paula E. "Culture and Gender: Women in the Immigrant Jewish Community." In *The Legacy of Jewish Migration: 1881 and Its Impact,* ed. David Berger. Brooklyn, N.Y.: Brooklyn College Press, 1983.

______. *Gender and Assimilation in Modern Jewish History: The Roles and Representations of Women.* Seattle, Wash.: University of Washington Press, 1995.

Idelsohn, A. Z. *Jewish Music in Its Historical Development.* New York: Tudor Publishing Co., 1944.

Ignatius, David. "Tension of the Times." *Washington Post,* 18 June 2004, A29.

Isenberg, Barbara. "Invitation to a Women-Only Dinner." *Los Angeles Times,* 6 April 1978, sec. 4, pp. 1, 12.

Iskin, Ruth E. "Female Experience in Art: The Impact of Women's Art in a Work Environment." *Heresies* 1, no. 1 (January 1977), 71–78.

Jablon, Robert. "Hope Rekindled in Murder Case: Police Reopen Probe Involving Boxing Trainer." *Pasadena Star-News,* 10 March 1999, A6.

Jack, Ian. "LOOK! Exit Judy, Struggling." *London Times,* May 1975, 32.

Jahnke, Art. "Oh Waiter, What's This Butterfly Doing in My Soup?" *Boston Phoenix,* July 1980.

Janson, H. W., Anthony F. Janson et al. *History of Art,* 7th ed. Saddle River, N.J.: Pearson Prentice-Hall, 2006.

Jay, Karla. "Through the Male Art World." *Lesbian Tide* (1975).

Johnson, Ken. "Offering Up Good Cheer and the Humanist Values, All Rendered in Clichés." *New York Times,* 4 August 2000, E36.

Jones, Amelia, ed. *Sexual Politics: Judy Chicago's* Dinner Party *in Feminist Art History.* Berkeley: University of California Press, 1996.

______, and Laura Meyer. *Feminist Directions: 1970/1996: Robin Mitchell, Mira Schor, Faith Wilding, Nancy Youdelman.* Riverside, Calif.: Sweeney Art Gallery, 1996.

Joselit, Jenna Weissman. "'A Set Table': Jewish Culture in the New World, 1880–1950." In *Getting Comfortable in New York: The American Jewish Home, 1880–1950,* ed. Susan L. Braunstein and Jenna Weissman Joselit. New York: Jewish Museum, 1990.

Joseph, Nadine. "A Special Kind of Art." *Cleveland Plain Dealer,* 13 June 1979.

Kamin, Ira. "Opening The Dinner Party." *San Francisco Sunday Examiner & Chronicle,* 3 June 1979, 32–34.

Kaplan, Judy, and Linn Shapiro, eds. "Red Diapers." In *Red Diapers: Growing Up in the Communist Left.* Champaign-Urbana: University of Illinois Press, 1998.

Karkabi, Barbara. "Specially Chosen Women Doing Needlework for Artist's Next Project." *Houston Chronicle,* 9 July 1981, sec. 5, 1, 5.

Kaufman, Betty. "Celebrating the History of Women." *Boston Globe,* 15 July 1980, letters to the editor.

Kaufmann, Aharon Ben Alexander. *Letter Regarding Education* (Translation from the Hebrew title). Pirhei Tzafon. Vilna, 1844.

Kauss, Linda. "Judy Chicago: Mona Lisa Is Not the Only Woman in Art." *Phoenix Gazette,* 12 April 1975, sec. A, 7.

Kelly, Alfred H., and Winfred A. Harbison. *The American Constitution: Its Origins and Development.* New York: W. W. Norton & Co., 1963.

Ketcham, Diane. "Judy Chicago's Dinner Party: Two Views of the First Feminist Epic Artwork: On the Table, Joyous Celebration." *Village Voice,* 11 June 1979, 47–50.

Kingsley, April. "The I-Hate-To-Cook 'Dinner Party.'" *Ms.,* June 1979, 30–31.

Kirsch, Jonathan. "The Flowering of the Artist." *Coast* 16, no. 6 (June 1975), 36–39.

Klehr, Harvey. *The Heyday of American Communism: The Depression Decade.* New York: Basic Books, 1984.

Klehr, Harvey, and John Earl Haynes. *The American Communist Movement: Storming Heaven Itself.* New York: Twayne Publishers, 1992.

Klein, Jennie. "Sexual/textual Politics: The Battle Over Art of the 70's." *New Art Examiner,* October 1996, 26–31.

Knight, Christopher. "More Famine Than Feast." *Los Angeles Times,* 2 May 1996, F1, F11.

Kobrin, Leon. *A Lithuanian Village.* Translated by Isaac Goldberg. New York: Brentano's, 1914.

Koch, Joanne. "The New Professionals." *Chicago Tribune,* 8 September 1974, G20, G22.

Koploy, Shirley. "The Woman's Building: Alive and Living in L.A." *Ms.* 3, no. 4 (October 1974): 100–3.

Korenak, Linda. "Judy Chicago: Opening of the Flower." *Amazon* 3, no. 6 (October 1974), 4.

Kramer, Hilton. "Judy Chicago's 'Dinner Party' Comes to Brooklyn Museum." *New York Times,* 17 October 1980, C1.

Krull, Craig. *Photographing the L.A. Art Scene 1955–1975.* Santa Monica, Calif.: Smart Art Press, 1996.

Kubitza, Anette. "Rereading the Readings of *The Dinner Party* in Europe." In *Sexual Politics: Judy Chicago's* Dinner Party *in Feminist Art History,* ed. Amelia Jones. Berkeley: University of California Press, 1996.

Kuby, Lolette. "Hoodwinking Women." *Cleveland Magazine* 10, no. 8 (August 1980), 83–85.

Kueter, Dale. "'Anniversary Prompts History Project: Temple Judah Commissions 'People Story' of Jews in Cedar Rapids.'" *Cedar Rapids Gazette,* 25 March 1989, 7A.

Kuperstein, Elana Eizak. "Judy Chicago: A Feminist Artist in Search of Her Jewish Self." *Women's World,* April/May 1987, 11.

Kusel, Heinz. *Heinz Kusel Between Experience and Reflection: The Story of a Painter as Told to Thomas Kusel.* Auburn, Calif.: Destiny Publishing, 2004.

Lacy, Leslie Alexander. *The Rise and Fall of a Proper Negro.* New York: Macmillan, 1970.

Lacy, Suzanne. Interview by Moira Roth. Archives of American Art Oral History Program, Smithsonian Institution. Berkeley, Calif., 1990. Online at http://www.aaa.si.edu/oralhist/lacy90.htm#top.

Lake View High Yearbook Staff. *Red and White.* Chicago: Lake View High, 1955–57.

Lancet, Barry. "Ben Cohen, American Potter in Echizen, Japan." *Ceramics: Art and Perception* [Sydney, Australia] 9 (1992), 56–59.

Larkin, Kathy. "Judy Chicago: Art Across the Gender Gap." *Post-Tribune* (Chicago), 2 December 1984, Today's Woman, 2, 4.

Larson, Kay. "Judy Chicago's Dinner Party: Two Views of the First Feminist Epic Artwork Under the Table: Duplicity, Alienation." *Village Voice,* 11 June 1979, 49–50.

______. "More (or Less) Awful Rowing Toward God." *Village Voice,* 17 December 1979, 113.

LeCocq, Karen. *The Easiest Thing to Remember: My Life as an Artist, a Feminist and a Manic Depressive.* Bloomington, Ind.: 1st Books, 2002.

Lee, Felicia R. "Arts Festival Next Front for 'Vagina Warrior.'" *New York Times,* 12 June 2006, E1.

Lehmann-Haupt, Christopher. "Her Struggle as a Writer." *New York Times,* 10 March 1975.

Leider, Philip. "The Cool School." *Artforum* 2, no. 12 (Summer 1964), 46–51.

Lerner, Gerda. *The Grimké Sisters from South Carolina: Pioneers for Women's Rights and Abolition.* New York: Shocken Books, 1971.

Levin, Elaine. "China Painting—Past and Present." *Artweek,* December 1977, 5.

______. "Judy Chicago: The Dinner Party." *Ceramics Monthly* 27, no. 6 (June 1979), 46–49.

Levin, Gail. "Beyond the Pale: Jewish Identity, Radical Politics, and Feminist Art in the United States." *Journal of Modern Jewish Studies* 4 (July 2005), 205–32.

______. *Edward Hopper: An Intimate Biography.* New York: Alfred A. Knopf, 1995.

______. "Learning to Appreciate Judy Chicago." *Women in the Arts* 20, no. 2 (Fall 2002), 12–17.

Levin, Nora. *While Messiah Tarried: Jewish Socialist Movements, 1871–1917.* New York: Schocken Books, 1977.

Levy, G. Rachel. *Religious Conceptions of the Stone Age and Their Influence Upon European Thought.* New York: Harper & Row, 1963.

Levy, Rebecca. "Judy Chicago's Holocaust Project: A Time to Heal." *Austin Chronicle* 14, no. 10, 4 November 1994, 34.

Lewis, Judith. "The Trouble with Judy: Reflections on The Dinner Party and the Artist Who Created It." *Los Angeles Weekly* 18, 26 April 1996, 26–35.

Liddick, Betty. "Emergence of the Feminist Artist." *Los Angeles Times,* 17 January 1972, sec. 4, 6. JCCSL, Box 11, Folder 37.

Lincoln, Liz. "Clearing the Table, Letter to the Editor Responding to Kuby's Article." *Cleveland Magazine* 10 (October 1981).

Lipinski, Ann Marie. "Public May Never Again Feast on Paean to Women." *Chicago Tribune,* 19 August 1979, L1, L2.

______. "An Invitation to 'The Dinner Party.'" *Chicago Tribune,* 6 September 1981, sec. 12, 1, 4.

Lippard, Lucy R. "Getting Hers." *Ms.* 4, no. 2, August 1975, 42–43.

______. *From the Center: Feminist Essays on Women's Art.* New York: E.P. Dutton & Co., 1976.

______. *Eva Hesse.* New York: New York University Press, 1976.

______. "Dinner Party a Four-Star Treat." *Seven Days,* 27 April 1979, 27–29.

______. "Judy Chicago's 'Dinner Party.'" *Art in America* 68, no. 4 (April 1980), 114–26.

______. "Born Again." *Village Voice,* 16 April 1985, 96. JCCSL, Box 2, Folder 18.

______. "Long Labor for the Birth Project." *In These Time* 1911, 29 (May/June 1985), 20–21. JCCSL, Box 2, Folder 18.

______. *The Pink Glass Swan: Selected Essays on Women's Art.* New York: New Press, 1995.

______. "Uninvited Guests: How Washington Lost 'The Dinner Party.'" *Art in America* 79 (December 1991), 39–47.

Litt, Stephen. "Chicago the Artist Paints with a Windy Brush." *Cleveland Plain Dealer,* 4 May 1996, 8E, 12E.

Logan, Paul. "Artists Trade Santa Fe for Historic Belen Hotel." *Albuquerque Journal,* 15 July 1993, A1, A9.

Longcope, Kay. "A Judy Chicago Project." *Boston Globe,* 8 May 1985, 77–78.

Lord, M. G. "The Table Is Set at Last, in a Home." *New York Times,* 8 September 2002, 78, 82.

Lott, Jane. "Women Put in Their Plate." *Observer* (London), 10 March 1985.

Lown, Bella. *Memories of My Life: A Personal History of a Lithuanian Shtetl.* Malibu, Calif.: Joseph Simon Pangloss Press, 1991.
Lozowick, Louis. *100 Contemporary American and Jewish Painters and Sculptors.* New York: YKUF Publishers, 1938.
Lucie-Smith, Edward. *Judy Chicago: An American Vision.* New York: Watson-Guptill Publications, 2000.
Lumpkin, Libby. "Unintended (PH)Allacies: A Feminist Reading of 'Sexual Politics.'" *Art Issues,* September/October 1996, 21–25.
Lyons, Harriet. "Organizing How 'The Dinner Party' Got to Houston, Boston, and New York." *Ms.,* November 1980, 91–92.
McColm, Del. "Artists Advised to Unite Against Gallery Controls." *Davis Enterprise,* 5 May 1978, Weekend.
McCormick, Ellen. "Judy Chicago: Feminist Art Show." *Portland Scribe,* 4–14 March 1976, 3.
McGiver, Ian. "American Civil Liberties Union." In *The Encyclopedia of Chicago,* ed. James R. Grossman and Ann Durkin Keating. Chicago: University of Chicago Press, 2004.
McGrath, Tom. *Witness to the Times: Poems by Thomas McGrath.* Los Angeles, 1953.
McGuigan, Cathleen. "A Shock Grows in Brooklyn." *Newsweek,* 11 October 1999, 68–70.
McMillan, Sue. "Women's Studies Courses." *Strait* 2, no. 8 (7 February 1973), 6–7.
McQuiston, Eleanor. *A History of Temple Judah of Cedar Rapids.* Cedar Rapids, Ia.: Temple Judah, 1989.
McShine, Kynaston. *Primary Structures: Younger American and British Sculptors.* New York: Jewish Museum, 1966.
Manger, Barbara. "Metamorphosis." *Midwest Art* 1, no. 1 (February 1975): 2.
Marder, Herbert. *Feminism and Art: A Study of Virginia Woolf.* Chicago: University of Chicago Press, 1972.
Marmor, Kalmon. *David Edelstadt.* New York: YKUF Farlag, 1950.
Marnham, Patrick. *Dreaming with His Eyes Open: A Life of Diego Rivera.* New York: Alfred A. Knopf, 1998.
Marsh, Ann. "A Theoretical and Political Context." In *Feminism-Art-Theory,* ed. Hilary Robinson. Oxford, U.K.: Blackwell Publishers, 1985.
Martin, Dale. "Birth Project Kept Needleworkers in Stitches." *San Mateo Times,* 17 April 1985, B1.
Mattera, Joanne. "The Dinner Party: A Symbol of Our Heritage (Review)." *East West Journal,* January 1980, 81–82.
May, Elaine Tyler. "Explosive Issues: Sex, Women, and the Bomb War." In *Recasting America: Culture and Politics in the Age of Cold War,* ed. Lary May. Chicago: University of Chicago Press, 1989.
Mays, John Bentley. "Epic Dinner Party Strikes to the Core." *Toronto Globe and Mail,* 22 May 1982, Entertainment sec., 11.
Mazur, Edward Herbert. *Minyans for a Prairie City: The Politics of Chicago Jewry, 1850–1940.* New York: Garland Publishing, 1990.
Mead, George Herbert. *Mind, Self and Society, from the Standpoint of a Social Behaviourist.* Chicago: University of Chicago Press, 1934.
Mendelsohn, Ezra. "Regional Factors in the Formation of the Jewish Labor Movement in Czarist Russia." In *Essential Papers on Jews and the Left,* ed. Ezra Mendelsohn. New York: New York University Press, 1997.
Mendes-Flohr, Paul, and Jehuda Reinharz. *The Jew in the Modern World: A Documentary History,* 2nd ed. New York: Oxford University Press, 1995.
Merzer, Meridee. "Art?" *Penthouse,* October 1975, 45–46.
Meyer, James. *Minimalism: Art and Polemics in the Sixties.* New Haven, Conn.: Yale University Press, 2001.
Meyer, Laura. "From Finish Fetish to Feminism: Judy Chicago's *Dinner Party* in California Art History." In *Sexual Politics: Judy Chicago's Dinner Party in Feminist Art History,* ed. Amelia Jones. Berkeley: University of California Press, 1996.
______. "A Monumental Meal." *Gadfly* 1, no. 7 (September 1997), 6–11.
Michaelson, Judith. "Time for L.A. to Feast on 'Dinner'?" *Los Angeles Times,* 24 December 1984, sec. 6, 1, 10.
Miller, Arthur. *A View from the Bridge: A Play in Two Acts.* London: Crescent Press, 1957.
Miller, Nory. "Judy Chicago, a Partisan Painter in Feminist Hues." *Chicago Daily News,* 14–15 September 1974, 13.
Millett, Kate. "Sexual Politics." In *Sexual Politics.* Garden City, N.Y.: Doubleday, 1970.
Mills, Paul C. *Spray.* Santa Barbara, Calif.: Santa Barbara Museum of Art, 1971.
Mishler, Paul C. *Raising Reds: The Young Pioneers, Radical Summer Camps, and Communist Political Culture in the United States.* New York: Columbia University Press, 1999.
Mogul, Susan. "Susan Mogul." In *Women of Vision: Histories in Feminist Film and Video,* ed. Alexandra Juhasz. Minneapolis: University of Minnesota Press, 2001.
Monk, Linda. "How Can Birth Be Embarrassing?" *Washington Post,* 8 June 1985.
Morgan, Robin. "No More Miss America!" In *Sisterhood is Powerful: An Anthology of Writings*

from the Women's Liberation Movement, New York: Vintage Books, 1970.
Morrison, Don. "Judy Chicago's Art Boils to Proclaim Judy Chicago, Woman." *Minneapolis Star,* 9 January 1975, 2C.
Muchnic, Suzanne. "An Intellectual Famine at Judy Chicago's Feast." *Los Angeles Times Book Review,* 15 April 1979, 3.
______. "Inside Look at Museum Policy." *Los Angeles Times,* 27 July 1981, sec. 4, 1, 4.
______. "Gallery Serves up Divergent Fare." *Los Angeles Times,* 25 February 1985, Sec. 6, 1, 9.
______. "The Galleries: Wilshire Center." *Los Angeles Times,* 8 April 1988, sec. 4, 22.
Munro, Eleanor. *Originals: American Women Artists.* New York: Simon & Schuster, 1979.
Murdock, Maureen. *Father's Daughters: Transforming the Father-Daughter Relationship.* New York: Fawcett Columbine, 1994.
Nelson, Robert. "Letters: Chicago Vs. Muchnic." *Los Angeles Times Book Review,* 29 April 1979, 1, 2.
Nemser, Cindy. "The Women's Conference at the Corcoran." *Art in America* 50 (January/February 1973), 86–90.
______. *Conversations with 12 Women Artists.* New York: Charles Scribner's Sons, 1975.
Nielsen, Nancy. "Show Chicago's Art." *Chicago Tribune,* 30 August 1979, B2.
Niger, Shmuel. "Yiddish Literature and the Female Reader." In *Women of the Word: Jewish Women and Jewish Writing,* ed. Judith R. Baskin. Detroit: Wayne State University Press, 1994.
Nin, Anaïs. *The Delta of Venus.* New York: Harcourt, 1969.
Nochlin, Linda. "Why Have There Been No Great Women Artists?" *ARTnews* 69, no. 9 (January 1971).
______. "Miriam Schapiro: Recent Work," *Arts Magazine* 48 (November 1973), 38–41.
Northrup, JoAnne Severns. "Judy Chicago." In *Finish Fetish: LA's Cool School,* ed. Frances Colpitt. Los Angeles: Fisher Gallery, University of Southern California, 1991.
Novak, Estelle Gershgoren, ed. *Poets of the Non-Existent City: Los Angeles in the McCarthy Era.* Albuquerque: University of New Mexico Press, 2002.
Nutkiewicz, Michael. "Watching Evolution of a Challenging Work." *Cleveland Jewish News,* 7 January 1994.
O'Hara, Frank. *Jackson Pollock.* New York: George Braziller, 1959.
Ohpir, Adi. "On Sanctifying the Holocaust: An Anti-Theological Treatise." In *Impossible Images: Contemporary Art After the Holocaust,* ed. Laura Levitt, Shelly Hornstein, and Lawrence J. Silberstein. New York: New York University Press, 2004.
Omer-Sherman, Ranen. " 'Thy People Are My People': Emma Lazarus, Daniel Deronda, and the Ambivalence of Jewish Modernity.' " *Journal of Modern Jewish Studies* 1, no. 1 (May 2002), 59–60.
Orvino, Jennie. "Judy Chicago: Opening of the Flower." *Amazon* 3, no. 6 (October 1974), 3.
Paffilas, Polly. "Folks Protest; Antiques Sale Returns." *Akron Beacon Journal,* 6 July 1983, B2.
Parker, Rozsika. *The Subversive Stitch.* London: Women's Press, 1984.
Pascal, Julia. "Judy Chicago." *City Limits,* 22–28 March 1985.
Patai, Raphael. *The Hebrew Goddess,* 3rd ed. Detroit, Mich.: Wayne State University Press, 1990.
Patterson, Charles. *The Eternal Treblinka: Our Treatment of Animals.* New York: Lantern Books, 2002.
Patterson, David. *The Hebrew Novel in Czarist Russia.* Lanham, Md.: Rowman & Littlefield, 1964.
Perreault, John. "No Reservations." *SoHo News,* 22 October 1980, 19.
______. "Who's Afraid of Vagina Woolf?" *Nyartsmagazine.Com,* 15 April 2003. Online at http://nyartsmagazine.com/71/afraid.htm.
Pincus, Lily. *Death and the Family: The Importance of Mourning.* New York: Pantheon Books, 1974.
Plagens, Peter. "Judith Gerowitz, Rolf Nelson Gallery." *Artforum* 4, no. 7 (March 1966), 14.
______. "Judy Gerowitz, Rolf Nelson Gallery." *Artforum* 4, no. 8 (April 1966), 14.
Plett, Nicole. "Artist Attacks Stereotypes in Bronze Now." *Albuquerque Journal,* 13 July 1986. JCCSL, Box 2, Folder 20.
Pogrebin, Letty Cottin. "Anti-Semitism in the Women's Movement." *Ms.* June 1982, 66.
Pomrenze, Seymour Jacob. "Aspects of Chicago: Russian-Jewish Life, 1893–1915." In *The Chicago Pinkas,* comp. and ed. Simon Rawidowicz. Chicago: College of Jewish Studies, 1952.
Pratt, Norma Fain. "Culture and Radical Politics: Yiddish Women Writers in America, 1890–1940." In *Women of the Word: Jewish Women and Jewish Writing,* ed. Judith R. Baskin. Detroit: Wayne State University Press, 1994.
Prentice, Kathy. "Women's Work Comes to State: 'The Birth Project.' " *Detroit Free Press,* 20 February 1986, B1, B3.
Pruden, Walter. "A Big Dinner Bell, but No Groceries." *Washington Times,* 20 July 1990.
Quaintance, Alice. "Some Images of Judy Chicago Relating to Women and Women Relating to Judy Chicago." *Pandora,* June 1976, 9.
Rabbinical Assembly of America. *Sabbath and*

Festival Prayer Book. United Synagogue of America, 1946, reprinted 1955.

Raven, Arlene. "Feminist Content in Current Female Art." *Sister Magazine: West Coast Feminist Newspaper* 6 (October/November 1975), 10.

______. *Metamorphosis.* Minneapolis: College of St. Catherine, 1975.

______, and Susan Rennie. "The Dinner Party Project: An Interview with Judy Chicago." *Chrysalis* 1, no. 4 (1977), 89–101.

______. *At Home.* Long Beach, Calif.: Long Beach Museum of Art, 1983.

______. *Crossing Over: Feminism and Art of Social Concern.* Ann Arbor, Mich.: UMI Research Press, 1988.

______. "Judy Chicago: The Artist Critics Love to Hate." *On the Issues* 3, no. 3 (Summer 1994), 35–40.

Rice, Robin. "Having My Baby: It's Been a Tough Labor and Delivery for Judy Chicago's 'Birth Project.'" *Philadelphia City Paper,* 19–26 September 1986, 11–13.

Richard, Paul. "'Birth Project': Fetal Visions." *Washington Post,* 28 May 1985, D7.

Richards, Margaret. "Galleries: Judy Chicago." *Socialist Tribune,* May 1975.

Richardson, Bill. "The Dinner Party." *Congressional Record* 138 (19 February 1992), E333–34.

Rickert, Shirley Kassman. "Thoughts on Feminist Art." *Strait* 2, no. 8 (7–21 February 1973), 15–18.

Rico, Diane. "Project Gives Birth to Widespread Interest." *Los Angeles Daily News,* 27 March 1985, L.A. Life sec., 15, 18.

Rischin, Moses. *The Promised City: New York's Jews 1870–1914.* Cambridge, Mass.: Harvard University Press, 1962.

Robbins, Corinne. "Object, Structure or Sculpture: Where Are We?" *Arts Magazine* 40, no. 9 (September–October 1966), 36.

Robertson, Nan. "4,500 Guests, Most of Them Women, Answer 'The Dinner Party' Invitation." *New York Times,* 18 October 1980.

Robinson, Gaile. "The Man Behind Gauguin." *Dallas Star-Telegram,* December 2005.

Robinson, Hilary, ed. *Feminism-Art-Theory: An Anthology, 1968–2000.* Oxford: Blackwell Publishers, 2001.

Robinson, Nancy. "The Great Ladies." *Sister: Los Angeles Feminist Newspaper* 4, no. 11 (January 1974).

Rolf, Ida P. *The Integration of Human Structures.* New York: Harper & Row, 1977.

Rorty, James. "The Anti-Communism of Senator McCarthy: It Slays More Friends Than Foes." *Commentary* 16, no. 2 (August 1953), 122–29.

Rosch, Leah. "Hard Labor: Judy Chicago Delivers the Birth Project." *Boston Phoenix,* 14 May 1985, 6–7. JCCSL, Box 2, Folder 18.

Rose, Barbara. *Claes Oldenburg.* New York: Museum of Modern Art, 1970.

______. "Vaginal Iconography." *New York* 7 (11 February 1974), 59.

Rose, Martha. "Feminist Wants Women to See Art in Terms of Own Experience." *Minneapolis Star,* 5 April 1973.

Rosenberg, Harold. "Is There a Jewish Art?" In *Discovering the Present.* Chicago: University of Chicago Press, 1973.

Rosenfeld, Alvin H. "The Americanization of the Holocaust." *Commentary* 99, no. 6 (June 1995), 35–40.

Rosten, Leo. *The Joys of Yiddish.* New York: McGraw-Hill, 1968.

Roth, Moira. *The Shrine, The Computer and the Dollhouse: Miriam Schapiro.* La Jolla, Calif.: Mandeville Art Gallery, University of California at San Diego, 1975.

______. *The Amazing Decade: Women and Performance Art in America, 1970–1980.* Los Angeles: Astro Artz, 1983.

______, ed. *Conversations: Interviews with 28 Bay Area Women Artists.* Oakland, Calif.: Mills College, 1988.

Rountree, Cathleen. *Coming into Our Fullness. On Women Turning Forty:* Freedom, Calif.: Crossing Press, 1991.

Rowley, Hazel. *Richard Wright: The Life and Times.* New York: Henry Holt & Co., 2001.

Rubin, Sylvia. "The Birth Project." *San Francisco Chronicle,* 3 April 1985, 23.

Rubin, William S. *Frank Stella.* New York: Museum of Modern Art, 1970.

Ruchames, Louis. "Jewish Radicalism in the United States." In *The Ghetto and Beyond: Essays on Jewish Life in America,* ed. Peter I. Rose. New York: Random House, 1969.

Rudin, A. James. "Beersheba, Kan. 'God's Pure Air on Government Land.'" *Topeka, Kansas, Historical Society* 34 (1968), 282–98.

Rynn, Berry. *Hitler: Neither Vegetarian nor Animal Lover.* New York: Pythagorean Books, 2004.

Sabbath, Lawrence. "Dinner Party Serves Up History of Women's Struggle." *Montreal Gazette,* 20 March 1982, B7.

______. "The Tough, Fragile Artist Behind 'The Dinner Party.'" *Montreal Gazette,* 17 April 1982, A1, A4.

Sackler, Elizabeth A., ed. *Judy Chicago.* New York: Watson-Guptill, 2002.

Saltzstein, Katherine. "Judy Chicago Recreates Hill in Watercolor." *News-Bulletin* (Valencia County, N.M.), 9–10 June 1999, Weekend sec., 6A.

Sanchez, Arley. "Man Lends Talent to Art." *Journal South* (New Mexico), 11 May 2000, 1, 2.

Sanders, Ronald. *Shores of Refuge: A Hundred Years*

of Jewish Emigration. New York: Henry Holt & Co., 1988.

Schapiro, Miriam. "Miriam Schapiro Interviewed by Judith Dancoff." *Everywoman* 2, no. 7, issue 18 (7 May 1971), 3.

______. "Education of Women as Artists: Project *Womanhouse*." *Art Journal* 31, no. 3 (Spring 1972), 268–70.

Schillinger, Liesl. "Beyond the Flower: The Autobiography of a Feminist Artist." *New York Times*, 24 March 1996, sec. 7, 21.

Schneider, Susan Weidman. *Jewish and Female: Choices and Changes in Our Lives Today.* New York: Simon and Schuster, 1984.

Schor, Mira. "A Plague of Polemics." *Art Journal* 50, no. 4 (Winter 1991), 36–41.

Schrank, Sarah. "The Art of the City: Modernism, Censorship, and the Emergence of Los Angeles's Postwar Art Scene." *American Quarterly* 56, no. 3 (September 2004), 663–91.

Schwarz, Karl. *Jewish Artists of the 19th and 20th Centuries.* New York: Philosophical Library, 1949.

Seaman, Donna. "Beyond the Flower (Book Review)." *Booklist* 92 (1 March 1996), 1116.

Segal, Lewis. "Lewitzky's Feminist Statement." *Los Angeles Times*, 23 September 1996, F5.

Seitz, William C. *Art in the Age of Aquarius: 1955–1970.* Washington, D.C.: Smithsonian Institution, 1992.

Seldis, Henry J. "Technology for Art's Sake." *Los Angeles Times* (1967), 17–18, JCCSL, Box 43.

Selz, Peter, and William Wilson. "Los Angeles—A View from the Studios." *Art in America* (1969), 144.

Shepherd, Michael. "The Woman's Work That's Never Done." *Sunday Telegraph* (London), 14 April 1985.

Shinn, Dorothy. "The Gospel According to Judy Chicago." *Beacon, The Sunday Magazine of the Akron Beacon*, 5 July 1981, 4–7, 15.

Shirey, David L. "Visual Arts Hears from Women's Lib." *New York Times*, 23 April 1972, 63.

Shuldiner, David P. *Of Moses and Marx: Folk Ideology and Folk History in the Jewish Labor Movement.* Westport, Conn.: Bergin & Garvey, 1999.

Shulman, Irving. *The Amboy Dukes: A Novel of Wayward Youth in Brooklyn.* New York: Avon, 1946.

Silverman, William J. "Patient Care to the Community." In *The Sentinel's History of Chicago Jewry 1911–1961*, ed. Anita Libman et al. Chicago: Sentinel, 1961.

Simon, Clea. *The Feline Mystique.* New York: St. Martin's Press, 2002.

Sinclair, Molly, and Jo Ann Lewis. "UDC to Renovate Library for Controversial Artwork." *Washington Post*, 19 July 1990, D1, D5.

Smith, Barbara. "The Female Sexuality/Female Identity Exhibition." *Womanspace* 1, no. 2 (April/May 1973), 23–27, 34.

______. "Wanda Westcoast & Judy Chicago at 707." *Womanspace* 1, no. 2 (April/May 1973), 29–30.

Smith, Elizabeth A., ed. *Lee Bontecou.* Chicago: Chicago Museum of Contemporary Art, 2004.

Smith, Roberta. "For a Paean to Heroic Women, a Place at History's Table." *New York Times*, 20 September 2002, E34.

Smith, Wes. "Scraps from The Dinner Party." *Atlanta Journal*, 28 July 1982, 1B.

Sokolov, Raymond. "Ritual, Myth and Romance on the Santa Fe Trail." *Wall Street Journal*, 5 August 1983, 21.

Solanas, Valerie. *Scum Manifesto.* New York: Olympia Press, 1968.

Sorin, Gerald. *The Prophetic Minority: American Jewish Immigrant Radicals, 1880–1920.* Bloomington: Indiana University Press, 1985.

Sorkin, Jenni. *Minimal/Liminal: Judy Chicago and Minimalism: 1965–1973.* Santa Fe: Lew Allen Contemporary, 2004.

Spitalnick, Lou. "Judy Chicago's 'Dinner Party.'" *New York Post*, October 1980, D1, D4.

Stein, Judith. "Judy Chicago at Kenmore." *Art in America*, July–August 1974.

Steinberg, Peter L. *The Great "Red Menace": United States Prosecution of American Communists, 1947–1952.* Westport, Conn.: Greenwood Press, 1984.

Stern, Sydney L. *Gloria Steinem: Her Passions, Politics, and Mystique.* New York: Birch Lane Press, 1997.

Stevens, Elisabeth. "'Dinner Party' Is Essentially a Political Statement." *Baltimore Sun*, 11 May 1980, D13.

Stevens, Mark. "Guess Who's Coming to Dinner." *Newsweek*, 2 April 1979, 92.

Stocking, Susan. "Through the Looking Glass with Judy Chicago." *Los Angeles Times*, 9 July 1972, 18.

Stofflet-Santiago, Mary. "Judy Chicago Ceramics." *Artweek*, 26 January 1976.

Storch, Randi. "Communist Party." In *The Encyclopedia of Chicago*, ed. James R. Grossman and Ann Durkin Keating. Chicago: University of Chicago Press, 2004.

Sutinen, Paul, and Catherine Wood. "Judy Chicago Explodes Feminine Mystique in Art." *Williamette Week*, September 8, 1975, 12.

Sweets, Ellen. "The Chicago Story: Artist's 'Dinner Party' Was Going Well in D.C.,

Until Congress Crashed It." *Dallas Morning News,* 16 September 1990, 1C.
Swift, Harriet. "Judy Chicago Delivers Her 'Birth Project.'" *Tribune* Oakland, California, 1 April 1985, C1, C3.
Sword, Judy. "Feminist Art-Leader Seduces Crowd." *ATHAPASCAN* (Southwestern College) 2 (24 March 1972), 1.
Szajkowski, Zosa. *Jews, Wars, and Communism.* New York: Ktav, 1972.
Tarzan, Deloris. "Artists Have 'Psychic Relati[onship].'" *Seattle Times,* 18 May 1976, B8.
Taylor, Robert. "'The Dinner Party' Somewhat Unappetizing." *Boston Globe,* 3 July 1980, 18.
Temin, Christine. "Judy Chicago's Unintended Horror; *Holocaust Project: From Darkness into Light by Judy Chicago with Photography by Donald Woodman.*" *Boston Globe,* 22 September 1995, 51.
Tennant, Donna. "A Monumental Work of Art." *Houston Chronicle,* 9 March 1980, 14.
______. "'Right Out of History': A Remarkable Story." *Houston Chronicle,* 9 March 1980, 14.
Terbell, Melinda. "Judy Chicago at Grand View One." *ARTnews,* February 1974.
Terwoman, Beverly. "The Dinner Party." *Pacific Sun,* 20–26 April 1979, 5–7, 27.
Thompson, Christina. "The Dinner Party." January 1988. JCCSL, Box 2, Folder 25.
Tousley, Nancy. "Judy Chicago's Dinner Party Rewrites Women's History." *Calgary Herald,* 22 November 1980.
Traver, Nancy. "Judy Chicago's Art Stands Test of Time." *WOMANNEWS,* 11 December 2002, 1, 8.
Trilling, James. "Judy Chicago: A Beacon Letter to the Editor." *New York Times,* 22 September 2002, Arts & Leisure sec., 4.
Tuchman, Maurice. "Introduction." In *American Sculpture of the Sixties,* ed. Maurice Tuchman Los Angeles: Los Angeles Museum of Art, 1967.
Tucker, Marcia. *The Structure of Color.* New York: Whitney Museum of American Art, 1971.
Viera, Ricardo, and Laurence J. Silberstein. *Holocaust Project: From Darkness into Light.* Bethlehem, Pa.: Zoellner Arts Center, Lehigh University, 2000.
Vital, David. *Zionism: The Formative Years.* Oxford: Clarendon Press, 1982.
von Buchau, Stephanie. "The Dinner Party." *Pacific Sun,* 20–26 April 1979, 5.
Wadler, Joyce. "Public Lives: Uncovering Art in the Act of Being Spied Upon." *New York Times,* 2 October 2002, 2.
Wald, Alan M. *The New York Intellectuals: The Rise and Decline of the Anti-Stalinist Left from the 1930s to the 1980s.* Chapel Hill: University of North Carolina Press, 1987.
Wald, Lillian D. *Windows on Henry Street.* Boston: Little, Brown, & Co., 1936.
Walker, Alice. *In Search of Our Mother's Gardens.* San Diego: Harcourt, Brace, Jovanovitch, 1983.
Walker, Margaret. *Richard Wright: Daemonic Genius.* New York: Warner Books, 1988.
Weiler, N. Sue. "State of the Union: A Brief History of Jewish Involvement in Chicago's Labor Movement From 1886." *Western States Jewish History* 31, no. 1 (Fall 1998).
Weinstein, Natalie. "After 'Dinner Party,' Judy Chicago Feasts on Judaism." *Northern California Jewish Bulletin,* 14 June 1996, 29, 31.
Welch, Tom. "Socialists Stir at UCLA, Radicals Pass Out Colored Circulars." *UCLA Daily Bruin,* 7 October 1957, 7.
Welland, Sasha S. "The Long March to Lugu Lake: A Dialogue with Judy Chicago." *Yishu Journal of Contemporary Chinese Art* 1, no. 3 (November 2002).
Wells, Maureen. "Interview with Diane Gelon." *What She Wants* 8, no. 10 (May 1981), 6, 12.
Wiegand, Kate. *Red Feminism: American Communism and the Making of Women's Liberation.* Baltimore: Johns Hopkins University Press, 2001.
Wiesel, Elie. "Art and the Holocaust: Trivializing Memory." *New York Times,* 11 June 1989, sec. 2.
Wilding, Faith. *By Our Own Hands: The Woman Artist's Movement in Southern California, 1970–1976.* Santa Monica, Calif.: Double X, 1977.
______. "The Feminist Art Programs at Fresno and Cal Arts, 1970–75." In *The Power of Feminist Art,* ed. Norma Broude and Mary Garrard. New York: Harry N. Abrams, 1994.
Willis, Ellen. "Ellen Willis." *Village Voice,* 5–11 November 1980, 32.
Wilson, Sharon Rose. *Margaret Atwood's Fairy-Tale Sexual Politics.* Toronto: ECW Press, 1993.
Wilson, William. "Judy Gerowitz Sculpture in Pasadena." *Los Angeles Times,* 18 May 1969, 48.
______. "Judy Chicago Exhibition at Cal State Fullerton Gallery." *Los Angeles Times,* 2 November 1970, sec. 4.
______. "A Vague Unfreedom in Feminist Works." *Los Angeles Times,* 9 April 1972, 56.
______. "China Painting: A Revived Craft." *Los Angeles Times,* 5 December 1977, sec. 4, 3.
______. "Art Walk: La Cienega Area." *Los Angeles Times,* 28 January 1977, sec. 4, 6.
Withers, Josephine. "Feminist Performance Art: Performing, Discovering, Transforming Ourselves." In *The Power of Feminist Art,*

ed. Norma Broude and Mary Garrard. New York: Harry N. Abrams, 1994.
Wolfe, Clair. "Los Angeles; Painted Sculpture." *Artforum* 2, no. 11 (May 1954), 12.
Wolff, Janet. *Postmodernism and Society.* London: Macmillan, 1990.
" 'Womanhouse' Opens." *Los Angeles Free Press.* 4 February 1972.
Wong, Edward. " 'Brutality as a Performance Art'." *New York Times,* 27 January 2002.
Woo, Elaine. "Discrimination Behind the Brush: Women Artists Complain of Second-Class Status." *Los Angeles Herald Examiner,* 12 March 1978, E9.
Woolf, Virginia. *To the Lighthouse.* New York: Harcourt, 1927.
______. *Orlando: A Biography.* New York: Harcourt Brace, 1928.
______. 1929. *A Room of One's Own.* New York: Harcourt, Brace, & World.
______. *Three Guineas.* London: Hogarth Press, 1938.
Wootten, Dick. "Judy Chicago Show Is Profitable Dinner Party." *Cleveland Press,* 7 August 1981, D24.
Wortz, Melinda. *Beth Ames Swartz Inquiry into Fire.* Scottsdale, Ariz.: Scottsdale Center for the Arts, 1978.
Wright, Richard. "Lawd Today!" In *Early Works: Lawd Today! Uncle Tom's Children, Native Son.* Notes by Arnold Rampersad. New York: Library of America, 1991.
Wylder, Viki D. T. *Trials and Tributes.* Tallahassee, Fla.: Florida State University, 1999.
Yezierska, Anzia. *Breadgivers.* New York: Persea Books, 1925.
Zack, Margaret. "China Painting and Feminism?" *Picture Magazine* (Minneapolis Tribune), 16 February 1975, 10–17.
Zinberg, Israel. *A History of Jewish Literature,* vol. 11, *The Haskalah Movement in Russia.* New York: Ktav., 1978.
Zolotow, Maurice. "The 78 Most Interesting People in Los Angeles." *Los Angeles Magazine* 59 (November 1979), 201–7.
Zucker, Bat-Ami. "American Jewish Communists and Jewish Culture in the 1930s." *Modern Judaism* 14 (1994).

SELECTED FILMOGRAPHY

Amend, Kate. *From Darkness Into Light: The Making of the Holocaust Project.* 1994. 29 minutes.
Dancoff, Judith. *Judy Chicago and the California Girls.* 1970.
Demetrakas, Johanna. *Womanhouse.* Phoenix Films, 1974. 47 minutes.
______. *Right Out of History: The Making of Judy Chicago's Dinner Party.* Phoenix Films, 1980. 60 minutes.
Kupcinet, Irv. *The Kup's Show.* Guests Roy Cohn, Judy Chicago, and Christopher Anderson. WTTW, Chicago, 1981. Video.

NOTES

Introduction: What's in a Name?

1. Edward Wong, "Brutality as a Performance Art," *New York Times,* 27 January 2002, 20.
2. Judy Chicago, *Through the Flower: My Struggle as a Woman Artist* (New York: Doubleday, 1975), 63; Judy Chicago, *Beyond the Flower: The Autobiography of a Feminist Artist* (New York: Viking Penguin, 1996), 20.
3. Vicky Chen Haider, "Chicago's Butterfly," *Chicago Sun-Times,* 19 June 1975, sec. 2, 81.
4. Anonymous, "Judy Gerowitz, Rolf Nelson Gallery," *Artforum* 4, no. 8 (April 1966), 14.
5. Chicago, *Beyond the Flower,* 16.
6. Joe Goode, interview by author, 2 February 2005.
7. Judy Chicago to author, 21 July 2004.
8. Alona Hamilton Cooke, interview by author, 14 January 2004, Venice, Calif.
9. Chuck Arnoldi, interview by author, 8 January 2004, Venice, Calif.
10. Jerry McMillan, interview by author, 31 January 2005.
11. Craig Krull, *Photographing the L.A. Art Scene, 1955–1975* (Santa Monica, Calif.: Smart Art Press, 1996), 78.
12. McMillan interview.
13. Agnes Diggs, "Clue Offers New Hope for Solving 1977 Murder," *Los Angeles Times,* 9 March 1999. When it opened in 1933 at 318 South Main Street in L.A., it was called the Spring Street Newsboys' Gym. Later, known as the Main Street Gym, it remained the most important training ground for L.A. boxers until Steindler's murder in 1977, which is still unsolved. See also http://www.lapdonline.org/press_releases/2002/03/pr02137.htm.
14. Robert Jablon, "Hope Rekindled in Murder Case: Police Reopen Probe Involving Boxing Trainer," *Pasadena Star-News,* 10 March 1999, A6.
15. Lisa Bloom, "Ethnic Notions and Feminist Strategies of the 1970s," *Jewish Identity in Modern Art History,* ed. Catherine M. Soussloff (Berkeley: University of California Press, 1999), 136, 139. This article appeared three years after I began my research. I agree with Bloom about the importance of Jewish ethnicity for feminist art, if not with many of her particulars, among them her inclusion of Carolee Schneemann as a Jewish feminist artist. My interview with Schneemann, 10 August 2002, confirms that she was born in Fox Chase, Pennsylvania, of Protestant parents and raised in the Quaker tradition. Joe Goode says that Judy "couldn't have tried to deny who she was," that it wouldn't have been her character.
16. George Eliot, *Daniel Deronda,* as quoted by Judy Chicago on her drawing in the series *Compressed Women Who Yearned to Be Butterflies,* 1973.
17. Chicago, *Through the Flower,* 3.
18. Goode interview. The photograph of Joe Goode on the cover was taken in January 1970. See Krull, *Photographing,* 63.
19. Krull, *Photographing,* 78.

Early Childhood in Chicago 1

1. William J. Silverman, "Patient Care to the Community," in *The Sentinel's History of Chicago Jewry, 1911–1961,* ed. Anita Libman et al. (Chicago: Sentinel, 1961), 196.
2. Irving Cutler, *The Jews of Chicago* (Urbana: University of Illinois Press, 1996), 235.
3. Irving Cutler, *Chicago: Metropolis of the Mid-Continent* (Dubuque, Ia.: Kendall/Hunt), 73.
4. Irving Cutler, "West Side Story: Remembering the Days When Lawndale Was Where It, and We, Were At," *Jewish United Fund News,* May 1988, 16.
5. This date, which Chicago no longer recalls, is according to the FBI file for Judy Sylvia Cohen, 3-6-59, Los Angeles, Calif. Their marriage license number is 1480-416. May Levinson Cohen was born April 3, 1911. Arthur Melvin Cohen was born July 23, 1909.
6. Judy Chicago, *A Jewish Journal,* unpublished handwritten manuscript, (1985–93), 71, October 1986. JCCSL, Box 72, Folders 23–38. Judy

wrote in her *Jewish Journal* that Bertha came from Vilna, and "she came over here alone as a young woman." According to the U.S. Census for both 1920 and 1930, Bertha Cason Levinson was born in Poland and came to the United States in 1906.

7. Judy Chicago to author, 22 March 2001. The U.S. census for 1920 documents that Harry Levinson was the proprietor of a leather goods shop. May was then eight and Dora (Dorothy) was five. The family lived on Cortez Street in the Humboldt Park neighborhood of Chicago.
8. See Shaul Lipschitz, "Jewish Communities in Kurland," in *The Jews in Latvia,* ed. M. Bebe et al. (Tel Aviv: Association of Latvian and Estonian Jews in Israel, 1971), 276–85. See excerpt on Internet site: www.jewishgen.org/Courland/lipschitz.htm.
9. See Erich Haberer, *Jews and Revolution in Nineteenth-Century Russia* (Cambridge, England: Cambridge University Press, 1995), and Benjamin Harshav, *Language in Time of Revolution (Contraversions: Jews and Other Differences)* (Palo Alto, Calif.: Stanford University Press, 1993), 134.
10. Judy Chicago to author, letter of 22 March 2001.
11. Moses Rischin, *The Promised City: New York's Jews, 1870–1914* (Cambridge, Mass.: Harvard University Press, 1962), 27.
12. Bella Lown, *Memories of My Life: A Personal History of a Lithuanian Shtetl* (Malibu, Calif.: Joseph Simon Pangloss Press, 1991), 10.
13. Leoni Zverow McVey to author, 21 October 2002.
14. Judy Chicago, *Through the Flower: My Struggle as a Woman Artist,* 2nd ed. (New York: Penguin Books, 1975), 3.
15. Judy Chicago, *Beyond the Flower: The Autobiography of a Feminist Artist* (New York: Viking Penguin, 1996), 4; Howard Rosen to author. The U.S. Census for 1910, 1920, and 1930 offer varied data on ages and dates of immigration that are somewhat inconsistent with dates accepted by the extended Cohen family. There may have been reasons to predate immigration, and, for women, to postdate the year of birth. Equally, claiming a U.S. birth rather than a foreign birth offered advantages. The 1910 census lists Rose Cohen, Ben and Anna's second daughter, as born in Iowa in 1890, long before the parents moved there.
16. The musician Elyokum Zunser, native of Vilna, wandered to Kovno, where he engaged in the embroidery trade before 1861. A. Z. Idelsohn, *Jewish Music in Its Historical Development* (New York: Tudor, 1944), 444.
17. Robert Colby, Meyer Cohn's son, interview by author, July 2000. Some of the Cohens spelled their name Cohn; Meyer's two sons changed their name to Colby.
18. Haberer, *Jews and Revolution,* 40.
19. Lown, *Lithuanian Shtetl,* 82.
20. Haberer, *Jews and Revolution,* 40. Salanter's many articles were published in collections such as *Imrei Binah* (Sayings of Wisdom), *Or Yisrael* (Light of Israel), and *Even Yisrael* (Rock of Israel).
21. Immanuel Etkes, *Rabbi Israel Salantner and the Mussar Movement: Seeking the Torah of Truth* (Philadelphia: Jewish Publication Society, 1993), 318.
22. Etkes, *Rabbi Israel Salantner,* 170–71.
23. After Salanter's death, the question of whether Mussar should become part of the yeshiva curriculum led to disputes, with many of the rabbis considering such study a waste of time that could better be spent studying the Talmud, and warning against too much moral introspection as psychologically unhealthy. The dispute among the pro- and anti-Mussar forces sometimes led yeshivas to split into two over the issue. In Slobodka the Yeshiva split into two in 1897, one Kneseth Yisrael, which emphasized Mussar, and the other Kneseth Yitzchak, which did not.
24. Haberer, *Jews and Revolution,* 40.
25. Arye Landau was later called [Arthur David] Landau by Enid Cohen Rosen, his granddaughter. Enid Cohen Rosen, interview by author, 14 August 2000. Judy Chicago to author, 18 December, 2005, says she always thought that her paternal grandparents' marriage was a love match but "that there were problems with the family reaction because they were first cousins." However, in practice, first cousins often married in Eastern European Jewish culture.
26. Israel Cohen, *Vilna* (Philadelphia: Jewish Publication Society of America, 1943), 339.
27. David Vital, *Zionism: The Formative Years* (Oxford: Clarendon Press, 1982), 168–69. Jews worked in the garment, food, wood, and metal trades.
28. Cohen, *Vilna,* 339. See also Nora Levin, *While Messiah Tarried: Jewish Socialist Movements, 1871–1917* (New York: Schocken Books, 1977), 228.
29. Vital, *Zionism: Formative Years,* 171.
30. Cohen, *Vilna,* xxiii.
31. I. Cohen and Louis Cohen appear in the Topeka City Directory beginning in 1890–91. Louis's son was the baseball player Sam Bohne (born in San Francisco in 1896 as Samuel Arthur Cohen; died 1977), who

played for the St. Louis Cardinals beginning in 1916.

32. A. James Rudin, "Beersheba, Kan. 'God's Pure Air on Government Land,'" *Topeka, Kansas, Historical Society* 34 (1968), 282–98.
33. Benjamin Peixotto, author of *Anglo-Jewish History,* in *American Israelite,* Cincinnati, February 18, 1887, as quoted ibid., 283.
34. Leon Kobrin, *A Lithuanian Village,* trans. Isaac Goldberg (New York: Brentano's, 1914), 156.
35. The first, B'nai Israel, was not founded until 1905, when the congregation numbered only fifteen members, presumably representing fifteen families, for only the men would be counted.
36. Ages according to the late Enid Cohen Rosen, interview by author, 14 August 2000.
37. Norma Fain Pratt, "Culture and Radical Politics: Yiddish Women Writers in America, 1890–1940," in *Women of the Word: Jewish Women and Jewish Writing,* ed. Judith R. Baskin (Detroit: Wayne State University Press, 1994), 121.
38. Susan A. Glenn, *Daughters of the Shtetl: Life and Labor in the Immigrant Generation* (Ithaca, N.Y.: Cornell University Press, 1990), 12.
39. Rose's daughter Ruth Levinson Psundstein told me that she was still afraid of cats because her mother told her this story as a child. Interview by author, 15 August 2000. On the old wives' tale, see Clea Simon, *The Feline Mystique* (New York: St. Martin's Press, 2002), 73.
40. Cohen, *Vilna,* 290–91.
41. Ibid., 341.
42. Rischin, *Promised City,* 45.
43. Cohen, *Vilna,* 342.
44. Ibid., 343. Ezra Mendelsohn, "Regional Factors in the Formation of the Jewish Labor Movement in Czarist Russia," in *Essential Papers on Jews and the Left,* ed. Ezra Mendelsohn (New York: New York University Press, 1997), 3.
45. Ronald Sanders, *Shores of Refuge: A Hundred Years of Jewish Emigration* (New York: Henry Holt & Co., 1988), 194.
46. This group probably included someone who knew of Benjamin Cohen from the yeshiva in Lithuania, then part of the Russian Empire, unless he responded from Topeka to an advertisement in a Yiddish newspaper.
47. Dale Kueter, "Anniversary Prompts History Project: Temple Judah Commissions 'People Story' of Jews in Cedar Rapids," *Cedar Rapids Gazette,* 25 March 1989, 7A.
48. Eleanor McQuiston, *A History of Temple Judah of Cedar Rapids* (Cedar Rapids, Ia.: Temple Judah, 1989), 5.
49. The drawing was in the synagogue until 1964, when the Original orthodox congregation merged with Temple Judah, a Reform congregation, and moved into a newly constructed temple. Judy Chicago visited and recalled seeing a drawing of praying hands, which she did not think was very well done.
50. See Cedar Rapids city directories for 1896, p. 64, which lists Mrs. Annie Cohen, notions; listing repeated in 1897, p. 64; 1900, p. 75. The 1901 directory lists "B.G. Dry Goods, as well as Gertrude, Rosa, and Tillie." The 1903 directory, p. 94, repeats this listing, but identifies Annie as an "agt.," presumably an agent for real estate, and their street number has changed from 43 to 46, which may just represent a renumbering.
51. Glenn, *Daughters of the Shtetl,* 86–87.
52. Shirley's son, Julian Schwartz, to author, 24 February 2005.
53. The *Gazette*'s Cedar Rapids City Directory 1904–5, 89.
54. The *Gazette*'s Cedar Rapids City Directory, 1906–7, 84. The *Gazette*'s Cedar Rapids City Directory, 1906, 94.
55. Chíah Pippa Landau Cohen was the daughter of Haskell (Chatzkill) Landau.
56. Howard Rosen, interview by author, 6 July 2004. Judy Chicago quoted in Robert A. Cohn, "Judy Chicago Describes Her Struggle as a Woman Artist," *St. Louis Jewish Light,* 9 April 1980, 7.
57. Quoted in Vivian Gornick, *The Romance of American Communism* (New York: Basic Books, 1977), 34.
58. Enid Cohen Rosen, interview by author, 27 February 2001. In *Chicago City Directory* for 1928–29, Arthur M. Cohen is listed as a "roomer" there. Judy's aunt Enid seems to have recalled a house on Rice Street that was always very noisy; Judy Chicago, *A Jewish Journal,* unpublished handwritten manuscript, JCCSL (1985–93), 11. JCCSL, Box 72, Folders 23–38.
59. Kobrin, *Lithuanian Village,* 80. Nahum Meyer Shaikevich Shomer (1849–1905) was the author of *shund* (trashy) novels written for a female readership. See also Shmuel Niger, "Yiddish Literature and the Female Reader," in *Women of the Word: Jewish Women and Jewish Writing,* ed. Judith R. Baskin (Detroit: Wayne State University Press, 1994), 82.
60. Kobrin, *Lithuanian Village,* 185.
61. Zosa Szajkowski, *Jews, Wars, and Communism* (New York: Ktav, 1972), 115.

62. Melech Epstein, *Jewish Labor in U.S.A., 1882–1914* (Miami Beach, Fla.: Ktav, 1969), ix.
63. Sholem Aleichem, "We Strike," in *The New Country,* ed. and trans. Henry Goodman (New York: YKUF, 1961), 85, as cited in Paul Buhle, *From the Lower East Side to Hollywood: Jews in American Popular Culture* (New York: Verso, 2004), 28.
64. Howard Rosen interview.
65. Julian Schwartz, son of Shirley Cohen Schwartz, interview by author, 11 August 2000.
66. Enid Cohen Rosen, interview by author, 27 February 2001. The name "Grand Avenue Synagogue" comes from Ruth Levinson Psundstein, daughter of Rose Cohen Levinson, Judy Chicago's aunt. Its location (across from the building at 1820 South Ridgeway in Chicago where his daughter, Shirley Cohen Schwartz [1902–1989], and her family lived) was told to me by her son, Julian Schwartz.
67. Ruth Levinson Psundstein, daughter of Shirley Cohen Schwartz, interview by author, 12 August 2000.
68. Ruth Levinson Psundstein, Rose Cohen Levinson's daughter, interview by author, 15 August 2000.
69. Seymour Jacob Pomrenze, "Aspects of Chicago Russian-Jewish Life, 1893–1915," in *The Chicago Pinkas,* comp. and ed. Simon Rawidowicz (Chicago: College of Jewish Studies, 1952), 127.
70. Mrs. Benjamin Davis, "Religious Activity, Chicago," quoted in Pomrenze, " 'Chicago Russian-Jewish Life,' " 128.
71. Ibid.
72. Buhle, *Jews in American Popular Culture,* 38–39.
73. Ibid., 161.
74. Ruth Levinson Psundstein, interview by author, 13 August 2000.
75. The Chicago city directory for 1928–29 lists James C. Curtis & Co., which sold undertaker supplies and was located at 1214–22 Van Buren. According to the FBI, the company that employed Arthur Cohen was James S. Curts Company, 1232 West North Avenue, Chicago.
76. Hazel Rowley, *Richard Wright: The Life and Times* (New York: Henry Holt & Co., 2001), 58.
77. Howard Rosen, son of Enid Cohen Rosen, Arthur's sister, interview by author, 9 August 2000.
78. Cutler, *Chicago: Metropolis,* 72.
79. Richard Wright, "Lawd Today!" in *Early Works: Lawd Today! Uncle Tom's Children, Native Son,* notes by Arnold Rampersad (New York: Library of America, 1991), 129.
80. Ibid., 149.
81. Ibid.
82. Cutler, *Jews of Chicago,* 129.
83. Edward Herbert Mazur, *Minyans for a Prairie City: The Politics of Chicago Jewry, 1850–1940* (New York: Garland, 1990), 309.
84. Ibid.
85. Ibid., 310.
86. Louis Ruchames, "Jewish Radicalism in the United States," in *The Ghetto and Beyond: Essays on Jewish Life in America,* ed. Peter I. Rose (New York: Random House, 1969), 245.
87. Bat-Ami Zucker, "American Jewish Communists and Jewish Culture in the 1930s," *Modern Judaism* 14 (1994): 182.
88. Randi Storch, "Communist Party," in *The Encyclopedia of Chicago,* ed. James R. Grossman and Ann Durkin Keating (Chicago: University of Chicago Press, 2004), 190.
89. Margaret Walker, *Richard Wright, Daemonic Genius* (New York: Warner Books, 1963), 63.
90. Richard Wright, "What Happens at a Communist Party Branch Meeting in the Harlem Section?" *Daily Worker,* 15 August 1937, as quoted in Rowley, *Richard Wright,* 128.
91. Paul C. Mishler, *Raising Reds: The Young Pioneers, Radical Summer Camps, and Communist Political Culture in the United States* (New York: Columbia University Press, 1999), and "Red Diapers," in *Red Diapers: Growing Up in the Communist Left,* ed. Judy Kaplan and Linn Shapiro (Champaign-Urbana: University of Illinois Press, 1998).
92. Henry L. Feingold, *The Jewish People in America* (Baltimore: Johns Hopkins University Press, 1992), 196.
93. Gornick, *Romance of American Communism,* 14–15.
94. Karl Baarslag, *History of the National Federation of Post Office Clerks* (Washington, D.C.: National Federation of Post Office Clerks, 1945), 179.
95. David P. Shuldiner, *Of Moses and Marx: Folk Ideology and Folk History in the Jewish Labor Movement* (Westport, Conn.: Bergin & Garvey, 1999), 141.
96. N. Sue Weiler, "State of the Union: A Brief History of Jewish Involvement in Chicago's Labor Movement from 1886," *Western States Jewish History* 31, no. 1 (Fall 1998), 69.
97. Pratt, "Culture and Radical Politics," 121.
98. Saul Bellow, "Writers, Intellectuals, Politics: Mainly Reminiscence," *National Interest* (Spring 1993), 124.
99. Ibid.
100. Ibid.

101. Ibid., 125.
102. Cutler, "Lawndale," 16.
103. Judy Chicago, scrapbook about childhood, 1971 and 1973, 1.
104. She told Leoni Zverow McVey that she and Leoni's mother had studied with the same teacher. Leoni McVey to author, 21 October 2002.
105. Jessica Fizdale Radin to author, 27 February 2005.
106. Leoni Zverow McVey to author, 4 April 2004.
107. Buhle, *Jews in American Popular Culture,* 42.
108. Pratt, "Culture and Radical Politics," 129–30.
109. Judy Chicago, childhood scrapbook.
110. Ibid.
111. Ibid.
112. Ibid. See also Chicago, *Through the Flower,* 1–2.
113. Chicago, childhood scrapbook, 1. See also Chicago, *Through the Flower,* 2.
114. Nancy Traver, "Judy Chicago's Art Stands Test of Time," *Womannews,* 11 December 2002, 8.
115. Judy Chicago, *Personal Journal,* vol. 1, 134. Italics have been used where Chicago underlines for emphasis.
116. Chicago, childhood scrapbook, 2. *Chicago, Through the Flower,* 3.
117. Chicago, childhood scrapbook, 13.
118. Joe McCarthy and Harry Tierney, "Alice Blue Gown," from the 1919 Broadway musical *Irene.*
119. Chicago, childhood scrapbook, 1.
120. Ibid., 4.
121. Judy Chicago, *Kitty City: A Feline Book of Hours* (New York: Harper Design, 2005), 5.
122. Chicago, childhood scrapbook, 4.
123. Ibid., 2.
124. Judy Chicago, interview by author, 13 June 2004.
125. Harvey Klehr, *The Heyday of American Communism: The Depression Decade* (New York: Basic Books, 1984), 410–11.
126. Ian McGiver, "American Civil Liberties Union," in *The Encyclopedia of Chicago,* ed. James R. Grossman and Ann Durkin Keating (Chicago: University of Chicago Press, 2004), 18.
127. Kate Wiegand, *Red Feminism: American Communism and the Making of Women's Liberation* (Baltimore: Johns Hopkins University Press, 2001), 98.
128. Ibid., 98–99.
129. Chicago, childhood scrapbook, 3.
130. Chicago, *Personal Journal,* vol. 3, 1 November 1972, 132–33.
131. Chicago, *Jewish Journal,* 30 December 1985, 11.
132. Second-grade report card dated 1947, when she received the grade of E (excellent) for all subjects. JCCSL, Box 1, Folder 1.
133. Chicago, childhood scrapbook, 3.

Daddy's Little Girl 2

1. Judy Chicago, childhood scrapbook, 3.
2. Ibid.
3. Ibid.
4. Judy Chicago, *Beyond the Flower: The Autobiography of a Feminist Artist* (New York: Viking Penguin, 1996), 5.
5. Leoni Zverow McVey to author, 4 April 2005.
6. Chicago, *Beyond the Flower,* 5.
7. Chicago, childhood scrapbook, 3.
8. Chicago, *Beyond the Flower,* 5; Chaim Freedman, *Eliyahu's Branches: The Descendants of the Vilna Gaon and His Family* (Teaneck, N.J.: Avotaynu, 1997), 79.
9. Louis Greenberg, *The Jews in Russia: The Struggle for Emancipation* (New Haven, Conn.: Yale University Press) 1944, 17.
10. Paul Mendes-Flohr and Jehuda Reinharz, *The Jew in the Modern World: A Documentary History,* 2nd ed. (New York: Oxford University Press, 1995), 390.
11. Israel Abrahams, comp. and ed., *Hebrew Ethical Wills* (Philadelphia: Jewish Publication Society of America, 1948), 316, 318; Chaim Freedman, *Eliyahu's Branches,* 14.
12. Abrahams, *Hebrew Ethical Wills,* 321.
13. Hirsz Abramowicz, *Profiles of a Lost World* (Detroit: Wayne State University Press, 1999), 31.
14. Ibid., 21.
15. Immanuel Etkes, "The Gaon of Vilna and the Haskalah Movement: Image and Reality," in *BINAH Studies in Jewish History, Thought, and Culture,* ed. Joseph Dan (New York: Praeger, 1889), vol. 2.
16. Robert A. Cohn, "Judy Chicago Describes Her Struggle as a Woman Artist," *St. Louis Jewish Light,* 9 April 1980, 7.
17. Judy Chicago, *A Jewish Journal,* unpublished handwritten manuscript, (1985–93), 23 September 1986, 57. JCCSL, Box 72, Folders 23–38.
18. Judy Chicago, *Through the Flower: My Struggle as a Woman Artist,* 2nd ed. (New York: Penguin Books, 1975), 5.
19. Cohn, "Judy Chicago Describes."
20. Chicago, childhood scrapbook, 3. Chicago, *Through the Flower,* 5.
21. Chicago, *Jewish Journal,* 23 September 1986, 56.
22. Ibid., October 1986, 71.
23. Chicago, childhood scrapbook, 3.

24. Chicago, *Jewish Journal,* 24 September 1986, 58.
25. Judy Chicago quoted in Natalie Weinstein, "After 'Dinner Party,' Judy Chicago Feasts on Judaism," *Northern California Jewish Bulletin,* 14 June 1996, 29.
26. Chicago, childhood scrapbook, 2.
27. Ibid.
28. Chicago, *Through the Flower,* 6–7.
29. Ibid., 4–5.
30. Chicago, *Beyond the Flower,* 7.
31. Judy Chicago, *Personal Journal,* vol. 1, 135.
32. C. S. Howlett (Head, Junior School of the Art Institute of Chicago), letter to Judy Cohen, 9 September 1950, JCCSL.
33. Judy Cohen to her mother, 5 February 1959, JCCSL.
34. Junior School of the Art Institute of Chicago to Judy Cohen, 1 September 1951, and 17 November 1956, JCCSL, Box 1, Folder 1.
35. Edithe Jane Cassady (Junior School of the Art Institute) to Judy Cohen, 19 March 1956, JCCSL.
36. Leoni Zverow McVey and Esther Boroff Charbit to author, 4 April 2005. Decades later, on the occasion of the hundredth anniversary of the Junior School of the Art Institute, McVey recalled speaking to Emanuel Jacobson, who was honored at the event, noting that he "began to rhapsodize about Judy's talent and accomplishments"; Leoni Zverow McVey to the author, 21 October 2002.
37. Walt Disney was in the Junior School of the Art Institute of Chicago before leaving for Kansas City in 1917 at the age of fifteen or sixteen. In 1971, Judy Chicago would go to teach at the California Institute of the Arts, the new art school Disney had founded in 1961.
38. Chicago, *Through the Flower,* 6.
39. Ibid., 7. Judy's cousin Helen Whitebook remembers that, as a teenager, Judy continued to come from Chicago to visit during summers.
40. Howard Rosen, interview by author, 9 August 2000.
41. Chicago, *Through the Flower,* 4.
42. Richard M. Fried, *Nightmare in Red: The McCarthy Era in Perspective* (New York: Oxford University Press, 1990), 3.
43. Howard Rosen, Helen Whitebook, and Lilian Tart, interviews by author, August 2000. Ruth Levinson Psundstein called Arthur "a great man" who was "kind to everybody, educated"; interview by author, 13 August 2000.
44. May Cohen to Pearl Cassman, 5 February 1970, JCCSL.
45. Chicago, childhood scrapbook, 2.
46. Chicago, *Beyond the Flower,* 3.
47. Chicago, *Jewish Journal,* 23 September 1986, 56–57.
48. Chicago, *Beyond the Flower,* 3.
49. Harvey Klehr and John Earl Haynes, *The American Communist Movement: Storming Heaven Itself* (New York: Twayne Publishers, 1992), 85.
50. Julian Schwartz to author, 24 February 2005.
51. Zosa Szajkowski, *Jews, Wars, and Communism* (New York: Ktav, 1972), 431–32.
52. See Dov Levin, *The Lesser of Two Evils: Eastern European Jewry Under Soviet Rule, 1939–41* (Philadelphia, Pa: Jewish Publication Society, 1995), 179.
53. FBI file for Arthur M. Cohen.
54. Karl Baarslag, *History of the National Federation of Post Office Clerks* (Washington, D.C.: National Federation of Post Office Clerks, 1945), 186.
55. Ibid., 134.
56. Peter L. Steinberg, *The Great "Red Menace": United States Prosecution of American Communists, 1947–1952* (Westport, Conn.: Greenwood Press, 1984), 19–20, 25.
57. Ibid., 25.
58. Ibid., 27.
59. Fried, *Nightmare in Red,* 68.
60. Steinberg, *Great "Red Menace,"* 30.
61. Fried, *Nightmare in Red,* 70.
62. Morris Fine, ed., *American Jewish Yearbook* (New York: American Jewish Committee, 1951), vol. 52, 23.
63. FBI file for Arthur M. Cohen.
64. Alfred H. Kelly and Winfred A. Harbison, *The American Constitution: Its Origins and Development* (New York: W. W. Norton & Co., 1963), 896.
65. Cited in the FBI file, as in the records of the House Committee on Un-American Activities.
66. Klehr and Haynes, *American Communist Movement,* 93.
67. FBI file for Arthur M. Cohen.
68. Albert Fried, ed. "Communism in America," in *Communism in America: A History in Documents* (New York: Columbia University Press, 1997), 359.
69. Alexander M. Campbell (assistant attorney general) memo to FBI director, 27 December 1948, 146-200-1174.
70. Chicago, *Through the Flower,* 5. Chicago, *Beyond the Flower,* 6.
71. FBI office memorandum, 6 March 1959, found in the FBI file for Judy Sylvia Cohen [Chicago].
72. Judy Chicago, childhood scrapbook, 3.
73. Griffin Fariello, *Red Scare: Memoirs of the*

American Inquisition, An Oral History (New York: W. W. Norton & Co., 1995), 131.

74. Chicago, childhood scrapbook, 3.
75. Ibid.
76. Harvey Klehr, *The Heyday of American Communism: The Depression Decade* (New York: Basic Books, 1984), 75.
77. Patrick Marnham, *Dreaming with His Eyes Open: A Life of Diego Rivera* (New York: Alfred A. Knopf, 1998), 259, 277–94. Rivera gave Trotsky safe harbor in his home in Mexico until he discovered that Trotsky had betrayed him by having an affair with his wife; at that point Rivera turned on the exiled Russian leader.
78. Paul Buhle, *From the Lower East Side to Hollywood: Jews in American Popular Culture* (New York: Verso, 2004), 111.
79. Chicago, childhood scrapbook, 3.
80. Chicago, *Through the Flower,* 6.
81. Vivian Gornick, *The Romance of American Communism* (New York: Basic Books, 1977), 12.
82. Chicago, *Through the Flower,* 9. See also Joyce Wadler, " 'Public Lives: Uncovering Art in the Act of Being Spied Upon,' " *New York Times,* 2 October 2002, 2, which discusses the comments of artist Arnold Mesches, who publicly acknowledged that he had been a Communist Party member. He emphasized here and elsewhere that being a Communist meant that he was for peace, for rights for black people, and for women and that it was never about overthrowing the government.
83. Chicago, *Beyond the Flower,* 10.
84. Chicago, *Through the Flower,* 11.
85. Arthur M. Cohen died in Michael Reese Hospital of acute intestinal obstruction. Death Certificate state file #49326, Cook County, Ill.
86. See Maxine Harris, *The Loss That Is Forever: The Lifelong Impact of the Early Death of a Mother or Father* (New York: Penguin Books, 1996), 85.
87. Chicago, *Beyond the Flower,* 9.
88. Ibid., 8.
89. Chicago, *Jewish Journal,* 30 December 1985, 12; she noted that "now it's complicated by her age & increasing senility & incapacity."
90. Harris, *Loss That Is Forever,* 51.

Inklings of Identity 3

1. Judy Chicago, *Beyond the Flower: The Autobiography of a Feminist Artist* (New York: Viking Penguin, 1996), 8–9.
2. There is a huge body of literature on this subject. See, for example, Maureen Murdock, *Father's Daughters: Transforming the Father-Daughter Relationship* (New York: Fawcett Columbine, 1994), 209–12.
3. Chicago, *Beyond the Flower,* 9.
4. Ibid., 11.
5. Maxine Harris, *The Loss That Is Forever: The Lifelong Impact of the Early Death of a Mother or Father* (New York: Penguin Books, 1996), 4–6.
6. Ibid.
7. Robert A. Cohn, "Judy Chicago Describes Her Struggle as a Woman Artist," *St. Louis Jewish Light,* 9 April 1980, 7.
8. Rabbinical Assembly of America, *Sabbath and Festival Prayer Book* (United Synagogue of America, 1946; reprinted 1955), 225.
9. As quoted in Leo Rosten, *The Joys of Yiddish* (New York: McGraw-Hill, 1968), 442.
10. Chicago, *Beyond the Flower,* 3.
11. Judy Chicago, *Personal Journal,* vol. 3, 60.
12. Philip Krone, interview by author, 22 June 2004.
13. Marjorie (Marjie) Kaplow Ross Kaplan to author, 11 February 2005.
14. Gladys Nilsson to author, 2 March 2005. After graduation she attended the School of the Art Institute of Chicago. Nilsson is an accomplished artist associated with Chicago's *Hairy Who.* She recalls that she and Judy Cohen traveled in different circles at Lake View.
15. Anita Nelson Dickson to author, 7 February 2005.
16. Judy Chicago, *Personal Journal,* vol. 2, 53.
17. Lake View High yearbook staff, *Red and White* (Chicago: Lake View High, 1955), 47. Judy Cohen was in Division 2B8.
18. Cecilia Honet Bethe, interview by author, 4 February 2005.
19. James Rorty, "The Anti-Communism of Senator McCarthy: It Slays More Friends Than Foes," *Commentary* 16, no. 2 (August 1953), 123–25.
20. Gladys Nilsson to author, 2 March 2005.
21. Tom Mitchel to author, 22 August 2006.
22. Judy Chicago, *Through the Flower: My Struggle as a Woman Artist,* 2nd ed. (New York: Penguin Books, 1975), 13.
23. Chicago, *Beyond the Flower,* 11.
24. Tom Mitchel to author, 22 August 2006.
25. Chicago, *Through the Flower,* 14.
26. Ibid., 12–13.
27. Judy Chicago, interview by author, 13 June 2004.
28. Irving Shulman, *The Amboy Dukes: A Novel of*

Wayward Youth in Brooklyn (New York: Avon, 1946), 4.
29. Ibid., 5–6.
30. Lake View High yearbook staff, *Red and White* (Chicago: Lake View High, 1956), 114.
31. Ibid., 137.
32. Chicago to author; Gladys Nilsson to author, also commented that she had no cashmere sweaters, which were beyond the means of her working-class Swedish-immigrant parents.
33. Some of these still exist: one with Judy in curlers, another with her saluting, several of her and Tommy, including one dressed for the prom, which she included on the dust jacket for *Through the Flower.*
34. Leoni Zverow McVey to author, 6 April 2005.
35. Judy Chicago to author, 15 February 2005.
36. Philip Krone, interview by author, 27 October 2004.
37. Judy Chicago, *A Jewish Journal* (1985–93), unpublished handwritten manuscript, 14 November 1986, 79. JCCSL, Box 72, Folders 23–38.
38. Ibid., 78.
39. Louise Abdell Holland, interview by author, 3 February 2005. Holland would later become president of the village of Winnetka, Illinois. Mrs. McMillan's anti-Semitism was confirmed by Carol Milner, who was then another student at Lake View High.
40. Lake View High Yearbook Staff, *Lake View High 1956,* 135.
41. Lake View High Yearbook Staff, *Lake View 1955,* 28–29.
42. Chicago, *Through the Flower,* 8.
43. Chicago, *A Jewish Journal,* 14 November 1986, 78.
44. Judy Chicago, *Through the Flower,* 14.
45. Allen Podet to Judy Chicago, 3 July 2004.
46. Allen Podet to Judy Chicago, 9 February 2005.
47. Lake View High yearbook staff, *Red and White* (Chicago: Lake View High School, 1957), 145. Under Judy Cohen's senior picture is the following list: "GAA 500 Point Letter, All-School Council Vice-President, French Club, Graduation Aide Co-Captain, Red and White Art Staff, Red and White Advertising Staff, Junior Chorus, Scholastic Art Award-Gold Key, Decoration Committee, Hi-Q, Gold Pin, National Honor Society, Who's Who Among Student Leaders."
48. Anita Nelson Dickson to author, 22 February 2005.
49. Judy Chicago to author, 25 February 2005.
50. Anita Nelson Dickson to author, 7 February 2005. Judy Chicago suggested that she took it from somewhere, maybe the novel *Amboy Dukes.* Interview by author, 9 February 2005.
51. Anita Nelson Dickson became a graphic designer and educator.
52. Kathy Larkin, "Judy Chicago: Art Across the Gender Gap," *Post-Tribune* (Chicago), 2 December 1984, 2. JCCSL, Box 2, Folder 15.
53. Paul Buhle and Nicole Schulman, *Wobblies: A Graphic History of the Industrial Workers of the World* (New York: W. W. Norton & Co., 2005).
54. Chicago, *Beyond the Flower,* 12.

Out West: Contending with Men 4

1. Judy Chicago, *Through the Flower: My Struggles as a Woman Artist,* 2nd ed. (New York: Penguin Books, 1975), 15.
2. Judy Chicago. Interview by Jane Collings. Oral History Program. Transcript, 26. UCLA, 2004.
3. Judy Cohen to May Cohen, 27 September 1957, JCCSL. She wrote this Yiddish word transliterated from the Hebrew letters with which Yiddish is normally written.
4. Judy Cohen to May and [Ben] Bob Cohen, n.d. (fall 1957), JCCSL.
5. Ibid.
6. Judy Cohen to her family, 15 December 1957, JCCSL.
7. Judy Cohen to May Cohen and Ben Cohen, 17 November 1957, JCCSL.
8. Albert Boime and Paul Arden, *The Odyssey of Jan Stussy in Black and White: Anxious Visions and Uncharted Dreams* (Los Angeles: Jan Stussy Foundation, 1995), 55–56.
9. Jonathan Kirsch, "The Flowering of the Artist," *Coast* 16, no. 6 (June 1975), 38.
10. Estelle Gershgoren Novak to author, February 2005, recalled that this was UCLA's nickname.
11. Tom Welch, " 'Socialists Stir at UCLA/ Radicals Pass Out Colored Circulars,' " *UCLA Daily Bruin,* 7 October 1957, 7.
12. Sharon Schuchet, "Socialist Workers Cited 'Subversive,' " *Daily Bruin,* 11 October 1957, and "Socialist Workers Tie-up with Communists Shown," 14 October 1957. See the 10 December 1956 issue on the investigation of subversion on campus. All are online at http://www.ulwaf.com/Daily-Bruin-History/15_Epilogue.html.
13. C. Scott Littleton to author, 22 February 2005. The following descriptions of campus life are also his.

14. See http://www.naacphouston.org/history.htm.
15. Judy Chicago to May Cohen, n.d., early November 1957, JCCSL.
16. Judy Cohen to May Cohen, 7 December 1957, mentions that she will be going to the studio of Milton Gershgoren the next day.
17. Judy Cohen to her family, 17 November 1957, JCCSL. The Westwind International Folk Ensemble, legacy of the late Mike Janusz, has pursued its original dedication to the preservation of folk cultures through traditions of dance, music, song, and custom. It began in the summer of 1959 when UCLA instructor Michael Janusz organized the Los Angeles International Folk Chorus, whose first full concert was a part of the second annual UCLA Folk Festival in the summer of 1960. Mike later married Leslie Fizdale, Jessica's younger sister.
18. Judy Cohen to May Cohen, 17 November 1957.
19. Griffin Fariello, *Red Scare: Memoirs of the American Inquisition: An Oral History* (New York: W. W. Norton & Co., 1995), 18–19.
20. Judy Cohen to May Cohen, 1 November 1957.
21. Judy Cohen to May Cohen, 7 September–7 December 1957, JCCSL.
22. Sara Evans, *Personal Politics: The Roots of Women's Liberation in the Civil Rights Movement and the New Left* (New York: Alfred A. Knopf, 1979), 49.
23. Stan Evans, "People, Places & Problems in the News," *UCLA Daily Bruin,* 1 October 1957, 3.
24. Judy Cohen to May and [Ben] Bob Cohen, 1 November 1957, JCCSL.
25. Judy Cohen to her family, n.d., fall 1957, JCCSL.
26. Estelle Gershgoren to author, 28 February 2005.
27. Judy Cohen to May Cohen, letter of December 7, 1957, JCCSL.
28. Evans, *Personal Politics,* 24.
29. Kate Wiegand, *Red Feminism: American Communism and the Making of Women's Liberation* (Baltimore: Johns Hopkins University Press, 2001), 1.
30. Judy Cohen to May Cohen, 1 November 1957, JCCSL.
31. Judy Cohen to May and [Ben] Bob Cohen, 15 December 1957, JCCSL.
32. Judy Cohen to May Cohen, 1 November 1957, JCCSL.
33. Judy Cohen to May Cohen, n.d., early 1960, JCCSL.
34. UCLA transcript for Judith S. Cohen.
35. Judy Cohen to May Cohen, 23 March 1958, JCCSL.
36. Judy Cohen to May Cohen, 25 March 1958, JCCSL. The next references are also from this letter.
37. Leslie Alexander Lacy, *The Rise and Fall of a Proper Negro* (New York: Macmillan, 1970), 19.
38. Chicago, *Through the Flower,* 16.
39. Judy Cohen to May Cohen, 16 January 1958, JCCSL.
40. Evans, *Personal Politics,* 25.
41. Lacy, *Proper Negro,* 85.
42. Ibid., 92.
43. Chicago, *Through the Flower*, 16.
44. Lacy, *Proper Negro,* 100.
45. Ibid., 96.
46. Ibid., 95.
47. Ibid., 95.
48. Paul C. Mishler, *Raising Reds: The Young Pioneers, Radical Summer Camps, and Communist Political Culture in the United States* (New York: Columbia University Press, 1999), 7.
49. Sid Gershgoren to author, 13 February 2005.
50. Paul Buhle, *From the Lower East Side to Hollywood: Jews in American Popular Culture* (New York: Verso, 2004), 17–18.
51. Author obtained this file under the Freedom of Information Act.
52. Fariello, *Red Scare,* 216.
53. Estelle Gershgoren Novak to author, 13 February 2005.
54. Judy Cohen to May Cohen, 31 January and 16 January 1958, JCCSL.
55. Judy Cohen to May Cohen, 16 January 1958.
56. Judy Cohen to May Cohen and [Ben] Bob Cohen, 25 March 1958, JCCSL
57. Judy Cohen to May Cohen, 9 December 1958, JCCSL.
58. Julie Ross to author, 23 February 2005.
59. Sid Gershgoren to author, 13 February 2005; confirmed by Estelle Gershgoren Novak to the author, 28 February 2005.
60. Estelle Gershgoren Novak to author, 13 February 2005.
61. Lacy, *Proper Negro,* 100.
62. Ibid.
63. Ibid.
64. Ibid.
65. Chicago, *Through the Flower,* 16.
66. Ibid.
67. Ibid., 17.
68. Judy Cohen to May Cohen, 2 April 1958, JCCSL.
69. Ibid.
70. Ibid. The following unattributed quotations are also from this letter.

71. Judy Cohen to May Cohen, 4 November 1958 [SLRC].
72. Judy Cohen to May Cohen, 23 October 1958, JCCSL.
73. Judy Cohen to May Cohen and [Ben] Bob Cohen, 9 October 1958, JCCSL.
74. Ibid.
75. Julie Ross to author, 22 February 2005.
76. Judy Cohen to May Cohen and [Ben] Bob Cohen, 14 November 1958, JCCSL.
77. Julie Ross to author, 23 February 2005. The following recollections are also from this source.
78. Judy Cohen to May Cohen, n.d., fall 1958, JCCSL.
79. Ibid.
80. Ibid.
81. Ibid.
82. Judy Cohen to May Cohen, n.d., early 1959, JCCSL.
83. Lloyd Hamrol to author, 3 April 2004.
84. Ibid.
85. Ibid.
86. Judy Cohen to May Cohen, n.d., fall 1958, JCCSL.
87. Judy Cohen to May Cohen and [Ben] Bob Cohen, 4 November 1958, JCCSL.
88. Julie Ross to author, 27 February 2005.
89. Judy Cohen to May Cohen, 9 October 1958, JCCSL.
90. Marv Bornstein to author, 27 February 2005.
91. Judy Chicago to her family, 25 October 1958, JCCSL.
92. Judy Cohen to May Cohen, 25 October, 28 November, and 9 December 1958, JCCSL. Chicago, *Through the Flower,* 17.
93. C. Scott Littleton to author, 21 and 22 February 2005. Further references are from this source.
94. Judy Cohen to her family, 25 October 1958, JCCSL.
95. Ibid.
96. Tom McGrath, statement to the House Un-American Activities Committee, 1953, reprinted in *North Dakota Quarterly* (Fall 1982).
97. Estelle Gershgoren Novak, ed., *Poets of the Non-Existent City Los Angeles in the McCarthy Era* (Albuquerque: University of New Mexico Press, 2002), 25. See also Tom McGrath, *Witness to the Times: Poems by Thomas McGrath* (Los Angeles, 1953). "Published" by his students, Kent State University Library and Brown University Library possess copies.
98. C. Scott Littleton to author, 26 February 2005.
99. Ibid.
100. Ibid.
101. Judy Cohen to May Cohen and [Ben] Bob Cohen, 9 December 1958.
102. C. Scott Littleton to author, 22 February 2005.
103. Judy Cohen to May Cohen, 9 December 1958, JCCSL.
104. Ibid.
105. Ibid.
106. George Herbert Mead, *Mind, Self and Society, from the Standpoint of a Social Behaviorist* (Chicago: University of Chicago Press, 1934), 216.
107. Ibid.
108. Ibid., 218.
109. Ibid.
110. Judy Cohen to May Cohen, 7 February 1958, JCCSL.
111. Judy Cohen to May Cohen, 14 November 1958, JCCSL.
112. Judy Cohen to May Cohen, 9 December 1958, JCCSL.
113. Mike Davis, *City of Quartz: Excavating the Future in Los Angeles* (New York: Verso, 1990), 65.
114. Judy Cohen to May Cohen, 24 December 1958, JCCSL.
115. Judy Cohen to May Cohen, n.d., December 1958, JCCSL.
116. Ibid.
117. Arthur Miller, *A View from the Bridge: A Play in Two Acts* (London: Crescent Press, 1957), 17.
118. Judy Cohen to May Cohen, 31 December 1958, JCCSL. Julie Ross to author, 26 February 2005. According to Estelle Gershgoren Novak (to author 13 February 2005,), the late Bob Kaufman, who went on a Freedom Ride journey to campaign for civil rights, was once badly beaten in a Texas jail cell.
119. Judy Cohen to May Cohen, 5 March 1959, JCCSL.
120. Judy Cohen to May Cohen, n.d., late December 1958, JCCSL.
121. Judy Cohen to May Cohen and [Ben] Bob Cohen, 5 February 1959, JCCSL.
122. Chicago, *Through the Flower,* 27–28.
123. Ibid.
124. Ibid., 28.
125. Lloyd Hamrol to author, 3 April 2004.
126. Judy Cohen to May Cohen, 5 March 1959, JCCSL. The following references are from this source.
127. Ibid.
128. Ibid.
129. Judy Cohen to May Cohen and [Ben] Bob Cohen, 25 March 1959, JCCSL.
130. Judy Cohen to May Cohen and [Ben] Bob Cohen, 31 March 1959, JCCSL.

131. Judy Cohen to May Cohen, 5 March 1959, JCCSL.
132. Judy Cohen to May Cohen and [Ben] Bob Cohen, 31 March 2005, JCCSL.
133. Judy Cohen to May Cohen and [Ben] Bob Cohen, 25 March 1959, JCCSL.
134. Ibid.
135. Ibid.
136. Ibid.
137. Judy Chicago to author, May 2006.
138. Judy Cohen to May Cohen and [Ben] Bob Cohen, 25 March 1959, JCCSL.
139. Ibid.
140. Judy Cohen to May Cohen and [Ben] Bob Cohen, 31 March 1959, JCCSL.
141. Judy Cohen to May Cohen, 7 May 1959, JCCSL.
142. Judy Cohen to May Cohen and [Ben] Bob Cohen, 14 May 1959, JCCSL. The quotations that follow are also from this letter.
143. Judy Cohen to May Cohen, 30 June 1959, JCCSL.
144. Judy Cohen to May Cohen, 9 June 1959, JCCSL.
145. Chicago, *Through the Flower,* 18.
146. Judy Cohen to May Cohen, 14 May 1959, JCCSL.
147. Judy Cohen to May Cohen, 9 June 1959, JCCSL.
148. Judy Cohen to May Cohen, 30 June 1959, JCCSL. The following information is from this source.
149. Judy Chicago, *Beyond the Flower: The Autobiography of a Feminist Artist* (New York: Viking Penguin, 1996), 12. Judy Cohen to May Cohen, 30 June 1959, JCCSL. Gerowitz was born on 2 April 1935.
150. Paul Gerowitz, Jerry's younger brother, to author, 4 January 2004.
151. Lloyd Hamrol to author, 3 April 2004.
152. Frank Mecoli to author, 2 March 2005. The following comments are from this source.
153. Judy Cohen to May Cohen, 30 June 1959, JCCSL.
154. Lew Merkelson to author, 25 February 2005.
155. Paul Gerowitz to author, 4 January 2004.
156. Seeger was sentenced to a year in prison for contempt, although the verdict was reversed in 1962. See http://www.historymatters.gmu.edu/d/6457.
157. Chicago, *Through the Flower,* 18.
158. Ibid.
159. Judy Cohen to May Cohen and [Ben] Bob Cohen, 14 May 1959, JCCSL.
160. Judy Cohen to May Cohen, 14 July 1959, JCCSL.
161. Ibid.
162. See Henry Adams, *Thomas Hart Benton: An American Original* (New York: Alfred A. Knopf, 1989), 180–81.
163. Judy Cohen to May Cohen, 14 July 1959, JCCSL.
164. Ibid.
165. Judy Cohen to May Cohen, n.d., early 1960, JCCSL.
166. May Cohen to Pearl S. Cassman, 23 August 1959, JCCSL.
167. Judy Cohen to May Cohen, 9 June 1959, JCCSL.
168. Chicago, *Through the Flower,* 18–19.
169. May Cohen to Pearl Cassman, 17 January 1960, JCCSL.

Rebellious Odyssey 5

1. Judy Chicago, *Through the Flower: My Struggle as a Woman Artist,* 2nd ed. (New York: Penguin Books, 1975), 19.
2. Judy Cohen to May Cohen and [Ben] Bob Cohen, 7 September 1959, JCCSL.
3. Judy Cohen to May Cohen, 28 September 1959, JCCSL.
4. Judy Cohen to May Cohen and [Ben] Bob Cohen, 22 September 1959, and Judy Cohen to May Cohen, 31 October 1959, JCCSL.
5. Judy Cohen to May Cohen, 28 September 1959, JCCSL.
6. Judy Cohen to May Cohen, 20 October 1959, JCCSL.
7. Judy Cohen to May Cohen, 18 September 1959, JCCSL.
8. Ibid.
9. Ibid.
10. Judy Cohen to May Cohen, 5 March 1960, JCCSL.
11. Judy Cohen to May Cohen and [Ben] Bob Cohen, 22 September 1959, JCCSL.
12. Judy Cohen to May Cohen, n.d., September 1959, JCCSL.
13. Raphael Soyer to author, March 1985, while posing for a portrait.
14. For the story of this journal, see Gail Levin, *Edward Hopper: An Intimate Biography* (New York: Alfred A. Knopf, 1995), 445–73.
15. Judy Cohen to May Cohen, 9 October 1959, JCCSL.
16. Judy Cohen to May Cohen and [Ben] Bob Cohen, 22 September 1959, JCCSL.
17. Judy Cohen to May Cohen, 20 October 1959, JCCSL.
18. Judy Cohen to May Cohen, 31 October 1959, JCCSL.
19. Judy Cohen to May Cohen, 2 October 1959, JCCSL.
20. Judy Cohen to May Cohen, n.d., 1959, and

Judy Cohen to May Cohen, 9 October 1959, JCCSL. For the history of such groups at Henry Street, see Lillian D. Wald, *Windows on Henry Street* (Boston: Little, Brown, & Co., 1936), 156–57.
21. Judy Cohen to May Cohen, 9 October 1959, JCCSL.
22. Judy Cohen to May Cohen, 31 October 1959, JCCSL.
23. May Cohen to Pearl S. Cassman, 10 November 1959, JCCSL.
24. Judy Cohen to May Cohen, 31 October 1959, JCCSL.
25. Judy Cohen to May Cohen, 31 October 1959, JCCSL.
26. Ibid.
27. Judy Cohen to May Cohen, 12 November 1959, JCCSL.
28. Judy Cohen to May Cohen and [Ben] Bob Cohen, 22 September 1959, JCCSL.
29. Judy Cohen to May Cohen, 8 December 1959, JCCSL.
30. Judy Cohen to May Cohen, 31 October 1959, JCCSL.
31. May Levinson to Pearl S. Cassman, 30 December 1959, JCCSL.
32. Judy Cohen to May Cohen, 28 September 1959, JCCSL.
33. Judy Cohen to May Cohen, 23 February 1960, JCCSL.
34. Judy Cohen to May Cohen, 20 February 1960, JCCSL.
35. Judy Cohen to May Cohen, 20 October 1959, JCCSL.
36. Lucy Lippard to author, 9 June 2004.
37. Chicago, *Through the Flower,* 19–20.
38. Judy Cohen to May Cohen, 20 October 1959, JCCSL.
39. Judy Chicago, *Beyond the Flower: The Autobiography of a Feminist Artist* (New York: Viking Penguin, 1996), 14, and Judy Cohen to May Cohen, 9 November 1959, JCCSL.
40. Judy Cohen to May Cohen, 28 December 1959, JCCSL.
41. Julie Ross to author, 1 March 2005.
42. Judy Cohen to May Cohen, 8 December 1959, JCCSL.
43. Chicago, *Through the Flower,* 18–19.
44. Ibid.
45. Judy Cohen to May Cohen, n.d., late December 1959 or very early January 1960.
46. Judy Cohen to May Cohen, 12 December 1959, JCCSL.
47. Ibid.
48. Ibid.
49. Judy Cohen to May Cohen, 8 December 1959, JCCSL.
50. Ibid.
51. Judy Cohen to May Cohen, 25 December 2005, JCCSL.
52. Judy Cohen to May Cohen, January 1960, JCCSL.
53. Ibid.
54. Judy Cohen to May Cohen, January 30, 1960, JCCSL.
55. Judy Cohen to May Cohen, 28 December 1959, JCCSL.
56. Judy Cohen to May Cohen, 12 December 1959, JCCSL.
57. Chicago, *Through the Flower,* 28.
58. Judy Cohen to May Cohen, 2 March 1960, JCCSL.
59. Judy Cohen to May Cohen, 12 December 1959, JCCSL.
60. Ibid.
61. Judy Cohen to May Cohen, 28 December 1959, JCCSL.
62. Judy Cohen to May Cohen, n.d., early January 1960, JCCSL.
63. Judy Cohen to May Cohen, 20 January 1960, JCCSL.
64. Ibid.
65. Judy Cohen to May Cohen, 23 February 1960, JCCSL.
66. Judy Cohen to May Cohen, 20 March 1960, JCCSL.
67. Ibid.
68. Judy Cohen to May Cohen, 25 April 1960, JCCSL.
69. Judy Cohen to May Cohen, 20 January 1960, JCCSL.
70. Judy Cohen to May Cohen, 29 February 2000, JCCSL.
71. Emily Walker of West Redding, Conn., is listed as a collector in the catalog raisonné of Jackson Pollock, vol. I.
72. Judy Cohen to May Cohen, 29 February 1960, JCCSL.
73. Judy Cohen to May Cohen and [Ben] Bob Cohen, 22 September 1959, JCCSL.
74. Judy Cohen to May Cohen, 22 September 1959, and 30 January 1960, JCCSL. She was reading Miller's *Tropic of Cancer, Tropic of Capricorn,* and *Rosy Crucifixion,* loaned to her by a friend named Frank.
75. Albert Camus, *The Rebel,* as quoted in Vivian Gornick, *The Romance of American Communism* (New York: Basic Books, 1977), 265.
76. Ibid.
77. Judy Cohen to May Cohen, 20 February 1960, JCCSL.
78. Todd Gitlin, *The Sixties: Years of Hope, Days of Rage* (New York: Bantam Books, 1987), 84.
79. Ibid., 84.
80. Judy Cohen to May Cohen, n.d., early 1960, JCCSL.

81. Judy Cohen to May Cohen, n.d. early 1960, JCCSL.
82. Judy Cohen to May Cohen, 29 February 1960, JCCSL.
83. Ibid.
84. Judy Cohen to May Cohen, 20 March 1960, JCCSL.
85. Ibid.
86. Ibid.
87. Ibid.
88. Judy Cohen to May Cohen, 25 April 1960, JCCSL.
89. Judy Cohen to May Cohen, 7 and 29 May 1960, JCCSL. The producers decided that "12 year olds wouldn't understand the lyrics" and backed out the day the contract was to be signed. Evidently these singers were not Paul Simon and Art Garfunkel, who also recorded with Columbia a few years later.
90. Judy Cohen to May Cohen, 7 May 1960, JCCSL. Judy does not recall if she ever got paid.
91. Judy Cohen to May Cohen, 7 and 29 May 1960, JCCSL.
92. Julie Ross to author, 23 February 2005.
93. Judy Cohen to May Cohen, 29 May 1960, JCCSL.
94. Judy Cohen to May Cohen, 14 June 1960, JCCSL.
95. Judy Cohen to May Cohen, 29 May 1960, JCCSL.
96. Judy Cohen to May Cohen, 14 June 1960, JCCSL.
97. Judy Cohen to May Cohen, 20 March 1960, JCCSL.
98. Judy Cohen to May Cohen, 14 June 1960, JCCSL.
99. Judy Cohen to May Cohen, 9 August 1960, JCCSL.
100. Ibid.
101. May Levinson to Pearl S. Cassman, 3 September 1960, JCCSL.
102. Ibid. *Hocks a chinek* literally means "beat a tea kettle."
103. Chicago, *Through the Flower,* 20.
104. Ibid.
105. Ibid.
106. George M. Goodwin, interviewer, "Oliver Andrews Oral History," Los Angeles Art Community: Group Portrait, UCLA (Los Angeles, 1977), 131.
107. Chicago, *Through the Flower,* 31.
108. Lloyd Hamrol to author, 3 April 2004.
109. Joan (Giovanna) D'Angelo Brennan to author, 14 March 2005.
110. Lloyd Hamrol to author, 3 March 2004.
111. May Cohen to Pearl S. Cassman, 2 November 1960, JCCSL.
112. Ibid.
113. Chicago, *Through the Flower,* 21.
114. May Cohen to Pearl S. Cassman, 12 December 1960, JCCSL.
115. May Cohen to Pearl S. Cassman, 31 December 1960, JCCSL.
116. May Cohen to Pearl S. Cassman, 2 February 1961, JCCSL.
117. Ibid.
118. May Cohen to Pearl S. Cassman, 28 March 1961, JCCSL.
119. Ibid.
120. May Cohen to Pearl S. Cassman, 6 May 1961, JCCSL.
121. May Cohen to Pearl S. Cassman, 29 October 1961, JCCSL.
122. Dr. Renee Kaplan of UCLA Student Psychological Services to author, June 23, 2006.
123. Judy Chicago to author, 24 June 2006.
124. Chicago, *Through the Flower,* 21.
125. Ibid.
126. Ibid.
127. Ibid., 21–22.
128. Ibid., 22.
129. Joan (Giovanna) D'Angelo Brennan to author, 4 and 14 March 2005.
130. Frank Mecoli to author, 2 March 2005.
131. Ralph Gibson to author, 1 September 2006.
132. May Cohen to Pearl S. Cassman, 29 October 1961, JCCSL.
133. Paul Gerowitz to author, 4 January 2004.
134. William W. Melnitz to Judith Sylvia Cohen, 21 July 1961, JCCSL, Box 1, Folder 1.
135. Class of 1961 yearbook staff, *UCLA Southern Campus Yearbook* (Los Angeles: UCLA, 1961), 42:84.
136. May Cohen to Pearl S. Cassman, 7 February 1962, JCCSL.
137. She had been on dean's honors list for six semesters. Dean William W. Melnitz to Judith S. Cohen, August 7, 1962, JCCSL, Box 1, Folder 1.
138. Judy Chicago, "Two Artists, Two Attitudes: Judy Chicago and Lloyd Hamrol Interview Each Other," *Criteria: A Review of the Arts* 1, no. 2 (November 1974): 9.
139. Joan (Giovanna) D'Angelo Brennan to the author, 14 March 2005.
140. Chicago, *Through the Flower,* 22.
141. Lloyd Hamrol to author, 3 April 2004.
142. Janice Johnson to author, 13 February 2005.
143. Chicago, *Beyond the Flower,* 15.
144. Chicago, *Through the Flower,* 23.
145. Janice Johnson to author, 13 February 2005.
146. Chicago, *Through the Flower,* 23.
147. Ibid., 24.
148. Ibid.
149. Ibid.

150. Ibid.
151. Ibid., 25.
152. Maxine Harris, *The Loss That Is Forever: The Lifelong Impact of the Early Death of a Mother or Father* (New York: Penguin Books, 1996), 223. Lily Pincus, *Death and the Family: The Importance of Mourning* (New York: Pantheon Books, 1974), 171.
153. Harris, *Loss That Is Forever,* 141.

The Dance of Loss and Love 6

1. Judy Chicago, *Kitty City: A Feline Book of Hours* (New York: Harper Design, 2005), 5.
2. Judy Gerowitz to Janice Johnson, 16 June 1963.
3. Ibid.
4. Ibid.
5. She taught as a teaching assistant, 1963–64; then as an instructor in the UCLA Extension division from 1963 to 1966; and then in the UCI (Irvine) Extension Division from 1966 to 1969.
6. Judy Chicago, *Through the Flower: My Struggle as a Woman Artist,* 2nd ed. (New York: Penguin Books, 1975), 33.
7. Frank O'Hara, *Jackson Pollock* (New York: George Braziller, 1959), pl. 56.
8. Judy Chicago, "Two Artists, Two Attitudes: Judy Chicago and Lloyd Hamrol Interview Each Other," *Criteria: A Review of the Arts* 1, no. 2 (November 1974), 9.
9. Judy Chicago to Edward Lucie-Smith (January 1999), quoted in Edward Lucie-Smith, *Judy Chicago: An American Vision* (New York: Watson-Guptill, 2000), 17.
10. Elaine Tyler May, "Explosive Issues: Sex, Women, and the Bomb War," in *Recasting America: Culture and Politics in the Age of Cold War,* ed. Lary May (Chicago: University of Chicago Press, 1989), 165.
11. Alexander King quoted in David Allyn, *Make Love Not War: The Sexual Revolution: An Unfettered History* (Boston: Little, Brown & Co., 2000), 21.
12. Betty Friedan, *The Feminine Mystique* (New York: W. W. Norton & Co., 1963).
13. Ibid., 261.
14. Ibid.
15. Meridee Merzer, "Art?" *Penthouse,* October 1975, 45. JCCSL, Box 1, Folder 42.
16. Lloyd Hamrol to author, 3 April 2004.
17. Joan (Giovanna) D'Angelo Brennan to author, 5 March 2005.
18. Sam Amato to author, 20 March 2005.
19. Elliot Elgart to author, 20 March 2005.
20. Vija Celmins to author, July 24, 2005.
21. For the entire story of Berman's arrest, see Sarah Schrank, " 'The Art of the City: Modernism, Censorship, and the Emergence of Los Angeles's Postwar Art Scene,' " *American Quarterly* 56, no. 3 (September 2004), 682.
22. Judy Chicago to author, 29 November 2005.
23. Yet when this same work was shown at the Los Angeles County Museum of Art in 1966, city officials reacted negatively to erotic art exhibited in a publicly funded space. See Schrank, "Art of the City," 685.
24. May Cohen to Pearl Cassman, 28 April 1964, SLRC.
25. May Cohen to Pearl Cassman, 15 December 1963, SLRC.
26. Judy Gerowitz to Janice Johnson, 4 June 1964.
27. Judy Gerowitz to Janice Johnson, n.d., late spring 1964.
28. Judy Gerowitz to Janice Johnson, 4 June 1964.
29. Judy Gerowitz to Janice Johnson Lunetta, n.d., June 1964.
30. Judy Gerowitz to Janice Johnson, 4 June 1964.
31. Chicago, *Through the Flower,* 35. Lloyd Hamrol to author, 20 March 2005.
32. Judy Chicago, "Judy Chicago Talking to Lucy Lippard," *Artforum* 13, no. 1 (September 1974), 60.
33. Bereal holds a slice of watermelon. Others include Larry Bell, holding a bagel to indicate that he is Jewish, Joe Goode, and Ron Miyashiro.
34. Ed Bereal to author, 10 February 2006.
35. Ibid.
36. Judy Sword, "Feminist Art-Leader Seduces Crowd," *ATHAPASCAN* (Southwestern College) II (24 March 1972), 1.
37. Judy Gerowitz to Janice Johnson, 4 June 1964.
38. June Wayne to author, 5 December 2005.
39. Judy Gerowitz to Janice Johnson, 4 June 1964, and n.d., late spring 1964.
40. Judy Gerowitz to Janice Johnson, n.d., late spring 1964.
41. John Coplans, "Oral History." Interview by Paul Cummings. Archives of American Art (New York: Smithsonian Institution, 1975), online at http://archivesofamericanart.si.edu/oralhist/coplan75.htm.
42. Chicago, *Through the Flower,* 37.
43. Judy Gerowitz to Janice Johnson, n.d., late spring 1964.
44. Anonymous, "Critic," *Neworld* 2, no. 1 (Fall 1975), 13. JCCSL, Box 1, Folder 42.
45. Ibid.
46. Clair Wolfe, " 'Los Angeles; Painted Sculpture,' " *Artforum* 2, no. 11 (May 1964), 12.

47. Judy Gerowitz to Janice Johnson, 4 June 1964.
48. Gail Levin, *Edward Hopper: An Intimate Biography* (New York: Alfred A. Knopf, 1995).
49. Judy Gerowitz to Janice Johnson, 4 June 1964.
50. Ibid.
51. Judy Gerowitz to Janice Johnson, 8 June 1964.
52. Judy Gerowitz to Janice Johnson and Louis Lunetta, n.d., late June 1964.
53. Judy Gerowitz to Janice Johnson Lunetta, n.d., June 1964.
54. Ibid.
55. Chicago, *Through the Flower*, 37.
56. Ibid.
57. The author has documented in conversations with many female partners Harold Rosenberg's womanizing, despite the fact that he remained married.
58. Chicago, *Through the Flower*, 37.
59. Ibid., 38.
60. Judy Gerowitz to Janice Johnson and Louis Lunetta, n.d., mid-June 1964.
61. Ibid.
62. Ibid.
63. Ibid.
64. Judy Gerowitz to Janice Johnson Lunetta, n.d., June 1964.
65. Judy Gerowitz to Janice Johnson and Louis Lunetta, n.d., mid-June 1964.
66. Judy Gerowitz to Janice Johnson and Louis Lunetta, n.d., late June 1964.
67. Judy Gerowitz to Janice Johnson and Louis Lunetta, n.d., late June 1964.
68. Judy Gerowitz to Janice Johnson, 4 October 1964.
69. Ibid.
70. Ibid.
71. Ibid.
72. Ibid.
73. Philip Leider, "The Cool School," *Artforum* 2, no. 12 (Summer 1964), 47.
74. Stanley Grinstein to author, 9 January 2004.
75. Chicago, *Through the Flower*, 35.
76. Laura Meyer, "A Monumental Meal," *Gadfly* 1, no. 7 (September 1997), 8.
77. Judy Gerowitz to Janice Johnson, 4 October 1964.
78. Judy Chicago to author, February 2005.
79. Chicago, *Through the Flower*, 36–37.
80. Chicago, "Talking to Lucy Lippard," 60.
81. Catalog of same name by director Donald J. Brewer. Gerowitz's *Carhood* is number 30. Hamrol showed *T.F.*, a polychrome wood piece lent by Henry Hopkins.
82. Judy Gerowitz to Janice Johnson and Louis Lunetta, 8 June 1964.
83. Judy Gerowitz to Janice Johnson, 4 October 1964.
84. Clair Wolfe, "Arts and Architecture: Los Angeles," *Artforum* 81 (September 1964), 7.
85. Judy Gerowitz to Janice Johnson and Louis Lunetta, n.d., October 1964.
86. Ibid.
87. Ibid.
88. Joe Goode, interview by author, 2 February 2005. Goode remembered the party on the night that Cooke died, 11 December 1964. More likely what he remembers was the big party that Judy gave on Christmas Eve 1964, noted in her letter to Janice Johnson and Louis Lunetta, 29 December 1964.
89. Judy Gerowitz to Janice Johnson and Louis Lunetta, 29 December 1964.
90. Ibid.
91. Ibid.
92. Ibid.
93. Ibid.
94. Judy Gerowitz to Janice Johnson and Louis Lunetta, n.d., October 1964.
95. Judy Gerowitz to Janice Johnson and Louis Lunetta, 28 January 1965.
96. James Plotkin to author, 7 January 1994.
97. Judy Gerowitz to Janice Johnson, 3 March 1965, collection of Janice Johnson.
98. Judy Gerowitz to Janice Johnson and Louis Lunetta, 28 December 1964.
99. Judy Gerowitz to Janice Johnson and Louis Lunetta, 29 December 1964.
100. Judy Gerowitz to Janice Johnson and Louis Lunetta, 28 December 1964.
101. Judy Chicago to author, 6 December 2005. This has been incorrectly documented elsewhere as taking place in 1972, after Chicago no longer resided in Pasadena. The artist cited in the same source is Barbara Smith, then known as Barbara Turner. See Jay Belloli et al. *Radical Past: Contemporary Art and Music in Pasadena, 1960–1974* (Pasadena, Calif.: Armory Center for the Arts, 1999), 100, 106.
102. Elyse Grinstein to author, 9 January 2004.
103. Chicago, *Through the Flower*, 38.
104. Judy Gerowitz to Janice Johnson, 3 March 1965, collection of Janice Johnson.
105. Ibid.
106. Ibid.
107. Clare Spark Loeb to author, 6 December 2005.
108. Judy Gerowitz to Janice Johnson, 3 March 1965, collection of Janice Johnson.
109. Suzanne Muchnic, "Inside Look at Museum Policy," *Los Angeles Times*, 27 July 1981, sec. 4, 4. JCCSL, Box 81, Folder 29. Documents list protesters, who included Diane Gelon and Judy Baca, among others.
110. Judy Gerowitz to Janice Johnson and Louis Lunetta, 29 December 1964.

111. Ibid.
112. Judy Gerowitz to Janice Johnson and Louis Lunetta, n.d., 1965. Judy Gerowitz to Janice Johnson, Louis Lunetta, and family, 24 May 1965.
113. Judy Gerowitz to Janice Johnson, 3 March 1965, collection of Janice Johnson.
114. Ibid.
115. Ibid.
116. Ibid.
117. Ibid.
118. Billy Al Bengston to author, 12 January 2004.
119. Ibid.
120. Judy Chicago, interview by author, 13 June 2004.
121. Judy Gerowitz to Janice Johnson and Louis Lunetta, 24 May 1965.
122. See Frank Stella's *Sinjerli II* or *Takht-i-Sulayman I,* both of 1967, in William S. Rubin, *Frank Stella* (New York: Museum of Modern Art, 1970), 139, 144.
123. Peter Plagens, "Judith Gerowitz, Rolf Nelson Gallery," *Artforum* 4, no. 7 (March 1966), 14.
124. Peter Plagens, "Judy Gerowitz, Rolf Nelson Gallery," *Artforum* 4, no. 8 (April 1966), 14.
125. Ibid.
126. James Meyer, *Minimalism: Art and Polemics in the Sixties* (New Haven, Conn.: Yale University Press, 2001), 13.
127. When Chicago dug this work out of storage decades later, she had lost its title. She both repainted and retitled it *Trinity.* The piece was subsequently shown in *Judy Chicago Minimalism, 1965–1973,* in 2004 at LewAllen Contemporary in Santa Fe.
128. Raphael Patai, *The Hebrew Goddess,* 3rd ed. (Detroit, Mich.: Wayne State University Press, 1990), 221–54.
129. Ibid., 252.
130. Ibid., 237.
131. Fidel Danieli, "Los Angeles: Judy Gerowitz," *ARTnews* 65, no. 1 (March 1966), 20.
132. Ann Goldstein, *A Minimal Future? Art as Object 1958–1968* (Los Angeles: Museum of Contemporary Art/MIT Press, 2004), 17.
133. John Coplans, "The New Abstraction on the West Coast U.S.A.," *Studio International* 169, no. 865 (May 1965), 199.
134. Chicago, *Beyond the Flower,* 16.
135. Judy Gerowitz to May Cohen, 29 June 1966, JCCSL.
136. Judy Gerowitz to May Cohen, 29 January 1966.
137. Kynaston McShine, *Primary Structures: Younger American and British Sculptors* (New York: Jewish Museum, 1966), 17,
138. Meyer, *Minimalism: Art and Polemics,* 22.
139. Kynaston McShine to Allene Talmey, 18 March 1966, quoted in James Meyer, "Another Minimalism," in Goldstein, *Minimal Future?* 34.
140. Anonymous, "Engineer's Esthetic," *Time,* 3 June 1966, 65.
141. Corinne Robbins, "Object, Structure or Sculpture: Where Are We?" *Arts Magazine* 40, no. 9 (September–October 1966), 36.
142. Meyer, *Minimalism: Art and Polemics,* 24–25.
143. William C. Seitz, *Art in the Age of Aquarius, 1955–1970* (Washington, D.C.: Smithsonian Institution, 1992), 109–10.
144. Lloyd Hamrol quoted in Chicago, "Two Artists, Two Attitudes," 8.
145. Barbara Rose, *Claes Oldenburg* (New York: Museum of Modern Art, 1970), 185.
146. Willaim Wilson, "Geometric Forms Float as a Cloud," *Los Angeles Times,* 29 August 1966, 14.
147. Ray Duncan, "An Artist Feathers Her Nest," *Pasadena Star-News,* 1966, 17.
148. Ibid.
149. Ibid.
150. Ibid.
151. Ibid.
152. May Cohen to Pearl Cassman, 30 August 1966, SLRC.
153. May Cohen to Pearl Cassman, 25 January 1967, SLRC.
154. Irving Petlin to author, 30 January 2006.
155. Lloyd Hamrol to author, 20 March 2005.
156. Henry Hopkins to author, 6 January 2004.
157. Francis Frascina, *Art, Politics and Dissent: Aspects of the Art Left in Sixties America* (Manchester, U.K.: Manchester University Press, 1999), 17.
158. Art Berman, "Art Tower Started as Vietnam Protest," *Los Angeles Times* (1966), 3, 24.
159. Johanna Demetrakas to author, 21 October 2002.
160. *L.A. Times* photo with caption beginning "A Rising Protest Sculptor Mark di Suvero prepares . . . ," JCCSL, Box 1, Folder 34.
161. Judy Chicago and Dextra Frankel, "Invisible Twenty-One Artists Visible," in *Twenty-One Artists—Invisible/Visible* (Long Beach, Calif. Long Beach Museum of Art, 1972), 9.
162. Dextra Frankel to author, 14 January 2004.
163. Henry T. Hopkins, "Strong Hands and Sneakers: Monumental Sculpture at Century City," *Century City Centurion,* November–December 1967, 8. JCCSL, Box 1, Folder 35.
164. Chicago, *Kitty City,* 5.
165. Chicago, "Talking to Lucy Lippard," 60.
166. John Coplans, "The New Sculpture and

Technology," in *American Sculpture of the Sixties,* ed. Maurice Tuchman (Los Angeles: Los Angeles County Museum of Art, 1967), 24.
167. Maurice Tuchman, "Introduction," in *American Sculpture of the Sixties,* ed. Maurice Tuchman (Los Angeles, Calif.: Los Angeles Museum of Art, 1967), 10.
168. Henry J. Seldis, "Technology for Art's Sake," *Los Angeles Times* (1967), 16.
169. Anonymous, "Sculpture Evaporating Environments," *Time,* 12 January 1968, 30.
170. Henry Hopkins with Evris Tsakirides, *Lloyd Hamrol: Works, Projects, Proposals* (Los Angeles: Los Angeles Municipal Art Gallery, 1986), 6.
171. Seldis, "Technology for Art's Sake," 16.
172. Ibid.
173. Lloyd Hamrol quoted in Chicago, "Two Artists, Two Attitudes," 8.
174. See Chicago, *Through the Flower,* 38–54.
175. May Cohen to Pearl Cassman, 26 February 1968, SLRC.
176. Peter Selz and William Wilson, "Los Angeles—A View from the Studios," *Art in America* (1969), 144.
177. Ibid.
178. Judy Gerowitz, Los Angeles FM Radio on Fine Arts, May 1968, JCCSL, Box 1, Folder 36.
179. Clare Spark Loeb to author, 6 December 2005.
180. William Wilson, "Aspects of Modernity in Orange County Shows," *Los Angeles Times,* 27 October 1968, 52.
181. Judy Chicago, "Interview by Hazel Slawson," typescript, (n.d., c.1973), 9. JCCSL.
182. Chicago, "Talking to Lucy Lippard," 60.
183. Chicago, *Through the Flower,* caption following 72 in 2nd ed.
184. Keith Sonnier to author, 2 February 2006.
185. Chicago, *Through the Flower,* 58.
186. Chicago, "Talking to Lucy Lippard," 60.
187. Chicago, *Through the Flower,* 52.
188. See Alice Echols, *Daring to Be Bad: Radical Feminism in America, 1967–1975* (Minneapolis: University of Minnesota, 1989), 9.
189. Chicago, "Talking to Lucy Lippard," 60.
190. Judy Chicago, *Beyond the Flower: The Autobiography of a Feminist Artist* (New York: Viking Penguin, 1996), 29.
191. JoAnne Severns Northrup, "Judy Chicago," in *Finish Fetish: LA's Cool School,* ed. Frances Colpitt (Los Angeles: Fisher Gallery, University of Southern California, 1991), 42.
192. Selz and Wilson, "Los Angeles," 144.
193. Judy Gerowitz, *Judy Gerowitz* (Pasadena, Calif.: Pasadena Art Museum, 1969), n.p.
194. Chicago, "Talking to Lucy Lippard," 60.
195. Laura E. Cogburn, "PLAstics," in *Finish Fetish: LA's Cool School,* ed. Frances Colpitt (Los Angeles: Fisher Gallery, University of Southern California, 1991), 12–13.
196. William Wilson, "Judy Gerowitz Sculpture in Pasadena," *Los Angeles Times,* 18 May 1969, 48.
197. Selz and Wilson, "Los Angeles," 144.
198. Ibid.
199. Neither Judy Chicago nor James Turrell, in separate conversations with the author, recalls this event.
200. See http://w201.nl/~kazil/advartoo.html.
201. Elyse and Stanley Grinstein to author, 9 January 2004.
202. Jack Rhyne to author, 9 August 2005.

Feminist Class 7

1. Jack Rhyne to author, 1 August 2005.
2. Frank Laury to author, 14 February 2006.
3. Dal Henderson to author, 28 August 2005.
4. Judy Chicago to author, 12 December 2005.
5. Dal Henderson to author, 28 August 2005.
6. Vanalyne Green to author, 19 December 2005.
7. Heinz Kusel, *Heinz Kusel Between Experience and Reflection: The Story of a Painter as Told to Thomas Kusel* (Auburn, Calif.: Destiny, 2004), 297.
8. Ibid., 293.
9. Jack Rhyne, who studied with Kusel, to the author, 1 August 2005.
10. Kusel, *Heinz Kusel,* 22. He had previously belonged to D.J. 1-11, another youth group that had opposed Hitler.
11. Oliver Andrews, "Los Angeles Art Community: Group Portrait." Interview by George M. Goodwin. Oral History Program Transcript, 82. UCLA, 1977. He referred to her by the name Judy Chicago. Her first surviving résumés, however, list "California State University (1969–1971)," JCCSL, Box 1, Folder 2; she again listed it on an early résumé as, "Fresno State College, Asst. Professor 1969–71," JCCSL, Box 16, Folder 8, for the Guggenheim grant application. Chicago may have believed that she had started in Fresno the fall of 1969 (as on her CV for the "Lively Word" speakers' bureau, on which she listed "1969 Married Lloyd Hamrol. Became assistant professor at Fresno State College [until 1971]. Performed her first *Atmospheres.*") She may also have decided that starting her job in the fall of 1969 made her look better. This is also the date in the catalog Judy Chicago and Dextra Frankel, "Invisible Twenty-One

Artists Visible," in *Twenty-One Artists—Invisible/Visible* (Long Beach, Calif.: Long Beach Museum of Art, 1972), 22. It may be that she wanted to indicate concisely that she had taught in Fresno for more than one school year.

12. Kusel, *Heinz Kusel,* 32.
13. Ibid., 305.
14. Ibid., 11.
15. Judy Chicago and Judith Dancoff, "Judy Chicago Interviewed by Judith Dancoff," *Everywoman* 2, no. 7, issue 18 (7 May 1971), 4.
16. Chicago, *Through the Flower: My Struggle as a Woman Artist,* 2nd ed. (New York: Penguin Books, 1975), 59.
17. Valerie Solanas, *Scum Manifesto* (New York: Olympia Press, 1968), excerpted in *Feminism–Art–Theory: An Anthology, 1968–2000,* ed. Hilary Robinson. (Oxford: Blackwell Publishers, 2001), 12.
18. Judy Chicago, "Two Artists, Two Attitudes: Judy Chicago and Lloyd Hamrol Interview Each Other," *Criteria: A Review of the Arts* 1, no. 2 (November 1974), 9.
19. Ibid.
20. Judy Chicago, "Judy Chicago Talking to Lucy Lippard," *Artforum* 13, no. 1 (September 1974), 60.
21. May Cohen to Pearl Cassman, 5 February 1970, JCCSL.
22. See CV from 1975 in JCCSL, Box 1, Folder 2.
23. Guy Dill to author, 11 June 2006.
24. Nancy Youdelman to author, 6 December 2005. Youdelman recalls Faith Wilding (who was there) saying that there were hecklers—guys who were threatened and became angry and vocal. Youdelman is now a sculptor; Wilding is a performance artist.
25. Suzaan Lacy to author, 9 January 2004.
26. Judy Chicago, "Interview by Hazel Slawson," typescript (c.1972), 3, JCCSL.
27. Judy Chicago, *Personal Journal,* vol. 1, 3.
28. Jack Rhyne to author, 1 August 2005.
29. Vanalyne Green to author, 19 December 2005. Part of her communication to me was previously published: Vanalyne Green, "The Feminist Art Program," in *Women of Vision: Histories in Feminist Film and Video,* ed. Alexandra Juhasz (Minneapolis: University of Minnesota Press, 2001), 156.
30. Vanalyne Green to author, 19 December 2005.
31. Laurel Klick to author, 8 February 2006.
32. Ibid.
33. Jack Rhyne to author, 1 August 2005.
34. May Cohen to Pearl Cassman, 19 May 1970, JCCSL.
35. Jack Rhyne to author, 3 August 2005. He would become a friend of the family and go on to work for Chicago at other sites.
36. Ibid.
37. Mark di Suvero to author, 3 January 2006.
38. Judy Chicago, *Through the Flower,* 62–63.
39. May Cohen to Pearl Cassman, 5 November 1970, JCCSL.
40. This ad appeared in *Artforum* 9, no. 2 (October 1970), 20.
41. Boxing photo ad, *Artforum* 9, no. 4 (December 1970), 36.
42. Judy Chicago quoted in Jonathan Kirsch, "The Flowering of the Artist," *Coast* 16, no. 6 (June 1975), 37. JCCSL, Box 1, Folder 42.
43. Ibid.
44. Ibid.
45. William Wilson, "Judy Chicago Exhibition at Cal State Fullerton Gallery," *Los Angeles Times,* 2 November 1970, pt. 4.
46. Ibid.
47. Ibid.
48. Ibid.
49. Copy in archives at JCCSL.
50. Gerda Lerner, *The Grimké Sisters from South Carolina: Pioneers for Women's Rights and Abolition* (New York: Shocken Books, 1971), 193, 161–62; see also Sara Evans, *Personal Politics: The Roots of Women's Liberation in the Civil Rights Movement and the New Left* (New York: Alfred A. Knopf, 1979), 26.
51. Shulamith Firestone, *The Dialectic of Sex: The Case for Feminist Revolution* (New York: William Morrow & Co., 1970), 29.
52. Judy Chicago, *Painting Sculpture Photographs of Atmospheres by Judy Chicago* (Fullerton: California State Gallery, 1970).
53. Thomas H. Garver, "Judy Chicago, Art Gallery, California State College, Fullerton," *Artforum* 9, no. 5 (January 1971), 92.
54. Ibid., 92–93.
55. Ibid., 93.
56. Judy Chicago to Phil Leider, n.d., January 1971, published March 1971, JCCSL, Box 9, Folder 8.
57. Ibid.
58. Ibid.
59. Ibid.
60. Ibid.
61. Chicago, *Through the Flower,* 64.
62. Ibid., 56.
63. Miriam Schapiro, conversation with author, July 1997.
64. Judy Chicago, *Beyond the Flower: The Autobiography of a Feminist Artist* (New York: Viking Penguin, 1996), 64. Though not named in this text, Chicago identified him

to author, 24 January 2006, saying that she found his Pasadena loft for him.

65. Mark di Suvero to author, 30 January 2006.
66. Chicago, *Beyond the Flower*, 57.
67. Chicago, "Talking to Lucy Lippard," 61.
68. Paul C. Mills, *Spray* (Santa Barbara, Calif.: Santa Barbara Museum of Art, 1971), 18.
69. Chicago, *Through the Flower*, 70–92; Chicago, *Beyond the Flower*, 23.
70. Chicago, *Personal Journal*, vol. 1, 3.
71. Nancy Youdelman to author, 6 April 2004.
72. Ibid.
73. Chicago, *Personal Journal*, vol. 1, 4.
74. Dori Atlantis and Chris Rush to author, 1 April 2004.
75. Ibid.
76. Chris Rush to author, 1 April 2004.
77. Suzanne Lacy to Moira Roth, Archives of American Art, 16 March 1990.
78. Ibid.
79. Green, "Feminist Art Program," 156.
80. Vanalyne Green to author, 19 December 2005.
81. Faith Wilding, *By Our Own Hands: The Woman Artist's Movement in Southern California, 1970–1976* (Santa Monica, Calif.: Double X, 1977), 10.
82. Chicago, "Chicago Interviewed by Slawson," 8.
83. Judy Chicago to author, 25 July 2005.
84. Ibid. See also Susan Stocking, "Through the Looking Glass with Judy Chicago," *Los Angeles Times*, 9 July 1972, 44. JCCSL, Box 1, Folder 39.
85. Chicago, "Chicago Interviewed by Slawson," 8–9.
86. Vanalyne Green to author, 19 December 2005.
87. Suzanne Lacy, "Interviewed by Moira Roth," Archives of American Art Oral History Program, Smithsonian Institution (Berkeley, Calif., 16 March 1990), tape 1, side A, online at http://www.aaa.si.edu/oralhist/lacy90.htm#top.
88. Ibid.
89. Karen LeCocq to author, 6 April 2004.
90. Stocking, "Through the Looking Glass," 44. JCCSL, Box 1, Folder 39.
91. Chicago, "Chicago Interviewed by Slawson," 17.
92. Chicago, *Personal Journal*, vol. 1, 7.
93. Boston Women's Health Book Collective, *Our Bodies, Ourselves: A Book By and For Women* (New York: Simon & Schuster, 1971).
94. Nancy Youdelman to author, 28 May 2006. Judy Chicago to author, 28 May 2006. She assigned *Our Bodies, Ourselves* only this first year, because it then became so popular that everyone had already read it.
95. Karen LeCocq, *The Easiest Thing to Remember: My Life as an Artist, a Feminist, and a Manic Depressive* (Bloomington, Ind.: 1st Books, 2002), 54.
96. Karen LeCocq to author, 6 April 2004.
97. LeCocq, *Easiest Thing*, 62.
98. Karen LeCocq to author, 6 April 2004.
99. Ibid.
100. Ibid.
101. Chris Rush to author, 1 April 2004.
102. Jan Lester Martin to author, 7 April 2004.
103. Nancy Youdelman to author, 6 April 2004; Shawnee Wollenman to author, 29 July 2006; and Cheryl Zurilgen to author 29 July 2006.
104. Chicago, *Personal Journal*, vol. 1, 25–26.
105. Nancy Youdelman to author, 6 April 2004.
106. Vanalyne Green to author, 19 December 2004.
107. Ibid.
108. Ibid. Green's testimony rules out once and for all a recent guess about Chicago's change of name: ignoring its roots in her growing feminist consciousness and imputing it to a supposed wish to conceal and escape her Jewish heritage. See Lisa Bloom, " 'Ethnic Notions and Feminist Strategies of the 1970s,' " in *Jewish Identity in Modern Art History*, ed. Catherine M. Soussloff (Berkeley: University of California Press, 1999), 135–63. Bloom's guess has no basis in Chicago's attitude toward her Jewishness, but it may unconsciously betray some of Bloom's own feeling.
109. Vanalyne Green to author, 19 December 2005.
110. Suzanne Lacy to Moira Roth, AAA, oral history, 16 March 1990.
111. Unidentified "Tape of a Conversation with Judy Chicago," JCCSL.
112. Ibid.
113. Shawnee Wollenman Johnson to author, 3 September 2006.
114. Linda Nochlin, "Why Have There Been No Great Women Artists?" *ARTnews* 69, no. 9 (January 1971), 23–39+. See Faith Wilding, "Women Artists and Female Imagery," *Everywoman* 2, no. 7 (7 May 1971), 18. Wilding notes that their research on women artists began "from the beginning of the [school] year."
115. Wilding, *By Our Own Hands*, 13. Karen LeCocq to author, 6 April 2004.
116. Suzanne Lacy to author, 9 January 2004.
117. Chicago, "Chicago Interviewed by Slawson," 15–16.
118. Chicago, *Personal Journal*, vol. 1, 4.
119. Ibid., 5.
120. Judy Chicago to May Cohen, 18 November 1970, JCCSL.

121. Chicago, *Through the Flower,* 93.
122. Chicago, "Chicago Interviewed by Slawson," 12–13. Years later Schapiro recalled bringing Chicago to La Jolla to have her speak about the Fresno program, which she described as a "stirring" talk "Conversations with Judy Chicago and Miriam Schapiro," in *The Power of Feminist Art,* ed. Norma Broude and Mary D. Garrard [New York: Harry N. Abrams, 1994], 74.) Chicago had indeed lectured at La Jolla but not about the Fresno FAP, because by the time she began it in fall 1970, Schapiro had already left La Jolla to join her husband at CalArts. Chicago does not recall ever lecturing about the FAP for Schapiro in either La Jolla or Valencia, and it is contrary to how she operates; she does not speak about something before she does it or even before she finishes a project. So it would have been completely out of character for her to have gone to Schapiro's class to talk about the Fresno program when she was so uncertain of its success. (Chicago to author, 25 July 2005. She does recall giving a talk about her art at U.C. San Diego at La Jolla.)
123. Chicago, "Chicago Interviewed by Slawson," 13.
124. Miriam Schapiro, "Miriam Schapiro Interviewed by Judith Dancoff," *Everywoman* 2, no. 7, issue 18 (7 May 1971): 3. Chicago, "Chicago Interviewed by Slawson," 14.
125. Chicago, "Chicago Interviewed by Slawson," 12.
126. Nancy Youdelman to author, 6 April 2004.
127. Ibid.
128. LeCocq, *Easiest Thing,* 59.
129. Faith Wilding, "The Feminist Art Programs at Fresno and Cal Arts, 1970–75," in *The Power of Feminist Art,* ed. Norma Broude and Mary Garrard (New York: Harry N. Abrams, 1994), 36.
130. This image was first reproduced in Schapiro, "Schapiro Interviewed by Judith Dancoff," 3, and then on the cover of Moira Roth, *The Shrine, The Computer and the Dollhouse: Miriam Schapiro* (La Jolla, CA: Mandeville Art Gallery, University of California at San Diego, 1975). There are several photographs of Schapiro in this costume, one of which is frontal and another that shows a three-quarter view of her face.
131. Chris Rush to author, 1 April 2004.
132. Chicago, *Personal Journal,* vol. 1, 6–7.
133. Simone de Beauvoir, *The Second Sex* (New York: Alfred A. Knopf, 1953), 348.
134. Ibid.
135. Suzanne Lacy to author, 9 January 2004.
136. Jan Lester Martin to author, 7 April 2004.
137. Vanalyne Green to author, 19 December 2005.
138. Ibid.
139. Jan Lester Martin to author, 7 April 2004.
140. Chicago, "Chicago Interviewed by Slawson," 15.
141. Chicago, *Personal Journal,* vol. 1, 8 March 1971, 1.
142. Chicago, *Personal Journal,* vol. 1, 8 March 1971, 1. Historians have not yet identified who first used this phrase. Instead, Hilary Robinson postdated Chicago's article in the Feminist Art Program's issue of *Everywoman* 7 from the spring of 1971 to 1972, making it seem a year later than it actually was. Hilary Robinson, *Feminism–Art–Theory: An Anthology, 1968–2000,* 294.
143. *Everywoman* 2, no. 7, 1971, 3. Clearly Miriam Schapiro and Judy Chicago had by this time agreed to bring Chicago's program to CalArts under this name.
144. Chicago, *Personal Journal,* vol. 1, 8 March 1971, 2.
145. Ibid.
146. Chicago, "Chicago Interviewed by Slawson," 2.
147. Chicago, *Personal Journal,* vol. 1, 9 March 1971, 11.
148. Ibid., 13 March 1971, 14.
149. Ibid., 22 March 1971, 15.
150. Ibid., 13 March 1971, 12.
151. Ibid., 22 March 1971, 15.
152. Wilding, "Feminist Art Programs at Fresno," 35.
153. Chicago, *Personal Journal,* vol. 1, 13 March 1971, 14.
154. Nancy Youdelman and Jan Lester Martin to author, 31 May 2006.
155. Chicago, *Personal Journal,* vol. 1, 22 March 1971, 16.
156. Roxanne Dunbar-Ortiz, *Outlaw Woman: A Memoir of the War Years, 1960–1975* (San Francisco: City Lights, 2001), 317.
157. Chicago, *Personal Journal,* vol. 1, 23 March 1971, 16–17.
158. Nancy Youdelman to author, 6 April 2004. Cay Lang to author, 22 June 2006. Lang is now a photographer.
159. Lacy, "Interviewed by Moira Roth," tape 1, side A.
160. Chicago, *Personal Journal,* vol. 1, 24 March 1971, 17.
161. Ibid. Suzanne Lacy to author, 9 January 2004.
162. Chicago, *Personal Journal,* vol. 1, 24 March 1971, 18.
163. Ti-Grace Atkinson, *Amazon Odyssey: The First Collection of Writing by the Political Pioneer of the Women's Movement* (New York: Link Books, 1974), xxii.
164. Ibid., 90.

165. Chicago, *Personal Journal,* vol. 1, 26 March 1971, 20.
166. Larry Bell to author, 14 January 2004.
167. Jan Lester Martin to author, 7 January 2004.
168. Vanalyne Green to author, 19 December 2005.
169. Shawnee Wollenman Johnson to author, 29 July 2006.
170. Chicago, *Personal Journal,* vol. 1, 24 March 1971, 18–19.
171. Judy Chicago to the Admissions Committee (California Institute of the Arts), 27 March 1971, JCCSL, Box 11, Folder 17.
172. Ibid.
173. Ibid.
174. Chicago, *Personal Journal,* vol. 1, 28 March 1971, 22–23.
175. Ibid., 28 March 1971, 23.
176. Ibid., 30 March 1971, 23.
177. Jack Rhyne to author, 3 August 2005.
178. Chicago, *Personal Journal,* vol. 1, 6 April 1971, 33–34.
179. Ibid., 11 April 1971, 44.
180. Ibid., 14 April 1971, 47.
181. Judy Chicago and Ruth Iskin, "Judy Chicago in Conversation with Ruth Iskin," *Visual Dialog* 2, no. 3 (May 1977), 14.
182. Chicago and Dancoff, "Chicago Interviewed by Dancoff," 4.
183. LeCocq, *Easiest Thing,* 59–60.
184. Chicago, *Personal Journal,* vol. 1, 51. Wilding, *By Our Own Hands,* 15.
185. Chicago to author, 21 December 2005.
186. Vicki Hall to author, 16 November 2005. The following references are also from this date.
187. Chicago, *Personal Journal,* vol. 1, 53.
188. Ibid.
189. Ibid., 54.
190. Author interviewed this student, who wishes to remain anonymous.
191. Chicago, *Personal Journal,* vol. 1, 26 April 1971, 57.
192. Ibid., 26 April 1971, 55–56.
193. Ibid., 26 April 1971, 57–58.
194. Ibid.
195. Ibid., 26 April 1971, 58.
196. Ibid., 26 April 1971, 59.
197. Ibid., 27 April 1971, 62.
198. Ibid., 27 April 1971, 64.
199. Ibid., 27 April 1971, 65.
200. Ibid., 26 April 1971, 59.
201. Lucy R. Lippard, *Eva Hesse* (New York: New York University Press, 1976).
202. Chicago, *Personal Journal,* vol. 1, 2 May 1971, 69.
203. Ibid., 6 May 1971, 75.
204. Sarah Petlin to author, 1 February 2006.
205. Chicago, *Personal Journal,* vol. 1, 2 May 1971, 70.
206. Ibid.
207. Ibid., 2, 6 May 1971, 70–71.
208. Ibid., 6 May 1971, 70.
209. Ibid., 6 May 1971, 72–73.
210. May Cohen to Pearl Cassman, 15 April 1971, JCCSL.
211. Ibid.
212. Chicago, *Personal Journal,* vol. 1, 6 May 1971, 73.
213. Jackie Winsor to author, 1 February 2006.
214. Chicago, *Personal Journal,* vol. 1, 6 May 1971, 73–74.
215. Ibid., 11 May 1971, 77–78.
216. Lee Bontecou, quoted in Elizabeth A. T. Smith et al., Museum of Contemporary Art, Chicago, 2004.
217. Chicago, *Personal Journal,* vol. 1, 11 May 1971, 78–79.
218. Ibid.
219. Ibid., 11 May 1971, 79.
220. Ibid., 11 May 1971, 80.
221. Grace Glueck, "The Ladies Flex Their Brushes," *New York Times,* 30 May 1971, D20.
222. Chicago, *Personal Journal,* vol. 1, 11 May 1971, 80.
223. Grace Glueck to author, 6 December 2005. Glueck assured me that no editor imposed this language. Although at the time the idea of "feminism" turned her off, before too long she was engaged in a sex-discrimination lawsuit by women at the *New York Times,* chronicled by Nan Robertson in *The Girls in the Balcony: Women, Men, and the New York Times* (New York: Random House, 1992).
224. Glueck, "Ladies Flex," D20.
225. Chicago, *Personal Journal,* vol. 1, 11 May 1971, 81.
226. Grace Glueck, "No More Raw Eggs at the Whitney?" *New York Times,* 13 February 1972, D21.
227. Chicago, *Personal Journal,* vol. 1, 11 May 1971, 80.
228. Ibid., 11 May 1971, 81.
229. Ibid., 13 May 1971, 82.
230. Ibid., 13 May 1971, 84.
231. Ibid., 13 May 1971, 84–85.
232. Ibid., 13 May 1971, 85.
233. Ibid.
234. Ibid., 13 May 1971, 86.
235. Ibid.
236. Ibid., 18 May 1971, 92.
237. Ibid., 20 May 1971, 96.
238. Ibid., 27 May 1971, 96–97.
239. Allan Kaprow to author, 10 March 1999.
240. Suzanne Lacy to Moira Roth, 16 March 1990.
241. Chicago, *Personal Journal,* vol. 1, 27 May 1971, 98–99.

242. Ibid., 27 May 1971, 99–100.
243. Ibid., 28 May 1971, 101.
244. *Everywoman,* 7 May 1971, special issue written by the women of the Fresno Feminist Art Program.
245. Jan Lester Martin to author, 7 April 2004.
246. Paula Harper to author, 30 January 2004.
247. Chicago, *Personal Journal,* vol. 1, 1 June 1971, 104.
248. Ibid., 1 June 1971, 106–09.
249. Vicki Hall to author, 7 December 2005.
250. Chicago, *Personal Journal,* vol. 1, 1 June 1971, 109.
251. Chicago to author, 24 January 2006.
252. Chicago, *Personal Journal,* vol. 1, 110.
253. Ibid., 111.
254. Paula Harper to author, 30 January 2004.
255. Chicago, *Personal Journal,* vol. 1, 112.

Beyond the Abstract: *Womanhouse* 8

1. Judy Chicago, *Personal Journal,* vol. 1, 25 June 1971, 126.
2. Paula Harper to author, 30 January 2004.
3. Chicago, *Personal Journal,* vol. 1, 12 June 1971, 114–15.
4. Ibid., 12 June 1971, 122.
5. Ibid., 21 June 1971, 115.
6. Ibid., 25 June 1971, 124.
7. Ibid., 25 June 1971, 125.
8. Chicago, *Personal Journal,* vol. 3, 29 July 1972, 82. She noted "as my brilliant friend, Arlene [Raven], observed . . ."
9. Chicago, *Personal Journal,* vol. 1, 25 June [2 July] 1971, 127.
10. Ibid., 2 July 1971, 128.
11. Ibid., 2 July 1971, 128–29.
12. Ibid., 2 July 1971, 129.
13. Ibid., 2 July 1971, 128.
14. Ibid., 6 August 1971, 136.
15. Ibid., 6 August 1971, 137.
16. Ibid.
17. Ibid., 6 August 1971, 137–38.
18. Ibid., 6 August 1971, 138.
19. Carol Ockman to Mimi, Judy, Paula, 30 January [1972], JCCSL, Box 11, Folder 34.
20. Chicago, *Personal Journal,* vol. 1, 6 August 1971, 134.
21. Shulamith Firestone, *The Dialectic of Sex: The Case for Feminist Revolution* (New York: William Morrow & Co., 1970), 169.
22. Ibid.
23. Chicago, *Personal Journal,* vol. 1, 6 August 1971, 135.
24. Ibid., 6 August 1971, 135–36.
25. Ibid., 9 August 1971, 139–40.
26. Ibid., 9 August 1971, 140.
27. Term 1, 1972 CalArts, Schedule of Classes—School of Art.
28. Chicago, *Personal Journal,* vol. 1, 16 August 1971, 141.
29. Paula Harper to author, 30 January 2004.
30. Gail Levin, "Beyond the Pale: Jewish Identity, Radical Politics, and Feminist Art in the United States," *Journal of Modern Jewish Studies* 4 (July 2005): 205–32.
31. Chicago, *Personal Journal,* vol. 1, 23 August 1971, 144.
32. Ibid., 27 August 1971.
33. Ibid., 23 August 1971, 143.
34. Ibid., 23 August 1971, 144.
35. Ibid., 23 August 1971, 145. Brach is known as an entertaining raconteur; students who prefer not to speak in class might prefer his style.
36. Ibid.
37. Ibid.
38. Ibid., 23 August 1971, 146.
39. Ibid., 23 August 1971, 146–47.
40. Clare Spark to author, 6 December 2005.
41. Judy Chicago, *Fragments from the Delta of Venus* (New York: PowerHouse Books, 2004), 8.
42. Chicago, *Personal Journal,* vol. 1, 23 August 1971, 146.
43. Chicago, *Fragments,* 11.
44. Ibid.
45. Ibid.
46. Judy Chicago quoted in Noël Riley Fitch, *Anaïs: The Erotic Life of Anaïs Nin* (Boston, Mass.: Little, Brown & Co., 1993), 399. Fitch garbles some details about *Womanhouse.*
47. Chicago, *Fragments,* 8.
48. Marcia Tucker, *The Structure of Color* (New York: Whitney Museum of American Art, 1971); the other women were Ellen Cibula, Helen Frankenthaler, and Jane Kaufman.
49. Ibid., 18.
50. Judy Chicago, *Personal Journal,* vol. 2, 13 September 1971, 7.
51. Ibid., 15 September 1971, 9.
52. Ibid., 15 September 1971, 10–11.
53. Ibid., 15 September 1971, 11, about visit of the previous day.
54. Ibid., 15 September 1971, 12.
55. Ibid.
56. Ibid., 15 September 1971, 12–13.
57. Ibid., 15 September 1971, 13.
58. Ibid., 13 September 1971, 8.
59. Ibid., 15 September 1971, 14.
60. Ibid., 15 September 1971, 42.
61. Emma Goldman, *Living My Life* (New York: Alfred A. Knopf, 1931).
62. Arlene Raven, "Feminist Content in Current Female Art," *Sister Magazine: West Coast Feminist Newspaper* 6 (October/November 1975): 10.

63. Paula Harper to author, 30 January 2004.
64. Ibid.
65. Chicago, *Personal Journal,* vol. 1, 9 September 1971, 151.
66. Ibid.
67. Chicago to author, 7 December 2005.
68. June Wayne to author, 6 December 2005.
69. Chicago to author, 7 December 2005.
70. Chicago, *Personal Journal,* vol. 2, 8 September 1971, 5.
71. Ibid.
72. Ibid., 18 September 1971, 17–18.
73. Ibid., 26 September 1971, 20–21.
74. David Allyn, *Make Love Not War: The Sexual Revolution: An Unfettered History* (Boston: Little, Brown & Co., 2000), 29.
75. Ibid., 46, 25–29.
76. Chicago, *Personal Journal,* vol. 2, 26 September 1971, 21–22.
77. Chicago, *Personal Journal,* vol. 2, 30 September 1971, 26–27.
78. Gore Vidal review appeared in *Los Angeles Times,* 26 September 1971. Chicago wrote her letter on 28 September, 1971, JCCSL, Box 9, Folder 8.
79. Chicago, *Personal Journal,* vol. 2, 24.
80. Ibid., 30 September 1971, 28.
81. Chicago, *Personal Journal,* vol. 1, 9 September 1971, 150.
82. Chris Rush to author, 1 April 2004.
83. Chicago, *Personal Journal,* vol. 2, 10 October 1971, 30.
84. Ibid., 23 October 1971, 35.
85. Ibid., 23 October 1971, 34.
86. Ibid., 23 October 1971, 35.
87. Ibid., 25 October 1971, 40–41.
88. Ibid., 4 November 1971, 45.
89. Ibid., 7 November 1971, 52.
90. Ibid., 4 November 1971, 42–43.
91. Ibid., 7 November 1971, 48.
92. Ibid., 7 November 1971, 49–50.
93. Ibid., 7 November 1971, 49.
94. Ibid., 7 November 1971, 50.
95. Ibid., 7 November 1971, 51.
96. Ibid., 7 November 1971, 52–53.
97. Ibid., 7 November 1971, 54.
98. Ibid., 11 November 1971, 55.
99. Ibid., 11 November 1971, 57.
100. Ibid.
101. Ibid., 1 December 1971, 63.
102. Ibid., 1 December 1971, 64.
103. Ibid., 1 December 1971, 64–65.
104. Ibid., 1 December 1971, 65.
105. Ibid., 1 December 1971, 65–66.
106. Ibid., 1 December 1971, 66–67.
107. Ibid., 1 December 1971, 67–68.
108. Ibid., 1 December 1971, 72.
109. Ibid., 10 December 1971, 73.
110. Ibid., 1 December 1971, 74.
111. Ibid., 1 December 1971, 76.
112. Ibid., 1 December 1971, 77.
113. She did have a show at his gallery in Corona del Mar, Calif., in 1972. CV from 1975, when she was living at 1651B 18th Street in Santa Monica, JCCSL, Box 1, Folder 2.
114. Chicago, *Personal Journal,* vol. 2, 17 December 1971, 78–79.
115. Ibid., 17 December 1971, 79.
116. Ibid., 17 December 1971, 80.
117. Ibid., 17 December 1971, 80–81.
118. Ibid., 17 December 1971, 81.
119. Ibid., 27 December 1971, 83.
120. Ibid.
121. Ibid., 27 December 1971, 83–84.
122. Ibid., 27 December 1971, 86–87.
123. Priscilla English, "An Interview with Two Artists from Womanhouse," *New Woman,* April–May 1972, 36.
124. " 'Womanhouse' Opens," *Los Angeles Free Press,* 4 February 1972, JCCSL.
125. Judy Chicago and Miriam Schapiro, *Womanhouse,* exhibition catalog (Los Angeles, 1972), n.p.
126. Ibid.
127. Chicago, *Personal Journal,* vol. 2, 6 January 1972, 94.
128. English, "Interview with Two Artists," 40.
129. Robin Mitchell to author, 12 January 2004. Mitchell is now an artist.
130. Faith Wilding to author, 18 December 2005.
131. Judy Chicago, *Through the Flower: My Struggle as a Woman Artist,* 2nd ed. (New York: Penguin Books, 1975), 213–17.
132. Faith Wilding to author, 18 December 2005.
133. Robin Mitchell to author, 13 January 2004.
134. Mira Schor to author, 28 May 2002. Schor is now an artist.
135. Robin Weltsch Storie to author, 23 December 2005. Storie, now a wife and mother, works in her own interior design business.
136. Robbin Schiff to author, 22 December 2005. Jan Oxenberg to author, 11 February 2006, says that she worked on *Womanhouse* part-time, had a car, and never knew that Schiff needed a ride home. Oxenberg is now a film producer, writer, and director.
137. Mary Beth Edelson to author, 26 January 2006. Edelson claimed that she heard that women in *The Dinner Party* studio had to get permission to use the bathroom—a falsehood that persists despite testimony from the workers themselves.
138. Robbin Schiff to author, 22 December 2005. Schiff now works as a graphic designer in the book industry.
139. Betty Liddick, "Emergence of the Feminist

Artist," *Los Angeles Times,* 17 January 1972, sec. 4, p. 6. JCCSL, Box 11, Folder 37.
140. Grace Glueck, "Winning the West," *New York Times,* 16 April 1972, D19.
141. Jan Oxenberg to author, 11 February 2006.
142. Chicago, *Personal Journal,* vol. 2, 1 January 1972, 88–89.
143. Ibid., 1 January 1972, 89.
144. Ibid., 1 January 1972, 91.
145. Ibid., 6 January 1972, 92.
146. Ibid., 12 January 1972, 96.
147. Ibid., Leslie Alexander Lacy, *The Rise and Fall of a Proper Negro* (New York: Macmillan, 1970).
148. Chicago, *Personal Journal,* vol. 2, 12 January 1972, 96.
149. Ibid., 12 January 1972, 98.
150. Ibid., 19 January 1972, 98–99.
151. Sara Evans, *Personal Politics: The Roots of Women's Liberation in the Civil Rights Movement and the New Left* (New York: Alfred A. Knopf, 1979), 179.
152. Chicago, *Personal Journal,* vol. 2, 19 January 1972, 99.
153. Ibid.
154. Glueck, "Winning the West," D19.
155. Chicago, *Personal Journal,* vol. 2, 19 January 1972, 105.
156. Anonymous, "Bad Dream House," *Time,* 20 March 1972, 77.
157. Ibid.
158. Chicago, *Personal Journal,* vol. 2, 4 February 1972, 112.
159. Clare Spark Loeb to the author, 6 December 2005.
160. Carol Ockman to Mimi, Judy, and Paula, 30 January [1972], JCCSL, Box 11, Folder 34.
161. Carol Ockman to author, 3 February 2006.
162. Chicago, *Personal Journal,* vol. 2, 16 February 1972, 114–15.
163. Ibid., 4 February 1971, 107.
164. Ibid., 4 February 1972, 108–09.
165. Ibid., 4 February 1972, 109.
166. Ibid., 18 February 1972, 117–18.
167. Ibid., 18 February 1972, 118.
168. Ibid., 28 February 1972, 119.
169. Ibid., 28 February 1974, 126.
170. Johanna Demetrakas to author, 21 October 2002.
171. Chicago, *Personal Journal,* vol. 2, 28 February 1972, 123.
172. Ibid., 28 February 1972, 124.
173. Ibid., 28 February 1972, 124–25.
174. Ibid., 5 March 1972, 129.
175. "Situation Report," *Time,* 20 March 1972.
176. Chicago, *Personal Journal,* vol. 2, 5 March 1972, 130.
177. Ibid.
178. Copy of this letter from Judy Chicago to Mr. and Mrs. Klick supplied to the author by Laurel Klick, 8 February 2006. Laurel Klick's work in special effects for film has won Emmy awards.
179. Laurel Klick to author, 8 February 2006.
180. Laurel Klick to author, 9 February 2006.
181. Ibid.
182. Susan Mogul to author, 2 February 2006. Mogul is a performance and video artist.
183. Ibid.
184. Ibid.
185. Nancy Youdelman to author, 6 April 2004.
186. Nancy Youdelman, interview by author, 6 September 2004. Rachel Youdelman to author, 28 January 2006.
187. Chicago, *Personal Journal,* vol. 2, 6 March 1972, 131, 133.
188. Ibid., 13 March 1972, 136.
189. Ibid., 15 March 1972, 139.
190. Ibid., 18 March 1972, 139–40.
191. Ibid., 18 March 1972, 142.
192. Ibid., 18 March 1972, 143.
193. Ibid., 23 March 1972, 142.
194. Ibid.
195. Judy Sword, "Feminist Art-Leader Seduces Crowd," *ATHAPASCAN* (Southwestern College) II (24 March 1972), 1. JCCSL, Box 1, Folder 39.
196. Ibid.
197. Chicago, *Personal Journal,* vol. 2, 29 March 1972, 146–47.
198. Ibid., 29 March 1972, 148.

Working Through Feminism 9

1. Anonymous, "Bad Dream House," *Time,* 20 March 1972, 76–77.
2. Judy Chicago, *Personal Journal,* vol. 3, 6.
3. Ibid., 5 April 1972, 6.
4. Judy Chicago and Dextra Frankel, "Invisible Twenty-One Artists Visible," in *Twenty-One Artists—Invisible/Visible* (Long Beach, Calif.: Long Beach Museum of Art, 1972), 9.
5. William Wilson, "A Vague Unfreedom in Feminist Works," *Los Angeles Times,* 9 April 1972, 56.
6. Chicago, *Personal Journal,* vol. 3, 14 April 1972, 15.
7. The organizers were Cynthia Bickley, Mary Beth Edelson, Barbara Frank, Enid Sanford, Susan Sollins, Josephine Withers, and Yvonne Wulff.
8. Judy Chicago, "Statements of Participants," artists' statements, Conference for Women in the Visual Arts, Corcoran Gallery of Art, Washington, D.C., 1972.

9. David L. Shirey, "'Visual Arts Hears from Women's Lib,'" *New York Times,* 23 April 1972, 63.
10. Ibid.
11. Ibid.
12. Cindy Nemser, "The Women's Conference at the Corcoran," *Art in America* 50 (January/February 1973): 87.
13. Judy Chicago quoted in ibid.
14. Ibid.
15. Ibid.
16. Ibid.
17. Without specifying precisely why, Schapiro told the author in interviews in 1997 and 1998 that the Corcoran conference marked the ending of her relationship with Chicago.
18. See Mary Beth Edelson, *The Art of Mary Beth Edelson* (New York: Distributed Art Publishers, 2002), 32b.
19. Mary Beth Edelson to author, 26 January 2006.
20. O'Keeffe would hold one of the thirty-nine place settings in Chicago's *The Dinner Party,* but none of the other eighty-two women in the poster reappear at Chicago's table.
21. Chicago, *Personal Journal,* vol. 3, 23 April 1972, 21.
22. Shirey, "Visual Arts Hears," 63. Nemser, "Women's Conference at the Corcoran," 88.
23. Shirey, "Visual Arts Hears," 63.
24. See Diana Fuss, *Essentially Speaking: Feminism, Nature and Difference* (New York: Routledge, 1989), 1–21.
25. Shirley Kassman Rickert, "Thoughts on Feminist Art," *Strait* 2, no. 8 (7–21 February 1973): 17.
26. Ibid.
27. Ibid.
28. Ibid.
29. Judy Chicago, "Judy Chicago Talking to Lucy Lippard," *Artforum* 13, no. 1 (September 1974): 64.
30. Ibid.
31. Judy Chicago, "Two Artists, Two Attitudes: Judy Chicago and Lloyd Hamrol Interview Each Other," *Criteria: A Review of the Arts* 1, no. 2 (November 1974): 11.
32. Nemser, "Women's Conference at the Corcoran," 87–88.
33. Chicago, *Personal Journal,* vol. 3, 23 April 1972, 21.
34. Ibid.
35. Ibid., 25.
36. Ibid., 8 May 1972, 32.
37. Ibid.
38. Arlene Raven to author, 24 July 2005.
39. Chicago, *Personal Journal,* vol. 3, 37.
40. Arlene Corkery Raven to Judy Chicago, 17 May 1972.
41. Chicago, *Personal Journal,* vol. 3, 23 May 1972, 39.
42. Guy Dill to author, 6 October 2006. Dill recalls that the event took place in his studio while he was out of town.
43. Judy Chicago, *Through the Flower: My Struggle as a Woman Artist,* 2nd ed. (New York: Penguin Books, 1975), 219.
44. Jan Oxenberg to author, 11 February 2006.
45. Shawnee Wollenman to author, 29 July 2006.
46. Clare Spark Loeb to author, 6 December 2006.
47. Judy Chicago to author, 24 January 2006.
48. Chicago, *Personal Journal,* vol. 3, 32.
49. Ibid., 25 June 1972, 64.
50. Susan Stocking, "Through the Looking Glass with Judy Chicago," *Los Angeles Times,* 9 July 1972, 18. JCCSL, Box 1, Folder 39.
51. Judy Chicago quoted in ibid.
52. Chicago, *Personal Journal,* vol. 3, 64.
53. Judith Solodkin to author, 12 December 2005.
54. Chicago, *Personal Journal,* vol. 3, 10 July 1972, 72.
55. May Cohen to Pearl Cassman, 18 October 1972, JCCSL.
56. Chicago, *Personal Journal,* vol. 3, 17 July 1972, 75.
57. Chicago, *Personal Journal,* vol. 1, 16 August 1971, 141.
58. Judy Chicago, *The Dinner Party: A Symbol of Our Heritage* (New York: Anchor Books/Doubleday, 1979), 8.
59. Chicago, *Personal Journal,* vol. 3, 24 July 1972, 80.
60. Judy Chicago, "Interview with Judy Chicago by Jan Butterfield," *City of San Francisco,* 20 January 1976, 44.
61. Ibid., 45.
62. Ibid.
63. Chicago, *Personal Journal,* vol. 3, 24 July 1972, 80.
64. Judith Solodkin [signed in jest Judith Manhattan] to Judy Chicago, 20 August 1972, JCCSL, Box 9, Folder 8.
65. Chicago, *Personal Journal,* vol. 3, 5 August 1972, 85.
66. Judith Solodkin to author, 12 December 2005.
67. June Wayne to author, 5 December 2005.
68. Chicago, *Personal Journal,* vol. 3, 17 August 1972, 89.
69. Ibid., 24 August 1972, 91.
70. Ibid.
71. Ibid., 28 September 1972 account of visit of 27–28 August 1972, 96.
72. Ibid.
73. Ibid., 105–6.

74. Ibid., 13 September 1972, 107.
75. Ibid., 109.
76. Ibid., 110.
77. Ibid., 112.
78. Ibid., 112.
79. Ibid., 114.
80. Ibid., 13 November 1972, 116–17.
81. Ibid., 94.
82. Ibid., 95.
83. Ibid., 1 November 1972, 130.
84. Felicia R. Lee, "Arts Festival Next Front for 'Vagina Warrior,'" *New York Times,* 12 June 2006, E1.
85. Chicago, *Personal Journal,* vol. 3, 131.
86. Chicago, *Personal Journal,* vol. 3, 1 November 1972, 132. For years, neither Schapiro nor Chicago would speak on the record about their relationship. Only after Schapiro organized artists to boycott the exhibition did Chicago share her journals and speak to me about what took place. See Amelia Jones, ed., *Sexual Politics: Judy Chicago's* Dinner Party *in Feminist Art History* (Berkeley: University of California Press, 1996).
87. Nancy Youdelman to author, 6 April 2004. Betty Liddick, "Emergence of the Feminist Artist," *Los Angeles Times,* 17 January 1972, sec. 4, p. 6. Miriam Schapiro, in conversation with the author, repeatedly raised the issue of her lifelong struggle with her weight.
88. Karen LeCocq, *The Easiest Thing to Remember: My Life as an Artist, a Feminist and a Manic Depressive* (Bloomington, Ind.: 1st Books, 2002).
89. Chris Rush to author, 1 April 2004.
90. Miriam Schapiro, interview by author, 6 July 1997.
91. Ibid.
92. Theodore Schapiro, interview by author, 1997.
93. Chicago, *Personal Journal,* vol. 3, 1 November 1972, 132.
94. Ibid., 5 November 1972, 134.
95. Ibid., 5 November 1972, 134–35.
96. Ibid., 5 November 1972, 135.
97. Ibid., 5 November 1972, 136.
98. Ibid., 22 November 1972, 137.
99. Ibid.
100. Ibid., 30 November 1972, 140.
101. Ibid., 30 November 1972, 142–43.
102. Ibid., 30 November 1972, 146.
103. Paul Brach, dean of arts, to Judy Chicago, 28 November 1972, JCCSL.
104. Robin Mitchell to author, 12 January 2004.
105. Ibid.
106. Chicago, *Personal Journal,* vol. 3, 141.
107. Nemser, "The Women's Conference," 87.
108. Judy Chicago to Cindy Nemser, n.d., c. November 1972.
109. Ibid.
110. Ibid.
111. Ibid.
112. Ibid.
113. Ibid.
114. Ibid.
115. Ibid.
116. Ibid.
117. Ibid.
118. Ibid.
119. Ibid.
120. Ibid.
121. Ibid.
122. Ibid.
123. Chicago, *Personal Journal,* vol. 3, 28 December 1972, 148.
124. Ibid., 28 December 1972, 148–49.
125. Deloris Tarzan, "Artists Have 'Psychic Relati[Onship],'" *Seattle Times,* 18 May 1976, B8.
126. Chicago, *Personal Journal,* vol. 4, 6.
127. Ibid., 15 January 1973, 8.
128. Ibid., 20 January 1973, 9–10.
129. Susan Hardy, "Judy Chicago—Artist, Woman," *Strait* 2, no. 8 (7 February 1973), 13.
130. Sue McMillan, "Women's Studies Courses," *Strait* 2, no. 8 (7 February 1973): 6. This article drew from one published in *Current* magazine in November 1972, which said that some six hundred courses in women's studies were now offered across the country.
131. Ibid., 7.
132. Chicago, *Personal Journal,* vol. 4, 20 January 1973, 9–10.
133. Ibid., 20 January 1973, 12–13.
134. Ibid., 20 January 1973, 11–13.
135. May Cohen to Pearl Cassman, 5 March 1973, JCCSL. May writes that *Womanspace* was even mentioned in the *Center for Democratic Studies* magazine.
136. Vicki Hodgetts, "Womanspace: Rezoning the L.A. Art Scene," *Ms.* 2, no. 1 (August 1973), 24.
137. Judy Chicago to author, 21 July 2003. Chicago confirms that she read this book shortly after its 1959 publication.
138. Norman O. Brown, *Life Against Death: The Psychoanalytical Meaning of History* (Middletown, Conn.: Wesleyan University Press, 1959), 63.
139. Chicago told this publication that she had had a female audience in mind. Anonymous, "Judy Chicago," in *Current Biography* (Bronx, N.Y.: H.W. Wilson Co., 1981), 63.
140. Chicago, *Personal Journal,* vol. 4, 6 March 1973, 17–18.
141. Boston Women's Health Book Collective, *Our Bodies, Ourselves: A Book By and For Women* (New York: Simon & Schuster, 1971), 14.

142. Barbara Smith, "The Female Sexuality/ Female Identity Exhibition," *Womanspace* 1, no. 2 (April/May 1973), 24.
143. Shirley Koploy, "The Woman's Building: Alive and Living in L.A.," *Ms.* 3, no. 4 (October 1974), 102.
144. Barbara Smith, "Wanda Westcoast & Judy Chicago at 707," *Womanspace* 1, no. 2 (April/ May 1973), 30.
145. Ibid., 29.
146. Chicago, "Talking to Lucy Lippard," 62.
147. Smith, "Wanda Westcoast & Judy Chicago at 707," 30.
148. Hunter Drohojowska-Philp, "Prints of the City," *Los Angeles Times,* 15 October 1995, 63. JCCSL, Box 2, Folder 32. This reporter recounted incorrectly that the print appeared on the cover of Chicago's book *Through the Flower.*
149. Martha Rose, "Feminist Wants Women to See Art in Terms of Own Experience," *Minneapolis Star,* 5 April 1973, JCCSL, Box 1, Folder 40.
150. Ellen Lanyon to author, 8 January 2006. Emilio Cruz (1938–2004) was a visual and performance artist and a writer.
151. Chicago, *Personal Journal,* vol. 4, 10 April 1973, 31. Undated letter describing this event from Eileen Van Vlack (of Cleveland Heights, Ohio) to Judy Chicago, JCCSL, Box 9, Folder 7.
152. Chicago, *Personal Journal,* vol. 4, 22 April 1973, 36–37.
153. Ibid., 16 April 1973, 34–35.
154. Herbert Marder, *Feminism and Art: A Study of Virginia Woolf* (Chicago: University of Chicago Press, 1972), 3.
155. Feminist Studio Workshop brochure, collection of the author.
156. Sheila de Bretteville to author, 7 December 2005.
157. Chicago, *Personal Journal,* vol. 4, 6 March 1973, 20.
158. Ibid., 13 May 1973, 39.
159. Ibid., 41.
160. Ibid., 1 April 1973, 27.
161. Ibid., 1 April 1973, 28.
162. Ibid., 28.
163. Arlene Raven, *Metamorphosis* (Minneapolis: College of St. Catherine, 1975), n.p.
164. Judy Chicago to Lucy Lippard, n.d., entitled *NOTES FROM A RETROGRADE ARTIST,* summer 1973, collection of Lucy Lippard.
165. Ibid.
166. Ibid.
167. Jonathan Kirsch, "The Flowering of the Artist," *Coast* 16, no. 6 (June 1975), 39.
168. Chicago, *Personal Journal,* vol. 4, 41.
169. Ibid., 13 May 1973, 42–43.
170. Ibid., 4 June 1973, 49.
171. Ibid., 16 May 1973, 45.
172. Ibid., 16 May 1973, 46.
173. Ibid.
174. Ibid.
175. Ibid., 4 June 1973, 51.
176. Ibid., 22 June 1973, 51–52.
177. Virginia Woolf, *To the Lighthouse* (New York: Harcourt, 1927), 159.
178. Chicago, *Personal Journal,* vol. 4, 22 June 1973, 51.
179. Ibid., 4 July 1973, 53.
180. Priscilla English, "An Interview with Two Artists from Womanhouse," *New Woman,* April–May 1972, 36.
181. Chicago, *Personal Journal,* vol. 4, 58.
182. Ibid., 18 July 1973, 59.
183. Ibid., 1 August 1973, 62–63.
184. Ibid., 18 August 1973, 68.
185. Ibid., 18 August 1973, 66.
186. Ibid., 18 August 1973, 67.
187. Ibid., 10 September 1973, 70.
188. Ibid., 10 September 1973, 72.
189. Arlene Raven, *At Home* (Long Beach, Calif.: Long Beach Museum of Art, 1983), x.
190. Maria Karras to author, 11 February 2006.
191. Cheryl Swannack to author, 9 February 2006.
192. Criste Kruse to author, 8 February 2006.
193. Maria Karras to author, 11 February 2006.
194. Susan Mogul, "Susan Mogul," in *Women of Vision: Histories in Feminist Film and Video* (Minneapolis: University of Minnesota Press, 2001), 187.
195. Linda Yaven to author, 12 February 2006.
196. Ibid.
197. Laurel Klick to author, 8 February 2006.
198. Chicago, *Personal Journal,* vol. 4, 7 October 1973, 73.
199. Ibid., 7 October 1973, 74.
200. Ibid., 7 October 1973, 75.
201. Ibid., 7 October 1973, 76.
202. Ibid., 7 October 1973, 77.
203. Ibid.
204. Chicago, "Two Artists, Two Attitudes," 9.
205. Ibid.
206. Chicago, *Personal Journal,* vol. 4, 21 October 1973, 81.
207. Ibid.
208. Doris Bry to Margaret A. Willard, 15 October 1973, JCCSL, Box 8, Folder 35. This folder contains the complete correspondance.
209. Susan Rennie to author, 12 February 2006, and Kirsten Grimstad to author, same date.
210. Nancy Robinson, "The Great Ladies," *Sister: Los Angeles Feminist Newspaper* 4, no. 11 (January 1974), JCCSL, Box 1, Folder 41.
211. Ibid.

212. Chicago, *Personal Journal,* vol. 4, 10 December 1973, 90–91.
213. Ibid., 10 December 1973, 92.
214. Robinson, "The Great Ladies."
215. Melinda Terbell, "Judy Chicago at Grand View One," *ARTnews,* February 1974, 73. Cited in Anonymous, "Judy Chicago," 63–64.
216. Paul and Catherine Wood Sutinen, "Judy Chicago Explodes Feminine Mystique in Art," *Willamette Week,* 8 September 1975, 12.
217. Chicago, *Personal Journal,* vol. 4, 10 December 1973, 91.
218. Ibid., 10 December 1973, 93.
219. Betty Prashker to author, 15 December 2005.
220. Ibid.
221. Chicago, "Two Artists, Two Attitudes," 9.
222. Ibid.
223. Ibid.
224. Chicago, *Personal Journal,* vol. 4, 6 February 1974, 95.
225. Chuck Chesnut to author, 14 February 2006.
226. Chicago, *Personal Journal,* vol. 4, 6 February 1974, 96–97.
227. Ibid., 6 February and 28 April 1974, 102, 105.
228. Chicago, "Talking to Lucy Lippard," 63.
229. Chicago, *Personal Journal,* vol. 4, 6 February 1974, 101.
230. Ibid.
231. Ibid., 28 April 1974, 107.
232. Ibid.
233. Judy Chicago, *Beyond the Flower: The Autobiography of a Feminist Artist* (New York: Viking Penguin, 1996), 108.
234. Barbara Manger, "Metamorphosis," *Midwest Art* 1, no. 1 (February 1975), 2. JCCSL, Box 1, Folder 42.
235. Linda Korenak, "Judy Chicago: Opening of the Flower," *Amazon* 3, no. 6 (October 1974), 4. Unknown to the reviewer, this quotation is actually from a print made from the center drawing of the *Rejection Quintet.* Manger, "Metamorphosis," 2.
236. Judy Chicago quoted in Manger, "Metamorphosis," 2.
237. Chicago, "Interview with Judy Chicago by Jan Butterfield," 45.
238. Ibid.
239. Chicago, "Two Artists, Two Attitudes," 9.
240. Chicago, *Beyond the Flower,* 28 April 1974, 109.
241. Ibid.
242. Chicago, *Personal Journal,* vol. 4, 9 May 1974, 112. "Women's Work," featuring the work of forty-five artists, including Lee Krasner, Louise Nevelson, Eleanor Antin, Faith Ringgold, Nancy Grossman, and Elaine de Kooning, among others, was curated by Marcia Tucker, Adelyn Breeskin, Anne d'Harnoncourt, Lila Katzen, and Cindy Nemser.
243. Ibid., 9 May 1974, 113.
244. Ibid., 9 May 1974, 114.
245. Judith Stein, "Judy Chicago at Kenmore," *Art in America,* July–August 1974.
246. Ibid.
247. May Cohen to Pearl Cassman, 23 May 1974: "New York, where a party was held in her honor and 150 people attended." JCCSL, Box 8, Folder 12.
248. Chicago, *Personal Journal,* vol. 4, 9 May 1974, 116–17.
249. Janet Bajan to author, 27 June 2004.
250. Kirsch, "The Flowering of the Artist," 39.
251. Miriam Schapiro to Margaret A. Willard, 10 May 1974, and Miriam Schapiro to Judy Chicago, 11 May 1974, JCCSL.
252. Chicago, *Personal Journal,* vol. 4, 9 May 1974, 112–13.
253. Ibid., 9 May 1974, 117.
254. Ibid., 9 May 1974, 117–18.

To *The Dinner Party* and History 10

1. Judy Chicago, *Personal Journal,* vol. 4, 28 April 1974, 104.
2. Barbara Isenberg, "Invitation to a Women-Only Dinner," *Los Angeles Times,* 6 April 1978, 12.
3. Jenna Weissman Joselit, "'A Set Table': Jewish Culture in the New World, 1880–1950," in *Getting Comfortable in New York: The American Jewish Home, 1880–1950,* ed. Susan L. Braunstein and Jenna Weissman Joselit (New York: Jewish Museum, 1990), 53.
4. Judy Chicago, *Beyond the Flower: The Autobiography of a Feminist Artist* (New York: Viking Penguin, 1996), 47.
5. Chicago, *Personal Journal,* vol. 4, 29 April 1974, 104.
6. Pat Colander, "Judy Chicago: Midwife to a Female Art Renaissance," *Chicago Tribune,* 16 June 1975, B2.
7. Chicago, *Personal Journal,* vol. 4, 9 May 1974, 110.
8. Ibid., 9 May 1974, 111.
9. Ibid., 28 April 1974, 105.
10. Ibid., 111.
11. Ibid., 2 June 1974, 121.
12. Judy Chicago, "Judy Chicago: World of the China Painter," *Ceramics Monthly* 26, no. 5 (May 1978), 40.
13. Chicago, *Personal Journal,* vol. 4, 2 June 1974, 119.
14. Virginia Woolf, *Orlando: A Biography* (New York: Harcourt Brace, 1928).
15. Chicago, *Personal Journal,* vol. 4, 14 June 1974, 123–24.

16. Ibid., 14 June 1974, 124.
17. Ibid., 14 June 1974, 126–27.
18. Ibid., 14 June 1974, 127–28.
19. Ibid., 14 June 1974, 128.
20. Ibid., 14 June 1974, 129.
21. Chicago, *Personal Journal,* vol. 4, 9 July 1974, 133, and Arlene Raven to author, 8 June 2005.
22. Ibid., 9 July 1974, 132–33.
23. Ibid., 9 July 1974, 134.
24. Ruth E. Iskin, "'Female Experience in Art': The Impact of Women's Art in a Work Environment," *Heresies* 1, no. 1 (January 1977), 71, 73. JCCSL, Box 1, Folder 44.
25. Elyse Katz Flier, "Open Wall Show," *Artweek,* 13 July 1974, 8.
26. Ibid.
27. Chicago, *Journal,* book 4, 27 August 1974, 143.
28. Judy Chicago, "Judy Chicago Interviewed," *Northwest Passage* 14, no. 12 (May 1976), 14–15.
29. Chicago, *Journal,* book 4, 27 August 1974, 143.
30. Ibid.
31. Ibid., 27 August 1974, 146.
32. Ibid., 27 August 1974, 147.
33. Ibid., 27 August 1974, 149.
34. Joanne Koch, "The New Professionals," *Chicago Tribune,* 8 September 1974, G20.
35. Chicago, *Personal Journal*, vol. 5, 8 October 1974, 5.
36. Ibid.
37. May Cohen to Pearl Cassman, 3 October 1974, JCCSL, Box 8, Folder 12.
38. Chicago, *Personal Journal,* vol. 5, 8 October 1974, 6.
39. Nory Miller, "Judy Chicago, a Partisan Painter in Feminist Hues," *Chicago Daily News,* 14–15 September 1974, 13.
40. Linda Korenak, "Judy Chicago: Opening of the Flower," *Amazon* 3, no. 6 (October 1974), 4.
41. Jennie Orvino, "Judy Chicago: Opening of the Flower," *Amazon* 3, no. 6 (October 1974), 3.
42. Arlene Raven, "Feminist Content in Current Female Art," *Sister Magazine: West Coast Feminist Newspaper* 6 (October/November 1975), 10.
43. Chicago, *Personal Journal,* vol. 5, 8 October 1974, 6–7.
44. Ibid., 4 August 1974, 140–41.
45. Ibid., 4 August 1974, 141.
46. Michele Kort to the author, 7 February 2006.
47. Chicago, *Personal Journal,* vol. 5, 8 October 1974, 8–9.
48. Ibid., 8 October 1974, 9–10.
49. Judy Chicago quoted in Melinda Wortz, *Beth Ames Swartz: Inquiry into Fire* (Scottsdale, Ariz.: Scottsdale Center for the Arts, 1978), 17.
50. Chicago, *Personal Journal,* vol. 5, 18 October 1974, 14–15.
51. Ibid., 18 October 1974, 15–16.
52. Ibid., 8 October 1974, 11.
53. Ida P. Rolf, *The Integration of Human Structures* (New York: Harper & Row, 1977).
54. Chicago, *Personal Journal,* vol. 5, 18 October 1974, 16.
55. Ibid., 18 October 1974, 18. In fact, many of Chicago's most successful students work in performance or video: for example, Suzanne Lacy, Faith Wilding, Susan Mogul, and Vanalyne Green.
56. Ibid.
57. May Cohen to Lydia and Fred Grady, 14 October 1974, JCCSL.
58. Chicago, *Personal Journal,* vol. 5, 12 November 1974, 25.
59. Ibid., 12 November 1974, 20–21.
60. Ibid., 12 November 1974, 23.
61. Ibid., 12 November 1974, 26.
62. Bruce to Judy Chicago, handwritten undated letter in JCCSL, Box 9, Folder 7.
63. Chicago, *Personal Journal,* vol. 5, 32.
64. Ibid., 3 December 1974, 32.
65. Ibid., 3 December 1974, 29.
66. Ibid., 3 December 1974, 30.
67. Ibid., 3 December 1974, 30–31.
68. Ibid., 3 December 1974, 32–33.
69. Ibid., 7 December 1974, 36–37.
70. Ibid., 7 December 1974, 38.
71. James Champy, "The Residue of Leadership: Why Ambition Matters," *Leader to Leader* summer (2000), 14–19. Online at http://leadertoleader.org/leaderbooks/L2L/summer2000/champy.html.
72. Chicago, *Personal Journal,* vol. 5, 7 December 1974, 38.
73. Ibid.
74. Ibid., 22 December 1974, 40.
75. Ibid.
76. Barbara Rose, "Vaginal Iconography," *New York* 7 (11 February 1974), 59.
77. Cheryl Swannack to author, 9 February 2006.
78. Chicago, *Personal Journal,* vol. 5, 22 December 1974, 42–43.
79. Ibid., 22 December 1974, 42.
80. Ibid., 22 December 1974, 43–44.
81. Cheryl Swannack to author, 9 February 2006.
82. Ibid.
83. Judy Chicago quoted in Mary George-Geisser, "Judy Chicago: Artist and Feminist," *Gold Flower* 6, no. 7 (February 1975), 1. JCCSL.
84. Ibid.
85. Ibid.
86. Judy Chicago quoted in caption in Margaret Zack, "China Painting and Feminism?" *Picture Magazine, Minneapolis Tribune,* 16 February 1975, 14. JCCSL, Box 1, Folder 32.
87. Ibid.

88. Arlene Raven, *Metamorphosis* (Minneapolis: College of St. Catherine, 1975), n.p.
89. Chicago, *Personal Journal,* vol. 5, 12 November 1974, 20–21.
90. George-Geisser, "Judy Chicago: Artist and Feminist," 1.
91. Zack, "China Painting and Feminism?" 11.
92. Don Morrison, "Judy Chicago's Art Boils to Proclaim Judy Chicago, Woman," *Minneapolis Star,* 9 January 1975, 2C.
93. Cindy Battis, "Reviews," *The Wheel* (The College of St. Catherine) 42, no. 6 (17 February 1975), JCCSL, Box 1, Folder 42.
94. Chicago, *Personal Journal,* vol. 5, 7 January 1975, 5.
95. Sandra Taylor to author, 2 February 2006.
96. Chicago, *Personal Journal,* vol. 5, 7 January 1975, 53.
97. Ibid.
98. Chicago even stayed for most of the visit at the home of Carol Fisher and her companion, the painter Warren Knight.
99. Chicago, *Personal Journal,* vol. 5, 7 January 1975, 53–54.
100. Ibid., 7 January 1975, 54.
101. Ibid., 7 January 1975, 63.
102. Sandra Taylor to author, 2 February 2006.
103. Annotated program, JCCSL, Box 11, Folder 20.
104. Chicago, *Personal Journal,* vol. 5, 2 February 1975, 66.
105. Ibid., 2 February 1975, 62.
106. Zack, "China Painting and Feminism?" 10. Chicago may have made an unconscious reference to Jewish prayer books in Hebrew, which open from the left. She would also have seen such books in the synagogue that she attended after her father's death. A sense of difference fits the outsider identity of both the woman and the Jew.
107. Chicago, *Personal Journal,* vol. 5, 12 January 1975, 60.
108. Judy Chicago to Lucy Lippard, March 1, 1975.
109. Feminist Art Workshop documentation, folding brochure published 1975, St. Paul, Minn., JCCSL, Box 11, Folder 20. Participants included in the brochure: Laura Blew, Cindy Petersen, Nancy S. Hanily, Cindy Jacobson, Carole Fisher, Ruth Iskin, Arlene Raven, Myrna Williams, Christine Frank, Gail Summerskill, Anne Weslowski, Jo Nonnemacher, Judy Chicago, and Sister Ann Jennings.
110. Judy Chicago to Lucy Lippard, March 1, 1975.
111. Carol Fisher to Judy Chicago, 7 April 1975, JCCSL, Box 11, Folder 20.
112. Chicago, *Personal Journal,* vol. 5, 21 February 1975, 72.
113. Ibid., 2 February 1975, 63.
114. Ibid., 21 February 1975, 70.
115. Ibid.
116. Ibid., 21 February 1975, 71.
117. Ibid., 21 February 1975, 71–72.
118. Ibid., 17 March 1975, 79.
119. Chicago, *Personal Journal,* vol. 5, 17 March 1975, 78–79.
120. Ibid.
121. Ibid., 17 March 1975, 79.
122. Paul Sutinen and Catherine Wood, "Judy Chicago Explodes Feminine Mystique in Art," *Willamette Week,* 8 September 1975, 12. JCCSL, Box 83, Folder 16.
123. Ibid.
124. Judy Chicago, "Judy Chicago: The Artist Views Herself and a World of Love, Death and Longshots," *Playgirl* 2, no. 12 (May 1975), 80–81, 102.
125. Meridee Merzer, "Art?" *Penthouse,* October 1975, 45. JCCSL, Box 1, Folder 42.
126. Judy Chicago, "Breaking the Silence, Interview by Su Braden," *Time Out Limited,* May 1975, JCCSL, Box 1, Folder 42.
127. Christopher Lehmann-Haupt, "Her Struggle as a Writer," *New York Times,* 10 March 1975.
128. Karla Jay, "Through the Male Art World," *Lesbian Tide* (1975), 20.
129. Ibid.
130. Judy Chicago, *Through the Flower: My Struggle as a Woman Artist,* 2nd ed. (New York: Penguin Books, 1975), 4.
131. Lucy Lippard, "Getting Hers," *Ms.* 4, no. 2 (August 1975), 42.
132. Frances Chapman, "Judy Chicago: Vaginal Iconographer," *off our backs,* July 1975, 16.
133. Ibid.
134. Ibid., p. 17.
135. Vera Goodman, "Judy Chicago, Trendsetter," *New Directions for Women* (Spring 1976), 15.
136. Judy Chicago quoted in Jonathan Kirsch, "The Flowering of the Artist," *Coast* 16, no. 6 (June 1975), 38, 39.
137. Vicky Chen Haider, "Chicago's Butterfly," *Chicago Sun-Times,* 19 June 1975, sec. 2, 81. JCCSL, Box 1, Folder 42.
138. Ibid.
139. Ibid.
140. Ibid.
141. Ibid.
142. Chicago, *Personal Journal,* vol. 5, 17 March 1975, 77–78.
143. Anaïs Nin, *The Delta of Venus* (New York: Harcourt, 1969).
144. Adrienne Rich to Judy Chicago, 6 May 1975, JCCSL, Box 8, Folder 36.
145. Adrienne Rich to Judy Chicago, 14 August 1975, JCCSL, Box 8, Folder 36.
146. Judy Chicago to Lucy Lippard, envelope postmarked March 1, 1975.

147. Ibid.
148. Zack, "China Painting and Feminism?" 17.
149. Ibid.
150. Chicago, *Personal Journal,* vol. 5, 14 April 1975, 85.
151. Ibid., 14 April 1975, 87–88.
152. Ibid., 14 April 1975, 88.
153. Ibid., 14 April 1975, 89.
154. Ibid., 19 May 1975, 98.
155. Ibid., 19 May 1975, 99.
156. Ibid., 19 May 1975, 100.
157. Ian Jack, "LOOK! Exit Judy, Struggling," *London Times,* May 1975, 32. JCCSL, Box 1, Folder 42.
158. Margaret Richards, "Galleries: Judy Chicago," *Socialist Tribune,* May 1975, JCCSL, Box 1, Folder 42.
159. Chicago, "Breaking the Silence," JCCSL, Box 1, Folder 42.
160. Judy Chicago to Lucy Lippard, 22 April 1975.
161. Chicago, *Personal Journal,* vol. 5, 4 May 1975, 93.
162. Ibid., 19 May 1975, 102.
163. Judy Chicago to Lucy Lippard, 22 April 1975, JCCSL.
164. Chicago, *Personal Journal,* vol. 5, 5 June 1975, 109.
165. Ibid., 15 June 1975, 119.
166. Ibid., 15 June 1975, 111.
167. Ibid., 25 July 1975, 120.
168. Ibid., 25 July 1975, 124.
169. Judy Chicago to Lucy Lippard, n.d., July 1975.
170. Ibid.
171. Barry Lancet, "Ben Cohen, American Potter in Echizen, Japan," *Ceramics: Art and Perception* [Sydney, Australia] no. 9 (1992), 56.
172. Rob Barnard, "Ben Cohen, 46, American Ceramist in Japan," *American Craft,* June/July 1992, 17.
173. Julia Cassim, "Stricken Ceramist in Fukui Shapes Skills of His Successor," *Japan Times,* 21 January 1992, 4.
174. Chicago, *Personal Journal,* vol. 5, 11 August 1975, 135.
175. Ibid., 9 September 1975, 137.
176. Ibid., 9 September 1975, 139.
177. Sutinen, "Judy Chicago Explodes Feminine," 12.
178. Ibid.
179. Ibid.
180. Ibid.
181. Isenberg, "Invitation to a Women-Only Dinner," 14.
182. Judye Keyes to author, 30 January 2006.
183. Ibid.
184. Isenberg, "Invitation to a Women-Only Dinner," 12.
185. Susan Hill to author, 19 September 2002.
186. When Gelon attended the College Art Association meeting in Detroit in 1974, she photographed Judy and Arlene Raven on an excursion to the Art Institute of Chicago, standing in front of Grant Wood's *American Gothic.*
187. Diane Gelon, "Defining Jewish Feminism," *UCLA Daily Bruin,* supplement in November 1974, 4. JCCSL, Box 84, Folder 4.
188. "Women's Day: Chicken Soup, Sisterhood and Then What?," *B'nai B'rith Messenger,* 25 May 1973, JCCSL, Box 84, Folder 4.
189. Diane Gelon to author, 27 May 2003.
190. Judy Chicago quoted in "Judy Chicago Interviewed," *Northwest Passage,* 15. JCCSL, Box 1, Folder 43.
191. Ibid.
192. Judy Chicago, *Personal Journal,* vol. 6, 21 November 1975, 4.
193. Chicago, *Personal Journal,* vol. 6, 10 December 1975, 18.
194. Lucy Lippard to Bill Lacey (National Endowment for the Arts), 24 November 1976, JCCSL, Box 83, Folder 20.
195. Ibid.
196. Judy Chicago to Lucy Lippard, 11 December 1975, JCCSL, Box 83, Folder 20.
197. Judy Chicago to Lucy Lippard, n.d., envelope postmarked March 1, 1975, JCCSL.
198. Cindy Nemser to author, 14 January 2006.
199. Judy Chicago to Cindy Nemser, 16 March 1975; Cindy Nemser to author, 14 January 2006. Cindy Nemser, *Conversations with 12 Women Artists* (New York: Charles Scribner's Sons, 1975). Chicago was not among the twelve artists interviewed.
200. Goodman, "Judy Chicago, Trendsetter," 15.
201. Ibid.
202. Judy Chicago quoted in ibid.
203. Diane Gelon to author, 27 May 2003.
204. Chicago, *Personal Journal,* vol. 6, 27 December 1975, 30.
205. Ibid., 4 January 1976, 33–34.
206. Ibid., 18 January 1976, 44.
207. Mary Stofflet-Santiago, "Judy Chicago Ceramics," *Artweek,* 26 January 1976.
208. Tom Albright, "Judy Chicago," *San Francisco Chronicle,* 10 January 1976, JCCSL, Box 1, Folder 43.
209. Judy Chicago to Sylvia Brown, Quay Gallery, San Francisco, carbon copy of a letter of 19 January 1976, JCCSL, Box 9, Folder 9.
210. Chicago, *Personal Journal,* vol. 6, 4 January 1976, 35.
211. Ibid., 18 January 1976, 45.
212. Manuel Neri to author, 9 January 2004.
213. Chicago, *Personal Journal,* vol. 6, 18 January 1976, 45.
214. Ibid., 4 January 1975, 38.

215. Ellen McCormick, "Judy Chicago: Feminist Art Show," *Portland Scribe,* 4–14 March 1976, 3.
216. Chicago, *Personal Journal,* vol. 6, 11 March 1976, 59.
217. Ibid., 11 March 1976, 59–60.
218. Ibid., 11 March 1976, 56.
219. Ibid., 18 May 1976, 82.
220. Ibid., 17 May 1976, 75.
221. Judy Chicago, "Two Artists, Two Attitudes: Judy Chicago and Lloyd Hamrol Interview Each Other," *Criteria: A Review of the Arts* 1, no. 2 (November 1974), 14.
222. Alice Quaintance, "Some Images of Judy Chicago Relating to Women and Women Relating to Judy Chicago," *Pandora,* June 1976, 9. JCCSL, Box 1, Folder 43.
223. Chicago, "Judy Chicago Interviewed," *Northwest Passage,* 15.
224. Ibid.
225. Quaintance, "Some Images of Judy Chicago," 9.
226. Ibid.
227. Ibid.
228. Judy Chicago quoted in Susan Finkel, "The Art of Judy Chicago: Female and Feminist," (21 May 1976), 7. JCCSL Unidentified Clipping Box 1, Folder 43.
229. Chicago, *Personal Journal,* vol. 6, 18 May 1976, 83–84.
230. Ibid., 17 May 1976, 79.
231. Ibid., 9 May 1976, 65–66.
232. Ibid., 9 May 1976, 72–73.
233. Copies of letters from Judy Chicago to Arlene, Ruth, and Sheila with copies to Susan and Kirsten, 21 May 1976; letters of response by Arlene Raven and Ruth Iskin dated 23 May 1976; Chicago's letters of response to Raven and Iskin of 26 May 1976; Sheila de Bretteville's response on 24 May 1976; Chicago's response to her letter and a last letter from de Bretteville to Chicago, dated 27 May [1976], JCCSL, Box 11, Folder 48.
234. Kirsten Grimstad to author, 12 February 2006.
235. Michele Kort to author, 7 February 2006.
236. Goodman, "Judy Chicago, Trendsetter," 15.
237. Ibid.
238. Ibid.
239. Sheila de Bretteville to Judy Chicago, 27 May 1976, 5. JCCSL, Box 11, Folder 48.
240. Sheila de Bretteville to author, 12 July 2005.
241. Ibid.
242. Chicago, *Personal Journal,* vol. 6, 7 June 1976, 86–87.
243. Ibid., 7 June 1976, 87.
244. Sheila de Bretteville to author, 7 December 2005.
245. Diane Gelon to author, 19 April 2002.
246. Chicago, *Personal Journal,* vol. 6, 15 June 1976, 91.
247. Ibid., 27 June 1976, 102.
248. Ibid., 8 July 1976, 105.
249. Ibid., 21 July 1976, 109.
250. Isenberg, "Invitation to a Women-Only Dinner," 12.
251. Chicago, *Personal Journal,* vol. 6, 21 July 1976, 107.
252. Audrey Cowan to author, 6 January 2004.
253. Isenberg, "Invitation to a Women-Only Dinner," 14.
254. Audrey Cowan quoted in Judith Lewis, "The Trouble with Judy: Reflections on The Dinner Party and the Artist Who Created It," *Los Angeles Weekly* 18, 26 April 1996, 28.
255. Isenberg, "Invitation to a Women-Only Dinner," 14.
256. Chicago, *Personal Journal,* vol. 6, 1 August 1976, 110.
257. Kathy Erteman to author, 30 January 2006.
258. Sharon Kagan to author, 30 January 2006.
259. Ibid.
260. Ibid.
261. Ibid.
262. Ibid.
263. Ann Isolde to author, 6 January 2004.
264. Isenberg, "Invitation to a Women-Only Dinner," 14.
265. Ann Isolde quoted in Jan Castro, "Jan Castro Interview with Kate Amend and Ann Isolde. The Dinner Party Talks," *River Styx* 9 (1981), 68–69.
266. Obituary, "Dorothy K. Goodwill, 62, Church Embroidery Artist," *Cleveland Plain Dealer,* 2 November 2000, 9B.
267. Chicago, *Personal Journal,* vol. 6, 1 August 1976, 113.
268. Ibid., 9 August 1976, 117.
269. Ibid.
270. Chicago, *Personal Journal,* vol. 6, 7 September 1976, 123.
271. Juliet Myers to author, 10 June 2004.
272. Ibid. In 1990 Juliet cofounded Fine Arts for Children and Teens (FACT), an organization that provides quality visual arts education to local young people, ages 8 to 18, regardless of family income.
273. Ibid.
274. Judy Chicago, *The Dinner Party: A Symbol of Our Heritage* (New York: Anchor Books/Doubleday, 1979), 237.
275. Juliet Myers to author, 10 June 2004.
276. Christina Thompson, "The Dinner Party," unnamed Australian publication, January 1988, JCCSL, Box 2, Folder 25.
277. Chicago, *Personal Journal,* vol. 6, 30 September 1976, 129.

278. Ibid., 16 October 1976, 140–41.
279. Ken Gilliam to author, 9 January 2006.
280. Chicago, *Personal Journal,* vol. 6, 18 November 1976, 163.
281. Judy Chicago to Lucy Lippard, n.d., c. December 1976, JCCSL, Box 83, Folder 20.
282. Ibid.
283. Ibid.
284. Ibid.
285. Ibid.
286. Chicago, *Personal Journal,* vol. 6, 27 November 1976, 163.
287. Ibid., 27 November 1976, 11 December 1976, 165.
288. Ibid., 4 December 1976, 172–73.
289. May Cohen to Lydia and Fred Grady, December 1976, JCCSL, Box 8, Folder 15.
290. Ibid.
291. Chicago, *Personal Journal,* vol. 6, 26 December 1976, 180–81.
292. Ruth Askey, "Judy Chicago: Pride in Women and in Herself," *Artweek* (January 1977), JCCSL, Box 1, Folder 33.
293. Ibid.
294. William Wilson, "Art Walk: La Cienega Area," *Los Angeles Times,* 28 January 1977, sec. 4, p. 6.
295. Chicago, *Personal Journal,* vol. 6, 13 January 1977, 188.
296. Ibid., 13 January 1977, 185.
297. Chicago, *Dinner Party,* 38–39.
298. Judy Chicago to Lucy Lippard, 31? May 1977, JCCSL, Box 83, Folder 20.
299. Chicago, *Dinner Party,* 39; Chicago, *Personal Journal,* vol. 7, 8 June 1977.
300. Chicago, *Dinner Party,* 40; Chicago, *Personal Journal,* vol. 7, 10 July 1977.
301. Chicago, *Dinner Party,* 41; Chicago, *Personal Journal,* vol. 7, 16 July 1977, 29 July 1977, and 16 August 1977.
302. Chicago, *Dinner Party,* 41; Chicago, *Personal Journal,* vol. 7, 4 August 1977 and 8 August 1977.
303. Chicago, *Dinner Party,* 44; Chicago, *Personal Journal,* vol. 7, 21 October 1977.
304. Chicago, *Dinner Party,* 45; Chicago, *Personal Journal,* vol. 7, 30 November 1977. Leonard Skuro to author, 8 January 2004. Skuro declined to say anything more about *The Dinner Party,* claiming that he had talked about it enough.
305. Kathy Erteman to author, 30 January 2006.
306. Chicago, *Dinner Party,* 45; Chicago, *Personal Journal,* vol. 7, 30 November 1977 and 21 December 1977.
307. Chicago, *The Dinner Party,* 46; Chicago, *Personal Journal,* vol. 7, 14 January 1977.
308. Isenberg, "Invitation to a Women-Only Dinner," 14.
309. Ibid.
310. Diane Gelon to author, 19 April 2002.
311. William Wilson, "China Painting: A Revived Craft," *Los Angeles Times,* 5 December 1977, sec. 4, 3.
312. Elaine Levin, "China Painting—Past and Present," *Artweek,* December 1977, 5.
313. Diane Gelon, journal (begun 1 November 1977) of the final year of making *The Dinner Party,* verso page 31. JCCSL, Box 81, Folder 5.
314. Judith Anderson, "The Ultimate in Female Art," *San Francisco Chronicle,* 13 February 1978, 21.
315. Ibid.
316. Ibid.
317. Ibid.
318. Ibid.
319. Ibid.
320. Judy Chicago, "A Date with Judy: A Dialogue with Judy Chicago, Suzanne Lacy and Faith Wilding," manuscript for article in *Images and Issues* (1980), 2. JCCSL, Box 6, Folder 3.
321. David Hale, "Dinner Party Will Honor 1,038 'Significant' Women," *Fresno Bee,* 23 March 1978, D1. JCCSL Box 1, Folder 45.
322. Ibid.
323. Ibid.
324. Elaine Woo, "Discrimination Behind the Brush: Women Artists Complain of Second-Class Status," *Los Angeles Herald Examiner,* 12 March 1978, E9.
325. Judy Chicago quoted in Del McColm, "Artists Advised to Unite Against Gallery Controls," *Davis Enterprise* (5 May 1978), Weekend, 8.
326. Ibid.
327. Anderson, "The Ultimate in Female Art," 21.
328. Ibid.
329. Ibid.
330. Isenberg, "Invitation to a Women-Only Dinner," sec. 4, 1.
331. Ibid., 14.
332. Judy Chicago to Lucy Lippard, 28 September 1978, JCCSL, Box 83, Folder 23.
333. Ibid.
334. Ann Isolde to Judy Chicago, n.d. (c. 1978), JCCSL, Box 9, Folder 7.
335. Judy Chicago to Lucy Lippard, 28 September 1978, JCCSL, Box 83, Folder 23.
336. Ibid.
337. Diane Gelon, journal of the last year of *The Dinner Party,* 43. JCCSL, Box 81, Folder 5.
338. Judy Chicago, *Personal Journal,* vol. 8, 4 December 1978, 30.
339. Ibid., 30 December 1978, 39.
340. Ibid., 30 December 1978, 36.
341. Ibid., 5 February 1979, 70–71.

The Dinner Party Makes Waves 11

1. Susan Rennie and Arlene Raven, "The Dinner Party Project: An Interview with Judy Chicago," *Chrysalis* 1, no. 4 (1977): 91.
2. Henry Hopkins quoted in Elaine Levin, "Judy Chicago: The Dinner Party," *Ceramics Monthly* 27, no. 6 (June 1979), 49.
3. Judy Chicago, *The Dinner Party: A Symbol of Our Heritage* (New York: Anchor Books/Doubleday, 1979).
4. Rennie and Raven, "Dinner Party Project," 97.
5. Edward Lucie-Smith, *Judy Chicago: An American Vision* (New York: Watson-Guptill, 2000), 66; Lucie-Smith makes the comparison to Blake.
6. Lucy Lippard, "Dinner Party a Four-Star Treat," *Seven Days,* 27 April 1979, 29.
7. Ben Cohen to Judy Chicago, 5 March 1979.
8. Program for "A Celebration of Women's Heritage," 17 March 1979. JCCSL, Box 83, Folder 22.
9. Ira Kamin, "Opening The Dinner Party," *San Francisco Sunday Examiner and Chronicle,* 3 June 1979, 32.
10. Ibid.
11. Judy Chicago, *Beyond the Flower: The Autobiography of a Feminist Artist* (New York: Viking Penguin, 1996), 67.
12. "A Feminist Sculptures 'Dinner Party,'" *New York Times,* 1 April 1979, 52.
13. Mark Stevens, "Guess Who's Coming to Dinner," *Newsweek,* 2 April 1979, 92.
14. Ibid.
15. Alfred Frankenstein quoted in Thomas Albright, "Primarily Biological," *ARTnews* 78, no. 6 (Summer 1979), 156.
16. Beverly Terwoman, "The Dinner Party," *Pacific Sun,* 20–26 April 1979, 6.
17. Ibid.
18. Stephanie von Buchau, "The Dinner Party," *Pacific Sun,* 20–26 April 1979, 5.
19. Blue Greenberg, "'The Dinner Party' Captures Essence of Women's History," *Durham Morning Herald,* 13 April 1979, Women Today, 1B.
20. Charlotte Harmon, "A Generous Helping of Feminism on 'Dinner Party' Plates," *Los Angeles Times Book Review,* 15 April 1979, 3.
21. Suzanne Muchnic, "An Intellectual Famine at Judy Chicago's Feast," *Los Angeles Times Book Review,* 15 April 1979, 3. JCCSL, Box 2, Folder 1.
22. Ruth Askey, "Letters: Chicago vs. Muchnic," *Los Angeles Times Book Review,* 29 April 1979, 1.
23. Robert Nelson, "Letters: Chicago vs. Muchnic," *Los Angeles Times Book Review,* 29 April 1979, 1.
24. Sandy Ballatore, "Letters: Chicago vs. Muchnic," *Los Angeles Times Book Review,* 29 April 1979, 1.
25. Judy Chicago to author, 24 January 2006.
26. Grace Glueck, "Judy Chicago and Trials of 'Dinner Party,'" *New York Times,* 30 April 1979, D10.
27. Ibid.
28. Clare B. Fischer, "Reviewed: Judy Chicago's The Dinner Party," *Newsletter: The Center for Women and Religion of the Graduate Theological Union* [Berkeley, Calif.] 5, no. 3 (Spring 1979), 14–15.
29. Ibid., 15.
30. Ibid., 15. Chicago, *Dinner Party.*
31. Lippard, "Dinner Party a Four-Star Treat," 27, 29.
32. Diane Ketcham, "Judy Chicago's Dinner Party: Two Views of the First Feminist Epic Artwork: On the Table . . . Joyous Celebration," *Village Voice,* 11 June 1979, 47–48. JCCSL, Box 1, Folder 2.
33. Kay Larson, "Judy Chicago's Dinner Party: Two Views of the First Feminist Epic Artwork Under the Table: Duplicity, Alienation," *Village Voice,* 11 June 1979, 50. JCCSL.
34. Kay Larson to author, 12 February 2006.
35. Ibid.
36. April Kingsley, "The I-Hate-To-Cook 'Dinner Party,'" *Ms.,* June 1979, 31.
37. Chicago quoted in Rennie and Raven, "Dinner Party Project," 96.
38. Diane Elvenstar, "Into the Heart and Soul of Creativity," *Los Angeles Times,* 3 December 1979, sec. 4, p. 1. JCCSL, Box 79, Folder 33.
39. Judy Chicago to author, 24 January 2006.
40. The author has interviewed this woman and agreed to her wish that her identity be kept secret.
41. Mildred Hamilton, "'The Dinner Party' Left Without a Second Sitting," *San Francisco Examiner and Chronicle,* 1 July 1979, Scene 6.
42. Harriet Lyons, "Organizing: How 'The Dinner Party' Got to Houston, Boston, and New York," *Ms.,* November 1980, 91.
43. Chicago, *Personal Journal,* vol. 8, 130.
44. Hamilton, "Left Without a Second Sitting," 6.
45. Kay Larson, "More (or Less) Awful Rowing Toward God," *Village Voice,* 17 December 1979, 113. JCCSL, Box 2, Folder 1.
46. Jan Adams, "Chicago's Dinner Party: A Feminist Feast," *Lesbian Tide,* May–June 1979, 4.
47. Albright, "Primarily Biological," 156.
48. Hal Fischer, "San Francisco," *Artforum* 17, no. 10 (Summer 1979), 77–78.

49. Hamilton, "Left Without a Second Sitting," 6.
50. Ibid.
51. Typescript account in JCCSL, Box 83, Folder 23.
52. Ann Marie Lipinski, "Public May Never Again Feast on Paean to Women," *Chicago Tribune,* 19 August 1979, L1.
53. Diane Gelon to author, 19 April 2002.
54. Lucy R. Lippard, "Judy Chicago's 'Dinner Party,' " *Art in America* 68, no. 4 (April 1980), 124.
55. Lipinski, "Public May Never Again Feast," L2.
56. Nancy Nielsen, "Show Chicago's Art," *Chicago Tribune,* 30 August 1979, B2.
57. Lipinski, "Public May Never Again Feast," L1.
58. Lyons, "Organizing How 'The Dinner Party,' " 92.
59. Ann Rockefeller Roberts to author, 1 February 2006. Harriet Lyons to author, 25 January 2006. Lyons recalls attending the event.
60. This quotation is from the museum's own website: www.moma.org/about_moma/history/.
61. "Situation Report," *Time,* 20 March 1972.
62. The recent hiring of women curators, including Connie Butler, organizer of the forthcoming exhibition of feminist art for the Museum of Contemporary Art (MoCA) in L.A., seems to suggest a much-needed change of direction. The inaugural installation of MoMA's permanent collection in the new building in November 2003 featured far too few historic women artists (documented at only 5 percent), even failing to hang the museum's own works by such major women artists as Sonia Delaunay and Gabrielle Münter.
63. Lyons, "Organizing How 'The Dinner Party,' " 92.
64. Ibid.
65. Invitation, JCCSL, Box 83, Folder 23.
66. Ibid. Lippard's typescript is annotated by hand.
67. Maurice Zolotow, "The 78 Most Interesting People in Los Angeles," *Los Angeles Magazine* 59 (November 1979), 203.
68. Adele Freedman, "Judy Chicago: The Artist as Full-Scale Feminist Myth," *Montreal Globe and Mail,* 23 February 1980, Entertainment, 5.
69. Ibid.
70. Ibid.
71. Judy Chicago quoted in Kathy Larkin, "Judy Chicago: Art Across the Gender Gap," *Post-Tribune* (Chicago), 2 December 1984; Today's Woman, 2, JCCSL, Box 2, Folder 15.
72. Judy Chicago to author, 24 January 2006.
73. Ibid.
74. Judy Chicago, "A Date with Judy: A Dialogue with Judy Chicago, Suzanne Lacy and Faith Wilding," manuscript for article in *Images and Issues,* (1980), 4. JCCSL, Box 6, Folder 3.
75. Ibid.
76. Chicago, *Personal Journal,* vol. 8, 3 June 1979, 141.
77. Marta Hallowell to Judy Chicago, 24 October 1980, JCCSL, Box 7, Folder 38.
78. Eva S. Jungermann to Judy Chicago, 6 January 1986, JCCSL, Box 7, Folder 38, writing for the *Contemporary Forum* newsletter, Phoenix Art Museum, Winter 1985, 1–2.
79. Chicago, *Personal Journal,* vol. 8, 17 June 1979, 151.
80. Chicago, *Beyond the Flower,* 75.
81. Calvin Cannon quoted in Mimi Crossley, "The Men in the Kitchen of 'The Dinner Party,' " *Houston Post,* 25 March 1980, B1.
82. Deborah Lipton to author, 11 April 2005, and Ann Sutherland Harris to Deborah Lipton, 12 March 1980.
83. Elisabeth Stevens, " 'Dinner Party' Is Essentially a Political Statement," *Baltimore Sun,* 11 May 1980, D13; accompanied by note of 11 May 1980 from Stevens to Judy Chicago, JCCSL.
84. Donna Tennant, "A Monumental Work of Art," *Houston Chronicle,* 9 March 1980, 14.
85. Donna Tennant, " 'Right out of History,' a Remarkable Story," *Houston Chronicle,* 9 March 1980, 14.
86. Lippard, "Chicago's 'Dinner Party,' " 115.
87. Ibid., 124.
88. Carlene Hill, "Dressing for 'Dinner' A Woman's Work Is Never Done," *Boston Phoenix,* 1 July 1980, sec. 3, 2.
89. April Hankins to author, 2 January 2006.
90. Ibid.
91. Ibid.
92. Diane Gelon, "The Critic's Voice: Who Speaks for Us?" *Sojourner,* October 1980, 5.
93. Robert Taylor, " 'The Dinner Party' Somewhat Unappetizing," *Boston Globe,* 3 July 1980, 18.
94. Betty Kaufman, "Celebrating the History of Women," *Boston Globe,* 15 July 1980, letters to the editor.
95. Gelon, "Critic's Voice: Who Speaks for Us?" 5.
96. Chicago, *Beyond the Flower,* 87.
97. Darrah Cole, "The Dinner Party: Judy Chicago," *Vision,* September/October/November 1980, 12.
98. Art Jahnke, "Oh Waiter, What's This Butterfly Doing in My Soup?" *Boston Phoenix,* July 1980.

99. Judy Chicago to Lucy Lippard, letter entitled *"NOTES FROM A RETROGRADE ARTIST,"* summer (late June?) 1973, collection of Lucy Lippard.
100. Kathie Beals, "'The Dinner Party' a Feminist Feast," *Gannett Westchester Newspapers*, 28 October 1980, B1; includes a notice in a box with this review/feature article.
101. Judy Chicago, "An Enquiry Into the Relationship Between Art and Politics," manuscript for lecture at Harvard (1980), 1. JCCSL. Box 6, Folder 23.
102. Lou Spitalnick, "Judy Chicago's 'Dinner Party,'" *New York Post*, October 1980, D1. See also Nan Robertson, "4,500 Guests, Most of Them Women, Answer 'The Dinner Party' Invitation," *New York Times*, 18 October 1980, JCCSL, Box 2, Folder 8.
103. Judy Chicago, "Long Distance: Judy Chicago Interviewed by Kelley Loftus," *Artlies* 1, no. 4 (May 1994), 12.
104. Alan M. Wald, *The New York Intellectuals: The Rise and Decline of the Anti-Stalinist Left from the 1930s to the 1980s* (Chapel Hill: University of North Carolina Press, 1987), 360. During the 1970s and early 1980s Kramer consistently reviewed my writings and exhibitions that I curated as positive. As long as he perceived my work as apolitical, he liked it. When my feminist sympathies became evident, he was completely taken aback and slammed my biography of Edward Hopper, which featured his artist-wife Josephine Verstille Nivison Hopper. See Gail Levin, *Edward Hopper: An Intimate Biography* (New York: Alfred A. Knopf, 1995) and Gail Levin, "Learning to Appreciate Judy Chicago," *Women in the Arts* 20, no. 2 (Fall 2002), 14.
105. Hilton Kramer, "Judy Chicago's 'Dinner Party' Comes to Brooklyn Museum," *New York Times*, 17 October 1980, C1.
106. Ibid.
107. Ibid.
108. Ellen Willis, "Ellen Willis," *Village Voice*, 5–11 November 1980, 32.
109. Ibid.
110. Joanne Mattera, "The Dinner Party: A Symbol of Our Heritage (Review)," *East West Journal*, January 1980, 82.
111. John Perreault, "No Reservations," *SoHo News*, 22 October 1980, 19.
112. Lawrence Alloway, "Judy Chicago Philip Guston," *Nation*, 15 November 1980, 525.
113. Sheryn Goldenhersh, "Judy Chicago Hosts Her 'Dinner Party' at the Brooklyn Art Museum," *St. Louis Jewish Light*, 5 November 1980, 7.
114. Letty Cottin Pogrebin, "Anti-Semitism in the Women's Movement," *Ms.*, June 1982, 66.
115. Susan Weidman Schneider, *Jewish and Female: Choices and Changes in Our Lives Today* (New York: Simon and Schuster, 1984), 199.
116. Nancy Tousley, "Judy Chicago's Dinner Party Rewrites Women's History," *Calgary Herald*, 22 November 1980, JCCSL. See also Candas Jane Dorsey, "Women, Art, and Celebration," *Interface* (1980), 15.
117. Helen Corbett, "A Woman's Work: Rewriting History Through Her Art," *Edmonton Journal*, 29 November 1980, H1.
118. Laura Green, "Finally, We're Invited to Judy Chicago's 'Dinner Party,'" *Chicago Sun-Times*, 6 September 1981, 6. This fantasy would have been difficult but not impossible to realize, thanks to microsurgery, through which some have had their tubes untied so that they could become pregnant.
119. Jean Barlow Hudson, "The Dinner Party," *Wimmin's Voices*, 2 July 1981.
120. Judith Lewis, "The Trouble with Judy: Reflections on The Dinner Party and the Artist Who Created It," *Los Angeles Weekly* 18, 26 April 1996, 32.
121. Faye Dambrot and Robert Zangrando, "The Dinner Party: A Reply," *Beacon: The Sunday Magazine of the Akron Beacon Journal*, 2 August 1981.
122. David Evett, "Moveable Feast," *Northern Ohio Live* 1, no. 16 (4–17 May 1981), 28.
123. Robert Zangrando to author, 12 January 2006. Polly Paffilas, "Folks Protest; Antiques Sale Returns," *Akron Beacon Journal*, 6 July 1983, B2. Dick Wootten, "Judy Chicago Show Is Profitable Dinner Party," *Cleveland Press*, 7 August 1981, D24. Ursuline College master's student Ann Macklin is currently writing "Values through Voices: Judy Chicago's The Dinner Party (Cleveland Exhibit)—The Audience Speaks," "to investigate whether there is a link/correlation between the language used by the institutions (art world, politicians, media) and the language used by the audience (attendees)." She reports that the visitors' books from the Cleveland showing reveal a majority of positive responses.
124. Dambrot and Zangrando, "The Dinner Party: A Reply."
125. Nadine Joseph, "A Special Kind of Art," *Cleveland Plain Dealer*, 13 June 1979.
126. Helen Cullinan, "Judy Chicago 'The Dinner Party' Is in Keeping with Feminist Style," *Cleveland Plain Dealer*, 7 May 1981, E1.
127. Cynthia Dettebach, "'Dialogue, Controversy' Served at Dinner Party," *Cleveland Jewish News*, 8 May 1981, 31.

128. Dorothy Shinn, "The Gospel According to Judy Chicago," *Beacon: The Sunday Magazine of the Akron Beacon,* 5 July 1981, 4.
129. Lolette Kuby, "Hoodwinking Women," *Cleveland Magazine* 10, no. 8 (August 1980), 83–84.
130. Liz Lincoln, "Clearing the Table, Letter to the Editor Responding to Kuby's Article," *Cleveland Magazine* 10 (October 1981), 10.
131. Evett, *Northern Ohio Live,* 28.
132. Helen Cullinan, "Feminist Art Esprit Creates a Cleveland-Chicago Bond," *Cleveland Plain Dealer,* May 1979.
133. Diane Gelon quoted in Maureen Wells, "Interview with Diane Gelon," *What She Wants* 8, no. 10 (May 1981), 6, 12.
134. Ann Marie Lipinski, "An Invitation to 'The Dinner Party,'" *Chicago Tribune,* 6 September 1981, sec. 4, 1.
135. "Hot Type: The Dinner Party's Hosts," *Chicago Reader,* 11 September 1981, 4.
136. Lipinski, "Invitation to 'The Dinner Party,'" 4. Others involved in the Chicago effort were Bette Cerf Hill, Jean Hunt, and Hedy Ratner.
137. Gerber, "People," *Skyline Newspapers,* 7 January 1982, sec. 1, 2.
138. John Grod, "Plastic Artist Under Attack?" *Chicago Reader,* 2 October 1981.
139. Ibid.
140. Alan G. Artner, "Inanity Outweighs the Controversy of 'Dinner Party,'" *Chicago Tribune,* 14 September 1981, B8.
141. Judy Chicago on Irv Kupcinet, *The Kup's Show,* guests Roy Cohn, Judy Chicago, and Christopher Anderson, WTTW (Chicago, 1981), video.
142. Judy Chicago to author, 24 January 2006.
143. John Bentley Mays, "Epic Dinner Party Strikes to the Core," *Toronto Globe and Mail,* 22 May 1982, "Entertainment," 11. Adele Freedman, "Dinner Party: Art or Exhumation?" *Toronto Globe and Mail,* 19 April 1982. Susan Crean, "The Dinner Party: Indigestion for the Establishment," *Broadside: A Feminist Review* 3, no. 10 (September 1982), 8. JCCSL.
144. "Audacieuse . . . éclate de sensibilité et de rigueur, de sensualité, de passion et de tendresse." "Des milliers de visiteurs recueillis défilent presque religieusement devant les trois tables que formant un triangle équilatéral—symbole de la femme." "'The Dinner Party' une Oeuvre Colossale," *Le Céramiste* 1, no. 4 (July 1982), 10.
145. Lawrence Sabbath, "Dinner Party Serves Up History of Women's Struggle," *Montreal Gazette,* 20 March 1982, B7.
146. Mays, "Epic Dinner Party," 11.
147. Crean, "Indigestion for the Establishment," 8. "'Dinner Party' Draws 50,000 in Toronto," *Montreal Gazette,* 8 July 1982.
148. Crean, "Indigestion for the Establishment," 8.
149. Natalie Veiner Freeman, "Revelations of a Private Female World," *Maclean's,* 5 April 1982, 44.
150. Mays, "Epic Dinner Party," 11.
151. Ibid.
152. Ibid.
153. Crean, "Indigestion for the Establishment," 8. JCCSL, Box 2, Folder 13.
154. Robert Fulford, "Dinner Party's Sweep Is Breathtaking," *Toronto Star,* 12 June 1982.
155. http://microformguides.gale.com/Data/Download/9023000C.rtf as of June 1, 2006, in the timeline of the Atlanta Lesbian Feminist Alliance (ALFA), now in Atlanta Lesbian Feminist Alliance Archives, c. 1972–94, Rare Book, Manuscript, and Special Collections Library, Duke University, Durham, N.C.
156. Flyer in Atlanta Lesbian Feminist Alliance Archives, c. 1972–94, Rare Book, Manuscript, and Special Collections Library, Duke University, Durham, N.C.
157. Wes Smith, "Scraps from The Dinner Party," *Atlanta Journal,* 28 July 1982, 1B.
158. Catherine Fox, "Guess Who's Coming to Dinner?" *Atlanta Constitution,* 27 July 1982, 1B. JCCSL, Box 2, Folder 13.
159. Ibid., 3B.

New Ventures 12

1. Judy Chicago, *Personal Journal, No. 8,* Collection of Judy Chicago (1978–80), 4 July 1979, 158.
2. Lucy Lippard, "Long Labor for the Birth Project," *In These Times,* 1911, 29 (May/June 1985), 20. JCCSL.
3. Judy Chicago, *The Birth Project* (New York: Doubleday, 1985), 26.
4. Ibid., 19.
5. Edward Lucie-Smith, *Judy Chicago: An American Vision* (New York: Watson-Guptill, 2000), 98.
6. Chicago, *Birth Project,* 17.
7. Mary Ross Taylor, interview with author, 11 January 2004.
8. Ibid.
9. Postcard sent by Mary Ross Taylor, 1980. Collection of Judy Chicago.
10. Chicago, *Personal Journal,* vol. 9, 21 September 1980; only this excerpt was provided by Judy Chicago.
11. Mary Taylor to Judy Chicago, 20 March 1981, Collection of Judy Chicago.

12. Mary Ross Taylor to Judy Chicago, 7 July 1982, Collection of Judy Chicago.
13. Mary Ross Taylor to Judy Chicago, 18 August [1982], Collection of Judy Chicago.
14. Sally Babson to author, 29 January 2006.
15. Judy Chicago to author, 18 December 2005.
16. Mary Ross Taylor to author, 11 January 2004.
17. Judy Chicago, *Beyond the Flower: The Autobiography of a Feminist Artist* (New York: Viking Penguin, 1996), 144.
18. Lawrence Sabbath, "The Tough, Fragile Artist Behind 'The Dinner Party,'" *Montreal Gazette,* 17 April 1982, A4. JCCSL, Box 2, Folder 13.
19. In interviews with the author, various friends of Chicago's, for example, Suzanne Lacy (9 January 2004), have mentioned her onetime intimacy with Taylor. Chicago herself has made available to the author documentary evidence of this and other relationships.
20. Raymond Sokolov, "Ritual, Myth and Romance on the Santa Fe Trail," *Wall Street Journal,* 5 August 1983, 21.
21. Mary Ross Taylor to author, 10 January 2004.
22. Lippard, "Long Labor for the Birth Project," 21.
23. Ibid.
24. Lucy Lippard, "Born Again," *Village Voice,* 16 April 1985, 96. JCCSL, Box 2, Folder 18.
25. Michele Maier to author, 2 June 2006.
26. Ibid.
27. Ibid.
28. Barbara Karkabi, "Specially Chosen Women Doing Needlework for Artist's Next Project," *Houston Chronicle,* 9 July 1981, sec. 5, p. 5.
29. Ibid.
30. Kathy Larkin, "Judy Chicago: Art Across the Gender Gap," *Post-Tribune* (Chicago), 2 December 1984, Today's Woman, 4.
31. Pamella Nesbit to author, 15 January 2006.
32. Ibid.
33. Ibid.
34. Chicago, *Birth Project,* 66.
35. Pamella Nesbit to author, 15 January 2006.
36. Sally Babson to author, 29 January 2006.
37. Ita Aber to author, 13 August 2002. Aber wrote this unsolicited letter upon reading the author's article, "Learning to Appreciate Judy Chicago," in *Women in the Arts,* 2002.
38. Ida Aber to author, 18 December 2005.
39. Chicago to author, 24 January 2006.
40. Ita Aber to author, 13 August 2002.
41. Ida Aber to author, 18 December 2005.
42. Chicago to author, 24 January 2006.
43. Chicago, *Birth Project,* 230.
44. Ita Aber to author, 18 December 2005.
45. Chicago credited Faith Wilding with this insight. Judy Chicago, "Judy Chicago: The Second Decade 1973–1983," *Women Artists News* 9, no. 5–6 (Summer 1984), 13. JCCSL, Box 2, Folder 16.
46. Judy Chicago quoted in Guy Cross, "An Interview with Judy Chicago," *Santa Fe's Monthly,* September 1996, 43. JCCSL, Box 2, Folder 35.
47. Steve Carrell, "The Birth Project," *American Medical News,* 24 September 1982, 9.
48. Suzanne Muchnic, "Gallery Serves up Divergent Fare," *Los Angeles Times,* 25 February 1985, Calendar, 9.
49. Sylvia Rubin, "The Birth Project," *San Francisco Chronicle,* 3 April 1985, 23. JCCSL, Box 2, Folder 18.
50. Muchnic, "Gallery Serves up Divergent," 9.
51. Paul Richard, "'Birth Project': Fetal Visions," *Washington Post,* 28 May 1985, D7.
52. Linda Monk, "How Can Birth Be Embarrassing?" *Washington Post,* 8 June 1985.
53. Diane Rico, "Project Gives Birth to Widespread Interest," *Los Angeles Daily News,* 27 March 1985, L.A. Life, 15. JCCSL, Box 2, Folder 18.
54. Ibid., 15, 18.
55. Harriet Swift, "Judy Chicago Delivers Her 'Birth Project,'" *Tribune* [Oakland, Calif.], 1 April 1985, C3.
56. Ibid.
57. Kay Longcope, "A Judy Chicago Project," *Boston Globe,* 8 May 1985, 78.
58. Leah Rosch, "Hard Labor: Judy Chicago Delivers The Birth Project," *Boston Phoenix,* 14 May 1985, 7. She is today Jacqueline Moore Alexander.
59. Ibid.
60. Anita Creamer, "Celebrating Women's Creativity," *Dallas Times Herald,* 20 June 1984, 1F.
61. Ibid., 8F.
62. Kathy Prentice, "Women's Work Comes to State: 'The Birth Project,'" *Detroit Free Press,* 20 February 1986, B1, B3.
63. Edward Sozanski, *Philadelphia Inquirer,* September 1986. JCCSL.
64. Robin Rice, "Having My Baby: It's Been a Tough Labor and Delivery for Judy Chicago's 'Birth Project,'" *Philadelphia City Paper,* 19–26 September 1986, 11. JCCSL, Box 2, Folder 19.
65. Sandy Ballatore, "'Dinner Party' Needs a Host," *Albuquerque Journal,* 20 August 1989, G1. JCCSL, Box 2, Folder 26.
66. Anette Kubitza, "Rereading the Readings of *The Dinner Party* in Europe," in *Sexual Politics: Judy Chicago's* Dinner Party *in Feminist Art History,* ed. Amelia Jones (Berkeley: University of California, 1996), 155.

67. Judy Chicago to Bill Harpe, 23 July 1984, JCCSL, Box 6, Folder 30.
68. Judy Chicago, "A Tribute to Virginia Woolf," Blackie, 21 October 1982, 3. JCCSL, Box 6, Folder 27.
69. Edward Gage, "Impeccable 'Dinner Party,'" *Edinburgh Newspaper* August 1984, JCCSL, Box 2, Folder 15.
70. Judith Michaelson, "Time for L.A. to Feast on 'Dinner?'" *Los Angeles Times,* 24 December 1984, sec. 6, 1.
71. Ibid., sec. 6, 10.
72. Richard Cork, "Monumental," *Listener,* 21 March 1985.
73. Michael Shepherd, "The Woman's Work That's Never Done," *Sunday Telegraph* [London], 14 April 1985.
74. Julia Pascal, "Judy Chicago," *City Limits,* 22–28 March 1985, JCCSL, Box 2, Folder 24.
75. Judy Chicago quoted in Pascal, "Judy Chicago."
76. Jane Lott, "Women Put in Their Plate," *Observer* [London], 10 March 1985.
77. Judy Chicago to author, 16 December 2005.
78. Romona Scholder to the author, 10 June 2004. Chicago, *Beyond the Flower,* 165–67.
79. Chicago, *Beyond the Flower,* 170.
80. Judy Chicago to author, 24 January 2006.
81. Swift, "Judy Chicago Delivers Her 'Birth Project,'" C1.
82. Dale Martin, "Birth Project Kept Needle-workers in Stitches," *San Mateo Times,* 17 April 1985, B1.
83. Donald Woodman to author, 6 June 2004.
84. Donald Woodman to author, 17 December 2005.
85. Romona Scholder to author, 10 June 2004.
86. Donald Woodman to author, 6 June 2004.
87. Chicago, *Beyond the Flower,* 172.
88. Chicago, *Personal Journal,* vol. 14, 17 September 1985, 87–88.
89. Ibid., 17 September 1985.
90. Ibid., 17 September 1985.
91. Chicago, *Beyond the Flower,* 173.
92. Donald Woodman to author, 6 June 2004.
93. Chicago, *Personal Journal,* vol. 14, 26 September 1985, 95–96.
94. Ibid., 26 September 1985.
95. Romona Scholder to author, 10 June 2004.
96. Donald Woodman to author, 6 June 2004.
97. Ibid.
98. Donald Woodman to author, 17 December 2005.
99. Ibid.
100. Ibid.
101. Agnes Martin quoted in John Gruen, *The Artist Observed: 28 Interviews with Contemporary Artists* (New York: A Cappella Books, 1991), 85–86, based on 1976 interview held in New York.
102. Matt Schudel, "Influential Abstract Painter Agnes Martin Dies at 92," *Washington Post,* 18 December 2004, B06.
103. Gruen, *Artist Observed,* 78.
104. That Martin was a lesbian appears in Harmony Hammond, *Lesbian Art in America: A Contemporary History* (New York: Rizzoli, 2000), 186, n. 3. See also Laura Cottingham, *Seeing Through the Seventies: Essays on Feminism and Art* (Padstow, Cornwall, U.K.: G + B Arts International, 2000), 158, n. 23.
105. Lee Seldes, *The Legacy of Mark Rothko: An Exposé of the Greatest Art Scandal of Our Century* (New York: Holt Rinehart & Winston, 1978).
106. Gruen, *Artist Observed,* 82.
107. Donald Woodman to author, 17 December 2005.
108. Ibid.
109. Judy Chicago, *A Jewish Journal,* unpublished handwritten manuscript, (1985–93), 1. JCCSL. Box 72, Folder 23.
110. Ibid.
111. Ibid., 12 November 1985, 5.
112. Sally Eauclaire, "The Holocaust Project: A Controversial Artist's New Work Parallels Her Own Bittersweet Journey to Self-Discovery," *Chicago Tribune Magazine,* 17 October 1993, 18.
113. Chicago, *Jewish Journal,* 12 November 1985, 5.
114. Judy Chicago, drawing, dated November 1985, JCCSL, Box 72, Folder 23.
115. Yaffa Eliach, *Hasidic Tales of the Holocaust* (New York: Oxford University Press, 1982).
116. Chicago, *Jewish Journal,* 3 January 1986, 16.
117. Ibid., 21 November 1985, 8. This poem is printed in the back of the *Dinner Party* book.
118. Chicago, *Jewish Journal,* 3 January 1986, 14.
119. Ibid., 3 January 1986, 19.
120. Ibid., 3 January 1985, 23.
121. Donald Woodman to author, 17 December 2005.
122. Ibid.
123. Ibid.
124. Caption in Judy Chicago, *Powerplay,* catalog, Paula Harper, ed. Sidney L. Bergen (New York: ACA Galleries, 1986), 18.
125. Judy Chicago, *Powerplay, Three Faces of Man,* press statement for event "sponsored by Lawrence Properties in coordination with Women in the Arts," JCCSL, Box 72, folder 15.
126. Judy Chicago, Interview with Cathleen Rountree for *Coming Into Fullness: On Women Turning Forty,* typescript, (1991), n.p., JCCSL,

Box 7, Folder 39. Cathleen Rountree, *Coming into Our Fullness: On Women Turning Forty* (Freedom, Calif.: Crossing Press, 1991), 28.

127. Judy Chicago, "Being in the Presence of the Truth: An Interview with Judy Chicago," interview by Nancy Jo Hoy, *From the Ear* (Spring 1994), 42.
128. Chicago, *Jewish Journal,* 22 April 1986, 34.
129. Ibid., May 1986, 36.
130. Ibid., 1 April 1986, 27.
131. Ibid., 22 April 1986, 22.
132. Ibid., September 1986, 48.
133. Elizabeth Bernstein, "Chicago View of Holocaust," *JUF* [Jewish United Fund] *News,* October 1993, 68. JCCSL, Box 72, Folder 42.
134. Contract and lecture text are in JCCSL, Box 6, Folder 33. Caroline Fetsher, "Frauenkunst Soll aus Blut und Milch Sein," *Spiegel* 25 (16 June 1986), 166. Dagmar von Garnier to author, 18 September 2002.
135. Kubitza, "Rereading the Readings," 164.
136. Dagmar von Garnier to the author, 18 September 2002. Von Garnier heard about this biography and sought out the author to defend her point of view.
137. Chicago, *Jewish Journal,* May 1986, 39.
138. See Kubitza, "Rereading the Readings," 165.
139. Fetsher, "Frauenkunst Soll aus Blut und Milch Sein," 166.
140. Nicole Plett, "Artist Attacks Stereotypes in Bronze Now," *Albuquerque Journal,* 13 July 1986, JCCSL, Box 2, Folder 20.
141. Paula Harper, *Powerplay,* ed. Sidney L. Bergen (New York: ACA Galleries, 1986), 19.
142. Ibid.
143. Chicago, *Powerplay,* 2.
144. Chicago, "Being in the Presence of the Truth," 37.
145. Ann Marsh, "A Theoretical and Political Context," in *Feminism-Art-Theory,* ed. Hilary Robinson (Oxford, U.K.: Blackwell, 1985), 98.
146. Chicago, *Jewish Journal,* October 1986, 68.
147. Ibid., October 1986, 73.
148. Ibid.
149. Ibid., October 1986, 70.
150. David Galloway, "From Bankfurt to Frankfurt: A Cash and Carry Renaissance," *Art in America,* September 1987.
151. Kubitza, "Rereading the Readings," 166.
152. Ibid., 166–69.
153. Ibid., 169; Lippard, "Long Labor for the Birth Project."
154. Bernstein, "Chicago View of Holocaust," 69.
155. Adi Ohphir, reprinted from *Tikkun* 2, no. 1 (1987), as Adi Ohpir, "On Sanctifying the Holocaust: An Anti-Theological Treatise," in *Impossible Images: Contemporary Art after the Holocaust,* ed. Laura Levitt, Shelly Hornstein, and Lawrence J. Silberstein (New York: New York University Press, 2004), 195.
156. Ibid., 197.
157. Ibid., 199–200.
158. Ibid., 203.
159. Anonymous, "New York's Avant-Garde School: Daring New Lincoln Strives for Student Self-Assertiveness," *Ebony* 34–44 (May 1965): 40.
160. Elizabeth Sackler to author, 16 January 2006. Anonymous, "New York's Avant-Garde," 34.
161. Elizabeth Sackler to author, 16 January 2006.
162. Elizabeth Sackler to author, 9 February 2005.
163. Judy Chicago, *Holocaust Project: From Darkness Into Light* (New York: Penguin Books, 1993), 78.
164. Ibid.
165. Ibid., 79–80.
166. Judy Chicago, *Israel Journal,* November 1988.
167. Chicago, *Holocaust Project,* 82.
168. Bernstein, "Chicago View of Holocaust," 69.
169. Ibid.
170. Elana Eizak Kuperstein, "Judy Chicago: A Feminist Artist in Search of Her Jewish Self," *Women's World,* April–May 1987, 11.
171. Bernstein, "Chicago View of Holocaust," 69.
172. Ibid., 70.
173. Judy Chicago, "Judy Chicago: Artist's Statement," *Gallerie Women's Art* 1, no. 1 (Annual/June 1988), 38.
174. Ibid.
175. Ibid.
176. Ricardo Viera and Laurence J. Silberstein, *Holocaust Project: From Darkness into Light* (Bethlehem, Penn.: Zoellner Arts Center, Lehigh University, 2000), n.p.
177. Chicago, *Holocaust Project,* 88.
178. Ibid.
179. Eauclaire, "The Holocaust Project," 20.
180. Donald Woodman to author, 29 January 2006.
181. Judy Chicago to author, 17 January 2006.
182. Chicago, *Holocaust Project,* 126.
183. Judy Chicago, "Exploring the Significance of the Holocaust Through Art," *Holocaust Project Newsletter,* no. 6 (Winter 1991–92), 1. Maddy was battling cancer at the time but chose to make this work.
184. Judy Chicago to Michael Caudle, 5 August 1989, JCCSL.
185. Eauclaire, "The Holocaust Project," 20.
186. Suzanne Muchnic, "The Galleries: Wilshire Center," *Los Angeles Times,* 8 April 1988, sec. IV, p. 22. JCCSL, Box 2, Folder 25.
187. Christina Thompson, "The Dinner Party," January 1988, JCCSL, Box 2, Folder 25.
188. Chicago, *Beyond the Flower,* 207.

Resolution: Finding a Home 13

1. Barry Lancet, "Ben Cohen, American Potter in Echizen, Japan," *Ceramics: Art and Perception* [Sydney, Australia], no. 9, (1992), 56.
2. Ben Cohen, "Joyous Flame," *Ceramics Monthly* 38, no. 6 (June–July–August 1990), 60.
3. Lancet, "Ben Cohen, American Potter," 56.
4. Ibid., 58.
5. Julia Cassim, "Stricken Ceramist in Fukui Shapes Skills of His Successor," *Japan Times,* 21 January 1992, 4.
6. Julia Cassim, "Friends Rally to Help Potter with Lou Gehrig's Disease," *Japan Times,* 24 September 1990.
7. Judy Chicago, *Hana Motsu Onna: Wesuto Kosuto Ni Hanahiraita Feminizumu Ato no Kishu, Judi Shikago Jiden* (Through the Flower), Kazuko KOIKE (Tokyo: Parco Shuppan Co., 1979).
8. Judy Chicago, *Beyond the Flower: The Autobiography of a Feminist Artist* (New York: Viking Penguin, 1996), 221.
9. Ben Cohen to his family and friends, 20 October 1991, Collection of Reiko Kakiuchi-Cohen.
10. Chicago, *Beyond the Flower,* 222.
11. Lancet, "Ben Cohen, American Potter," 59.
12. Reiko Kakiuchi-Cohen has continued to make pottery and shows in Japan and at the Touching Stone Gallery in Santa Fe, N.M.
13. Judy Chicago quoted in Cathleen Rountree, *Coming into Our Fullness: On Women Turning Forty* (Freedom, Calif.: Crossing Press, 1991), 31.
14. Lucy R. Lippard, "Uninvited Guests: How Washington Lost 'The Dinner Party,'" *Art in America* 79 (December 1991), 39.
15. Jonetta Rose Barras, "UDC's $1.6 Million 'Dinner' Feminist Artwork Causes Some Indigestion," *Washington Times,* 18 July 1990, A1.
16. David Ignatius, "Tension of the Times," *Washington Post,* 18 June 2004, A29. *The Washington Times,* which was founded in 1982, is currently overseen by the Rev. Chung Hwan Kwak, a close adviser to the church's founder, the Rev. Sun Myung Moon. See also the *Columbia Journalism Review* website as of 20 June 2006: http://www.cjr.org/tools/owners/newsworld.asp.
17. Barras, "UDC's $1.6 Million 'Dinner,'" A1.
18. Molly Sinclair and Jo Ann Lewis, "UDC to Renovate Library for Controversial Artwork," *Washington Post,* 19 July 1990, D1.
19. Lippard, "Uninvited Guests," 41.
20. See the Parris amendment in *Congressional Record—Daily Digest,* 26 July 1990, D506, 19742.
21. Pete Domenici quoted in Katie Hickox, "Work by Santa Fe Artist Stirs Congressional Fray," *Santa Fe New Mexican,* 28 July 1990, A1.
22. Walter Pruden, "A Big Dinner Bell, but No Groceries," *Washington Times,* 20 July 1990. Lippard, "Uninvited Guests," 43.
23. Lippard, "Uninvited Guests," 43.
24. Ellen Sweets, "The Chicago Story: Artist's 'Dinner Party' Was Going Well in D.C., Until Congress Crashed It," *Dallas Morning News,* 16 September 1990, 1C.
25. Gaile Robinson, "The Man Behind Gauguin," *Dallas Star-Telegram,* December 2005.
26. Staff, "Dallas Museum Director Gets Probation," *Houston Chronicle,* 3 November 1992, News Briefs, 3.
27. Lippard, "Uninvited Guests," 45.
28. Ibid.
29. Katie Hickox, "Santa Fe Artist's Sculpture Gift Brings Controversy to University," *Santa Fe New Mexican,* 5 August 1990, B1. Hickox, "Work by Santa Fe Artist," A2.
30. Riane Eisler, "Sex, Art and Archetypes," *Women's Review of Books* 8, no. 6 (March 1991).
31. Lippard, "Uninvited Guests," 43.
32. Ibid., 47.
33. Judy Chicago to the editor of *ARTnews,* 18 December 1990.
34. Lippard, "Uninvited Guests," 39–47.
35. Betsy Baker to Lucy Lippard, n.d., summer 1991.
36. Bill Richardson, "The Dinner Party," *Congressional Record* 138 (19 February 1992), E333–34.
37. Rountree, *Coming into Our Fullness.*
38. Judy Chicago, Interview with Cathleen Rountree for *Coming Into Fullness: On Women Turning Forty*, typescript, (1991), JCCSL, Box 7, Folder 39. Judy Chicago to Cathleen Rountree, n.d., January 1991.
39. Judy Chicago quoted in Judith Lewis, "The Trouble with Judy: Reflections on The Dinner Party and the Artist Who Created It," *LA Weekly* 18, 26 April 1996, 32.
40. Judy Chicago quoted in ibid.
41. Tom Freudenheim to author, 30 August 2006.
42. Janet Bajan to author, 9 June 2004.
43. Kate Millett, "Sexual Politics," in *Sexual Politics* (Garden City, N.Y.: Doubleday, 1970), 39.
44. Susan Brownmiller, "In Our Time: Memoir of a Revolution," in *In Our Time: Memoir of a Revolution* (New York: Random House, 1999), 173.

45. Janet Bajan to author, 9 June 2004.
46. Ibid.
47. Elizabeth Sackler to author, 9 February 2005. See also "No More Miss America!," August 1968, reprinted in Robin Morgan, ed., "No More Miss America!" in *Sisterhood Is Powerful: An Anthology of Writings from the Women's Liberation Movement* (New York: Vintage Books, 1970), 584–88.
48. Elizabeth A. Sackler to author, 18 January 2006.
49. Elizabeth A. Sackler to author, 9 February 2005.
50. Ibid.
51. Elizabeth A. Sackler to author, 18 January 2006.
52. Janet Bajan to author, 9 June 2004.
53. Chicago, *Beyond the Flower,* 254.
54. Edward Lucie-Smith, *Judy Chicago: An American Vision* (New York: Watson-Guptill, 2000), 154.
55. Peter Goddard, "Southern Revival," *Toronto Star,* 29 January 2005, H1.
56. Paul Logan, "Artists Trade Santa Fe for Historic Belen Hotel," *Albuquerque Journal,* 15 July 1993, A9. JCCSL, Box 2, Folder 30.
57. Judy Chicago quoted in Katherine Saltzstein, "Judy Chicago Recreates Hill in Watercolor," *News-Bulletin* (Valencia County, N.M.) 9–10 June 1999, Weekend, 6A.
58. Mary Abbe, "Judy Chicago Says That Fame Doesn't Remove Sexist Obstacles to Art," *Minneapolis Star Tribune,* 14 January 1994, 4E.
59. Although an early draft of a contract with the Spertus proposes that the artists would receive 25 percent of "the excess of exhibition revenues over exhibition costs" instead of a fee, in fact all revenues from the exhibition itself went to Through the Flower; contract draft is in JCCSL, Box 74, Folder 1.
60. This list is printed on the stationery from "Holocaust Project/1990."
61. Sally Eauclaire, "The Holocaust Project: A Controversial Artist's New Work Parallels Her Own Bittersweet Journey to Self-Discovery," *Chicago Tribune Magazine,* 17 October 1993, 18.
62. Judy Chicago, "Exploring the Significance of the Holocaust Through Art," *Holocaust Project Newsletter,* no. 6 (Winter 1991–92), 1.
63. Eauclaire, "Holocaust Project," 17–18.
64. Chicago, *Beyond the Flower,* 168. Virginia Woolf, *Three Guineas* (London: Hogarth Press, 1938).
65. Judy Chicago to author, 16 January 2006.
66. Eauclaire, "Holocaust Project," 17.
67. Elie Wiesel, "Art and the Holocaust: Trivializing Memory," *New York Times* 11 June 1989, sec. 2.
68. Fred Camper, "The Banality of Badness," *Chicago Reader,* 21 January 1994, sec. 1, 22.
69. Eauclaire, "Holocaust Project," 19.
70. Observed by the author in a class at Lehigh University, May 2000.
71. Arlene Raven quoted in Letty Cottin Pogrebin, "Anti-Semitism in the Women's Movement," *Ms.,* June 1982, 69.
72. Elizabeth Hess, "Planet Holocaust: From Feminism to Judaism: Meet the New Judy Chicago," *Village Voice,* 2 November 1993, 44.
73. Hess, "Planet Holocaust," 44.
74. Michael Nutkiewicz, "Watching Evolution of a Challenging Work," *Cleveland Jewish News,* 7 January 1994, 11.
75. Philip Gourevitch, "Washington's Holocaust Theme Park," *Harper's,* July 1993, 56.
76. Philip Gourevitch, *We Wish to Inform You That Tomorrow We Will Be Killed with Our Families: Stories from Rwanda* (New York: Farrar, Straus and Giroux, 1998).
77. Ibid.
78. Harry Kriesler, "Reporting the Story of a Genocide, Conversations with Philip Gourevitch, Staff Writer, *The New Yorker,*" 11 February 2000. Conversations with History, Institute of International Studies, University of California at Berkeley. Online at http://globetrotter.berkeley.edu/people/Gourevitch/gourevitch-con0.html.
79. Arlene Raven, "Judy Chicago: The Artist Critics Love to Hate," *On the Issues* 3, no. 3 (Summer 1994): 40.
80. Nick Charles, "Project's Not on Critics' List," *New York Daily News,* 22 April 1994.
81. Judy Chicago and Michele Spirn, "An Interview with Judy Chicago on the Holocaust Project," *NCJW Journal* 17, no. 1 (Fall 1994): 18.
82. Rebecca Levy, "Judy Chicago's Holocaust Project: A Time to Heal," *Austin Chronicle* 14, no. 10 (4 November 1994): 34.
83. Alvin H. Rosenfeld, "The Americanization of the Holocaust," *Commentary* 99, no. 6 (June 1995): 36.
84. Ibid., 37.
85. Ibid.
86. Eauclaire, "Holocaust Project," 19.
87. Isaiah Kuperstein to author, 28 July 2005.
88. Christine Temin, "Judy Chicago's Unintended Horror; Holocaust Project: From Darkness Into Light by Judy Chicago with Photography by Donald Woodman," *Boston Globe,* 22 September 1995, 51.
89. Renee Graham, "Why Judy Chicago Is the Artist the Art World Loves to Hate," *Boston Sunday Globe,* 24 September 1995, B27.

90. Ibid.
91. Quoted in ibid.
92. Judy Chicago to Renee Graham, 25 September 1995, Collection of Judy Chicago.
93. Fran Heller, "Journey of Identity," *Cleveland Jewish News,* 3 May 1996, 16.
94. Stephen Litt, "Chicago the Artist Paints with a Windy Brush," *Cleveland Plain Dealer,* 4 May 1996, 8E, 12E. JCCSL, Box 2, Folder 36.
95. Stephen Feinstein to Judy Chicago, 6 May 1994, JCCSL.
96. Charles Patterson, *The Eternal Treblinka: Our Treatment of Animals* (New York: Lantern Books, 2002), gives proof that Hitler was not a vegetarian. See also Rynn Berry, *Hitler: Neither Vegetarian Nor Animal Lover* (New York: Pythagorean Books, 2004), 1–3.
97. Patterson, *Eternal Treblinka.* Italian, German, Polish, Czech, Croation, and Hebrew translations have since been published.
98. Isaac Bashevis Singer, "The Letter Writer," in *The Seance and Other Stories* (New York: Farrar, Straus and Giroux, 1968), 270.
99. Jyl Lynn Felman, "Judy Chicago's Holocaust Project," *Lilith* 19, no. 2 (30 June 1994), 15–16.
100. Miriam Schapiro to author, 1995, 1996.
101. Lewis, "Trouble with Judy," 30.
102. Amelia Jones, ed., *Sexual Politics: Judy Chicago's* Dinner Party *in Feminist Art History* (Berkeley: University of California Press, 1996), 7.
103. Amelia Jones to author, August 2005.
104. Libby Lumpkin, "Unintended (PH)Allacies: A Feminist Reading of 'Sexual Politics,'" *Art Issues,* September–October 1996, 24.
105. Jones, *Sexual Politics: Judy Chicago's,* 23.
106. Lewis, "Trouble with Judy," 30.
107. Jones, *Sexual Politics: Judy Chicago's,* 24.
108. Laura Meyer, "From Finish Fetish to Feminism: Judy Chicago's *Dinner Party* in California Art History," in Jones, *Sexual Politics,* 46–74.
109. Christopher Knight, "More Famine Than Feast," *Los Angeles Times,* 2 May 1996, F11.
110. Robin Abcarian, "The Lesson of Judy Chicago: Fame Has Its Detractions,'" *Los Angeles Times,* 28 April 1996, E2.
111. Jennie Klein, "Sexual/Textual Politics: The Battle over Art of the 70's," *New Art Examiner,* October 1996, 30.
112. Lewis, "Trouble with Judy," 30.
113. Ibid.
114. Susan Bickelhaupt and Maureen Dezell, "Chicago Comes to Cambridge," *Boston Globe,* 5 June 1996, 34. JCCSL, Box 2, Folder 33.
115. http://www.radcliffe.edu/schles/collections_overview.php.
116. Chicago, *Beyond the Flower.* While selectively omitting, Chicago has reported her life with remarkable integrity.
117. Donna Seaman, "Beyond the Flower (Book Review)," *Booklist* 92 (1 March 1996), 1116.
118. Liesl Schillinger, "Beyond the Flower: The Autobiography of a Feminist Artist," *New York Times,* 24 March 1996, sec. 7, 21.
119. Schillinger, "Beyond the Flower," 21.
120. Lewis Segal, "Lewitzky's Feminist Statement," *Los Angeles Times,* 23 September 1996, F5.
121. Scarlet Cheng, "A Future Defined by Needle and Thread," *Los Angeles Times* 21 January 2001, Calendar, 76.
122. Unidentified writer, "Art: On View," *Time,* 20 February 1928, 21–22, quoted in Barbara Buhler Lynes, ed., *O'Keeffe, Stieglitz, and the Critics, 1916–1929* (Chicago: University of Chicago Press, 1989), 283.
123. Judy Chicago to author, 21 June 2006.
124. The women who produced Chicago's needlework designs for *Resolutions* included Helen Eisenberg, Gerry Melot, Pat Rudy-Bease, Mary Ewanoski, Pamella Nesbit, Lisa Maue, Alise Anima, Louise Otewalt, Penny Harris, Jane Thompson, Tamara Norrgard, Lynda Patterson, Betsy Smullen, Joyce Gilbert, Candis Duncan Pomykala, Joan Palmer, Audrey Cowan, Paula Daves, and Jacquelyn Moore.
125. Judy Chicago quoted in Michele Hewitson, "Missing the BIG Picture," *Weekend Herald* [Auckland, New Zealand] 10–11 July 1999, J4.
126. Pamella Nesbit to the author, 15 January 2006.
127. Ibid.
128. Ibid.
129. Ibid.
130. Ibid.
131. Jane Thompson to author, 16 December 2006.
132. Jackie Moore to Judy Chicago, 20 June 1997, copy made available by Jackie Moore Alexander.
133. Patricia Rudy-Baese to author, 4 January 2006.
134. Arley Sanchez, "Man Lends Talent to Art," *Journal South* [New Mexico], 11 May 2000, 1, 2.
135. Pamella Nesbit to author, 15 January 2006.
136. Paula Harper, "The Chicago Resolutions," *Art in America,* June 2000, 113.
137. Ken Johnson, "Offering Up Good Cheer and the Humanist Values, All Rendered in Clichés," *New York Times,* 4 August 2000, E36.
138. Nancy Berman quoted in Cheng, "A Future Defined by Needle," 77.

139. Elizabeth A. Sackler to author, 18 January 2006.
140. Judy Chicago to author, 7 February 2006. Lucie-Smith, *Judy Chicago: An American Vision.*
141. Elizabeth A. Sackler to author, 23 January 2006.
142. Ibid.
143. Cathleen McGuigan, "A Shock Grows in Brooklyn," *Newsweek,* 11 October 1999, 70.
144. Elizabeth A. Sackler to author, 9 February 2005.
145. Arnold Lehman to author, 19 January 2006.
146. Brooklyn Museum press release for the Elizabeth A. Sackler Center for Feminist Art, n.d. (January 2006).
147. Arnold Lehman to author, 18 January 2006.
148. Paul Buhle, *From the Lower East Side to Hollywood: Jews in American Popular Culture* (New York: Verso, 2004), 235.
149. Roberta Smith, "For a Paean to Heroic Women, a Place at History's Table," *New York Times,* 20 September 2002, E34.
150. Ibid.
151. Ibid.
152. Ibid.
153. James Trilling, "Judy Chicago: A Beacon," *New York Times,* 22 September 2002, letter to editor, Arts & Leisure, 4. The article he responded to was M. G. Lord, "The Table Is Set At Last, in a Home," *New York Times,* 8 September 2002, 78.
154. Ibid.
155. Leslie Camhi, "Dinner Is Served: Reassessing Judy Chicago and Other Feminist Avatars," *Village Voice,* 16–22 October 2002, 55.
156. John Perreault, "Who's Afraid of Vagina Woolf?" *Nyartsmagazine.com,* 15 April 2003, nyartsmagazine.com/71/afraid.htm.
157. John Perreault to author, 29 January 2006.
158. Brooklyn Museum of Art press release, August 2002, 1.
159. H. W. Janson et al., *History of Art,* 7th ed. (Saddle River, N.J.: Pearson Prentice Hall, 2006), 621–22.
160. Ibid.
161. Michael Botwinick to author, 6 September 2006.

Postscript

1. S. L. Berry, "Art with Attitude," *Indianapolis Star,* 26 September 1999, sec. 1, 2.
2. Sasha S. Welland, "The Long March to Lugu Lake: A Dialogue with Judy Chicago," *Yishu Journal of Contemporary Chinese Art* 1, no. 3 (November 2002), 69.
3. Arlene Raven died August 1, 2006, at the age of sixty-two. Chicago lost a close friend and a strong advocate for her work and for feminist art. For her remembrance of Raven, see the Jewish Women's Archives website: www.jwa.org/discover/inmemoriam/raven.
4. The Feminist Art Project: Call for Participation, n.d. (January 2006).

ACKNOWLEDGMENTS

Research for this book has benefited from grants by the Hadassah-Brandeis Institute at Brandeis University; the Research Foundation of the City University of New York; the Elizabeth and Arthur Schlesinger Library, Harvard University; and the National Endowment for the Humanities. Neither the content nor the conclusions of this book, however, represent anyone's views other than my own.

Although this is in no sense an authorized biography, I wish to thank Judy Chicago for trusting me to tell the story of her life and interpret her art. She allowed me free access to her friends and family as well as to some of her personal papers and private journals still in her possession. In exchange, I agreed only to let her read an early draft of this book and comment upon it. I was then free to write what I wanted, having received in advance photographs as well as written permissions to reproduce her artwork and quote from her writing. Her response upon reading was to ignore her critics and to offer only a few factual corrections and the comment: "It was very painful for me to relive so much—nevertheless, it was my life." I have pried deeply and found in Chicago a person of integrity and strength. Her relaxed attitude about privacy, her probing intelligence, her contributions as an artist and as an educator, and her sense of history make her an ideal subject for biography, a genre in which she herself reads widely.

For leading me to Judy Chicago, I wish to thank Miriam Schapiro, who in 1971 teamed up with her to bring Chicago's Feminist Art Program from Fresno to CalArts. I came to know Schapiro well through my search for a strong female artist who was not a victim. After writing the biography of Edward Hopper and discovering in the diaries of his wife, Josephine Nivison Hopper, the suffering of a woman artist, I was looking for an artist who had been able to better the lot of women artists. I had discovered that almost all of Jo Hopper's art had been discarded by the Whitney Museum of American Art, which received it in her bequest in 1968, along with her husband's artistic estate. Therefore I was determined to find a woman artist who would not be erased from history.

It has been my good fortune to make contact with more than two hundred and fifty people who crossed paths with Chicago. Although she was quite surprised by the number and variety of witnesses I located, she made no effort to censor my contact with any of them: not her ex-husband; nor her former lovers, students, or employees; nor disaffected relatives; nor those who panned her work. I interviewed family members, friends, and classmates from elementary school, high school, and college; her students in the Feminist Art Program and in the Feminist Studio Workshop; and fellow artists, critics, art dealers, museum directors, and art collectors. On occasion I even found those who recalled Judy Cohen and knew of Judy Chicago but had no idea that they were the same person. My conversations included taped interviews in person that lasted for hours, e-mail exchanges that went on for months, phone conversations, and brief talks at parties or other events. All were valuable in helping me to better understand my subject.

I wish to thank all of those who gave so generously of their time and memories, including: Ita Aber, Jacquelin Moore Alexander, Peter Alexander, Sam Amato, Kate Amend, Eleanor Antin, Chuck Arnoldi, Ruth Askey, Dori Bigger Atlantis, Nancy Azara, Sally Babson, Judy Baca, Beth Bachenheimer, Janet Bajan, John Baldessari, Molly Barnes, Loretta Barrett, Larry Bell, Carl Belz, Billy Al Bengston, Ed Bereal, Dorian Bergen, Jeffrey Bergen, Nancy Berman, Cecelia Honet Bethe, Terry Blecher, Cheryl Bookout, Michael Botwinick, Paul Brach, Ruth Braunstein, Joan (Giovanna) D'Angelo Brennan, William Brice, Norma Broude, John Bullard, Nancy Downey Caddick, William Calvin Cannon, Judy DeVita Carlson, Vija Celmins, John Chamberlain, Esther Boroff Charbit, Phyllis Chesler, Chuck Chesnut, Becky Cohen, Elijah Cohen, Harold Cohen, Reiko Kakiuchi Cohen, Robert Colby, Alona Hamilton Cooke, Audrey Cowan, Bob Cowan, Judith Dancoff, Marlene Deane, Sheila Levrant De Bretteville, Johanna Demetrakas, Agnes Denes, Anita Nelson Dickson, Guy Dill, Laddie John Dill, Mary Ann Dill, Mark di Suvero, Mary Beth Edelson, Elliot Elgart, Kathy Erteman, Cindy Ewing, Carole Fisher, Noël Riley Fitch, Susie Fitzhugh, Audrey Flack, Doug Flanders, Travis Foote, Llyn Foulkes, Dextra Frankel, Faiya Fredman, Tom Freudenheim, Nancy Fried, Penny Friedberg, Everett Frost, Vivien Green Fryd, Charles Gaines, Paige Gardner, Mary D. Garrard, Diane Gelon, Paul Gerowitz, Sid Gershgoren, Ralph Gibson, Ken Gilliam, Tina Girouard, Connie Glenn, Carl Gliko, Grace Glueck, Joe Goode, Vanalyne Green, Blue Greenberg, Kirsten Grimstad, Elyse Grinstein, Stanley Grinstein, Susan Grode, John Gruen, Vicki A. Hall, Lloyd Hamrol, Harmony Hammond, April Hankins, Paula Harper, Penny Harris, Helen Harrison, Newton Harrison, Dal Henderson, Suzanne Henderson, Susan Hill, Louise Holland, Henry Hopkins, Shelley Hornstein, Ruth Iskin, Ann Isolde, Leslye Janusz, Ann S. Jennings, Janice Johnson, Shawnee Wollenman Johnson, Amelia G. Jones, Sharon Kagan, Marjorie Kaplow Ross Kaplan, Allan Kaprow, Maria

Karras, Karen Keifer-Boyd, Judye Keyes, Susan E. King, Laurel Klick, Michele Kort, Sarah Kovner, Joyce Kozloff, Sandra Kraskin, Philip Krone, Christe Kruse, Lolette Kuby, Elena Kuperstein, Isaiah Kuperstein, Suzanne Lacy, Cay Lang, Ellen Lanyon, Kay Larson, Frank Laury, Karen LeCocq, Arnold Lehman, David Leibold, Vicki Leon, Marcia Levine, Francine Geselter Liebold, Lucy R. Lippard, Deborah Lipton, Scott Littleton, Carey Lovelace, Edward Lucie-Smith, Libby Lumpkin, Evy Lutin, Harriet Lyons, Michele Maier, Isabel (Welsh) Marcus, Ruth Solomon Markowitz, Jan Lester Martin, Jerry McMillan, Leonie Zverow McVey, Frank Mecoli, Lew Merkelson, Deena Metzger, Lanny Meyers, Tom Mitchel, Robin Mitchell, Susan Mogul, George Moore, Honor Moore, Charles Moskos, Suzanne Muchnic, Juliet Myers, Rolf Nelson, Cindy Nemser, Manuel Neri, Pamella Nesbit, Gladys Nilsson, Linda Nochlin, Estelle Gershgoren Novak, Carol Ockman, Dennis O'Connor, Jan Oxenberg, Logan Palmer, John Perreault, Irving Petlin, Sarah Petlin, Herman Pevner, Jeanne Phillips, Clare Pierson, Edie Hopkins Pistolesi, Peter Plagens, James Plotkin, Allen Podet, Betty Prashker, Ruth Levinson Psundstein, Jessica Fizdale Radin, Aviva Rahmani, Arlene Raven, Susan Rennie, Jack Rhyne, Ann Rockefeller Roberts, Enid Cohen Rosen, Howard Rosen, Julia Ross, Moira Roth, Pat Rudy-Baese, Chris Rush, Janet Russek, Cheryl Zurilgen Rutter, Elizabeth A. Sackler, Miriam Schapiro, Theodore Schapiro, David Scheinbaum, Robbin Schiff, Christina Schlesinger, Romona Scholder, Mira Schor, Alan Schwartz, Julian Schwartz, Barbara Seaman, Joan Semmel, Sandy Shannonhouse, Alix Kates Shulman, Suzanne Siegel, Laura Silagi, Ruth Silverman, Marilyn Skinner, Judith Solodkin, Keith Sonnier, Clare Loeb Spark, Nancy Spero, Lael Stegall, Judith Stein, Louise Steinman, Robin Weltsch Storie, Cheryl Swannack, Lilian Tart, Mary Ross Taylor, Sandra Taylor, Jane Thompson, Billie Tsien, Marcia Tucker, James Turrell, Bella Zweig Vivante, Judith Von Euer, Dagmar Von Garnier, Patricia Watkinson, June Wayne, Wanda Westcoast, Helen Whitebook, Faith Wilding, Jane Wilson, Jackie Winsor, Donald Woodman, Viki Wylder, Linda Yaven, Nancy Youdelman, Rachel Youdelman, and Robert Zangrando. I hope that anyone whom I may have forgotten to include here will forgive my unintentional oversight.

For supplying photographs for this book, I wish to thank Mary Beth Edelson, Susie Fitzhugh, Paul Gerowitz, Lloyd Hamrol, Paula Harper, Maria Karras, Michele Maier, Jerry McMillan, Jack Rhyne, Elizabeth A. Sackler, John B. Van Sickle, and especially Donald Woodman, who has photographed Chicago's work so well for the last twenty years. For help in locating photographs, I wish to thank Cheri Gaulke, Carol Chen, and Mayumi Nishida.

For their welcome insights and advice upon reading parts of this manuscript, I wish to thank Patricia Hills, who gave so generously of her time and read the entire book in an early stage; John Babcock Van Sickle, who read much of this book; Lauri Umansky, who read an early version of the chapter on the sixties; and the members of Women Writing Women's Lives, a seminar of biographers, who read an early draft of the introduction and a chapter about Chicago's ancestors, especially Kathy Chamberlain, Dorothy Helly, Patricia Laurence, and Victoria Olsen.

For extending their hospitality and facilitating my research trips, I am especially grateful to Judith Tick and Steve Oleskey, Audrey and Bob Cowan, Patricia Hills and Kevin Whitfield, Laura and David Meyer, and Steven and Ann Sunshine. The late Fred Karl and his wife, Dolores Karl, gave me important early encouragement. I wish to thank especially Loretta Barrett, Judy Chicago's literary agent, for all of her help.

In my research, I have received assistance from many libraries and generous librarians. At Baruch College of the City University of New York, Art Downing, Katherine Shelfer, Lisa Ellis, and especially Louisa Moy have been very helpful. I also wish to thank: Jean Coffey at California State University, Fresno; Elizabeth Dunn, Special Collections Library, Duke University; Althea Greenan of Goldsmith's University Library of London; Teresa Barnett of the oral history program at UCLA and Cherry Williams of the UCLA library; Coco Halverson at the CalArts library; Jim McMasters at the Northwestern University library; Sandy Slater, Special Collections Library at the University of North Dakota; Jo Pearson of the Cedar Rapids Public Library; Beverly Redford of the Historical Center in Cedar Rapids; Warren Taylor of the Topeka and Shawnee County Public Library; the Edward P. Taylor Research Library and Archives, Art Gallery of Ontario; and the entire staff of Elizabeth and Arthur Schlesinger Library, Harvard University, where I received a research grant. My work on the Judy Chicago papers at the Schlesinger was interrupted by both the closing of the library for renovation and the closing of Chicago's papers for cataloging. Thus, I first examined some papers in uncataloged boxes and reexamined them again in neat, numbered folders.

In a class by himself is Dan Sharon, librarian at the Spertus Institute in Chicago, who encountered me when I first began to research my subject's Jewish ancestry and Chicago roots. Without his extraordinary encouragement and frequent suggestions, I might have abandoned that quest. Later on, I benefited from the work of Simon Zalkind of the Mizel Center for Arts and Culture in Denver, who invited me to participate in the exhibition *Upstarts and Matriarchs: Jewish-American Feminists,* which opened in January 2005. More recently, I have found helpful discussions with both Laura Kruger and Jean Rosensaft of the

Hebrew Union College–Jewish Institute of Religion Museum in New York, who have invited me to co-organize a show called *Judy Chicago: Jewish Identity.*

I also received generous help in my research from many others, including distinguished scholars who took time out from their own work to answer my queries. I wish to thank Joyce Antler, Elissa Auther, Nancy Downey Caddick, Louis Cohen, M.D., Penny Franklin, Elizabeth Gong-Guy, Clare ("Chaikey") Greenberg, John Hardy, Martin Jacobs, Renee Kaplan, M.D., Elaine A. King, Joy Kingsolver, Craig Krull, Ann Mackin, Yuko Nakama, James Oles, Jo Pearson, Beverly Redford, Alexandra Schwartz, David Sokol, Lisa Thrower, and Barbara Wolanin. I also appreciate Jason Belland for helping me with digital images. At Baruch College of the City University of New York, I am very grateful to Dean Myrna Chase, who has consistently been so supportive of my research and writing. I also wish to thank Philip Lambert, the chairperson of my department of fine and performing arts and all my Baruch colleagues for their encouragement. At the Graduate Center of the City University of New York, many colleagues have been supportive, especially Mary Ann Caws and Marc Dolan, who heads the program in American studies.

At Harmony Books, I gratefully acknowledge Shaye Areheart, whose early insight and enthusiasm allowed this book to become a reality. I am very happy to thank my editor, Julia Pastore, who has in every way lived up to her name, serving as the good shepherd, coaxing me to conform to a schedule too short for my comfort, asking all the right questions, and making valuable suggestions, always with good cheer, tact, and sensitivity. Thanks also to the care given this manuscript by editorial assistant Kate Kennedy; production editor Camille Smith; copy editor Janet Biehl; Laura Duffy, the designer of the cover; Suzanne Brown and Walter Friedman in production; and Barbara Sturman, who designed the book's interior.

To my husband, John B. Van Sickle, I dedicate this book. He sacrificed his vacations to accompany me on research trips to California, driving me around Los Angeles and Fresno so that I could conduct interviews in person. He documented those interviews with photographs, which I treasure. As always, his generosity in sharing with me his many abilities—including as a wordsmith and as a solver of software glitches—have made this a better book and writing it much more pleasant. Had I not had his help, this book would not have made its deadline, but his translation and commentary on Virgil's *Eclogues* might have been finished sooner.

ILLUSTRATION CREDITS

INTERIOR

All photographs courtesy of Through the Flower Archives except:

Pages 1 and 101 used by permission of Jerry McMillan.
Page 79 courtesy of Paul Gerowitz.
Page 174 used with permission of Lloyd Hamrol.
Pages 175 and 249 used with permission of Maria Karras.
Page 206 used with permission of Susie Fitzhugh.
Page 303 used with permission of Jack Rhyne.
Page 333 used with permission of Michele Maier.
Page 369 courtesy of Elizabeth A. Sackler.
Page 397 used with permission of Donald Woodman.
Page 400 courtesy of John Babcock Van Sickle.

INSERT

Figures 1, 5, 6, 7, 8, 10, 11, 13, 16, 18, 19, 20 and 21 courtesy of Through the Flower Archives.
Figure 12 photograph by Paula Harper.
Figure 25 photograph by Michele Maier.
All other photographs of Judy Chicago's artwork by Donald Woodman.

INDEX

Page numbers in *italics* signify black-and-white photographs in the text. Figure numbers in brackets refer to artwork in the color insert.

ABOUT THE AUTHOR

GAIL LEVIN is an art historian, curator, and biographer who is internationally recognized for her scholarship on twentieth-century and contemporary art. The preeminent authority on Edward Hopper, she served from 1976 to 1984 as first curator of the Hopper Collection at the Whitney Museum of American Art, where she organized several major exhibitions, created the Hopper archives, and wrote eight books, including the catalogue raisonné of Hopper's oeuvre. Among her other books, two feature her own photographs, which have been exhibited in museums and galleries around the United States and published both here and abroad.

Levin's 1976 doctorate was the first granted in art history by Rutgers University, and Simmons College conferred on her an honorary Doctorate of Humane Letters in 1996. Her work has been recognized with numerous fellowships and awards. She served as the founding president of the Catalogue Raisonné Scholars Association, an affiliate of the College Art Association. Currently, she holds the Pollock-Krasner/Stony Brook Research Fellowship and is writing a biography of the abstract expressionist painter Lee Krasner, whom she first met while conducting research for her dissertation. She is professor of art history, American studies, and women's studies at Baruch College and the Graduate Center of the City University of New York.